A TWENTY-FIRST CENTURY GUIDE TO ALDERSONIAN MARKETING THOUGHT

A TWENTY-FIRST CENTURY GUIDE TO ALDERSONIAN MARKETING THOUGHT

Edited by
BEN WOOLISCROFT
University of Otago

ROBERT D. TAMILIA
University of Quebec at Montreal

STANLEY J. SHAPIRO
Simon Fraser University

Kluwer Academic Publishers
Boston/Dordrecht/London

Library of Congress Cataloging-in-Publication Data

A C.I.P. Catalogue record for this book is available
from the Library of Congress.

ISBN-10: 0-387-26175-3   e-ISBN-10: 0-387-28181-9   Printed on acid-free paper.
ISBN-13: 978-0387-26175-1   e-ISBN-13: 978-0387-28181-0

Printed in the United States of America.

9 8 7 6 5 4 3 2 1   SPIN 11330455

springeronline.com

This book is dedicated to the memory of Wroe Alderson, the most important figure in the development of theory of marketing.

Contents

Contents   ix

List of Figures

List of Tables

Authors Contributing Original Works

Dennis B. Arnett, Ph.D. Associate Professor of Marketing, Rawls College of Business Administration, Texas Tech University. darnett@ba.ttu.edu

Michael Halbert Retired consultant/teacher, mike-halbert@juno.com

Shelby D. Hunt, Ph.D. Jerry S. Rawls & P.W. Horn Professor of Marketing, Rawls College of Business Administration, Texas Tech University, sdh@ba.ttu.edu

James C. McKeon, Ph.D. Executive in Residence, School of Business, Western New England College, jmckeon222@comcast.net

Robert Rothberg, Ph.D. Director of the MBA Program, Faculty of Management, Rutgers Business School, RRothberg@aol.com

Stanley J. Shapiro, Ph.D. Professor-Emeritus of Marketing, Faculty of Business, Simon Fraser University, sshapiro@sfu.ca

Robert D. Tamilia, Ph.D. Professor of Marketing, Ecole des Sciences de la Gestion, University of Quebec at Montreal, tamilia.robert@uqam.ca

Alf H. Walle, Ph.D Associate Professor of Business, Department of Business and Economics, Erskine College, walle@erskine.edu

Ian Wilkinson, Ph.D. Professor of Marketing, School of Marketing, University of New South Wales, i.wilkinson@unsw.edu.au

Ben Wooliscroft, Ph.D. Lecturer, Department of Marketing, University of Otago, bwooliscroft@business.otago.ac.nz

Louise Young, Ph.D Professor of Marketing, School of Marketing, University of Technology, louise.young@uts.edu.au

Preface

We put this book together for one very simple reason—to familiarize a new generation of marketing scholars with the life, the writings and the intellectual legacy of Wroe Alderson, unquestionably the pre-eminent marketing theorist of the mid-twentieth century. Had a Hall of Fame for marketing academics been established at the time, Alderson might well have been a unanimous choice the first year nominations were accepted. The Editors consider him as important to the marketing discipline as Keynes was to economics or Taylor to early management thought. Nevertheless, Alderson currently receives little or no attention in marketing classes whether these be offered at the BBA, the MBA or the Ph.D. level. There are a number of possible explanations for this neglect, some discussed in the pages that follow. However, our major objective as editors was not to chastise others for their errors of omission but rather to assemble in a single publication a selection of material written by and about Wroe Alderson that would serve as a twenty-first century guide to Aldersonian marketing thought.

The book itself is divided into six Parts each with its own brief introduction. There's a biography in Part I and in Part II a fairly extensive set of what, both now and previously, appeared to be Alderson's most important theoretical contributions. Alderson as consultant is also represented in Part III by practitioner-oriented material on marketing management and on marketing ethics. The fourth Part contains a number of previously published articles that either build on Alderson's work or show the interdisciplinary nature of his thinking by relating it to that of leading academics from other areas. In the fifth Part, six newly written contributions provide additional insights into Wroe Alderson's life, his work, his character and his intellectual impact. Finally, one finds at the end of this volume a complete listing of publications both by Alderson (over a forty year period) and about him.

This information belongs on the historical record both because of its past importance and its current relevance. We believe a careful reading of what follows will show that Alderson's work still continues to provide, decades after it was first published, many important conceptual building blocks. These are components which contemporary marketing scholars can use in their own efforts to improve both the theory and the practice of marketing. Phrased another way, we believe Wroe Alderson deserves to be recognized both as a seminal thinker and as a still very relevant figure in the intellectual history of the marketing discipline. That's our position and it is an opinion we believe that many others who read the material found in this volume will come to share.

THE EDITORS

Acknowledgments

A great many individuals and organizations assist the editors of any publication but never more than when the volume in question contains material originally published over half a century ago. The accompanying Exhibit identifies the publishing firms and other organizations that kindly gave us permission to reprint material either by or about Wroe Alderson. We are most grateful for this assistance since, literally, without such permission this book could not have been published.

However, that Exhibit merely begins the identification of all those deserving our thanks. Close to half of the material in this book originally appeared in publications by Wroe Alderson on which the Richard D. Irwin Company held the original copyright. The current publisher of the successor organization to Richard D. Irwin, Mr. Andy Winston, Publisher of McGraw-Hill/Irwin, kindly informed us that, given the date of the original publications, the copyrights in question had by now reverted to the Alderson family. Professor Alderson's three children, Asia Alderson Bennett, Maya Alderson Schulze and Evan Alderson, had from the very beginning of the project been supportive of this initiative. They were thus more than willing to allow us to select whatever material we wished from the books their father had originally published with Richard D. Irwin.

Exhibit: Organizations that Provided Permission to Reprint Material

The Editors wish to thank the following organizations for granting us permission to reprint the material identified below:

1 The American Marketing Association for permission to reprint:

 a Alderson, Wroe and Cox, Reavis (1948). Towards a Theory of Marketing. *Journal of Marketing*, 13(October:137-152.

 b Alderson, Wroe (1950). Survival and Adjustment in Organized Behavior Systems. In Cox, Reavis and Alderson, Wroe, editors, *Theory in Marketing*, pages 65-87. Richard D. Irwin, Inc., Chicago.

 c Alderson, Wroe (1952). Ethics, Ideologies and Sanctions. In *Report of the Committee on Ethical Standards and Professional Practices*, pages 1-20. American Marketing Association, Chicago.

 d Amstutz, Arnold (1968). Book Review *Planning and Problem Solving in Marketing. Journal of Marketing Research*, 5(February):109-111.

e Lusch, Robert (1980). Alderson, Sessions and the 1950s Manager. In Lamb, Charles and Dunne, Patrick, editors, *Theoretical Developments in Marketing*, pages 4-6. The American Marketing Association, Chicago.

f Hunt, Shelby D., Muncy, James A. and Ray, Nina (1981). Alderson's General Theory of Marketing: A Formalization. In Enis, Ben and Roering K., editors, *Review of Marketing 1981*, pages 314-324. The American Marketing Association, Chicago.

2 Emerald Group Publishing Limited for permission to reprint:

a Reekie, W. Duncan and Savitt, Ronald (1982). Marketing Behaviour and Entrepreneurship. *European Journal of Marketing*, 16(7):55-66. Available at: http://www.emeraldinsight.com/ejm.htm.

b Dixon, Donald and Wilkinson, Ian (1989). An Alternative Paradigm for Marketing Theory. *European Journal of Marketing*, 23(8):59-69. Available at: http://www.emeraldinsight.com/ejm.htm.

c Priem, Richard, Rasheed, Abdul M. A. and Amirani, Shahrzad (1997). Alderson's transvection and Porter's value system: a comparison of two independently developed theories. *Journal of Management History*, 3(2):145-165. Available at: http://www.emeraldinsight.com/jmh.htm.

3 Crain Communications Inc. for permission to reprint:

a Alderson, Wroe (1957). Advertisers Urged to Follow Path of Rational Problem Solving Rather Than of Instinctive Drives. *Advertising Age*, 28(March, No. 4):83-84.

b Alderson, Wroe (1958). A Basic Guide to Market Planning. *Industrial Marketing*, (July):53-57.

4 John Wiley and Sons, Inc. for permission to reprint:

a Grether, E. T. (1967). Chamberlin's Theory of Monopolistic Competition and the Literature of Marketing. In Kuenne, Robert, editor, *Monopolistic Competition Theories: Studies in Impact*, pages 315-318. Wiley, New York.

5 Walter A. Haas School of Business, University of California, Berkeley for permission to reprint:

a Alderson, Wroe (1958). The Analytical Framework for Marketing. In Duncan, Delbert, editor, *Proceedings: Conference of Marketing*

Teachers from Far Western States, pages 15-28. University of California, Berkeley.

6 The Christian Association, the University of Pennsylvania, for permission to reprint:

    a Alderson, Wroe. (1964). The American Economy and Christian Ethics. A paper first presented to a student group in June of 1964.

The material found in Parts I and V of this volume, in contrast, was newly written for inclusion in it. The editors are most grateful to Mike Halbert, to Shelby Hunt and Dennis Arnett, to Ian Wilkinson and Louise Young and to Alf Walle for finding time in their already crowded schedules to prepare such outstanding contributions. The Editors' own original contributions are also to be found in Parts I and V.

We also wish to thank Jag Sheth for his efforts to help us find a publisher for this important heritage volume. We are grateful, as well, to Len Dawson who kindly shared with us materials assembled for a project, unfortunately aborted in the early 1980s, that would have seen the American Marketing Association publish a complete set of *Cost and Profit Outlooks*. Included in this material from Dr. Dawson, and subsequently drawn upon in this publication, was an unpublished paper by Ed McGarry on the history of the annual Marketing Theory Seminars and the text of the eulogy Orin Burley delivered at Wroe Alderson's funeral.

When thanks are being given out, an especially generous portion belongs on the plates of our Editor, Sean Lorre, and his employer, Springer Science and Business Media. Springer recognized that our proposed publication would be of considerable academic value and shared our belief that it would prove commercially attractive as well.

The initial impetus for this book was the doctoral dissertation on Wroe Alderson that Ben Wooliscroft wrote at the University of Otago under the supervision of Professor Rob Lawson. We are most grateful both to Professor Lawson and to the Business School of the University of Otago for creating an academic climate in which high quality conceptual and theoretical dissertations, as well as methodologically driven ones, are acceptable. Would that this were now the rule and not the exception!

We would also like to thank the interlibrary loan staff at UQAM for their help in locating publications reviewed for the book. Thanks to Raymond Laliberté, research associate at UQAM's Business School, for his assistance.

Finally, we wish to thank two spouses, Roberta Shapiro and Sanna Ganglmair-Wooliscroft, both for the encouragement they provided throughout the project and for the assistance they willingly offered at various stages of this undertaking.

So ends our listing of the "thank you's" due up to the time of publication. Of course, we are also grateful to each and every reader of this book for taking the time and trouble to become familiar with the work of Wroe Alderson. Professor Alderson was, unquestionably and indisputably, the preeminent marketing theorist of the mid-twentieth century. He provided much of the intellectual foundation of our discipline, a foundation on which so many others, some knowingly but others not, have built. After you have read the book, we trust you will agree that there was indeed intellectual justification for this effort to provide both the current and future generations of marketing scholars with a twenty-first century guide to Aldersonian marketing thought.

Ben Wooliscroft
Robert D. Tamilia
Stanley J. Shapiro

I

WROE ALDERSON: THE MAN

Chapter 1

WROE ALDERSON A LIFE[*]

Ben Wooliscroft
University of Otago

Abstract   Wroe Alderson was a scholar and a man of many talents. A Renaissance man in the truest sense of the term, he was a practitioner, scholar, theorist, philosopher, theologian, mentor, and good friend to many who knew him. Alderson rose from simple beginnings to be one of the leading marketing consultants in America, and the leading marketing theorist and father of modern marketing thought.

1.   Who was Wroe Alderson?

Wroe Alderson (see Figure 1.1) was born near St Louis, Missouri September 27, 1898, into a family of limited means. Wroe was the eldest child of a large Southern Methodist family. Unusual for the times, Alderson's mother had attended college and worked as a teacher.

Wroe Alderson's father, Walter Alderson, had been an impressively strong man who was rumoured, likely apocryphally, to have lifted train wheel assemblies for entertainment at a circus (Hollander, 2001). Walter had travelled widely in the United States as a young man. In 1897 he had gone to Alaska to prospect for gold, unsuccessfully. While he had no formal education, he was a voracious reader and strong debater, a pastime his son would also enjoy in the years to come. For a time, Walter Alderson served as U.S. Marshall in a small Missouri town (Bennett and Bennett, 2003).

From these somewhat simple beginnings Wroe Alderson rose to the pinnacle of marketing practice and theory. He has been lauded as the father of the modern

---

[*] This biography relies heavily on interviews with Alderson's children, Asia Bennett and Evan Alderson, and those who worked with/for Alderson, particularly Stanley J. Shapiro, Michael Halbert, Patrick J. Robinson, and Robert Rothberg, who all generously gave their time. It was a pleasure to meet so many people who share a passion for a great marketing thinker.

Figure 1.1. Wroe Alderson circa 1899

era of marketing (Jones and Shaw, 2002). Smith (1966) considered Alderson's four contributions to the marketing discipline to be:

- He brought an interdisciplinary approach to marketing theory formation which attracted many scientists from other fields to the study of marketing.

- His work provides an illustration of the "importance and usefulness of marketing theory" (p. 65).

- He bridged the gap between practitioner and academic communities.

- He stimulated the minds of others while his "own specific contributions to marketing were monumental" (p. 65).

There is no doubt that Alderson is a very influential figure in the history of marketing thought (Bartels, 1988, Holbrook, 1998, Holbrook, 2001, Hollander, 1998, Jones and Shaw, 2002, Sheth et al., 1988). In spite of his importance to the marketing discipline, and unlike other disciplines' approach to their leaders, his life has received relatively little attention.

This biography follows Alderson's life through a number of themes, arranged in chronological order based on their starting date, but overlapping due to some of the themes continuing their importance through Alderson's life.

2. Alderson: the Early Years

Wroe Alderson graduated eighth grade and left school at the age of 15 (Bennett and Bennett, 2003). As a young man, he left home in Missouri and took to the rails, living as a hobo[1] and travelling as far as Washington State (Bennett and Bennett, 2003). Pre-World War I he held many manual and menial jobs, including a job in a tannery (Bennett and Bennett, 2003). While he travelled around the country working, he would send money home to help support the family each month (Alderson, nd). He then taught school for a while in backwoods Missouri, where he would have to fight his, often considerably larger, pupils to get their attention (Bennett and Bennett, 2003). Alderson was an able fighter and was involved in a number of prize fights. Later he would regale his family and friends with stories of him outwitting larger opponents in the ring (Bennett and Bennett, 2003). He was to continue to do a number of predominantly manual jobs until World War I broke out, when he enlisted in the army.

---

[1]A *hobo* is defined as "a wandering workman or tramp" (Brown, 1993, p. 1243). In America they often rode the railways illegally to get between places, facing the wrath of rail police, who were known to exact vicious beatings on those caught riding the rails for free.

3.   Alderson: World War I

In 1919, while Alderson was in the army his father, 16 year old sister and 3 year old brother died in the influenza epidemic, which is estimated to have taken 675 000 American lives, more than the combined combat casualties of World War I, World War II, Korea and Vietnam for America (Crosby, 1989). Alderson had not seen them since leaving home, to seek his fortune, and he felt terribly guilty (Bennett and Bennett, 2003). As the eldest son, Wroe took on the mantle of man of the house, looking after his mother and siblings financially — which he was to continue to do for many years.

Being "severely left-handed" during his time in the army, Alderson was not suited to using a rifle with a sight designed for right-handed soldiers and was posted to Washington State where he was trained as a typist and journalist and given the job of clerk/typist for the army (Bennett, 2001). It was probably the last time that Alderson ever typed — he always hand wrote his papers, books and reports and then had a typist translate his generously flowing hand writing into a readable form.

4.   Alderson: Studying between the Wars

After leaving the armed services, Alderson worked in a number of casual jobs in the Washington area, including as a lumberjack. It was during this time while working in Washington that Alderson met Professor Selden Smyser of Ellensburg Teachers College (currently, after a number of different names, called Central Washington University) (Bennett, 2001). Smyser noticed in Alderson an able mind and encouraged him to undertake study. Alderson was to later repay Smyser's support by sponsoring the Smyser Award, a $50 award for the "best paper in some phase of social communication or relationship" each year (Hogan, 2003). Alderson played college football while at Ellensburg Teacher College, in spite of being only 5 foot 6 inches tall. He was very proud of his ability to tackle and outplay players considerably larger than himself (Bennett and Bennett, 2003). The post war years were a tumultuous time for Alderson, including a brief marriage, of which little is known. He did not complete his studies at the Ellensburg Teachers College (Bennett, 2001).

In 1923 Alderson enrolled at George Washington University, in Washington D.C. — bringing with him credits from his previous studies — where he graduated in 1925, aged 27, with a degree in economics and statistics. While at George Washington University, Wroe courted Elsie Star Wright. Elsie was born in 1898 in Bedford County, Virginia (Philadelphia Inquirer, 1989). Before meeting Wroe, she taught at rural schools in Virginia and Oklahoma. An enthusiastic suitor and a devoted husband, Alderson wrote books of love poems to his wife, whom he called "Star". They were married while Alderson worked on a project for the Department of Commerce in the Southern States (his influential study into the efficiency of drug store purchasing policies, among others). He was so busy that Christmas Day 1927 was the only day he could be sure to have off for the wedding. They married in a church, with the Alderson crest on it, in the town of Alderson, West Virginia.

Wroe was busy working, studying and supporting his mother and siblings. He worked for the Department of Commerce, originally under Herbert Hoover, from 1925 until 1934, producing a number of important reports (i.e. Alderson, 1928, Alderson and Miller, 1930, Alderson and Bromell, 1930, Alderson and Haag, 1931, Alderson and Aiken, 1932, Alderson and Meserole, 1932, Alderson and Miller, 1934). Wroe Alderson is listed on the editorial board of the *American Marketing Magazine*[2] as a representative of a federal agency, which can be assumed to be the Department of Commerce (Tamilia, 2002). He was also on the editorial board of the *Journal of Marketing* in later years.

His wife, Elsie, continued her studies and eventually was only one course in German, which she struggled with, and a thesis short of completing her doctorate in genetics and embryology at Johns Hopkins University. She undertook research at the Marine Biological Laboratory in Woods Hole, Massachusetts on two separate occasions. He may have been not entirely regretful that she didn't finish — "there was room for one professional in the Alderson household" (Bennett, 2001).

Each time Elsie returned to her doctoral studies seems to coincide with her falling pregnant with another child and abandoning study once more (Bennett and Bennett, 2003). Alderson struggled with the liberation of women at a personal level, while being in favour of it at a societal level (Bennett, 2001). He was the dominant figure in his household and his wife provided the stability and moderation for the family (Alderson, 2001). In 1933 Asia Alderson, later Asia Bennett, was born to the couple — the first of three children: Maya, 1936, later Maya Schulze; and Evan, 1938.

Wroe was a dedicated and loving father and husband, but was not always patient with his family, having very firm views about how things should be done and when they should be done. He was very interested in people and delighted in discussing and philosophising, but, when he was finished with someone, he was completely finished with them. An ex-friend would be dead to him and his family would be expected not to mention the name again (Alderson, 2001).

5.   Quakerism

In 1936 Alderson joined Curtis Publishing Company, leaders in marketing research (Sheth et al., 1988). In August 1939 the Aldersons moved to Haverford Pennsylvania for Alderson's work. A colleague found a house for them and

---

[2]established in 1934 and merged to become the *Journal of Marketing* in 1936.

introduced them to the Friends school for Asia. It was the start of their interest in Quakerism. Wroe and Elsie wanted their children to be brought up in a church and this Quaker meeting, with its intellectually lively congregation, suited the Aldersons. They became involved in the life of the Haverford Friends Meeting. Wroe really took to Quakerism and was made a member of the congregation in 1940 — very swiftly, when most members have gone through long periods of contemplation and consideration that typically take over a year. Elsie was not released by her Southern Baptist church to join the Quakers and was required to "enter on her own recognisance" (Bennett, 2001). Attracted to the Quaker church because of its emphasis on nature and equality — as Wroe was — she was active in the church, including teaching in First School (the Quaker Sunday school). Alderson took his commitment as a Friend very seriously and often spent considerable time preparing for worship so that he could make a meaningful contribution. He was very quickly to become a well respected and influential member of the Meeting (Bennett, 2001).

Wroe Alderson was very aware of being an imperfect human being and trying to improve himself through the *inward teacher* — the Quaker practice of finding guidance from God within themselves (Bennett, 2001).

In 1948, Alderson visited Mexico as a delegate of the American Friends Service Committee (AFSC) to survey the service projects there as a part of the AFSC's peace work (Bennett, 2001). Apart from visits to Canada during his travels as a youth, it was his first international travel and he relished his experiences with Mexicans and their culture (Bennett, 2001).

In 1955 Alderson joined a delegation of Friends to the Soviet Union as an economist, in an attempt to open a productive dialogue with the Cold War enemy and to find different ways of considering the relationship between the two superpowers. Alderson's passport of the time includes the special permit allowing him to enter the USSR, a country that America banned its citizens from visiting. The delegation included Clarence Pickett, emeritus AFSC Executive Secretary and friend of Eleanor Roosevelt. Alderson was very proud of being asked to go and was the lead author of a booklet published by the AFSC (Alderson et al., 1956). On returning to the United States, Alderson had a full schedule of speaking engagements to share his experiences in the Soviet Union. Unfortunately his health gave out and not for the last time (Bennett, 2001).

Though he was physically vigorous and athletic as a young man, with brown hair and blue eyes, by the mid 1950s he was seriously overweight and was often short of breath (Bennett, 2001). During 1955 he suffered his first heart attack. A man who liked his food and drink (Robinson, 2001, Robinson, 2003, Shapiro, 2001), Alderson tried to moderate his diet, with limited success (Bennett, 2001). He ate a lot of meat and had very high cholesterol and blocked arteries.

During the height of McCarthyism the Aldersons campaigned, ultimately unsuccessfully, for a noted Chinese actress, who had become a family friend when a graduate student at Bryn Mawr College, and her journalist husband who were being deported to China. They were arrested and imprisoned on return to Communist China and died in prison (Bennett and Bennett, 2003).

Wroe Alderson was very involved in the AFSC — which had been formed in 1917 to promote peace and justice — and served for some time on its Board of Directors. The AFSC received the Nobel Prize for Peace in 1947 for its work during World War II. The award was accepted on behalf of the organisation by Professor Henry J. Cadbury, renowned Harvard University theologian and friend of Wroe Alderson. Wroe's daughter, Asia was later to work as executive secretary of the AFSC and the Friends World Committee. Alderson was also active in the Philadelphia Yearly Meeting Social Order Committee, a group concerned with racial issues, housing, industrial relations and opportunities for the poor. Alderson's two daughters often spent weekends in the Philadelphia slums painting and renovating.

Quakerism was important to Alderson and to his marketing theory. His concept of double searching, he suggested, came to him while in worship contemplating man's search for God and God's search for man (Bennett, 2001). Wroe was capable of beautiful turns of phrase, as was evident when he spoke in a Friends' Meeting and then wrote of the beauty in the Chesapeake Bay, see Figure 1.2.

6.   Alderson and World War II

Before and during the early days of the the United States' entry into World War II, the Aldersons had refugees from Germany and Austria staying with them. Both Wroe and Elsie were active in Quaker efforts to assist refugees from Nazism (Bennett, 2001, Philadelphia Inquirer, 1989).

In 1943 Alderson took leave from Curtis Publishing to work in Washington, as a part of the war effort. It is somewhat ironic that Alderson a Quaker, and thus a pacifist, was a member of the American war effort. There is, however, a suggestion from his daughter that his strong Quaker beliefs would have required him to be a conscientious objector had he been of an age to fight (Bennett, 2001). During World War II Alderson worked for the Office of Price Administration (OPA), lead by John Kenneth Galbraith, as well as the Bureau of Economic Warfare and the Foreign Economic Administration, based in Washington D.C. (Bennett, 2001, Galbraith, 2002, The New York Times, 1965).

There were several hundred economists and other scholars working in the OPA and it is unclear what Alderson's duties were (Galbraith, 2002). Given his previous government employment and expertise in market research — particularly the fact that he set up Alderson Consulting immediately after the war, with its primary focus on market research, pricing and distribution — it is likely that he was involved in market research for the OPA.

We have just had a week of golden October days beside the Chesapeake, with Heaven waiting in every sunset.

The hoarse cry of the wild goose is like a brute reaction to beauty too bright to be borne. A world in flames, over land and water, re-enacts the ancient and tragic mystery of Death-in-Life and Life-in-Death.

The dogwood leaves are dying in a burst of battle red. Oak and maple strew the lane with the vivid hues of passion and the soft shades of memory. And soaring there on a high stark limb is the scarlet banner of ivy.

On the water, where life first found its home, life is still harvesting life: a fisherman out in the chilly dawn; the sails of the oystermen at noon; a belated woman crabber poling her skiff through the ripples along the shore. Underneath the surface the living still feeds on the living — or faces death in the stab of the heron or the swoop of the osprey.

A philosopher speaking for the pantheism of the East has said that life is perpetual perishing. What we see now shall never be seen again. What we love most, even now is slipping away. We weep for beauty vanishing but beauty is its heir. The flower fading on its stalk will cast its seed for flowers to scent tomorrow.

A poet once prayed to be released from too much love of living. Let us rather pay to love life freely and to spend it freely. Time is our sovereign currency but let us not grasp it with a miser's hand.

And let no puny man fancy himself an Atlas, bearing the world on his shoulders. The world will not fall apart without us because God holds it together. Individually we are held and jointly we endure within the magnificent fabric of his grand design. The notes are transient — the symphony eternal. Our faith in a loving and eternal God is faith in the abundance of life.

Figure 1.2. Alderson's Letter to the Haverford Meeting

As well as being concerned with price controls (Galbraith, 2003), the OPA was involved in advertising campaigns aimed at keeping inflation in check during and after the war. The OPA was successful in its mission and inflation was kept under control during and after the war, in stark contrast to the rampant inflation after World War I (Galbraith, 2002).

It is likely that while working for the OPA Alderson spent time with E. T. Grether, who was a special consultant to the OPA in 1944. Certainly Alderson and Grether were to remain fast friends until Alderson's death (Bennett and Bennett, 2003). While working in Washington, Alderson stayed away from the family for long periods of time, coming back to Haverford infrequently (Bennett, 2001).

In 1944 the Pabst Brewing Company Postwar Employment Awards for maintaining full employment were decided. Almost 36 000 papers had been sent in on the topic of how to maintain full employment after the war (Fitch and Taylor, 1946). Herbert Stein won the first prize and Alderson received one of 17 awards, being given a grant of $1000.00 and a medal in recognition of the value of his entry.

7.   Alderson: The Consultant

In 1944 Alderson set up a consulting business, which was to become the Alderson and Sessions consulting company in 1945, with the addition of Robert E. Sessions, who he had met at the OPA, as a partner. In 1949 the firm was known briefly as Alderson, Simons and Sessions (Alexander et al., 1949). Alderson was not, particularly, interested in money and used the company to sponsor the development of theory and his social concerns. While employed by Alderson and Sessions, William Baumol developed the ideas which he published in *Business Behavior, Value and Growth* (Shapiro, 2001). Baumol wrote in his foreword, "I owe profound gratitude to Wroe Alderson. . ." (Baumol, 1959, p. viii). Charles Sevin also further developed his earlier work on distribution cost accounting while employed by Alderson and Sessions (Shapiro, 2001).

The consulting company published the *Cost and Profit Outlook* periodical which was to contain many of the ideas that then appeared in Alderson's books and articles. *Cost and Profit Outlook*, and *Growth and Profit Planner*, a similar newsletter produced by Behavior Systems (Alderson, 1964b), had a major impact on the relationship between academia and practising marketers (Lusch, 1980) and are, if not frequently, significantly referenced.

Because of, or in spite of this, Alderson and Sessions was to grow into an internationally successful consulting company with many important clients (see Table 1.1). Alderson was imaginative, idealistic and a risk taker, which occasionally lead to tight finances for the family, such as when in 1948 the firm's office moved to Lewis Tower in the commercial heart of Philadelphia.

He did, though, earn more money than it may have appeared by looking at him, typically dressed in a suit which had seen better days (Bennett, 2001). Alderson also spent a great deal of time travelling, giving speeches and writing. Alderson and Sessions grew the company and its reputation for excellence can be seen in the quote from Crisp in 1957, when discussing marketing research in the United States (see Figure 1.3).

E. I. du Pont de Nemours & Co., Inc.	Smith, Kline & French Laboratories
Standard Oil Company of New Jersey	National Dairy Products Corporation
The York Corporation	Bigelow-Sanford Carpet Company, Inc.
Bendix Aviation Corporation	The Publicker Industries
The United States Rubber Company	The National Association of Retail Grocers
Zellerbach Paper Company	The American National Retail Jewellers Association
Sharp and Dohme, Inc.	Paraffined Carton Association
Laminated Bakery Package Association	Farm Journal, Pathfinder, Inc.
Curtis Publishing Company	The Philadelphia Evening Bulletin
The Traffic Audit Bureau	The Advertising Research Foundation
J. Walter Thompson Co.	McKee and Albright, Inc.
Lamb, Smith and Keen, Inc.	The Rockefeller Foundation
Haverford College	The Western Saving Fund Society
The Real Estate Trust Company	John Wanamaker, Philadelphia
Bailey, Banks and Biddle Co.	Sixty-ninth Street Merchants Association
White and Case	Morgan, Lewis and Bockius
Blenko, Hoopes, Leonard & Glenn	Carl Seiler & Co.
Joseph E. Lewis & Co.	Scripto, Inc.

Table 1.1. Clients of the Alderson and Sessions Consulting Company
(Alderson and Sessions, 1955, pp. 6-7)

When Robert E. Sessions left the company, it became Alderson Associates. Alderson felt betrayed by Sessions leaving the firm at a time which put considerable pressure on the firm and Alderson financially (Bennett and Bennett, 2003).

Alderson enjoyed the high life and made sure that those friends, colleagues and clients who were with him were having a good time (Robinson, 2001). He enjoyed fine drink and food and entertained generously. Alderson knew the best restaurants in major cities around America and the world. He was proud to be known to the owners and chefs of these establishments (Robinson, 2003). Alderson is frequently described by those close to him as combining the attributes of a *gourmet* and a *gourmand* (Alderson, 2003, Halbert, 2003, Robinson, 2001, Robinson, 2003, Shapiro, 2001). He was a notoriously fast eater, downing his whole meal before his first time meal companion, Michael H. Halbert, had finished adjusting his serviette (Halbert, 2003), but that is not to say that he did not greatly enjoy his food.

Major Types of Consulting Organizations in the Marketing Research Field

Here are the major types of consulting organizations active in the marketing research field:

Complete Marketing Research Service Organizations

These are organizations headed by one or more individuals with broad experience in the marketing research field. Their activities, like the marketing research field itself, are problem-oriented. They are called in for aid with a marketing and/or marketing research problem. They recommend the approach which, in the light of their experience, seems to offer the client the greatest promise of making a profit contribution far in excess of its cost. They work in a world in which the three dimensions of the problem—the time dimension, the profit dimension, and the facilities dimension—are extremely important guides in their day-to-day activities.

Within this category there is a size distinction to be noted. A very few relatively large organizations belong in this grouping, along with a much larger number of middle-sized firms. In the case of the very large organizations—such as Alfred Politz Research, Inc. in New York or Alderson & Sessions in Philadelphia—a single assignment is likely to be handled on a team basis. The team will be under the guidance of one of the principals or partners in the firm but will represent the allocation to a single client or client's problem of only a moderate proportion of the organization's total personnel.

Figure 1.3. Description of Alderson and Sessions Consulting Company
(Crisp, 1957, pp. 765-766)

The consulting company was later sold to John Diebold and Associates, when Alderson was advised by his doctor to leave the stressful life of consultancy (Middleton, 1964, Sass, 1982). Alderson joined the staff of the Wharton Business School, but the academic life was not enough for Alderson and he set up Behavior Systems Research Company, in 1963 (Alderson, 1964a, Robinson, 2001). It was "a vehicle for his research and consulting interests" (Middleton, 1964, p. 2). Behavior Systems was run using functionalism as the basis for its consulting and research (Middleton, 1964). Upon Alderson's death, Behavior Systems was taken over by his partners and eventually sold (Alderson, 1965a).

One Hand Clapping

When times were good in the late 1950s, Wroe and Elsie built their home, *One Hand Clapping* in Royal Oak, Maryland, on Chesapeake Bay. The house on Chesapeake Bay was a special place for Wroe and his family, connecting them to nature. It was here that Wroe wrote much of his poetry. Alderson was heavily involved in designing the changes to the building and extensions to the meagre house and two cottages that were on the grounds at Royal Oak when he bought them (Bennett and Bennett, 2003). Alderson also had a boat channel dredged and a harbour shored up for his boats. He was not a particularly practical man and tools never lasted long around him, being neglected and falling into disuse (Bennett and Bennett, 2003).

There had been some tension in the Alderson house as Wroe had earlier purchased a farm for his mother and brothers to live on, before providing Elsie with a home that they owned, initially in Haverford (Bennett and Bennett, 2003). When his son Evan read Packard's *The Hidden Persuaders* (1958), it lead to many arguments, with Wroe defending business against what he saw as slurs (Alderson, 2001). Evan had the same moral strength as his father and, while studying at Berkeley, was involved in the free speech movement, to his father's discomfort. Evan spent a year in Vienna, Austria during his undergraduate studies, funded by Wroe, with whom he had an at times difficult relationship.

Wroe and Elsie sold their family home in Haverford in 1962 and commuted between an apartment close to Wharton, and the Maryland home, where Wroe had a boat, which was his pride and joy. It was a sign of having reached Alderson's inner sanctum to be invited on to the 'yacht' — a rather unspectacular 26 foot Trojan motor boat named *3rd Haven*, which allowed Alderson to live out his desire to be a 'country gentleman' (Bennett, 2001). Those who were invited onto the boat were his closest friends and colleagues (Fisk, 2001). He owned a number of other smaller yachts and boats, but his lack of maintenance lead to them rotting or falling into general disrepair (Bennett and Bennett, 2003). Alderson enjoyed entertaining and his students and colleagues were frequent guests to *One Hand Clapping*. Russell Ackoff, one of Alderson's colleagues, fondly remembers visiting *One Hand Clapping* with his wife and children and not seeing the children again until they left. Alderson would have been busy entertaining them with energy and enthusiasm (Ackoff, 2003).

8.   Alderson and Academia

In 1940, while a member of the Commercial Research Department of Curtis Publishing Company, Alderson was a contributing author to *Marketing* — with Ralph S. Alexander, Frank M. Surface and Robert F. Elder — an undergraduate textbook on marketing, considered to be one of the first managerial marketing textbooks (Bartels, 1962, Bartels, 1970). In contrast to the majority of textbooks, the chapters are identified with the individual authors (Alexander et al., 1940). The textbook was reprinted in 1944 (Alexander et al., 1949). Later editions were published, in 1949 and 1953, without the assistance of Robert F. Elder, who was unable to contribute due to pressures of work.

1948 saw Alderson take on the mantle of President of the American Marketing Association (AMA). Alderson was also heavily involved in The Institute of Management Sciences (TIMS) — later to become INFORMS — among a number of professional bodies (Bennett, 2001, Robinson, 2001).

Moving office and the pressures of business did not stop Alderson from his academic contributions and in 1948 he authored a paper, titled "Towards a Theory of Marketing", with Reavis Cox in the *Journal of Marketing* (Reprinted in Chapter 3 on page 39).

"Towards a Theory of Marketing" is undoubtedly one of Alderson's most influential articles and its influence can be seen in all of Alderson's published marketing theory. It sets out the building blocks for a theory of marketing, noting where theory can be borrowed and adapted to suit the needs of marketing. This paper notes the previously limited nature of marketing theory and research and calls for more research and theory in:

- problems of price discrimination

- spatial aspects of marketing

- temporal aspects of marketing

- attitudes and motivations of buyers and sellers. (Alderson and Cox, 1948)

The call for research into price discrimination is an early indicator of Alderson's ethical concerns with marketing.

In 1949 Reavis Cox and Wroe Alderson organised a symposium where invited authors presented papers on *Theory in Marketing*[3] — theory of how to

---

[3]It is clear from the contents of the book that the editors were concerned with the development of theory *of* marketing — a theory of how the market works — as well as theory *in* marketing.

do marketing — which was published as an American Marketing Association sponsored book in 1950. A second edition was published in 1964, with Stanley J. Shapiro as the third, and most active, editor, based on the papers from another invited symposium (Shapiro, 2001).

In the late 1940s Alderson demonstrated his social concern, setting up *Interns in Industry* in Chicago. It was a programme which involved college students spending time working on production lines and learning about the people that they would end up managing when they had graduated (Bennett and Bennett, 2003).

Alderson undertook graduate study at MIT and the University of Pennsylvania (Alderson, 1957a), but never gained a Ph.D.. According to Asia Alderson Bennett, Alderson, an otherwise confident man, was always aware of his lack of a doctorate, perhaps because of his wife's education (Bennett, 2001). However, to his colleagues in later years, he expressed a certain satisfaction at not having a doctorate and being a successful academic (Halbert, 2003). Alderson was offered at least a half dozen honorary doctorates, but turned them down because "those who have them [doctorates] have worked so hard to get them" (Halbert, 2003). Perhaps because he lacked a doctorate, Wroe was particularly proud of the awards he received in marketing and the reception of his books. His association with Wharton — the business school founded by a Quaker benefactor — also gave him pleasure (Bennett, 2001).

During the 1940s and 1950s, Alderson enjoyed membership in a philosophy club based around the faculty of Bryn Mawr, Swathmore and Haverford colleges. Most of the members were philosophers and Alderson delighted in sharing ideas with them and the philosophical discussions. In 1951 Alderson was published in *Philosophy of Science*, a hard journal for a philosopher to get into and a considerable achievement for someone with a background in business management. He also published in *Law and Contemporary Problems*, *Annals of the American Academy of Political and Social Science*, *Explorations in Entrepreneurial History*, *American Statistician*, and *Advanced Management*, along with a host of marketing periodicals and conferences throughout his career.

Alderson was a voracious reader and would "often buy one or more books a day", mainly history, philosophy, theology, fiction, psychology, behavioral psychology or mathematics (Bennett, 2001). Requiring little sleep, he was known to read several books in an evening. Alderson's writing often assumes that the reader is familiar with the basics, at least, of several of these disciplines, in part leading to the all too common complaint about his readability (Holbrook, 1998, Sheth et al., 1988).

In 1953, Alderson taught for the first time as a visiting professor at the Massachusetts Institute of Technology (MIT). He was also to teach or lecture at "the Universities of Illinois, Ohio State, Buffalo, Toronto, North Carolina,

Miami, Princeton, Johns Hopkins, Wisconsin and New York, at Case and Drexel Institutes," and to "have served as an Associate at the Harvard Business School and on the Advisory Council to the Department of Economics at Princeton" (Alderson, 1957a, Alderson, 1959). In 1953 he was inducted into the hall of fame for distribution, recognition of his work with the Department of Commerce and as a consultant, particularly on distribution cost accounting. Alderson was very proud of his association with MIT (Bennett, 2001).

In 1954 Alderson was awarded the Charles Coolidge Parlin award, sharing the award with Donald M. Hobart, vice president of the Curtis Publishing Company, for his contribution to the "application of a theoretical perspective for marketing derived by them from the general science of human behavior" (Robinson et al., 1976, p. 11). Alderson and Hobart had been friends before they worked together at Curtis Publishing Company and remained friends (Bennett and Bennett, 2003). The approval of his peers was very important to Alderson and to receive the award named after his mentor in marketing research was particularly appropriate. He wrote a short biography of Charles Coolidge Parlin in the 1956 *Journal of Marketing*.

Alderson was the only person to receive the Paul D. Converse prize for contribution to marketing twice. The first was in 1955 for his work on the Louisville Grocery survey, published in 1932, and general leadership in the development of marketing theory. The second award was given posthumously in 1967 for *Marketing Behavior and Executive Action* and Alderson's work on theory in marketing (Converse Award Committee, 2003).

Alderson was the father and director of the *Marketing Theory Seminars* (Wales and Dawson, 1979). The seminars were 'conferences as they should be' and, in some ways, influenced the early Macromarketing Seminars (Shapiro, 2001). Alternating between Boulder, Colorado, hosted by the University of Colorado, and Burlington, Vermont, hosted by the University of Vermont, the seminar attendees were invited to bring their families. Mornings were spent in discussion of 'issues' in marketing theory and afternoons were spent recreating together, often sailing or walking (Bennett, 2001). He was a friend to a number of very well known thinkers, including Russell L. Ackoff, William Baumol, Kenneth Boulding, C. West Churchman, Joel Dean, and Herbert A. Simon, who all visited the *Marketing Theory Seminars* at one time as Alderson's guest. Attendants, who were by invitation only, at the *Marketing Theory Seminars* included P.D. Converse, Donald Dixon, Al Doody, George Fisk, Bill Lazer, Stanley J. Shapiro, Monty Somers and Hugh Wales (Shapiro, 2001, Wales and Dawson, 1979).

No formal papers were presented, though Alderson would often prepare at length to present his latest thoughts, and no proceedings were produced. There was an attempt one year to record the discussion, but it broke down when an argument reached the level where the language could not be recorded (Dixon,

2001). The seminars could be both boring and exhilarating, but they built a community of scholars with interests in marketing theory and its development.

At one time the Alderson family was due to fly out of Denver and Wroe did not know where the airport was. The family sat white knuckled as Wroe 'found' the airport by watching where the planes were landing, as he drove through the city at exciting speeds (Bennett, 2001). He was known for his driving, enjoying fast driving and covering considerable distances by car. There was much relief that Alderson wasn't driving when he had his heart attack in 1965 (Bennett and Bennett, 2003).

Alderson was not always an easy man to get along with. He could be very generous with his ideas, as when he gave his notes on segmentation to Wendell Smith to write up. These were to become the award winning article 'Product Differentiation and Market Segmentation as Alternative Marketing Strategies' in the 1956 *Journal of Marketing* (Robinson, 2001, Monroe, 2001). Or he could be very protective of 'his' ideas. When Alderson picked up a new book, the first thing that he would do is go to the back to see if he was referenced, such was the confidence of the man (Robinson, 2001).

Wroe Alderson was a very intellectually vibrant man. He has been described as both a filter of ideas and a distributor of ideas (Robinson, 2001, Shapiro, 2001). He had an ability to bring to whatever he was thinking about relevant material from other disciplines in a way that surprised those around him (Alderson, 2001, Shapiro, 2001). Whether he was the originator of ideas or the person who saw their value in a wider, or other, situation, he was widely recognised as a genius (Ackoff, 2003, Fisk, 2001, Robinson, 2001, Shapiro, 2001).

Wroe Alderson formulated his theories in the functionalist paradigm, a paradigm which is almost unheard of today in marketing, but which he felt offered the only real possibility for fruitful marketing theorising in the 1950s (Alderson, 1957). Because of its rarity today, a definition is provided below.

Functionalism — or structural functionalism as it is also known — has been defined as:

> A theoretical perspective that views societies as integrated, harmonious, cohesive 'wholes' or 'social systems', where all parts ideally function to maintain equilibrium, consensus and social order. Rather like an organism, or body, societies are analysed in terms of their constituent parts, or 'sub-systems', all of which have to function efficiently if the overall 'health' and well-being of the organism or society are to be maintained. Thus the functionalist perspective on any feature of society or group, would question what function that feature performs for the social 'whole'. For example, what are the functions of language, of mass media systems and so on, how do they serve to maintain equilibrium and consensus, and how are they functionally interrelated to other social systems? (O'Sullivan et al., 1983, p. 95)

By seeking to understand the whole system, Alderson was looking at how the system could be improved (Alderson, 2001). In looking at society through functionalism, a number of sociologists, particularly Emile Durkheim (1858-1917) and Talcott Parsons (1902-1979), identified that often parts of the system may be functioning well, but at the cost of other parts of the system (society) (O'Sullivan et al., 1983). Functionalism as a research paradigm lends itself particularly to those with concern for ethics and marginalised members of society.

In 1957 Alderson's best known book, *Marketing Behavior and Executive Action*, was published to rave reviews (Mitchell, 1959, Mulvihill, 5859). It remains his most cited work. The functionalist/biological/systems approach that Alderson applied to the problem of how marketing works was justified in the first part of the book, before being expounded upon in the second part. The third part of the book applies that theory to the problems of the marketing manager.

In his recent review, Holbrook (2001) glowingly recommends Alderson's *Marketing Behavior and Executive Action* to a new generation of marketing scholars saying:

> So why do I recommend Wroe Alderson as the seminal source of a world-changing moment? It strikes me, in retrospect, that Alderson was far ahead of his time in the formulation of marketing theory generally and especially in expounding (1) the ecological view and (2) the experiential perspective. First, with respect to (1) the ecological view, Alderson was the earliest writer in my recollection to call attention to the importance of fitting into the environment and pursuing a niche that confers a selective advantage. In this, he anticipated ideas that later came to full flower under the headings of environmentalism, the ecological imperative, the systems view, and (more generally) macromarketing. Only a fine line separates Alderson's insights from the more elaborately formulated epiphanies preached by the most recent advocates of complexity theory such as Axelrod and Cohen (Harnessing Complexity,1999), John Holland (Emergence,1998), Kelly and Allison (The Complexity Advantage,1999), Roger Lewin (Complexity,1999), or Lewin and Regine (Weaving Complexity and Business,2001). In reading the contemporary works on chaos, fractals, complex adaptive systems, and how these concepts apply to the management of organizations, I frequently find myself wondering, "But isn't this what Alderson was saying back in the 1950s?" Second, regarding (2) the experiential perspective, Alderson was the first in our discipline to stress the importance of what Beth Hirschman and I came to call the "consumption experience." Clairvoyantly, Alderson recognized that customer value is derived not from an object itself but rather from the experience-providing service(s) that the object performs. This insight has served as the primary justification for about 90 percent of the work I have done in consumer research. Subsequently, I have found that various important economists, starting with Adam Smith and extending through Alfred Marshall and Lord Keynes, have voiced similar views — most articulately in the powerful writing of Lawrence Abbott (Quality and Competition,1955). Further, my work with Beth has been pre-dated and updated by that of other authors well worth reading such as Walter Woods (Consumer Behavior,1981) and Bernd Schmitt (Experiential Marketing,1999) or Pine and Gilmore (The Experience Economy,1999). Somewhere in Heaven, Wroe Alderson must be smiling (Holbrook, 2001, online).

In 1959 Alderson joined the faculty of the Wharton Business School where he was to work until he died. Alderson, in spite of his magnificent insights in writing, was not an inspiring teacher, at least not in the class room (Shapiro, 2001). He was known to teach in a monotone and to reserve his best insights for the staff club once he had had a couple of drinks. Those students who attended the bar with him found a lively man who was willing to share his wide knowledge and to challenge their point of view, whatever it may be.

He was not a great manager of people and when his assistant at Wharton, Stanley J. Shapiro, was absent from the office for a couple of weeks while moving, he returned to the office expecting to be questioned about that absence and found that Alderson had not even noticed. On one occasion Alderson rushed around the office preparing to get to a conference over the weekend only to return on Monday having gone a week early (Shapiro, 2001).

Alderson was, however, a great organizer, networker and visionary. In 1962 Alderson approached Thomas McCabe, Sr., former president of the Scott Paper company, and convinced him to invest in the setting up of the Marketing Science Institute (MSI), which was based next to the Wharton campus (Marketing Science Institute, 2001, Robinson, 2001). McCabe had the reputation to pull many corporate sponsors into the project and it was successfully run near Wharton for five years, before being moved to Harvard Business School in 1968 (Bloom, 1987, Robinson, 2001). Each of the companies sponsoring MSI was committed to $50 000 over 5 years (Robinson, 2003). Alderson was instrumental in hiring Wendell R. Smith as the first president and Patrick J. Robinson as the first research director (Robinson, 2001). Robinson had been employed by Alderson to work for Alderson Associates, but when he moved to Philadelphia Robinson found that Alderson Associates had been taken over by John Diebold and Associates (Robinson, 2001). Robinson left Alderson Associates and worked for a number of companies, including Mobil Oil, before renewing his working relationship with Alderson at the MSI (Robinson, 2001). Michael H. Halbert was another of Alderson's hirings to the MSI (Halbert, 2003). In the same year Paul Green joined the faculty at Wharton. He was to to work alongside Alderson and be heavily influenced by him (Green, 2001a).

In 1962 Alderson was also instrumental in setting up the Management Science Center at the University of Pennsylvania, which he directed, and the migration of the Case group, with director Russell L. Ackoff, to the University of Pennsylvania (Robinson, 2001).

After his second heart attack, in 1963, he decided that he wanted to live his life, even if it was to be shorter, and continued to enjoy those things which gave him pleasure (Bennett, 2001). Alderson threw himself into his work once more. While in his hospital bed he attempted a proof for Fermat's last theorem. The proof was considered plausible by qualified reviewers and he even considered submitting it towards a doctoral degree (Bennett and Bennett,

2003). On leaving hospital he was eager to complete his work on marketing theory and he redoubled his work rate for his remaining years.

The Analytical Framework for Marketing (1963) (reproduced in Chapter 4 on page 61) was a conference paper presented by Alderson at the *Conference of Marketing Teachers from Far Western States*, in Berkeley, which has appeared in the leading compilation of marketing articles, *Marketing Classics* since the first edition (1961) to the current edition, eighth (Enis et al., 1990). That this paper has been the lead article in every edition of *Marketing Classics*, until it was moved to the second chapter to accommodate Levitt's *Marketing Myopia* indicates its importance to marketing scholarship.

Alderson organised a symposium to gather the leading minds on the relatively new business topic of computing and published *Marketing and the Computer* in 1963 as a collection of the papers presented at the meeting. Alderson was a Ford Foundation Visiting Professor at New York University during part of 1963 (Sheth et al., 1988). He also visited Japan to share his business theory with the Japanese people as they sought to rebuild their country. Alderson was invited to give a number of seminars in Japan on marketing theory (Bennett, 2001). At the same time that the Japanese were listening to W. Edwards Deming on quality control, they were listening to Alderson on marketing (Wren, 1994). Japan was to have a lasting impression on Alderson and he collected Japanese ink drawings and garden sculpture on his return to America (Bennett, 2001). His students in Japan were to correspond with Wroe, and his wife Elsie after his death, for many years, sending letters and *haiku* — a three line poem syllables, see Figure 1.5 for one of the haiku sent to the Aldersons (Bennett, 2001). He was very pleased that his ideas had value across cultures (Bennett, 2001). In 1984, Alderson's *Marketing Behavior and Executive Action* was translated and published in Japanese (Alderson, 1984).

A deeply moral man, Alderson wrote "Ethics, Ideologies, and Sanctions" for the *Report of the Committee on Ethical Standards and Professional Practices* published in 1964 (Reprinted in Chapter 21 on page 301). He also gave speeches on ethics and business, including "The American Economy and Christian Ethics" a talk given to the Christian students association at the University of Pennsylvania (Reprinted in Chapter 22 on page 313), a topic of particular interest to him.

In 1964 Alderson (see Figure 1.4) also authored *Planning and Problem Solving in Marketing*, an expanded version of the third part of his 1957 *Marketing Behavior and Executive Action* with his Wharton colleague Paul Green (Alderson, 1963a). Another of Alderson's invited symposia lead to *Patents and Progress* which was published in 1965, addressing the topic of intellectual property long before it became the popular topic it is now.

Alderson's theories were heavily influenced by his strong Quaker beliefs (Alderson, 2001, Bennett, 2001, Green, 2001b). They were also formed, in large

Figure 1.4. Wroe Alderson circa 1964

SHORAIYA MINATSUTSUGANAKU TOSHITACHINU

The breeze over the pine tree
Everyone healthy and happy
Welcomes a new year

Kuninosuke Igarashi

Figure 1.5. Haiku sent to the Aldersons after Wroe's visits to Japan

part, during his years working for the Department of Commerce, preparing major studies, with very large datasets. His work as a consultant after World War II impacted on his view of the marketing system and he used his consulting projects to develop marketing theory (Rothberg, 2004). Alderson was somewhat unusual in that he spanned academic marketing and practical marketing and was so successful in both.

Additionally, Alderson's (1968) concern for those not benefiting from the marketing economy was likely to be a reflection of his early life, when he road the rails and undertook a series of menial jobs. His family was poor and didn't own a home, until he bought his mother and siblings one. He retained an active interest in those less fortunate throughout his life, working through Quaker organisations on behalf of the poor (Bennett, 2001).

Alderson's ethical concerns did not rest with the poor alone. He was explicit in his calls for fair pricing and accurate and honest promotion, all of which can be linked to the teachings of leading Quaker writers (Wooliscroft, 2000).

Alderson was among the first to call for the study of consumer behaviour to extend beyond the purchase, to include consumption of the product. He called for the study of hedenomics, the pleasure involved in consumption, to further understanding of the market system (Alderson, 1957, Alderson, 1965). He both read and published widely.

Alderson produced theory *of* marketing using his practical experiences and his wide reading of literature from philosophy and the social sciences to provide the basis for the theories. He was in a position to be labelled an *action researcher* because through his consulting and business activities he was able to change factors and see what happened (Gummesson, 2001). Action research is defined by Gummesson as:

> The concept of action research (or action science) is reserved for the situations when researchers assume the role of change agents of the processes and events they are simultaneously studying. In contrast to the mainstream researcher who is

> serenely detached, the action researcher is deeply involved. Applied to the study of business corporations and marketing, the action researcher can be a person who is both an academic researcher and either a marketing practitioner or an external consultant, a consumer or a citizen (Gummesson, 2001, p. 37).

Alderson filled all five roles that Gummesson proffers for an action researcher. He was an academic member of staff and researcher, a marketing practitioner (for his own firm Alderson Associates), an external consultant (for many clients) and both a consumer and a citizen.

He was also a *grounded theoretician* in that he came across the evidence of marketing and formed his theories, theories which were a departure from standard marketing thought. This departure from standard thought supports the suggestion that he was a grounded theorist — before grounded theory was made popular (Glaser and Strauss, 1967, Glaser, 1988, Glaser, 1992, Strauss and Corbin, 1990, Gummesson, 2001).

Alderson had the opportunity to use intuition in the way Gummesson uses the term,

> It is an elaborate integration of huge amounts of data, in a good sense subjectively processed in a nanosecond; it can be specified as 'implicitly systematic' (Gummesson, 2001, p. 34).

Wroe Alderson's works have continued to have influence on the discipline of marketing, though they are often not referenced. Alderson was certainly ahead of his times in many ways, a true visionary.

It was Memorial Day in 1965 when Alderson died on the shuffle board court in Maryland, he was not quite 67 years old. He had gathered gathered some of the doctoral students from Wharton for the weekend and was entertaining them when he suffered his final heart attack. His funeral was well attended and deeply moving (Robinson, 2001). An extract from his eulogy is reprinted in Chapter 32 on page 450.

He was a dedicated Quaker until his death (Green, 2001a). There are two Quaker magazines in Alderson's papers stored in the Wharton archives, which appear to be the current contents of his desk when he died, a token of his abiding and active interest in Quakerism and its beliefs.

Alderson was "the most influential marketing theorist to date" (Wooliscroft, 2003, p. 484). He has highly influenced almost all the schools of thought, as defined by Sheth et al. (1988) in marketing since 1960 (Wooliscroft, 2003). And yet he is rarely, if significantly, referenced today (Wooliscroft, 2003).

Elsie Star Wright Alderson survived her husband for 24 years before dying at the age of 91, on the 25th July 1989 (Philadelphia Inquirer, 1989, Bennett, 2001).

Asia Alderson Bennett rose to the position of executive secretary for the Philadelphia-based American Friends Service Committee, which Wroe had been a member of the board of before his death. She was very active in humanitarian aid and social justice projects, both in the United States and around the world. She is currently retired and living in Snohomish, Washington with her husband Lee, a retired geologist.

Maya Alderson Schulze, Wroe's youngest daughter lives with her husband in Ohio. In spite of Wroe's attitudes to women's roles he was disappointed when she married younger than he would have liked and abandoned her studies, in spite of showing an aptitude for things academic (Bennett, 2001).

Evan Alderson went on to be a professor and Dean of Arts at Simon Fraser University (Alderson, 2001). He continues to be involved in education and lives in Vancouver with his wife Ingrid.

9.   After Alderson's Death

After Alderson's death two books were published with him as author. Three signed book contracts were left in his personal effects. The contracts for the books — *Technological Change and Government Policy in Marketing*, *Theory and Practice of Advertising*, with Paul E. Green, J. W. Millard and Jack Rosenthal, and *Business and Society*, with Alfred Watson — were never fulfilled.

Wroe's three colleagues, Paul E. Green, Patrick J. Robinson and Michael Halbert, provided minor editing to the manuscript that Alderson had already sent to the publisher and *Dynamic Marketing Behavior*, an expanded version of the second section of Alderson's 1957 *Marketing Behavior and Executive Action*, was posthumously published in 1965. It was to be the pinnacle of Alderson's published theory *of* marketing (Alderson, 1963a).

In *Dynamic Marketing Behavior* Alderson left 150 falsifiable propositions. Those propositions have received very little attention. The shift from academic marketing being concerned with theory *of* marketing to theory *in* marketing has meant that many of those propositions have not been of interest to mainstream marketing research over the last 50 years (Wooliscroft, 2003).

Michael Halbert also authored *Men, Motives, and Markets*, based on Alderson's notes, in 1968 (Bennett and Bennett, 2003). Kernan, while reviewing *Men, Motives and Markets*, sums up Alderson's approach to theory and marketing.

> The late Wroe Alderson was the archtype of avant garde thinkers in marketing. For some three decades prior to his untimely death, he was the principal advocate of *theory* in[4] marketing, a fact which at first seems incongruous since his was one of the best known consulting firms. Theory that could not underpin action, however, was bad theory to him. Consequently, theory and policy were hardly antithetical (Kernan, 1970, p.96).

---

[4]Kernan uses the term theory in marketing to represent what has been defined in this biography as theory *of* marketing.

Kernan further finds that *Men, Motives and Markets*, while it is introductory, "seeks to display marketing's role in the economy. In the simplest of terms, it is about how the marketing process works and why" (Kernan, 1970, p.96). It is exactly this which Alderson sort to explain throughout his career and writing. "Wroe believed studying how business could operate better was part of making the world a better place" (Alderson, 2001).

He also indicates the ease of reading Alderson when he states:

> . . . it is exactly what one has come to expect of Alderson and Halbert. What *is* surprising is the craftsmanship brought to bear on such a broad and sweeping panorama of topics. Even the likes of these gentlemen are not *expected* to be so succinct (Kernan, 1970, p. 96).

Men, Motives and Markets is Alderson's last publication, other than reprints. As such it has a special place when considering the direction that he took over his publishing career. An extract from *Men, Motives and Markets* was published in *Marketing and Social Issues: An Action Reader*, edited by John R. Wish and Stephen H. Gamble (1971). The introduction to the section, in which Alderson's extract is included, notes Alderson's strong social responsibility and his call for:

1 *Finding better ways to move goods to the market.* Our urban ghettos and rural markets are two major population segments that require improved quality and lower cost of the goods they desire.

2 *Product innovation that meets the needs of our population.* We must place more effort on anticipating the application of new technologies to meet present and future needs.

3 *Bringing new people into the market economy.* Many persons in the United States are not really participating in the "affluence" that some enjoy (Wish and Gamble, 1971, p. 8).

Wish and Gamble's (1971) three goals of Alderson's theory building highlight Alderson's strong social conscience and his overriding desires for a theory of marketing, the betterment of society. It is no surprise that Alderson, a man who left home to ride the rails and with a deep conviction to the Quaker faith, retained a concern for those not as well off as himself.

References

Ackoff, Russell L. (2003). Personal Interview in his offices near Philadelphia on the 5th August.

Alderson, Evan (2001). Personal Interview conducted in his office at the Downtown campus of Simon Fraser University, Vancouver on the 5th of September.

Alderson, Evan (2003). Personal Interview conducted in his office at his home in Vancouver on the 19th of August.

Alderson, Wroe (1928). Advertising for Community Promotion. Technical Report Domestic Commerce Series No. 21, United States. Bureau of Foreign and Domestic Commerce (Department of Commerce), Washington. U. S. Government Print Office.

Alderson, Wroe (1932). Louisville Grocery Survey, pt. III, A-C; pt. IV. Technical Report Distribution Cost Studies, No. 11-14, United States. Bureau of Foreign and Domestic Commerce (Department of Commerce), Washington. U. S. Government Print Office.

Alderson, Wroe (1937). The Effect of Price Controls on Non-price Competition. *Law and Contemporary Problems*, 4(3):356–362.

Alderson, Wroe (1940). The Consumer Market - Income, Expenditure, and Savings. *Annals of the American Academy of Political and Social Science*, 209(1):1–13.

Alderson, Wroe (1951). A Systematics for Problems of Action. *Philosophy of Science*, 18(1):16–25.

Alderson, Wroe (1953a). Social Adjustment in Business Management. *Explorations in Entrepreneurial History*, 6(1):20–29.

Alderson, Wroe (1953b). Statistical Training for Marketing Research. *American Statistician*, 7(February):9–11.

Alderson, Wroe (1955). Operations Research And Management Problems. *Advanced Management*, 20(4):14–17.

Alderson, Wroe (1956). Biography of Charles Collidge Parlin. *Journal of Marketing*, 21(1/4):1–2.

Alderson, Wroe (1957a). Basic Research and The Future of Marketing Theory. In Bass, Frank M., editor, *The Frontiers of Marketing Science: Proceedings of the 1957 American Marketing Association Conference*, pages 170–178. American Marketing Association, Chicago.

Alderson, Wroe (1957b). *Marketing Behavior and Executive Action: A Functionalist Approach to Marketing*. Richard D. Irwin Inc., Homewood, Ill.

Alderson, Wroe (1959). Paper prepared for expert testimony.

Alderson, Wroe (1963a). Application for Ford Foundation Funding to Support PhD Students under Wroe Alderson, Ford Foundation Archives, Reel R1643, Grant number PA 64-14.

Alderson, Wroe (1963b). The Analytical Framework for Marketing. In Bliss, Perry, editor, *Marketing and Behavioral Sciences*, pages 25–40. Allyn and Bacon, Inc., Boston.

Alderson, Wroe (1964a). Needs, Wants and Creative Marketing. In Westing, Howard and Albaum, Gerald, editors, *Modern Marketing Thought: An Environmental Approach to Marketing*, pages 18–21. The MacMillan Company, New York. Reprinted from Cost and Profit Outlook, Vol. 8, No. 9, September, 1955.

Alderson, Wroe (1964b). The Strategy of Marketing Research. *Growth and Profit Planner*, 2(1):1,3.

Alderson, Wroe (1965b). *Dynamic Marketing Behavior: A Functionalist Theory of Marketing*. Richard D. Irwin Inc., Homewood, Ill.

Alderson, Wroe (1984). The Analytical Framework for Marketing. In Brown, Stephen W. and Fisk, Raymond, editors, *Marketing Theory: Distinguished Contributions*, pages 45–53. John Wiley & Sons, New York.

Alderson, Wroe (Circa 1965a). Correspondence from Alderson's partners in Behavior Systems after his death to Elsie Alderson.

Alderson, Wroe (n.d.). Letter sent home while travelling around explaining his inability to send money this month. Held in his personal papers.

Alderson, Wroe and Aiken, B. B. (1932). Merchandising Requirements of the Drug Store Package. Technical Report Domestic Commerce Series, No. 73, United States. Bureau of Foreign and Domestic Commerce (Department of Commerce), Washington. U. S. Government Print Office.

Alderson, Wroe and Bromell, John R. (1930). Problems of Wholesale Paint Distribution. Technical Report Distribution Cost Studies No. 8[a], United States. Bureau of Foreign and Domestic Commerce (Department of Commerce), Washington. U. S. Government Print Office.

Alderson, Wroe, Cary, Stephen G., Edgerton, William B., Moore, Hugh W., Pickett, Clarence E., and Zelliot, Eleanor (1956). *Meeting the Russians. American Quakers Visit the Soviet Union*. American Friends Service Committee, Philadelphia.

Alderson, Wroe and Cox, Reavis (1948). Towards a Theory of Marketing. *Journal of Marketing*, 13(October):137–152.

Alderson, Wroe and Green, Paul (1964). *Planning and Problem Solving in Marketing*. Richard D. Irwin Inc., Homewood, Ill.

Alderson, Wroe and Haag, Jr., Frederick (1931). Problems of Wholesale Electrical Goods Distribution. Technical Report Distribution Cost Studies No. 9, United States. Bureau of Foreign and Domestic Commerce (Department of Commerce), Washington. U. S. Government Print Office.

Alderson, Wroe and Halbert, Michael H. (1968). *Men, Motives and Markets*. Prentice-Hall Inc., Englewood Cliffs, N.J.

Alderson, Wroe and Martin, M. W. (1965). Toward a Formal Theory of Transactions and Transvections. *The Journal of Marketing Research*, 2(May):117–127.

Alderson, Wroe and Meserole, W. H. (1932). Drug Store Arrangement. Technical Report Domestic Commerce Series No. 57, United States. Bureau of Foreign and Domestic Commerce (Department of Commerce), Washington. U. S. Government Print Office.

Alderson, Wroe and Miller, N. A. (1930). Problems of Wholesale Dry Goods Distribution. Technical Report Distribution Cost Studies No. 7, United States. Bureau of Foreign and Domestic Commerce (Department of Commerce), Washington. U. S. Government Print Office.

Alderson, Wroe and Miller, Nelson A. (1934). Costs, Sales, and Profits in the Retail Drug Store. Technical Report Domestic Commerce Series, No. 90, United States. Bureau of Foreign and Domestic Commerce (Department of Commerce), Washington. U. S. Government Print Office.

Alderson, Wroe and Sessions, Robert E. (circa 1955). Advertising pamphlet.

Alderson, Wroe and Shapiro, Stanley J., editors (1963). *Marketing and the Computer*. Prentice-Hall Inc., Englewood Cliffs, N.J.

Alderson, Wroe, Terpstra, Vern, and Shapiro, Stanley J., editors (1965). *Patents and Progress: The Sources and Impact of Advancing Technology*. Richard D. Irwin Inc., Homewood, Ill.

Alexander, Ralph S., Surface, Frank M., and Alderson, Wroe (1949). *Marketing*. Ginn & Company, Boston.

Alexander, Ralph S., Surface, Frank M., and Alderson, Wroe (1953). *Marketing*. Ginn & Company, Boston, 3rd edition.

Alexander, Ralph S., Surface, Frank M., Elder, Robert F., and Alderson, Wroe (1940). *Marketing*. Ginn and Company, Boston.

Bartels, Robert (1962). *The Development of Marketing Thought*. Richard D. Irwin, Homewood, Ill.

Bartels, Robert (1970). *Marketing Theory and Metatheory*. Richard D. Irwin, Homewood, Ill.

Bartels, Robert (1988). *The History of Marketing Thought*. Publishing Horizons, Inc., Columbus, Ohio.

Baumol, W. J. (1959). *Business Behavior, Value and Growth*. The MacMillan Company, New York.

Bennett, Asia (2001). Personal Interview conducted in her home in Snohomish, Washington, on the 4th of September.

Bennett, Asia and Bennett, Lee (2003). Personal communication [email] received 24th of March.

Bloom, Paul N. (1987). *Knowledge Development in Marketing: The MSI Experience*. Marketing Science Institute and Lexington Books, Lexington, Massachusetts.

Brown, Lesley (1993). *The New Shorter Oxford English Dictionary: On Historical Principles. Volume 1, A-M*. Clarendon Press, Oxford.

Converse Award Committee (2003). Previous Converse Award Winners.

Cox, Reavis and Alderson, Wroe (1950). *Theory in Marketing*. Richard D. Irwin, Chicago.

Cox, Reavis, Alderson, Wroe, and Shapiro, Stanley J., editors (1964). *Theory in Marketing: Second Series*. Richard D. Irwin, Homewood, Ill.

Crisp, Richard D. (1957). *Marketing Research*. McGraw-Hill Book Company, New York.

Crosby, Alfred W. (1989). *America's Forgotten Pandemic, The Influenza of 1918*. Cambridge University Press, Cambridge.

Dixon, Don (2001). Personal Interview conducted in his home near Philadelphia on the 14th of August.

Enis, Ben M., Cox, Keith K., and Mokwa, Michael P., editors (1990). *Marketing Classics*. Prentice Hall, Upper Saddle River, eighth edition.

Fisk, George (2001). Personal Interview conducted at his home in the Jordan apartments, Philadelphia on the 14th of August.

Fitch, Lyle and Taylor, Horace, editors (1946). *Planning for Jobs: Proposals Submitted in the Pabst Postwar Employment Awards*. The Blakiston Company, Philadelphia.

Galbraith, John Kenneth (2002). Personal Communication dated 24 June, 2002.

Galbraith, John Kenneth (2003). Personal Interview conducted at his home in Cambridge Massachusetts on the morning of the 16th of August.

Glaser, B. G. (1988). *Theoretical Sensitivity*. Sociology Press, Mill Valley, California.

Glaser, B. G. (1992). *Basics of Grounded Theory Analysis*. Sociology Press, Mill Valley, California.

Glaser, B. G. and Strauss, A. L. (1967). *The Discovery of Grounded Theory*. Aldine, New York.

Green, Paul E. (2001a). Personal Interview conducted at the Washington D.C. Hilton on the 11th of August.

Green, Paul E. (2001b). The Vagaries of Becoming (and Remaining) a Marketing Research Methodologist. *Journal of Marketing*, 64(July):104–108.

Gummesson, Evert (2001). Are Current Research Approaches in Marketing Leading Us Astray? *Marketing Theory*, 1(1):1–27.

Halbert, Michael (2003). Personal Interview conducted in his home near Philadelphia on the 6th August.

Hogan, Gerard (2003). Personal Communication [email] dated 26th of February.

Holbrook, Morris B. (1998). Closely Read Books - Marketing Literature, Consumption as Text, and the Leaves from Our Lives: Slow, Slower, and Slowest. *Journal of Marketing*, 62(July):141–151.

Holbrook, Morris B. (2001). Wroe Alderson (1957) Marketing Behavior and Executive Action. *ACR News*, pages 37–38.

Hollander, Stanley C. (1998). Lost in the Library. *Journal of Marketing*, 62(January):114–123.

Hollander, Stanley J. (2001). Personal Interview conducted in his office at Michigan State University, East Lansing, on the 20th of August.

Jones, D. G. Brian and Shaw, Eric H. (2002). A History of Marketing Thought. In Weitz, Barton A. and Wensley, Robin, editors, *Handbook of Marketing*, pages 39–65. Sage Publications, Thousand Oaks, Ca.

Kernan, Jerome B. (1970). Men, Motives, and Markets, By Wroe Alderson and Michael H. Halbert (Book review). *Mississippi Valley Journal of Business and Economics*, 5(2):96–97.

Lusch, R. F. (1980). Alderson, Sessions, and the 1950s Manager. In Lamb, C., editor, *Theoretical Developments in Marketing*, pages 4–6. American Marketing Association, Chicago.

Marketing Science Institute (2001). Marketing Science Institute Featured Academic: Paul Green: Mastering Tradeoffs. http://www.msi.org/msi/facad-pg.cfm.

Middleton, Kenneth A. (1964). Why Behavior Systems? *Growth and Profit Planner*, 2(1):2.

Mitchell, Glen H. (1959). Wroe Alderson, Market Behavior and Executive Action: A Functionalist Approach to Marketing Theory (Book Review). *Journal of Farm Economics*, 41(4):853–855.

Monroe, Kent (2001). Personal Interview conducted in his office at the University of Illinois, Urbana Champagne on the 23rd of August.

Mulvihill, Donald F. (1958/59). Book Reviews: Marketing Behavior and Executive Action. *Southern Economic Journal*, 25(1/4):113–114.

O'Sullivan, Tim, Hartley, John, Saunders, Danny, and Fiske, John (1983). *Key Concepts in Communication*. Methuen & Co. Ltd, London.

Packard, Vance (1958). *The Hidden Persuaders*. Pocket Books, Inc., New York.

Philadelphia Inquirer (1989). Elsie Alderson, 91; Active in Friends. Obituary column, August 6.

Robinson, Patrick J. (2001). Personal Interview conducted in his home near Philadelphia on the 14th of August.

Robinson, Patrick J. (2003). Personal Interview conducted at the Aronimink Golf Club, Newton Square Pennsylvania on the 5th of August.

Robinson, Patrick J., Blazovic, Vincent P., Green, Paul E., Buell, Victor P., Linnemann, Robert E., Corbin, Arnold, and Michner, Walter W. (1976). *The Charles Coolidge Parlin Awards: Thirty Years of Achievements in Marketing*. The Parlin Board of Governors and the Philadelphia Chapter of the American Marketing Association, Philadelphia.

Rothberg, Robert (2004). Interview conducted in the boardroom, Fairmont Vancouver Hotel, Vancouver, Canada on the 30th of May.

Sass, Steven A. (1982). *The Pragmatic Imagination. A History of the Wharton School 1881-1981*. University of Pennsylvania Press, Philadelphia.

Shapiro, Stanley J. (2001). Personal Interview conducted in his room at the Delta Suites Hotel, Vancouver on the 6th September.

Sheth, Jagdish N., Gardner, David M., and Garrett, Dennis E. (1988). *Marketing Theory: Evolution and Evaluation*. John Wiley and Sons, Inc., New York.

Smith, Wendell R. (1956). Product Differentiation and Market Segmentation as Alternative Marketing Strategies. *Journal of Marketing*, 21(July):3–8.

Smith, Wendell R. (1966). Leaders in Marketing: Wroe Alderson. *Journal of Marketing*, 30(January):64–65.

Strauss, Anselm and Corbin, Juliet (1990). *Basics of Qualitative Research*. Sage, Newbury Park, California.

Tamilia, Robert (2002). Personal Communication, received 27 September, 2002.

The New York Times (1965). Wroe Alderson, 66, of Wharton School. Obituary column, June 2.

Wales, Hugh G. and Dawson, Jr., Lyndon E. (1979). The Anomalous Qualities Between Present-Day Conferences and Alderson's Marketing Theory Seminars. In Ferrell, O. C., Brown, Stephen W., and Lamb, Jr., Charles W., editors, *Conceptual and Theoretical Developments in Marketing*, pages 222–227. American Marketing Association, Chicago.

Wish, John R. and Gamble, Stephen Holland (1971). *Marketing and Social Issues: An Action Reader*. John Wiley and Sons, Inc., New York.

Wooliscroft, Ben (2000). Examining a Case for Quaker Influence on Modern Marketing Theory. In Shultz, C. J. II and Grbac, B., editors, *Marketing Contributions to Democratization and Socioeconomic Development Proceedings of Macromarketing 2000*, pages 326–336. University of Rijeka.

Wooliscroft, Ben (2003). Wroe Alderson's Influence on Marketing Theory through His Textbooks. *Journal of the Academy of Marketing Science*, 31(4):481–490.

Wren, Daniel A. (1994). *The Evolution of Management Thought*. John Wiley & Sons, Inc., New York, fourth edition.

II

ALDERSON'S THEORY OF MARKET BEHAVIOR — SELECTED WRITINGS

Chapter 2

INTRODUCTION TO PART II: WROE ALDERSON'S THEORY OF MARKET BEHAVIOR — SELECTED WRITINGS

Ben Wooliscroft

Wroe Alderson sought to provide the marketing discipline with a theory of how marketing works (theory of marketing), with the benefit of allowing marketers to improve the marketing system. His writings on how a manager should act, or theory in marketing, were always couched in his theory of marketing. When deciding which selections we should provide the reader, the editors were confronted with many difficult decisions. Alderson wrote richly and widely and these selections are not intended to replace reading Alderson's works, merely to provide an introduction to the richness that those pages hold. We have selected the papers and concepts which we see as being key to gaining an understanding of Alderson's theory of marketing.

The first paper included in this part is Alderson and Cox's (1948) "Towards a Theory of Marketing". This paper is a stepping off point for Alderson's concerted effort to develop a theory of marketing. It is a paper which details from where the authors saw the possibility to draw theory from other disciplines and the need for and purposes of a theory of marketing. Alderson was to spend the rest of his life working on this project, developing a theory of marketing.

The second item included, "An Analytical Framework for a Theory of Marketing" is by virtue of its continued inclusion in *Marketing Classics* one of Alderson's most reproduced papers. It is a paper originally presented at a late 1950s conference of marketing educators. It details how Alderson believed marketing should be taught and provides an easily understandable introduction to Alderson's thoughts on how marketing works.

The next two chapters deal with Alderson's organized behavior systems, the unit of analysis of his theories. The first chapter reproduces his paper in *Theory in Marketing* (1950) and provides an introduction to his organized behavior system concept, rationality in those systems and their goal of survival. The second chapter is from *Marketing Behavior and Executive Action* (1957) and focuses on the firm as an organized behavior system. It provides a more in depth treatment of the survival of the firm as an organized behavior system, and of the ways that survival can be accomplished, notably through growth.

The fifth chapter in this part, from *Marketing Behavior and Executive Action* (1957), discusses the "power principle", the necessity of organized behavior systems seeking power in order to continue to survive and grow. The power principle is not the unbridled seeking of power, rather the appropriate use and development of power to maximise the future opportunities of the organized behavior system in its environment.

The chapter "The Principle of Postponement", from *Marketing Behavior and Executive Action* (1957), is one of Alderson's temporal concepts. In taking a medium to long-run view on efficiency in the market place, he observes the possibility for the reduction in risk associated with postponing decisions about a product's final form until the latest practical time. This approach has obvious parallels in just-in-time production management.

In the next chapter, from *Marketing Behavior and Executive Action* (1957), Alderson's theory of the firm is built around the search for differential advantage as a means to firm survival. This chapter, "Competition for Differential Advantage", provides Alderson's thoughts on firms operating in a heterogeneous marketplace and the ways in which they can achieve a differential advantage. The opportunities for firms, or organized behavior systems, to compete in the market place are expounded upon comprehensively. Later in this book Alderson's differential advantage theory is compared with the more recent Resource-advantage theory (see Chapter 33 on page 453).

In the chapter "Matching and Sorting: The Logic of Exchange", from *Marketing Behavior and Executive Action* (1957), Alderson explains the purpose of exchange in the heterogeneous market place. He outlines the sorting processes involved in matching heterogeneous demand and supply in a market place. This represents an important departure from mainstream economic thought with its reliance on the underlying assumption of homogeneity of supply and demand. The sorts (sorting out, accumulation, allocation, assortment) combined with transformations provide a means to understand the processes of the market place in providing a finished product which has the appropriate form, time and space utility for the end consumer.

There follow two chapters on functionalism, the paradigm in which Alderson prepared his theory of marketing. The first chapter, from *Dynamic Marketing Behavior* (1965), is Alderson's introduction to the use of the functionalist paradigm, providing a justification for functionalism over the alternative paradigms he considered. In this chapter Alderson also discusses the levels of theory of marketing that could be prepared in a functionalist paradigm. The following chapter "Functionalism: Descriptive and Normative" justifies Alderson's provision of a normative — rather than descriptive as he is often accused of providing — theory of the market place in *Dynamic Marketing Behavior*

One must conclude that something has gone wrong with the method of attack — that a new and creative analysis is required.

Northrop, in his stimulating study of the logic of research,[2] holds that the most difficult part of an inquiry usually is its initiation. As he sees matters, inquiry begins with a problem circumstances have called to someone's attention. Ordinarily the problem arises because newly discovered facts upset accepted explanations.

The first step is to analyze the problem imaginatively, since its nature will dictate the methods that must be used to solve it. From the analysis of the problem springs an understanding of the sorts of fact that must be assembled to answer it and of the methods by which they can be assembled. After this come the actual assembly of the facts required, description and classification of these facts, derivation from them of fruitful and relevant hypotheses, and verification of the hypotheses thus deductively derived by inductive appeal to further facts.

Apparently what marketing men now seek in their appeal to theory is imaginative guidance into such a creative analysis of the problems of marketing. This can be put another way. Events in recent years have forced students of marketing to put a heavy emphasis upon problems of private management and public policy. One result has been to reveal the inadequacy of the earlier years of study in the field, which proceeded by almost haphazard accumulation of facts. It has become evident that if the difficulties raised by events in the areas of public and private policy as applied to marketing are to be solved, they must be put into a framework that provides a much better perspective than is now given by the literature. Only a sound theory of marketing can raise the analysis of such problems above the level of an empirical art and establish truly scientific criteria for setting up hypotheses and selecting the facts by means of which to test them.

3.   Specific Reasons for the Interest in Marketing Theory

The nature of the demand students of marketing are making upon their would-be theorists can be clarified further by considering some of the specific problems they feel need to be treated inadequately in the existing literature. Northrop, as we have seen, suggests that a problem calling for the initiation of some systematic inquiry usually makes its appearance when existing theories fail to satisfy students because they do not account for or take into consideration all of the relevant observed facts. In essence, this is today's situation in the study of marketing.

Conclusions as to policy and procedure in the field of marketing, and particularly those derived from the so-called principles stated in manuals of man-

---

[2]F. S. C. Northrop, The Logic of the Sciences and the Humanities, Macmillan Co., New York, 1947.

agement or in the great body of general economic theory, often seem not to jibe with the observable facts. Furthermore, a good many such problems are thrown at marketing men where the facts have not been collected or, even more important, where no one has a clear understanding of the sorts of facts that must be assembled and analyzed. A few illustrations will serve to make clear the present less-than-satisfactory position of marketing theory.

(1) Problems of Price Discrimination

Difference in the prices competing buyers pay for goods bought from a common supplier or in the prices they receive from a common buyer raise critical problems of managerial and public policy. Here, as in other aspects of economic life, we come up against the twentieth century's version of an ancient problem—that of the just or fair price. Laws have been enacted and the courts have rendered judgments under these laws that alter profoundly prevailing views as to what is socially desirable in pricing and what is not.

Among marketing men there exists an uneasy feeling that at least some of the policies thus being established would be substantially different if the facts of marketing as they ought to be known to marketing men were included in the supporting theories. In particular, it seems to be felt that the policy decisions rest upon a careless acceptance of mere conventions as objective facts. Thus the conventional definition of price in narrow terms as a ratio between quantities of money and quantities of goods, rather than in terms of completely negotiated sales transactions, is taken to denominate price in connotations where only the broader definition can be valid.[3] Yet marketing men have done virtually nothing to correct the situation by defining a completely negotiated sales transaction and proceeding to work out theories based upon it.

(2) Spatial Aspects of Marketing

Students of the economics of land utilization have given much attention to problems raised by the location of various kinds of economic activity. Students of marketing have made very little contribution to that discussion. This is true despite the fact that repeatedly they must give attention to related managerial problems. For example, they often help business men determine how large a trading area is served by a particular store or by a particular cluster of stores. They advise operators as to where within a particular trading area a retail or wholesale enterprise should locate its physical facilities.

---

[3]Some aspects of this problem were considered in an earlier article by one of the present authors: Reavis Cox, "Non-Price Competition and the Measurement of Prices," Journal of Marketing, Vol. X, No. 4, April 1946, pp 370-383.

Neither the marketing man nor the analyst of land utilization had received much help from the general economist, with his theories of pure rent and his tendency simply to assume rather than to explain the existence of a spatial distribution of marketing activities such that forces of supply and demand can in some significant sense be brought to a focus in price. Hence, it appears that marketing men should assume the task of working out concepts that have true significance in analyzing the nature of the distributive space through which goods and services are marketed and the nature of the force that have brought the existing distributive pattern into existence.

(3) Temporal Aspects of Marketing

Economic theory has sometimes evaded problems raised by time through analyzing instantaneous relationships instead of utilizing period analysis. This procedure in effect reduces the economy to a timeless universe in which other problems become more amenable to analysis. A market becomes an organization existing in full maturity at a given instant of time, rather than an organism growing and changing through time. Price becomes a unit of behavior taken at a particular instant and resulting from the interplay of forces that work themselves out instantaneously, rather than a structure or pattern extending over time. Consumption becomes an instantaneous process rather than one that requires appreciable periods of time.

Under some circumstances these distortions of fact do no harm and may be very helpful; but they also lead to erroneous results when the economist forgets to drop his rigid assumptions as he works with problems for which the passage of time is critically important, such as the negotiation of transactions, trading in futures, and the consumption of consumers' durables.

Unfortunately, many marketing people have themselves accepted uncritically conclusions resting upon such misleading assumptions. Only now are they coming to realize that theories built upon this kind of foundation fail to conform to what they know concerning the facts of price structures and price policies, of commodity exchanges, and of the use of consumer credit to finance the purchase of durables. It is clear that new concepts and new analyses based on new and more realistic assumptions are required if the nature and significance of market phenomena involving the passage of appreciable periods are to be explored thoroughly.

(4) Economic Entities

For purposes of economic analysis it is conventional to work with entities that are not always readily observable or measurable in the flesh. They are arbitrarily assumed to exist as identifiable units that make decisions and engage in economic behavior. They consequently are extremely important in analyses of the ways in which economic decisions are reached. The firm, the market, and the economy are excellent illustrations.

Exposure to day-to-day problems and processes in marketing has suggested to some students that there are purposes for which other entities may be more meaningful. Thus in working with the problems raised by marketing functions and the costs of performing them, perhaps the market channel is a more meaningful concept than any of these others. Again, the dispersion market may be singled out for meaningful analyses. Yet again, marketing men know that for some purpose the most meaningful analysis emerges when, contrary to the most usual custom among economists, emphasis is put upon cooperative rather than upon competitive behavior. Economics as a pattern of mutually interacting and supporting activities consciously directed toward accomplishing a common, over-all task, is a concept as valid as the one that emphasizes rivalry and competition in efforts to gain individual advantage. For an understanding of marketing as a social instrument, it may be the essential concept.

Despite the need, marketing men have made little progress toward setting up new fruitful concepts of economic entities derived from their experiences of economic activity or toward working out theoretical formulations based upon such concepts. In particular they have done little toward working out a theory of cooperation in the broad sense, although they have given much attention to formally organized enterprises that describe themselves as cooperative rather than as competitive businesses.

(5) Limitations upon the Alternatives Open to Economic Entities

Much of the prevailing economic theory and many of the public policies based upon it proceed upon the assumption that business management and the management of consumption both operate by making decisions intended to maximize results under a continuous function. Little or no weight is given to the fact that decisions are really discontinuous (made in "lumps" or "bundles," as it were) and that real choices must be made from specific alternatives of quite limited number and scope. Marketing men know these facts, yet they have done very little toward setting up alternative formulations based upon what they know concerning the limitations within which managers and consumers operate.

(6) Attitudes and Motivations of Buyers and Sellers

Every theory of management as well as every theory of economic behavior must rest upon some concept of human motivations and attitudes. The concepts, implicit or explicit, that underlie much of economic theory, clearly fall far short of conforming to the facts of human behavior. Although one turns first to psychologists for correctives, students of marketing themselves have a better

much of whose work consists of seeking out general patterns of group behavior, should find this approach particularly fruitful.

It should be remembered that marketing men call one of their traditional approaches to the study of marketing the institutional approach. As used by most marketing men (the recently published text by Edward A. Duddy and David A. Revzan being a conspicuous exception), the term has been restricted to efforts to describe what goes on in marketing by classifying, describing and analyzing the operations of the two million or so individual establishments that participate in marketing. This approach is not institutional in the sociologist's sense. It is nevertheless adaptable to a more fundamental and far-reaching approach that would treat retailers, wholesalers and other entities active in marketing as institutions in the true sociological usage of the term. In this view, the agencies of marketing would become patterns of human behavior and communication clustered about some physical facility, such as a store or warehouse, that can be identified and located for counting and measurement. Similarly the economic entities discussed about could be viewed as clusters or patterns of group behavior.

Individual economists of the institutional school also offer specific fruitful ideas for the development of marketing theory. Thus John R. Commons provides the basic inspiration for dividing transactions into routine and fully negotiated ones. Upon this idea can be built a meaningful analysis of changes in the ways buyers and sellers do business and of the significances of these changes for costs of marketing.

Von Neumann and Morgenstern have taken the fully negotiated transaction as their point of departure in a book that brings a new mathematical approach to the analysis of market behavior. This may turn out to be the genuine revolution in economic theory which has been presaged by such diverse developments as Keynes' challenge of Says' Law of Markets and the recasting of competitive theory by Chamberlin and others. Starting from an exhaustive analysis of the negotiated transaction they offer hope of a fresh attack on such problems as efficiency in distribution and monopolistic restriction.

Clark's pioneer work on overhead costs provided a source from which stems directly or indirectly, much of the fruitful effort of marketing men to work out definitions of cost and of the relations between cost and price from which in time will almost certainly come significant contributions to the theory of marketing.

Marketing is of necessity involved with competition and price. Therefore the core of marketing theory might well be modern price theory with its stress on different types of competitive situations.

The work of E. H. Chamberlin, Joan Robinson, Robert Triffin as well as such men as Bain and others in analyses of non-perfect competition, offers an especially vital challenge to marketing theorists. Marketing men will certainly follow their lead in questioning the validity as statements of fact of the assumptions underlying much traditional economic theory. As the same time, marketing men have every opportunity to advance monopolistic competition theory in providing alternative assumptions and hypotheses drawn from experience in the market.

Certainly the last word has not been said on product differentiation as a factor in what Triffin calls heterogeneous competition — a term, incidentally, which well might replace "monopolistic competition" as being more descriptive and not so weighed with objectionable connotations. Economic discussions tend to assume that product differentiation always represents a departure from uniformity but the reverse may be true with respect to units produced by a firm which differentiates. Suppose there is a field in which each producer is making a great many varieties of the same article in accordance with the diverse specifications demanded by purchasers. Then one enterprising firm has an opportunity to steal a march on competition by manufacturing only identical units. By adopting a standard formula within its own business it may achieve substantial advantages in mass production economies and be obliged to use only part of the savings in sales and advertising expenses to attract to itself the buyers who are willing to accept its standardized product.

More broadly it may be said that differentiation is a basic function of the market which is carried out primarily through the channels of distribution and which is intimately related to the problem of efficiency in marketing. Chamberlin recognizes time and place utility and all specialized services as aspects of product differentiation but does not treat the subject exhaustively. For marketing theory a crucial problem is the point in the flow at which differentiation does or should take place. As a general principle it seems clear that it should be avoided as long as possible to maximize the proportion of the distribution job which can enjoy the economics of minimum differentiation.

The relation of sales cost to competition has been touched upon by many writers but remains an item of unfinished business for marketing theory. The general assumption appears to be that the effect of competition in imperfect markets is to raise sales costs. This assumption needs to be tested against an analysis which starts from the negotiated sale transaction as the norm and recognizes that there may be many ways of achieving the relative economy of routine sales transactions. Advertising may help to perform for one class of products the simplification of transactions achieved through commodity exchanges in another. It is not likely that distribution can ever achieve the economics which arise from the use of power machinery in production. It is well to remember, however, that specialization and routinization provide the original basis for improving efficiency in both production and distribution.

One of the most profound questions with respect to the heterogeneous competition which prevails in our economy today is whether we can develop a theory of competition which has any real relevance for public policy on such matters as the regulation of marketing policy. The apparent willingness of many influential economists to throw over the benefits of mass production in order to achieve a closer approach to atomistic competition is surely unrealistic. Following J. M. Clark and Robert Triffen, a radical revision of competition theory may revolve around overhead costs and differentiated market position in a heterogeneous economy. Empirical studies of competition indicate that these two factors can provide the basis for dynamic equilibrium.

The direction for advance which is indicated here is an analysis of the process of price negotiation and the conditions for a balance of economic forces achieved through bargaining. Ordinarily there are limits observed by either side and principles by which their bargaining activities are guided which may result in a long-run outcome with respect to prices which is not too different from the long-run outcome under the supposition of pure competition. In a mass production economy the central consideration in negotiation may generally be expected to be the endeavor to balance access to markets through diversified channels against the need for enough volume to reach the breaking point in production costs.

The development of the so-called macroeconomics in recent years largely under the influence of Keynes has concentrated the attention of economists on national aggregates such as total consumer income, the level of employment, consumer expenditures, and capital formation. The results which may be hoped for in more reliable estimates and predictions of these aggregates have great practical significance for marketing research, which is quite generally concerned with evaluating the outlook for individual concerns or products. The theoretical significance of Keynes for marketing lies in other directions, as for example in underscoring the importance of market organization by advancing the thesis that the automatic functioning of the market mechanism cannot be taken for granted.

Work such as that exemplified in Bertil Ohlin's analysis of inter-regional trade has already provided the conceptual basis for one course in the theory of marketing.[5] It has also provided foundations for more meaningful analyses than have been widely attempted as yet of the economics of trading areas, economic regions within a national economy, and the various sections of a metropolitan community. Beginnings have been made towards these sorts of analyses; but

---

[5]This is a course in the theory of domestic commerce organized by E. T. Grether at the University of California. So far as the present writers have been able to discover, only three courses are currently given in the colleges of the country that specifically undertake a systematic presentation of a theory of marketing. In addition to Dean Grether's course, there is one given by E. D. McGarry at the University of Buffalo that builds upon an analysis of the functions of marketing. The third, given by Reavis Cox at the University of Pennsylvania, is built around analyses of the meaning and measurement of location in and flow through distributive space and time, problems of human behavior, patterns of social communications, prices and price structure, and problems of efficiency, waste and productivity.

they offer fruitful opportunities for more penetrating studies than have yet been made.

(2) Contributions from Systematic Studies of Group Behavior

A second possible source for contributions to the evolving theory of marketing will be found in studies of group behavior made by social scientists in fields other than economics, and notably in the work of anthropologists, sociologists and social psychologists. George Lundberg's application to marketing in his Parlin lecture of his concepts of measurable patterns and clusters of communication is an example of what can be done with ideas borrowed directly from sociology. It offers a promising device to be used in analyzing the economic significance of such entities as cities, towns, trading centers, trading areas and individual retailers with their customers and their sources of supply; of advertising media and those they reach; and of the multitude of other patterns of communication through which human wants are converted into economic demand, information is distributed among sellers and buyers, and transactions are negotiated and carried into effect.

Kenneth Boulding speculates in a recent article on the limitations of the principle of maximization of returns as the foundation of the theory of the individual business enterprise. He suggests that the principle of organizational preservation may turn out to be more fruitful. One of the authors of this article has pointed out that organizations act as if they had a will to survive and that this drive arises from the individual's struggle for socio-economic status.[6]

Among psychologists, the topological concepts developed by the late Kurt Lewin and expounded in somewhat simpler form by his former student Robert W. Leeper, offer some promise of setting up procedures that may lead to a more effective understanding of human motivation than has thus far been achieved. In the field of industrial relations, Elton Mayo at Harvard and E. W. Bakke at Yale have developed promising concepts and procedures for inquiries into the factors that determine how human beings behave in the relations of employer and employee and in the development of trade unions. Such concepts and procedures give some evidence of being applicable to problems of marketing with good effect.

Students of public opinion and consumer attitudes, among whom Hadley Cantril may be mentioned, are virtually within the field of marketing; but they have drawn heavily upon other disciplines in their work.

---

[6]Wroe Alderson, "Conditions For a Balanced World Economy," World Economics, Vol. II, No. 7, October 1944, pp. 3-25.

(3) Contributions from Ecological Studies

Research by a wide variety of students into problems of human geography, population, traffic and city planning has offered many opportunities for enriching the theory of marketing. R. M. Haig's early essay on the economic functions of the metropolis and Harold Meyer's classification and analysis of the patterns of growth exhibited by secondary shopping centers in Chicago, are examples of useful analyses derived from the work of city planners.

W. J. Reilly's law of retail gravitation probably fits best into the ecological classification, although it would also be placed in the next section among the examples of work done in marketing research that is leading to a more fundamental understanding of the nature and function of marketing. Long neglected, Reilly's law has again begun to attract notice. After some revisions, it has provided the basic procedure used by Paul D. Converse to determine the directions and distances people go to shop for certain types of goods in Illinois. Still further revised, it has provided a system worked out in detail by the Curtis Publishing Company for dividing the entire country into trading areas for shopping goods. Although the immediate application has thus been made to the problems faced by individual merchants and individual communities in building their trade, this law as revised provides one starting point for a theory of the relationships of individual retailers or clusters and their customers.

Even more significant have been the efforts of John Q. Stewart to apply to the distribution of the population, and to the influences individual people and clusters of people exert upon each other at a distance, concepts much like those he has used in his work as a physicist and astronomer. His method, which he has summed up under the term social physics, may well lead to the clearest understanding yet attained and the most precise measurement thus far made of the forces that determine how people assemble themselves into markets and the ways in which they exert influence upon each other. It may thus provide a procedure for reducing to quantitative measurement the concept of patterns of social communication or influence devised by the sociologists.

(4) Contributions in Marketing Literature Itself

Tentative beginnings towards a meaningful theory of marketing may also be found scattered through the literature of marketing itself. It is impossible to make a complete listing here of the many significant contributions; but a few names may be mentioned so as to indicate the nature of these beginnings:

Melvin T. Copeland's early work in the classification of commodities on the basis of shopping methods used by the consumers who acquire them.

The work done in defining and describing the functions of marketing by such men as A. W. Shaw, Paul T. Cherington, Fred E. Clark and, more recently, E. D. McGarry.

E. T. Grether's use, noted above, of the concept of interregional trade as a frame upon which to build a theory of marketing, and his work with price discrimination and price structures.

The effort of Charles F. Phillips, since widely copied, to work the ideas and principles of value developed by neoclassical and monopolistic-competition economists into the body of marketing principles.

Robert W. Bartels' attempt to cull out of the literature of marketing all the principles or theories it contains.

Ralph W. Breyer's pioneer effort to struggle with the problem of space and time in marketing, with the concept of marketing as a social institution, and with the influence of changes in costs imposed at one level of the channel upon costs incurred at other levels.

The work done by John Paver, Victor H. Pelz, and others in using traffic flows and pedestrian movements as indicators of the structure of markets and trading areas.

Ralph Cassady's analyses of price discrimination and its legal significance, and the work done by Cassady and others with problems of decentralization in the retail trade of large cities.

The work of Roland S. Vaile and, more recently, Neil H. Borden in the study of the economic effects of advertising. This is supplemented by William B. Ricketts' work with procedures for evaluating the business effects of advertising.

Many other examples could be given; but these will suffice for present purposes. They make it clear that students who undertake to build a systematic theory of marketing will find stones at hand for the purpose. The stones must be dug out of the existing literature, reshaped, and supplemented by many others that remain to be discovered. They nevertheless provide material for a start.

5.   A Possible Approach to an Integrated Theory of Marketing

Any comprehensive approach to the development of a marketing theory would need to meet several tests:

1 It should give promise of serving the variety of needs that have created the current interest in marketing theory.

2 It should be able to draw in a comprehensive way upon the starting points for theory already available in the literature, such as those listed above;

3 It should provide a consistent theoretical perspective for the study of all the major classes of significant entities in marketing.

Such a viewpoint would appear to be available in what may be called group behaviorism as it has been developing in the social sciences. This view differs from the narrower use of the term behaviorism by Pavlov and Watson in that it gives a sociological emphasis to the analysis. The basic concept of group behaviorism is the organized behavior system.

Marketing theory may be said to consist of making clear what we mean by behavior, what we mean by system, and what we mean by organization, all as applied to marketing. Application to marketing implies that principles pertaining to these basic concepts should be given specific form and content in relation to all of the types of organized behavior systems that are significantly involved in the marketing process. These types of behavior system include, as we have seen, the firms engaged in buying or selling, the family as an earning and consuming unit, the local dispersion market, the channel of distribution, the industry supplying a phase of consumer or industrial need, and the economic system as a whole.

Group behaviorism differs from institutionalism that it is basically concerned with the concrete entities that interact within a behavior system. It differs from the approach to systems that has generally been followed in mathematical economics in that it takes account of the patterns of group behavior developed within specific systems as qualifying their operations. Thus, while it may make use of equilibrium concepts, it does not depend primarily on analogies drawn from the equilibrium systems discussed in physics.

Group behaviorism has the further distinction that it emphasizes those aspects of individual behavior that tend to perpetuate organized behavior systems and thus to render them at least semiconservative in the technical sense. Economic theory tends to assume that the systems under consideration do not obey the laws of conservation.

The approach through group behaviorism is most closely allied to what is usually called the functional approach in marketing. It would undertake to analyze marketing processes by taking primary account of the objectives they are designed to serve. Thus it retains the emphasis of the general economists on the forces of supply and demand but must go further in order to throw light on specific problems and situations in marketing. Eventually it should enable the market analyst to formulate the way in which market forces interact at any point in the system he has under investigation.

Marketing is still in what Northrop described as the first stage of scientific study, namely that of the gathering of vast compilations of fact. It was Francis Bacon, at the very beginning of modern scientific awakening, who felt that all problems would be solved if only enough facts were accumulated. Economic theory in the main has remained one step further back in a prescientific or metaphysical stage. It has occupied itself with the effort toward logical deductions from assumptions.

Neither economics not marketing can lay much claim to being scientific until they attain the stage of continuous interaction between theory and research.

The assumptions on which theory rests must more and more spring from careful empirical generalization. The facts which research gathers must more and more be relevant to hypotheses adopted on theoretical grounds.

6.   An Application of Group Behaviorism to Marketing Research

The feasibility and significance of approaching a theory of marketing through group behaviorism will be tested in an exploratory survey of the productivity of marketing in Philadelphia being organized this summer (1948). For purposes of this survey, the economic entity chosen is the Philadelphia dispersion market. Tentatively this has been defined as an organized behavior system embracing a group of people to whom goods and services flow through points of entry located within the Philadelphia area in so far as they do not originate within the area itself; the formal organizations, agencies or entities that do the work required to effectuate the flow in so far as the consumers do not do it for themselves; and the patterns of social communication, physical flow and movement through time by means of which the work is arranged and effectuated. For purposes of quantitative analysis, some arbitrary departures from the details of this definition doubtless must be made because of limitations upon the sorts of data to be had within limits of feasible financial expenditure. These concessions to practical difficulties will be held to the narrowest possible limits.

The specific objective of the project is to test the feasibility and significance of a long list of tentative formulas devised by one of the authors. These formulas are intended to serve as indicators of degrees of efficiency in dispersion marketing. The project will also give some indications, however, as to whether the basic theoretical approach being made is valid. In so doing it will, if it succeeds, meet the first of the tests suggested in the preceding section for the validity of approaches to the development of a marketing theory. That is, it will help satisfy the two basic needs underlying the demand for such a theory: First, it will provide a way of stating theoretical problems in marketing that, in the terms used by Northrop, permits the initiation of really meaningful inquiries. Second, it will make possible the drawing up of generalizations that have meaning and significance because they can be subjected to the test of relevant facts.

The project, if it succeeds, will also satisfy the test of making comprehensive drafts upon the literature for approaches, concepts and procedures. For example, the frame of reference that treats the dispersion market as the unit for observation comes from the developing realization already noted that new types of economic entities must be visualized.

The treatment of any such entity as an organized system of group behavior derives from the sociological concept of institutions as patterns of social communication. Emphasis will be placed upon the cooperative, as contrasted with the competitive aspects of the market, the objective being to determine what the market as a whole accomplishes for the people who compose it.

In setting up the formulas, which are essentially ratios between units of input and units of output, heavy reliance has been placed upon the functional approach to a study of marketing. "Functions" have been redefined for the purposes of analysis at this particular level; but the survey will hold closely to the basic concept of measuring the output or product of marketing in units of work defined by reference to the functions the dispersion market is supposed to perform.[7] A kind of equilibrium analysis will be achieved through establishing a concept of unit or optimum efficiency for each task the market performs. Against this unit efficiency, taken as a goal, the actual performance of the market in each particular can be evaluated. Instead of being looked upon as a device to introduce imperfections into an otherwise perfect market, the behavior system under analysis will be taken as designed to reduce the degree of imperfection already present.

The specific measures to be used derive in the last analysis from the numerous studies of which a few examples were given above under the headings "Ecological Studies" and "Marketing Literature Itself." Present indications are that the ecological studies will be particularly useful. In order to measure some aspects of effort expended and work done, reliance can best be put upon concepts of movement and flow through some one or more varieties of space and time against the resistance of some one or more varieties of obstacle. To use these concepts effectively, clear definitions will be required of distributive space and time, locations or position, and flow or movement. The definitions will have to be so set up that the terms lend themselves to quantitative measurement. For these purposes, studies of the sort illustrated above by reference to Lundberg, Paver, Palz, Reilly, Converse and Stewart will be particularly helpful. For the analysis of other aspects of effort expended and work done, reliance can perhaps best be made on other sources illustrated by Commons' suggestion of the contrast between fully negotiated and routine transactions, various studies of retail mortality, and struggles by many economists with problems of price differential and price structure.

There is every likelihood that this sort of comprehensive analysis of any entity such as the dispersion market will lead to significant formulations of theory, as this term has been defined above; that is, this sort of study should provide clear, detailed and specific statements of what is meant by behavior in marketing, what is meant by a system or pattern of behavior, and what is

---

[7] For a statement of some views held by the present writers concerning ways of measuring productivity n marketing, see Reavis Cox, "The Meaning and Measurement of Productivity in Marketing," and Wroe Alderson, "A Formula for Measuring Productivity in Distribution," Journal of Marketing, Vol. XII, April, 1948, pp. 433-448.

meant by organized or group patterns. It should be particularly useful in so far as it provides a procedure for reducing these various matters to quantitative measurement.

Furthermore, there are good prospects that what is worked out in this sort of survey will provide a theoretical perspective applicable to the study of other identifiable and significant entities in marketing. Thus it gives promise of meeting the third test suggested above. It bids fair to be not merely an isolated empirical study but a unit in something much larger. Should it prove successful, it will contribute substantially to creating the general theory so earnestly wanted by students of marketing.

7.   Marketing Theory and Economic Theory

An issue requiring the most careful consideration is whether the marketing field can satisfy its needs for a marketing theory until reformulation of economic theory has progressed further. Any market analyst who sees his role as that of facilitating adjustments of private and public policy in a world of change must grow impatient with the faltering attempts of economic theorists to deal with the dynamic aspects of an enterprise economy. The most acute marketing problems are precipitated by the facts of technological change. The market analyst is bound to wonder how the economists can expect to cope with change so long as he is so generally inclined to consider technology outside his proper field of interest.

The market analyst does not have the luxury of choice as to whether he will adopt a dynamic view. At the very least he must take account of technological change in marketing. Progressive changes in the technology of distribution, in the methods and channels of marketing, are surely significant for economic theory. They are of the essence of any perspective which might be distinguished as marketing theory. Thus the marketing theorist is obliged to break the economist's taboo on the discussion of technology at least as it applies to the techniques of marketing.

There is another aspect of the dynamics of market organization which is fundamental for marketing theory and eventually inescapable, it would appear, for economic theory. That is the fact that an organized behavior system is not a neutral framework or container for the actions and evaluations which take place within it. That is to say that a market changes day to day through the very fact that goods are bought and sold. While evaluation is taking place within a marketing structure, the structure itself is being rendered weaker or stronger and the changes in organization which follow will have an impact on tomorrow's evaluations. Marketing theory will not provide an adequate approach if it ignores this interaction between the system and the process which takes place within it. Whether economic theory can dispense with such considerations is another question.

N. B. The ideas credited to the various authors mentioned in Section 4 may be found in the following sources:

References

Bain, Joe S. (1942). Market Classifications in Modern Price Theory. *The Quarterly Journal of Economics*, 56(4):560–574.

Bakke, E. W. (1946). *Mutual Survival: The Goal of Unions and Management.* Yale University Labor and Management Center, New Haven.

Bakke, E. W. (n.d.). Principles of Adaptive Human Behavior. A mimeographed preliminary draft privately circulated.

Barnard, Chester I. (1948). *Organization and Management.* Harvard University Press, Cambridge.

Bartels, Robert (1944). Marketing Principles. *Journal of Marketing*, 9(2):151–157.

Borden, Neil H. (1942). *The Economic Effect of Advertising.* Richard D. Irwin, Inc., Chicago.

Boulding, Kenneth E. (1942). Samuelson's Foundations: The Role of Mathematics in Economics. *Journal of Political Economy*, 56(3):187–199.

Bowden, William K. and Cassady, Jr., Ralph (1941). Decentralization of Retail Trade in Metropolitan Marketing Area. *Journal of Marketing*, 5(3):270–275.

Breyer, Ralph F. (1934). *The Marketing Institution.* McGraw-Hill Book Co., New York.

Breyer, Ralph F. (1944). *Bulk and Package Handling Costs.* American Marketing Association, New York.

Cantril, Hadley (1944). *Gauging Public Opinion.* Princeton University Press, Princeton.

Cassady, Jr., Ralph (1944). Shifting Retail Trade within the Los Angeles Metropolitan Market. *Journal of Marketing*, 8(4):398–404.

Cassady, Jr., Ralph (1946a). Some Economic Aspects of Price Discrimination Under Non-Perfect Conditions. *Journal of Marketing*, 11(1):7–20.

Cassady, Jr., Ralph (1946b). Techniques and Purposes of Price Discrimination. *Journal of Marketing*, 11(2):135–150.

Chamberlin, E. H. (1933). *The Theory of Monopolistic Competition: A Reorientation of the Theory of Value.* Harvard University Press, Cambridge, Massachusetts. Frequently revised since then.

Cherington, Paul T. (1920). *The Elements of Marketing.* Macmillan Co., New York.

Clark, Fred E. (1922). *Principles of Marketing.* Macmillan Co., New York, first edition. Revised at intervals since.

Clark, J. M. (1923). *Studies in the Economics of Overhead Costs*. University of Chicago Press, Chicago.

Clark, J. M. (1948). *Alternative to Serfdom*. Aldfred A. Knopf.

Commons, John R. (1934). *Institutional Economics*. Macmillan Co., New York.

Converse, Paul D. (1946). *Retail Trade Areas in Illinois*. University of Illinois, Urbana.

Copeland, Melvin T. (1923). The Relation of Consumer's Buying Habits to Marketing Methods. *Harvard Business Review*, 1(April):282–289.

Doherty, Richard P. (1941). The Movement and Concentration of Retail Trade in Metropolitan Areas. *Journal of Marketing*, 5(4):395–401.

Doherty, Richard P. (1942). Decentralization of Retail Trade in Boston. *Journal of Marketing*, 6(3):281–286.

Duddy, Edward A. and Revzan, David A. (1947). *Marketing: An Institutional Approach*. McGraw-Hill Book Co., New York.

Grether, E. T. (1939). *Price Control Under Fair Trade Legislation*. Oxford University Press, New York.

Grether, E. T. (1944). Geographical Price Policies in the Grocery Trade, 1941. *Journal of Marketing*, 8(4):417–422.

Haig, Robert Murray (1926). Toward an Understanding of the Metropolis. *Quarterly Journal of Economics*, 40(February and May):179–208,402–434.

Keynes, J. M. (1936). *The General Theory of Employment, Interest and Money*. Harcourt, Brace & Co., New York.

Knauth, Oswald (1948). *Managerial Enterprise*. W. W. Norton.

Leeper, Robert W. (1943). *Lewin's Topographical and Vector Psychology: A Digest and a Critique*. University of Oregon, Eugene.

Lewin, Kurt (1936). *Principles of Topological Psychology*. McGraw-Hill Book Co., New York.

Lewin, Kurt (1938). The Conceptual Representation and the Measurement of Psychological Forces. *Contributions to Psychological Theory*, 1(5). Published by Duke University Press, Durham.

Lundberg, G. A. (1945). *Marketing and Social Organization*. Curtis Publishing Co., Philadelphia. This was the first Parlin Memorial Lecture.

Lundberg, George and Steele, Mary (1938). Social Attraction Patterns in a Village. *Sociometry*, 1(January-April):375–419.

Mayer, Harold M. (1942). Patterns and Recent Trends of Chicago's outlying Business Centers. *Journal of Land and Public Utility Economics*, 18(1):4–16.

Mayo, E. (1946). *The Human Problems of an Industrial Civilization*. Harvard University Bureau of Business Research, Cambridge, second edition.

McGarry, E. D. The Functions of Marketing. Manuscript.

Ohlin, Bertil (1935). *Interregional and International Trade*. Harvard University Press, Cambridge.

Paver, John and McClintock, Miller (1935). *Traffic and Trade*. McGraw-Hill Book Co., New York.

Pelz, Victor H. (1946). *Traffic Audit Bureau, Methods for the Evaluation of Outdoor Advertising*. Traffic Audit Bureau, New York.

Phillips, Charles F. (1938). *Marketing*. Houghton Mifflin Co., Boston.

Reilly, William J. (1929). *Methods for the Study of Retail Relationships*. University of Texas, Austin.

Ricketts, William B. Testing and Measuring Advertising Effectiveness. Manuscript.

Robinson, Joan (1933). *The Economics of Imperfect Competition*. Macmillan and Co. Ltd, London.

Shaw, A. W. (1912). Some Problems in Market Distribution. *Quarterly Journal of Economics*, (August):703–765.

Stewart, John Q. (1947). Empirical Mathematical Rules Concerning the Distribution and Equilibrium of Population. *Geographical Review*, 37(3):461–485.

Stewart, John Q. (1948). Concerning 'Social Physics'. *Scientific American*, (May):20–23.

Strohkarck, Frank and Phelps, Katherine (1948). The Mechanics of Constructing a Market Area Map. *Journal of Marketing*, 21(4):493–496. A description of the method used by the Curtis Publishing Company in constructing its map, "Market Areas for Shopping Lines".

Triffin, Robert (1940). *Monopolistic Competition and General Equilibrium Theory*. Harvard University Press, Cambridge.

Vaile, Roland S. (1927). *Economics of Advertising*. Ronald Press Co., New York.

von Neumann, John and Morgenstern, O. (1944). *Theory of Games and Economic Behavior*. Princeton University Press, Princeton, first edition.

Chapter 4

THE ANALYTICAL FRAMEWORK FOR MARKETING*

Wroe Alderson

Mr. Alderson is President of Alderson Associates, Inc., Philadelphia.

My assignment is to discuss the analytical framework for marketing. Since our general purpose here is to consider the improvement of the marketing curriculum, I assume that the paper I have been asked to present might serve two functions. The first is to present a perspective of marketing which might be the basis of a marketing course at either elementary or advanced levels. The other is to provide some clue as to the foundations in the social sciences upon which an analytical framework for marketing may be built.

Economics has some legitimate claim to being the original science of markets. Received economic theory provides a framework for the analysis of marketing functions which certainly merits the attention of marketing teachers and practitioners. It is of little importance whether the point of view I am about to present is a version of economics, a hybrid of economics and sociology, or the application of a newly emergent general science of human behavior to marketing problems. The analytical framework which I find congenial at least reflects some general knowledge of the social sciences as well as long experience in marketing analysis. In the time available I can do no more than present this view in outline or skeleton form and leave you to determine how to classify it or whether you can use it.

An advantageous place to start for the analytical treatment of marketing is with the radical heterogeneity of markets. Heterogeneity is inherent on both the demand and the supply sides. The homogeneity which the economist assumes for certain purposes is not an antecedent condition for marketing. Insofar as it is ever realized it emerges out of the marketing process itself.

The materials which are useful to man occur in nature in heterogeneous mixtures which might be called conglomerations since these mixtures have only a

---

*This paper was originally printed in Delbert, Duncan Ed. (1958) *Proceedings: Conference of Marketing Teachers from Far Western States* Berkeley, University of California, pages 15-28.

random relationship to human needs and activities. The collection of goods in the possession of a household or an individual also constitutes a heterogeneous supply, but it might be called an assortment since it is related to anticipated patterns of future behavior. The whole economic process may be described as a series of transformations from meaningless to meaningful heterogeneity. Marketing produces as much homogeneity as may be needed to facilitate some of the intermediate economic processes but homogeneity has limited significance or utility for consumer behavior or expectations.

The marketing process matches materials found in nature or goods fabricated from these materials against the needs of households or individuals. Since the consuming unit has a complex pattern of needs, the matching of these needs creates an assortment of goods in the hands of the ultimate consumer. Actually the marketing process builds up assortments at many stages along the way, each appropriate to the activities taking place at that point. Materials or goods are associated in one way for manufacturing, in another way for wholesale distribution, and in still another for retail display and selling. In between the various types of heterogeneous collections relatively homogeneous supplies are accumulated through the processes of grading, refining, chemical reduction and fabrication.

Marketing brings about the necessary transformations in heterogeneous supplies through a multiphase process of sorting. Matching of every individual need would be impossible if the consumer had to search out each item required or the producer had to find the users of a product one by one. It is only the ingenious use of intermediate sorts which make it possible for a vast array of diversified products to enter into the ultimate consumer assortments as needed. Marketing makes mass production possible first by providing the assortment of supplies needed in manufacturing and then taking over the successive transformations which ultimately produce the assortments in the hands of consuming units.

To some who have heard this doctrine expounded, the concept of sorting seems empty, lacking in specific behavioral content, and hence unsatisfactory as a root idea for marketing. One answer is that sorting is a more general and embracing concept than allocation which many economists regard as the root idea of their science. Allocation is only one of the four basic types of sorting all of which are involved in marketing. Among these four, allocation is certainly no more significant than assorting, one being the breaking down of a homogenous supply and the other the building up of a heterogeneous supply. Assorting, in fact, gives more direct expression to the final aim of marketing but allocation performs a major function along the way.

There are several basic advantages in taking sorting as a central concept. It leads directly to a fundamental explanation of the contribution of marketing to the overall economy of human effort in producing and distributing goods. It provides a key to the unending search for efficiency in the marketing function itself. Finally, sorting as the root idea of marketing is consistent with the assumption that heterogeneity is radically and inherently present on both sides of the market and that the aim of marketing is to cope with the heterogeneity of both needs and resources.

At this stage of the discussion it is the relative emphasis on assorting as contrasted with allocation which distinguishes marketing theory from at least some versions of economic theory. This emphasis arises naturally from the preoccupation of the market analyst with consumer behavior. One of the most fruitful approaches to understanding what the consumer is doing is the idea that she is engaged in building an assortment, in replenishing or extending an inventory of goods for use by herself and her family. As evidence that this paper is not an attempt to set up a theory in opposition to economics it is acknowledged that the germ of this conception of consumer behavior was first presented some eighty years ago by the Austrian economist Boehm-Bawerk.

The present view is distinguished from that of Boehm-Bawerk in its greater emphasis on the probabilistic approach to the study of market behavior. In considering items for inclusion in her assortment the consumer must make judgments concerning the relative probabilities of future occasions for use. A product in the assortment is intended to provide for some aspect of future behavior. Each such occasion for use carries a rating which is a product of two factors, one a judgment as to the probability of its incidence and the other a measure of the urgency of the need in case it should arise. Consumer goods vary with respect to both measures. One extreme might be illustrated by cigarettes with a probability of use approaching certainty but with relatively small urgency or penalty for deprivation on the particular occasion for use. At the other end of the scale would be a home fire extinguisher with low probability but high urgency attaching to the expected occasion of use.

All of this means that the consumer buyer enters the market as a problem-solver. Solving a problem, either on behalf of a household or on behalf of a marketing organization means reaching a decision in the face of uncertainty. The consumer buyer and the marketing executive are opposite numbers in the double search which pervades marketing; one looking for the goods required to complete an assortment, the other looking for the buyers who are uniquely qualified to use his goods. This is not to say that the behavior of either consumers or executives can be completely characterized as rational problem-solvers. The intention rather is to assert that problem-solving on either side of the market involves a probabilistic approach to heterogeneity on the other side. In order to solve his own problems arising from heterogeneous demand, the marketing executive should understand the processes of consumer decision in coping with heterogeneous supplies.

The viewpoint adopted here with respect to the competition among sellers is essentially that which is associated in economics with such names as Schumpeter, Chamberlin and J. M. Clark and with the emphasis on innovative competition, product differentiation and differential advantage. The basic assumption is that every firm occupies a position which is in some respects unique, being differentiated from all others by characteristics of its products, its services, its geographic location or its specific combination of these features. The survival of a firm requires that for some group of buyers it should enjoy a differential advantage over all other suppliers. The sales of any active marketing organization come from a core market made up of buyers with a preference for this source and a fringe market which finds the source acceptable, at least for occasional purchases.

In the case of the supplier of relatively undifferentiated products or services such as the wheat farmer differential advantage may pertain more to the producing region than to the individual producer. This more diffused type of differential advantage often becomes effective in the market through such agencies as the marketing cooperative. Even the individual producer of raw materials, however, occupies a position in the sense that one market or buyer provides the customary outlet for his product rather than another. The essential point for the present argument is that buyer and seller are not paired at random even in the marketing of relatively homogeneous products but is related to some scale of preference or priority.

Competition for differential advantage implied goals of survival and growth for the marketing organization. The firm is perennially seeking a favorable place to stand and not merely immediate profits from its operations. Differential advantage is subject to change and neutralization by competitors. In dynamic markets differential advantage can only be preserved through continuous innovation. Thus competition presents an analogy to a succession of military campaigns rather than to the pressures and attrition of a single battle. A competitor may gain ground through a successful campaign based on new product features or merchandising ideas. It may lose ground or be forced to fall back on its core position because of the successful campaigns of others. The existence of the core position helps to explain the paradox of survival in the face of the destructive onslaughts of innovative competition.

Buyers and sellers meet in market transactions each side having tentatively identified the other as an answer to its problem. The market transaction consumes much of the time and effort of all buyers and sellers. The market which operates through a network of costless transactions is only a convenient fiction which economists adopt for certain analytical purposes. Potentially the cost of transactions is so high that controlling or reducing this cost is a major objective in market analysis and executive action. Among economists John R. Commons has given the greatest attention to the transaction as the unit of collective action.

He drew a basic distinction between strategic and routine transactions which for present purposes may best be paraphrased as fully negotiated and routine transactions.

The fully negotiated transaction is the prototype of all exchange transactions. It represents a matching of supply and demand after canvassing all of the factors which might affect the decision on either side. The routine transaction proceeds under a set of rules and assumptions established by previous negotiation or as the result of techniques of pre-selling which take the place of negotiation. Transactions on commodity and stock exchanges are carried out at high speed and low cost but only because of carefully established rules governing all aspects of trading. The economical routines of self-service in a super market are possible because the individual items on display have been pre-sold. The routine transaction is the end-result of previous marketing effort and ingenious organization of institutions and processes. Negotiation is implicit in all routine transactions. Good routines induce both parties to save time and cost by foregoing explicit negotiation.

The negotiated transaction is the indicated point of departure for the study of exchange values in heterogeneous markets. Many considerations enter into the decision to trade or not to trade on either side of the market. Price is the final balancing or integrating factor which permits the deal to be made. The seller may accept a lower price if relieved from onerous requirements. The buyer may pay a higher price if provided with specified services. The integrating price is one that assures an orderly flow of goods so long as the balance of other considerations remains essentially unchanged. Some economists are uneasy about the role of the negotiated transaction in value determination since bargaining power may be controlling within wide bargaining limits. These limits as analyzed by Commons are set by reference to the best alternatives available to either partner rather than by the automatic control of atomistic competition. This analysis overlooks a major constraint on bargaining in modem markets. Each side has a major stake in a deal that the other side can live with. Only in this way can a stable supply relationship be established so as to achieve the economics of transactional routines. Negotiation is not a zero sum game since the effort to get the best of the other party transaction by transaction may result in a loss to both sides in terms of mounting transactional cost.

In heterogeneous markets price plays an important role in matching a segment of supply with the appropriate segment of demand. The seller frequently has the option of producing a streamlined product at a low price, a deluxe product at a high price or selecting a price-quality combination somewhere in between. There are considerations which exert a strong influence on the seller toward choosing the price line or lines which will yield the greatest dollar volume of sales. Assuming that various classes of consumers have conflicting claims on the productive capacity of the supplier, it might be argued that the price-quality combination which maximized gross revenue represented the most constructive compromise among these claims. There are parallel considerations with respect to the claims of various participants in the firm's activities on its operating revenue. These claimants include labor, management, suppliers of raw materials and stockholders. Assuming a perfectly fluid situation with respect to bargaining among these claimants, the best chance for a satisfactory solution is at the level of maximum gross revenue. The argument becomes more complicated when the claims of stockholders are given priority, but the goal would still be maximum gross revenue as suggested in a recent paper by William J. Baumol. My own intuition and experience lead me to believe that the maximization of gross revenue is a valid goal of marketing management in heterogeneous markets and adherence to this norm appears to be widely prevalent in actual practice.

What has been said so far is doubtless within the scope of economics or perhaps constitutes a sketch of how some aspects of economic theory might be reconstructed on the assumption of heterogeneity rather than homogeneity as the normal and prevailing condition of the market. But there are issues raised by such notions as enterprise survival, expectations, and consumer behavior, which in my opinion cannot be resolved within the present boundaries of economic science. Here marketing must not hesitate to draw upon the concepts and techniques of the social sciences for the enrichment of its perspective and for the advancement of marketing as an empirical science.

The general economist has his own justifications for regarding the exchange process as a smoothly functioning mechanism which operates in actual markets or which should be taken as the norm and standard to be enforced by government regulation. For the marketing man, whether teacher or practitioner, this Olympian view is untenable. Marketing is concerned with those who are obliged to enter the market to solve their problems imperfect as the market may be. The persistent and rational action of these participants is the main hope for eliminating or moderating some of these imperfections so that the operation of the market mechanism may approximate that of the theoretical model.

To understand market behavior the marketing man takes a closer look at the nature of the participants. Thus he is obliged, in my opinion, to come to grips with the organized behavior system. Market behavior is primarily group behavior. Individual action in the market is most characteristically action on behalf of some group in which the individual holds membership. The organized behavior system is related to the going concern of John R. Commons but with a deeper interest in what keeps it going. The organized behavior system is also a much broader concept including the more tightly organized groups acting in the market such as business firms and households and loosely connected systems such as the trade center and the marketing channel.

The marketing man needs some rationale for group behavior, some general explanation for the formation and persistence of organized behavior systems. He finds this explanation in the concept of expectations. Insofar as conscious choice is involved, individuals operate in groups because of their expectations of incremental satisfactions as compared to what they could obtain operating alone. The expected satisfactions are of many kinds, direct and indirect. In a group that is productive activity is held together because of an expected surplus over individual output. Other groups such as households and purely social organizations expect direct satisfactions from group association and activities. They also expect satisfactions from future activities facilitated by the assortment of goods held in common. Whatever the character of the system, its vitality arises from the expectations of the individual members and the vigor of their efforts to achieve them through group action. While the existence of the group is entirely derivative, it is capable of operating as if it had a life of its own and was pursuing goals of survival and growth.

Every organized behavior system exhibits a structure related to the functions it performs. Even in the simplest behavior system there must be some mechanism for decision and coordination of effort if the system is to provide incremental satisfaction. Leadership emerges at an early stage to perform such functions as directing the defense of the group. Also quite early is the recognition of the rationing function by which the leader allocates the available goods or satisfactions among the members of the group.

As groups grow in size and their functions become more complex functional specialization increases. The collection of individuals forming a group with their diversified skills and capabilities is a meaningful heterogeneous ensemble vaguely analogous to the assortment of goods which facilitates the activities of the group. The group, however, is held together directly by the generalized expectations of its members. The assortment is held together by a relatively weak or derivative bond. An item "belongs" to the assortment only so long as it has some probability of satisfying the expectations of those who possess it.

This outline began with an attempt to live within the framework of economics or at least within an economic framework amplified to give fuller recognition to heterogeneity on both sides of the market. We have now plunged into sociology in order to deal more effectively with the organized behavior system. Meanwhile we attempt to preserve the line of communication to our origins by basing the explanations of group behavior on the quasi-economic concept of expectations.

The initial plunge into sociology is only the beginning since the marketing man must go considerably further in examining the functions and structure of organized behavior systems. An operating group has a power structure, a communication structure and an operating structure. At each stage an effort should be made to employ the intellectual strategy which has already been suggested.

That is, to relate sociological notions to the groundwork of marketing economics through the medium of such concepts as expectations and the processes of matching and sorting.

All members of an organized behavior system occupy some position or status within its power structure. There is a valid analogy between the status of an individual or operating unit within the system and the market position of the firm as an entity. The individual struggles for status within the system having first attained the goal of membership. For most individuals in an industrial society status in some operating system is a prerequisite for satisfying his expectations. Given the minimal share in the power of the organization inherent in membership, vigorous individuals may aspire to the more ample share of power enjoyed by leadership. Power in the generalized sense referred to here is an underlying objective on which the attainment of all other objectives depends. This aspect of organized behavior has been formulated as the power principle, namely, "The rational individual will act in such a way to promote the power to act." The word "promote" deliberately glosses over an ambivalent attitude toward power, some individuals striving for enhancement and others being content to preserve the power they have.

Any discussion which embraces power as a fundamental concept creates uneasiness for some students on both analytical and ethical grounds. My own answer to the analytical problem is to define it as control over expectations. In these terms it is theoretically possible to measure and evaluate power, perhaps even to set a price on it. Certainly it enters into the network of imputations in a business enterprise. Management allocates or rations status and recognition as well as or in lieu of material rewards. As for the ethical problem, it does not arise unless the power principle is substituted for ethics as with Macchiavelli. Admitting that the power principle is the essence of expediency, the ethical choice of values and objectives is a different issue. Whatever his specific objectives, the rational individual will wish to serve them expediently.

If any of this discussion of power seems remote from marketing let it be remembered that the major preoccupation of the marketing executive, as pointed out by Oswald Knauth, is with the creation or the activation of organized behavior systems such as marketing channels and sales organizations. No one can be effective in building or using such systems if he ignores the fundamental nature of the power structure.

The communication structure serves the group in various ways. It promotes the survival of the system by reinforcing the individual's sense of belonging. It transmits instructions and operating commands or signals to facilitate coordinated effort. It is related to expectations through the communication of explicit or implied commitments. Negotiations between suppliers and customers and much that goes on in the internal management of a marketing organization can best be understood as a two-way exchange of commitments. A division sales manager, for example, may commit himself to produce a specified volume of sales. His superior in turn may commit certain company resources to support his efforts and make further commitments as to added rewards as an incentive to outstanding performance.

For some purposes it is useful to regard marketing processes as a flow of goods and a parallel flow of informative and persuasive messages. In these terms the design of communication facilities and channels becomes a major aspect of the creation of marketing systems. Marketing has yet to digest and apply the insights of the rapidly developing field of communication theory which in turn has drawn freely from both engineering and biological and social sciences. One stimulating idea expounded by Norbert Wiener and others is that of the feedback of information in a control system. Marketing and advertising research are only well started on the task of installing adequate feedback circuits for controlling the deployment of marketing effort.

Social psychology is concerned with some problems of communication which are often encountered in marketing systems. For example, there are the characteristic difficulties of vertical communication which might be compared to the transmission of telephone messages along a power line. Subordinates often hesitate to report bad news to their superiors fearing to take the brunt of emotional reactions. Superiors learn to be cautious in any discussion of the subordinate's status for fear that a casual comment will be interpreted as a commitment. There is often a question as to when a subordinate should act and report and when he should refer a matter for decision upstream. Progress in efficiency, which is a major goal in marketing, depends in substantial part on technological improvement in communication facilities and organizational skill in using them.

The third aspect of structure involved in the study of marketing systems is operating structure. Effective specialization within an organization requires that activities which are functionally similar be placed together but properly coordinated with other activities. Billing by wholesaler grocers, for example, has long been routinized in a separate billing department. In more recent years the advances in mechanical equipment have made it possible to coordinate inventory control with billing, using the same set of punch cards for both functions. Designing an operating structure is a special application of sorting. As in the sorting of goods to facilitate handling, there are generally several alternative schemes for classifying activities presenting problems of choice to the market planner.

Functional specialization and the design of appropriate operating structures is a constant problem in the effective use of marketing channels. Some functions can be performed at either of two or more stages. One stage may be the best choice in terms of economy or effectiveness. Decision on the placement of a function may have to be reviewed periodically since channels do not remain static. Similar considerations arise in the choice of channels. Some types of distributors or dealers may be equipped to perform a desired service while others may not. Often two or more channels with somewhat specialized roles are required to move a product to the consumer. The product's sponsor can maintain perspective in balancing out these various facilities by thinking in terms of a total operating system including his own sales organization and the marketing channels employed.

The dynamics of market organization pose basic problems for the marketing student and the marketing executive in a free enterprise economy. Reference has already been made to the competitive pursuit of differential advantage. One way in which a firm can gain differential advantage is by organizing the market in a way that is favorable to its own operations. This is something else than the attainment of a monopolistic position in relation to current or potential competitors. It means creating a pattern for dealing with customers or suppliers which persists because there are advantages on both sides. Offering guarantees against price declines on floor stocks is one example of market organization by the seller. Attempts to systematize the flow of orders may range from various services offered to customers or suppliers all the way to complete vertical integration. Another dynamic factor affecting the structure of markets may be generalized under the term "closure." It frequently happens that some marketing system is incomplete or out of balance in some direction. The act of supplying the missing element constitutes closure, enabling the system to handle a greater output or to operate at a new level of efficiency. The incomplete system in effect cries out for closure. To observe this need is to recognize a form of market opportunity. This is one of the primary ways in which new enterprises develop, since there may be good reasons why the missing service cannot be performed by the existing organizations which need the service. A food broker, for example, can cover a market for several accounts of moderate size in a way that the individual manufacturer would not be able to cover it for himself.

There is a certain compensating effect between closure as performed by new or supplementary marketing enterprises and changes in market organization brought about by the initiative of existing firms in the pursuit of differential advantage. The pursuit of a given form of advantage, in fact, may carry the total marketing economy out of balance in a given direction creating the need and opportunity for closure. Such an economy could never be expected to reach a state of equilibrium, although the tendency toward structural balance is one of the factors in its dynamics. Trade regulation may be embraced within this dynamic pattern as an attempt of certain groups to organize the market to their own advantage through political means. Entering into this political struggle to determine the structure of markets are some political leaders and some administrative officials who regard themselves as representing the consumer's interests. It seems reasonable to believe that the increasing sophistication and buying skill of consumers is one of the primary forces offsetting the tendency of the free market economy to turn into something else through the working out of its inherent dynamic forces. This was the destiny foreseen for the capitalistic system by Schumpeter, even though he was one of its staunchest advocates.

The household as an organized behavior system must be given special attention in creating an analytical framework for marketing. The household is an operating entity with an assortment of goods and assets and with economic functions to perform. Once a primary production unit, the household has lost a large part of these activities to manufacturing and service enterprises. Today its economic operations are chiefly expressed through earning and spending. In the typical household there is some specialization between the husband as primary earner and the wife as chief purchasing agent for the household. It may be assumed that she becomes increasingly competent in buying as she surrenders her production activities such as canning, baking and dressmaking, and devotes more of her time and attention to shopping. She is a rational problem solver as she samples what the market has to offer in her effort to maintain a balanced inventory or assortment of goods to meet expected occasions of use. This is not an attempt to substitute Economic Woman for the discredited fiction of Economic Man. It is only intended to assert that the decision structure of consumer buying is similar to that for industrial buying. Both business executive and housewife enter the market as rational problem solvers, even though there are other aspects of personality in either case.

An adequate perspective on the household for marketing purposes must recognize several facets of its activities. It is an organized behavior system with its aspects of power, communication, and operating structure. It is the locus of forms of behavior other than instrumental or goal-seeking activities. A convenient three-way division, derived from the social sciences, recognizes instrumental, congenial, and symptomatic behavior. Congenial behavior is that kind of activity engaged in for its own sake and presumably yielding direct satisfactions. It is exemplified by the act of consumption as compared to all of the instrumental activities which prepare the way for consumption. Symptomatic behavior reflects maladjustment and is neither pleasure giving in itself nor an efficient pursuit of goals. Symptomatic behavior is functional only to the extent that it serves as a signal to others that the individual needs help.

Some studies of consumer motivation have given increasing attention to symptomatic behavior or to the projection of symptoms of personality adjustment which might affect consumer buying. The present view is that the effort to classify individuals by personality types is less urgent for marketing than the classification of families. Four family types with characteristically different buying behavior have been suggested growing out of the distinction between the instrumental and congenial aspects of normal behavior. Even individuals who are fairly well adjusted in themselves will form a less than perfect family if not fully adapted to each other.

On the instrumental side of household behavior it would seem to be desirable that the members be well coordinated as in any other operating system. If not, they will not deliver the maximum impact in pursuit of family goals. On the congenial side it would appear desirable for the members of a household to be compatible. That means enjoying the same things, cherishing the same goals, preferring joint activities to solitary pursuits or the company of others. These two distinctions yield an obvious four-way classification. The ideal is the family that is coordinated in its instrumental activities and compatible in its congenial activities. A rather joyless household which might nevertheless be well managed and prosperous in material terms is the coordinated but incompatible household. The compatible but uncoordinated family would tend to be happy-go-lucky and irresponsible with obvious consequences for buying behavior. The household which was both uncoordinated and incompatible would usually be tottering on the brink of dissolution. It might be held together formally by scruples against divorce, by concern for children, or by the dominant power of one member over the others. This symptomology of families does not exclude an interest in the readjustment of individuals exhibiting symptomatic behavior. Such remedial action lies in the sphere of the psychiatrist and the social worker, whereas the marketer is chiefly engaged in supplying goods to families which are still functioning as operating units.

All of the discussion of consumers so far limits itself to the activities of the household purchasing agent. Actually the term consumption as it appears in marketing and economic literature nearly always means consumer buying. Some day marketing may need to look beyond the act of purchasing to a study of consumption proper. The occasion for such studies will arise out of the problems of inducing consumers to accept innovations or the further proliferation of products to be included in the household assortment. Marketing studies at this depth will not only borrow from the social sciences but move into the realm of esthetic and ethical values. What is the use of a plethora of goods unless the buyer derives genuine satisfaction from them? What is the justification of surfeit if the acquisition of goods serves as a distraction from activities which are essential to the preservation of our culture and of the integrity of our personalities?

It has been suggested that a study of consumption might begin with the problem of choice in the presence of abundance. The scarce element then is the time or capacity for enjoyment. The bookworm confronted with the thousands of volumes available in a great library must choose in the face of this type of limitation.

The name hedonomics would appear to be appropriate for this field of study suggesting the management of the capacity to enjoy. Among the problems fo hedonomics is the pleasure derived from the repetition of a familiar experience as compared with the enjoyment of a novel experience or an old experience with some novel element. Another is the problem of direct experience versus symbolic experience, with the advantages of intensity on the one hand and on the other the possibility of embracing a greater range of possible ideas and sensations by relying on symbolic representations. Extensive basic research will probably be necessary before hedonomics can be put to work in marketing or for the enrichment of human life through other channels.

This paper barely suffices to sketch the analytical framework for marketing. It leaves out much of the area of executive decision-making in marketing on such matters as the weighing of uncertainties and the acceptance of risk in the commitment of resources. It leaves out market planning which is rapidly becoming a systematic discipline centering in the possibilities for economizing time and space as well as resources. It leaves out all but the most casual references to advertising and demand formation. Advertising is certainly one of the most difficult of marketing functions to embrace within a single analytical framework. It largely ignores the developing technology of physical distribution. Hopefully what it does accomplish is to show how the essentially economic problems of marketing may yield to a more comprehensive approach drawing on the basic social sciences for techniques and enriched perspective.

Chapter 5

SURVIVAL AND ADJUSTMENT IN ORGANIZED BEHAVIOR SYSTEMS*

Wroe Alderson

1. The Basic Concept of the Organized Behavior System

Marketing behavior embraces a wide range of organized activities in the distribution and exchange of goods and services. In the American economy, distribution provides the link between mass production and individualized consumption. Marketing must adjust itself to continuous changes in production techniques and in patterns of consumer demand. Marketing specialists administer a dynamic segment of economic life. Paralleling the day-to-day administration and control of marketing processes, marketing analysis and planning are directed toward constant improvement. The forms of market organization must be altered to serve new objectives or to meet established needs with greater efficiency.

Effective performance of such an exacting role requires a rich perspective. Marketing practice needs to be oriented to the principles of group behavior developing out of such fields as social psychology and cultural anthropology. It needs to be aware of the main lines of thought that have emerged in economics as a more abstract and generalized approach to the study of markets. Marketing needs an ordered framework for a broader and more significant organization of its own empirical findings. In short, marketing theory is essential to the scientific approach that has long been the guiding ideal of the professional marketing specialist.

Marketing theory that will meet these requirements is not the same thing as economic theory. The science of marketing must progress through constructive interaction between fact finding and deductive analysis. Economic theory in its purest form has not been contaminated by contact with fact finding. Marketing necessarily concerns itself with the organizing effort that makes possible the orderly flow of goods. Economics assumes as already given the results labori-

---

*Originally appeared as Chapter 4 in *Theory in Marketing* (1950), pages 65-87.

ously achieved through market organization. Marketing is obliged on the basis of its own empirical findings to regard much of consumer demand in the light of acquired behavior. No theory can illustrate the facts about demand unless it has come abreast of the modern psychology of learning (Miller and Dollard, 1941).

The branch of economics known as the "theory of the firm" does not satisfy the growing demand for marketing theory. The theory of the firm could be more appropriately labeled the "entrepreneurial theory of price." The entrepreneur under this theory manipulates the firm and its resources with complete flexibility and unrestricted control over allocation. The firms of the real world are stubborn entities which tend to maintain persistent identity over time. It is an ironic paradox that so-called "firm theory" eliminates real firms and most of their real problems in its attempt to reduce the analysis of entrepreneurial judgment to the single issue of price determination (Boulding, 1942).

This is not to deny that marketing has much to learn from the various schools of economic thought. Monopolistic competition theory, for example, has been highly suggestive from the beginning, and is believed to point ultimately to the kind of treatment presented here concerning the internal and external adjustments of individual firms and other behavior systems[1]. Marketing owes a debt to Keynes for his challenge to Say's law of markets and for the developments in forecasting methods growing out of the Keynesian emphasis on national aggregates such as consumer income and employment. Any theoretical perspective for the study of marketing institutions is bound to rely heavily upon the work of economists following the institutionalist approach — (for example Commons, 1934, Weber, 1947, Clark, 1923).

Marketing theory may never attain the precise formulation of economic theory, but it needs a broader and richer approach than is currently offered by any school of economics. Marketing already has its own method of fact finding and analysis and its own standards of performance in scientific research (Churchman, 1948). It must be ready to draw on any division of the social sciences that can contribute to the solution of marketing problems. Its need for theory is a need for the kind of perspective that can guide the selection methods in specific problem situations and that can facilitate the integration of research findings into a growing body of scientific marketing principles.

Some basic concepts are required to facilitate the kind of integration in the social sciences that appears urgent from the marketing viewpoint. This essay presents the concept of the organized behavior system and some theorems concerning those behavior systems which are of greatest interest to marketing. Samuelson (1947) employs the concept of the causative or equilibrium system, and asserts that the same analysis of maximizing behavior can be applied in ev-

---

[1] See the discussion of pluralistic competition by R. G. Gettell elsewhere in this volume

ery system. The present view also undertakes to state some general principles that are true for all types of action in these group behavior patterns. The concept of the organized behavior system resembles Commons' concept of the going concern, but deals more directly with the problem of survival as it confronts the system.

Internal balance in the system is of special interest in itself and also in relation to external equilibrium. The analysis of internal balance resembles in some degree the discussion of homeostasis in biology beginning with Cannon in 1929. "Homeostasis" is defined as the conditions for stable internal equilibrium that are necessary to the survival of an organism. The achievement of these conditions is directly related to the adjustment of the organism to its environment, but is not determined in any simple mechanical way by environmental pressures. Lundberg (1948) has recently suggested that the term "sociostasis" be used when social systems rather than biological organisms are involved. Since there is no direct analogy with the homeostatic processes in the animal body, the term "internal balance" will generally be employed, except when referring to the concept of homeostasis as used in recent publications. The survival of behavior systems depends upon internal balance, but the maintenance of this balance lies in the realm of social process and is accomplished by quite different means than its counterpart in physiology.

2.   The Structure of Behavior Systems

The concept of an organized behavior system is broader than Commons' conception of a going concern. Any set of activities that tends to persist for more than a moment and that has certain other characteristics, to be enumerated shortly, may be taken as an organized behavior system. The range is from the world economy at one end to what Commons calls a "strategic transaction" at the other. A transaction or bargaining situation may persist for days if it goes beyond routine buying and selling and involves decisions of crucial importance. Between these extremes, there are several types of organized behavior systems of interest to marketing. These types include the firm, the industry, the marketing channel, the dispersion market, and the ultimate consuming unit.

Each type of organized behavior system has its specific characteristics which need to be determined through empirical investigation. Certain formal attributes tend to apply universally among all types of organized behavior systems. The foundation for the proposed theoretical position is a statement of what these general characteristics are. The description of an organized behavior system will be developed along two lines. The first step is to discuss the formal character of systems in general. After that, restrictions will be imposed in order to limit the theory to the field of organized human behavior.

A system is, first of all, composed of parts. This attribute of a system may be called *componency*. Other formal attributes correspond to the most universal relationships existing between a system and its components, and among the components themselves. One fundamental relationship is that one or more of the components of a system may qualify as subsystems with their own inherent tendencies toward persistent identity. Many of the most important phenomena in marketing grow out of the fact that some of the types of systems that have been named are commonly found to be components of other systems. Linton (1945) says that "every society from the primitive band to the modern state is really an organized aggregate of small organized groups." He calls this phenomenon "cellular organization."

A second formal attribute is that components may be arranged in series and each may function in turn in a process or reaction involving the whole series. In marketing terms, an obvious example is the distribution channel through which goods may flow from the producer through one or more types of intermediaries — for instance, wholesalers and retailers — and finally reach the ultimate consuming unit. This formal attribute may be called *seriality*.

An important special case of seriality is that in which the series returns upon itself and the flow continues in circular fashion. Circularity is present in all economic activity that is not designed to achieve a single nonrecurring objective. Schumpeter (1934) takes the circular flow as fundamental for his theory of economic development.

Another formal characteristic is that of concurrence. More commonly, concurrence is discussed in terms of the two separate aspects of *divergence* and *convergence*. In either case, concurrence may be regarded as a set of vectors running to or from a common point. In marketing, it may represent the alternatives for choice on the one hand or the joint impact of competitive efforts on the other. A sales executive considering different channels for the distribution of his goods represents the divergent aspect of concurrence. The same buyer being solicited by several competing salesmen is an example of convergence from the standpoint of the sellers.

There is an important special case of concurrence which characterizes many systems. The system may have one center of concurrence dominating all others. That is to say, the vectors running to or from this center are more numerous and connect directly or indirectly with more components than is true for any other center in the system. The characteristic of possessing a dominant center may be designated as centrality. It is a commonplace that centrality in some degree is found in nearly all formal organizations. Lundberg (1945) and other sociologists have found a high degree of centrality in informal organizations such as the set of friendly relationships in a community. The significance of this type of centrality for marketing was pointed out in the first Parlin Memorial Lecture.

It is believed that the structure of any system can be reduced to the primitive attributes of componency, seriality, and concurrence. In organized behavior systems, seriality and concurrrence will also appear in the special forms of *circularity* and *centrality*. Without these two attributes, it is difficult to conceive of an organized behavior system manifesting persistent identity over any considerable period of time. These structural attributes of a system provide a basis for analyzing the fundamental aspects of group behavior.

First, there is the phase of behavior that is directly concerned with the place of the components in the system. This may be called membership or positional behavior. Components extend recognition to each other as members of a system. The membership bond may arise in conjunction with mutual protection in the animal herd or savage tribe. At a later stage, the group determines and enforces property rights among its members. In the most advanced behavior systems, the desire to belong still implies that the aggregation of the components serves some purpose for the individual components. Where the system is not engaged in the production of goods to be shared, the association may serve chiefly as a congenial environment for self-expression. Clubs and fraternities are examples of systems based partly on this desire for congeniality.

Even a purely social group offers its members a form of security. While protection from physical harm may not be involved in a significant way, the group may provide prestige or help to preserve a member's self-esteem. Defense against a common enemy, recognition and enforcement of rights, and the enhancement of the individual sense of status through belonging to a preferred group provide strong motivations for positional behavior. Circularity is present in full measure, since each component of the system is both the agent exhibiting positional behavior and the object of such behavior on the part of the other components.

Membership activity tends to keep a system going. New members are accepted from time to time, as in the puberty rites of primitive tribes whereby the adolescent is admitted to adult society. Members may be ejected for various offences which threaten the integrity of the system.

Positions within the system are graded in power and prestige (Warner and Lunt, 1942). A number of members often aspire to the higher places, and the needs of the system demand that these places be filled as they become vacant through death or other causes. Rivals sometimes fight and kill each other off unless the group has developed less violent methods of choosing between them. Other members may accept subordinate rank and seek favor of the victorious leaders. Positional behavior normally tends to maintain a working balance among the status expectations of the members, and thus tends to keep the system intact. Centrality is an almost universal structural attribute which facilitates and controls positional adjustment in both formal and informal systems. Leadership identifies its destiny with the survival of the system, and tends to become an instrumentality of the system in reconciling the aspirations of other members.

The second fundamental aspect of group behavior is *communication*. The process of positional behavior for most of the systems that are of interest to marketing utilizes elaborate forms of communication. At the most elementary level, as in an ant colony or a herd of cattle, membership is probably established and perpetuated through such outward marks as characteristic sounds, smells, or movements. Language is essential to organization at the human level since it involves the formulation and enforcement of rules of membership. Given an ample means of communication, individuals no longer need to look alike or smell alike to be members of the same club. Criteria not open to direct perception can determine eligibility for membership — for example, grandfather's place of residence or acceptance of a religious creed.

Communication opens up possibilities for co-operative behavior other than membership activities. Operating systems arise in which components perform specialized functions in the production of goods and services. These differentiated activities may be co-ordinated through market exchange or through instructions and operating signals emanating from a control center. In either case, communication is the essential instrument of co-ordination in the development of functional specialization within operating systems.

Communication should not be regarded as the integrative factor through which internal balance is maintained, but only as a tool that may be used for that purpose. Social solidarity does not arise as a mechanical result of the number of telephones or the number of television sets in use. Language can be employed to express dislike and disagreement as well as concord. Nevertheless, the possibilities for expanding the size of systems and the scope of systemic activities are increased in direct proportion to the advance in techniques and facilities for communication. A marketing system — for instance, a distribution channel — may exhibit a strong membership bond, even though its components are scattered throughout the United States. The operations of the distribution channel may consist of many specialized processes carried out through subsystems known as retailers, wholesalers, and national sales companies. These marketing organizations perform their functions through staff members with diversified skills and training. An extremely complex network of communication is utilized in the course of the diversified marketing activities that start with the cotton or wool on the farm and end with the purchase of a dress in a retail store. The flow of communication is circular because it moves in both directions along the channel. It is highly centralized in the way in which it flows in and out of the centers of co-ordination.

In addition to positional behavior and communication, the third broad aspect of group activity is *operational behavior*. The operating system utilizes materials and resources and turns out goods or services. The product of a system may be regarded as the joint product of its components. Each component contributes its part to production and receives some share or claim upon the joint product. The structure of operations is concurrent and often highly centralized. The system of distribution as a whole is convergent in the way that raw materials move to central markets or manufacturing plants. It is divergent in the normal flow of the finished product to the ultimate consumer. The structure of distribution is serial in the way in which separately organized steps follow one another in the movement of goods. The economy as a whole is circular in structure, since each component gives up its own product and receives other products in return.

The development of differentiated operating systems affects positional behavior in a number of ways. The operating structure of the system provides status opportunities for individuals or subsystems. A component achieves status by fitting into the series of differentiated steps in a process. It achieves membership security by becoming part of the circular flow. Positions at or near a center of convergence are relatively advantageous and provide goals for an intensified status drive. A subsystem — for example, a business firm — may achieve position through technical competence in a function. Entry may be free and membership informal, as it is ideally under the theory of perfect competition, or the newcomer may have to be passed by the admissions committee of a guild or profession. In any case, the balance of status expectations within the subsystem is conditioned by the requirement that the subsystem must achieve position within the larger system. If no restrictions on entry are imposed by competitors, there may still be restrictions on entry arising from other causes. A retailer may be free to establish himself in a dispersion market, for example, but be limited by availability of sites, by the licensing and zoning regulations of the community, and by the distribution policies of the manufacturers whose goods he desires to sell.

The superior effectiveness of an operating system places a premium on the achievement of status within it. The more productive system has a larger output to share. The desire for goods reinforces the desire for status. The possession of goods contributes to the enhancement of membership status and prestige. Effective operation in the use of materials and resources generally enables a firm to enjoy a strong position in the market and to choose between alternatives for continuing to strengthen its position. The components of the system experience increasing confidence in the position of the system and hence in the satisfaction of their own status expectations through the system.

The specific character of techniques employed in using materials and resources is part of the subject matter of marketing to the extent that these techniques determine the effectiveness of an organization in making marketing adjustments. All of the details of marketing techniques are within the scope of marketing theory by this definition plus the critical aspects of production techniques. The techniques and facilities for communication in the market are involved in every aspect of marketing theory and practice. Marketing should follow with interest the new developments in the study of control and communication recently reported by Weiner (1948). They key problems discussed are those of the maximum amount of information that can be transmitted through a channel in a stated period of time. A distinction is drawn between pertinent message and noise. A message that is pertinent from one viewpoint might, of course, constitute noise in relation to another message competing for the use of the same channel. Some insights here may suggest new methods of evaluating advertising and other forms of communication in marketing. Wiener, incidentally, is pessimistic about the social outlook, finding no adequate mechanism for homeostasis in society. He feels that private ownership of the means of mass communication frustrates homeostatic adjustments, but he is left with the problem of explaining the historical fact of the survival of organized behavior systems.

3.   Rationality and Routines

In its day-to-day manifestations, the behavior system is a complex of established patterns or routines. The role of rationality may appear restricted within this framework, but it is nevertheless a vital role. Although each participant may have learned these routines largely through imitation, the pattern as a whole must be instrumental in order to be continued. In the more advanced behavior systems, each routine is likely to have been adopted to meet a recognized need or to replace another routine which was judged to be less efficient. The existing set of routines thus holds a dual relationship to rationality. It is both the end result of past exercise of rationality and the structure through which rationality operates currently to achieve conscious ends. The place of rationality and routine in the business firm has been analyzed in a luminous essay by Whitehead (1931).

Routines are liberating if they are rationally related to the goals to be served and if the administration of routines is rational and effective. The reduction of detailed activities to routine leaves time and energy for the considerations and calculations required to make strategic decisions. Some writers — for example, Mannheim (1940) — have held that the rationalization of economic activities necessarily narrows the range of freedom and rationality for the individual. A distinction is drawn between following a rational routine and truly rational behavior on the part of participants. This view may represent a reaction to some of the excesses of the scientific management movement in the United States and Europe. Under the modern theory of management growing out of the work of Mayo (1945, 1946), Barnard (1938), Bakke (1947), and others, a routine would not be considered genuinely rational if it needlessly restricted the individual's sense of participation or frustrated his status expectations.

placed if the system is to last. Neither does the persistent identity of the system rest on fixed habits or conditioned responses according to the formula of Watsonian behaviorism. There is no question of the reality of group discipline and the social pressure directed toward preserving the standard patterns. The individual, however thoroughly conditioned to start with, forgets the patterns, loses his skill in executing it, or diverges from it willfully. What most needs to be explained is why social pressure and the exercise of rationality combine to preserve the complex of activities that is continued through the survival of the behavior system.

> 1. An organized behavior system will tend to survive as long as the footing it occupies endures because of the collective action arising out of the status expectations of its components.

The individuals or subsystems that comprise a behavior system have a stake in its survival because it serves them as a ground of status. If it is an operating system, their expectations in relation to the system pertain also to the income or goods derived from it. These expectations are dependent upon status expectation, since shares in output are correlated with status. The portion of collective action oriented toward status expectations can thus be set up as the main factor in the preservation of the system. This view concerning the role of status expectations in group behavior is supported by recent developments in social psychology (Bakke, 1940, Bakke, 1946, Bakke, 1947).

Because the system is the ground for status, individuals work for it, scheme for it, and, upon occasion, are prepared to die for it. They will accept small returns over a long period if they feel that their status expectations will eventually be gratified. Most remarkable of all, perhaps, is the extent to which they will accept group discipline in the remolding of customary behavior to conform to the requirements of the system. An expanding system tends to require increasing specialization of its members in order to maintain the effective functioning of the system as a whole. Thus, group discipline may impose a differentiated pattern of rights and duties upon its members but with the whole complex oriented toward the preservation of the system.

The drive for place and recognition is believed by Wiener and others to be an antisocial factor that frustrates movements towards homeostasis. The present view is directly contrary, namely, that the status drive is the ultimate basis for internal balance in organized behavior systems. The stronger individuals struggle for dominant positions, while others play a more submissive role in order to continue as components of the system. The leaders, in their struggle for power, are obliged to court the loyalty of followers. The choice of leadership by followers depends on their estimate of how the choice will affect the future status pattern. Whatever stresses arise, the components tend to modify their relationships to maintain a workable pattern as long as each component continues to value its status in the system. That homeostasis is generally operative in behavior systems is indicated by the actual survival of systems over long periods of time.

While the stimulus of status expectations may explain persistent efforts to preserve the system, additional principles are needed to explain survival under certain circumstances. The second survival theorem is as follows:

> 2. An organized behavior system may survive the most aggressive attacks of competitors, because it is able to exist on the core of its position even though losing ground at the fringes, and meanwhile mature its own campaign that may utilize strategies that have been overlooked.

The competition of large business firms may be more intense and ruthless that the competition of small firms, as pointed out by Nourse and others. The problem then becomes that of explaining why firms can survive this kind of competition. The Marxian principle of capitalist accumulation is constantly being refuted in modern economies like that of the United States. Marx (1867) believed that capitalism was inevitably cannibalistic. However large enterprises became, some would be stronger than others, and the weak would always be devoured by the strong.

To understand modern marketing, it is necessary to recognize that selling takes the form of campaigns and strategies that must be effectuated over considerable periods of time. The importance of alternative strategies in economic behavior has been pointed out by von Neumann and Morgenstern (1947). The fact that a company may be fifth in a field of five is likely to be interpreted as a challenge by the marketing strategist rather than as a portent of doom. Even though the company is steadily losing in its relative position, the strategist may gamble on reversing the trend if he feels that the firm can hang on until his program had had time to take effect.

In particular, he will examine the activities of competitors, in the hope of finding his own opportunity in some weakness of their position. In order to succeed, they have been obliged to take definite stands in their relationships with customers and others. Thus, their choice of certain strategies may make other strategies unavailable to them. For example, the leaders may have differentiated their products in directions that make them more acceptable to one segment of the market but less acceptable to others. If often happens in modern competitive situations that a new firm arises to challenge the leadership in a field because, in reversing some of the policies of the leaders, it is fulfilling a demand that is not being met by the leaders.

There remains the situation in which an organized behavior system might be expected to disappear because of radical environmental disturbance affecting its functions. The third survival theorem, pertaining to this type of situation, is as follows:

> 3. An organized behavior system may survive despite severe functional disturbance resulting from environmental changes if sufficient plasticity remains so that

life of a business firm often depends directly on the life of the founder and owner. Today the corporate form of business organization prevails, and there is a presumption of immortality concerning the corporation. It is not likely that any of the firms now in existence will really last forever, but many large corporations have been in existence far longer than the lives of any of their present executives or owners.

The struggle for survival among organized behavior systems of all types has transcended some of the limitations of individual competition for survival. Earlier versions of economic theory were modeled directly on the struggle for survival in nature. In any given field many firms were engaged in competition, and the least efficient ones perished like unsuccessful individuals or animal species. New firms were constantly entering wherever opportunity existed, and economic evolution was presumed to parallel the emergence of new species under the law of the jungle.

Actually, a firm does not have to die because it is inefficient in its original function. It can be reorganized so that it can perform more effectively, or it can take on new functions. It may persist for a number of years without such internal adjustments through sheer inertia or momentum. A firm or any other organized behavior system is an expression of the expectations of individuals. Even though the surplus of goods or psychic satisfactions which the behavior system provides have diminished or disappeared, individuals may still cling to it because they have no better alternative. The momentum which keeps a firm going sometimes resides in large part in the energy and determination of the leader or of a small group of policy makers and investors. Expectations in business involve a weighing of risk against possible gains. Thus a firm with only a small chance of success can be kept intact over a long period by the hope of large gains in case that one chance prevails. These are some of the reasons why the outcome of competition with respect to survival and growth is not always what might be predicted on the basis of the theory of pure competition.

Survival through Status Expectations of Subsystems

In ecology an individual or species is presumed to survive because there is a place for it in the scheme of things. That means that the environment offers an opportunity which cannot be exploited so successfully by any other individual or species. This position in the web of life has been variously called a niche, a foothold, or a footing. The importance of this chance for survival in life and in society was dramatically expressed by the sociologist Robert Park in saying that even a blade of grass must have a place to stand. Similarly, a business firm or any other organized behavior system must have a footing or a place to stand in order to survive and prosper. In an earlier statement the writer expressed this condition of survival in what he called the first survival theorem, which reads as follows: *An organized behavior system will tend to survive as long as the footing it occupies endures because of the collective action arising out of the status expectations of its components.*

The individuals or subsystems that comprise a behavior system have a stake in its survival because it serves them as a ground of status. If it is an operating system, their expectations in relation to the system pertain also to the income or goods derived from it. These expectations are dependent upon status expectations, since shares in output are correlated with status. The portion of collective action oriented toward status expectations can thus be identified as the main factor in the preservation of the system. This view concerning the role of status expectations in group behavior is supported by recent developments in social psychology.

Because the system is the ground for status, individuals work for it, scheme for it, and upon occasion are prepared to die for it. They will accept small returns over a long period if they feel that their status expectations will eventually be gratified. Most remarkable of all, perhaps, is the extent to which they will accept group discipline in the remolding of customary behavior to conform to the requirements of the system. An expanding system tends to require increasing specialization of its members in order to maintain the effective functioning of the system as a whole. Thus, group discipline may impose a differentiated pattern of rights and duties upon its members but with the whole complex oriented toward the preservation of the system.

Survival through Competitive Strategy

Another shortcoming of the traditional picture of economic competition is that it deals only with the tactics of competition and ignores its strategy. In other words, it portrays a continuous and unrelenting battle in which the weaker contestants are constantly failing and disappearing and reinforcements are constantly entering the fray. Actually, when a competitor has gained a foothold, he begins to think in terms of campaigns by which he can expand his position. Often it is only the campaign which fails rather than the firm itself. After an unsuccessful campaign a firm is able to draw back into its original position and await another opportunity to launch a better-prepared attack. It is in the nature of any ecological niche or position in the market to have a core and a fringe. The core is that part of the environment which is most completely suited to the operations of the individual organism or group. Often the core is relatively free from attack, since no competitor can invade it without operating at a disadvantage. The fringe is that part of the environment in which the individual or group can still operate but at a lower efficiency. The fringe extends out to the point where the particular entity loses its differential advantage and must compete on equal terms and, at the outside limit, would suffer a disadvantage in attempting to expand any further. The writer has previously discussed this phenomenon in what he called the second theorem of survival: *An organized behavior system may survive the most aggressive attacks of competitors because it is able to exist at the core of its position even though losing ground at the fringes and, meanwhile, mature its own campaign which may utilize strategies that have been overlooked by competitors.*

To understand modern marketing, it is necessary to recognize that selling takes the form of campaigns and strategies that must be effectuated over considerable periods of time. The importance of alternative strategies in economic behavior has been pointed out by von Neuman and Morgenstern. The fact that a company may be fifth in a field of five is likely to be interpreted as a challenge by the marketing strategist rather than as a portent of doom. Even though the company is steadily losing in its relative position, the strategist may gamble on reversing the trend if he feels that the firm can hang on until his program has had time to take effect.

In particular, he will examine the activities of competitors in the hope of finding his own opportunity in some weakness of their position. In order to succeed, they have been obliged to take definite stands in their relationships with customers and others. Thus, their choice of certain strategies may make other strategies unavailable to them. For example, the leaders may have differentiated their products in directions that make them more acceptable to one segment of the market but less acceptable to others. It often happens in modern competitive situations that a new firm rises to challenge the leadership in a field because, in reversing some of the policies of the leaders, it is fulfilling a demand that is not met by the leaders.

Survival through Plasticity

The third type of situation is that in which an organized behavior system persists despite the fact that its original function has disappeared. An effective organization comes to be an important asset itself to all the individuals who have participated in its activities. Continued group coherence at the human level may rest in moderate degree on the fact that the individuals who make up the group have come to trust each other and to enjoy working together. An organization can grow out of some temporary need. It may persist by taking on another function. One of our greatest universities was founded because a group of men who had been working together selling Liberty Bonds in the First World War were reluctant to disband. Having enjoyed working as a team in raising money, they looked around for another good cause and decided to collect a fund to establish a university in their city. There are some remarkable examples among business firms of passing through a series of transformations. One well-known New England firm began many years ago in the manufacture of pumps. During the Civil War it turned to the manufacture of rifles because it was one of the few firms with an adequate knowledge of metalworking. It never got back to manufacturing pumps. The manufacture of rifles took the firm still further in the direction of precision metalworking. Today it is one of the leading machine-tool builders in the United States and seems likely hereafter to expand on that base rather than going through any further radical transformations. The third survival theorem, intended to characterize this situation, is as follows: *An organized behavior system may survive despite severe functional disturbance resulting from environmental changes if sufficient plasticity remains so that new functions may develop or new methods may be adopted for performing existing functions.*

It is in a fact of common observation that organized behavior systems frequently survive after their original functions have disappeared. This is true of business firms and government bureaus, among other types of behavior systems. To survive under such conditions requires that the system be able to remain intact during a difficult transition period. This may happen if there is an overlapping between the gradual disappearance of the old function and the establishment of the new function. In some cases the resources of the system are such as to enable it to persist for a time without functioning at all. In any case such a transition calls for a high degree of plasticity on the part of the components of the system.

"Plasticity" may be defined as the capacity for undergoing a reshaping of behavior patterns. A greatly expanded conception of the range of plasticity in human behavior has emerged from the modern approach in cultural anthropology. The fact that such radical transformation in the functioning of a system can happen at all is striking proof of the vitality of systems and the strength of the drive for survival. The more highly specialized the behavior system, the more serious does functional disturbance become. Specialization necessarily arises with the expansion of the system and the increasing range of its activities. In times of stress or unavoidable contraction of activity, versatility is at a premium as compared with specialization. In complex systems, rational planning emerges as a response to the need for accelerating specialization without aggravating vulnerability.

Survival through Growth

The second systematic goal is that of continuous growth. That is to say that systems often behave as if they were driving toward the goal of becoming larger and larger. Sometimes rapid growth seems to be taking advantage of a vacuum in the ecological setting, as in the case already mentioned of rabbits when first introduced into Australia. In human organizations growth may occur in spite of major obstacles or may even seem to be stimulated by them. Here the rate of growth depends on the force of the drive behind it. The expectations of the individuals involved may be heightened by hopes for great gains or relative ease of growth once initial obstacles are overcome. In general, there are two sources of growth for an operating organization. It may expand the volume of its present activities, or it many engage in new activities. In marketing terms this usually means selling more of the same product or adding more products to the line.

The drive for growth is often reinforced by the conviction that growth is necessary for survival. A truism widely accepted in American business it that it is necessary to go forward in order not to fall backward. A firm that becomes overshadowed by its rivals may lose out altogether unless it is content to compete for a very restricted part of the total market. In the early history of man, it is probable that large organizations wiped out many small ones or in some cases absorbed their remnants. Marx assumed the same thing would necessarily happen in free competition among business firms, with an inevitable trend toward concentration and monopoly. The worst results predicted by Marx have not been borne out by history. In the United States the total number of firms continues to increase as fast as the total population, although there have been some important changes in the size distribution, which will be analyzed later.

American business firms range from giant corporations to one-man operations, but growth is an essential aspect of competition for all. Vitality is required even for survival; but vitality is difficult to maintain without growth, at least in the American business climate. The vitality of a firm depends on the vigor and ambition of its members. The prospect of growth is one of the principal means by which a firm can attract able and vigorous recruits. Thus, management in a typical firm is caught in a cycle in which growth is essential even though management may not have an intense desire for expansion. If the firm does not grow, it cannot compete for the more able candidates among executives and workers. If the character of its membership deteriorates, it is likely to lose out altogether in competition.

The growing firm also attracts favorable attention from customers and from suppliers. Suppliers tend to give favorable treatment to any customer firm which is growing rapidly, hoping to retain it as a customer when it has attained a larger size. New types of marketing institutions which have appeared from time to time, such as chain stores, have profited materially from this attitude on the part of producers supplying them with goods. Similarly, the customer who has ventured to buy from a relatively new firm is confirmed in his judgment by its continued growth and is inclined to recommend it to others. Another aspect of growth in operating organizations is its relation to commitments between the top executive and his subordinates. Often he has had to hold out the lure of company expansion in order to get the men he wants. He and they must work together successfully to achieve these goals if the organization is to hold together.

The emphasis on growth is not peculiar to America or to business but applies to many societies and many types of organized behavior systems in which new possibilities are constantly being opened up through technological advance. In fact, the principle would have to be modified only slightly in a completely static society. In this case the commitment between superior and subordinate would relate to the maintenance of the present level of activity and the security of the individual's status rather than the improvement in his position. Even in our own dynamic society, rates of change vary by industry and among firms, as do the relative values placed by individuals upon security and growth.

1.   Stages in Business Growth

The life history of a typical business can be divided into three stages, differing as to rate of growth. The middle stage is the period of most rapid growth, with slower growth in the earlier and later stages. These three stages in business history provide a convenient starting point for consideration of the strategy of growth. The stages in growth can be labeled as those of establishment, expansion, and stabilization. These words characterize a central focus for business policy in each stage. In simpler terms the most urgent goal in each successive stage might be described as getting started, getting ahead, and getting set. It is not desirable to overemphasize the difference from stage to stage, since the general pattern of daily operation is identical in many respects for large and small business. From the viewpoint of strategy, however, there is a real difference in the relative importance of policy issues as a business passes from one stage to the next. These issues pertain to promotion, pricing, distribution policy, product development, and investment in plant capacity to meet anticipated demand. To simplify the discussion, the subject will be presented primarily from the standpoint of the company producing and selling a single product. These observations about the growth process are believed to hold for all types of organized behavior systems. The discussion will proceed in terms of the business firm in order to make it more vivid for the marketing student, even at the risk of anticipating matters which will be treated in more detail later on.

Stage 1: Establishment

Many of the most difficult problems of business strategy are those facing a company which is just entering business. That is one reason why so few survive beyond their initial effort to get started. In the past it might be said that management was either very farsighted or very lucky in any enterprise that succeeded in getting a foothold. Today it is much more feasible to estimate in advance the prospects of success. The company with a meritorious product and some experience in normal business operation can obtain answers through scientific methods that were at one time available only at the costly basis of trial and error.

The most urgent requirement with respect to the new business or the new product is knowledge of the market. Ideally, the investigation of the market should take place before the final design of the product has been determined. Even though a product meets a definite need, it may fail to achieve acceptance through some minor flaw which might have been corrected. Intimate and detailed knowledge is needed as to the way in which such products are used and as to educational problems in teaching people to use an improved product.

The first and most basic question to be answered is that of how demand for the product is to be promoted. If the idea is new, people will have to be told about it in order to buy the product. The drive to succeed whatever the cost is also a major factor. An operation that was otherwise promising may fail, just before it turns the corner, through the exhaustion of either its assets or the confidence of its management.

Stage 2: Expansion

During the period of expansion the emphasis in the firm's objectives generally shifts from securing a place in the market to excelling and outdistancing competition. The goal of maximum sales is gradually substituted for that of minimum risk. Competitive efficiency in promoting sales and in other aspects of distribution becomes the touchstone of success.

The natural sales trend is sharply upward during this period. The chief goal of management is to accelerate this rate of growth without permitting a corresponding increase in costs per unit. Advertising through mass media may be relied upon increasingly to reach an ever-broader public. If so, there will be an attempt to find an advertising formula which fits the product and its market. Numerous experiments may be necessary to find an application of the power of mass media to the selling methods through which the product gained a foothold.

Increasing sales should lead to lower costs per unit. Savings in distribution costs do not arise in altogether automatic fashion from larger volume. The increased scale of operation offers an opportunity for savings through adoption of appropriate methods. Management may or many not discern these opportunities throughout the period of expansion. This applies to production as well as distribution processes. Faster assembly and packaging lines, more specialized use of labor, new devices for increasing the productivity of salesmen, and a greater reliance on mass-distribution channels are among the changes which may be introduced to keep pace with increasing volume.

This is the period in which there is the maximum opportunity to use price as an instrument of sales strategy. Generally speaking, prices on manufactured products tend to be downward over the period. Prices are reduced in the hope of attracting all the new customers who are now ready to buy. Any slower rate of adjustment will encourage competition to enter the field. To reduce prices any faster is to forego gross income which is essential to the fullest expansion of the business.

Many marketing organizations during the period of greatest expansion follow the financial policy of keeping profits down to a moderate rate and plowing the bulk of earnings back into promotional expenditures or other activities directed toward expansion, such as technical and economic research. The chief limitation of this viewpoint is that it may be necessary to pay out some profits as a means of attracting new investors. It may not be possible for the entire increase in working capital to come out of earnings. In many cases, borrowing or new stock issues provide most of the new funds required. The business may have to show steady though moderate profits in order to obtain loans or new equity capital.

Stage 3: Consolidation

In the third stage of business growth the objective is the most favorable outlook as to stable and continuing profits. The well-established company does not point toward the greatest possible earnings this year or next. The ideal aim is to make a good showing year after year, meanwhile preserving and expanding the assets of the company.

It is not suggested that the company which has reached this stage in its life history will give up all hope of further rapid expansion. Some change in demand or in the technological possibilities of production may initiate a whole new cycle. Management should be ever alert to such eventualities. The established company occupying such a position of leadership is usually obliged to work for two broad objectives. One is to improve conditions for its industry, and the other is to maintain its relative position within the industry. Its requirements as to volume of sales are so large that it directs its promotion to all possible customers. Its advertising is almost certain to create customers for its smaller competitors as well as for itself. Its product quality and its prices set up standards which others may strive to meet in the one case and cut under in the other. Meanwhile, as more and more competitors enter the field, its percentage share of the total market inevitably declines, even though its dollar volume may continue to increase.

The two great periods in the history of a firm are the initial stage in which it is struggling for a foothold and the period when it has attained its major growth and a slowing-down of expansion appears imminent. Some firms which have had a meteoric rise go into an equally dramatic decline. Executives who looked good when they were being carried along by the momentum of steady growth may prove unable to cope with the problems of business maturity. Junior executives and other valued employees may become disaffected because the chances for personal advancement no longer appear so bright. Trouble starts even before the turn occurs if management fails to recognize the approaching change in the trend or chooses to ignore the warning signals. Millions of dollars can be spent in a vain effort to pierce the ceiling on the assumption that the old rate of growth can be maintained. Large advance commitments for advertising and sales organization can be built up on this assumption, resulting in disastrous cutbacks when the change in trend finally becomes apparent.

The stages of growth for the firm have been described in ordinary business terms, but the dynamics of growth arise from the inherent nature of organized behavior systems. A system survives because of the expectations it creates in its members. A system grows in order to meet their expectations more fully, and growth itself creates still greater expectations. The members or at least the leaders within a system are oriented toward growth by means of the power principle. However, they must act to maximize the outputs of the system. There is an overriding rationality in promoting the power to act. With respect to the firm the power principle has direct application to the three stages of its life history. First, there is the objective of gaining a foothold in order to be able to act at all. Next, there is an enhancement of the power to act through expansion. Finally, there is the attempt to maintain it through consolidation.

References

Clements, F. E. and Shelford, V. E. (1939). *Bio-ecology*. John Wiley & Sons, Inc., New York.

Homans, George C. (1950). *The Human Group*. Harcourt, Brace Co., New York.

Lundberg, G. A. (1945). *Marketing and Social Organization*. Curtis Publishing Co., Philadelphia. This was the first Parlin Memorial Lecture.

Moreno, J. L. (1934). *Who Shall Survive?* Nervous and Mental Diseases Publishing Co., Washington, D. C.

Shannon, Claude E. and Weaver, Warren (1949). *Mathematical Theory of Communication*. University of Illinois Press, Urbana.

Wiener, N. (1948). *Cybernetics or Control and Communication in the Animal and the Machine*. Wiley & Sons, Inc., New York.

Some of the key concepts of this book are drawn from the interplay between economics and biology. Darwin's great hypothesis about evolution was inspired in part by the writings of Malthus, an economist and population theorist. Today ecology is a recognized branch of biology and might be loosely defined as the economics of plant and animal societies. Ecology in turn is currently contributing to a deeper understanding of organized behavior systems in human society.

Moreno's book was one of the first to analyze the membership bonds which characterize group structure. He is one of the founders of the branch of sociology known as sociometry. The book by Homans reports several more recent studies of the structure and function of small groups.

Shannon and Weaver developed their theory as an aid to designing telephone circuits and similar communication channels. Wiener adapted these ideas to a consideration of the human nervous system. They can also be applied to communication within a social system.

The lecture by Lundberg is one of the first formal applications of sociometry to marketing. It initiated a series of annual lectures honoring Charles Coolidge Parlin, marketing pioneer who made use of some of the same notions in an intuitive but effective fashion.

Chapter 7

THE POWER PRINCIPLE*

Wroe Alderson

The power drive finds dynamic expression through what may be called "the power principle." An individual or an organization, in order to prevail in the struggle for survival, must act in such a way as to promote the power to act. The power principle is especially important in relation to the expansion of a growing system. As a system grows, it is increasing its power or capacity to carry on its regular processes on a greater scale. The existence of power is a necessary condition for the continuance of many of these activities. Therefore the maintenance and the enhancement of power is an inherent goal for any organized behavior system. A cohesive behavior system operates as if it were animated by the power principle, even though this is only a reflection of the behavior of its leading members. The power principle has a number of specific applications or corollaries which can be observed in group behavior.

Some of the corollaries of the power principle pertain to the control and use of energy or capacity for action. A system may attempt to extend its control over additional sources of energy or to increase its capacity for the various aspects of its operation. In business terms this may mean either buying or selling a new plant or acquiring new mineral or other natural resources. There are also frequent attempts, in line with the power principle, to increase the efficiency of the organization in the use of energy or capacity already under its control. All of these possibilities with respect to greater control or increasing efficiency apply to marketing just as much as to production.

Other consequences of the power principle pertain to executive decision as a general principle governing the choice among alternatives. Economic theory centers attention on alternatives which represent a greater or smaller return in relation to the value of inputs involved. Marketing is also concerned with alternatives which will determine the course of action over a longer period of time and where results of choice cannot be measured in immediate monetary returns. The application of the power principle requires that choice in the current

---

*Originally appeared in *Marketing Behavior and Executive Action* (1957), pages 51-52.

situation will be such as to broaden freedom of choice in the future. The strategy of marketing is concerned with situations in which the wrong choice of method in entering a market may in effect block the opportunity and narrow the range of choice which can be exercised by management thereafter. In developing a new market, the first goal is to establish a beach-head or a foothold, but it is equally important to select the beach-head in such a way that it is possible to move forward thereafter. The best market strategist is usually the one who is able to project his vision further into the future and to foresee the consequences of the initial steps. He is also able to evaluate opportunity more accurately, seeing it as an opportunity for growth in a given area rather than the prospect for immediate sales. Since he is looking forward to the development of a growing market, he tries to avoid rash steps in the beginning which would foreclose this prospect.

The power principle can also be interpreted in relation to risk and the executive function of weighing alternative risks. The greatest risk of all for anyone exercising power is that of losing it by pushing it too far. The power principle suggests a reasonable restraint in the exercise of power, both as to the goals for which it is to be used and as to the form in which it is exerted. This consequence of the power principle should result in prudence but not excessive caution. No system of action can be directed successfully by making avoidance of risk the principal aim. The difficulty is that there is no escape from risk because the risks associated with inaction are often more severe than the risks of action.

Chapter 8

MARKETING EFFICIENCY AND THE PRINCIPLE OF POSTPONEMENT*

Wroe Alderson

Marketing efficiency within a complete system of distribution can be promoted through application of the principle of postponement. Distribution cost analysis has been successfully applied in the past to problems of efficiency for individual marketing units. Less progress has been made in evaluating the efficiency of a complete system or marketing flow such as the movement of a major agricultural crop from grower to consumer.

1. Postponement in Product Differentiation

Changes in form may occur along the way, varying from elaborate fabrication and combination of raw materials to mere cleaning or packaging of a product which is to reach the consumer in essentially the same form as that in which it was produced. Changes in location of inventory occur as the product moves from farm to elevator, to factory, to warehouse, to retail store. Efficiency in the basic marketing processes depends on a proper ordering of these related steps involving changes in form, identity, or place.

The marketing process, like any other process, is extended in time. It can be viewed as a series of steps which need to be arranged in the most effective sequence. The process is marked by a definite direction which can be defined in terms of what is happening to the product along the way. The product starts out as materials which are relatively raw and unspecialized. It ends up as a relatively refined and specialized article, shaped to a type of need and fitted to the specific requirements of the individual consumer who buys it. To serve the individual consumer, the product must assume a special character as to its use qualities; these qualities must be adequately identified in relation to the proposed use; and it must be available at a convenient place when the consumer wants it.

---

*Originally appeared in *Marketing Behavior and Executive Action* (1957), pages 423-427.

All of these changes in form, identity, and location of the product are bracketed by the economist under the term "product differentiation." The closer the product is to the point of consumer purchase, the more differentiated it becomes. For many kinds of products the demand of the individual consumer is unique, or nearly so, when all of his special requirements are taken into account — including basic use, special features, color, size, and place of purchase. Mass production is made possible by the vast and intricate system of sorting which lies between the standardized output of farm or factory and the unique requirements of individual consumers.

Sorting as carried on by marketing agencies lays the foundation for mass production but raises its own problems of efficiency. How can the cost of sorting be controlled, so that it will not absorb all the savings in production costs made possible by sorting? One general method which can be applied in promoting the efficiency of a marketing system is the postponement of differentiation. As already stated, the principle of postponement requires that changes in form and identity occur at the latest possible point in the marketing flow; and changes in inventory location occur at the latest possible point in time.

The first aim of postponement is to permit sorting to occur to the greatest possible extent while the product is in a relatively undifferentiated state. Sorting by large lots is less costly per unit of product than sorting in small lots. Grading and refining of a product sets up separate identities which must be recognized in subsequent sorting. Dispersion of supply to a number of places reduces the scale on which sorting can proceed thereafter.

In addition to reducing the cost of sorting, postponement serves to reduce marketing risk. Every differentiation which makes a product more suitable for a specified segment of the market makes it less suitable for other segments. If a pair of shoes is to be purchased by the author of this book, it must be shaped to the size of 8 double E. That differentiation makes the product unsuitable for purchase by the great majority of consumers. It must also be stocked by a store in Philadelphia, which eliminates it from practical consideration by men in San Francisco or New Orleans. To make up shoes to a certain size or last is to assume a marketing risk related to the reliability of the estimate of demand for that size. To take the additional step of shipping the shoes to Philadelphia involves a further risk as to the share of the market represented by this city. Each step in differentiation is taken on the basis of some prediction concerning demand for that differentiation at some future time. Postponement cuts down that risk by moving the differentiation nearer to the time of purchase.

The principle of postponement might be reduced to absurdity by concluding that it pointed to the complete postponement of every step in the process. Thus, materials would be turned over to the consumer in the raw state; and he would be asked to make the best of them. This absurdity is avoided because the product must at least be moved from its original source to the place of purchase.

and that movement must be completed in time for the product to be available when the consumer expects to buy it. Similarly, there are other limits as to the postponability of each step in the process. Fabrication cannot be postponed beyond the point in the marketing process at which the necessary plant equipment and labor skills are available. Preservative processes for perishable goods must be applied soon enough in the marketing flow to be effective. Processes of refinement which greatly reduce the weight of raw material must be applied soon enough to avoid wasteful expenditure for transportation. Postponement as a technical concept is an aid in allocating the scarce resource of time and has no resemblance to wasting it through procrastination.

Orderly application of the principle of postponement means the separate consideration of limits for each step in the process. Each step in turn is regarded as a candidate for postponement. The limits of postponability with respect to each step are taken into account. The final outcome of this analysis is the arrangement of the steps in the most effective sequence. Each step has been postponed to the latest feasible point in the sequence.

2.   Postponement of Changes in Inventory Location

With respect to the postponement of changes in inventory location, the analyst works back from the anticipated time of consumer purchase. Retail stocks should be replenished often enough to maintain adequate displays and to provide some margin of safety for unexpected variations in demand. Wholesale stocks should provide against similar contingencies, and wholesale purchases should allow for time in transit. A marketing agency that engaged in any form of processing would also have to allow for its normal production time. During any remaining time that the designated goods are in existence, the efficiency of the system would be enhanced by holding them as far back in the marketing flow as possible.

When the analyst is examining a going system of marketing for any product, he will usually find a partial but imperfect adherence to the principle of postponement. Some steps in the process are handled in a particular manner and at a particular place because the business grew up that way. Such a pattern often persists even though important changes have occurred in sources of raw materials, the character of demand, and technological possibilities as to processing and transportation. The principle of postponement provides a starting point for a critical examination of the present pattern and recommendations of changes which will promote efficiency.

Analysis and planning can speed up adjustments in a marketing system; but the principle of postponement tends to work itself out by less formal means, given enough time. Many of the changes in marketing in recent years can readily be interpreted as applications of this principle. The tremendous emphasis on rapid turnover of inventory in wholesale and retail establishments is one obvious application. This movement has been carried to extremes at times by merchants who made the highest possible turnover an end in itself. The correct rate of turnover could be determined in each case by a move conscious and precise application of the principle of postponement. Starting from the goal of postponing the replenishment of stocks, and giving due consideration to the factors limiting postponability, the question of turnover rate would answer itself.

Postponement of differentiation has brought about large savings in the marketing and handling of basic raw materials. The development of petroleum pipe lines capitalizes upon the fluid character of the original raw material and postpones as long as possible the breaking-down of supply into separate lots which must be loaded and unloaded into tank cars and trucks. Manufacturers of many products made of steel, from refrigerator cabinets to carpet tacks, purchase steel in relatively undifferentiated form from the rolling mills, with fairly uniform requirements as to physical handling in transportation and storage.

3.   Elimination through Postponement

Another advantage in examining the postponability of a step is that it may turn out that it can be eliminated entirely. If a step is not performed prematurely, it may never have to be performed at all. Many years ago the author "bucked wheat" in the Palouse country of eastern Washington. That meant following a combine which was leaving sacks of wheat behind it and throwing the sacks onto a truck. Today the grain is not bagged at all. A truck with an open box body travels with the combine, and the loose grain pours directly into the box. When one truck is full and leaves for the elevator, another truck pulls into line. The same kind of change is now occurring in the case of dry edible beans and peas. At one time the whole crop was bagged in the field and then had to be dumped out at the elevator for cleaning. Today, about half the crop moves from farm to elevator in bulk.

The development of self-service food markets proves that differentiation can sometimes be avoided by passing certain steps on to the consumer. At first it seemed unlikely that the majority of consumers would want to give up the service of having groceries delivered to their homes or undertake the extra work assembling their own orders in the store. It must always be kept in mind that the consumer is engaged in sorting also and may prefer an opportunity for effective selection to further differentiations undertaken by the seller. In the supermarket the urban housewife is able to make a rapid and efficient selection of the items she wants for one or more meals for her family. At one time, she may have made a similar selection from a well-stocked home larder. Like the retailer, she has reduced the size of her working stocks by postponing purchase now tha the self-service store offers such a convenient assortment from which she can make her selection.

The principle of postponement is not presented as an answer to all planning problems in marketing. It is only one major analytical tool that can be derived from the view that sorting is the essential marketing function. This view, in turn, has its limitations, pertaining as it does to the external relations of exchange among marketing units. There are other problems which can best be approached from the standpoint of the internal unity of systems and the survival values inherent in organized systems. For this type of problem, it is appropriate to employ a different set of tools, derived from such concepts as market position and market organization, market opportunity and marketing effort.

Chapter 9

COMPETITION FOR DIFFERENTIAL ADVANTAGE*

Wroe Alderson

The application of ecology to marketing organizations provides a new starting
point for the study of competition. It begins with the assumption of heterogeneity
in the market as the normal or prevailing condition, rather than building on an
assumption of homogeneity as the ideal condition. The emergence of relatively
homogeneous conditions at certain stages of the competitive process is treated
as a tendency which can be functionally useful for some aspects of marketing
operations rather than as an essential aspect of effective competition.

Starting as it does with an analysis of organized behavior systems, the functionalist
approach tries to understand how competition of the prevailing type can contribute
to the effective operation of behavior systems. This is in sharp contrast to the
approach that starts with a competitive ideal and finds itself obliged to reduce
behavior systems such as firms to bloodless and abstract entities because the going
concern of real life does not fit the pattern. There is no desire, however, to detract
from the great achievement of economists in developing their deductive analytical
apparatus to the point where it approximates the view of competition which is
obtained more directly by making a fresh start from ecology. The substance
of the functionalist approach is very similar to what Chamberlin implied by
"monopolistic competition" and what J. M. Clark has recently designated as "the
economics of differential advantage."

1.   The Economics of Differential Advantage

The functionalist or ecological approach to competition begins with the assumption that every firm must seek and find a function in order to maintain itself
in the market place. Every business firm occupies a position which is in some
respects unique. Its location, the products it sells, its operating methods, or the
customers it serves tend to set if off in some degree from every other firm. Each
firm competes by making the most of its individuality and its special character. It is constantly seeking to establish some competitive advantage. Absolute
advantage in the sense of an advanced method of operation is not enough if all

---

*Originally published in *Marketing Behavior and Executive Action* (1957), pages 101-120.

competitors live up to the same high standards. What is important in competition is differential advantage, which can give a firm an edge over what others in the field are offering.

Differential Advantage and Dynamic Competition

It is the unending search for differential advantage which keeps competition dynamic. A firm which has been bested by competitors according to certain dimensions of value in products or services always has before it the possibility of turning the tables by developing something new in other directions. The company which has the lead is vulnerable to attack at numerous points. Therein is a strong incentive for technical innovation and other forms of economic progress, both for the leader who is trying to stay out in front and for others who are trying to seize the initiative.

Departures from previous product designs or patterns of practice will not be successful unless they appeal to needs or attitudes of the buyer. Differentiation by the seller is an adaptation to differences in taste and requirements among consumers. Demand is radically heterogeneous or diversified and quite independent of the actions of the seller. Supply also breaks down into heterogeneous segments according to differences in location, raw materials, plant equipment, and the skills of management and labor. The processes of exchange in the market place are directed toward matching up segments of supply and demand to provide the best fit.

This conception of an economics of differential advantage has important consequences for the analysis of monopoly and competition and for the choice of criteria to determine the degree of competitiveness in a given industry. New firms enter a field because of an expectation of enjoying differential advantage. Their chance for survival depends on whether their expectations were realistic in the first place and whether the original advantage is maintained or wrested from them by others. The profit incentive provides the drive for vigorous competition, but this drive is directed toward differential advantage because of the fundamentally heterogeneous character of markets. The enterpriser accepts the risks of innovation in his search for differential advantage. Success may be rewarded by profits until other enterprisers overtake him. Later sections will develop further implications of this view for both market structure and market behavior.

The term "differential advantage" is currently being used by J. M. Clark, who developed the concept of workable competition. It is adopted here as the term which best characterizes the dynamics of competitive advantage. Much of the underlying analysis was developed by E. H. Chamberlin, who inaugurated a new era in the theory of the firm something over twenty years ago.

Differential Advantage and Monopolistic Competition

In his formulation of the theory of monopolistic competition, Chamberlin was applying to a wider field and developing with a greater elegance methods of analysis which, in their essentials, are already to be found in earlier economists such as Walras and Marshall. The roots of the economics of differential advantage go back still further, to the treatment of the division of labor and regional specialization by Adam Smith and Ricardo. J. M. Clark makes a fresh start by dealing directly with the struggle for differential advantage as the essence of competition. Chamberlin reaches a similar position in his later discussions of monopolistic competition by beginning with the traditional concepts of monopoly and pure competition and showing how they are usually blended in concrete situations.

Not a few economists join with Chamberlin in the advancement of a theory blending monopoly and competition. Arthur R. Burns in 1936 wrote: "The elements of monopoly . . . can no longer be regarded as occasional and relatively unimportant aberrations from competition. They are such an organic part of the industrial system that it is useless to hope they can be removed by law." W. A. Joehr points out that bilateral monopolies and oligopolies form a part of the competitive system. "Thus even if the existing structure of the present market economy could be called a 'world of monopolies,' its system of coordination could nevertheless be termed a competitive mechanism." It is the opinion of another contemporary, Kurt Rothschild, that the more realistic models of competition advanced by Chamberlin and Joan Robinson seemed to destroy the last nimbus which the idea of competition had managed to save through all the years of skepticism and criticism, by showing that so many adverse features were not occasional blemishes but were a part and parcel of the way competition works in our world.

Such terms as "pure competition" and "pure monopoly" have little relevance except for tracing the transition from an atomistic model to what is essentially an ecological view of competition among business firms. If Chamberlin had been the first major student of the subject, he might have moved more directly toward the creation of an appropriate theory. That would have meant starting with a recognition that markets are radically heterogeneous on both the supply side and the demand side. Under this approach, pure competition is nothing more than a limiting case in which there is a tendency to approach homogeneity. It is only an analytical reference point; and the true norm is effective competition, or that state of affairs which will facilitate the flow of goods in heterogeneous markets.

The fact that Chamberlin started from the traditional view led him to apply the slightly invidious term of "monopolistic competition" to what we recognized as the normal situation.

Preoccupied as they were with the problem of resource allocation, economists of the classical school devised an ingenious framework for the solution of the allocation problem. In the classical system, market structures were classified under either of two mutually exclusive categories, pure monopoly or perfect competition. In capsule form, a perfectly competitive market situation is one in which large numbers of atomistic buyers and sellers exchange an identical product. Since by assumption the quantities purchased or offered by any one buyer or seller do not represent a significant portion of the total amount being exchanged, no individual has an appreciable influence on the selling price. And since in any market the product is homogeneous, buyers are indifferent as to the source of their supply. It is assumed, moreover, that all productive resources are completely mobile and will move promptly to industrial sectors where money rewards are highest. Finally, in a perfectly competitive market all buyers and sellers and productive services are fully informed of available alternatives.

The Functionalist Approach

Within these assumption (and taking the distribution of income as given), the allocation of resources will be "ideal." Consumer want-satisfaction will be maximized. All productive services will be compensated according to their contribution to the national income. Business firms will be compelled to produce at lowest costs per unit of output in the short run and to adopt the most efficient size of plant in the long run. Should an innovation create economic rents (excess profits), additional resources will flow into the industry until the rents are dissipated. In brief, under static conditions, changes in demand or costs will set in motion adjustments which will bring about a new position of equilibrium.

2.   Business Expectations in Heterogeneous Markets

Chamberlin formulated the principle that the market for every competitor is in some degree unique, thus initiating a drastic revision in competitive theory. This "market uniqueness" he believed to be due mainly to the phenomenon known as "product differentiation," a concept involving both monopoly and competition. Grether and his associates, pursuing this lead from a marketing viewpoint, have suggested the equally helpful concept of enterprise differentiation which is implicit in the present treatment. Chamberlin writes that "a general call of product is differentiated if any significant basis exists for distinguishing the goods (or services) of one seller from those of another." The basis may be real or fancied, so long as it is of any importance to buyers and leads to a preference for one variety of the product over another. The market for each seller is unique, for "where such differentiation exists, even though it be slight, buyers will be paired with sellers, not by chance and at random as under pure competition, but according to their preferences."

Product Differentiation

Product differentiation takes various forms. It may be based upon certain characteristics of the product itself: patented features; trade-marks; trade names; peculiarities of the package or container; singularity in quality, design, color, or style. Product differentiation may also exist with respect to the conditions surrounding its sale. Examples of this are convenience of the seller's location, reputation and good will of the seller, services provided by the seller, and various other links which attach the customers to the seller. Product differentiation, broadly interpreted, represents a control over supply in the sense that only one seller offers a product of that exact name and identity. The seller offering a product different from others actually does occupy a monopoly position in that limited sense. A seller in a particular location is a monopolist in more ways than merely the obvious sense that two physical bodies cannot occupy the same space, for his geographical location ties certain customers to him. This is often called "spatial monopoly." The customer's approach and attitude are essential, for it is noteworthy that buyers take the product differences into account when purchasing.

Behind the acceptance of differentiation are differences in tastes, desires, incomes, locations of buyers, and the uses for the commodities. It may safely be generalized that such differences among buyers have always existed, and it follows that products have differed. Of course, the merchandising tools of advertising and promotion, plus technological advances, have emphasized and widened the scope of product differentiation. This differentiation, which is a reality in the economy, leads Chamberlin and others to point out the necessity of substituting for the concept of a "competitive ideal" an ideal involving both monopoly and competition. In the economist's role, and in the immediate situation of public policy, it would be advantageous to measure and evaluate activities in the economy against an ideal which represents something more readily approaching reality. Pure monopoly, on the one hand, is impossible because of substitutability. Pure competition is not possible because of the presence of heterogeneous products and markets.

Differentiation and Monopoly

With heterogeneous products each seller has a "complete monopoly" of his own product. This type of monopolist, however, is not free from outside competition, but only partially insulated from it. The monopolist's demand curve is vitally affected by competing substitutes. Control over total supply of all related products is impossible. Recognition and acceptance of Chamberlin's concept that the real world evidences a complex of monopoly and competition, based on product diversity — a natural consequence of the system of demands — leads to several useful analytical concepts. These include market segmentation, local oligopoly, and multilevel competition.

The economics of differential advantage, building on the foundations laid by Chamberlin, holds that no one enters business except in the expectation of some degree of differential advantage in serving his customers, and that competition consists of the constant struggle to develop, maintain, or increase such advantages. In large part, these efforts in any industry or area, of course, offset each other and cancel out; and to the extent that they do, a kind of "equilibrium" results, consisting of the offsetting of various differential advantages. It is possible under certain restricted assumptions to define with precision an equilibrium situation where a general and complete "balance" of such efforts would be achieved. But in real life, conditions are constantly changing, so that at any particular time some firms will be gaining and others falling back. Any concept of competition which does not include its dynamic aspects would have little relevance to reality.

This summary of the economics of differential advantage suggests several aspects of the theory which require further explanation. It is necessary to examine the following areas: (1) bases on which a differential advantage may be obtained; (2) risk and uncertainty involved in the expectation and exploitation of a differential advantage; (3) entry and exit of firms; (4) industry structure, "balance," and equilibrium; and (5) problem solving by firms and by public administration.

Differential Advantage and the "Product"

From the broad definition of "product" it is possible to determine these general bases for differential advantage. Differential advantage today rest on technological as well as on legal or geographical grounds. The legal and geographical grounds account for differential advantages due to trademarks, patents, and to location (spatial monopoly). The technological basis for obtaining a differential advantage receives increased emphasis in the American economy, in which there has been a shift in relative importance away from geographical advantage to technological advantage. The various aspects of technological advantage are in general related to use requirements, production processes, and marketing methods. An advantage may be obtained by styling a product to meet a particular consumer taste or desire, such as the production of golf clubs for left-handed players. Advantages based on production processes may be exploited by use of unique assembly-line methods, new equipment, or application of results from a time and motion study. Marketing methods offer and ever-widening basis for exploiting an advantage. A differential advantage may be obtained by a

with there being ample gains to diffuse." Such neutralization in our terms is the offsetting or destroying of rivals' differential advantages. It may take away the sales gains the innovator has made, or it may merely stop further gains. It may stop further gains quickly and encroach more gradually on gains already made, so that a residue of these gains may last a fairly long time. "If such a residue is expected, it is the innovator's chief incentive, since small but long-lasting gains outweigh large temporary ones."

3.   Conditions of Entry and Survival

Entry can best be understood as an aspect of the allocation of resources or the appropriate matching of segments of supply and demand through the processes of the market. The ability and desire to assume entrepreneurial responsibility is a scarce resource no less then labor, raw materials, or capital. Entry is an important aspect of the allocation process for all of these resources. This very complex allocation process starts out with the enterpriser who wants to go into business, who discerns an opportunity and then undertakes to collect and organize the facilities required for the purpose of exploiting this opportunity.

Barriers to Entry

Ease of entry means freedom from artificial barriers which might obstruct this allocation process in the market. Ease of entry does not arise as a problem except as there is a need for new entrants on the one hand and prospective entrants ready to fulfill the need on the other. Lack of entry in a given field does not constitute proof of barriers to entry. Among the barriers to entry most frequently cited are patents, secret skills and processes, monopoly of raw materials, cartel restrictions, and capital requirements.

The desire to become an independent businessman may be considered in two separate phases. One is the general desire to head a separate enterprise. The other is the intention to go into a particular industry in a given location and under other specified conditions. It is useful to consider the sequence of steps which a prospective entrant might follow. Initially, he looks around for an appropriate opportunity, typically an industry in which there is an unusual outlook for growth and profits. According to the economics of differential advantage, he would then consider what he had to offer that was unique or that would give him an edge over established competitors. Then, having defined the opportunity, he would determine whether the costs of acquiring the necessary resources, including a suitable location, raw materials, and labor with the necessary skills, are commensurate with the capital rewards from entry. When he has satisfied himself on all of these points, he would finally approach the problem of the necessary capital. If the capital were his own, he would have to make a decision as to whether the returns in this particular opportunity would be greater than in alternative uses. If the money is to come wholly or in part from other investors, he would have to persuade them to have confidence in his expectations as to differential advantage.

Persuading investors to put money into a prospective enterprise is a marketing operation similar to persuading customers to buy a product. There is no way of compelling the investor or the customer to part with his money if he does not have confidence in what is offered. In appealing to investors, the promoter must provide the kind of evidence which is acceptable to them regarding the reality of the differential advantage on which he expects to found his business. If the advantage is real, the amount of the funds required is not an insurmountable barrier. It is expensive to put up a steel mill, but if the enterpriser can show a real need — such as a market region which can be served more economically or an innovation in production methods which would assure an edge over existing producers — that kind of money would be available.

In brief, as far as capital requirements are concerned, the only valid barrier to prospective entrants is that the enterpriser or his potential backers do not have sufficient confidence in the expectation of differential advantage. This is the means by which the market allocates both entrepreneurial skill and other resources to the fields where there is the greatest expectation of differential advantage.

A related aspect of the problem of entry is that the optimum size of plant may be very large in the field under consideration, so that the prospective entrant would suffer an initial cost disadvantage if he could not start off working at capacity. The effect of optimum size on entry is complex, and the prevailing type of entry depends in part on this factor. If the optimum is large, there is likely to be a stimulation of entry for complementary firms rather than directly competitive firms. A company turning out a basic raw material, for example, needs an adequate number of fabricators to realize its full market potential and, in fact, often promotes the establishment of such complementary firms. If some of the fabricators get large enough, they may then integrate backward into the production of the basic raw material, provided that they are not obstructed by patents or other barriers to entry.

The Strategy of Entry

If small units can operate effectively, the way is open for competitive firms to enter by direct simulation of the established firms. That means trying to be as much as possible like the successful firms in the hope of sharing in their success. Simulation is especially common in the retail and wholesale trade, where the successful pattern of operation cannot be kept secret and cannot be protected by patent or trade-mark. When economists talk about economies of scale as a barrier to entry, their comments should be taken as applying generally to a single type of entry — namely, entry by direct simulation.

Entry by differentiation is usually possible, despite economies of scale in existing operations. To achieve great economies of scale, the seller must induce customers to accept a highly uniform product which is susceptible to mass-production methods. To the extent that he succeeds, the demand for individual variations is partially unsatisfied, even though some of these prospective customers might be willing to pay more in order to get something that was more precisely what they wanted. Loss of volume by the mass producer through further differentiation is constantly going on in industry. The production of upholstery fabrics is only one example of a type of production in very large plants where there has been a large amount of new entry through differentiation and dissipation of economies of scale previously enjoyed.

A significant form of entry is that of the existing firm going into a new field. Entry through diversification may well serve the ends of public policy, since it tends to assure the intensification of competition in a given industry even where new firms are not available to enter the field. Not all opportunities are susceptible, however, to exploitation by existing firms. That is a major reason why the number of firms continues to increase from year to year. A firm will hesitate to go into a field if this step may endanger what it already has. The two fields, that is, may be quite inconsistent and incompatible. A firm that competes primarily on the basis of efficiency in distribution tries to avoid the dissipation of this advantage which can arise from accepting orders for too many divergent products. The existing company may be restrained from exploiting a new opportunity because of established sales policy. Thus a company which has made a virtue of selling only through wholesalers faces serious hazards in taking on a line to sell direct to retailers. Those who have confined their sales to the drug trade often feel that they must pass up opportunities in the grocery trade. There are many cases of firms which operate under restrictions intended to preserve good trade relations and who therefore must leave the opportunity to differentiate to others.

The same considerations hold to some degree with respect to consumer good will. A manufacturer of a product which enjoys great prestige with the consumer may feel barred from bringing out a cheaper item under the same name. Examples could readily be cited, ranging all the way from face cream to automobiles. This consideration also restricts manufacturers in their choice of retail outlets and hence in the extent to which they can develop the market. The prestige of a product is related to the standing of the stores in which it is offered. All of these considerations help to keep opportunity open to the new entrant who differentiates either in product or in marketing methods.

From the viewpoint of antitrust law, the existence of barriers to entry is, then, a question of fact which can and should be determined by investigation rather than inference. For, as previously pointed out, it is highly improper to conclude that such barriers exist simply because of a low rate of entry. That may mean simply that there is no need for new entrants because, for example, product demand may be constant or falling. Again, lack of entrants may merely mean that there is no desire to enter this field on the part of prospective entrants into business.

Expectations of Differential Advantage

Entry into business is made on the basis of an advance estimate of the opportunity or the differential advantage which the entrant will enjoy. After entry has been effected, the expectations of the entrant may turn out to have been either unduly optimistic or unduly pessimistic. To have underestimated the opportunity creates some problems, but the entrant may be able to adjust to the unexpected opportunities. We are concerned more at this point with those cases in which realized opportunity barely equals or falls short of expectations. What are the factors governing survival and final exit if the firm does not survive?

Effectuating entry into business involves a number of steps and may require a considerable period of time. Exit may be even more protracted, even if it is clear from the first that the conditions for survival cannot be met. In extreme cases the entrant recognizes on the day he opens for business that he has made a mistake. Backing out may be more difficult than plunging in, whatever the problem he faced in entry. One aspect of business entry is that relatively liquid assets are transformed into relatively specialized and frozen assets. This process is not an easy one to reverse. The beginning stage in any new business is one of testing whether the conditions of survival can be met and if they cannot, planning to withdraw with minimum loss.

Conditions of Survival

Successful entry implies as a minimum result that the firm can survive for the indefinite future. That means that the realized opportunity is at least sufficient to yield an income that will defray the current operating costs of the business. To achieve this result, the business must attract customers whose purchases will provide the required revenue. Any business selling goods or services may be regarded as a link between certain suppliers on the one hand and customers on the other. To survive, a firm must offer a preferred route for a part of this flow of goods or services and for the transformation of goods which may occur in the process. The going concern many be said to close the circuit in this flow of economic values. Ability to survive rests ultimately on the fact of closure and whether the volume of goods involved and the margin on these goods are sufficient to meet the minimum operating requirements.

Ability to survive must be combined with the will to continue. Even a profitable business may suspend operations if its owners do not wish to go on. An unprofitable business may continue for an indefinite period if its owners are willing and able to meet its deficits. There are intermediate cases in which a business fails to show a profit in the accounting sense, but can survive for a considerable period without any additions to capital. The owner may be willing to forego all or part of the wages of management and may be using up his original capital by failing to accumulate any reserves for depreciation.

Most fundamentally, what is happening when business firms survive despite their failure to live up to expectations is that their backers have accepted a write-down for their expectations. A new entrant who puts $50,000 into his business and expects to earn a return on that amount may begin to behave shortly thereafter as if he expected a return on only $10,000. The write-down of expectations influences competitive behavior both of those already in the business and of those who might consider entering later. In a stagnant or declining industry their only alternative to accepting a write-down is withdrawal. In the example cited, the owner of the business might withdraw if he could recover $15,000 of his original investment but might accept the write-down to $10,000 if the amount he could hope to pull out was less than that. Such decisions would also be affected by judgments of the future trend in the value of assets. Thus the owner might accept a write-down to $10,000 rather than attempt recovery of a larger amount through liquidation because of a conviction that asset value will eventually equal or exceed the amount of the original investment.

Avenues of Exit

There are several well-marked avenues of exit from an overcrowded or otherwise unattractive field. Among these are outright liquidation of a firm, movement from one field into another, and sale as a going concern. Outright liquidation is the form of exit which has been implied so far. It may occur even in the case of a prosperous business which has remained the vehicle for the activities of a single individual or partnership. There may be no means of securing continuity for the business upon the death or retirement of the principals.

An organization may enter new fields and then gradually drop out of the older fields altogether. Jones and Lamson, which makes machine tools today, was once engaged solely in the manufacture of firearms and is the direct successor to a company which manufactured pumps. The U.S. Leather Company is really in the oil business. The Huron Milling Company does no milling; it is concerned with the chemistry of wheat flour.

Census statistics may show a largely fictitious exit from one field which should be balanced against apparent entry into another field. The extermination of hundreds of firms by reclassification on their census returns can greatly exaggerate the adverse trends in some industries. For example, let us look at two branches of the grain products industries such as flour and formula feeds. A firm reporting 50 per cent of its volume in flour in one census would drop out of the classification in the next census if its flour business were down to 49 per cent of its total, since the census classifies a firm according to where 50 per cent or more of its business falls. Thus, in related fields the change between successive census years might show a big drop in one and a gain in the other, while the true figures on both exit and entry would be much smaller.

The third way out is sale as a going concern. The prospective purchasers may not be very numerous, particularly in a declining industry. Outside capital is likely to look more favorably on expanding industries. Aside from exceptional cases, outside management would not expect to be able to do better with a company than the experienced people who were trying to get rid of it. The consequence is that the chances to sell as a going concern are most likely to apply to prospective purchasers in the same or related lines. A statute which was interpreted as a ban on all mergers of related companies would thus close off one of the principal opportunities for orderly exit, especially where stagnant or declining industries were concerned. It would be equivalent to blocking the normal process of reducing the number of firms in fields where the firms were too numerous.

4.   The Proliferation of Opportunity

Entry for a firm, like new employment for an individual, depends on the successful exploitation of opportunity. As economic activity expands, opportunity proliferates. That means that potential openings increase in number and variety and in direct relation to what has gone before. An open system is one in which openings are steadily being created, and open competition is a state of affairs in which all qualified aspirants can compete to fill the vacancies. It does not mean that every aspirant will attain the position of his first choice.

The proliferation of opportunity has been discussed in other papers as an inherent aspect of a free-enterprise economy. It has been contrasted with the Marxist principle of capitalist accumulation. Marx assumed that capitalism by its very nature was cannibalistic, that strong firms would necessarily get stronger and thus gobble up their weaker competitors until a single firm dominated each major segment of industry. More conservative economists than Marx have difficulty in avoiding this conclusion for industries with increasing returns to scale. At least one attempt has been made to show that the American economy is experiencing a long-run "decline in competition."

To say that opportunity proliferates is to say that there is an opportunity for the entry and survival of new firms precisely because of the success of existing firms. The firms already in the field help to determine the character of opportunity for the newcomer as well as to make opportunity available.

Proliferation through Simulation

The success of the established firm creates opportunities for new firms in several ways. The newcomer may enter the identical field after the first firm has pioneered production methods and product acceptance by the market, thus reducing uncertainty for those who follow. The original firm makes entry still easier if it abuses the privilege of being first in the field through high prices or otherwise takes its customers for granted. It may not be willing to increase its investment fast enough to take care of increasing demand. The new firms may make the same product but exploit a different segment of the market such as another region or community. Even if the pioneer follows an aggressive marketing program directed at the maximum rate of growth, common experience indicates that his advertising tends to create demand for all products of the given type and not merely the one bearing his brand name.

Proliferation through Deviation

The second aspect of proliferation is the opportunities created for the firm which deviates in strategic ways from the pattern set by the first firm. The pioneer generally assumes some definite position as to product characteristics and sales policies. This brings corresponding expectations from consumers and the trade, so that he is not free to deviate from the pattern. The dentifrice manufacturer who puts peppermint in his tooth paste is at a disadvantage with respect to those consumers who prefer wintergreen. If he has built his business on distributing his products through drugstores, he is vulnerable to attack by the newcomer who discovers that the same product can be marketed efficiently through grocery channels. Thus the original firm, by taking one specific stand as to products and policies, opens the way for others who are free to deviate from these policies. There is little the first firm can do to prevent others from gaining a foothold in this way.

Proliferation through Complementation

In the third type of opening, the established firm relinquishes a part of its activity to another firm which can serve it better than it can serve itself. In the field of marketing intermediaries, in particular, entry is achieved by successful competition with the new firm's prospective customers. A food broker exists because he can sell the goods of some manufacturers more efficiently than they can perform this function for themselves. The wholesaler has to cope with potential competition both from the manufacturer and from the retailer. Each would usually prefer to deal directly with the other unless the wholesaler can show substantial economies in bringing them together. In this third type of opening, the new firm is relating itself to existing firms by performing complementary functions. While this phase of proliferation is prevalent in the creation of marketing channels, it appears in many other fields as well. One example would be the numerous independent parts manufacturers producing components for automobile manufacturers.

The three aspects of proliferation may be summarized by saying that the success of an established firm may create opportunity for its simulant, its deviant, and its complement. These are characteristic types of openings by the requirements of an expanding system. Attention may now be turned to the way in which the system expresses these requirements or, in effect, lines up new firms to fill these openings.

5.   Operating Closure and Open Competition

The concept of closure as developed in communication theory can give somewhat greater precision to the treatment of self-sufficient systems. A system which is closed with respect to a given operation comprises all the parts and processes which are necessary to complete the operation. An operating system such as a telephone circuit may be interrupted by the incident of a broken wire and become a closed system again when the wire is repaired. The concept of closure with respect to an operating system is more or less analogous to concepts in topology and psychology. In set theory a closed set is one which contains all of its limit points. In Gestalt psychology the attempt to accomplish closure, to provide the missing link, is said to be characteristic both of perception and of problem solving. With respect to operating systems, the property of closure is fundamental, since the system cannot function at all without it. To the extent that we regard the national economy as an operating system and not merely a set of random variables arbitrarily selected for study, it is a system only to the degree that it achieves closure. The fact is recognized by economists in such phrases as "the circular flow of economic activity."

Closure for Efficient Routine

The operating significance of closure goes beyond the completeness of the system for the flow of economic processes. Within a closed system it is possible to work out and adopt efficient routines for handling these processes. If the system is made up of independent units, the established routines emerge more gradually from trade negotiation and the general adoption of the procedures which seem to work best. Among the characteristics of a routine that is working well is the economy of attention needed to maintain it. Repetitive operations proceed in accordance with expectations and with a minimum of effort being required to keep them under control. The value of a good working routine in human affairs is so great that it usually is better to let it alone unless a proposed change can effect a very material improvement. Certainly it cannot be kept in fluid state with endless small modifications, or it ceases to be a working routine. The importance of closure for the system as a whole is partly that it permits closure in the more detailed aspects of the operating structure. Performance of each individual in an operating system rests in large measure on his confidence that others will act in accordance with his expectations. Reliance on expected behavior characterizes relations among business firms as well as parts of the same company.

Openness for Free Competition

If closure is the fundamental characteristic of an operating system, competition must be regarded as a supplementary factor contributing to the efficiency of the system. It is more than a coincidental paradox that free and open competition is generally regarded as a desirable state of economic systems. At first glance it may be moderately disturbing to think that a system must be open in order to be competitive and closed in order to operate at all. Systems may be closed in one sense and open in another. It is more than a play on words to say that an economic system must be open for change even though it is a closed circuit for the flow of economic processes. The system may be closed in the sense that it has all the necessary parts to operate at the present level and open in the sense that its parts may be replaced or supplemented in such a way as to improve the operation of the system. Certainly no one requires that it be open to the extent of permitting random replacements or free entry of additional firms without reference to the requirements of the system.

The desirable state with respect to closure and openness can be suggested by the sign which is frequently displayed by a retail store that is being remodeled. The message reads "No interruptions to business while alterations are in progress."

The paradox of operating closure versus openness to change pertains to all machines and not merely to systems characterized by competition. A machine must retain a fixed structure for some period of time in order to complete an operating cycle. If the machine is to be rebuilt or adjusted, it usually has to be taken out of operation. There are modern machines capable of moderate adjustment or even self-adjustment with no interruption of operating processes. That is the kind of machine that the economic system is assumed to be. Yet the system is subjected to strains from time to time which appear to transcend its built-in power of adjustment. Some economists would prescribe an extreme degree of competitive flexibility to facilitate adjustment, even at the sacrifice of the operating closure required to maximize production. In fact, the model of perfect competition which is usually adopted as the ideal would largely disrupt operating closure in many places where it seems to be essential for the conduct of business. In a theoretically perfect market, buyer and seller would be paired on a random basis, transaction by transaction, rather than by customary and continuous association.

Resolution of the Paradox

The resolution of the paradox which has been under discussion lies in the fact that the same system may achieve closure at different operating levels. A plant which has been turning out 10,000 units of a given product may be capable of turning out 20,000 units if additional capacity is provided at a critical point in the production process which heretofore has acted as a bottleneck. The management continues to operate the plant at the lower level until conditions are auspicious for moving to the higher level. There is a minimum of disruption to operating closure in making the change, since the move is from one definite level to another. In the economic system as a whole, changeovers do not occur by the deliberate choice of an executive exercising control over the system, but through the interaction of independent elements which are members or potential members of the system. One function of competition is to effectuate changeovers from one operating level to another in the economic system as a whole, or in its various subsystems.

An obvious model for a system which has the potentiality for closure at various operating levels is the structure of the atom as pictured in quantum physics. An electron revolves around the nucleus in one orbit but appears to shift instantaneously to a different orbit when the energy level changes. There seems to be a finite number of orbits available with a discontinuous step or jump from one orbit to the next. The energy level over time is not a smooth variable but a step function.

Step-Function Corrections and Closure

The fact that the atom behaves in this way is still a mystery, but there is no mystery as to the fact that most adjustments in small segments of the economy take the form of step-function corrections. In building a bridge across a river, we are not willing to paraphrase the old proverb and say: "Half a bridge is better then none." Since the function of the bridge is closure, exactly one whole bridge is the right amount. Meeting the requirement of increased demand for a product usually takes place in discrete steps, whether the action is taken by established firms or by new firms entering the field. The established firm must build a new plant, broaden its channels of distribution, or adopt new operating methods which are appropriate to a larger volume of business. The new firm must create corresponding facilities and procedures subject to additional uncertainties as to both market acceptance and the operating efficiency of a new organization.

More and more it is the accepted practice to spend months in staff planning, trying to make the changeover in one jump when everything is ready. Good planning decisions often make a far greater difference in selling prices than willingness to forego profit. The difference between the best and the worst technologies might make it possible to drop a price by 25 to 50 per cent as compared with the few percentage points usually represented by profit.

6. The Network of Competition

The economics of differential advantage helps to explain why the vigor of competition is a function of the number of levels at which rivals operate. If there were to be only one level of competition, the most intensive rivalry would result if all firms operated on a national level. If there are a number of local companies as well, they are bound together competitively by the fact that they are all in competition with the national firms.

Local and National Competition

The national distributor of any given product may be regarded as a local competitor in each market. His product goes on the shelf beside the products made by local manufacturers. Consumers are free to choose one or the other. If the national brand is chosen, it is because the consumer has weighed its price and quality against the other brands and ended up giving it an edge. The national manufacturer is trying to realize certain sales goals nationally, but he is perfectly aware that he must achieve them market to market in the face of local competition. It is common practice for the national company to analyze its sales territory by territory and to put pressure on its sales force for better performance in territories that seem to be lagging.

The total effect of what is happening to a national firm, market by market, is what determines its national sales policies. Thus, vigorous competition by local firms in half of its sales territories forces the national firm to adopt policies which, when adopted, bring heavier competitive pressure to bear on the less vigorous competitors in its other territories. The national firm is a very effective channel for transmitting competitive pressures from one market to another. With respect to the competition between national firms and local firms, there are some ways in which the local firm has the best of it. The national firm is obliged, both legally and economically, to adopt a policy which is in some respects uniform for every territory. The local firm can adapt itself to its immediate market, deviating from the policies of that national firm in directions which take advantage of the most vulnerable points of the national competitor, but which the latter is not free to meet. This is unquestionably one of the reasons why only two or three firms in an industry may have discovered a pattern which enables them to compete nationally against local competition.

Geographic and Technological Competition

Often there may be more than two distinct levels of competition corresponding to different dimensions of differential advantage. Some firms compete largely on a combination of geographic advantage with the minimum technical facilities for turning out an acceptable product. Some succeed in competing over a greater geographical area by specializing in some dimension of technological advantage. The general trend in the United States has been toward diminishing importance for geographical advantage and the proliferation of various aspects of technical advantage. This is not a one-way trend, however, since some technical developments such as the transmission of electrical power and industrial air conditioning have opened up new possibilities for geographical specialization.

The flour industry in the Southeast is an excellent example of a three-level structure competition. In addition to local and national millers, the area has the unique development of flour-blenders not found anywhere else in the country. The flour-blender buys flour instead of wheat and blends it to specification. His product competes both in the bakery trade and on the grocery shelves with those manufactured directly from wheat by other millers. The average plant capacity of the blender is much larger in terms of end product than that of the local miller, but less capital is needed for entry into the blending business than to establish a modern flour-milling plant.

Multilevel Competition

Multilevel competition is the Southeast is a good illustration of what Chamberlin has called "the network of competition." In a differentiated industry each type of firm is competing for the consumer's dollar by using distinctive methods. Any one competitor has to meet the onslaught of several different types rather than competing only with others like himself. In the simpler and more homogeneous type of competition, a leading firm might be able to rest on its oars if it felt that it was the best in the field. In multilevel competition it might excel along one dimension but be definitely outclassed along other dimensions.

There is a further hazard that the relative importance of the dimensions of competition is steadily changing with changes in consumer preferences and in the technical possibilities. Using flour milling in the Southeast to show how a network of competition operates, four separate groups might be identified, since local millers in the region and millers of less than national scope shipping into the region have a different place in the network. For ease of reference, consider local millers in Alabama and Kansas, blenders in Alabama, and national millers in Minneapolis. The national miller competes with the Kansas miller in selling flour to the blender in Alabama, and also in selling packaged products to Alabama consumers. The national miller also competes with the

Alabama miller both in sales to blenders and in sales to the consumer. He competes with the blender as well as with other national millers in sales to the consumer. Here are six competitive fronts facing the national miller, even though only three types of competitors are involved. To complete the network, all the competitive relations, involving the other types, but not involving the national miller, would have to be listed. The Kansas miller competes with the blender as well as supplying him, and also competes with the Alabama mill. The Alabama mill also competes with the blender as well as supplying him. Altogether there are nine competitive relations which serve to integrate supply and demand throughout the market. Thus the competitive network is far more complicated and far more effective in transmitting competitive pressures than is immediately apparent from the conception of multilevel competition.

7.   Price Competition and Cost Reduction

Competition among sellers is the unending process of trying to attract customers by giving the consumer the same satisfaction for less money or by providing greater satisfaction without a corresponding increase in price. This section deals with the first aspect of competition, in which firms compete by lowering price, either absolutely or in relation to costs. The next section deal with the second aspect, in which the competitive emphasis is upon giving the buyer a better or more acceptable product. This second phase of competition has been discussed under the rather unfortunate label of "nonprice competition." It would be more accurate to call it product competition. Actually, product and price rivalry are opposite sides of the same coin, since both price and product enter into every transaction. Both are ways of giving the consumer a better value, one by taking something out of the price side of the balance and the other by putting more in on the product side.

Minimization of Costs

Competition based on price rests fundamentally on the minimization of costs. Cost reduction depends heavily, in turn, on the realization of economies of scale — that is, the progressive reduction of costs per unit of output. The most dramatic of these economies are achieved in production-line assembly and in the mass production of materials or component parts. But, in addition, there may be economies in distribution and marketing; a large organization can enjoy rewards from specialization. Moreover, the larger the average size of customers' orders, the lower is the ratio of sales to the fixed costs of billing and customer contact. Equally, the greater the sales volume, the lower will be the unit costs of staff functions such as technical and economic research. It must be remembered, however, that economies do not arise automatically with a greater volume of business. Large-scale operations provide the opportunity for the adoption of efficient methods, but resourcefulness and good judgment must still be employed in selecting the appropriate techniques. A highly specialized piece of equipment may, for example, represent efficient production if volume has been estimated correctly, but a very high cost of production if it must stand idle much of the time.

The impact of price competition may differ in detail on the various products made by the same company. That is true even when all the products of the firm are joint products of the same process and are derived from the same or related raw materials. The flour-milling industry is a good example, since it is basically engaged in the processing of wheat, although other ingredients are included in some of its products.

Grain product prices are highly responsive to short — as well as long-run — changes in the cost of wheat. That is not so true of prepared cake mixes as for flour for the very good reason that wheat flour is only one — and the least expensive — of the ingredients in a cake mix. It is clear that the prices of grain products are interrelated. They compete with each other, so that the price obtained for the major product is a controlling factor in the price that can be obtained for the minor products. The major product is bakery flour, which accounts for 75 per cent of the tonnage of all flour. The lower the price to the baker, the lower the prices at which he can sell bakery products. Family flour has to compete for consumer favor against the alternative of buying the finished product (bread or cake). Family flour has been losing out steadily over the years in its competition with commercial bakery products. That creates a downward pressure on the price of family flour which bears heavily on those millers who have a higher-than-average stake in family flour. Cake mixes must compete with commercial cakes on the one hand and with the separate ingredients on the other. The consumer of mixes would presumably expect to pay something less than the corresponding price for cake and something more than the price of the raw materials. If the price of the mix should get close to the upper end of this range, customers would be lost in two directions. Some would buy cake because the savings in buying the mix was too small. Others would go back to the separate ingredients because the savings to be obtained in that way was so large. Formula feeds compete with mill feeds and whole grain which would be readily substitutable in many feeding programs, if formula feeds did not enjoy an economic advantage. Thus, while the four product groups are in partially isolated fields of use, all of these fields are alternative users of wheat and hence part of a broader competitive network.

8. Product Competition and Consumer Choice

An active competitor is always striving to give the consumer a value as good or better than any other seller who strives to satisfy the same need. Measuring competition would be relatively simple if this effort were all expended on identical and unchanging products and took the sole form of initiating changes on the price side of the bargain. The dynamic character of modern competition arises in large part from the fact that sellers also initiate changes on the product side, attempting to outguess each other as to the improvements which induce a favorable consumer response.

Product Differentiation

Product competition tends to create a gradient in market response to each seller's product. To the extent that a product differs from what existed before, it is bound to suit some people better than others. This market gradient is expressed as the demand curve for the individual product. At the left and higher end of the curve are those consumers who, other things equal, get enough extra value out of the product to be willing to pay more for it. Further to the right are consumers who consider it directly interchangeable with other products for the same use, so long as there is no difference in price. Finally, at the extreme right are people who customarily place a very low value on the product but who may purchase it in an emergency if they cannot find their regular product.

The established producer or the prospective entrant with any knowledge of marketing does not embark on product differentiation casually. While he may be anxious to give his product some distinguishing characteristic, he is foolish to do it if the feature selected has no possible interest to the consumer. Only a minor fraction of the differentiations introduced are crowned with lasting success. Both market and technical research are directed toward improving the ratio. One result of research is to eliminate some of the possible differentiations by analysis rather than by trial and error in the market. By whatever means new product features are developed, it is clear that product competition is by no means the easy escape from price competition that it has seemed to some critics of modern merchandising.

Product Competition

Product competition supplements rather than supplants price competition. Suppose a competitor does not see any way to produce his present product for less in order to sell at a lower price. If, instead of improving his production process, he is able to improve his product, he is still competing but along a different dimension. Such a competitive move does not lessen price competition but may increase its intensity directly. If the producer making the innovation succeeds in giving the consumer more for her money, his competitors may have to reduce prices on the older product to meet this competition. Later on they will probably find a way to meet him on the product side too by introducing the same or a similar feature. The weighing of price against product still goes on, even through the process is more complicated that that implied by simpler models of competition.

In this context, advertising takes on a meaning quite different from that implied under perfectly competitive conditions. For where product differentiation is regarded as the essence of competition, advertising serves two functions, each of which is consistent with an optimum allocation of resources. On the one hand the advertisement is a means for enhancing the general dissemination of knowledge as to available products and their relative prices. On the other hand, as an alternative method of selling, it may reduce costs to the extent that fewer salesmen, wholesalers, and retailers may be required. In the latter case there may be secondary effects as well, since the use of advertising may compel rivals to reduce their own marketing costs or improve their products, or both.

Expanding Range of Consumer Choice

Product competition tends to assure an adequate or expanding range of consumer choice. Price competition alone cannot accomplish this. Certain products may have been acceptable under past conditions, but consumer requirements are constantly changing. To get new products promptly before the prospective user once they have been introduced is to speed the consumer verdict and to facilitate the continuous adaptation of products and production facilities to the market. The enrichment of consumer choice is illustrated by the case of the consumer who wishes to serve cake to her family. She is presented with a variety of commercially baked cakes by her grocer. He also has available mixes she can use to produce many different types of cake with the minimum of effort on her own part. Finally, she can reject any of these alternatives and purchase a uniform and dependable family flour with which to turn out a cake according to her own special recipe.

The producer accepts basic business risks in taking the initiative in product competition. The projected improvement in the product may not make enough difference to get a response from the consumer market. The added costs of the new feature may be greater than the added value to the average consumer. The new product may be superior to what is on the market, but inferior to what competitors are about to bring out. The market test of a new product may cause the project to be abandoned, but it may be that the real difficulty was with some phase of the marketing program rather than with the product itself. To bring about one new differentiation may be to encourage the demand for variety and hence to undermine the basis for mass production. In the early days of the Ford Motor Company, its reluctance to depart from mass-produced specifications was caricatured in the statement that you could "buy a Ford in any color, so long as it was black."

To assume that the manufacturer is concurrently engaged in a tacit collusion with other tire manufacturers to maximize joint profits is utterly unrealistic. It involves the old fallacy of trying to maximize two quantities at the same time. The major efforts at maximizing joint profits are clearly conformed to joint opportunity, which means that they usually run in the vertical direction embracing the successive stages in a trade channel.

References

Abbot, Lawrence (1955). *Quality and Competition*. Columbia University Press, New York.

Boulding, K. E. (1950). *A Reconstruction of Economics*. John Wiley & Sons, Inc., New York.

Chamberlin, E. H., editor (1950a). *Monopoly and Competition and Their Regulation*. John Wiley & Sons, Inc., New York. From the International Economic Association.

Chamberlin, E. H. (1950b). *The Theory of Monopolistic Competition*. Harvard University Press, Cambridge, Massachusetts, sixth edition.

Clark, J. M. (1923). *Studies in the Economics of Overhead Costs*. University of Chicago Press, Chicago.

Fellner, William John (1949). *Competition among the Few*. Alfred A. Knopf, New York.

Chamberlin has been the leading figure in the contemporary movement toward a more realistic theory of competition. His book, in its successive editions, has been very influential in marketing circles.

Clark's contributions are more diffuse but equally significant for marketing. The writer has utilized his work on overhead costs, his concept of workable competition, and his treatment of the economies of differential advantage which is one of the essays in the volume of essays on monopoly and competition edited by Chamberlin.

Boulding, in the reference cited, has a chapter on the ecological approach to competition. Abbot analyzes the competition on the product or quality side which is supplementary to price competition in what he calls "complete competition." Fellner is cited in the discussion of oligopoly at the end of the chapter.

Chapter 10

MATCHING AND SORTING: THE LOGIC OF EXCHANGE*

Wroe Alderson

> Exchange is essentially the act of improving the assortments held by the two parties to the exchange. Without the aid of organized marketing facilities, an individual seeking to acquire a product which could enhance the potency of his assortment was typically faced with a long and difficult search. Exchange was costly in human effort and confined to a very limited range of economic goods so long as the matching of small segments of supply and demand had to take place through such individual pairings.
>
> Economic progress has consisted largely in finding more efficient ways of matching heterogeneous supply and heterogeneous demand. Matching can be divided into the three phases of shaping, fitting, and sorting, the first two concerned with the form and the specific application of a product. Sorting as a means of accomplishing effective matching is roughly equivalent with the domain of marketing as compared with production. Four aspects of sorting are discussed, each playing an essential part in marketing processes. Among these four aspects of sorting, economics has emphasized allocation or the breaking-down of a homogeneous supply. Marketing theory gives relatively greater emphasis to assorting or the build-up of assortments. An assortment is a heterogeneous collection of products designed to serve the needs of some behavior system.

1. The Function of Exchange

It is commonly stated that exchange takes place because each party to the transaction has a surplus of one product and a deficit of another. In marketing terms, it is somewhat more precise to say that exchange takes place in order to increase the utility of the assortments held by each party to the transaction. That is to say that the assortment held by A can be improved by adding to it a product in the hands of B. At the same time the assortment held by B gains greater utility from the product received in exchange than it loses from the product which it gives up. Exchange under this conception is a creative function. It creates value in the sense that there is greater value in use for all of the products involved

---

Originally published in *Marketing Behavior and Executive Action* (1957), pages 195-217.

after the exchange than before the exchange. This is directly contrary to the conception held by some that exchange can only represent a transfer of values, and that any gain on one side must reflect a loss on the other. This doctrine of creative exchange is based on the notion that value pertains to assortments in use and not merely to individual products.

The notion of an assortment and its significance for the theory of marketing has already been presented in a preliminary way. The reader will observe that there is an analogy between the term "group" as applied to individuals and the term "assortments" as applied to goods. As with all analogies, it is important to understand its limitations as well as its valid application. A group regarded as an operating system performs many functions which are beyond the scope of the individual. Its entire performance is motivated by what it can contribute toward achieving the goals of the individual participants. A group has a structure and operating functions, but its apparent aims and objectives are entirely derivative.

Assortment of Goods

An assortment of goods has a kind of structure and internal consistency, but it has no purpose except to serve the purposes of the individuals of the group to whom the assortment belongs. A product may have a place in an assortment which is vaguely similar to the status which an individual enjoys in a group. There is, of course, no sense of belonging as in the case of the individual, and no attempt to achieve status as a means of promoting other goals. It is only from the viewpoint of some interested observer that a product fits into an assortment. In the case of the assortment of goods in the possession of a consumer, it is natural to adopt the viewpoint of this consumer in considering whether a given product will contribute to the utility of the assortment.

In some respects it is more precise to speak of the potency of the assortment, since the value of the assortment as a whole lies in providing against future contingencies facing the consumer. As described in the previous chapter, each consumer unit, such as a household, tries to be prepared for the appropriate type of behavior in view of future contingencies. The contingencies facing the individual vary both as to their likelihood of occurring and as to the degree of urgency in case they should occur. The value or utility of a product is related to both the urgency and the probability of the contingency to which it is related. Between two products, the one of greatest utility to the consumer is the one which will make the greatest contribution to the potency of the assortment. In other words, the product to be next acquired is the one which will most greatly reduce the risks of being unprepared to meet an urgent situation.

Closure of Assortment

Another parallel between group and assortment is that the concept of closure applies in both cases. A closed group is the one which is complete in the sense that all of the necessary positions are occupied in order to permit the group to function. A closed assortment is one which is complete in the sense that it provides for all of the contingencies for which the owner of the assortment is consciously attempting to be prepared. The closure of assortments is achieved only rarely and temporarily in our type of economy. An assortment which appears complete may quickly reach the stage where one or more of the products essential to closure are exhausted. Thus, consumers are constantly engaged in replenishing an assortment to restore the original state of potency. Assortments are also extended by adding items which they did not contain previously. The extension of an assortment may mean that the consumer for the first time is economically able to provide for some future occasion, or it may mean that for the first time he recognizes the urgency or the probability of some future contingency. A major function of selling and advertising is to bring consumers to recognize contingencies which were previously ignored.

Enhancing Potency of Assortment

The creative aspect of exchange in enhancing the potency of assortments can be seen most directly in the case of barter. Where one group has more wheat than it needs and the other group has more wool than it needs, the survival of both groups can be promoted by exchange. In a monetary economy the mutual enhancement of assortments is partially obscured. It is clear enough in the case of the buyer who is obtaining some product necessary to sustain his standard of life or to promote some particular objective. In the case of the seller the eventual result is the same, but the process is more roundabout. That is to say that the seller is compensated in a medium of exchange representing a general token of value. He will eventually use these returns to replenish the supplies needed to continue his operations, or will disburse them to the various participants in the process. Thus, they ultimately enable these participants to replenish or extend the assortments in their possession.

The marketing process as the creation of assortments is essentially irreversible. That is to say that at each step along the way a product is approaching the point at which it will become a part of some ultimate assortment. Costs are incurred at each step which cannot be recovered by reversing the process. When goods have finally reached the consumer, they have gained use value but have lost most of the commercial value they had in the channels of trade. That is because of the costs and the other factors which would stand as barriers to any reverse flow of good from consumer back into the market.

of mixture which occurs in nature is usually less suitable for human use than if the different elements occurred in pure form. The facts of heterogeneity of markets were discussed by the British economist, G.F. Shove. He used the example of a jigsaw puzzle to illuminate the process of matching up supply and demand. This figure of speech is interesting both as to the way in which it applies and the way in which the parallel breaks down. In solving a jigsaw puzzle, an individual starts with a conglomeration of pieces and must try to fit them together in a meaningful pattern which resembles the concept of an assortment. Jigsaw puzzles are usually solved on a rather naïve trial-and-error basis. The solver may either pick up a piece and look for all the openings where it might fit or observe an opening in the developing pattern and start looking for a piece to fit it. This type of procedure would resemble an unorganized market, in which the consumer searches for goods and the suppliers search for ultimate consumers, without benefit of the intervening marketing channels and processes. Suppose that the individual solver were confronted with a much larger jigsaw puzzle, in the completion of which he could make use of several helpers. Perhaps the picture to be put together was that of a wheat field beside a forest, with a stretch of sky beyond. There might therefore be a large area of the pattern made up respectively of yellow pieces, green pieces, and blue pieces. The solver and his helpers would probably start out by sorting the pieces into three piles, and then one or more persons would specialize in putting together pieces which represented the field, the forest, and the sky. The economics of marketing is concerned with the possibilities of using such intermediary steps in moving from the conglomeration on the one side to the assortment on the other.

The Four Aspects of Sorting

There are four aspects of sorting, which all enter into these intermediate processes and which result in economies that would be impossible if it were necessary to match every small segment of supply with every small segment of demand. The term "sorting" applies either to the practice of breaking down collections or to the building-up of collections. Sorting also has both its quantitative and qualitative aspects. These two basic distinctions result in four separate types of operations under the general heading of sorting. Starting with a conglomeration, we can perform the operation of sorting out, which breaks the collection into various types of goods. Sorting out results in a set of separate supplies which may be regarded as homogeneous in terms of the classification being used by the sorter. Given small homogeneous supplies, it is possible to create larger supplies by adding one to another. This building-up of a larger supply may represent the accumulation over a period of time from a single sorting operation, or it may represent the bringing together in a single place products which meet standard specifications but are drawn from different localities. In the latter case it may be that the large demand of a single plant is being matched by the accumulated supply. Once a large homogeneous supply has been accumulated, it may, on the other hand, be broken down by a process of apportionment or allocation. Division of the total supply is made in terms of the requirements of various operating units whose claims are to be met. Allocation may take place within a single organization in terms of planning and control, or it may take place through the market and be determined by such a consideration as price. Finally, there is the step of using supplies to build up assortments. This process may de designated as assorting, or the putting together of unlike supplies in accordance with some pattern determined by demand.

The four stages of sorting out, accumulation, allocation, and assorting have been introduced in the order in which they most frequently occur in marketing processes. There are, of course, many exceptions and variations; and the sequence is also complicated by manufacture or other changes in form, such as fitting, which may take place at various points along the way. The four types of sorting might also be grouped according to their logical relationships. Sorting out and assorting may be placed together as pertaining to the qualitative aspects of collections. Accumulation and allocation pertain to purely quantitative changes in what is taken to be a homogeneous supply. An alternative method of classification is to group sorting out and allocation together because the both apply to the breaking-down of a collection or a supply. The contrary process of building up a collection or supply is represented by accumulation and assorting.

Assorting in Marketing Theory

Marketing is concerned with all of these aspects of sorting as they appear in the process of matching supply and demand. Marketing theory necessarily places the greatest emphasis on assorting as the final step in meeting the needs of consumers, for which all the other types of sorting are merely preliminary.

Economics, with its emphasis upon scarcity rather than the unique character of individual needs, has paid most attention to allocation among the four types of sorting. Allocation has a special fascination for the mathematically inclined, since some problems of allocation are subject to precise solution through calculus and other mathematical techniques. The main hope for analyzing sorting in general, with some precision, seems likely to lie in the direction of symbolic logic. These possibilities will be discussed briefly in a later section of this chapter.

3.   Problems of Sorting Operations

There are some special problems pertaining to each of the four basic sorting operations. Marketing efficiency rests in part on a successful handling of these sorting problems. The four basic processes will be discussed in the order in which they were first introduced, starting with sorting out. The over-all organization of the sorting process will be discussed in the following section.

Sorting Out

Sorting out requires that standard classifications be established in advance. The sorter must have a definite set of criteria by which he is guided in inspecting units and throwing each into one class or another. He must decide how many classes to use and frequently must allow for a miscellaneous class to cover items which do not fit into any of the specified classes. Some characteristics of products or materials are more objective and measurable than others and lend themselves more readily to distinguishing one class from another. Sorting out by grades is one of the foundation stones of agricultural marketing as it has developed in the United States. Apples, for example, are graded by size as well as by color and freedom from blemishes. The culls go into other uses, such as vinegar making or the feeding of animals. Only the best-looking fruit goes to market for household consumption, but it is easier to assure eye appeal than flavor. The effort to maintain useful standards for agricultural produce is fraught with difficulties. Experts in nutrition say that beef with yellow fat should represent first grade because of the vitamin content. Actually, beef with white fat is classified as first grade because it has greater eye appeal for the consumer. Similarly, potatoes are graded by the smoothness of their skins rather than by any measure of their nutritional content. Grades once established are hard to maintain because of the shifting geography of production. It is scarcely feasible politically to administer a grading system which would put the product of one state in first grade and the comparable product of another state in second grade. Anyone familiar with the produce business can testify to the distressing lack of uniformity and quality labeled as first grade that sometimes gets through to the consumer.

Some years ago there was an active agitation for placing all canned or preserved foods under a system of grade labeling to supplement brand names or to take the place of such trade terms as "fancy," "choice," and "standard." Many obstacles developed, aside from the desire of packers to maintain the prestige of their brands. One is the variation in the quality of the crop which may occur from year to year, so that in a poor year no part of the crop might qualify according to rigid specifications. Yet it might be better to place some percentage of the crop in first grade, since some consumers are prepared to pay a premium for the best available. In products like coffee or flour, limitations are imposed by the desire for uniformity in flavor or performance. The standard is maintained by using whatever blend will produce the desired result rather than by sticking to a rigid formula related to the source or grade of the ingredients.

Grading is always having to be adjusted to the realities of supply and to the changing requirements of consumer use or of manufacture. Lumber is typical of the products in which the best available today might not have passed muster as first grade a few years ago. Grades for Douglas fir plywood are enforced by an industry association, but the declining quality of peeler logs makes it very difficult to maintain these standards. At the other extreme, there are cases of companies which built too much quality into their products in terms of durability or other physical characteristics. In the case of industrial raw materials, it quite often becomes possible to use those previously discarded as sub-standard because of improvements in processing. On the other hand, uniformity of materials often has a major impact on plant operations. The substitution of synthetic materials for such natural materials as leather has been accelerated by the greater uniformity of the synthetic product.

There are certain industrial processes which are scarcely more than an extension of the sorting out which can sometimes be performed by direct inspection of the units constituting the supply. Smelting is a process by which metal is separated out of the ore, leaving such residues as slag. The slag may have some use value also, but usually for very inferior uses and at much lower prices. The entire chemical and petroleum industries in a sense represent a sorting out or a separation of products which cannot be separated by merely physical means. Common salt is indeed composed of sodium and chlorine. The bond between the two elements can be broken down by electrolysis. The commercial incentive at one point might be to serve an active market for caustic soda and at another time to serve the market for chlorine. One constitutes the main product and the other the by-product which must be disposed of in many cases. In principle, this is no different from the sorting out of first-grade apples, leaving the culls to be disposed of for whatever they will bring. The apples, of course, can be left on the land to rot, while chemical by-products create a more serious disposal problem if there is no market for them. It is rather startling to be reminded in these days of automobiles that gasoline was once a troublesome waste product created in the process of producing the kerosene needed for domestic lighting. The still unsolved problems of disposing of industrial waste are reflected in the poisoning of streams and the fouling of the atmosphere in many communities.

Accumulation

The accumulation of the smaller homogeneous supplies into a larger supply serves several economic purposes. Possibly the simplest case is that of promoting the ease of transportation. Copra might be accumulated on a Pacific Island until a shipload was ready to be carried away. Coal might be loaded at a mine until a string of cars was ready to move. A similar reason for accumulation is to utilize storage space especially adapted for the purpose. Wheat moves to grain elevators, eggs and other produce to cold storage warehouses, whiskey into bonded warehouses for a certified period of aging.

Many raw materials, after being sorted out or refined, move to manufacturing plants for processing. Accumulation for a large plant must be a continuous flow rather than the periodic gathering of large lots. The working inventory on hand is steadily being used up and must be just as continuously replaced. Supplies may come in from a number of locations, but all must fall within certain limits as to product specifications in order to be suitable for processing. Industrial procurement has the task of enforcing technical standards on a steady flow of materials produced under varying conditions from a number of locations. The economies of procurement often require that minimum levels be maintained in the stocks of raw materials. These stocks constitute insurance against interruption in the flow of materials and allow the plant to continue to operate for a period until the flow is resumed. Such accumulations of materials can also minimize market risk as to price fluctuations. Materials may have been bought in large lots to obtain a favorable price. Some raw materials are highly seasonal in production, resulting in the need for accumulating inventory either at the source or at the plant. The decision as to where the accumulation will take place will depend on relative ability to carry the investment, on the degree of perishability of the material, and on the availability of suitable storage space. The final determination will be worked out through the price mechanism. The seller may take a lower price to speed up the movement of materials. The buyer may be willing to pay a higher price in return for a delay in taking possession of the materials.

The greatest urgency is typically on the side of the raw materials producer. The material he produces often has little or no use value to him or others in his immediate community. It may be highly perishable, as in the case of some agricultural products. He may be concerned that others will exhaust their supply first, as in the case of competitively developed oil fields. This urgency of the raw materials producer to sell is responsible for many types of economic regulation in the United States and elsewhere. The problem of farm surpluses had led to vast accumulations of various products either owned directly by the government or financed by the government. The purpose of such devices is to hold supplies off the market and allow for a more orderly movement later on. The difficulty is that these government arrangements create a new artificial market for the material involved, so that supplies are created to satisfy this market as well as the genuine market.

Raw materials countries provide even more spectacular examples of this abnormal type of accumulation. Coffee has been held off the market by such countries as Brazil until there appeared to be no solution except to dispose of great quantities by burning. Competition among raw materials countries nearly always places a bargaining advantage in the hands of the more industrialized countries buying the raw materials.

Good industrial procurement policies can give more stability to raw materials markets than artificial controls, at least for some favored products. The manufacturer who is trying to maximize his market by producing a uniform-quality product is in turn anxious to obtain raw materials of uniform quality. The soup manufacturer contracts in advance for the entire output of farmers producing tomatoes or other crops for his use. Skilled help is provided to the farmers in producing crops of the quality desired. Dairies rely on selected farms to provide milk which meets their standards, and enforce regulations as to sanitation and the care of dairy herds. Large marketing organizations such as chain stores often have standing arrangements with certain farms or farm communities to supply the fresh produce to be sold in their stores. Large printers have long-term contracts with paper mills or even sources of pulpwood. The requirements of mass production thus provide a secure and profitable niche for the raw materials producer in many cases. This runs contrary to the notion that free and open competition make for superior adjustment. The point is that highly specialized and massive requirements can best be met in some cases by tying up the most favorable sources, with resulting advantages to the producer as well. Here the full force of Shove's jigsaw puzzle is exemplified with the direct matching of a segment of demand and a segment of supply.

This discussion tends to qualify the original statement about the greater urgency on the part of the raw materials producer. The manufacturer has his urgencies also, but they are not served by an open market for raw materials in which much of the supply is not really suited to his needs. Sometimes the manufacturer integrates all the way back to raw materials sources to get the quantity and quality he needs. The intermediate stage of using selected suppliers on a contractual basis represents one of the many variations in the matching and sorting procedures which constitute marketing.

It should be noted that industrial procurement in most firms is concerned with many goods rather than a single material. The industrial purchasing agent may be regarded as building up an assortment to support his firm's operations in somewhat the same way that a household builds up end-use assortment. The purchasing agent tries to foresee future contingencies, taking account of their urgency and probability. He may stock certain parts or even whole machines because of the urgency of minimizing down-time in the case of breakdown. He may increase his stocks of certain raw materials because of an estimated increase in his company's sales or because or rumors of a strike or price increase affecting the supply. He is not free to judge each source of supply separately, but must sometimes choose one alternative over another in terms of what seems required by balance in the whole assortment.

Allocation

The third type of sorting, allocation, has had extensive theoretical treatment in economics. In fact, some economists define their field of study as that of determining the best allocations of scarce supplies. Allocation in the economic sense takes place both internally as a function of business management and externally through transactions in the market place. Both internal and external allocation mean the breaking down of a homogeneous supply into smaller quantities determined by the requirements of each use situation.

Internal allocation is guided, according to economists, by the principle of marginal productivity. That is to say that where there are two or more possible uses, each unit is assigned to the most productive use until productivity is equal at the margin. In other words, if this principle if followed effectively, the last unit assigned to each of several uses will be equally effective. In the operation of a marketing organization, internal allocation applies primarily to the deployment of workers or the appropriation of dollars for advertising or other types of promotion. It can apply also to the assignment of such facilities as office equipment, or the time of electronic computing machines. It enters into decisions concerning the use of the end product for such purposes as display, sampling, or actual sale.

The external allocation of the goods produced and marketed by a given firm is guided by the marginal revenue principle. If a company has several sales territories, it will distribute its products among these territories so as to obtain the same revenue from the last unit sold in each territory. Under the marginal revenue principle, the seller will be encouraged to expand his sales in all directions, until the last unit sold produces a revenue which barely covers all the costs of production and selling. This principle might induce him to expand the total area covered, until he reached a point on the perimeter of his sales region where delivery costs were just sufficient to absorb the margin between price and all other costs. He might be induced on the other hand, to intensify his sales effort closer to home, until the added costs of selling absorbed the available margin. Similarly, the pursuit of profit may induce the seller to make various adjustments to the demands of customers. He may give a price concession in recognition of the economy of a large order. He may vary his price according to the terms of delivery and payment which are convenient to the customer. In the free market the allocation of goods is assumed to be adjusted automatically to all of these varying conditions, and the goods are assumed to come into the possession of just those customers for whom they have the greatest utility.

In an earlier chapter, there was a discussion of rationing as a primitive operation taking place within an organized behavior system. Rationing is a process which is not necessarily guided by marginal principles but may be greatly affected by such considerations as maintaining the power structure. Internal allocation in a business firm is not carried out on a purely mathematical basis but necessarily takes account of the power and capacity of various operating units. In allocating the means of production, the chief executive receives back commitments concerning performance from each of his subordinates. Similarly, rationing is never entirely absent from the external allocation of products. It took the period of wartime scarcity to reveal the fact that the flow of goods is guided by many considerations other than price. There has scarcely been a time since the Second World War when one group or another of major commodities was not in short supply. That means that the people who were willing to buy at the stated price had total demands exceeding the supply. Whenever this happens, something other than price is involved in making the allocations.

The need for rationing under peacetime conditions arises partly from the existence of intermediary sellers. Assume that a manufacturer has only a certain quantity of a new product to sell in a given market, and it is clear in advance that consumers will be eager to buy it. The manufacturer may have been selling his other products to two leading dealers in this city, and either one of them might be able and willing to take the entire initial supply of his new product. It would not be rational for him to settle his problem by selling the entire amount to the highest bidder, since what he wants is an established and continuous business on this product rather than maximum profit from the initial sale. Forced with having to allocate on a basis other than price, the seller will consider such factors as stability and growth for his business. On grounds of stability, he is likely to favor the customer who has given him the most business in the past and thus might be expected to be most loyal in the future. On grounds of growth, he will be inclined to favor the customer who shows the greatest future promise or who has plans for featuring the new product effectively. Sometimes the allocation is made on less rational grounds and represents nothing more than a compromise with the relative amount of pressure exerted by one customer or the other. Each customer may offer reasons why he should be favored, which will presumably relate to the immediate or long-run interest of the seller. Thus, allocation may be brought about neither by the impersonal mechanism of price nor by the deliberate decision of the seller, but become a matter of negotiation.

There are other restrictions on the use of marginal principles for rational allocation. The developing techniques of linear programming are designed to cope with some of these difficulties. Programming techniques can take account of limitations of capacity or other structural features of an operation. There are, of course, the perennial problems of joint costs and division of returns among joint products. The importance of the joint-cost problem in marketing led to the development of the techniques of distribution cost analysis.

There is another fundamental limitation on marginal analysis which is of special concern to marketing. That is the fact that it is possible to approach the margin in many different ways. Thus, in an earlier example, a seller was pictured as having the alternatives of extending his territory so long as he could absorb the increased delivery costs or of intensifying promotion so long as he could absorb the increased sales costs. The theoretical answer is that a businessman should approach the margin in both of these ways or in any other ways that are open. The difficulty is that correct allocation becomes extremely complex when action is open in various directions and imposes a heavy burden on either business judgment or mathematical analysis. The allocation problem cannot be analyzed in terms of simple continuous functions when there is a choice of direction in approaching the margin. There is also the serious risk that the businessman is not even aware of some of the possible directions and may be missing his best opportunity in choosing among the directions in which he can allocate efforts or products.

Assorting

The fourth type of sorting, which has been designated as "assorting," has already been discussed in a preliminary way in the chapter on consumer behavior. It was pointed out that the function of the household purchasing agent is to build up use combinations in anticipation of patterns of behavior the family desires to follow. Here, as in the case of the industrial purchaser, the assortment may be regarded as a set of supplies, each consisting of one or more units of a particular type of goods. Each of these supplies is matched against a possible use, while the assortment as a whole represents the purchasing agent's best judgment as to the pattern of use. Some of the supplies in the assortment are simple complements of each other — as, for example, the collection of ingredients needed in baking a cake. The balance within the assortment as a whole goes beyond the relation of simple complementarity. Some of the products in the assortment may be used every day or may be consumed quickly and have to be replaced. Others are there only because of the outside possibility that the occasion for use will arise. A balanced assortment is one in which the last unit of each supply makes the same contribution to the potency of the assortment. In applying this principle to a household assortment, the difficulty arises that may of its constituent supplies consist of a single unit. Nevertheless, in a balanced assortment the cost of this unit will have been carefully weighed against other possible uses of the money, in relation to the criteria of the urgency and probability of the anticipated occasions of use.

It has already been suggested that assortments and problems of creating balanced assortments are encountered at various points in the economy and not merely in the household. Retailers, standing next to the consumer in the channels of trade, are especially conscious of the need for balanced assortments. The assortment carried by a retailer does not correspond to the assortment owned by any single household among his customers. The retail assortment is designed to provide a satisfactory range of choice for a class of customers served by his store. However, the same principle applies as to being guided by preparation for future contingencies. In this case the events anticipated with varying degrees of probability are purchases by customers of the store. In some lines of trade, such as groceries, many items are stocked with little risk because of the repeat demands of customers. In other lines, such as style goods, the risks are high, with an increasing premium on good judgment as to what to stock. Perhaps one of the most hazardous lines of retailing is that represented by the bookshop. When a book is expected to be a hit, the publisher is obliged to ration the supply. Unless the retailer gets a good initial supply, he is likely to lose out on many sales. If he overestimates his demand or the publisher has overestimated the salability of the book, the retailer will be left with remainders which are hard to move at any price.

A fundamental issue concerning retail stocks is that of breadth of line versus depth of line. A broad line provides a choice among a wide range of products, many of them having basically different purposes. A broad line may attempt to reflect a way of life or conception of contemporary life for a particular class of customers. It is no longer possible for even the largest stores to carry all of the types of goods which are offered to consumers. The entire range of goods available to consumers in a given economy might be designed as the "cultural inventory." The goods carried by any one store or purchased by any one consumer necessarily constitute only a selection from this cultural inventory.

There are other types of stores which carry a relatively narrow line, such as linens or photographic supplies, but provide a depth of assortment for the buyer with a special interest in this field. The narrow-line store attempts to give the consumer a more precise fit for particular requirements, while the broad-line store attempts to give him greater scope in satisfying all his requirements. Good retail assortments help to minimize the amount of consumer effort that must be expended in searching for desired items. Shopping is also facilitated through advertising sponsored by both the retailer and the manufacturer. These aspects of marketing will be treated more fully in discussing the evolution of the market transaction. The special problems of the wholesaler in maintaining effective assortments will be discussed in the next section, which deals with the various aspects of sorting which constitute marketing.

4.   Sorting and the Development of Intermediaries

An advanced marketing economy is characterized by intermediary sellers who intervene between the original source of supply and the ultimate consumer. These middlemen include retailers and wholesalers and many specialized types of merchants, brokers, and sales agents. The present view is that the number

and character of these intermediaries is determined primarily by the requirements of sorting and by the opportunity to effect economies by suitable sorting
arrangements. This chapter so far has dealt with the various types of sorting
and the characteristic problem of each type. The present section will show
their application in the channels of trade in minimizing the various elements of
marketing cost. The development of intermediate sorting will be traced from a
hypothetical beginning in a primitive society.

Decentralized Exchange

In a primitive culture, most of the goods used within a household are produced by members of the household. The term "produce" should be interpreted
broadly enough here to include not only fabrication but also the collection of
natural objects not already in the possession of someone else. At an early stage
in the development of economic activities, it is found that some of the needs of
a household or a tribe can be met more efficiently by exchange than by production. One family might be more skilful in making pots and another in making
baskets. The first might be able to make two pots and the second two baskets
faster than either could make one of each. If both families produce a surplus
of the article they can make best and then engage in exchange, both may get
better-quality goods at lower cost.

This is a very elementary example of the advantage of specialization in production and of the way specialization is promoted through exchange. The
purpose here is to show why exchange takes place through intermediaries and
to consider the additional advantages which are gained through the development of middlemen and their alignment into marketing channels. To that end,
we may picture a slightly more complex exchange economy consisting of five
households. Each is producing a surplus of some article used by all five. These
articles might be pots, baskets, knives, hoes, and hats. In each case a surplus of
four units is produced, and these units are then exchanged with the other households to obtain needed articles. Ten separate exchanges would be required, in
accordance with the simple mathematical fact that a pair of households could
be chosen in just ten ways from a total of five households.

Centralized Exchange

Now suppose that this pattern of decentralized exchange is replaced by a
central market. All come together at an appointed place on the second Thursday
in April, each bringing his surplus. This may be a time when they are coming
together anyway to celebrate the spring festival of their rain god. The exchange
is accomplished with greater convenience by bringing all five traders together
at the same time and place, rather than having individuals seek each other out
to conclude each transaction.

Only five trips are required instead of ten. Each participant has his surplus in readiness for exchange. This may not always be true in the case of decentralized exchange. When the potmaker visits the basketmaker to offer his wares, there may not be any finished baskets on hand and ready for exchange. Thus, it might require more than ten trips to complete the distribution of goods. In a primitive culture, the goods and the parties to the transaction must be brought together at the same time and place in order that exchange may occur. The example given shows how much more easily this is accomplished through a central market. Here in its most elementary form is the creation of time and place utility, a concept which is generally associated with marketing. Time utility and place utility have held little interest for the general economist but deserve a more intensive analysis from the viewpoint of the marketing economist. That which is accomplished through the central market is a decrease in the cost of creating these utilities. From the marketing viewpoint, nothing has utility unless it is present at the right time and place for use. The process of creating these necessary conditions for utility can be more or less efficient just as much as the process of production.

The Intermediary

The next step in the evolution of exchange is for the market to be operated by an individual who may be called a dealer. The five producers now engage in exchange with the dealer rather than with each other. The basketmaker, for example, trades his surplus to the dealer and receives from him the items he requires to replenish his assortment. He may acquire a pot, a knife, a hoe, and a hat in a single transaction rather than through four separate transactions with the respective producers of these articles. In this way he saves time either to make more baskets or to devote to other pursuits. Possibly he will make six baskets instead of five, and the dealer will retain one basket in payment for his services.

Our simplified model of exchange now embraces what has been called "possession utility" as well as time and place utility. Effort is involved in the act of exchange itself. The dealer has created possession utility by bringing about the transfer of goods from producer to consumer with less effort than would be involved in direct trading. Economic analysis of the factors in price equilibrium generally rests on the assumption that exchange transactions are costless. Marketing analysis directed toward an understanding of trade channels must begin with a recognition of the costs involved in the creation of time, place, and possession utility. It must be emphasized again that it is a highly artificial procedure to distinguish these separate aspects of utility or to regard them as the product of marketing effort. An alternative formulation is to interpret the above example as illustrating the economy in the cost of contact achieved through intermediaries. This is accomplished by reducing the number of transactions involved in creating complete assortments for every household.

The Ratio of Advantage of Intermediary Exchange

The saving might not be very important in the example given of a primitive economy consisting of only five producers. Cutting the number of transactions in half might not make a perceptible increase in productivity, and trading with each other might be valued in itself as a congenial form of social intercourse. The number of transactions necessary to carry out decentralized exchange is $\frac{n(n-1)}{2}$, where n is the number of producers and each makes only one article. Since the number of transaction required is only n if the central market is operated by a dealer, the ratio of advantage is $\frac{n-1}{2}$. Thus, if the number of producers is raised from 5 to 25, the ratio of advantage in favor of an intermediary increases from 2 to 12. With 125 producers the ratio of advantage is 62. The figure 125 is a tiny fraction of the number of articles which must be produced to maintain satisfactory assortments in the hands of all of the consuming units in our complex modern culture. Even at this preliminary level of analysis, the ratio of advantage in favor of intermediary exchange is overwhelming. Exchange arises out of considerations of efficiency in production. Exchange through intermediaries arises out of considerations of efficiency in exchange itself.

Intermediaries can increase the efficiency of exchange even when the producers and consumers under consideration are located in the same compact community. The advantages are greatest when large distances intervene. Place utility takes on new aspects when the potmaker and the basketmaker are hundreds or even thousands of miles apart. When buyer and seller are so far apart, one or the other must take the initiative in closing the gap; one of them must call on the other if they are to negotiate face to face. One side or the other must assume the cost of moving the goods; transportation and communication systems arise to bridge the distance. The railroads and trucking companies are, in effect, new types of specialized intermediaries serving buyer and seller more cheaply than they could serve themselves. It was no less an authority than Alfred Marshall who said that economic progress consists largely in finding better methods for marketing at a distance. The number of intervening marketing agencies tends to go up as distance increases. Many eastern companies who sell directly to wholesalers in other parts of the country sell through manufacturers' agents on the Pacific coast. This type of arrangement was even more common in the past but has been dropped in some instances as communication with the Pacific region has improved. Distance, for the present purpose, is not to be measured in miles but in terms of the time and cost involved in communication and transportation. In this sense there are points 300 miles inland in

China which are further away from Shanghai than is San Francisco. Tariffs and the formalities of customs clearance are also a form of distance. As a result, specialized import and export firms in addition to other types of intermediaries commonly enter into foreign trade.

Specialized Intermediaries

Production and consumption may also be separated widely in time. The wheat crop which is harvested in June is destined to be consumed as bread or other foodstuffs over a period of a year or more thereafter. To bridge this gap in time is to create utility for both producer and consumer. One wishes to be paid as soon as the crop is harvested. The other wants bread as needed, without having to maintain a stock of wheat in the meantime. Specialized intermediaries, such as grain elevators and warehouses, enter the picture and help to create time utility through storage. Banks, insurance companies, and other specialized institutions help to minimize the costs and the risks of owning goods in the period between production and consumption. Retailers and wholesalers create time utility simply by holding stocks of goods available to be drawn upon by buyers. Without these facilities the only course open to the buyer would be to place an order with the producer and wait until the article could be produced and delivered. To be able to obtain the article at once instead of waiting is the essence of time utility. Another way of creating time utility is by selling on credit either to consumers or to other types of buyers. Through the installment purchase of an automobile, for example, the consumer is able to begin enjoying the use of the car long before it would be possible for him to pay for it in full. An automobile used partly for business, or other items entering into a further stage of production, may help to raise the money needed for purchasing the product. Thus the production good in question starts creating value for both the maker and the user without waiting for the time when the user can pay cash for it.

5.   Technological Distance and the Discrepancy of Assortments

Producer and consumer are often a long way apart not only in time and space but also in other ways. A product has very different meanings for its producer and for the ultimate consumer buyer. The consumer judges the product in relation to anticipated patterns of behavior and considers how it will fit in with other products he expects to use. If the product is a mechanical refrigerator, it must fit into the space available for it in his kitchen or pantry and be equipped to utilize the supply of electricity or domestic gas. If the product is a tie, the wearer does not want the color to clash with the colors of his other clothing. The specifications of the ideal product from the consumer viewpoint are determined by use requirements, including the requirements of not detracting from the value in use of other items already in the assortment.

Association of Goods

The goods that a producer has for sale are the expression of his skills and resources. Ideal specifications from his viewpoint would be those which made most effective use of his plant capacity and of the available labor and raw materials. If he makes more than one product, his stock of finished goods may be regarded as an assortment in the sense that it constitutes a supply with diverse characteristics. In some cases the separate items will be quite unrelated from the viewpoint of the uses they serve. They may have nothing in common except that they were produced from the same materials or by similar processes. Two items many be linked even more closely, one being a primary product and the other a by-product. In any case it is a wholly different thing for goods to be found together because of convenience in production as compared to an assortment of goods that are all complementary in use.

The most convenient or constructive association of goods changes at each stage in the flow of merchandise from producer to consumer. This fact has been generalized as the "discrepancy of assortments." Goods are associated for transportation because of physical handling characteristics and common origin and destination. Goods are associated for storage in terms of the length of time they are to be stored and the conditions needed to preserve them. Between the producer's stock of finished goods and the assortment in the hands of the consumer, there may be other stocks or assortments maintained by retailers and wholesalers. The composition of these intermediate stocks is determined by the requirements of the functions performed.

The discrepancy of assortments places severe limitation on vertical integration of marketing agencies. A retail grocer typically relies on different wholesale sources for meat, produce, and packaged groceries. The requirement for storage, handling, and other aspects of the wholesale function are quite different in these three product fields. The retailer may provide the consumer who wants to buy peaches with a choice of fresh, canned, or frozen. Yet the routes by which the three items reached the grocery store would normally be quite different at both the wholesale and the production levels. If it were not for the discrepancy of assortments, marketing channels might be more frequently integrated from top to bottom. Most fundamental of these discrepancies is that between producer of stocks and consumer assortments. The product appears in a very different setting at these two levels and may be said to belong to the technology of production at one stage and the technology of use at the other. In addition to distance in time and space, marketing channels serve to bridge the technological gap (which may be regarded as a third form of distance between production and consumption.).

Intermediate Sorting

The ultimate in intermediate sorting is seen in the freight classification yard. Trains of cars arrive over various routes. These trains are broken up and re-combined according to the routes over which they will depart. Let us assume a simplified case in which five railroads come into the same terminal point. There are five production centers on each line or twenty-five in all. A train coming in over route A consists of one hundred loaded cars. Twenty cars are picked up at each production center on route A, each destined for one of the centers on other lines. The same volume of freight originates on each of the other routes. Each of the production centers ships and receives twenty carloads of freight. Yet, because of re-sorting at the central interchange, the entire movement of five hundred cars is completed by each of the five trains making a round trip over its own line. Note that there are no two cars for which both origin and destination coincide. Great improvements are currently being made in the operation of classification yards through application of automatic controls to this sorting process.

Chapter 11

INTRODUCTION TO FUNCTIONALISM*

Wroe Alderson

Theory and research are the major aspects of science. The interaction between theory and research is a necessary condition for scientific advancement. Marketing research, as the systematic collection of facts about markets, is commonly dated from 1911. For the first thirty-five years there was little interest in marketing theory. The primary goal of fact-finding was to aid marketing executives in understanding and solving specific marketing problems. Surveys were not designed to test theoretical propositions and very little explicit theory existed.

Marketing Behavior and Executive Action, published by this author in 1957, was the first book-length effort to lay the groundwork for a separate theory of marketing. This book was divided into three parts, the first two attempting to sketch a general theory of marketing, and the third suggesting principles of executive action oriented to the marketing theory. This third part has now been augmented, or supplanted, by the publication in 1964 of *Planning and Problem Solving in Marketing* by Alderson and Green. The present volume is a greatly expanded and completely rewritten version of the statement on marketing theory contained in the first two parts of *Marketing Behavior and Executive Action*.

This book attempts to pick up some of the loose ends left dangling in the earlier work and to round out a more comprehensive and logically consistent theoretical perspective. The author has enjoyed the advantage of presenting successive drafts to graduate classes at the University of Pennsylvania and to a faculty seminar at New York University under the Ford Distinguished Professorship. Some introductory comments about the nature and meaning of theory may serve to clarify the task which the author has undertaken and will hopefully indicate how much remains to be done in this exciting intellectual enterprise.

---

*Originally published in *Dynamic Marketing Behavior* (1965), pages 1-22.

1.   Theory and Marketing Science

The development of theory is the inevitable outcome of any concerted effort to improve practice. We must become more theoretical in order to become more practical. A major event in marketing was the founding in 1962 of the Marketing Science Institute. This non-profit organization is supported by a list of stellar American companies, with the direct participation of a group of executives primarily concerned with marketing practice. The philosophy of the founder of the Institute was that the initial effort to apply scientific methods in marketing had shown such promise as to justify a continuous program for the deliberate creation of a full-fledged science of marketing.

The Institute has launched on a series of studies unlike anything that practical business men had sponsored before. All of the firms involved spend millions of dollars annually for studies designed to shed light on their individual marketing problems. Now they are engaged through the research committees and seminars of the Institute in planning studies which can contribute to the solution of whole classes of individual problems. General studies have been published. The most recent one is called *The Sources and Meaning of Marketing Theory*, a book which will be considered in more detail shortly. Suffice it to say at this point that it is a remarkable experience to be present at meetings of the business supporters of the Institute and to observe the major concern with questions of marketing theory. Some of the events which have led to this change in the intellectual climate can be identified.

The explosion of the atomic bomb at Hiroshima on August 6, 1945 was a shocking reminder of the vast practical consequences of theoretical science. An equally rude awakening, from an American viewpoint, occurred with the launching of Sputnik I by the Russians in 1957. Even marketing professors had not discussed marketing theory in public until 1946; yet in 1965 a treatise on marketing theory appears with the full support of the leading marketing organizations in the United States.

Actually there are several roads to the recognition of the importance of theory even for the marketing executive who is primarily concerned with the solution of his own problems. It is a common experience in marketing research that after a survey has been made the executive or the researcher can usually think of ways in which the study could have been improved. These afterthoughts are one of the roots of marketing theory. One aspect of theory pertains to the nature of scientific methodology and the other to the conceptualization of the underlying reality which the science undertakes to study.

Consider a marketing executive who is looking over the results of a questionnaire to determine the weight the results should be given in reaching a decision. His first concern may be as to whether the questions were asked of the right people or of enough people. By the right people he means a sample that is truly representative of the population to which he expects to direct his marketing effort. By enough people he means a sample sufficiently large to keep sampling error within acceptable limits. The demise of the Literary Digest, and its political poll, had dramatically demonstrated that even a sample running into the millions could give the wrong answer because of hidden bias. The limited budgets for marketing research heretofore required that reliable answers be obtained using much smaller samples. An intensive interest in applied sampling theory developed, and area probability sampling emerged as a practical answer for many market research problems.

The marketing executive might also be concerned about the questions that were asked and the whole technique of obtaining answers. Survey questions are generally intended to obtain some measure of consumer behavior such as frequency of purchase of product, or to place those sampled in qualitative categories such as consumers who like or dislike the product. The executive may wonder whether the questions actually are valid measurements. Can the information on consumption be projected to the population as a whole? Can the number who express a favorable reaction to a new product be safely used to predict the degree of success when the product is introduced? Whether the executive knows it or not, he is putting pressure on the researcher to develop a more defensible theory concerning the measurement of marketing variables. This pressure has resulted in a vast amount of work with slow but steady progress in measurement techniques. The criteria by which one technique is judged to be better than another is in the realm of theory.

A method of sampling or measurement may have general superiority over another or it may be the most appropriate method in a given situation. Thus there is a strategy in the choice of methods which carries marketing research beyond the range of the general scientific methodology embodied in sampling theory and measurement theory. In all these areas the marketing researcher is compelled to develop better theory in order to provide the marketing executive with answers to the more sophisticated questions he is asking.

2.   Conceptual Models of Marketing Reality

This book deals primarily with a conceptual model of marketing reality rather than with an account of scientific methodology in marketing. *Planning and Problem Solving in Marketing*, by contrast, was largely methodological in character. Alderson's chapters presented some principles and procedures for planning in marketing and Green's chapters demonstrated the application of Bayesian decision theory to marketing problems. The present volume presents a conceptual model of markets and marketing processes and suggests some of the initial steps toward dealing with aspects of marketing in quantitative terms. This book explores the relationships among marketing variables, attempting to identify the variables which make up systems of marketing behavior and which merit the full attention of the scientific methodologist.

Admittedly this version of marketing theory is speculative and in that sense is similar to the successive versions of economic theory from Adam Smith to Alfred Marshall. It is based on years of observation from the vantage point of the market researcher and consultant. Unlike many economic theorists whose systems were purely deductive, the present volume culminates in one hundred and fifty propositions to be tested by research. This is in contrast with economists who have held that theirs was a deductive rather than an empirical science and that research designed to test their theoretical assertions was irrelevant.

This writer has had a few opportunities to engage in basic research in marketing and to deal with more general questions than those related to the specific problems of a specific client. These experiences have demonstrated that it is possible to discover general truths in marketing which transcend the scope of job-to-job analysis of marketing data. Also, hundreds of projects for individual clients, manufacturers, wholesalers and retailers, and for public agencies at all levels have helped to shape the view of marketing reality presented here.

In a mature science each proposition derived from theory is tested by research. If the proposition is not sustained by the test, it is usually reformulated and tested again, serving to give direction to a new research project. While only a small part of the propositions stated in this book have been tested by research, an earnest effort has been made to state them as falsifiable propositions. Without the continuous interplay of theory and research, it can scarcely be denied that accidents of temperament and social philosophy have helped to determine the character of the conceptual framework presented here. The remainder of this introduction will deal with functionalist theory as defined by the author, with other versions of functionalism, with alternative approaches to theory outside the functionalist school, with the requirements for valid marketing theory as expounded by M.H. Halbert of the Marketing Science Institute, and with the broad purposes, limitations and methodological commitments of functionalist theory in marketing.

3.   What is Functionalist Theory?

A recent monograph published by the American Academy of Political and Social Science is entitled "Functionalism in the Social Sciences." In his foreword the editor states that the functionalistic point of view has been "manifest" in all of the social sciences. He includes psychology, sociology, political science, economics, anthropology, geography, jurisprudence, and linguistics. He says, "Most primary theoretical and methodological debates in postwar social science have centered on functionalism and alternatives to it." From his reading in the behavioral sciences this author has long been aware that functionalism s the only school of thought which provides a common thread in all these various fields. One of the alternatives in each of the behavioral sciences is unctionalism.

The other alternatives reflect historic issues or special problems in the given ield and tend to preserve the barriers between fields rather than to favor integration. In anthropology, for example, there are at least four other major theoretical positions. The first pair places heavy emphasis respectively on evolution and diffusion to explain culture change. The early evolutionists like Lewis Morgan and some contemporaries such as Lester White have held that there was a fixed sequence of stages through which cultures advanced and that this sequence, with little difference except in timing, was repeated in one culture after another. Those who took an extreme position with respect to diffusion held that the emergence of new culture traits was an extremely rare occurrence. Elliott Smith, for example, held that the general pattern of culture everywhere has been transmitted by diffusion from its source in ancient Egypt.

The other two alternatives to functionalism might be labeled the psychological and the historical. Most generally the psychological group seems to have a leaning toward the Freudian and psychoanalytic type of psychology. In fact, Frazer in his *The Golden Bough* might be regarded as one of the forerunners of Freud. Some modern anthropologists such as Abram Kardiner have adopted the psychoanalytic approach because of their special interest in the problem of personality development in a cultural setting.

Several contemporary anthropologists have given attention to historical trends in connection with their developmental work in relatively primitive cultures. Margaret Mead has attempted historical reconstruction with emphasis on the role of the individual leader in her treatment of the Paliau movement among the Manus of the South Pacific. Miss Mead, however, has too much diverse talent to attempt to classify and indeed reflects a strong functionalist and interventionist base, particularly in her applied work with surviving primitive cultures. Julian Steward has been led by his emphasis on multilinear evolution to attempt some historical reconstructions in various culture areas.

Ralph Linton, while he did not call himself a functionalist, represented a considerable advance over Malinowski's dependence on an instinct theory in his development of an interaction model among various sub-cultures and cultural trends in a dynamic society. The purpose here is not to venture an opinion of anthropological theory as to point out the diversity and lead up to a similar statement on functionalism and its alternatives in marketing and economics.

In psychology, a book by A.A. Roback several years ago enumerated 47 separate theoretical positions in that science. Of these, only four dominant schools will be mentioned, including functionalism. The other three which have been most influential in American psychology are behaviorism, psychoanalysis and Gestalt. Actually these three labels each cover a broad area with man variants under each heading.

Behaviorism in the strictest sense, as applied to a school of psycholog holds that the only proper study of the psychologist is overt behavior whic can be observed, recorded and measured. The term *mind* drops out of th vocabulary of a behaviorist like John B. Watson. Introspective reports by th subject which had been relied upon by earlier psychologists were barred as method of research. This school has made the most notable contribution t learning, relying on its image of the nervous system as a collection of refle arcs which could be affected by processes of conditioning and reinforcement

Psychoanalysis is much more theoretical and speculative than psychologic behaviorism. Its great field of concentration has been motivation and pa ticularly the difference between conscious motives and hidden or suppresse motives. It is commonly agreed that Sigmund Freud was the great genius wh opened up all of this field for exploration; yet the divisive forces in depth psy chology have been so extreme that Freud broke off with all of his immediat disciples during his lifetime. These disciples included Jung, Adler and Ranl all of whom established distinctive schools of their own.

No purpose would be served in following all these variations, but it can be sai in general that depth psychology contrasts very sharply with behaviorism, bot in concept and method. Rather than banish the mind or soul from psychologic discussion, psychoanalysis presents a highly structured picture of the self wit the id, the ego and the super ego, and with the conscious, subconscious an unconscious levels in the mind.

Gestalt psychology grew out of interest in problems of perception, althoug Gestalt and its offshoots currently present a more rounded-out picture of th principal topics in psychology. The problems of perception studies initiall were of a direct and simple kind, dealing with questions of what we see o the way in which we become aware of the external world through the othe senses. A basic doctrine of the founder was that we perceive reality in orga nized wholes and only later begin to break an object or a total scene down int its constituent elements. Gestalt means *configuration*, and the early Gestalt ex periments concentrated on showing the dominant role of configuration in visua perception.

By natural extension of the term *perception* Gestalt has come to be the psy chology most useful to the student of insight and problem solving. Etymologi cally, insight means *a kind of seeing*. A few Gestaltists such as Max Wertheime have taken the extreme position that if you do not see into a problem imme diately you cannot solve it. Kohler made a more realistic allowance for th selective exploration by which the problem solver gives insight a chance t work.

Some offshoots of Gestalt, such as the field psychology of Kurt Lewin and the perceptional or phenomenological psychology of Coombs, Rogers and others, provide a more adequate framework for topics such as learning or motivation. Lewin in what he calls topological psychology pictures the self as operating in an environment which is polarized by recognition of elements which are favorable or unfavorable to the achievements of the objectives of the self. The self can gradually achieve mastery of an environment through increased knowledge of its structure and through the gradual acquisition of technical skills. This essential framework was evidently adopted in "Psychologists," an unpublished work of Churchman and Ackoff, and will also be evident in the basic outlines of the theory presented in Chapter 1 of this book.

Phenomenologists, such as Coombs and Rogers, have erected general psychology on a Gestalt basis but incorporating many of the special insights of behaviorism and psychoanalysis. It is indeed a kind of neo-functionalism which is recommended elsewhere in this book for the marketing man who does not trust his own judgment in the eclectic use of concepts and techniques from various schools of psychology.

With further respect to functionalism in psychology, it is often asserted that functionalism has been the dominant thread throughout the history of American psychology. It was a natural complement in psychology to the philosophical pragmatism of Dewey and James. Woodworth chose to call his special view "dynamic psychology," but he is generally classed as a functionalist by other writers. This writer has been especially influenced by his emphasis on "capacity primacy" as contrasted with "need primacy" in basic motivation.

O.H. Mowrer, in his recent and monumental two-volume work on learning theory, embraced a type of equilibrium theory which psychologists call homeostasis. This means the tendency of the organism to maintain steady states at various levels such as in the temperature and salinity of the blood and tension reduction through proper response after a need has been aroused. Mowrer makes special mention of Woodworth as one psychologist whose views do not rest easily within this static framework.

This brings us up to the somewhat more ambitious classification scheme which Don Martindale undertakes in functionalism in the social science monograph mentioned earlier. He suggests that there are about a dozen quite distinct and separate theoretical viewpoints in contemporary sociology, to say nothing of earlier views such as environmentalism, racial determinism, and the radical emphasis on the struggle for survival by Herbert Spencer and William Graham Sumner. Martindale also gives us a hand in reducing his eleven or twelve types of theory down to four broad classifications. We will deal with only these broad groups as in the discussion of anthropology and psychology.

Martindale suggests a four-way table based on two dichotomies. One has to do with the underlying conception of the nature of reality which is expressed

Table 11.1.

	Physical Sciences Methods	Life Sciences Methods
Basic Reality — Systemic Wholes	Dialectical Materialism *Karl Marx*	Functionalism *Talcott Parsons*
Basic Reality — Elements	Pluralistic Behaviorism *F. Stuart Chapin*	Existentialism *Kurt Jaspers*

in a theory. He divides sociologists into those who see social reality in terms of systematic wholes and those who see it in terms of separate distinguishable elements. This division will be accepted for the moment, but a three-way break will be suggested later.

In the other direction he divides sociologists according to their basic conception of scientific method. This is essentially a division between those who take physical science as their ideal for scientific method and those who adhere to some other ideal drawn from the life sciences or directly from the behavioral sciences themselves. He calls these two attitudes toward method positivism and anti-positivism. The four-way table developed in this way is shown in Table 11.1, with some attempt to simplify the terminology.

The name of a sociologist and the school he represents is shown in each of the four cells of the table. It will be seen that functionalism appears in the upper right-hand cell along with the name of Talcott Parsons, who is generally regarded as the outstanding exponent of contemporary functionalism. This means that functionalism is the school which is interested in systematic wholes and applies methods for their study derived from biology or directly from the behavioral fields themselves.

Similarly, the name of Karl Marx is associated with the study of systems by physical science methods, the name of F. Stuart Chapin with the study of separate elements using physical science methods, and the name of Kurt Jaspers with the study of separate elements but using methods not derived from the physical sciences. This classification device, which is so simple in essence, becomes moderately technical in the hands of Martindale, and interested readers are urged to refer to the monograph itself.

The present writer is not sure that the issue between positivism and anti-positivism is an enduring one so far as the behavioral sciences are concerned. It is likely that science will become unified in its methodology before it becomes unified in its ontology, or the underlying conception of the nature of reality. In biology, for example, there has been a tremendous revolution in the last fifteen years, with some of the most far-reaching research going on along the borderline of biochemistry. In the behavioral fields, including marketing, there is strong and continuing pressure for the adoption of quantitative methods.

The fight over positivism versus anti-positivism in methodology was more important to a generation that is passing, with people like George Lundberg and Stuart Dodd on one side, and Talcott Parsons and Robert K. Merton on the other. While the writer is prepared to see the methodological distinction obliterated, he would be happier about a trichotomy rather than a dichotomy with respect to ontology.

In between the emphasis on whole systems and individual elements, there would appear to be a group that is inclined to start with Gestalts, or configurations. It is quite conceivable that one using this starting point will immediately proceed in one of two directions — either toward building on the configuration to form a systematic whole, or breaking it down into its individual elements. In one of his essays, Bertrand Russell places considerable emphasis on this middle ground. Translating Russell into this writer's preferred terminology, he seemed to be asserting that any intellectual enterprise often begins with the search for significant structure. Possibly there is also some relation with the emphasis adopted by Merton in recent years calling for generalizations or principles of the middle range. This three-way division seems to the author a more suitable basis for classifying theoretical positions in the area of marketing and economics. Theory in these fields inevitably centers in some type of equilibrating system, equilibrium being approached either on a very short-run or very long-run basis.

There are three basic types of equilibrating systems. One is the atomistic in which there is a tendency toward equilibrium among separate elements. This is the kind of atomistic determinism which the physicist studies in the case of particles contained in a closed chamber. At the other extreme is the system regarded as an organic whole with structured components such as in the human body which are joined together in a fully determined and inflexible pattern. In between are the loosely coupled systems which might be regarded as consisting of semi-fabricated components but which bear in themselves the capacity to change or replace these components.

The theory which will be expounded in this book assumes that marketing systems are essentially of this latter type. A marketing system, like an ecological group, can adapt to the environment. It can do this by replacing its members, including replacements for such key members as its leaders. It is also capable of changing either its objectives or technologies through which it attempts to secure its objectives.

There would appear to be three broad alternatives for separate theoretical positions in marketing and economics. First is the atomistic model which has been well developed in classical economics. At the other extreme is the organismic model which this writer would associate with the genuine institutionalists such as Marx and Veblen. In the middle is the ecological model which this author regards as the home ground of functionalism. It can be observed in pseudo-institutionalists such as John R. Commons and J. R. Clark, and in pseudo-classicists such as J. M. Keynes. Functionalism is also the home ground for most contemporary writers on marketing theory.

The author hesitated about adopting the label of functionalism for his own views since it might be a source of some slight confusion in the marketing area. Earlier writers in marketing, seeking some ground of generalization, had emphasized the functions of marketing rather than the overall output of marketing systems in the sense that the term functionalism has been used in the behavioral sciences. While there is slight ambiguity, there is little outright conflict since the functions of marketing as listed by such writers as McGarry can be regarded as sub-functions which together constitute the function of marketing as a whole.

In the writer's particular version of functionalism there is the emphasis on system and system outputs which is shared by the functionalist in other fields. Functionalism looks at a systemic structure to determine the present relationship between inputs and outputs and to lay the groundwork for bringing about an improvement in these relationships. Functionalism is the position that comes naturally to those who are strongly oriented toward problem solving.

Marketing as it has developed concerns itself primarily with the movement of goods and, in fact, it might be well to designate the marketing specialist as a good economist. To the extent that he looks beyond the problems of individual clients with goods to sell, he is concerned with making imperfect markets more perfect and would usually favor intervention toward this end. Keynes was described as a functionalist above because of his interventionist proclivities as a monetary economist. He was concerned with one great marketing imperfection, namely, imperfection in investment markets, whereas the marketing man in his microeconomic studies becomes aware of specific imperfections in the markets for all of the major classifications of goods.

4.   Types of Functionalism

Another article appearing in the monograph already quoted has been very clarifying because it deals with a range of possible types within functional ism itself. This article by Ian Whitaker speaks in terms of sociology, but the distinctions drawn are equally applicable to functionalism in marketing and economics. Whitaker also employs the device of the four-way table, his major distinction being between those who are concerned primarily with large systems and those who are concerned primarily with small systems. He distinguishes these groups by the terms *macrofunctionalism* and *microfunctionalism*.

In the other direction he divides the field between those who are primarily concerned with a descriptive or factual approach and those who are primarily concerned to develop laws or generalizations. These he labels respectively

Table 11.2.

	Large Systems	Small Systems
Facts about Systems	*Malinowski*	*Lewin*
Laws Governing Systems	*Pfaff*	*Alderson*

with the terms *deographic* and *nomothetic*. Hereafter the distinction will be indicated by the simpler terms *fact* and *law*. Table 11.2 shows these distinctions and indicates the names of a writer or two who fit into these four cells.

In an unpublished doctoral dissertation recently completed by Martin Pfaff, there is a section heading, Functionalism, Malinowski to Alderson. Actually the student seems closer to Malinowski than to Alderson, but his name helps to fill out the table. Malinowski is described by Whitaker as being interested in large systems largely from a factual standpoint. This writer's view would go into the opposite cell, representing individuals who primarily are concerned with generalizations for small systems.

Kurt Lewin is described by Whitaker as being interested in facts for small systems. He points out, however, that both Malinowski and Lewin progressed from fact to law in the latter part of their careers. One suspects that the division of interest will continue to run more strongly between students of large and small systems than between those who are interested in fact and in law. As scientific methodology becomes more unified, one obvious trend is toward a greater interplay between fact and law even in the writings of a single author.

The distinction between large and small is rooted partly in the nature of the problems with which scholars are concerned and marketing men generally continue to think first of all of the behavior of households and business enterprises. There is likely, however, to be a philosophic cleavage that goes considerably deeper. Malinowski and such current followers as Pfaff have no hesitation in attributing functions to large systems, including entire cultures. The marketing man becomes a little uneasy in trying to think of a whole society or cultural complex as a system. The large system thinker talks functionalism in terms of complete integration, covering all the activities taking place in the environment. The small systems thinker is likely to be an incurable pluralist who can visualize systems operating in comparative isolation, perhaps with some continuous conflict at the fringes.

We may distinguish among various theoretical starting points on ontological grounds. The researcher's conception of reality is the determining consideration. Methodology should be adapted to conceptual content. The issue of fact versus law is really a methodological issue and this distinction will tend to disappear as well as the distinction between positivism and anti-positivism. We are left with a spectrum of approaches laid out along an ontological scale. Four of these have already been identified and two more remain to be introduced. The list of six is as follows:

1 Marketing systemics

2 Microfunctionalism

3 Macrofunctionalism

4 Institutionalism

5 Commodity flow theory

6 History of marketing thought

Each of these six approaches will be discussed in turn. The second is the one favored in this book, but some merit is found in all five alternative approaches.

Marketing Systemics

Marketing systemics is the term used to characterize what would now appear to be the most probably future stance of the Marketing Science Institute with respect to marketing theory. From an objective viewpoint, structure and function have an equal claim to the attention of the theorist. Both are aspects of marketing systems and cannot be neglected in a comprehensive explanation of marketing. The term systemics, suggested by members of the Institute staff, does not mean merely that both structure and function must be considered. Rather it suggests that they are inseparable aspects of a system and that it is futile to attempt to deal with either in isolation.

Marketing systemics would culminate in an atomistic theory, in this respect resembling neo-classical economics. It would differ from neo-classical economics in several respects, including the fact that it is potentially far more rigorous. The logical requirements for the deductive apparatus which Mr. Halbert prescribes for marketing would be of a higher order than those which have so far sufficed in economic theory. He evidently visualizes something similar to the analytical procedure suggested by Richard M. Martin in his article in *Theory in Marketing, Second Series*. This would be an approach to marketing theory which would exceed in logical rigor anything which now exists in physics or anywhere in the whole range of sciences with the exception of mathematics.

Marketing systemics would dispense with the assumption of rational behavior which has been relied upon in economic theory, at least until recently. Marketing systemics would be built on careful observation of marketing behavior and generalized descriptions of it without applying any normative term such as rational or irrational. The methods applied in this study of behavior would probably attempt to approximate those of clinical and experimental psychology.

For example, there is doubtful validity on any scientific grounds for the sweeping assumptions concerning profit maximization by a firm. Has a sufficiently large sample of business executives declared this to be their objective? If so, can this introspective report on their motivations be accepted at face value?

Marketing systemics would tend to reduce marketing behavior to the smallest practical elements such as purchasing decisions and the use of products in satisfying needs. At first it might limit its aims to predicting outcomes, only later attempting to specify conditions for control. The equilibrium discussed would be an equilibrium of abstract market forces rather than an equilibrium among the competitive efforts of problem solvers. In spirit marketing systemics would be similar to theoretical economics but with a much greater interplay between theory and research.

While scientific methodology is tending to become a seamless fabric, marketing systemics would place the greatest emphasis on methodology relative to concept and content. In particular it would transcend the other schools of thought in developing the possibilities for improved measurement in marketing. It would also be consistent with extensive use of mathematical system models and the use of such research tools as experimental games and computer simulation. The chief weakness of marketing systemics might lie in a preference for deterministic models and consequent tendency to dehumanize the active participants in the marketing process. It might have difficulty in dealing with values and with culture change. If structure and function are given equal weight, the analyst would find normative standards hard to come by. There would be circularity in asserting that a structure was functioning well and that a function was provided with an appropriate structure.

Microfunctionalism in Marketing

The view of theory espoused in this book is based on the functionalist approach to the study of small systems, primarily households and business enterprises. Such a system has a bond of solidarity because each member entertains expectations concerning the outputs of the systems. It can be said that the function of the system is to produce these preferred outputs. The structure of the system facilitates this desired outcome. The members need not have identical expectations. Perhaps the system has several outputs. The first participant may prefer one output and a second participant may prefer another. They can be tied together just as effectively as if they both desired the same output. Because of their joint expectations both members behave in such a way as to perpetuate the system. The apparent goal of system survival is based on the expectations of its members.

Microfunctionalism tends to be pluralistic. Each system is a center or power and decision. There can be external conflict between systems through their drive to achieve their goals and there can be internal conflict concerning the choice of goals. A later chapter on marketing and public policy introduces systems, which are radically different in kind from households and enterprises, into the pluralistic universe. The system concept tends to be a well defined group of participants with the resources they command rather than a set of abstract market forces. Accepted normative principles tend to be generated by the internal interaction of the group and by the resolution of external conflict.

The term *small system* here carries somewhat the same meaning as that employed by Ross Ashby. The size of a system depends on the complexity of its structure as much as on the number of its participants. A community containing only a few thousand people is regarded as a system, but with subsystems performing many functions, households, enterprises, political, social and cultural organizations, it would be large system analytically. General Motors with many thousands of participants but with automobiles as its chief output would be a smaller system in the functional sense.

The discussion of microfunctionalism can remain relatively brief at this point as it will be the subject of the remainder of this book. It is useful to here suggest some further comparisons with marketing systemics. A special virtue of functionalism is its power in developing testable hypotheses. For the problem solver in marketing, each new solution may suggest new theoretical implications for the problem solver who has adopted a functionalistic frame of reference. The conceptual richness of functionalism complements the methodological virtuosity of marketing systemics. The final chapter of this book presents 150 falsifiable propositions as some evidence of the resourcefulness of functionalism in this direction.

The conceptualist does not always provide the methodologist with statements cast in the most convenient form for testing. This is an old problem in science and will doubtless be a continuing one. What is called for is a series of transformations of conceptual statements in which the conceptualist and the methodologist can work together unless they are indeed one and the same person. This is a sort of pre-algebraic manipulation in which the aim is to produce a mathematical expression in which the unknowns can be replaced by numbers obtained through research. The relation between the conceptual sentence and the mathematical equation should be such that the sentence cannot be true unless the equation is true.

The vision here is one of scholars of rather different theoretical positions cooperating for the advancement of science in marketing. That is the only possible basis for cooperation in science since separate persons with precisely the same theoretical positions can rarely be found. This view in itself is good microfunctionalism, reflecting a belief that two persons do not have to have precisely the same goals in order for both to achieve satisfaction through the same project. The author has served in a modest way as a methodologist to Leo

Aspinwall in some aspects of his particular brand of microfunctionalism. M. I. Halbert, in turn, has served as a methodologist to the author in his slightly more mathematically oriented shopping studies in Boston and Philadelphia.

Macrofunctionalism in Marketing

This third view stands on the other side of microfunctionalism and, like marketing systemics, has close kinship with it. The microfunctionalist hesitates to set up system concepts unless he has empirical evidence that there is a set of components which interact in a persistent manner so as to form a system of action. A mere collection of components does not form a system. Thus he usually speaks in the plural of business enterprises as systems. He has some reservations as to whether the economy of a country can be referred to as the economic system, since often the subsystems which make it up are fully integrated. He will sometimes talk about the marketing system or the economic system in an advanced economy such as that of the United States, but he is troubled about the problem of relating these two system concepts to each other. The microfunctionalist asks, is the marketing system a subsystem of the economic system or does marketing reflect one set of systematic relations among firms while production and finance are a separate set of systematic relationships constituting the economic system?

Similar problems arise if we talk about the political system. There are political systems all the way up from a village administration to national governments and international agreements. A government, large or small, asserts its sovereignty over an area and performs the function of adjudicating disputes between individuals and groups within its domain. Yet there are organized groups within a society which resist this control as well as supra-governmental systems such as the church which try to induce their members to go beyond the law in recognizing duties and obligations. When someone speaks of the social system or the cultural system, anyone of pluralistic leanings becomes very troubled indeed. By what mechanism can individuals react within a social or cultural system which is distinct from their political and economic interactions, including face-to-face interaction in the market place? In what sense can a large and complex society be said to have objectives? By what means does a total culture containing many subcultures act to assure its survival as a culture?

Macrofunctionalists from Malinowski to Pfaff apparently have few qualms about such questions. Certainly there is something to be said for the strategy of starting from the top down and positing an integrated system for an entire society or culture. One might describe the ecological group as a population occupying a designated area. The population adapts itself through a series of systematic structures which facilitate the performance of functions. These can be regarded as parts of a total adaptive system even though some of them may be very loosely coupled so that effective interaction occurs only in the very long run. Strongly held behavior patterns reflecting fundamental values in the culture may require centuries for significant changes while changes in price and quantity may occur minute by minute in the market place.

To test the operations of such an integrated system model might require research on a grand scale. However, there is some evidence that at least a beginning can be made on some of the measurement problems involved. Given enough support from sponsors with vision, it is possible that faster progress could be made on large problems from the position of macrofunctionalism than from either a more limited functionalism or from marketing systemics. For the present it seems likely that the implications of the macrofunctionalist model will have to be worked out at the microfunctionalist level in order to generate testable propositions that sponsors will be willing to finance. While macrofunctionalism has the advantage of sweep and perspective, it may be handicapped from the viewpoint of ideology in appearing to favor monolithic social and political institutions. More pragmatic and pluralistic forms of functionalism may make faster progress on the American scene for the present.

5.   Institutionalism in Marketing and Economics

While most theoretical positions must take account of both function and structure, institutionalism is one of the views which places its primary emphasis on structure. The functionalist holds that structure must follow function but the primary interest of the institutionalist is to proceed from structure to structure. This view has strong roots in theories of biological evolution. The biologist and the paleontologist were long preoccupied with the mechanism of structural change and the succession of forms in any evolutionary line. The institutionalist in marketing has a similar interest in the changing forms of retailing and wholesaling and other marketing institutions.

Economics a few years ago witnessed the rise and fall of institutionalism as a major challenger to neo-classical theory. The influence of Marx and Veblen is still significant in some areas, but their influence on the central core of received theory has faded. The theoretical formulations of institutionalism have tended to lack quantitative precision and economists have shown a notable preference for elegance over relevance. Various types of institutionalism have carried more weight in labor economics, farm economics, anti-trust enforcement, and retailing. The issue has been further clouded by the fact that certain pseudo-institutionalists in economics have been among the leading functionalists.

Institutionalism might be an appropriate view for a scholar who was interested in marketing for the color and variety of ways in which people earn their living but with little concern for the daily problems of people actually engaged in marketing. A key problem in marketing is forecasting and especially the forecasting of structural change. If the market analyst could foresee the shape of the future, his company would have a great advantage in adapting its behavior within the new structural setting. An institutionalist approach might be justified in its own right to special problems of this type.

Any general use of institutionalist theory would almost inevitably rest on some type of dialectic such as Marx's analysis of the class struggle, Veblen's contrast between the instinct of workmanship as he attributed it to the engineers and the pecuniary motives of the business man, and the conflict between technological advance and ceremonialism as seen by Clarence Ayers. Hundreds of economists have worked within the limits of equilibrium theory and their contributions have been assimilated into the body of received theory. The leading institutionalists have each created a dynamic model of their own and have paid the price for their independence and originality. Functionalism stands in a better position to utilize the established techniques of equilibrium economics by employing it in the service of a functionalist vision of the way the system actually works and the ways in which system's functioning can be improved.

6.   Commodity Flow Theory

One possible position in marketing which has been present from the first may be called commodity flow theory. It was present in embryo in A. W. Shaw's dictum, marketing is movement, and was an organizing idea in the major projects undertaken by such early market researchers as Irving Paull and Sidney Anderson. Paull saw marketing as a flow sequence with pools or reservoirs along the way. Using this ordering idea, he and Anderson were able to cope with vast quantities of data in the Joint Agricultural Inquiry and draw some useful conclusions. This study formed part of the early background for the concept of the transvection that is discussed in Chapter 3.

A leading exponent of commodity flow theory today is Reavis Cox of the University of Pennsylvania. In his studies of the textile trade and in studies made with a group of associates for the Producers' Council, he has had an opportunity to test the organizing power of flow concepts. Trained as an economist and with a continuing interest in the efficiency of distribution, Cox doubtless views flow theory as a natural extension of economics in which received theory is largely taken for granted as the basic theoretical foundation for marketing. Also he has tended to have more interest in a general analytical interpretation of marketing which perhaps made him take less interest in functionalism as a perspective for problem solvers.

Commodity flow theory has two natural extensions in marketing. One is the comparative study of marketing in various countries. This study has already served its purpose in trying to understand the differences between the marketing of different classes of products in the United States. Commodity flow can also be applied to the study of communication in advertising and marketing generally. Halbert has discussed the analogy of information flows to commodity flows.

The informational revolution of the present era cries out for further progress in the theory of marketing communication. Leo Aspinwall, generally a fellow functionalist, implicitly recognizes the value of flow concepts in his parallel systems theory where he talks about the kinds of channels needed for the flow of goods and the flow of communication in different commodity classifications. Incidentally, a passing tribute to Aspinwall is in order as he derived his functionalism directly from his concern with practical problems rather than through borrowing from economics and the behavioral sciences.

The History of Marketing Thought

As marketing is a relatively new discipline, it has only a brief history, but one approach to the development of theory is to deal with the history of marketing thought. This several scholars have done. Marketing discussions do not go back to Aristotle, but one scholar has done so in searching for the roots of marketing theory. With a knowledge of how marketing is conducted today, it may be useful to reconstruct the methods that were probably used in primitive tribes and ancient times. Also, in looking at contemporary marketing some theoretical questions emerge which might repay careful study. For example, "How did the marketing concept emerge and what are its future consequences for marketing and business generally?"

Sufficient time has now elapsed to trace the spreading influence of some theoretical ideas in the marketing literature. Just to evaluate the evolving conceptions of marketing reality as they appear in successive generations of textbooks would be a useful service. This distillation of trends in theory or perspective might lead the student to undertake some extensions or refinements of theory on his own. This might begin on a purely deductive level, but the lapse of time in marketing would not be great until theoretical propositions would begin to be tested through research.

7.   The Methodological Commitments of Functionalism

The emergence of management science is likely to facilitate the development of a general theory of behavioral science. To manage means to control some system of action. The system models introduced by management science and operations research are more varied and flexible than those which have been identified with economics. Acceptance of the total systems approach is prescribed both by management science and by functionalist theory generally. Our concern to avoid sub-optimization confronts us with a more embracing problem. We must look at the whole system to learn about any of its parts. This would appear to be a counsel of despair telling us that we must know everything in order to learn anything.

Actually there are several legitimate approaches to piecemeal analysis within the systems framework. These include the following:

- Subsystems and their interactions

- The input-output approach

- Units of social action

- Comparative systems

- Analogous systems

Systems can be decomposed into subsystems. One escape from having to study everything at once is to decouple the operating groups which make up a system and study certain aspects of the interactions among subsystems or the processes which are going on within a subsystem. Methods of decomposition are developing as extensions of mathematical programming.

An operating system consumes inputs and produces outputs. The method formally known as input-output analysis traces the exchange among systems, each unit of production being an output of one system and an input for another. This method provides the groundwork for one class of dynamic models with the outputs of a contemporary system providing the inputs for a future system. There are other procedures in which one side or the other is held constant. Given a schedule of outputs, the analyst undertakes to determine how they can be produced at minimum cost. Or, given a schedule of available inputs, the analyst plots the feasibility boundaries for various combinations of outputs.

This book has suggested two units of action for a marketing system. One of these is the transaction, the focus of the negotiation which leads to exchange. A group engaged in bargaining is a small subsystem enduring over the period that the negotiation is in progress. The analyst can study the function and structure of these systems or he can draw generalizations showing contrasts and similarities over the range of a large number of transactions. In marketing cost analysis transactions are grouped to show the matching of classes of products with types of customers.

The transvection is a more embracing concept, representing a unit of action for the marketing system as a whole. Instead of matching buyers and sellers who are in immediate contact, it matches an original producer and an ultimate consumer through a series of sorts and transformations. The transvection concept can become a powerful planning tool in the task of making systems work better. It can illuminate the sorting problem which is central to marketing and guide the use of the various facilities through which transformations are performed.

The study of comparative systems is a field of growing promise. Comparing the way that marketing is carried out in the United States or in other countries, this study can point the way to improvement both here and abroad. The same opportunity holds for comparisons of marketing performance among firms in the same industry or from one industry to another. Studies can be made of the relative merits of private enterprise and public enterprise from the purely functional viewpoint of seeking the best channel for providing a particular product or service.

Finally, there is the study of analogous systems in which new vistas have been opened up through the possibilities of computer simulation. A system programmed for the computer can be made to behave in a way which is analogous to the behavior of a marketing system. The analyst can simulate different levels of operation, changes in competitive market structure, and alternative strategies projected over the year ahead. He can employ sensitivity analysis to determine which variables must be watched and which can be safely ignored.

Chapter 12

FUNCTIONALISM: DESCRIPTIVE AND NORMATIVE*

Wroe Alderson

This writer has characterized his theoretical position as functionalism and has accepted the implied commitment to the total systems approach. The functionalist in marketing engages in the study of systems with the aim of understanding how they work and how they can be made to work better. As a theorist he devises descriptive generalizations of marketing activities and institutions and finds a useful tool in the systems concept. He discovers a number of organized behavior systems in the world of marketing and finds that this recognition of systems of interacting forces aids him in explaining what is going on. He might note, for example, that systems have a tendency to persist over time, behaving as if they pursued a goal of survival.

This descriptive theory does not imply that systems are necessarily efficient in seeking any goal, including the goal of survival. The theory recognizes that systems cease to exist despite the efforts of participants to perpetuate them. The theory stresses environmental change and maladjustment which often occurs because of the lag in the adaptive processes of the system. In order to adapt, the control group in the system must be aware of the change which requires adjustment and must make the right choice among possible adaptations. The descriptive theory presents a picture of a number of systems occupying the same or an overlapping environment, all seeking goals including that of survival, but with varying degrees of adjustment to their opportunities and their problems. In each system there are decisions to be made about the level of aspiration and the technology employed. The decisions taken will vary with factors in the problem situation and with the characteristics of the decision makers.

The normative theory sketched herein deals with the question of how systems should operate to achieve their goals. This theory emphasizes the goal of survival as the means of relating the problem of adaptation in a given system to the larger systems of which it is part. It recognizes that freedom of choice exists at

*Originally published in *Dynamic Marketing Behavior* (1965), pages 318-321.

each level except for the economic sanctions of the market, the social sanctions imposed by a system on its subsystems or individual participants, ecological sanction inherent in the limitations of the ultimate environment. If a system fails because it violates some of these sanctions, than all of its subsystems must fail. The theory does not make the decision maker in a subsystem responsible for the success of the larger system since its management is not under his control. It does hold him responsible for avoiding actions which threaten the survival of the larger system since this obligation is a corollary of his role in perpetuating his own system.

Functionalism draws a sharper distinction between descriptive and normative theory than is customary among general economists. Some years ago a leading economist was asked whether he regarded his abstract model of the economy as descriptive or normative. More specifically, he was asked whether he regarded it as presenting an ideal of how the market economy should work or the best available description of how it actually works. He answered without the slightest reservation that the model was obviously both. He was not quite saying that the world we live in is the best of all possible worlds. He was asserting that economic activity is determined by market forces with only slight deviation from the pattern expressed in the model. The model should be taken as the norm and the aim of policy should be to eliminate these deviations from the norm. Under this view there is very little difference between descriptive theory and normative theory.

Functionalism opens a much wider gap between descriptive theory and normative theory, between things as they are and things as they should be according to criteria of rational conduct. There will always be room for improvement in marketing under the functionalist view of marketing theory. The policy maker at any level will be choosing among alternatives in the face of uncertainty generated by change and complexity. He may take account of ethical and esthetic considerations beyond anything which has been presented here. He may choose an action because it is right according to some social norm and not merely advantageous for his organization. His choice must be made with a set of limitations which rest on the fact that he must work through a system and act on behalf of a system. If he endeavors to promote his rational self-interest through a system, he is obliged to take account of the factors which affect the health of the system and its chances for survival.

The greater divergence between descriptive theory and normative theory asserted here with respect to functionalism is also observed in recent developments in dynamic economics. Samuelson and others have asserted that for any system with a goal of growth there is an optimal growth path over time. It does not follow that the control group in the system will discover this growth path or that it will be able to manage the system effectively in pursuing this path. Martin Shubik has given a formal treatment of games of survival among oligopolistic competitors. He shows that a wide range of choice is available to the players in such a game, and the formulation of normative rules for the players is by no means simple. He also stresses the factor of incomplete information in making the outcome indeterminate.

The proposed normative theory of marketing systems may be contrasted with Churchman's approach to a scientific ethics presented in a recent book. He formulates four imperatives which he feels show determinate decisions taken by the executive. The normative theory proposed here is probably most closely related to Churchman's discussion of the prudential imperative. The decision maker is advised to take this action or avoid that action in the pursuit of rational self-interest. The basic difference is the emphasis on sanctions rather than imperatives. Sanctions limit the scope of action rather then prescribing specific action. In this respect the normative theory is more in the spirit of J. M. Clark than of Churchman. Clark recognizes that the test of the market imposes constraints on competitors but that further constraints are necessary for the adequate functioning of a competitive system.

One reader, after seeing a draft of this chapter, said that it appeared to be an attempt to formulate ethical standards for marketing behavior. The author denies such an intention, but the denial rest on his own special conception of what constitutes an ethical choice. He holds that an ethical problem arises only at the point where the accepted rules no longer serve, and the decision maker is faced with the responsibility for weighing value and reaching a judgment in a situation which is not quite the same as any he has faced before. If there is a rule which tells the decision maker precisely what to do or a sanction which compels him to do it, he may be confronted with a moral or legal issue but not with an ethical problem.

Churchman as a scientist is inclined to believe that every decision would be completely determined if we knew enough to provide the decision maker with adequate rules. He readily admits that we are far from having such rules today. For the present Churchman is obliged to employ such sweeping principles as his ethical imperative which suggests that we should behave in the way that future generations would wish us to behave.

The view presented here is more libertarian, resting on a deep conviction of the reality of choice. This view relies on constraints imposed by the market, by organized society, and by the ecological structure of the environment. Within these constraints some area of free choice remains. One would hope that the responsible executive will use this freedom creatively. The executive is behaving ethically when he makes creative choices on behalf of the organization he directs and the culture to which he belongs.

The sanctions discussed in this version of normative theory are presumed to operate through rational self-interest. Hopefully the theory can support some normative judgments about marketing goals as well as marketing means without taking on the momentous task of creating a science of ethics.

Chapter 13

THE HETEROGENEOUS MARKET AND THE ORGANIZED BEHAVIOR SYSTEM*

Wroe Alderson

A theory of marketing explains how markets work. The ultimate purpose of theory is to find a way of making markets work better. Theory selects from the mass of marketing facts a set of events and activities which appear to hang together and to determine the outcome of the marketing process. A purely descriptive or historical treatment of marketing would not be marketing theory. Sheer curiosity about marketing institutions, past or present, doubtless has its own rewards. Reflection on one's own marketing experience or on the way that marketing was conducted in the past is a primary source of theoretical concepts. Theory emerges only when an attempt is made to predict the outcome of marketing activities. Marketing science advances by basing predictions on theory and then determining through observation or measurement whether the predicted events actually occurred. The ultimate application of marketing science is in the marketing plans designed to bring about improved marketing operations.

Marketing theory is not a new thing under the sun. Special theories of how advertising works or marketing channels work or consumer motivation works are presented every day in marketing classrooms throughout the country. Any attempt to explain a marketing phenomenon which will serve to explain other phenomena of the same class is a marketing theory. Marketing practitioners are equally addicted to theory. No advertising agency ever acquires a new account without predicting how advertising will work for its new client. The theoretical part of an agency's statement presents general arguments or a point of view on why advertising should work in cases of this kind. Some of these theories are not very good because the predictions turn out to be grossly unreliable, but they are theories nevertheless. One function of the marketing scholar is to generate more reliable theories and to find means for testing them.

Many scholars are content, at least for the present, to limit their efforts to specialized marketing theories dealing with a single phase of the subject —

Originally published in *Dynamic Marketing Behavior* (1965), pages 23-51.

often a very narrow phase. Only a few have been brash enough to propose a general theory of marketing. This book will be devoted to a further effort to present the elements of a general theory of marketing behavior. An earlier statement, published as *Marketing Behavior and Executive Action*, fell short of the ideal of a comprehensive and well-integrated theoretical structure. It now seems possible to remedy some of these defects, picking up loose ends which were left dangling and showing how they are connected in the total system.

The underlying viewpoint is the viewpoint of functionalism, which is likely to become the unifying thread in all the behavioral sciences. Functionalism has held a prominent place in sociology, psychology and anthropology. Several leading economists can be broadly classed as members of the functionalist school. Functionalism asks two characteristic questions about any set of phenomena which can be regarded as a system: "How does the system work?" and "How can it be made to work better?".

Functionalism implies a commitment to what is coming to be known as the total systems approach. To ask how marketing works is to ask how all its component parts and constituent activities work together to produce an end result. Fortunately it is possible to put the same question meaningfully about a subsystem such as a household or a firm. Any behavior system can be regarded as having an internal pattern of activities and external relations to the rest of the environment. However the behavior system is defined, the subject for study is the behavior of the system as a whole. This program of study is not quite as formidable as it sounds. The marketing theorist is interested in a set of problems called marketing problems. He pays primary attention to the marketing aspects of behavior and otherwise investigates the behavior of a system only as it may become involved in a marketing problem. The various divisions of the behavioral sciences are distinguished not so much by the phenomena they study as by the set of problems which are of special interest to each field.

1.   The Elements of Theory

In building a theory virtue is presumed to reside in using a very limited number of basic concepts. Obviously the larger this number becomes, the more difficult it is to explicate all their relationships and to produce a theoretical view that will really hang together. But if the theory is to have relevance as well as elegance, the choice of basic concepts is a fundamental and critical decision.

The logician calls his basic concepts the primitive terms of the theoretical language in which he will reason about his subject matter. Marketing theory has not yet reached the state of having a tight deductive apparatus in which theorems can be derived from axioms and then tested by empirical evidence. So far as the language of theory is concerned, however, it can now be asserted with confidence that all of its concepts can be defined in terms of three subject-matter primitives. These are sets, behavior and expectations.

The conceptual structure of marketing theory can be outlined in the form of three charts, each showing the successive derivation of other terms from the three primitive terms. A definition has been developed corresponding to each of the terms shown in these three charts. The immediate purpose is not the meticulous treatment of these definitions, which appear as an appendix to this chapter. The exposition of theory will follow a molar rather than an atomistic approach. That is to say, we will begin with some very broad and complex concepts which give the reader a more immediate grasp of the nature of the system we are building. There will be space given later on to delineate the foundations of these broad concepts. Meanwhile the charts will serve as a kind of a road map which may save the reader from getting lost as the discussion proceeds.

The two advanced concepts which project the essence of functionalist theory are the organized behavior system and the heterogeneous market. A complete definition of an organized behavior system draws on all of the primitive terms — namely, sets, behavior and expectations. A system is a set of interacting elements. A behavior system is a system in which the interactions take the form of human behavior. In an organized behavior system the organizing element is the expectations of the members that they as members of the system will achieve a surplus beyond what they could attain through individual and independent action. Among the elementary organized behavior systems are households and firms.

Organized behavior systems are the entities which operate in the marketing environment. The nature of that environment is suggested by the concept of the heterogeneous market. A perfectly heterogeneous market would be one in which there was a precise match between differentiated units of supply and differentiated segments of demand. It will be shown that there are some decisive advantages for marketing theorists to regard the market as heterogeneous.

At the same time it is recognized that partial homogeneities exist throughout the marketing system and that one of the functions of the system is to produce these partial homogeneities.

Having suggested that marketing consists of the activities of organized behavior systems, operating in heterogeneous markets, it is in order to be somewhat more specific about the nature of the marketing process. This process begins with conglomerate resources in the natural state and ends with meaningful assortments in the hands of consumers. The marketing process which brings about this change consists of an alternating sequence of sorts and transformations. Transformations relate to aspects of utility such as form, place and time, which are modified by the use of certain facilities. Sorting as seen by the

Figure 13.1. Definitions Derived from the Primitive Term—Sets

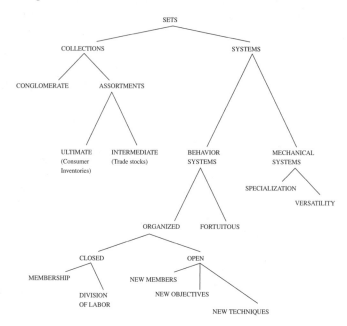

marketing operator is the assignment of goods, materials or components to the appropriate facilities.

It may appear to stretch the meaning of marketing to imply that it is concerned with changes in form utility. The choice of methods for changing the form is indeed within the realm of production technology. But the decision to change the form at all is explicitly or implicitly a marketing decision. The business of marketing is to place meaningful assortments in the hands of consumers and to accomplish this result the marketing executive makes a series of decisions concerning form, place and time utility with respect to the goods demanded by consumers.

We now have all the materials before us to make a very fundamental assertion about the nature of markets in an enterprise economy. Markets which are defined as heterogeneous can also be discrepant, since consumers may demand products which are not currently available and suppliers may undertake to sell products which are not currently demanded. Given markets which are both heterogeneous and discrepant, nothing is needed except adequate motive power to make them inherently dynamic. That motivation is provided by the expectations which lie at the heart of the organized behavior system. If a market is discrepant, the specific discrepancy can be removed by one of two forms of innovation. If the product is not currently available, it may be provided by

Figure 13.2. Definitions Derived from the Primitive Term—Behavior

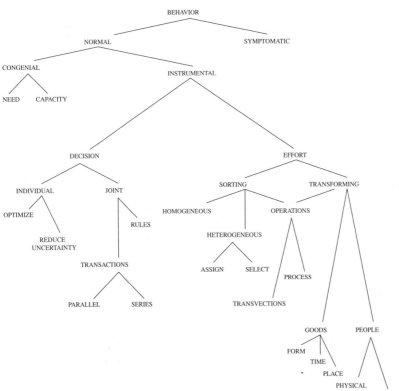

Figure 13.3. Definitions Derived from the Primitive Term—Expectations

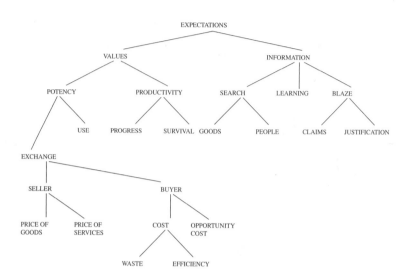

innovation in production. If the product is not currently demanded, demand may be made effective through innovation in marketing.

Markets which are defined as homogeneous are not inherently dynamic even if they are discrepant. In homogeneous markets the types of goods demanded are the same as the types of goods supplied. Hence, the market can be brought into balance by adjusting price and quantity and without innovation. Momentous theoretical consequences flow from the assumption that real markets are essentially heterogeneous and discrepant. Discrepancy can occur under either market expansion or market contraction. During expansion, discrepancy is likely to take the form of new products which the consumer has not yet learned to demand. During market contraction, as in an economic depression or wartime austerity, discrepancy takes the form of goods which are demanded but unavailable. Discrepancy is a radical form of market imperfection arising from demanded products without supply and available products without demand.

The title of this book, *Dynamic Marketing Behavior* is justified by the theory of marketing which has just been summarized. More broadly, marketing behavior is dynamic in three directions. First, there is the creation of product and marketing innovations. Secondly, there is a dynamic impact on the structure of the economy. Finally, the dynamic thrust of marketing in these directions brings about a profound transformation in marketing itself.

2.   The Perfectly Heterogeneous Market

It has been asserted that real markets are imperfect and advance occurs through efforts to remove the imperfections. This is another way of saying that markets are both heterogeneous and discrepant. A model of the market, abstracted from reality, might ignore these elements of diversity. The economist finds it useful for some purposes to use a model of a homogeneous market. This writer, for quite different purposes, presents a model of a perfectly heterogeneous market.

This model pictures an ideal situation which is abstracted from the real market. In the perfectly heterogeneous market each small segment of demand can be satisfied by just one unique segment of supply. The function of the market is to match these differentiated segments of demand with the corresponding segments of supply. The market is cleared when the matching is completed and each segment of demand has been satisfied. Markets in the real world are never wholly cleared. Some goods are left over which nobody wants. Some wants remain unsatisfied for lack of any corresponding goods. Some consumers accept goods which only partially satisfy their wants. This market imperfection results from a failure in market communication. It is the business of the marketing specialist to investigate these lapses and to institute remedial measures.

To digress at this point, marketing science is thoroughly pragmatic. The question, "How does the system work?" is closely linked to the question of "How can it be made to work better?" A failure in communication suggests that changes should be made in methods of communication if the added value is greater than the cost of change. It is within the realm of this science to predict that a system of communication will work better after change no less than to be able to predict the range of signal error before the change. The prediction of improved performance is based on the theory of how the system works. After the improvement is installed there may be a period of trial-and-error adjustment which corresponds to hypothesis testing in the usual scientific procedure. The final step is to measure the net gain from the improved performance.

To return to the heterogeneous market, it can be said to be cleared by information. The consumer must know that the appropriate segment of supply is precisely what he specified. Confusion of signals in the market place would result in mismatching. Marketing signals are often ambiguous. The woman who asks for a red dress may actually want crimson, scarlet, vermillion, maroon or some other of the innumerable shades of red. To specify a need does not mean providing a complete descriptive protocol of the product such as might be required to reproduce it. All that is required is for each consumer to designate the product he needs in such a way that it cannot be mistaken for any other. If there were less than a thousand products to be matched up in the heterogeneous market, a three-digit code would suffice to specify them unambiguously.

One purpose of the heterogeneous model is to take the measure of the information problem. One begins to see in terms of this model that a large but finite amount of information is required to clear the market. Just how much information is needed is a key question in marketing. An alternative form of this question is, "How much information will pay its way in contributing to the improvement of marketing processes?" One economist and perceptive student of marketing has neatly reversed the field by suggesting the need for a theory of optimal ignorance. In any case, information is not free. The cost of perfect information would be prohibitive. Since information has a cost, it is always pertinent to ask, "How much information is enough?"

The model of the perfectly homogeneous market is constructed for quite different purposes. In the homogeneous market it is assumed that the market is cleared by price. Perfect information in the market is taken for granted. Only price remains to be determined where thousands of suppliers are offering a homogeneous good to thousands of consumers who find a homogeneous good acceptable. Obviously the model of the perfectly homogeneous market has no counterpart in the real market. It is only a convenient fiction adopted by economists who want to think about the economic problem of price rather than the marketing specialist who wants to think about the marketing problem of information. While both the homogeneous model and the heterogeneous model are abstractions, the heterogeneous model impresses the marketing specialist as lying closer to the facts of the market place. It may be that the marketing specialist takes a microscopic view and hence is aware of differences which seem minor or irrelevant to the economist. It may also be true that the differences of viewpoints are appropriate to differences in the problems which each discipline sets out to study.

If the impression was given that price was not a marketing problem, this should be quickly corrected. Marketing is concerned with price, but it has a characteristic way of dealing with price phenomena. This is to reduce price to a datum and include it in the information that usually needs to be known about the product. Actually many purchases are made without inquiring about the price. When the consumer buys razor blades or cigarettes he is likely to assume that the price remains unchanged. If he is thinking about buying a new brand, he may ask about the new stainless steel blades or whether the new brand of cigarettes has a filter. He may return to his old brand if the new does not give him any added satisfaction and the comparative prices of the two brands may enter into that decision. In specifying a need for items such as wearing apparel, the consumer may have set a price limit rather than an exact price. There are other types of price information of interest to the regular consumer. Do prices fluctuate widely? Does the price include delivery or sales tax? Is there a quantity price? But there are often a number of variations in the qualities of the product offered which need to be compared with variations in the price.

The advocate of the homogeneous model might propose to reduce all information to price rather than reducing price to a datum of information. Taking the product as fixed and uniform, there is a cash price and a credit price, a carry-home price and a delivery price, a single-unit price and a quantity price. Since the product is taken to be standard and of known quality, the only missing datum is the variation in price according to the terms of sale. Actually there is no room in a truly homogeneous market for variations in the terms of sale. Consumers not only buy the same product but they buy it in the same way, leaving no place for imputing values to services whose costs cannot be precisely determined.

The solution of reducing information to price is obviously unsatisfactory for marketing. This approach could never provide an answer to the question of how much information is enough. In fact, it cannot answer the more fundamental question, "How much sorting is enough?" The answer to this question determines the activities which must be carried on in marketing channels. Reducing information to price cannot reveal the opportunities for substituting the flow of information for the flow of goods. It provides no handle for taking hold of the problem of partial homogeneities, an aid to marketing which will be discussed in the next section.

3.   The Sortability Scale

Heterogeneity and homogeneity are the extreme ends of a scale which ranges over many intermediate points. Any collection can be regarded as relatively heterogeneous or homogeneous. A question arises as to what the scale may be called. It is proposed that this scale be called the sortability scale. Only the simplest aspect of sorting is intended here, namely, the process which can be called sorting out. The process begins by establishing classes and then placing each item in the appropriate class.

Suppose a collection such as 1,000 packages of synthetic detergents are uniform so far as the naked eye can see. There is a single class of packages and in this sense they are not sortable. Sorting cannot occur unless there are two classes and at least two items. This fact is reflected in the ratio determining the sortability scale which is expressed as

$$\frac{(number\ of\ classes) - 1}{number\ of\ items - 1}.$$

In the example of the detergent packages the numerical solution would be

$$\frac{1 - 1}{1000 - 1} = \frac{0}{999} = 0.$$

Dividing zero by any number results in zero. Now suppose that there are a thousand items in a collection, but any two items can be clearly distinguished with the naked eye. The numerical solution would be

$$\frac{1000 - 1}{1000 - 1} = \frac{999}{999} = 1.$$

Thus, we have a scale running from 0 to 1. A sortability of zero would mean that the collection was perfectly homogeneous. A sortability of 1 would mean that the collection was perfectly heterogeneous. Degrees of sortability would be indicated by fractions lying between 0 and 1.

The sortability scale can be defined fairly precisely for the simple situation assumed. In other situations its accuracy would depend on the powers of discrimination of the sorter. In sorting colors one sorter might see two colors as different shades while a less discriminating eye would class the two colors together. Using unaided vision, a sorter might say that two objects were the same length while using a yardstick or a micrometer he would say that they were of different lengths.

Even more fundamentally, the outcome of sorting depends on purpose. A collection of potatoes might be judged to be homogeneous if they were all of good size and free of defects even though there were obvious differences in shape for the eye to distinguish. The potatoes are homogeneous in that each will be acceptable as a baked potato served to a guest. Collections can also be broken down into several classes according to purpose. On a recent trip to Japan I sent several packages home to Philadelphia. Some came by air mail and some came by sea mail. They were sorted into these two classes on the basis of weight and overall dimensions. While the objects they contained were quite different as to end-use, these two classes were homogeneous for the purpose at hand. Partial homogeneities are involved at various stages in the marketing process. Goods are classed together for temporary convenience in shipping, storage and display. Varying degrees of uniformity are called for at various stages in the production process. The market generates partial homogeneities along the way to facilitate the ultimate purpose of placing heterogeneous assortments in the hands of consumers.

There is no intention here of expressing a preference for either extreme or any point on the sortability scale. The heterogeneous model, however, is better adapted to the discussion of certain marketing problems. It is recognized that partial homogeneities are generated, particularly in mass production, which are beyond the powers of discrimination of the naked eye. Calipers and gauges of high precision and various physical and chemical tests are applied in quality control to sort out the defective pieces from the acceptable ones. From this high point of homogeneity the index of sortability rises as products move into the channels of distribution. Differences in branding, packaging, terms of sale, place and date of purchase, accessories and type of installation, and patterns of use once the item enters a consumer assortment largely dissipate the homogeneity which existed as the product came off the production line.

	Breaking Down	Building Up
Heterogeneous	Sorting Out	Assorting
Homogeneous	Allocating	Accumulation

4. Searching and Sorting in Heterogeneous Markets

The basic function in marketing is sorting. There are other functions in marketing such as transportation, storage, credit, display and promotion. But sorting is the decision aspect of marketing whether seen from the standpoint of the supplier or the consumer. The supplier assigns items to classes which are to be treated in different ways thereafter. The consumer selects an item into her assortment in relation to what the assortment already contains. While the marketing specialist is interested in all of the transformations which take place as goods move to market, including production transformations, his most vital concern is with the sorts intervening between successive transformations.

The term sorting may appear to cover so much territory as to be largely vacuous. Indeed, it resembles the general ideas of choosing or deciding in the stream of marketing activity. Sorting is not an empty term because it says something about the way choices are usually made in the market place. The assignment or selection which constitutes the act of sorting is always made with reference to some collection, or set, of goods. The farmer starts with a mixed lot of produce and sorts out the salable from the unsalable items. The central market assembles, or accumulates, goods of like grade and quality for convenience in distribution. The next step of distribution or dispersal to the ultimate market involves allocation of goods. Allocation may be based strictly on the flow of customer orders but sometimes it is modified or drastically altered by overriding considerations. Finally there is the characteristic action of the buyer of putting unlike things together to form an assortment. The name for this aspect of sorting is *assorting*.

The relations among these four aspects of sorting can be shown in a two-by-two table. The left-hand stub distinguishes between collections regarded as heterogeneous or homogeneous. The headings at the top indicate whether the sorting process is one of breaking down or building up.

The word sorting comes to mind most readily in sorting out, which means breaking down a heterogeneous collection into more homogeneous groups. Breaking down a homogeneous supply into smaller lots may be regarded as a special case. For some theoretical purposes sorting out and allocation can be combined under the term *assignment*. Turning to building up rather than breaking down, we are concerned with the collection which is the result rather than the one given initially. In the act of assorting, the sorter is building up a heterogeneous collection or assortment. In the act of accumulation the sorter is building up a homogeneous collection, or aggregated supply. Once again it is possible to combine assorting and accumulation under the term *selection* to cover sorting seen from the viewpoint of the buyer.

The use of the word allocation in this table suggests a way of relating the work of the general economist and the marketing specialist. The economist is concerned with the allocation of scarce resources for optimal results in producing goods and satisfactions. The economist deals with all of the resources of the economy or of a firm; investment capital, labor and operating expenditures for such inputs as raw materials. He prefers to deal with variables which can be regarded as homogeneous, at least in terms of their dollar values. He is less concerned with the schedule of outputs in the form of goods, particularly when he is dealing with such broad considerations as fiscal and monetary policy. The schedule of goods is affected by questions of taste and custom beyond his range of interest and competence as an economist.

The marketing specialist has no choice but to start with the detailed schedule of outputs since he tries not merely to understand demand but to influence it. As compared with the economist who is concerned with the allocation of scarce resources, the marketing specialist is concerned with all aspects of sorting as they determine the transformation of the raw products of nature into the final use goods found in consumer assortments. The same individual may be both an economist and a marketing specialist, but again different points of emphasis are appropriate in these two capacities.

In marketing, the aspect of sorting of greatest interest is assorting or the building of assortments. Assorting is the final step in taking products off the market. The other three aspects of sorting are not unimportant but their significance lies in what they can contribute to the final building of assortments. The marketing specialist must look at all the earlier sorts to make sure they were necessary for the end result. The accumulation of goods at central markets, for example, has been replaced in some instances by more adequate communication of information about goods. Until 1920 most steers went through the stockyards at Chicago mainly for the purpose of being graded. Since that time the livestock industry has learned that a steer does not have to be sent a thousand miles out of its way to have a price tag hung around its neck.

The terms searching and sorting appeared at the beginning of this section. It is readily possible to define searching as an aspect of sorting. Searching is a form of pre-sorting which can be carried out without the necessity of performing a physical sort. The function of searching is to locate items which belong in specified classifications. The pertinent consumer classes are those items which are broadly acceptable or unacceptable. Further sorts are performed in selecting the one item which can best be added to the consumer's assortment. This is largely a mental operation and does not usually involve moving the goods around. The consumer may set aside books, paintings, records, or suits he is considering buying and then make a final selection from this sub-collection. He is not free to move these items from store to store to make comparison more convenient. Possibly the abuse of the returned goods privilege has sometimes gone as far as making a sub-collection in one's home and then sending back the items not wanted.

The essential difference is that sorting involves a physical process which cannot be reversed without some loss. Searching is largely a mental process usually not involving physical movement of the goods. It generally means considerable movement on the part of the consumer or his agent in order to examine the various stocks of goods available. In one sense, search does not take place in real space but in an abstract-product space of many dimensions. The consumer may be looking for things which do not exist in the real world such as a combination of color, style and fabric which no dress manufacturer is producing. Sometimes the combination exists but not at the consumer's price level. Sometimes, as in gift shopping by a fastidious customer, the range of possibilities is wide but the list of items which meets standards in every particular is quite limited.

The vital distinction is that sorting is applied to a collection in existence at a single place, at least with respect to collections which are to be broken down into either heterogeneous or homogeneous parts. Searching is related to the building up of collections either into assortments or homogeneous supplies. In farm marketing a dealer, called a country buyer, travels about the country looking for livestock of a given grade. From the buyer's viewpoint, searching is an adjunct of assorting. It can be carried out by the consumer directly or as a vicarious search by the agent of the consumer.

Searching has been discussed from the viewpoint of the consumer searching for goods. It is equally important when seen from the viewpoint of the supplier who is searching for customers to buy his goods. The double search is fundamental to the whole process. The supplier develops more elaborate search methods than would be possible for the individual consumer. However, vicarious search on the part of large retailers looking for goods to satisfy their consumers can also be skillful and thorough. A more detailed discussion of the double search which precedes sorting will appear in Chapter 2.

5.   The Household as an Organized Behavior System

The one concept which is most fundamental for the whole theoretical structure is that of the organized behavior system. It provides the motive power which keeps the marketing process going. A basic type of organized behavior system is the household. A household even in the most primitive environment draws selectively on the resources of that environment. It chooses some stones as tools or weapons and discards others. It accumulates materials which can be used for shelter, clothing, or ornament, and classifies others as unusable.

The household persists over time because of its expectations concerning future behavior. These expectations must, on the whole, have a positive value for the individuals making up the household. Their expectations concerning the desired patterns of behavior are higher as members of the household than they would be otherwise. The behavior system offers a surplus to its participants which they would not expect to enjoy outside the system. These expectations of desired behavior patterns may not be fully realized. The theory only requires that these anticipations should persist, perhaps with occasional reinforcement, to show that conditions would be no better outside the system.

The household accumulates goods to sustain the expected patterns of behavior. At the lowest level of culture, as in the food-gathering Indian tribes of the western desert, food may be gathered and consumed at once. At this level of life the principal activity is almost a form of grazing. At higher levels nearly all goods are acquired for consumption at some future time. The time span may be relatively short, as in gathering supplies for a meal, or it may embrace a lifetime as in acquiring a house or permanent possessions. In advanced cultures most of the goods required are purchased in the market place. In many homes the only materials which experience further changes in form—for better or worse—are prepared as family meals. Home canning, sewing and baking are disappearing in our generation as spinning, weaving and soap making gradually disappeared from the rural economy of several generations ago.

The household today, or its primary purchasing agent, is engaged in creating or replenishing an assortment of goods to sustain expected patterns of future behavior. Items are added to the assortment because they increase the potency of the assortment. Potency may be described as the quality of the assortment which protects the household against unpleasant surprises. The unhappy event of being out of clean shirts or razor blades, failure to find a midnight snack in the refrigerator, or the unreliable performance of the refrigerator itself is likely to leave a marked effect on the housewife's inventory policy. Buying goods in generous quantities is not enough unless they are the right goods, consistent with the probable needs of the household.

The household purchasing agent is guided by two principles in making buying decisions. One is the conditional value of the good if used, and the other is the probability of use or the estimated frequency of use. Conditional value can vary greatly by products. A fire extinguisher might have very high value if there was occasion to use it on a house or on a boat. The failure to buy a package of cigarettes before going hunting might detract only moderately from the satisfactions of the trip. The story is quite different with respect to the incidence of use. The use of the fire extinguisher might occur once in a lifetime, if at all. The inveterate smoker knows that he will feel the urge to light a cigarette several times an hour. Taking both factors into account, the expected value of a good can be measured by the product of its conditional value and the probability of use. The fire extinguisher would have a very high value if heavy property damage or even loss of life were threatened without it, but the probability of needing it during the period it is owned is some very small fraction such as one over ten thousand. The package of cigarettes has a small value with respect to any given occasion of use, but the probability of use in any twenty-four hour period approaches one.

6.   The Firm as a Behavior System

Next to the household, the firm is the most significant organized behavior system in marketing. In the Middle Ages the firm was scarcely more than a household producing a surplus of some class of goods. The master craftsman and his apprentices constituted an extended household living under the same roof and sharing the same skills. The incentive to produce was the same as for the primitive household — to provide for the patterns of behavior expected in the future. The process was slightly more roundabout, the surplus being marketed and the proceeds used to acquire the products of other extended households.

The long process of removing production from the ordinary household was just beginning. Household industries grew into factory industries, involving further specialization and the application of mechanical power. The removal or production from the household is now largely complete in the United States. The economic function of the housewife is no longer to make things but to serve as the household purchasing agent in buying them. Farm families have been last to lose their generalized productive skills, but farm households now represent only 6.8 percent of total households. The vast majority of urban families live entirely within the money economy except for some backyard tomato vines and do-it-yourself Christmas presents. The economic process has become still more roundabout with the majority of adults selling their labor and using their labor income to purchase everything they require.

This tremendous transformation taking place in the way of life of the Middle Ages was a product of the heterogeneous market. As skills became specialized, exchange of goods gradually became more prevalent because the generalist could not compete with the specialist. These early markets were not national markets with thousands of suppliers selling homogeneous products. They were local or even neighborhood affairs in which a few extended households were trading with each other, thus transforming a household surplus into a social surplus and a household economy into a larger system of specialized production and exchange.

The basic dynamics of the transformation is self-evident. Part of the surplus produced in the effort to exploit the environment was additional skill. Generations of specialized effort brought an increase in technical knowledge which, in the long run, was more important than any immediate increase in outputs.

The markets were there because skills proliferated in various directions at once Heterogeneity provided the immediate basis for exchange. There was no possible route for passing directly to anything resembling the homogeneous market of pure and perfect competition. The underlying principle of market dynamics is that the existence of a market encourages the growth of a technology which gradually causes all products to flow through the market. For centuries the pace of change seemed slow and there have been setbacks even in modern times, but the outcome seems to have been inevitable from the first.

7.   Distributive Firms as Behavior Systems

An important aspect of technological advance is the advance in marketing technology. Learning how to market sometimes seems like the bottleneck restricting the potentials for mass production. As a matter of historic fact, the commercial revolution which had been under way for centuries preceded the industrial revolution of the 18th century. The merchant adventurer who gained or lost a fortune on a single cargo provided the pattern of great enterprise as the first exponent of vicarious search. They searched the world for goods which they knew were demanded at home. Gradually they evolved into wholesale merchants providing a regular service of supply to retailers and often financing the manufacturers who were smaller in scale. The wholesaler became the sorter par excellence. As his speculative background receded into the past, he discovered that his true role was to perform an intermediate sort between the manufacturer and the retailer.

The contours of the conventional marketing channel begin to appear. In the final stage it is the consumer who serves as a sink for the marketable goods he acquires in replenishing or extending his assortment. He is still motivated by the expectation of greater satisfactions inside the household than outside. The tangible manifestation of progress is the collection of goods and savings he acquires as time goes on. The requirements of the household for maintenance and for continued expansion provide the motive power for keeping the whole system running.

Just back of the consumer stands the retailer who maintains an assortment from which consumers make choices. While he maintains this assortment in the hope of profit rather than for his personal use, his calculations are similar to those of the consumer. He carries some items with a large conditional value to him in terms of gross profit. He carries other items with a smaller conditional value but a greater expectation of frequency of sale or turnover. He tries to avoid the extremes of large potential profit with little expectation of sale and rapid turnover with a negligible margin for profit. His expectations for future success are some combination of a hope for immediate profits and for long-range growth. If he survives at all, he will almost certainly grow as the experience ables for retailers indicate. In the present period his primary function appears to be display. Ordering by telephone is passé even for groceries. With five thousand items in a supermarket, the easiest way to be reminded of what to order is to use the supermarket itself as if it were a life-sized illustrated catalog.

The modern wholesaler exists as an exemplar of efficient distribution. He must compete with both his customers and his suppliers who never quite give up the idea of setting up a warehouse of their own. He enjoys some differential advantage with respect to other wholesalers in terms of his location. His real problem is the threat of potential competition from either end of the channel. He is there because they cannot perform the wholesale function as cheaply as he can. Nevertheless the wholesaler has lost ground in major areas and for a variety of reasons. The consolidation of retail organizations has cut in on his function in groceries. The preference of the pharmaceutical companies for selling prescription drugs directly to the retailer threatens his position in drugs.

Squeezed between large retailers and manufacturers with national advertising campaigns, the promotional function has almost disappeared in many wholesale lines. Suppliers continue to look for a shorter route to market and novel arrangements are emerging. The basic struggle will continue to lie between the superior economy in physical handling, where the wholesaler still has an edge, and the manufacturers felt need for closer and more direct relations with retailers and consumers in the areas of information and persuasion.

8. The Marketing Behavior of the Manufacturer

The manufacturer has emerged in a dominant role in marketing, and one of our primary concerns shall be to understand that role. One of its major aspects is the continual concern with new products. Manufacturers, both large and small, are under unremitting pressure to come up with something new. Newness means diversity and a steady thrust toward the heterogeneous end of the sortability scale. Every large company stakes its destiny on the new products coming out of its research and development laboratory. The time has come when creative destruction, as envisioned by Schumpeter, has full sway. We tear down in order to build up, and second best is swept away in the roaring tide of change.

The thrust toward heterogeneity strikes the dominant note in corporate policy. Companies which have had nothing new for years feel that they are standing uncertainly on the brink of insolvency even though they may still be earning modest profits. Companies of somewhat larger size relapse into also-rans when they fail to achieve a breakthrough. Companies merge themselves into conglomerate firms, hoping that somewhere around their horizon the lightning of innovation will strike. Almost universally growth is embraced as a goal, but profits and survival itself depend on the direction of growth. The differential

advantage derived from an innovation is rapidly neutralized and further innova
tions are required to stay in front. The road of progress is bumpy and the pace
is accelerating. The manufacturer leads the pack but glimpses the road ahead
but dimly.

The transfer of productive activities from the household to the factory ha
largely been completed. It is this transfer and the consequent advance in technol
ogy which has accelerated the pace of change. The manufacturing corporation
is a special type of behavior system which accounts for the unusual character o
our marketing economy. It is similar in basic structure to other organized behav
ior systems. Individuals seek membership in the corporation in the expectation
of greater rewards than they can find outside. Because of these expectations the
corporation acts as if it had a will to survive and, indeed, its members usually
take its immortality for granted.

The household by contrast is limited in size, growing only by natural increase
or by legal adoption of new members in the extended household of an earlie
time. The corporation can grow without limit, constantly restructuring itsel
to accommodate greater numbers and more specialized participants. The cor
poration selects ambitious individuals because of its inherent need for growth
and individuals of this type are likely to demand an even faster rate of growth
than their fellows. Most demanding of all is the chief executive who is held
responsible for profits as well as growth.

There seems to be little doubt that the center of aspirations has been trans
ferred in considerable measure from the household to the corporation. Wha
people ask of life is strongly influenced by the corporate setting. They are
taught to demand more of themselves and to expect more in return. Executive
and their wives are increasingly college bred and have enjoyed some extra year
for maturing their tastes and preferences. With productive activities removed
from the home, the woman's role as household purchasing agent is paramount
Confronted with all of the innovations the corporation can evolve, she under
takes to shape a style of living which is consistent with the scale of living he
husband can provide.

9.   Is the Marketing Channel a Behavior System?

Some difficulties arise in attempting to extend the concept of the organized
behavior system beyond the limits of the firm or the household as legal and
social entities. In particular, a question arises as to whether marketing channels
composed of firms, or perhaps of firms and households, can be regarded a
organized behavior systems. Interaction with the system is strong and wel
integrated in some channels and rather weak in others. The interaction between
an automobile manufacturing company and its dealers is constant. In some
respects, owners and prospective owners of the company's cars are part of the

system too. At the other extreme is the cotton textile industry in which the hazards have been so great that the industry has tended to follow the rule of every man for himself. One may wonder whether the appliance manufacturer or the car manufacturer can be regarded as part of an organized behavior system providing a channel for steel. The trademark policy and advertising of U.S. Steel appears to have proceeded on that assumption.

Some have made the touchstone the question of whether there was an effective channel captain present in the channel. A channel captain formulates the plans and programs that others in the channel generally accept and are guided by. There is no doubt that the car manufacturer is a channel captain in this sense, but the car manufacturer has his own exclusive dealers. The tire manufacturer is less successful in acting as a channel captain even though he has lavished millions of dollars in an effort to make his dealers strong. The prevalence of split accounts among dealers is one explanation, but lack of innovation in the product is another. In the textile industry the recent emergence of name brands of dresses with a positive style stance have brought some strength to the channel concept. In synthetic fabrics the manufacturer of the fiber has been a powerful influence for channel integration.

In operating terms a channel is tied together by orders and payments flowing in from the consumer and on back through the system. In the outward direction it is tied together by advertising, promotional plans and shipments. In some lines of trade, however, the orders for any one product line are a very small part of the total and the sense of working together toward a common end is weak. The retailer or wholesaler carries thousands of items and must stock many which are marginal, thus leaving him indifferent to any proposed promotional plans of the manufacturer. The large retailer, on the other hand, often serves as the channel captain and calls the signals for the channel participants farther upstream.

The test proposed here is that of a common stake in survival. This is obviously a strong motivation in the channel for automobiles. The manufacturer knows that his fate rests with his dealer organization. The dealer knows that he has a valuable franchise and that he will prosper as the manufacturer prospers. At the minimum, there is a reliance on customary sources of supply and on repeat purchases from regular customers. The real question is whether either side would assume any substantial costs or risks to ensure the survival of the other side. The answer would certainly be different from one line of trade to another. It is not sufficient that each side should count on the continued survival of the other in making its plans. The definition of the organized behavior system implicitly requires that strong action should be taken on behalf of the channel participant who is threatened. Sometimes action occurs almost by default as when a supplier becomes more and more deeply involved in extending credit

to his customer. The supplier is, in fact, assuming substantial risks and adde
costs on the customer's account.

There are situations in which rational self-interest would not prompt man
agement at one level to go very far toward ensuring the survival of firms a
another level. The channels may be very diffused so that little can be done t
strengthen them at a particular point. The customary channels may be graduall
breaking down and being replaced by a more direct route to market. In fact
there may be conflict in the channel with management eager to promote th
new channels while still using the old. These situations do not meet the tes
of a common stake in survival. The marketing channel exists but it would b
stretching the point to call it an organized behavior system with a tendency t
persist over a long period of time. At best it is a pseudo-system in which ther
is a fair amount of cooperation over a short interval but with no commitment
over the longer run.

If the common stake in survival is the touchstone, one wonders whethe
consumers should ever be included in the marketing channel as a behavio
system. In modern times the tie between the retailer and his customers is rathe
diffuse and depersonalized. A chain supermarket or a large department stor
could close its doors in most communities with no serious derangement of th
buying habits of consumers. They might mourn its passing briefly as a loca
institution but not be moved to action by word that the store was in trouble
The consumer cooperative might inspire this form of loyalty, but the appeal o
the cooperative movement is obviously not very strong in the United States
Consumers as against trade and industry may be forever on opposite sides o
the fence. The tie that binds business men together at successive levels is th
hope of profit. This is doubtless a good thing if the freedom of consumer choic
is to be preserved. It is probably healthier for choice to be preserved than fo
the consumer to eat what he regards as inferior fruits and vegetables sold unde
the co-op label out of loyalty to his consumer cooperative.

The arms length relationship between the consumer and suppliers has othe
advantages. It is important for consumers to insist on what they want withou
being sentimental or being overawed by a haughty clerk. It is well for th
supplier to adopt the position that he is helping the consumer to solve he
problems, but they need to be genuine solutions. The consumer can use advic
and counsel but in the last analysis the responsibility of choice is her own. Sh
must bear the leading part in deciding what is good for her.

The situation is rather different for the firm in which one or more members o
the household are employed. If employment is the sole source of their income
they may well feel that their own destiny and that of the firm are intimatel
bound together. It would not be unusual for individuals to loan money to th
firm or to go without salary for a time in the effort to save it. What they might b
willing to do in such a case depends, of course, on their status in the company

This comment is a digression for purposes of comparison, but the conclusion with respect to marketing channels is that the consumer may be included in the channel at the operating level but that he is not included in the channel as an organized behavior system.

10.   Other Systems

Other systems which are candidates for the designation of organized behavior systems are the retail center and the total marketing economy. The comments which have been made about the consumers as channel members would apply to the link between a consumer and a retail center. She may be accustomed to trade at Wibbleton but there is no recourse if she suddenly decides to shift to Wobbleton. However, the merchants of Wibbleton may be acting in concert in such areas as promotion and may be very much aware that Wibbleton must succeed if they are to succeed individually. It would be a question of fact whether this sense of a common stake in survival existed in a given case, but where it did, the trading center would qualify as an organized behavior system.

Finally, the question may be raised as to whether the whole marketing economy can be described as an organized behavior system. To qualify, the marketing economy should have certain operating characteristics with information circuits coordinating all parts of the system. It should also have a tendency to persist over time because the will of the majority is to have it persist. With respect to the first point, the market seems to be adequately interlinked, although this does not always appear on the surface where the thrust toward heterogeneity is a dominant trend. The market is segmented but the segments overlap. Thus, a national brand of wheat flour links two or more regional brands in the network of competition. They are in effective competition with the national brand.

The marketing economy has a tendency to persist over time partly because at this level of consideration we are not generally aware of alternatives. Active support of the system may be aroused when it is under attack. It might be described as a latent system for which support becomes manifest in times of stress. Some students have commented that the marketing economy may be gradually turning into something quite different, although the changes are not dramatic enough to make us spring to its support.

11.   Program

The elements have now been assembled for the development of marketing theory in what is to follow. The primitive terms of the theoretical language are sets, behavior and expectations. By building on these primitive terms to define other terms, we arrive at such complex concepts as the organized behavior system, the heterogeneous market and the sorting function. Various types of behavior systems have been discussed and the changing relations among them pointed out. Ultimately the whole scheme goes back to the organized behavior system. It is asserted that the environment in which the system operates can be characterized as a heterogeneous market. Searching and sorting are the fundamental procedures by which the system adapts itself to the market.

Considerations of cost and value control the application of searching and sorting to the problems of marketing. Searching which pertains to the movement of information leads to the question of how much information is enough. Sorting, which is more concerned with the movement of goods, raises questions about the usefulness of partial homogeneities and the interchangability of the movement of goods and the movement of information.

Several dynamic principles have been mentioned and attempts will be made later to knit them more closely together. Real markets are heterogeneous and discrepant and hence dynamic. The market is credited with opening the way for technological change, but technological advance is regarded as part of the surplus generated as the system adapts itself to its environment. Marketing effort changes the values in the cultures as well as the techniques employed in serving these values. Finally, in transforming society, the marketing system transforms itself.

12.   APPENDIX: Definitions

Sets

1 Sets are aggregates containing some class of components such as points in a plane, physical objects or human beings.

2 Collections are sets which can be taken as inert with no interaction among the components.

3 Systems are sets in which interactions occur that serve to define the boundaries of the set.

4 Conglomerates are collections as they occur in a state of nature and which may be regarded as random or neutral from the standpoint of human expectations.

5 Assortments are collections which have been assembled by taking account of human expectations concerning future action.

6 Ultimate assortments (consumer inventories) have been collected by the consumer in the hope and expectation of being prepared to meet future contingencies (probably patterns of behavior).

7 Intermediate assortments (trade stocks) have been collected to provide a choice of alternatives for (a) the consumer, (b) others in the trade.

8 A behavior system is a system in which persons are the interacting components. Broadly defined, a behavior system includes the assortment of assets which the members control and its point of contact with the environment which enable it to accept inputs and generate outputs.

9 An organized behavior system is one with these minimum characteristics:

    (a) A criterion for membership,

    (b) A rule or set of rules assigning duties,

    (c) A preference scale for outputs.

10 A fortuitous behavior system is one in which interactions are taking place, resulting in outputs with some positive or negative value, but without the degree of coordination suggested by the requirements for an organized behavior system.

11 An organized behavior system is closed in terms of current operations (all finite sets are closed).

12 An organized behavior system is open in terms of plans for future operation. (Plans involve the possibility of new goals, new techniques, new inputs, new members).

13 Rules of membership state rules of eligibility or exclude from membership specified classes in the general population.

14 Division of labor as specified by formal rules or a process is specified for choosing a leader who will assign duties to other members.

15 A behavior system is open if it is considering new objectives which generally offer many variations as to the direction in which the system is to move and the amount of effort to be expended.

16 A behavior system is open if it is currently engaged in revising its techniques or if it is generating techniques which are almost certain to require changes.

17 A behavior system may be regarded as open if it is seeking new members. This is particularly true of members higher up in the scale of responsibility who are likely to have an impact both on goals and techniques.

18 Mechanical systems are listed for the sake of completeness and contrast with behavior systems. Interactions occur among non-human components.

19 Some mechanical systems have highly specialized outputs and are structured with a view to maximum efficiency in producing these outputs.

20 Other mechanical systems have greater versatility with respect to potential outputs and are structured with a view to maintaining flexibility in meeting the demands of the market.

Behavior

21 Behavior is activity occupying time.

22 Normal behavior is that which is an end in itself or a means to an end.

23 Symptomatic behavior is that which is not functional in that it is neither an end or a means to an end.

24 Congenial — also called consummatory — behavior is that which is chosen because it is presumed to be an end in itself and is directly satisfying.

25 Instrumental behavior is that which is regarded as a means to an end. There may be a sequence of instrumental acts culminating in a desired state of affairs, one of which is the opportunity to engage in congenial behavior.

26 Some congenial behavior is satisfying because it reduces need — tension.

27 The same behavior can be both. It is directed toward gaining an end but also satisfying a basic need directly — that of manifesting skills or capacity.

28 Instrumental behavior consists of decision and the application of effort. It is convenient to think of decision as occurring instantaneously.

29 Effort occupies an interval of time.

30 Decision is choice among alternative ways of applying effort.

31 Individual decision involves allocation by an individual of the resources he controls.

32 An individual decision under certainty undertakes to optimize certain values.

33 An individual decision under uncertainty can be interpreted in terms of expected values.

34 Joint decision involves agreement between two or more individuals.

35 A decision can apply to a single event such as a transaction.

36 Transactions can be parallel, involving problems of coordination.

37 Transactions can be in series involving problems of optimal sequence.

38 A decision can mean the adoption of a rule governing many transactions.

39 Effort in marketing takes two primary forms — either sorting or transformation.

40 Sorting is reclassification and involves the creaction of subsets from a set or a set from subsets.

41 Homogeneity lies at the zero end of the sortability scale. That is to say, no further division into classes is possible at the level of discrimination applied.

42 Heterogeneity lies at the other end of the sortability scale. That is to say, the classes discriminated are as numerous as the units of the set.

43 The seller assigns products from heterogeneous sets to subsets. The assignment from homogeneous sets is taken as a special case.

44 The buyer selects products into heterogeneous sets or assortments. The selection into homogeneous sets is taken as a special case.

45 Transformation in marketing applies to goods or people.

46 Transforming changes the physical form of goods or their location in time and space.

47 Transforming changes the awareness or attitudes of people (their informational and motivational states) or their physical location.

48 Marketing operations can be defined as an alternating sequence of sorts and transformations.

49 A transvection is a unit of action of the marketing system resulting in placing a final product in the hands of the consumer but reaching all the way back to the raw materials entering into the product.

50 The marketing process is the marketing operation regarded as a total and continuous flow of marketing activities rather than the sum of all transvections.

Expectations

51 Expectations are attached to what the individual thinks may happen and the favorable or unfavorable results of these future events.

52 Values are based on the favorable or unfavorable consequences of an event or condition which the individual expects.

53 Information is expected in the three directions of probability — to an event occurring, instructions on reaction to the event, and whether the consequences will or will not be favorable.

54 Search is the sorting of information which precedes the sorting of goods or people.

55 Learning in marketing is the acquisition of information with particular reference to this impact on future searching and sorting.

56 Blaze is the obverse of search. It is the imparting of information by one party intended to influence search by the other party.

57 The consumer searches for goods and trade intermediaries engage in vicarious search on his behalf.

58 The seller searches for people who will buy goods or intermediaries who will sell them to consumers.

59 One aspect of blaze is the information incorporated in claims.

60 The second aspect of blaze is the justification for accepting these claims.

61 Potency is the expected value of an assortment or its anticipated effectiveness in meeting contingencies.

62 Exchange value is the anticipated potency relative to what is given in exchange.

63 Use value is the realized potency expressed as the product of the incidence of use and the conditional value if used, that value depending on the intensity of satisfaction with the product when used.

64 The seller of goods is generally giving them up for a more liquid or intangible asset.

65 The buyer of goods is generally accepting them in exchange for a more liquid or intangible asset.

66 The price of a good is measured by the asset the buyer gives up in exchange.

67 The price of a service such as that of a retailer is the difference between his purchase price and his selling price (gross profit).

68 The cost of a good to one person is the price he paid for it to another person.

69 Opportunity cost is measured by the alternative which was rejected in order to buy or sell the particular good.

70 Productivity is the capacity of a system to generate outputs.

71 Progress is the capacity to generate new techniques.

72 Survival is the capacity to retain potency over time.

Chapter 14

INFORMATION FLOWS IN HETEROGENEOUS MARKETS*

Wroe Alderson

The importance of information in heterogeneous markets was underscored in Chapter 1. This chapter will be devoted to a more detailed analytical treatment of information flows in heterogeneous markets. It has been asserted that demand and supply are matched, segment by segment, in the perfectly heterogeneous market. The detailed process of matching will now be considered in order to answer such questions as, "How much information is enough?"

The heterogeneous market is cleared by information. Either consumers must find the goods they want or suppliers must find the consumers who will accept the goods offered. The clearing of the market must involve some degree of initiative on both sides. To clarify further what is meant by clearing the market, three examples will be used in which matching would appear to be a paramount consideration. The examples are the matching of couples in marriage, the matching of homes and occupants, and the matching of jobs and workers. In each case our model of the market visualizes a Utopian society with one spouse per adult, one house per family and one place per worker. The examples were chosen because of the obviously predominant heterogeneity of the items to be matched and the general presumption favoring one-to-one matching in all three cases.

Suppose that in an isolated community there are precisely ten men and ten women who come to marriageable age at the same time. They all have unique characteristics which will qualify each person to enjoy connubial bliss with exactly one person of the opposite sex. In fact, this is a small scale model of the perfectly heterogeneous market. The market will be cleared when the matching is completed. Information is the means of clearing the market just as in the case of products and services. Let us suppose that by coincidence the appropriate mating is in alphabetical order but the couple do not know this in advance. Let us further suppose that the women represent the demand side and are actively

---

*Originally published in *Dynamic Marketing Behavior* (1965) pages 52-64.

Figure 14.1.

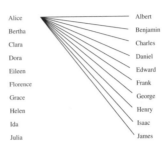

looking for husbands. They are confronted with a supply of potential husbands which is exactly the same number as the number of husband seekers. This is only a hypothetical situation and does not necessarily mean that we would be so unchivalrous as to make this assumption in real life.

Alice is first to do her shopping and after looking over all the men, settles for Albert. The chart (Figure 14.1) shows parallel columns for the two sexes and indicates by a series of lines the choice situation as it was presented to Alice. This, of course, takes Albert out of the market. Bertha is next in line but there are only nine men left for her to consider. She surveys her prospects and settles for Benjamin. From then on Clara has eight possibilities, Dora seven, Eileen six, and so on down to Julia. Julia has just one, but it turns out that only James possesses all of the traits she most admires. The couples are aware initially that this is a heterogeneous market so that each girl is content to wait her turn.

If they were not sure, each might want to shop for all of the men and the competition would doubtless become a little chaotic. At most, this would mean that each woman had ten possibilities to look over so that the total number of communications would be 10^2 or 100. for the more systematic procedure which has been imagined this number would be substantially reduced. In fact, it would be the triangular number obtained by summing 1 through 10. The formula for triangular numbers is

$$T = \frac{N(N+1)}{2}$$

In this case the total number of communications would equal 55.

Introducing a further assumption, it may be that there is some factor which divides the group sharply into two parts. Let us say that the girls from Alice through Eileen each wants to marry a farmer while the other five would not have a farmer. By convenient coincidence, the first five men in the list are farmers and the other five are not. The shopping rule stated previously is followed by the girls in each market segment separately. Breaking T down into the two market segments, t_1 and t_2 and using small n to represent the number in each segment, the formula would be as follows:

$$t_1 + t_2 = \frac{2n(n+1)}{2} = n(n+1)$$

In this case the total number of communications would be 30.

Finally, let us suppose that there is some one distinguishing feature which enables the girls to know at first sight who their appropriate mate is. Perhaps each wants to marry a man of the same nationality and there is exactly the right mix on each side of the market. In that case just 10 communications would suffice rather than 100, or 55, or 30. The purpose here is to show that a heterogeneous market can be cleared with a finite number of communications and that the possibility of economizing the use of information is always present.

The matching of homes and families is supported by our feeling that every family should have a home. Heterogeneity is obvious on both sides of the market. While there are real estate developments in which many homes are identical in floor plan and appearance, most consumers still resist this trend and insist that a home should be individual and unique. It is even more self-evident that families are different in the rent they can afford to pay, in size, age, religious and ethnic background and quirks of taste which affect the kind of home they would like to rent or buy.

Once more we visualize a community in which there are ten homes and ten families to be accommodated. The homes range a wide spectrum of size and rental value. It is quite likely that in this type of market the best fit would depend on a limited number of factors such as size of family and rental values. The maximum amount of information required was defined in connection with the previous example. In matching families and homes in such a small community it might easily happen that only two homes were within the price range of each family. Thus, at most there would be only 20 decisions to be made in getting everyone under cover. Actually only 15 decisions would be needed in a market with this structure. Families A and B are the available customers for homes 1 and 2. If A examines both and chooses 1, then the only choice left for B is 2. This means that three decisions would be made by each of five pairs.

The matching of couples in marriage might occur in a completely unstructured market. The matching of families and homes has at the very least the structured factor of location. People prefer locations which are more accessible or more remote, nearer to a school or nearer to a church or nearer to preferred neighbors. A serious complication as to the imperfection of the market is the existence of one-way attractions. That is to say, B would feel that his status was enhanced by living next door to A but A feels that his status would be undermined if B moved in next door. A Philadelphia realtor developed a hilltop with rather expensive homes. He found that homes sold quickly on the western slope but moved very slowly on the eastern slope. He had forgotten that an invisible line ran along the crest of the hill — namely, the boundary between two school districts, one with high prestige and the other with low prestige. He learned that the additional homes to be built on the eastern slope should be smaller and sold to families without children in school.

To clear the home market requires a large amount of information since the market is heterogeneous in a number of dimensions. The real home market is almost certainly discrepant since demand and supply could scarcely ever be in balance in terms of matching. Nevertheless the structure of the market would generally lead to workable solutions. Choices are interdependent in a market which is both heterogeneous and structured and the incompatibility of choices sometimes reduces the need for information.

A still more extreme case of a structured market is the employment market. Gunnar Myrdal, the Swedish economist, discusses the threat of structural unemployment in his *Challenge to Affluence*. Nevertheless it is useful to look at the perfectly heterogeneous model of this market since the need to match small segments of supply and demand is obviously its overriding feature. Let us take a small community in which there is only one small firm which needs ten employees and there are precisely ten people in the labor market. The firm requires the following staff:

1 President and general manager
1 Treasurer and controller
1 Production manager
1 Fabricator
1 Finisher
1 Handy man for maintenance, packaging and shipping
1 Sales manager
1 Sales manager for territory A
1 Sales manager for territory B
1 Sales manager for territory C

In the perfectly heterogeneous market the workers available precisely fit these requirements, but there is an information cost in accomplishing the process of matching. The president probably owns the company so that one place is already filled. The treasurer and controller may be his younger brother whose place is also secure. The other eight men do not choose their jobs since they are on the supply side of this market. Instead, they are selected into their positions by the officers of the company. If the officers act jointly there are only eight decisions to be made.

Filling out the organization structure in a firm is similar to what the consumer does in attempting to complete an assortment of goods. Possible patterns of organization are tested against the criterion of productivity, just as an assortment of goods is tested against the criterion of potency. Whether the market is cleared in the ideal sense of putting each man in the position which makes him most productive for the company depends on how well informed the two executives are about the eight men they are employing. The quality of their information will probably depend largely on their skill in asking questions of applicants and evaluating the answers.

Real employment markets are far over to the heterogeneous end of the sortability scale. They are also highly discrepant since employers are often looking for paragons who are unavailable, and applicants, even though highly skilled, may find there is no demand for their skills.

To avoid structural unemployment in an advanced economy there is need for the marketing viewpoint on the part of individuals or their representatives such as labor unions, colleges, executive placement agencies and government bureaus. People must be retrained or reconditioned so that they in effect become new products. Better forecasts must be made of the future markets for these reconditioned products. The capacity for growth and adjustment differs greatly by education and native endowment. Instead of trying to impart very advanced skills to people at the bottom, it may be easier to induce the people at the top to advance more rapidly. In any case, Myrdal has called attention to an imperfection in the labor market which may be as serious as for our time as the imperfection in the investment area which Keynes emphasized a generation ago.

1.   Specifying Consumer Needs

The consumer enters the market prepared to state her requirements with more or less precision. The specification of a daily need such as cigarettes is usually unambiguous. The consumer names the brand and specifies regular, king size, filter tip or menthol. The quantity is usually a pack but it may be two or three or even a carton. The goods are fully specified in the sense that the purchase order is unambiguous. A complete description is not required since the customer may merely point to the product wanted and ask the clerk to wrap it up. Fully specified goods are usually found at the end of Aspinwall's red-orange-yellow color scale.

One characteristic feature of the shopping goods which Aspinwall would place in the orange or yellow part of the spectrum is that these goods are only partially specified at the time that the customer enters the market. Some item is demanded such as a dress or a pair of shoes, but the consumer is not ready to say precisely what the item is. She may set a ceiling on the price she will pay and she may be looking for a red dress and red shoes. Beyond that she has fixed requirements as to size but a wide range of tolerance as to style and materials. Her specifications are likely to become more rigid as the shopping trip proceeds. Finally she is ready to designate the one item she is prepared to buy. Specification may be very loose indeed for the novice, whereas the experienced buyer has a pretty good idea of what the market affords and specifies the item needed more fully.

There are some needs which are in a sense unspecified. So-called impulse purchases are made by people who had no idea in advance that they were going to buy such an item. A man may go into a restaurant with nothing in mind except that mealtime has come around again. Presented with a menu, he sometimes makes a choice only with the greatest difficulty. Gift purchases may not be specified at all beyond the fact that the shopper has set broad limits on the price to be paid. The person receiving the gift may be expecting a present if it is an anniversary or other gift-giving occasion. From the receiver's viewpoint the gift is usually wholly unspecified, which adds to the uncertainty in the mind of the giver.

Finally, there are some goods which can fairly be called unspecifiable so far as the purchaser is concerned. An example is the prescription he buys in the drug store. The physician prescribes the drug on the basis of the patient's symptoms. The patient usually would not be competent or willing to prescribe for himself. An architect or contractor prepares specifications for a new home. The owner would usually feel that many of the items specified transcended his knowledge of what went into a house. An interior decorator is retained by homeowners who want certain effects but do not know how to obtain them.

These examples represent extreme cases of what might be called vicarious search. The physician, the architect and the decorator search for remedies, appropriate construction materials and furniture as well as accessories calculated to produce a satisfying esthetic appeal. Vicarious search is practiced far more broadly by retailers and wholesalers who search their source for the types of goods they expect their customers will buy. Manufacturers in effect are searching the technical possibilities when they bring out new products which they hope will appeal to consumers. Vicarious search is one of the ways of dealing with the information problem and keeping the cost within bounds.

While these various gradations of specifiability are recognized, the scheme needs to be simplified for convenient application. Everything which is not fully specified is regarded as partially specified. Convenience goods are fully specified in advance and shopping goods are specified at the moment of purchase.

2.   Identification by the Supplier

The supplier provides information about his product to facilitate his search for users. He is not sure who these users are or where they are to be found. His search is quite as eager and determined as the consumer's search for desired products. An interesting feature of information flows which takes place in marketing is the process of adjustment which marks this double search in which consumers are looking for products and suppliers are looking for customers.

Information provided by the supplier will be called identification. The consumer specifies his need and the supplier identifies his product. The convention adopted is to say that the consumer has fully specified his need when he designates a product and puts in his order. During the previous period of search the product may have been only partially specified, the consumer having only a generalized notion of what is required until finding the product with the particular qualities which are desired or acceptable.

The parallel convention on the supplier's side will not serve our purposes. The supplier can scarcely ever be said to identify his product completely. This would require a comprehensive descriptive protocol of the product. It would be hard to distinguish such a descriptive protocol from instructions for making the product. In fact, the nearest approach to full identification would be the do-it-yourself plans for building a desk or a boat.

The appropriate qualifier on the supplier's side is to say that the product is adequately identified. The question then arises as to purpose since the product may be adequately identified for one purpose but not another. A graded set of purposes will be presented shortly as they may be seen by the supplier. It may be said in general that the supplier's purpose is to sell goods and that he will provide the consumer with information which he believes is just adequate to that purpose. Since it costs money to transmit information, he cannot indulge in the luxury of information for its own sake. This limitation on information is valid because most consumers do not want to make a car or a suit of clothes. They merely want to buy one.

Identification is subject to other limitations even when the supplier feels the need to transmit information. It has been said that the consumer has some unspecified needs and that some of these needs may, in fact, be unspecifiable. Similarly on the supply side, some information may be regarded as uncoded or even uncodable. All information transmitted by any other means than direct vision is in a sense coded. Most information is coded in the form of words or pictures and often these fail to convey an accurate impression. The average consumer is not trained to receive and use quantitative data. Thus, the interior of a compact car may be described as "roomy" which may be about as helpful as defining its cubic space in feet and inches. When it comes to matters of taste and smell, vital qualities in some products, the common vocabulary fails us completely. The only available means of communication is what Frank Knight once called industrial poetry, which is the only recourse in suggesting to a teenager how good she will smell when doused with new Peach Blossom perfume.

Some of the information concerning products which the consumer would like to have is literally uncodable. Other information cannot be coded for reception by most consumers at the present time. Color is an attribute for which precise coding would be possible if consumers were equipped to receive it. A four-place

Figure 14.2.

code would identify all possible shades for any except the most discriminating eye. The consumer of course, would have to have a code book at hand and look up the color indicated by the code number. One color system in the paint industry lists 1,322 colors in its coded catalog. A sobering exercise for anyone who has no specialized knowledge of color is to see how long it would take him to write down as many as 25 names for colors.

3.   The Information Mismatch

The information consumers may want about a product and the information which suppliers give them may be represented by two overlapping circles (Figure 14.2). The circle on the left is designated as I, indicating the supplier's identification of his product.

The circle on the right is designated as S for consumer specification of the product desired. The overlap of the two circles is their logical product or intersection. In this area are those items of information which are both given and desired. The logical product is marked by the symbol I ∩ S, meaning the area common to both circles.

The minimum information which should appear in the overlap is its name, what it is claimed the product will do and usually the name of the maker or of the retailer who sells it. A product with this amount of information might be said to be barely identified. The consumer will need this data if he is to take any action at all after seeing an advertisement. Additional information may be provided to guide the consumer toward taking a particular action. If the supplier has guessed right, the product may be said to be adequately identified for the purpose at hand.

4.   The Purpose of Information

The suppler who is transmitting information through trade channels or through advertising media should start with an analysis of what purpose is feasibly accomplished through his message. While his ultimate aim is to sell goods, he must realize that consumers do not typically get an irresistible urge from seeing the advertisement and rush in to buy the product. The direct appeal of an old-time pitchman addressing a crowd on the Atlantic City Boardwalk will get this effect, but the advertiser usually has to settle for less. Here is a graded set of actions which it might be the purpose of the supplier to evoke:

1 To buy

2 To be reminded and then buy

3 To try and then buy

4 To shop and then buy

5 To have a demonstration and then buy

6 To recommend that others buy

With the exception of the first item, the supplier has a limited purpose in each case and is simply trying to move the consumer part of the way toward purchase. The supplier is presumed to have analyzed his situation and to have decided what is feasible for him to attempt. In selling a synthetic detergent, for example, the consumer is not likely to describe a product as her regular brand until she has bought her first trial package. The advertising says what needs to be said to get the consumer to try it in the hope that it will become her regular brand thereafter. A manufacturer gives away trial packages, offers them at reduced prices or at regular prices, but in every case he is hoping that the product can sell itself when it is given a trial. Ultimately the only thing worth knowing about the product is how it works. It may be put up in an attractive package, the color and odor of the material itself may be agreeable, but if it does not get clothes clean the consumer is not likely to try it again. Packaged products have the advantage that the consumer puts no great strain on her budget in buying a trial package. It is the final step in becoming informed on what she really wants to know, "Has the supplier made valid claims about performance?"

Once a product has made a place for itself in the consumer's assortment, information can be used to remind her of its virtues. This type of copy is often used for food products as compared to household supplies such as detergent. Appetite may be roused afresh by an attractive ad, and the housewife may be reminded to serve it to her family again. She does not have to be sold on the product idea since she is already familiar with it. The supplier wants to bring it back into the cycle of use as frequently as possible. The consumer is already familiar with its taste and appearance on the table and may remember a rare word of appreciation from her husband the last time it was served.

Another limited purpose of the supplier is that he hopes the consumer will shop and then buy. In the case of appliances, she frequently compares one make against another and takes her husband along to share in the final decision as to the price. In shopping for apparel she often enters the store in response to a store advertisement or that of the supplier of a name brand of dress or accessory. She rarely knows in advance just which item she will buy since she only knows the retailer's stock in a general way. She makes comparisons and ends up with a decision of what is best for her, which involves other decisions as to what would not look so well on her. The supplier only tries to get her into the store with some predisposition in favor of the goods displayed. The store's reputation may be more important than the supplier's reputation because she knows that the store has had a satisfactory assortment to choose from in the past.

Just as the housewife needs to know how a detergent works, so a buyer needs to know how a mechanical product works. Cameras, electric ranges, automobiles and business machines all have special features which usually require demonstration before the consumer is ready to buy. Sometimes a demonstration is nothing more than a ride around the block in the car of one's dreams, coupled with an explanation of its special features. Sometimes a demonstration means leaving an electric typewriter or a calculating machine at the customer's place of business for weeks or months while the employees are deciding whether they like it. In any case, the purpose of the supplier may be a limited purpose in arranging a demonstration if experience has shown that demonstration is a necessary condition of sale.

Finally, there is the situation in which a major objective is to induce consumers to recommend that other consumers buy the product. Refrigerators and other major appliances are bought only once in a term of years. Advertising might appear to be quite costly if it was directed only to those consumers who were considering buying a new one in the given year. If advertising can induce consumers to speak up for the make they prefer, it provides valuable reinforcement for the direct appeal. Of greatest value would be a word from recent buyers of similar models, shading off as the model is more and more outdated.

The supplier is counting on certain types of considerations being brought to mind in each of the purchasing situations. Some of the factors which are presumed to be at work are summarized below.

1 To buy	Immediate impulse
2 To be reminded and buy	Recall satisfactory experience
3 To try and then buy again	Validation of manufacturer's claims
4 To shop and then buy	Validation of manufacturer's claims
5 To have a demonstration and buy	Validation of manufacturer's claims
6 To recommend that others buy	Pride of ownership

To simplify, 1 and 2 might be classified as direct sale, 3, 4 and 5 as checking claims, and 6 as indirect sale. The list does not cover all of the limited purposes which advertising can have. Some retailers are selling credit terms rather than product, discounted prices on standard products, or prizes and premiums as features of the purchase. Some suppliers who see the face-to-face confrontation in the store as the key factor in the sale spend money to influence this encounter. One tire manufacturer, for example, suggests what the consumer should ask the dealer in order to get the service he needs. This manufacturer is convinced that the dealer will otherwise start nearly every interview as if the consumer were shopping for price rather than looking for the type of service indicated by the nature of his driving requirements.

5.   A Formula for Information Requirements

While there are a variety of selling situations with limited purposes, each calling for particular items of information, all needs can be reduced to a simple general formula. This formula takes account of the possibilities of making a sale, on the one hand, and the cost of providing the information, on the other. The evaluation of any particular advertising or promotional proposal would be made in accordance with an equation of the following form:

$$E_V = f(P_S, P_I, C_I, R_N)$$

This formula simply says that the expected value of the profit from sales is a function of the number of sales that will be made when the limited advertising purpose is achieved, the probability that consumers will act in accordance with the limited purpose, the cost of supplying the information, and the net revenue per sale exclusive of advertising. Suppose it has been determined that one out of four shoppers who come in for a demonstration will buy the new color Polaroid camera. Suppose that it can also be estimated that the advertisement will bring a stated number of customers into the store where the camera is to be had. It is assumed that the cost of the advertising message is known and that the net revenue per camera is known. Then any given advertising proposal could be evaluated by multiplying the estimated number entering the store by the probability of buying once they are there by the net revenue per camera and subtracting the cost of the advertising.

The calculation is somewhat more complicated in practice because there are other cost and revenue functions rather than single values. The advertising manager is not content to evaluate the particular program, but would like to pick the optimal program. The main point to be established here is that it is theoretically possible to get a numerical answer to the question of how much information is enough by taking account of the purpose that the information is intended to serve. The suggested calculation is an elementary exercise in the economics of information. The operator may arrive at his judgments on an intuitive basis, but in principle a limit can be placed on the amount of information required and a method for calculating this requirement

Chapter 15

TRANSACTIONS AND TRANSVECTIONS*

Wroe Alderson

A transaction is a product of the double search in which customers are looking for goods and suppliers are looking for customers. It is an exchange of information leading to an agreement concerning the marketing of goods. This agreement is a joint decision in which the customer agrees to take the goods offered and the supplier agrees to sell at the stated price and terms. There is always explicit or implicit negotiation in which each side measures the current opportunity by its next best alternative. In general, the customers can either accept or reject the good offered. In the latter case the customer is holding his money for some other use. The supplier can either sell or withhold his goods from the market, in the latter case hoping to find a more eager customer.

1. Routine and Negotiated Transactions

It is useful to divide transactions into fully negotiated transactions and routine transactions. A fully negotiated transaction is usually one of strategic importance to one or both parties. It can be strategic because it is controlling for a number of transactions which are to follow and which will take place within the framework established by the initial transaction. It can be strategic even though it is non-recurring because it is large in relation to the total pattern of activities on one side or the other. Both types of strategic transactions deserve to be fully negotiated, the large transactions because of the risks of being wrong, the controlling transaction because of the promise of economies over an indefinite period by reducing the cost of negotiation.

Routine transactions take place under the rules stated or implied in effectuating the initial strategic transaction. Supply contracts sometimes continue over many years and other supply arrangements are equally enduring, sanctioned only by custom rather than legal contract. Sometimes intricate institutional machinery is created to routinize large sets of transactions involving many buyers and sellers. The Stock Exchange is an excellent example. Representatives

---

*Originally published in *Dynamic Marketing Behavior* (1965), pages 75-97.

Agreement for	SW	WWS	CM	B	CP	CL
Transfer of sales responsibility	X	X	X	X		
Transfer of Ownership	X	X		X		
Transfer of Possession	X		X		X	X

of buyers and sellers have agreed on a set of rules for the protection of both sides. Millions of dollars change hands almost by the flick of an eyelash, but behind this instantaneous transaction lies one of the most carefully conceived bodies of regulations ever devised.

The same quality of foresight is in the background to facilitate trading on the grain and cotton exchanges or in the tobacco auctions. Consumer buying in a supermarket embodies the same principle. The consumer has become accustomed to her favorite store sometimes after some rather cautious trial purchases in which she pays close attention to price level and quantity of merchandise. Once she accepts the store with full confidence she is able to serve herself with no aid or interference from a sales person, the package and the price marked on it constituting the store's offer which she is free to accept or reject.

2.   The Substance of the Agreement

The agreement between the buyer and seller settles one or more issues about the movement of goods. The transfer may be complete and irrevocable or it may deal with a single aspect of the movement of goods. Considering transactions between business men at successive levels in the trade channels as well as transactions involving consumers, there are three main possibilities. These are transfer of sales responsibility, transfer of ownership and transfer of possession. The illustrations (X) in the table include transactions between various types of intermediaries as well as with the ultimate consumer.

The respective columns above pertain to transactions involving, in order, the service wholesaler (SW), the wholesaler without stocks (WWS), the commission merchant (CM), the broker (B), purchase by the consumer (CP), and leasing by the consumer (CL). The service wholesaler accepts sales responsibility and takes both ownership and possession of the goods. The wholesaler without stocks does not take possession of the goods but takes ownership. The commission merchant takes possession but not ownership. The broker does not take either ownership or possession but only sales responsibility. Since the consumer ordinarily is not buying for resale, sales responsibility is not ordinarily discussed with the consumer. In making a purchase the consumer takes both ownership and possession. In a rental or leasing arrangement the consumer takes possession only. However, sales responsibility is an important subsidiary consideration in the decision to buy or rent a home or an automobile. The conumer may prefer to pay a flat monthly charge on his automobile, for example, leaving the lessor responsible for sale at the end of the leasing period.

These various types of marketing institutions have evolved to meet particular marketing requirements. The service wholesaler originally flourished in the handling of standard products and performed a sorting function in "breaking bulk" because his customers typically bought in less than carload lots. The wholesaler without stocks is found in such product fields as coal and lumber. His customer buys in carload lots so that no purpose would be served by maintaining wholesale stocks with an added cost of loading and unloading. He deals in a standard product or at least one that is priced and sold by grades. Shipment is direct from the mine or sawmill and the wholesaler intervenes only to arrange transactions with the retail coal or lumber yard and to assume credit risks as the owner of the material.

The commission merchant is dealing in a non-standard product or at least one which cannot be finally graded until it comes into his possession. The commission merchant has been active in such fields as livestock and produce and in both cases grade is affected by the condition of the animals or produce on arrival at the terminal market. Better grading and better protection in transit has led to the rise of the service wholesaler in produce. Selection of breeds, more uniform feeding practices, and reliance on buyers in the growing areas has greatly reduced the role of the commission merchant in livestock and poultry. It is difficult for the commission merchant to retain the confidence of growers who may be thousands of miles away. In the early 19th century the commission merchants who handled the American tobacco crop in London were replaced by tobacco auctions at thousands of warehouses throughout the growing areas. The food broker, by contrast, is dealing with a standard product, selling to chains and wholesale grocers who can receive in carload lots and carrying their own credit. Though he does not take ownership or possession, he takes sales responsibility for manufacturers who individually could not afford to set up their own sales organizations.

The decision of whether to sell or lease to the consumer hangs on the consideration of whether the product is recoverable or non-recoverable. Mortgages on homes and instalment contracts on the sale of automobiles include provisions for repossession in case of default. Original paintings are especially suitable to leasing arrangements, and the practice will probably grow as people are more eager to possess them. The value of a good painting ordinarily does not decline during the lease period. A factor militating against leasing is pride of ownership. Incidentally, there are art centers such as San Francisco in which galleries have developed a lay-away plan for young couples who feel that it is as important to own a good painting or two as any item of furniture. The consumer's decision to buy or rent depends on such considerations as duration of the period of use, resale value and pride of ownership.

3.   The Discrepancy of Assortments

Goods are associated in different patterns at various levels in the channel. The basis of this association is the difference in technologies which apply at successive levels. Goods are associated at the manufacturing level because they can be made on the same equipment or in the same plant. They are associated at the wholesale level because of similarities among trade customers and similar requirements for shipment and storage. They are associated at the retail level because of consumer purchasing habits and convenience. The frequency of purchase, the frame of reference for making selections and the size of the average purchase relative to the consumer's budget are among the pertinent aspects of consumer buying habits. While in general there is some degree of resemblance between retail assortments and wholesale assortments in the same line of trade, the matching is far from perfect. The grocery retailer with a full line buys only about 40 percent of his requirements from the grocery wholesaler. His other needs are supplied by produce wholesalers, the wholesale division of the meat packer, the dairy, the wholesale baker and various manufacturers of packaged products selling directly.

This phenomenon in the channels of trade is called the discrepancy of assortments. While this phenomenon is prevalent in most lines of trade, it varies in relative importance from line to line. Discrepancy is low in the channels for automobiles or pianos. It is very high in groceries, drugs, hardware and department store lines. Discrepancy of assortments is associated with the cross currents which produce noisy channels. The paint manufacturer, for example, regards the hardware store as one of the channels available to him and asserts that the hardware dealer typically makes more money on paint than on any other line. This assertion does not make life any easier for the tool manufacturer who is trying to induce the retailer to do an adequate selling job on tools. The retailer has limited time and energy and cannot respond to all the pleas he hears from the suppliers of different products.

There might be some value in setting up a way to measure the degree of discrepancy in channels of trade. Any attempt by a manufacturer is rendered more difficult both by discrepancy and the number of steps in the channel. An index which would reflect both factors might be obtained for any manufacturer using a given trade channel. The diagram (Figure 15.1) illustrates the amount of discrepancy between the manufacturer's line and the retailer's line.

As the chart is drawn there is only the portion of the manufacturer's line labeled X which is common to the wholesaler and the retailer. Suppose that X is $\frac{1}{5}$ of the manufacturer's line, $\frac{1}{4}$ of the wholesaler's line and $\frac{1}{6}$ of the retailer's line. Perhaps a fair measure of discrepancy could be obtained by simply multiplying these ratios together to obtain the compound ratio $\frac{1}{120}$. A study in this area might result in some judgments as to the degree of discrepancy

Figure 15.1.

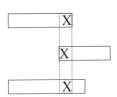

which is tolerable in this system. There would be many situations in which the discrepancy would be far greater than that represented by this ratio. A much more moderate approach to measuring discrepancy would be to take the average of the ratios rather than their product. In the present instance this would work out to $\frac{37}{180}$.

The discrepancy of assortments surely poses additional problems, whether viewed through the manufacturer's eyes or from some other standpoint. If the retailer receives merchandise from a wholesaler who is more interested in selling other types of accounts, he is likely to suffer real or fancied discrimination. If the retailer accounts for only a small part of the manufacturer's line, his type of store will receive a correspondingly small amount of attention from the manufacturer. The wholesaler is most vulnerable of all if he buys only a small part of what the manufacturer supplies and sells it to retailers for whom this is only a small part of what their customers demand. Most wholesalers need to be strongly anchored at one end or the other. Examples are the grocery wholesaler, supplying the full line of dry groceries to the retailer, and the appliance distributor providing an outlet for the full line of the appliance manufacturer.

4. Adjustment among Competitors

There are two opposing tendencies among competitors at any given level. One is to meet competition directly by offering an identical product. The other is to try to get some advantage over competitors by offering something different. These tendencies will be discussed more fully in the chapter on the search for differential advantage. The interest here is in the process of competitive adjustment, particularly as it works out at the retail level. The problem to be analyzed is the way in which retailers duplicate or differentiate the items handled. A hypothetical example will illustrate the main issues as to overlapping assortments at the same level compared to discrepancy of assortments among levels.

Suppose that each retailer in the market carries a thousand products, all under manufacturer brands. There are 2,000 manufacturer brands altogether. Retailer A enters the market first and makes a selection of the items he will carry. He

Figure 15.2.

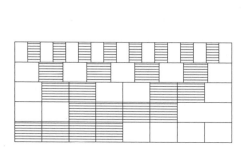

Figure 15.3.

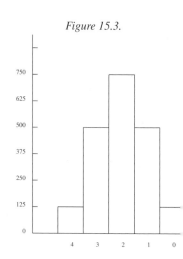

does not carry all brands of every product but tries to cover the full line b
carrying one or more brands in each category. Retailer B comes into the marke
next and feels obliged to carry many of the same brands because of the strengt
of their market position. He duplicates 500 of the brands carried by A and add
500 brands not carried by A. There are now 1,500 brands on the market. Th
third entrant is C who has the same views about meeting competition, but i
accomplishing this he has a somewhat different problem. He draws a sampl
from four quadrants into which all the available brands have been divided b
the combined choices of A and B. These are: first quadrant carried by A only
second quadrant, carried by both A and B; third quadrant, carried by B only
and fourth quadrant, carried by neither. Similarly, when D enters the market h
engages in a sampling process. There are now eight segments to be sampled an
he takes half of each segment. By now this sampling of the available brands b
four competitors would have produced a pattern something like the one in Figur
15.2. Most of the possible items are in some assortment and the majority are i
at least two assortments. The distribution by number of assortments, includin
these items, is shown in frequency distribution (Figure 15.3). Out of 2,00
items, 125 are carried by all four retailers, 500 are carried by three and 750 ar
carried by two. Thus, there are varying degrees of competition on 1,375 out c
1,875 items carried or over 70 percent. There is no direct competition on th
remaining items, 500 being carried by only one retailer and 125 carried by n
one.

While there is no direct competition on some of the items, all have bee
evaluated as competitive opportunities by four retailers. There is pressure o
each of the manufacturers whose product is not carried in the market to im
prove his product or lower his price in order to break in. There is unremittin
pressure from manufacturers to get retailers to stock their brands and to fin

ways of moving them at lower cost. These vertical interactions in the channel contribute significantly to the intensity of competition. They help to explain why it is possible to have vigorous competition in the midst of heterogeneity in several dimensions; heterogeneous items, heterogeneous retail assortments and discrepancy of assortments at the various supply levels backing up the retailer.

In the simple example given, there is only a moderate drive on the part of each retailer to meet competition directly. Yet with four retailers all but one-sixteenth of the available items are carried in the market. This means that the great majority of consumers would be able to find the specific item they wanted somewhere in the market. Other examples might have been used, assuming a greater drive toward direct competition. Suppose that each retailer in turn feels obliged to handle 1,500 out of the 2,000 items. By the same principle of sampling there would be only $\frac{1}{4}$ of 1 percent of the brands not carried by any retailer with four retailers in the market. This figure compares with $6\frac{1}{4}$ percent under the first example. The gain in completeness of stocks available to the consumer is not very material at this level. A market with very great urgency to meet competition directly would be one in which each retailer felt compelled to stock 1,800 out of the 2,000 items available. The number of brands not stocked by anyone would now be reduced to .0001. Only seven or eight items out of 2,000 are carried by a single retailer or about two each. It seems obvious that the competitive effort is too great in this market. Surely there is no local retail market which has to carry brand duplication to this point in order to be deemed competitive.

The frequency distribution for this last case is one in which each retailer stocks 9 out of 10 of the brands available (Figure 15.4). The distribution is derived from the binominal expansion under the sampling assumptions which have been made throughout. About two thirds of the brands would be carried by every retailer and nearly 30 percent by three out of four retailers. Just over 5 percent[1] would be carried by less than three retailers. It seems obvious that the competitive effort is too great in this market. Only seven or eight items out of 2,000 are carried by a single retailer or about two each. Certainly this would not provide any discernible differentiation of assortments such as is needed operationally to establish a following for each store among consumers. This tie which binds customers to particular stores for a large part of their business is an essential ingredient in an enterprise economy. Its significance will be discussed more fully in the chapter on advertising.

In real markets it is doubtful whether the drive to duplicate items is ever any greater than in the first example. There, it will be remembered, were 500 items carried by only one store. This would be an average of 125 per store

---

[1] In the 1965 printing this is erroneously written as "50 percent".

Figure 15.4.

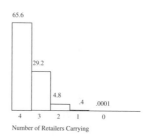

Number of Retailers Carrying

or 12.5 percent of the 1,000 items carried by each store. This would provide noticeable differentiation from store to store, coupled with opportunity for the consumer to compare prices in at least two stores on over 70 percent of all the items actually carried. On an intuitive basis this would appear to come close to an ideal state of competitive adjustment in which there would be a working balance between the costs of competition and the social value of competition. In theory an algorithm could be developed for computing the optimal relationship in competitive adjustment. One approach would be to make a marketing cost analysis for all the retailers in the market and have each give up items which were distinctly unprofitable. Some of the items given up by one retailer would turn out thereafter to be profitable for another. The ideal state of competitive adjustment might be defined as one in which each retailer was just breaking even on his marginal items. Retailers in every market exhibit excessive competition by this test. Long experience in marketing costs analysis shows that even profitable retailers lose money on many individual items.

5.   Formal Analysis of Transactions

The transaction is a fundamental building block which suggests possibilities for a more rigorous type of marketing theory. In the chart in Chapter 11 (Figure 11.2), showing concepts to be derived from the primitive term "behavior," transactions are shown as joint decisions between buyer and seller. The basis is also indicated for distinguishing between routine and negotiated transactions since a joint agreement can apply to a rule governing future transactions as well as to individual transactions.

The formal analysis of transactions will begin with a statement which might be called the Law of Exchange. This law states the conditions under which an exchange actually occurred since there are fortuitous factors which could interfere with the exchange in a given case. In the expression $x \backsimeq y$, it is merely asserted that x is exchanged for y. The sign of Libra, or the balance, being dopted to represent exchangeability. The Law of Exchange, stated verbally, would be as follows:

> Given that x is an element of the assortment A_1 and y is an element of the assortment A_2, x is exchangeable for y if, and only if, these three conditions hold:
>
>> (a) x is different from y (b) The potency of the assortment A1 is increased by dropping x and adding y (c) The potency of the assortment A2 is increased by adding x and dropping y
>
> In symbols the Law of Exchange would be stated as follows:

$$x \simeq y, \; if \; and \; only \; if \; x \neq y(x\epsilon A_1 \; and \; y\epsilon A_2)$$

$$P(A_1 - x + y) > PA_1 \; and \; P(A_2 + x - y) > PA_2$$

The previous formulation makes no explicit reference to the cost of executing an exchange transaction. For a complete statement of the Law of Exchange it should be stated explicitly that the increased potency for the assortment A_1 brought about by the transaction should be greater than the cost of the transaction and that the same thing should be true for the assortment A_2. This corollary of the Law of Exchange might be stated symbolically as follows;

$$x \simeq \; implies \; that \quad C[P(A_1 - X + Y) - P(A_1)] > C_{A_1}(Tr)$$
$$C[PA_2 + X - Y) - P(A_2)] > C_{A_2}(Tr)$$

At a first level of consideration, x and y might be regarded as two different products in a primitive economy such as a basket and a hat with exchange taking place on a barter basis. Given a medium of exchange, y might be regarded as an amount of money paid by the buyer to obtain the article. The definitions of buyer and seller need not detain us except to note a very general distinction. The buyer in a transaction is adding a less liquid item to his assortment, while the seller is adding a more liquid asset, very likely with the intent of exchanging his in turn for more specialized assets later on.

We are now in position to state three propositions with more obvious relevance to the problem of planning a marketing system. The first is concerned with the optimality of exchange in a particular exchange situation. Viewing exchange from the standpoint of one of the decision makers, we can say that exchange is optimal if he prefers it to any available alternative. Similarly, for the decision maker on the other side of the transaction, it will be optimal for him if he prefers it to any available alternative. It is assumed that if a concrete situation offers an exchange of opportunity, the number of alternatives realistically available to either side is not infinite in number but limited to only a few.

To summarize, it may be said that exchange is optimal if the individual decision maker I_1 prefers x to any of the available alternatives V_1 to V_n and if the decision maker I_2 prefers y to any of the available alternatives W_1 to W_n.

It is scarcely necessary to go through the procedure of stating this propositio symbolically since it would follow the pattern previously illustrated.

The principle of optimality rests on the Law of Exchange and its corollary The principle would hold only where the conditions were consistent with th previously stated propositions. The exchange of x for y is preferred by eac decision maker precisely because it offers the greatest increase in the potenc of his assortment.

The next proposition to be asserted is that a set of transactions in series ca replace direct sales by the supplier to the ultimate consumer if the transaction are optimal at each step. Let us assume initially that a sale is made directly b the supplier to the ultimate consumer. Now let us assume that a single interme diary intervenes between those two. If the exchange between the supplier an the intermediary is optimal, it means that he prefers this exchange to dealin directly with the consumer. Similarly, if the exchange between the consume and the intermediary is optimal, it means that the consumer prefers this trans action to a direct exchange with the supplier. This sequence of two transaction would therefore be eligible to replace the direct exchange between supplier an consumer.

If one intermediary can intervene between the supplier and the consumer, i follows that a second intermediary can intervene between the supplier and th first intermediary or between the first intermediary and the consumer, provide that the principle of optimality still obtains. Similarly, other intermediarie could be added to the chain as long as the principle of optimality was no violated.

Two major problems in planning the flow of transactions pertain to the cas of transactions in series, which has just been discussed, and the case of paralle transactions occurring at the same level of distribution as, for example, betwee the supplier and the first intermediary. One of the aims of planning is to reduc the cost of individual transactions, particularly the cost of negotiation. Th choices are to negotiate each of the parallel transactions separately or to nego tiate a rule under which all transactions of a given type can be routinized. Thi can be reduced to a clear-cut decision based on the relative costs of negotiatin individual transactions as compared to the cost of negotiating a rule plus th cost of negotiating the routinized transactions to be controlled by the rule. A formula for this might be as follows:

> Routinize if the cost of rule negotiation plus the cost of negotiating the routinized transactions while the rule holds is less than the total cost of negotiating the individual transaction without the rule.

The calculation would start by estimating the number of transactions whic will probably occur while the rule is in force and multiplying this number by the average cost of a routinized transaction. If this cost is less than the cos of negotiating the same number of individual transactions, it would be wortl while to negotiate the adoption of a rule. This, of course, is provided that the difference was greater than the cost of negotiating the rule. Generally, the saving would have to be substantial to force the decision maker on either side to initiate the process of negotiating a rule. There are, of course, many practical cases in which literally thousands of transactions are to be covered by the rule so that the condition of overall cost-saving would be fully satisfied.

6. The Transvection

The problems of competitive adjustment and of channel coordination call for a more powerful concept than the transaction. This is the concept of the transvection, a term invented by the author in 1958 for lack of an established English word with the same meaning. The word comes from the Latin roots trans and vehere. From its etymology the word was meant to convey the meaning of flowing through, with special reference to something which flows through a marketing system — in one end and out the other. A transvection is the unit of action for the system by which a single end product such as a pair of shoes is placed in the hands of the consumer after moving through all the intermediate sorts and transformations from the original raw materials in the state of nature. The choice of a word which would sound something like the word transaction was deliberate since the two ideas were obviously closely related.

A transvection is in a sense the outcome of a series of transactions, but a transvection is obviously more than this. The transactions as such are limited only to the successive negotiations of exchange agreements. A transvection includes the complete sequence of exchanges, but it also includes the various transformations which take place along the way. The pair of shoes in the hands of the consumer is obviously a very different thing from the raw materials in the state of nature. The student of transvections is interested in every step along the way by which this flow through the marketing system was accomplished.

Other contrasts can be drawn between a transaction and a transvection with respect to their uses in planning and decision-making. Transactions involve a transfer in ownership or use privileges covering not only sales but all forms of short-term rent and lease agreements. It is assumed that further transformations will take place under the new ownership, but ordinarily this is not required under the terms of the exchange agreement. In market planning there is necessarily substantial emphasis on means of motivating these further transformations following a transfer of ownership.

If planning is approached from the transvection standpoint, on the other hand, it is often convenient to consider first what might take place if the product remained under a single ownership throughout. This provides a way of specifying the transformations which are really essential in order to complete the transvection and the sorts of assignments which must intervene to link any pair of successive transformations. While the transaction concept is valuable for market planning, the transvection concept is more fundamental. Beginning from the perspective of the transvection, for example, will be useful in shaping the character of the transactions which need to occur at successive stages.

7.   The Shortest Route to Market

With the concepts of the transaction and the transvection in mind, we can now address ourselves to the problem of finding the shortest path to market. The original supplier, on one side, and the ultimate consumer, on the other, have a continuing stake in finding the shortest route to market available at any given time. The shortest route to market is not measured in either mileage or number of steps in the channel, although both of these are types of distance between producer and consumer. Rather the route to market is measured by cost or by some weighing of cost, time and risk. In a repetitive operation cost is the fundamental measure. Time is allowed for in part by the merchandise in the pipeline. In other words, time can be translated into cost. One of the savings in having fewer steps in the channel would be in reducing the amount of merchandise in the pipeline. Under other circumstances the lengthening of the pipeline can be accepted cheerfully because of offsetting savings in other directions. Risk or uncertainty can also be translated into expected costs or opportunity losses.

Transactions and transvections are two different ways of looking at the marketing process which starts with conglomerate resources as they occur in nature and ends with meaningful assortments in the hands of consumers. The concept of the transaction provides a means of attack on the problem of negotiation costs which is an important aspect of all costs in the process. The number of transactions in the sequence may appear to increase the total cost of negotiation but an additional intermediary may allow for a more homogeneous set of transactions and hence greater opportunities for routinization. From the viewpoint of the transvection, however, we are considering what is necessary for the total process, without regard to the successive changes in ownership or if the process was managed under a simple ownership throughout.

The various types of transactions already mentioned were devised by people searching for a shorter path to market. At one stage a manufacturer employs food brokers because it would cost him more to set up his own sales organization. At a later stage he has enough sales volume to maintain a direct sales force so that the broker would be superfluous and brokerage fees would constitute a needless cost. There is a kind of succession among types of intermediaries which is not unlike the succession of species in a forest, affected by climate and by changes which the species themselves produce in the environment.

Figure 15.5.

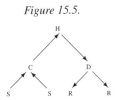

The concept of a transvection, on the other hand, is not concerned with the rise and fall of intermediaries but with something even more fundamental. Its concern is with what the marketing process would require even if only one intermediary intervened between the original source and the ultimate consumer. The marketing process consists of a series of sorts each time the goods change hands, interspersed with a series of transformations affecting the conditions under which the goods will eventually be brought to market. One of the simplest models for this process is provided by a system in which the intervening activities always consist of shipment from one point to the next. The model is derived from the operations of the United Parcel Company which is no longer solely concerned with deliveries from the retailer but competes with railway express and parcel post in the delivery of packages from a shipper to a receiver. This process is handled through a carefully engineered system in which a package is loaded into four or more successive vehicles and goes out of its way in terms of mileage to achieve the shortest route in terms of cost.

The structure of this system can be shown in a simple schematic diagram (Figure 15.5). Small trucks pick up packages from individual shippers and take them into a collection center. Here the packages go into much larger trucks to be carried a longer distance to a central hub. Packages are transferred to another large truck and are carried out to localized distribution centers. They are again transferred to smaller trucks for delivery along various routes. Note the perfect alternation of sorts and transformations. At the collection center the aspect of sorting involved is accumulation to form a load for the large truck with the hub as its destination. This is an example of partial homogeneity. The packages are alike in one operational aspect only, namely, they constitute the cargo of the same large truck headed for the hub. At the hub packages are sorted out according to distribution centers. At the distribution center they are sorted out again by the routes which will bring each package to its ultimate destination.

In this process each sort serves to facilitate the next transformation, all of the transformations in this system being simple changes in location. To find the lowest total cost (the shortest path to market) the analyst would minimize the expression $Y = C_s + C_t$, where C_s is the cost of sorting and C_t is the cost of transformations. Since the number of sorts and the number of transformations are discrete rather than continuous, the analyst would ordinarily be testing the proposition that one or more sorts would yield a lower cost or the reverse proposition that a system with one less sort would be more economical. To test either proposition would require an advance judgment of alternatives since there is usually more than one point in the system at which a sort could be inserted or eliminated. The United Parcel system was actually oversimplified for purposes of exposition.

There is another sort in the actual system of selecting packages for shipment from one hub to another hub. In this system a package can travel miles out of the way, coming back to a receiver who is not very far from the shipper. The system is justified by the fact that a package has to bear only a small part of the cost per mile of a truck along with hundreds of other packages. Obviously the cost would be prohibitive if each package was carried directly from shipper to receiver.

The marketing process is like this model except that activities intervene between the sorts, including transformations in form and storage which can be regarded as transferring goods from one point in time to a later point in time. They have greater utility at the later time because the demand for the goods is greater. A typical marketing sequence would be as shown:

| sort | Manufacture | sort | Ship | sort | Store | sort | Ship | sort | Display |

The first sort produces a partial homogeneity to facilitate production. At the end of the production line goods are sorted by destination and shipped to wholesalers. The wholesaler then sorts the shipment into his stock, keeping like goods together. Goods remain in storage over some period until ordered out by his retailers. The retailer adds the items received to his assortment which might be called assorting or selecting into his assortment. They remain on display until sold to consumers or removed from stock as unsalable.

It will be observed that the sequence of activities between the sorts accounts for the creation of form, space and time utility. Sometimes form utility is paired with production while marketing is credited with the creation of time and space utility. Actually the functions cannot be separated so neatly. The sorting operations which constitute the essence of marketing play precisely the same part in facilitating production through creating partial homogeneities as they do in facilitating shipment, storage or display.

There are five sorts in the sequence shown above, each related to the transformation which immediately follows. In seeking improvements in the system the analyst would once more try to minimize the sum of sorting costs and transformation costs. Not only would he test for inserting or eliminating sorts, but he might experiment with changing the sequence. Thus, raw materials might be shipped to terminal markets for storage and later fabrication rather than having manufacture take place near the beginning with shipment to terminal markets or distribution points later. The final stage in this sequence, the display function, does not quite fit the rubic of time, space and form utility. In a sense they are all brought back together again to facilitate choice from an assortment. Convenience in selection almost qualifies as another form of utility creating factor. It can take effect at various times and places within the locus of the consumer, including all the places where the consumer is likely to be in the widening circles of his travels rather than merely his home address.

8. The Logic of Sorting

The author has previously pointed out that the whole structure of marketing channels rests on the logic of sorting. If there are ten suppliers in a given market and ten customers, an intermediary always has the potentiality of intervening to reduce the cost of marketing. The intermediary does this by decreasing the number of trading relations required. If there are ten parties on either side of the market trading with each other, there are a hundred trading relations. If they trade through an intermediary there are only twenty since he is in contact with ten suppliers on one side and ten customers on the other. In general, his intervention reduces the trading relations from the product of the two numbers to the sum of the two numbers. The ratio between the sum and the product increases as the numbers increase. Assuming for convenience of illustration that suppliers and customers continue to be the same in number and that there are now one hundred of each, the sum of these two numbers is only one-fiftieth of the product of the numbers.

Theoretically the same calculation might be used to justify an indefinite number of steps. Given that a certain number of retailers is justified in reducing the number of trading relations involved in having manufacturers trade directly with consumers, a wholesaler is potentially capable of intervening between the manufacturer and the retailer. In some industries in the past a super-jobber has entered the picture to sell to sub-jobbers and the food broker continues to illustrate the possible economies provided by a third intervener.

In practice the sequence of successive interveners is soon brought to an abrupt halt. The sequence is terminated both because of the cost of the additional sorts and because of the decreasing efficiency of the channel as an information channel. Suppose that a market as originally constituted had forty suppliers and forty consumers. There is some justification for the first intervener who will reduce the number of trading relations by a factor of twenty, but now suppose that one or more intermediaries intervene between the first intervener and the suppliers and that others intervene between the first intervener and the customer. This would mean three sorts rather than one. There would have to be a much larger number on either side of the market to justify the additional sorts. One consideration which leads to additional sorts is geographic dispersion over a large territory. But successive steps in dispersion steadily reduces the number of parties on either side of the market until no further sorts could be justified.

The information passing through channels becomes less reliable as the channel grows longer. The noisy channel was discussed briefly in the last chapter. A channel is rendered noisy for marketing purposes by conflicting motivations which can enter at various points. There is a limit above which the noise level is no longer tolerable because of progressive declines in efficiency. The effect of conflict or inertia is to destroy motivation which in turn leads to the weakening or distortion of information signals in the channel.

9.   A Formal Analysis of Transvections

An effort will now be made to show how a theory of transvections could be cast in formal language. It has been said that the marketing process is the continuous operation of transforming conglomerate resources as they occur in nature into meaningful assortments in the hands of consumers. As will be seen from Figure 13.1 in Chapter 13, provision is made for defining conglomerates and assortments as types of collections, and a collection, in turn, as a type of set. Symbolically, the marketing process or operation might be shown as follows:

$$C(O_{t_1} - O_{t_0}) = \sum \triangle(A_1, A_2 \ldots, A_n + W)$$

In words, this proposition states that applying the operation O to the conglomerate C over the period from t_0 to t_1 results in increments to the assortments held by consumers, plus an allowance for waste.

A transvection by contrast refers to a single unit of action of the marketing system. This unit of action is consummated when an end product is placed in the hands of the ultimate consumer, but the transvection comprises all prior action necessary to produce this final result, going all the way back to conglomerate resources. The definition of a transvection can be shown symbolically as $T_V = STSTS \ldots TS$ where S is a sort and T is a transformation.

The statements so far about transvections indicate a need for two simple but fundamental proofs. The first is a proof that the sum of all transvections would correspond to an exhaustive description of the marketing process. The only difficulty here is in the selection of a long enough time period. By definition every sale of an end product has a transvection behind it. Thus, all the end products sold during a given year with their corresponding transvections would be approximately the same as the total marketing process for that year. Even if a four or five year period was considered, there would always be transvections terminating during the period which began in an earlier period and transvections beginning in the period which would terminate in a subsequent period. This is not so much a problem of proof as a problem of defining the marketing process and a transvection in such a way that they can be reconciled with each other.

The other problem is more clearly a problem of logical proof. That grows out of the definition of a transvection as shown in symbolic form. As shown in the formula, there is a continuous alternation between sorts and transformations. It will not be asserted that this alternation is inherent in the nature of a transvection.

The proposition that there is an alternation of sorts and transformations throughout the course of a transvection implies that a sorting action, or assignment, always intervenes between a transformation just completed and the one which is to follow. That this is necessarily true will become clear when the term transformation is more fully explained.

A transformation is a change in the physical form of a product or in its location in time and space which is calculated to increase its value for the ultimate consumer who adds the product to his assortment. In other words, transformations add form, space, and time utility. Marketing theory is not concerned with the techniques of creating form utility but only in their marketing implications. For example, marketing theory might need to distinguish between very broad categories of production such as refining and combining.

With respect to time and place utility, marketing is concerned with detailed techniques as well as broad perspective. Sorting might assign some goods to transportation equipment suitable for long hauls and other equipment designed for short hauls. Similarly, in the creation of time utility, some goods might be stored in one way while other similar or dissimilar goods could be stored more appropriately in a different type of facility. Credit is another way of creating time utility and again there is always an assignment problem prior to the selection of a mode of transportation.

Against this background, the formal proof of the alternating sequence might take the following form: Two sorts cannot follow each other in sequence in any significant sense since sorting out is the act of placing the members of a set in relevant subsets. If members are moved from one subset to another, it is to be regarded as inefficient or exploratory sorting and not successive sorts in a sequence.

Similarly, two transformations cannot appear successively without an intervening sort. Different facilities are required for fabrication, shipment, storage and credit. Thus, there has to be an intervening assignment to the appropriate facilities. In very rare cases facilities might be combined, as in further aging or agitation of a product while in transit. The point, however, is that assignment always precedes the use of a facility and that typically separate facilities are required for each transformation. There are, of course, possibilities for breaking the sequence of transformations down still further with additional intervening sorts, and this topic will now be treated briefly.

A distribution network quickly becomes too complicated for complete evaluation of marketing effectiveness. The concept of the transvection offers a means of piecemeal analysis for planning purposes without violating the principle of the total systems approach. Looking at a transvection in relation to a given end product, it can be bounded, or marked off, from other related transvections. A network may consist largely of divergent paths, particularly if the basic production process is one of refining with the end product distributed to thousands of consumers. A network may consist largely of convergent paths, particularly if the basic production process is one of combining materials and components and the ultimate consumer is government or a few large industrial buyers. In either case, there are a number of branching points on the main path along which the product flows through the network.

The bounding of the transvection means evaluation of additions or subtractions at each branching point along the way. Take the relatively simple case of a pair of shoes in which the principle component is leather. At each branching point at which lines converge, the costs of other components such as the shoemaker's findings must be added in. At each branching point where lines diverge there may be waste or by-products to be evaluated. Waste may carry a cost penalty for disposal while by-products may contribute some revenue to the main stream.

Optimal Number of Steps in a Transvection

Against this background a basic principle for the evaluation of transvections may be stated. A transvection has the optimal number of steps if costs cannot be decreased, either by increasing or decreasing the number of steps. Let us take a hypothetical case in which the only type of transformation pertains to spatial location. Assume that a natural product is being distributed and that it is snapped up immediately by consumers available at the terminal points. Even in this illustration, in which the creation of form and time utility are ruled out, there is still a problem of optimality for the number of steps in a transvection.

For any given system it is possible to compare two network plans. Suppose the following relationship holds—daily cost of transportation facilities plus daily cost of sorting under Plan A (4 sorts) > Plan B (5 sorts). It is clear that costs figures should be marshalled to test the possibility that Plan C (6 sorts) would cost still less. The number of possibilities is quite limited so that it would usually suffice to test only two plans against the network already in force, namely, those with one less sort and one more sort.

Actually the situation is not static but dynamic because of changing technologies both in transportation and sorting. Mechanical sorting equipment has made great strides recently, thus creating the possibility that more sorts would lead to greater efficiency. There are practical limits as to the length of a transvectional chain. At some point the cost of delay in the system would outweigh any further savings to be made through additional sorts.

When transformations are considered more generally, rather than dealing with transportation only, the same kind of reasoning still holds in principle. A detailed analysis might be required for the given network since the possible patterns may now be large though finite. For example, fabrication may involve both refining and combining. It may be efficient to separate these two by hundreds of miles even though additional sorts and transformations are introduced. An improvement in storage facilities may make it possible to store the product closer to the consumer or even to move it into the consumer's assortment more promptly. It is this last step in the forwarding of goods which may be accomplished through various forms of consumer credit.

Some networks and choices of technologies may involve hundreds of possibilities as to the design of the transvection. While a computer may be needed to test all the possibilities, including differences in number of warehouses and spatial dispersion of production, the test of optimality is in principle the same for all types of transvections.

Movement of Goods, Information, and People

Two further matters remain to be discussed very briefly, namely, the conditions under which the movement of information will facilitate the movement of goods and special situations in which people are physically moved as part of the marketing process. It will be useful to compare the three classes of movement with respect to the sequence of flows and inventories in the transvection. In movement, goods obviously cannot exist in two places at the same time. If goods move from one stocking point to another it reduces the inventory at one point and will presently show up as an addition to inventory at the other.

Information, on the other hand, can exist at two points at the same time. Mr Halbert has drawn some comparisons between the flows and and stocks of information. The parallel is suggestive but not perfect. A further set of principles is necessary to determine when a piece of information can safely be dropped from the first stock of data after having arrived at the second. These determinations must grow out of further analysis of the way in which the movement of information facilitates the movement of goods. For example, there is often a need to match the information on arrival in the second stock of information with information retained at the point of origin concerning the shipment of goods. Once the transaction is fully completed, including payment by the recipient, it may be possible to remove this piece of data from both stocks of information at the same time.

While there is certainly a factor of time utility with respect to information, it works in a reverse manner from time utility in the movement of goods. In the movement of goods, time utility is usually created by getting the goods to the ultimate destination as soon as possible. Time utility in the case of information is measured by decisions as to how soon it can be discarded, thus avoiding the continuing cost of storing it in retrievable form. There are also issues of form utility with respect to information relating to analytical transformation of data. No further analysis of these aspects of transformations as applied to data will be considered here. In general, the attempt is only to suggest that information flows as well as the flow of goods are involved in the complete description of a transvection. There are subtleties and distinctions involved in information flows which transcend the limits set here.

A similar brief reference can be made to the areas of marketing which involve the physical movement of people. People, like goods, can only exist in one point at a given time. The very interesting peculiarity of marketing which involves the movement of people is that individual persons become components of the purveyor's inventory. This can perhaps be seen most readily in the use of a facility such as a hospital. A patient might be treated in his own home but generally there are compelling considerations for treatment in a hospital. It is not entirely facetious to regard the individual patient as being kept in stock for periods ranging from a few hours to a number of months. The effort while he is in the hospital is to perform certain transformations which may change his condition from sick to well. Drugs and surgery are among the principal instruments which are used by the physician in the hope of effecting this transformation.

There are many other types of facilities in which the consumer enters into working inventory, including hotels, restaurants, barber and beauty shops, and places of entertainment. There are some special difficulties in applying the standard pattern of alternating sorts and transformations in these situations. Whereas a retailer or wholesaler builds up an assortment of goods so that the consumer may replenish or extend his allotment, the kind of institutions mentioned require a matching of facilities with the forecast of needs. The purveyor in such cases is assigning hours of occupancy or other units of service to individual consumers rather than goods. This statement must be qualified by the fact that there is a very wide range of demands placed on such institutions so that there is usually an assignment of heterogeneous goods or services to each customer.

Using the hospital illustration again, the complete description of a transvection would appear to require the splicing of two kinds of sequences. There is a series of alternating sorts and transformations leading up to the creation of the hospital environment and the appropriate stocks of drugs, foods, surgical appliances, etc. The individual is then assigned to the hospital by the admitting physician and usually to some specific part of the hospital. There is then a succession of sorts and transformations for the individual leading usually to discharge which is the final assignment to such subsets as the class of well people and the class which the hospital cannot help any further.

This chapter terminates with a final reminder to the reader of what it has attempted to accomplish. The author has tried to illustrate the molar approach to the development of formal theory in marketing and in a few cases has presented something resembling proof as a means of relating propositions to each other and showing that they are consistent. This author has also attempted to contribute more specifically to a theoretical treatment of transactions and transvections. In the case of transvections in particular, the effort has been to show both the extent of the difficulties and the promise of useful results in the development of formal theory.

Chapter 16

COOPERATION AND CONFLICT IN MARKETING CHANNELS*

Wroe Alderson

Cooperation is as prevalent in economic activity as competition. Internal cooperation is required if a behavior system is to act as a unit. Marketing channels cannot function without sustained cooperation in which each party knows what to expect from his opposite number. Economic processes involving marketing require cooperation and close coordination of marketing with other business functions such as production and finance. The cooperative aspect of economic behavior has been relatively neglected. Economists speak of competitive theory, of pure and perfect competition. There is no corresponding development of cooperative theory, no concepts of pure and perfect cooperation. Informally there is general recognition of the importance of team work and of the value of vertical coordination in the movement of goods and information through marketing channels. Marketing cries out for a theory of cooperation to match the theory of competition. This is an elementary attempt to sketch such a theory and then to apply it to the problem of marketing channels.

1. Monostasy and Systasy

One of the most fundamental tensions in human nature is the urge to stand alone as compared with the equally strong urge to stand together. The two coined words, drawn from Greek roots, are intended to designate these contrasting drives. *Monostasy* literally means standing alone and recalls the familiar word monopoly, meaning the only seller, or supplier, of a given product. The tendency toward monostasy represents the fundamental urge to be independent or to be different. It expresses the primitive need for separate identity and finds various outlets in marketing and economic activity. Monostasy normally leads to the exploitation of varied opportunities offered by the environment.

If every individual was motivated solely by the effort to find a separate place to stand, then competition would be a function of the density of population.

---

*Originally appeared as Chapter Ten in *Dynamic Marketing Behavior* (1965), pages 239-258.

The greater the number of people seeking a living in the environment, the more certain that multiple claims will be executed against the same or similar resources. In other words, competition in its most elemental form is a function of population pressure on scarce resources. Julian Steward describes the way of life of the Shoshone Indians in the Great Basin of the West with a single band gathering food over hundreds of square miles. Their territories were well separated so that they seldom came into colision with each other. Later on, the same area supported a much denser population with competition for limited supplies of precious metals or for fertile irrigated areas. The scale is from isolated individualism at one extreme to cutthroat competition at the other.

Systasy, the urge to stand together, would serve in some societies as an alternative explanation of human behavior. The urge to participate in common activities may be purely gregarious or it may spring from the recognition that men can accomplish tasks together which would be beyond the strength or skill of anyone individually. There are societies, including primitive tribes, which have been organized primarily on the basis of cooperation rather than competition. The basic urge toward systasy leads to the proliferation of social structure and sanctions, presumably over some period of adjustment. A cooperative society tends to be a closed society. Closure is essential if the group is in some sense to act as one. To cooperate is to work or act together.

The drive toward systasy can lead, at the extremes, to two quite different forms of organization. One is the relatively static situation with cooperative groups of moderate size acting in an unchanging environment. The other is the large tribal group or the modern nation organized on the basis of cooperation with a rapidly changing technology and an inevitable preoccupation with internal conflict. Rapid technological advance alone should suffice to produce tension and conflict in a cooperative society. Suppose there are at least two centers of power and that each controls some part of the resources that are theoretically at the disposal of the entire group. If, in addition, there is some difference of opinion as to the method of using the group's total resources, conflict can arise over differences in techniques even though it be assumed that both sides are fully committed to the stated group objectives. The scale of cooperative behavior runs from static cooperation to cooperation with active conflict.

2.   Competition and Cooperation among Primitive Peoples

The heading is the title of a book published in 1937, with Margaret Mead as editor and principal contributor. The thirteen tribes covered in this study were scattered over an immense area in North America, Africa and the South Pacific. These tribes are divided into three groups as to form of organization. Four are classified as individualistic, three as competitive, and six as cooperative. The editor, in the manner of a field anthropologist, stresses individual differences and anomalies which blur the sharp distinction suggested by the classification. Yet, there seems to be more room for gereralization in the summary of the material than was fully utilized by the editor. All of the cooperative societies are closed societies, which is not true of any of the competitive or individualistic societies. The need for a society to be closed in order to act as a unit has already been mentioned. A high sense of security for individuals is found in only the six cooperative societies and none of the others. This is scarcely surprising since the felt need for personal security is doubtless one of the main factors in the drive toward systasy which induces men to accept the limitations of a closed society.

In the three competitive societies, and in no others, there is a highly developed concept of status and emphasis upon rising in status. In all three competitive societies there is an educational system designed to prod children toward adulthood. But this type of educational system also exists in some of the societies of other types. In all three competitive societies there is an interest in property for individual ends, but this is also true for the two individualistic societies which lie closer to the competitive pattern. For five out of six cooperative societies there is faith in an ordered universe but also for the one individualistic tribe which lies closest to the cooperative pattern.

There are some attributes which bear little or no relation to the three-way classification. One of these is culturally institutionalized suicide which is found in eight of the thirteen tribes but occurs under all three forms of social organization. Another is the predominance of internal sanctions over external sanctions which occur in five of the thirteen societies and under each form of social organization. The third factor which exists under all forms of social organization is strong ego development which occurs in six of the thirteen societies, of which three are the three competitive societies. These three attributes were no doubt of some special interest to the anthropologists preparing this book, but there was no obvious correlation among the three. There were only two tribes which combined institutionalized suicide, predominance of internal sanctions, and strong ego development.

General diagrams are used in this book with the thirteen tribes laid out along the sides of a triangle, each side presenting a form of social organization. The one chart adopted here (Figure 16.1) from these materials shows the three factors for which there is a clear-cut correlation between a factor and a form of social organization.

The individualistic societies do not have any one trait in common. This may mean that living in the rugged mountains or in relative isolation in Canada and Greenland, they have greater freedom to vary in secondary attributes. Perhaps it is only after a certain density of population has been achieved that the community is forced to make the choice between regulated competition and positive

Figure 16.1.

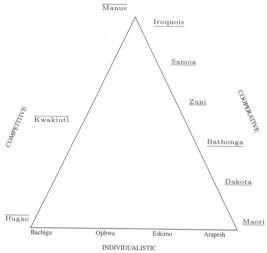

Overlined — Emphasis upon rising in status
Underlined — Closed societies and presence of high security for individuals

cooperation. Instead of a triangle the three types of society might be laid ou
on a hypothetical time scale as below.

The isolated bands which spread over the earth during the Old Stone Ag
may have lacked any explicit notions of either competition or cooperation
Implicitly cooperation doubtless existed on an instinctive basis in family groups
Externally these food gathering bands were in competition in the sense that the
drew upon the same supply of berries, roots and small animals. From time to
time accidental contact occurred, followed by an avoidance to maintain thei
isolation. If population grows, a critical density is reached, making frequen
contact inevitable. This "choice" was made so long ago that no trace of it ca
be found today. It was probably influenced by such factors as the distributio
of leadership ability within the larger population when the choice was made
An environmental factor was surely the relative importance of the scarcity o
food and the danger of attack from outside enemies. One case might call fort
individual effort to produce food and other products while the threat of attac
might lead more directly to a tight bond among the members of the group.

If the competitive route is chosen, competition presumably goes through var
ious stages from raw and primitive competition to rules governing competitio
between two or more groups. Finally, political control may be extended ove
the whole population when it becomes necessary to maintain the norms of com
petition. If the cooperative route is chosen, some other means for extendin
the scope of political systems might be visualized, such as the conquest and

pacification of an external group which was regarded as a threat. Within the cooperative society itself, conflict is always possible. Rival leadership will arise to dispute with the established leader as to the choice of means for achieving the goals of the system. If conflict develops with respect to the fundamental goals of the system, this may lead to revolutionary changes in the system itself rather than a mere change in leadership.

	Initial State	Changing State	Advanced State
Individualistic	*Isolation*	*Accidental Contact*	*Avoidance*
Competitive	*Raw Competition*	*Regulated Competition*	*Political Unity*
Cooperative	*Cooperation*	*Conflict of means*	*Conflict of goals*

There would appear to be strong tendencies toward convergence, starting either from the competitive or the cooperative form of organization. In the competitive society, as population increases, more and more constraints will be imposed on competition, including prohibitions of competing with government in the areas of operation it reserves to itself. As a cooperative society becomes larger, conflicts will appear until it is forced to recognize differences in techniques and goals in the wider population. Similarity of structure will emerge in the advanced state even though this result has been approached from opposite ends of the spectrum.

Margaret Mead's study was by definition limited to primitive tribes. If the transition to early civilization is included, as in the work of Julian Steward, the competitive and cooperative forms begin to merge in varying degrees. The nature of the environment and the rate of technological advance seem more controlling in the long run. Ancient Egypt was a closed society with nearly self-sufficient resources and a cooperative pattern imposed from the top. Mesopotamia generated an agricultural surplus but was obliged to buy many things from its neighbors and depended on competition among its enterprising capitalists, both at home and abroad.

3.   An Approach to the Theory of Economic Interaction

Competition and cooperation are alternative ways of organizing the use of resources to meet the needs of a society. Under both forms of organization there are several basic problems in the use of resources in relation to an organized flow of economic activities. The first is to make decisions on the allocation of resources as inputs into the process. This can be done either through a competitive price mechanism or by cooperative procedures. In practice, cooperative allocation means that a decision maker, acting on behalf of the group, attempts to make the allocation in a way that will further the objectives of the group.

The second basic problem arises in the allocation of the outputs of the system. Once more the sale-rationing mechanism may be the competitive prices at which individuals choose to buy or refuse to buy. The alternative cooperative method is for someone acting upon behalf of the group to use well established rationing rules, which in some sense have the consent and support of the group. Finally, there is the problem of assigning tasks to individual participants in the system. This may be accomplished through a competitive labor market or, alternatively, these decisions may be made by an individual acting on behalf of the group.

There are some theoretical arguments in favor of the competitive procedure for the entire allocation process as compared with the cooperative procedure, but these arguments make some rather drastic assumptions as to the character of the competitive market. There is an obvious elegance about permitting all these types of allocation to be made automatically by means of a single network of competitive prices, including allocation of the productive factors of capital equipment, raw materials, labor, and managerial skill, as well as the allocation of the end products among consumers. The only trouble is that the functioning of the competitive allocation process requires near perfect markets or at least workable competition at all of these separate decision points in the system. Under the situation prevailing when many primitive tribes rejected the competitive process in favor of the cooperative, these conditions with respect to pure and perfect markets obviously did not exist. In fact, many of these societies did not meet the minimum requirement of a standard medium of exchange or other organized means of stating relative values.

The cooperative society among primitive tribes could have a separate set of allocation rules at each decision point or it might attempt to relate these various decisions through some common policy or principle. The starting point in each of the cooperative societies studied by Margaret Mead seems to have been concern for the security of the individual. The individual was secure in his status in the society and secure in his expectations of rewards in relation to his status. His position may have been immutably fixed so that he was not free to improve his status, but neither was he free to starve to death so long as his tribe had goods to share with him. The individual might retain his independence in a tribe organized on a competitive basis but with all the risks inherent in environmental fluctuations.

The essential difference in the two forms of organization lay in the fact that the cooperative group first prescribed the individual's shares in the outputs of economic activity and then what it required of the individual in productive activity. In a competitive society the starting point was the inputs of effort and other productive factors into the system with share in the outputs depending to some degree on the inputs. The modern socialistic cliché is "To each according to his need, from each according to his ability." The reversal of this doctrine was put in a solder's blunt words by Captain John Smith, "He who does not work shall not eat."

An attempt will be made to state this contrast between types of systems a little more precisely in terms of definitions. The references are limited for the moment to primitive tribes in which fairly clear-cut examples of cooperative or competitive societies might be found. A cooperative society is one which recognizes a stated share in the outputs of economic activity as an inherent right according to status, and then endeavors to induce what is regarded as an appropriate contribution of effort to production. A competitive society is one in which individuals contribute their efforts to production in the expectation that their share in outputs will vary accordingly.

4.   Common Goals and Operating Structure

The cooperative form of organization is sometimes explained in terms of goals that are held in common by all members of the society. But even in a cooperative society there are minimum individual goals, such as the basic elements of subsistence. In fact, in an ultimate sense, only individuals have goals and not the social organization as such. A goal universally held would be a goal desired by all individual participants and not a super goal pertaining to the organization. There are some needs that can generally be attributed to all individuals in the group. Among these is defense against attack from external and hostile forces. The goal of defense could be a universal goal, particularly if the enemy group was hostile to all bearers of the particular culture as such and seemed determined to annihilate it or drive it out of its familiar habitat. The goal of protecting the group then becomes fully merged with the individual need for self-preservation.

The cooperative form of organization may serve to shift emphasis away from goals of more limited appeal to those which are universally held. It seems to be an easy transition in primitive society from the goal of defense to that of military success for an aggressive society and the satisfaction of belonging to a tribe or nation which is expanding its dominion over others. To the extent that cooperative societies guarantee subsistence in accordance with status, the individual would naturally be less preoccupied with this subject. By the same token, he might be more concerned with the goals which were universally held and which were the centre of attention for his fellows as well as for himself.

With less emphasis on goods, there is likely to be a greater emphasis on prestige and the means for attaining it in a cooperative society. Individuals work hard for the so-called social goals with no visible reward but with an obvious craving for recognition and enhanced standing within the group. Social standing is an important consideration in other societies, too, but its relative importance among possible rewards would appear to be greater in the cooperative society. There is the strange case of rivalry for prestige among highly competitive Kwakiutl which seems almost like a travesty on some aspects of our capitalistic society. In this case the concept of prestige is one in which property becomes a weapon for forcing a rival to admit one's own superiority. It is very different from the notion of earning public esteem through devotion to a shared goal.

The individual seeks a place in the operating structure of a cooperative society. In some cases he has so little room for mobility that he might be said to accept an assigned place rather than seeking it. In some primitive societies social position is hereditary but requirements are laid on the individual to measure up to his status. In other cooperative societies there is considerable room for specialization and for training individuals for these specialized roles. The individual finds security within the operating structure of the cooperative society, fitting into his position in somewhat the same way that an individual or group might fit into an ecological niche in the environment. In a cooperative society the opportunity for the individual is socially conditioned and there is an emphasis on social rewards. In a competitive society the individual's place is rooted more directly in his command of material resources and the emphasis is on material rewards or on social gains that are obtained through the use of material rewards.

5. Function and Structure in Social Organization

The competitive society in the primitive world could function more directly and more flexibily in the exploitation of the environment. The cooperative society tended to have a more elaborate structure, providing a greater degree of control over the functioning of the system. The cooperative society in effect imposed a formal set of values on the functioning system in order that it might function to achieve a set of socially approved ends. The cooperative society has a stronger orientation toward assuring the survival of the individual and of the culture itself through the individual.

The values recognized by the cooperative society could include an explicit or implicit recognition of constraints imposed on individual behavior by the environment. A general doctrine of conservation would fit into this value structure as would more specific limitations on the exploitation of the environment. It is possibly because of this intervening structure of values that cooperative societies are sometimes said to have something less than an objective view of the environment in which they operate. Nevertheless, adjustment to short-run environmental fluctuations such as in crop yields or the abundance of game might be eased by cooperative principles of sharing.

A cooperative society might pose some obstacles to the adoption of new technologies. The structure of such a society actually embodies a plan of operation in which the parts have been carefully adjusted to each other. Change affecting any one sector might be resisted because of the reaction of other sectors. Even though the new technology could lead to a greater surplus for the whole system, the control group might not be convinced of this conclusion. This group might exercise control subject only to the maintenance intact of the existing operating structure. Any proposed revision in a part of the system would then raise the issue of revision of the whole system. The barrier to fundamental change might approach the absolute.

It has been pointed out in an earlier section that society seems to be confronted by a choice as to form of organization at some point as it emerges from an isolated and relatively unorganized state. It may only behave as if a choice were being made because the full adjustment to the competitive model or the cooperative model may extend over years or even centuries. There is certainly no desire here to reinstate the social contract myth, which reasoned as if the social group had held a plenary session to decide how it would be governed. It is more likely that there were some environmental and social factors which tipped the scales toward one pattern or another. Among the factors which may have favored the cooperative solution are an environment which is nearly self-sufficient at the existing level of demand, a need for defense against outside enemies, as when a conquering race imposes its controls on a native population, a rich and varied culture, and strong and charismatic leadership during the period of transition from a diffuse and individualistic pattern to a cooperative society.

6.   Convergence and Conflict in the Modern State

The hypothesis was previously advanced that whether a society adopts the competitive or the cooperative solution at the primitive stage, there will be a steady convergence toward a mixed or balanced form of organization as the society develops into the stage of full civilization. If a primitive society elects the cooperative pattern, it will suffer some loss of efficiency in those areas which could best be treated through competitive interaction. If a primitive society elects the competitive pattern, it will be less effective in those areas of social value which depend on integration and coordination. Starting from a clearly defined pattern of either type, the growing complexity of emerging civilization will force the society to make some accommodations in the direction of the opposite type. It would be impossible to imagine a large modern nation which could suppress either competitive patterns or cooperative patterns over any considerable period of time. The two approaches to the allocation of resources and management of social and economic processes are bound to exist side by side.

The American economy is still a competitive economy as a matter of emphasis, just as the theoreticians of the Soviet Union stress the cooperative aspects of their society. The differences in ideology, however, are more marked than the basic preferences for competition or cooperation as such. There appears to be a growing and largely unacknowledged dependence on the competitive price mechanism in the Soviet Union. Currently there is active discussion in Russia concerning the value of profit incentives and some deliberate experiments have produced remarkably favorable results. There are many areas in our own economy in which we rely primarily on cooperative patterns rather than competitive patterns of activity.

The respective ideologies of capitalism and communism still stress independence, on the one hand, and security, on the other hand, as the more basic human values. So far as the Soviet system is concerned, the promise of security might continue to be an illusion for some time in a country which has endured so many bloody upheavals and purges. On our own side, we may begin to wonder as the frontier vanishes just how real independence can be. The comments of Gunnar Myrdal on structural unemployment in the United States raise some uncomfortable doubts about the nature of economic freedom. We may have already moderated the concepts of social Darwinism as advocated by William Graham Sumner to the point where the individual is no longer free to starve. The individual may still be free to stagnate or to suffer spiritual deterioration through loss of his identity.

This sketch for a theory of economic interaction may appear to have ranged far beyond the boundaries of marketing. The remainder of this chapter will return to a focus on marketing and closely related aspects of the American economy. Further comments will be made about the nature of cooperation as it is found in the marketing setting. The place of conflict will also be considered as it becomes involved in marketing processes and institutions. It has already been suggested that conflict is an inevitable part of continuing adjustment particularly for activities which are organized on a cooperative basis. In the American economy one place where cooperation plays a key role is in the marketing channel.

7.   The Role of the Intermediary

If channels are already established and strictly maintained, agencies at successive levels must of necessity cooperate. The wholesaler sells to the retailer because he has no other way of reaching the consumer. The retailer buys from the wholesaler because he has no other source of goods which he can resell to consumers. When a manufacturer like Eli Lilly and Co. adopts a policy of selling only to wholesale druggists, it is equivalent to a decision that Lilly will not try to reach the consumer except through the combined action of the wholesaler and the retailer.

In the process of cooperating, the wholesaler and retailer agree on many things. First, there is the implicit agreement to maintain a continuous trading relationship. The wholesaler also agrees that his salesmen will call at specified times, that merchandise will be delivered in securely packed cartons and at times when it is convenient for the retailer to receive it, that spoiled or damaged goods can be returned, and that merchandise is certified to be of the type and quantity ordered. The retailer agrees to check the merchandise promptly and, in the case of merchandise involving special deals, to carry out promotional plans specified by the wholesaler.

Quite a different issue is how the wholesaler came into being in the first place. What was there about the relationships between the manufacturer and the retailer which called a wholesaler into being? Was their urgency to cooperate with a wholesaler and through him with others so great as to create an economic niche which only a wholesaler could fill? The answer is in the affirmative and is detailed at some length in an article by this author entitled "The Development of Marketing Channels."

That article called attention to some simple but fundamental mathematical relations contrasting the state of affairs with and without an intermediary. Suppose that 100 manufacturers and 100 retailers have been trading with each other in a given market. The number of trading relationships which must be maintained is the product of the two numbers, or 10,000. Now suppose that an intermediary is introduced into the channel and that all manufacturers and all retailers trade through the intermediary. The number of trading relationships which must be maintained is the sum of the two numbers, or 200. The reduction in the number of trading relations is in the order of 50 to 1 and many of the costs of doing business would be reduced accordingly.

Offsetting the costs which have been reduced, it must be observed that some new costs have been introduced into the channel, including the costs of maintaining a wholesale inventory and the sorting cost associated with receiving goods into stock from the manufacturer and preparing goods for shipment to consumers.

Some analysts have raised the question of the possibility of infinite regress with respect to the length of a channel. If one intermediary is a good thing, why not another and another ad infinitum? The problem of infinite regress does not occur because of the offsetting costs of adding an intermediary which would presently be greater than any possible saving. Assume, for example, that the wholesale druggist delivered to half a dozen sub-wholesalers strategically located in his territory and these sub-wholesalers in turn delivered to the retail druggist. The added costs would be those of six warehouses with their warehousemen and deliverymen. The cost of an extra loading and unloading could only be justified if it represented a saving as compared with delivery direct from the main warehouse in the first instance. In fact, some element of progressive

differentiation would be required, such as a difference in demand among variou
subterritories or a difference in the type of transportation required to cover th
shipments to a sub-wholesaler as compared with his shipments to the retailer.

In actual situations it turns out that a channel is longer than need be for par
of the volume moving through the channel. Some retailers are large enougl
so that they receive merchandise in carload or truckload shipments and henc
are eligible to buy directly from the producer. Some local producers are smal
enough that they can dispose of their entire output to a few retailers in thei
immediate community and do not require the comprehensive coverage mad
available by the wholesaler. The wholesaler faces the constant threat of com
petition from his customers and his suppliers. His only safety is in efficien
cooperation with those who cannot serve themselves so well.

8.   The Behavior System and the Theory of Cooperation

To consider more specific application to marketing of our rudimentary theor
of economic interaction, we return to the concept of an organized behavio
system. The notion of cooperation is implicit in the concept of a behavio
system. Its internal structure is designed to facilitate cooperation. The critica
question is where to set the boundaries of the behavior system. Wherever thes
limits are set there is by definition a cooperative interaction, whether weal
or strong, taking place within these limits. This means that there is a contro
group within the system and that the control group projects a plan of operatio
and attempts to induce participation on its own terms. As discussed in earlie
chapters, this plan of operation may exert its full influence only within th
domain of a single company or its marketing organization. If the wholesaler
and retailers serving the company normally adhere to this plan, then they ar
properly included in the behavior system making up a marketing channel. They
are part of the system if it can be predicted that their behavior will tend t
perpetuate the system or serve the more detailed operating goals of the system

These considerations follow directly from the definition of a behavior system
It is a group of people held together by the expectation of some surplus in exces
of what they could obtain by working alone and who are concerned to preserv
the system so long as it supports these expectations. The expectation of a
surplus could pertain to a marketing channel no less than to the corporation
itself. This may be equivalent to saying that all internal allocation follows the
cooperative pattern and that the boundaries of what is considered internal can
be defined variously for different problems. So long as there is an attempt t
make allocations conform to a single yardstick, such as expected profits, the
allocator may work out his problem in terms of what might be called pseudo
competition. For example, he might set transfer prices among units within his
company, based on prices determined competitively in the open market.

The cooperative pattern permits the allocator to pass beyond the single crite-rion and to entertain multiple considerations in determining allocations either of finished goods or of inputs into the productive process. A plant organized on a cooperative basis might issue an extra ration of milk to under-nourished workers or their children. It might make appeals to the ablest workers, based on prestige rather than money, to get them to put forth their best efforts. In-centive programs for salesmen, distributors and dealers often rely heavily on non-monetary appeals. There are always at least three criteria for allocation within a cooperative framework which do not always lead to the same con-clusion. These are net profits, the growth rate, and the state of health of the organization or its capacity for survival. There are various ways of combining these factors either on the basis of intuitive judgment or seeking an optimal value under one criterion while viewing the others as limiting constraints.

When there are two or three separate agencies in a marketing channel, it may be assumed that there is usually a shared goal of making retail sales as large as possible. The larger the pot, the larger the share would tend to be for each. The several agencies in the channel observe their own constraints as to what they are willing to do to maximize retail sales. The manufacturer is not willing to spend advertising dollars to the point where he would incur a net loss in order to maximize the sales of the retailer. So far as prices are concerned, however, the manufacturer would generally favor retail prices which were set as if they were designed to maximize sales and, incidentally, to minimize sales resistance which might otherwise have to be overcome by increased advertising.

9. The Seeds of Conflict

Assume that each agency in the channel was acting in such a way as to maximize sales (subject to the appropriate constraints) and thus provide the largest total amount for sharing by all who contributed to the supply. This would not necessarily lead to harmony, since there might be unresolved issues as to the size of the shares. Ideally one might wish to match shares at each level with contribution to the end result. The difficulty, of course, is to find any defensible way of measuring separate contributions. Attempts have been made in marketing to break the total effort down into sub-tasks and to compensate the wholesaler or retailer for performing each of these tasks on the basis of its presumed value for the manufacturer. Even if the one agency in the channel serving as channel captain had perfect knowledge of the values to be assigned to each marketing task, and made his allocation accordingly, there would always be some for whom the basis of allocation was unacceptable.

Tensions build to a peak in times of change. Stress is created during the emergence of new forms of distribution or the reshuffling of functions within the channel. Volume is diverted into new channels, leaving less for traditional channels. One agency may take over a sub-task once performed by another absorbing this portion of the total revenue into its own share. Sometimes the element of conflict is so pronounced that an effective channel can scarcely be said to exist. It is obviously difficult for two parties to cooperate effectively in the execution of a plan and be engaged simultaneously in a bitter fight over the division of revenue. It might be hoped that each agency would perform its task effectively and then bargain over the amount it should be paid for its services. Too often a distribution service is withheld as a means of forcing a concession or performed in only a perfunctory fashion even after the concession is granted. The question might well be raised as to whether such a channel constitutes a behavior system. Nevertheless, the channel is certainly a system in the sense of persistent interaction. Even when this interaction is primarily in the form of conflict, hope continues that it will be resolved satisfactorily and that effective cooperative action will be resumed. So long as all parties feel that they have a stake in the survival of the channel, it may be regarded as a behavior system.

The channel ceases to be a usable behavior system when one or more participating agencies becomes disaffected. To withdraw from the conflict may mean that it has been concluded that the issues are no longer worth fighting for so that even the conflict situation might be healthier. The disaffected agency may have no other recourse for the time being but to continue to use the channel. If this agency has vigor and competence it may redouble its efforts to find a shorter road to market or to identify partners it would rather work with in performing the marketing function. A channel is ripe for drastic change when major participants decide that it is no longer effective.

10.   External Conflict versus Competition

There is a superficial resemblance between external conflict and competition but the distinction needs to be sharply drawn. Firms which recognize each other as competitors have achieved a working accommodation. They are engaged in trying to provide better products or to supply them more cheaply in the effort to take business away from each other. Within the recognized group there is rivalry but not hostility. There are other firms which stand beyond the pale, which do not compete in customary fashion and are regarded as inimical to the interests of the in-group. A trade or industry can be led to present a solid front of opposition to such outsiders in much the same way that a closed tribal society resists invasion by an alien tribe. The threatened will often use all available means, including political pressure and legislation, to curb or eliminate the new type of enterprise. External conflict resembles war more than it does competition regulated by law and business custom.

At the national level intolerance and suspicion of contrasting forms of organization reaches the extreme. The question of whether coexistence is possible s raised repeatedly and seriously by both capitalists and Communists. On the Communist side some have preached the doctrine of world revolution, holding that it is impossible to maintain a Communist state indefinitely, alone in a hostile world. On the capitalist side there are some who fear a perennial threat of subversion and who vacillate between the remedies of preventive war and rigid isolationism. There has been an earnest effort to promote interchange and to develop better understanding. Yet, many people on both sides have such fixed notions about the other that the attempt to improve communications sometimes seems to result chiefly in the exchange of ideological insults.

External conflict tends to be a conflict over values. Pushed to the extreme, it calls for the annihilation of those that hold other values. Internal conflict is more likely to be limited to a conflict over means. So long as a behavior system holds together at all, there is some presumption of shared goals. If we assume that in a competitive society each enterprise is simply trying to make a profit, then the only problem inside a behavior system is to maximize total returns and then decide how these returns are to be distributed. Goals are actually not so clear cut, however, and they become increasingly more complex with every advance in technology, with the corresponding increase in power over the environment and the consequent need for a greater sense of direction and control in exercising it. In periods of rapid change, business executives as well as other people become more concerned or even confused about their underlying objectives. Conflict over means can pass over into the more fundamental tension of conflict over ends. West Churchman has suggested that progress does not lie in the elimination of conflict but in focusing conflict on more precisely formulated and relevant issues.

11.   Rival Attempts to Organize the Market

Rivalry in organizing the market is a fundamental force in market dynamics. This drive is expressed in several ways, starting with the effort to induce adherence to a plan which has already been discussed. Assume that a manufacturing industry is highly competitive but must sell its consumer goods line through wholesalers and retailers. In a very real sense the critical point in competition is at the retail level. The effectiveness of each manufacturer in competition will depend not only on his own efficiency but on his ability to induce wholesalers and retailers to cooperate with him. Thus, Goodyear, together with its retailers and distributors, constitutes a team which competes with a corresponding team from Firestone in selling tires to consumers. So long as these companies are competing, tire by tire, for the consumers' dollar, it is difficult to conceive of them colluding with each other or with other tire companies in the sale of their products. In other words, it would be inconsistent for each tire company to serve as channel captain in the vertical direction and simultaneously collude in a horizontal direction. William Fellner in his discussion in *Competition Amon* *the Few* suggested that large firms must behave as if there was implicit collusio among them, but it is difficult to square this comment with cooperation in th vertical dimension.

In any case, the dynamic effect on the market would be substantial if Fireston were not able to stand up to Gooodyear in the process of inducing cooperatio from others in the channel. If one competitor after another should fail to measur up, a single firm might achieve dominance very rapidly. Competitors might b helpless to retaliate if they have been unable to maintain effective channe cooperation. It might be asserted that the dominant company had achieve unreasonable market power, according to the tests proposed by Carl Kayser Other economists feel that it is difficult to apply such tests in blanket fashio since what is really involved is relative market power. Power is related t capacity, including the capacity to induce channel cooperation. It might b unwise to deny the second firm in a field the chance to attain the capacit required to offset the power of the leader even though that capacity was attaine or strengthened through merger.

A second objective in attempts to organize the market is to be able to bu and sell goods through procedures convenient to one's self. Suppliers typicall set their own terms of sale, including cash discounts, datings, etc. There ma be quite a variety of terms of sale in an industrial field and hence for any on customer buying from these suppliers. Now suppose that some one custome was so important that he could require all suppliers to standardize on the base h preferred and to sell to him in a uniform way. If he can make this requiremen stick, it will mean substantial savings to him in processing paper work an reducing the routine complexities of his business. By the same token, th success of the dominant company in enforcing standardization on his bas would constitute a competitive handicap for others who where not able to d so. At this level the effort of this company in organizing the market results i organizing the market around the company or to its special advantage.

A still more profound expression of the drive to organize the market take as its goal the substitution of a new set of marketing processes and institution for what now exists. Some dramatic examples can be found in aspects of th food industry, such as the remarkable changes which have occurred in livestoc marketing. An outstanding case is the development in the broiler industry The farmer who once raised the chickens has stepped up his output but n longer owns them nor does he own the feed he provides for them. He runs chicken boarding house and is paid so much a week or so much per chicken fo providing their quarters and serving their meals. The hatcheries in the prim broiler country of the Delmarva Peninsula are operated as separate enterprise and in fact, bring their eggs in from New England. The chickens are slaughtere in packing houses that are far more modern than most of those engaged in mea packing and were engineered for maximum efficiency at a later time. The market moves on fractions of a cent in the sale of broilers to the supermarkets.

What is it that makes all of this system run? The man behind the scenes, unmentioned until now, is the manufacturer of mixed feeds. It is he who has organized the whole operation, providing finance or other support needed. The feeds manufacturer regards the production of broilers as a further stage in the processing of feed. He sells to poultry growers whose operations run in excess of half a million dollars of broilers a year. The eastern shore is not only close to the major markets, but it enjoys yields of corn, barley and soy beans. The crowning touch in this organization of the market for mixed feeds is that the eastern shore does not feed its own soy beans to its chickens. It has established a premium market for its soy beans in Europe. So the feed manufacturers supplying the Peninsula depend largely on soy beans shipped in from the Middle West.

The drive to organize the market has far greater dynamic effect than the horizontal competition taking place at any one level. The tension between centers of power is particularly great where there are both strong retailers in the channel and strong marketing organizations representing manufacturers. The manufacturer has product innovation on his side while large retailers engage in enterprise differentiation to supply consumers with new patterns of service. Consumer sovereignty is the controlling force in the long run. Whatever the interaction between large retailers and large producers, it must end eventually in giving the consumer more for less. The ultimate need in vertical cooperation is to cooperate with the consumer. As consumers become more knowing, the whole economy tends toward becoming an integrated consumer cooperative. The competition which really counts and is often expressed in sweeping and dynamic changes is competition for the privilege of cooperating with the consumer.

12.   Summary of the Theory of Market Interaction

The last three chapters have dealt with the way in which organized behavior systems interact in the market. Chapter 8 discussed the search for differential advantage with primary emphasis on the producer. Abbott's concept of complete competition was introduced, which takes account of both product competition and price competition. That thrust toward heterogeneity is the inevitable and dynamic result of competition between problem solvers who find differential advantage in one product improvement after another.

To understand competition among retailers requires appeal to the concept of enterprise differentiation. By ready extension this concept becomes the concept of enterprise assignment, which is a substantial qualification of the economic principal of resource allocation. The retailer, and multi-product firms generally, are still searching for differential advantages but not in the direction of differentiating individual products.

The final level of generality is attained in looking at economic interaction in the vertical dimension in marketing channels. It is no longer possible to explain the marketing process by reference to the competitive aspects of competition alone, since channels cannot perform their function except through coopera tion. The final area in which a firm can search for differential advantage is in competition to organize the market. A firm can differentiate its product to adjust to a segmented market, it can differentiate itself to facilitate assignmen to an operating niche, or it can reorganize the marketing structure of which i is a part to facilitate its own functioning in that structure.

III

WROE ALDERSON — WRITINGS ON MANAGE-MENT PRACTICE AND ETHICAL BEHAVIOR

Chapter 17

INTRODUCTION TO PART III: WROE ALDERSON — WRITINGS ON MANAGEMENT PRACTICE AND ETHICAL BEHAVIOR

Stanley J. Shapiro

Wroe Alderson wrote for managers. He often did this indirectly in the sense that he believed nothing was more managerially relevant than sound marketing theory. However, both as a long time consultant and concerned citizen, he also authored a considerable volume of more applied material, directed toward already practicing managers and appearing in publications such managers might be expected to read. The selections reproduced below provide a feel for Aldersonian thinking both as regards best management practice and, as well, acceptable ethical behavior.

The first selection in this section was written by Dr. Robert Lusch some 15 years after Alderson's death. It highlights the nature and scope of *Cost and Profit Outlook*, the newsletter published by Alderson and Sessions. That publication over time came to be widely read both by marketing practitioners and by academics. In most respects, the Lusch selection speaks for itself. However, the American Marketing Association subsequently decided not to proceed with publishing the complete set of *Cost and Profit Outlooks* unless it received a publishing subvention. That decision effectively killed the project. Hopefully, it will prove possible in this new era of web sites and Internet access to make complete sets — both of *Cost and Profit Outlook* and *Growth and Profit Planner*, a publication of Behavior Systems, the consulting firm Alderson established while at Wharton — generally available.

The Lusch article focuses attention on the *Cost and Profit Outlook* material that he believed had the greatest theoretical relevance. He did this because he felt, as early as 1980, that the material Alderson wrote describing "best practice" marketing management techniques for the 1950s was already dated and thus of only limited interest. In many respects, this was true when Dr. Lusch wrote and even truer today. However, the editors of this publication have other objectives in mind. Since we wished to demonstrate both the range and depth of Aldersonian thought, we decided this volume very definitely should contain examples of the "best practices" literature he directed toward the marketing managers of his day. Three such selections have been chosen with that objective in mind.

The first such article is one on marketing planning that appeared in a 1958 issue of *Industrial Marketing* magazine. The second, appearing in *Advertising Age* and written at about the same time (1957), described alternate psychological underpinnings to contemporary advertising and made a case for assuming consumer rationality. Our third selection, one that discussed the expected contribution of the then newly emerging field of Operations Research to marketing management, appeared in *Advanced Management* in 1955. However, we have chosen to include in this volume not this exact article but rather a marginally changed version that Alderson incorporated into *Marketing Behavior and Executive Action*.

In contemporary academic marketing, almost all professors focus on either the managerial, the behavioral or the quantitative dimensions of our discipline. Including these excerpts was an editorial approach we have chosen to demonstrate that Alderson in the middle to late 1950s was making contributions to all three of these dimensions. Within the managerial domain, the full range and final statement of Aldersonian thought as regards the nature and practice of marketing management is to be found in Parts I and III of *Planning and Problem Solving in Marketing*. But what would be the best way to provide readers with a full appreciation of that publication? We decided this should be done by publishing a review of the volume by Dr. Arnold Amstutz which appeared in a 1968 issue of the *Journal of Marketing Research*. This review provides a far better feel for the book than would the selection of a few short excerpts.

The last two articles appearing below highlight Alderson's concerns with marketing ethics. The first is taken from a report Alderson prepared as Chair of an AMA Task Force on Marketing Ethics. The final selection is the text of a speech that Alderson made in 1964 to students at the Christian Association of the University of Pennsylvania. This material was subsequently published in the August 1964 issue of *Growth and Profit Planner*. Wroe Alderson was for many years a practicing Quaker and this affiliation almost certainly influenced his views as to what would constitute ethical business behavior.

Other editorial teams might well have chosen a different mix of readings for this section of the publication. However, each such group would likely be approaching the selection task from its own, somewhat unique, perspective. And even if they weren't the case, space limitations would still require that difficult editorial choices be made. Because space was limited, we "shortlisted" but finally, decided not to include Alderson's Introduction to Frank, Kuehn and Massey's *Quantitative Techniques in Marketing Analysis*. This remains, however, a useful contribution in which Alderson discussed both the past history and likely future, of quantitative analysis in marketing. Also reluctantly excluded was Alderson's mid-1950s predictions as to the future of retailing. These are to be found in an article that appeared in a 1955 issue of *Nation's Business*.

More complete bibliographical information on these "almost" selections and a great many other references that should be of value to those interested in other dimensions of Aldersonian thought are to be found in the bibliography of writings by and about Wroe Alderson that appears at the end of this volume. Much of this material is already accessible to the persistent researcher. Hopefully, the two newsletters containing so much valuable information and providing so many insights into Alderson's thinking will also soon be accessible.

Chapter 18

ALDERSON, SESSIONS AND THE 1950S MANAGER*

Robert F. Lusch
University of Wisconsin, Madison

Abstract

An analysis of the newsletter, *Cost and Profit Outlook* that was published by Alderson & Sessions, Incorporated during the 1950s provides insights into how Wroe Alderson and Robert Sessions viewed the 1950s manager. Also it offers a perspective for how contemporary marketing academicians might view or interact with the 1980s manager.

1. Introduction

In 1944 a management consulting firm in Philadelphia, Pennsylvania was established. By 1955, after experiencing explosive growth this management consulting firm had attained national and in some respects international stature. The firm had offices in Philadelphia and Mexico City. It enlisted the expertise on both a part time and full time basis of leading professors across the United States for guidance on research projects of both a basic and applied nature. Some of the more well known associates of the firm were: Leo Aspinwall, William J. Baumol, William Bennett, C. West Churchman, C. Joseph Clawson, Michael Halbert, Harvey W. Huegy and Wendell Smith.

This management consulting firm was formed by Wroe Alderson and was initially called Wroe Alderson and Company. In 1945, when Robert E. Sessions joined the firm, the name was changed to Alderson & Sessions, Incorporated. In 1949 the corporation was liquidated and a partnership, Alderson and Sessions was formed. The partnership was wholly owned by Wroe Alderson and Robert E. Sessions. When Sessions left in 1958 to become executive vice president of Mead Johnson and Company the name was changed again, this time, to

---
*Originally published in Charles Lamb and Patrick Dunne eds. *Theoretical Developments in Marketing*, pages 4-6, American Marketing Association, Chicago.

Alderson Associates, Inc. In the early 1960s the company was sold to The Diebold Group.

Alderson & Sessions, Incorporated began publishing a newsletter in 1947 called *Cost and Profit Outlook*. This newsletter, typically 4-6 pages in length and usually published monthly, was circulated among existing clients, prospective clients and a select group in the academic community. Predictably the specific content of these newsletters is dated. Nonetheless the editorial content of the newsletters is suggestive of how Alderson & Sessions viewed the 1950s manager.

2.   Editorial Content

The articles that appeared in *Cost and Profit Outlook* can be categorized into three basic types: (1) those with immediate managerial implications; (2) those focusing on economic trends and developments; and (3) those dealing with the role of research, theory and science in business administration. Some examples of those articles with immediate managerial concern are: (a) "Marketing Audit for Industrial Advertisers" (November 1947); (b) "Getting the Most for Your Research Dollars:" (May-June 1949); (c) "Effective Use of Marketing Channels" (May 1952); (d) "Resolving Conflicts in Sales Policy" (February 1955); (e) "Management Support for Marketing Planning" (December 1957). A sampling of titles focusing on economic trends and developments are: (a) "Advertising and the Business Cycle: Newspapers vs. Magazines" (July 1947); (b) "The Changing Structure of the American Economy" (July 1950); (c) "The Outlook for the Expanding Economy" (February 1953); (d) "Construction's Contribution to the U. S. Economy" (September 1955); (e) "A Plan for the Middle East" (February 1957). Finally let's look at a few titles that explored the role of research, theory and science in business administration and typically in marketing. (a) "Marketing Efficiency and the Principle of Postponement" (September 1950); (b) "Experimental Methods in Motivation Research" (March 1954); (c) "The Development and Use of Models in Operations Research" (April 1955); (d) "Parallel Systems of Promotion and Distribution" (October 1956); (e) "Introducing Behavior Research" (January 1958).

The preceding sampling of titles should provide a flavor of the editorial content of the newsletter. Fortunately the American Marketing Association has agreed to republish the newsletter, along with other material in book form under the title *Cost and Profit Outlook: An Historical Compendium of Changing Marketing Perspectives* with Reavis Cox, Lyndon E. Dawson, Jr., and Hugh G. Wales as co-authors. This book should be released in early 1980 and will allow anyone interested in the newsletter to have easy access to them. It is also interesting to note that a considerable amount of the material in Alderson's

ast book (Alderson, 1965) — *Dynamic Marketing Behavior* — had appeared
earlier in *Cost and Profit Outlook*.

3. The A & S Viewpoint

The perspective of Alderson & Sessions that will be relayed is based upon
a careful reading of the articles published in *Cost and Profit Outlook* in category three above — those articles dealing with research, theory and science in
business. The focus is on this select group of articles for two major reasons.
First, this is a theory conference and therefore there is no rationale for depart-
ing from our reason for gathering. Second, most of the content of the articles
in categories one and two (those with immediate managerial implications and
those focusing on economic trends) are dated in terms of usefulness. Whereas
the basic message in the research, theory and science articles is still relevant
today.

A View of Theory

The philosophy that Alderson & Sessions expressed on research, theory and
science in their newsletter was being directly communicated to managers. The
newsletter was generally not circulated to, nor were the articles written for,
professors of business. As one might expect therefore not all business readers liked what they read, just as today not all business readers of the *Journal
of Marketing* like what they read. By discussing and exploring new issues in
research, theory and science Alderson & Sessions were not trying to maximize their consulting revenues. The author believes that by addressing these
issues Alderson & Sessions incurred considerable downside risk. For example
many managers in 1949 probably did not care to read about the principle of
postponement and/or the sorting process in marketing. Nonetheless the article,
"Marketing Efficiency and the Principle of Postponement" was published in
Cost and Profit Outlook in September 1950. Nor was it likely that the 1950s
manager wanted to read about operations research in 1950, motivation research
in 1953, mathematical programming in 1955, or Aspinwall's "Parallel Systems
of Promotion and Distribution" in 1956; and these are only a few representative
examples.

In short, Alderson & Sessions both explicitly and implicitly told the 1950s
manager, regardless of whether he liked it or not, that good theory and practice
are inseparable. Some didn't like it! In an issue of the newsletter (1954)
Alderson & Sessions state

> Reading the *Cost and Profit Outlook* has led some firms to retain our services,
> but it has doubtless discouraged others from doing so. Either way it may have
> served the purpose of matching our consulting firm with those clients who are
> interested in *our type of thinking*. [emphasis added].

As one might expect, therefore, Alderson & Sessions received a fair amount of editorial advice. In the same issue of the newsletter (1954) they comment on this advice: "The gist of all the editorial advice received is to make the material easier to read without watering down the technical content."

Finally in the March-April 1958 issue of the newsletter, Alderson & Sessions heed some of the editorial advice they had received over the years by changing the basic tone of the newsletter to make it more readable. In the May-June issue (1958) they reflect on their experiment.

> The character and format of the *Cost and Profit Outlook* has changed but little over the years except for the last issue and this one. Typically an issue has consisted of four solidly printed pages with two or three articles, serious in tone and analytical in approach. Many readers have expressed approval while others have suggested that the solid text be broken up with shorter items, sacrificing something in content for easier readability. The last issue was an experiment in accordance with these suggestions. We tried to add a dash of humor and even included a limerick of our own composition. As a research project this experiment was a failure. A number of spontaneous comments were received but they were about evenly divided among favorable and unfavorable comments.

It should be pointed out that Alderson & Sessions used the *Cost and Profit Outlook* as a vehicle to obtain invitations to bid on research projects. It would seem therefore that they believed that there were in the 1950s a sufficient number of managers that were searching for a new way to view marketing, that they would be receptive to new theories. The situation in the 1980s or even in the year 2000 will be no different and thus marketing academicians should not necessarily avoid communicating theory to the business executive.

A View On Consulting

In general Alderson & Sessions believed that research, theory and science played an important role in management and marketing consulting. An examination of some of their specific views however will enable us to better understand how they viewed this relationship.

Alderson & Sessions did not view marketing science and marketing consulting as the same thing. In an issue of the newsletter (1953) they express their view on the distinction between a market analyst (consultant) and a scientist.

> While the market analyst may employ scientific research techniques his immediate aim is not that of knowledge for its own sake, which is generally identified with science. The marketer is concerned with a problem of action which he tries to solve through organized knowledge. The marketing consultant shares the scientist's interest in facts but he approaches them from quite a different perspective. The scientist gathers facts to test hypotheses which are the consequences of a theory. His aim is to confirm or revise his theory. The market analyst gathers facts to test assumptions which are the necessary antecedents of a working plan. His aim is to assist in bringing about more effective action.

The preceding suggests that Alderson & Sessions felt that the marketing consultant could not be a scientist. However, they made it clear to the executive that marketing analysts can only solve problems if they have theory (Alderson & Sessions, 1951).

> Pressures exerted by the practical business executives are forcing the marketing analyst to become a better theorist. The more penetrating and exacting the questions asked by the businessman the greater the need for a theoretical background which will guide the researcher in collecting the right facts and subjecting them to the most fruitful forms of analysis.... The market analyst is turning to the marketing faculties of the universities and expecting something more from them than a purely descriptive and technical treatment of marketing. The pressure of business upon the market analyst for a judicious perspective in approaching problems is being translated into a pressure on the marketing teachers for the development of marketing theory.

Since the marketing consultant needed theory to perform his job Alderson & Sessions frequently urged executives to financially support or otherwise help develop basic science in marketing. At first Alderson was rather indirect in his view on this. In the October 1947 issue of *Cost and Profit Outlook* an excerpt of Alderson's reply to the official notification of being elected president of the American Marketing Association states that: "Marketing itself has a basic structure suggesting the possibility of setting up a standard framework for the analysis of any problem." Two years later in an issue of the newsletter Alderson & Sessions are much more direct and to the point. In the following quotes from an issue of the newsletter (Alderson & Sessions, 1949a, Alderson & Sessions, 1949b) their view on the development of basic research is expressed.

> It is high time that people in marketing — engaged as we are in an applied science — should develop a fundamental science as the basis for our profession... Much has been learned in the last forty years about the orderly collection and analysis of marketing information. The trouble is that marketing research has largely been conducted within the narrow perspective dictated by the urgency of immediate problems... If the marketing profession is genuinely interested in scientific foundations for its activities, it will have to play a major role in creating the underlying science.

It is also in this issue of the newsletter that Alderson & Sessions make an explicit appeal to companies to support basic research. In fact they set an example by announcing their commitment to funding basic research.

> The firm of Alderson & Sessions has launched a program of basic research dealing with the nature of consumer demand as expressed through market behavior. This program is being conducted at our expense rather than at the expense of our clients. It is directed toward the advancement of the science of marketing. It may be a long time before we obtain any significant findings in this program of exploratory research. However, as developments occur in this program the highlights will be reported in the *Cost and Profit Outlook*.

In summary, Alderson & Sessions held the view that marketing consultants and marketing scientists pursued different endeavors. But since the consultant needed theory to do his or her job it was in part the role of the consultant to foster the development of theory if they expected or wanted the discipline of marketing to advance.

A View On Theory And Practice

Often it has been suggested that the various publication vehicles published by the American Marketing Association must meet the needs of the theory builders, theory testers and the practitioners. Perhaps the most discussion on this subject has focused on the *Journal of Marketing*. It is difficult to say how Alderson & Sessions would stand on this continual controversy. The author however believes that they would view the needs of these two groups as compatible. That is they would probably view theory and practice as going hand in hand. In an article entitled "Perspectives for Marketing Practice" Alderson & Sessions (1950) state that: "Pressures exerted by the practical business executive are forcing the marketing analyst to become a better theorist." This view appears to be consistent with the explicit views expressed by recent editors of the *Journal of Marketing*. Consider the following quotes:

> "JM should serve as the leading marketing publication for the benefit and enhancement of members of the business and academic communities" (Wind, 1979). — "The Journal must continue to publish articles that represent contributions to the science of marketing. If we carry a half dozen or so articles per issue, we will be raising the level of marketing thought considerably" (Bursk, 1976). — "It is hoped that the placement of these articles in a separate theory section does not restrict their audience to only those readers interested in theory since, as editor, I believe they are of potential interest to all marketers" (Cundiff, 1973). — "Specific goals of the *Journal of Marketing* are to advance science in marketing ..." (Kelley, 1967).

It is interesting to speculate however about why if so many knowledgeable marketers agree on the need for a good fit between theory and practice that the controversy goes on. Perhaps it is because the concepts of theory and science mean different things to different marketers. And of course this suggests the possibility that Alderson & Sessions and recent editors of the JM as well as other marketers really don't know what is the true nature of theory and science.

4.   Concluding Comment

I have been forced, as all historians are, to make several inferences. The inferences may be incorrect. Nonetheless I believe that Alderson & Sessions held at least three views — (1) theory should be communicated to the manager, (2) marketing consultants are not marketing scientists but they do need theory and should therefore support basic research, and (3) the practical manager needs theory and thus theory and practice must go hand in hand. Even if these inferences about the views that Alderson & Sessions held during the 1950s are correct it is possible that in latter years after looking back upon their careers that their views may have changed.

References

Alderson & Sessions (1947). Question and Comment. *Cost and Profit Outlook*, 1(October).

Alderson & Sessions (1949a). A Personal Message to our Friends in Business and in the Marketing Profession. *Cost and Profit Outlook*, 2(May-June).

Alderson & Sessions (1949b). Foundations of Marketing Science: A Proposal for Basic Research. *Cost and Profit Outlook*, 2(May-June).

Alderson & Sessions (1950). The Alderson and Sessions Basic Research Program. *Cost and Profit Outlook*, 3(September).

Alderson & Sessions (1951). Perspectives for Marketing Practice. *Cost and Profit Outlook*, 4(September).

Alderson & Sessions (1953). How to Solve Marketing Problems. *Cost and Profit Outlook*, 6(August).

Alderson & Sessions (1954). Editorial Program for 1955. *Cost and Profit Outlook*, 7(December).

Alderson & Sessions (1958). A Plea for Editorial Help. *Cost and Profit Outlook*, 9(May-June).

Alderson, Wroe (1965). *Dynamic Marketing Behavior: A Functionalist Theory of Marketing*. Richard D. Irwin Inc., Homewood.

Bursk, Ed (1976). Editorial. *Journal of Marketing*, 40(October):11.

Cundiff, Edward W. (1973). Editorial. *Journal of Marketing*, 37(October):1.

Kelley, Eugene (1967). Editorial. *Journal of Marketing*, 31(July):11.

Wind, Yoram (1979). The Journal of Marketing at a Crossroad. *Journal of Marketing*, 43(January):9–12.

Chapter 19

A BASIC GUIDE TO MARKET PLANNING*

Wroe Alderson

Market planning is a race against time. The planning of any future activity is an exercise of foresight on behalf of the persons who are going to engage in that activity. The planner attempts to forecast the future possibilities and to design a program which will maximize the benefits to be obtained from these activities.

The time element is especially important in market planning because the market itself has a time dimension. A market is not simply a collection of people or of business firms who may buy our products over some future period. A market grows out of the consuming or producing behavior of these individuals or firms and the way in which our products can fit into these patterns of behavior over a stated operating period. If a given set of prospects do not use our product this year a significant part of our total market has disappeared. The potential market for next year and for subsequent years still lies ahead, but this year's market is gone forever. What may be even more serious is that the market for next year and thereafter is not as large as it should be because we did not get started this year.

This notion of the time dimension of markets may suggest such a breathless pace that it would be futile to try to plan. My conviction is quite the opposite. My first answer to the question of why to plan is that planning is a way of economizing time and time is the scarcest and most irrecoverable of all resources. We find in our research and consulting assignments for clients that it is desirable to spend one-fourth to one-third of the total time in planning. By this degree of emphasis on planning we are able to reduce substantially the total elapsed time from authorization of the assignment to delivery of the final report.

Planning in industrial marketing is planning for growth and technological change in the structure of American industry. Industrial marketing, of course, is concerned with the sale of producer's goods. Any plan to increase the sale of an industrial product can only succeed on the presumption that it will make the

*Originally appeared in *Industrial Marketing* (1958) 44(July), pages 53-57.

audit attempts to define or redefine the opportunity for the company to grow and prosper. The audit distinguishes between the core market which is the foundation of the company's market position and the fringe market in which it competes for supplementary volume. It distinguishes between segments of the market in which the needs of the customer may differ significantly both as to the characteristics of a product and as to the services which he requires in buying and using it.

In evaluating the effectiveness of a marketing organization the audit looks at its performance of its present task, and its capacity for taking on new or expanded marketing programs. Judgments need to be made as to the responsiveness of the market to various types of impact which the organization can deliver. The sales and advertising efforts of the company may already have passed the point of diminishing returns in some directions but still offer room for increasing productivity in other directions. The audit should report with candor on the weaknesses of the organization in carrying out its present marketing program or any that may have been under consideration. It should be equally forthright, however, as to what the organization is good at. It may be as important to give the organization the kind of a sales job it can do well as it is to change the organization to match a sales assignment determined on other grounds. In looking at competitors the market audit attempts a similar weighing of strengths and weaknesses. At what points are competitors vulnerable to a degree that might offer an opening for a new marketing attack? What are the sources of strength which may require defensive measures against future threats?

3.   Generation of Strategies

The heart of any marketing plan is a core idea which matches a general conception of a marketing program against the objective to be achieved. The term "strategy" is properly applied to the whole pattern of activity and not merely more or less activity within the same pattern. A marketing strategy is similar to a military strategy to the extent that it is the grand design which controls the selection of all the tactical details that will be involved in a comprehensive plan. It also differs from a military strategy in important respects. A business is usually in competition with a number of opponents rather than in mortal conflict with one. There is less room for outguessing the opponent in business strategy since very often the best course of action remains the same regardless of what competitors do. Competition is a continuous process rather than a single engagement, and the basic rule for the marketing strategist is to "play his ace." The process of playing one's ace, however, should not be confused with merely doing more of what the company has been doing all along.

Core ideas for marketing strategies can come from a number of places, including a flash of insight from an experienced marketing executive. The last thing that planning should do is place any damper on the free play of intuition. It should, however, provide a systematic way of looking for strategies, and that is one reason why this conception of the planning process starts with a marketing audit. The audit deals with the elements out of which strategies must arise. Whatever individual thought or conferences go into the generation of strategies, it is desirable to develop a comprehensive list rather than accepting the first good idea as necessarily the best strategy. Given a comprehensive list, systematic procedure can assist in the evaluation of alternative strategies and the eventual choice of a course of action. Alternatives need to be weighed in terms of the desirability of the objectives sought and the feasibility of achieving them with the means at hand. This is the first major step in clarifying the relationship between means and ends although this basic issue persists all the way through to the final stage in planning.

4.   Programming

To develop a marketing program means to devise a pattern of activity for carrying out the marketing strategy that has been selected. A comprehensive list of possible elements should first be developed. A starting point may be the elements making up the present marketing program supplemented by other elements known to be present in the marketing programs of competitors. If the company is entering an entirely new field, checklists are readily available to remind the planner of the various elements which should be given consideration.

The next step in programming is to arrange these elements in one or more sequences which must follow each other in a marketing operation. In the process of creating this pattern some elements will be eliminated because they do not seem consistent with others which are more essential. One device for testing a doubtful element is to see how far ahead in the proposed sequence of activities it can be pushed without embarrassment to the stages which preceded it. Sometimes this technique of successive postponements reveals that the element is not needed at all and can be eliminated. A marketing program generally specifies several separate sequences of activity which must go on concurrently such as advertising, selling, and the physical movement of goods. The final step of programming is the coordination of these concurrent sequences so that together they will provide the maximum impact on the market.

5.   Scheduling

Up to this point in the process the planner has been dealing largely with "rubber time" rather than calendar time. That is, in designing a sequence of activity he is chiefly concerned with what comes before or after rather than how long after or with specific calendar dates. Scheduling is the process of matching a program with the calendar. The planner works back from specified the stage of final review the executive who must accept and activate the plan is properly concerned about the relation between ends and means. The review provides a final test of fit between what is desirable and what is feasible.

The last review step is to state the objectives which will be pursued in no more than a paragraph and to summarize the means of achieving them in a page or two. A similar statement prepared at the beginning of the planning assignment would be likely to seem somewhat unrealistic when the assignment was completed and to fall short of establishing a sense of direction for all of the various activities of the marketing organization.

An organization is made up of a number of participants with diverse individual interests and often with conflicting views as to the precise objectives of the operation as a whole. The great virtue of an adequate plan is to enable the executive group to move together and not at cross purposes. As the net impact against the marketing target increases, the opportunity for achieving both company and individual objectives is enhanced.

The time is past in most companies for relying on the momentum of company growth as the organizing factor. The future must be planned and created in accordance with the growth prospects for the economy as a whole. This is particularly true in the industrial field, in which each firm is trying to fill an effective but changing role in a great productive machine. The necessary adjustments within this industrial structure are too complex and too dynamic to be made effectively without market planning as a systematic and orderly discipline.

Chapter 20

RESEARCHER FINDS A VOID IN FREUD... ADVERTISERS URGED TO FOLLOW PATH OF RATIONAL PROBLEM SOLVING RATHER THAN OF INSTINCTIVE DRIVES*

Wroe Alderson
Alderson & Sessions, Philadelphia

In trying to devise winning strategies, advertisers necessarily rely upon some theory or explanation of how consumers can be expected to react to products or to advertising appeals.

Many advertising experts are inveterate theorists themselves. Often the theories propounded are created on the spot to persuade clients to accept one campaign proposal or another. The great sums at stake and the growing sophistication of both clients and agency executive have created a demand for a more general theory of motivation with foundations in psychology and the other social sciences.

Despite real progress in motivation theory and research, the diversity of theoretical positions, particularly in psychology, has created a confusion of counsel. Motivation research is an essential aid to advertising strategy, but the advertising strategist would be well advised to assay the long range consequences of some of the proposed theoretical positions.

1.   A Start — Behaviorism

For more than a generation the psychological foundations of advertising theory were relatively simple, consistent, and widely accepted. The behaviorism of John B. Watson was distinctly an American product which seemed well adapted to the American scene and to advertising in particular.

According to this view a child entered the world with little except the capacity to receive impressions and to develop attitudes and habits implanted by its

---

*Originally appeared in *Advertising Age* (1957) March 4th, pages 83-84.

elders. Similarly, the consumer entering the market was like a clean state on which the advertiser could leave whatever impressions he pleased.

This view concerning the role of advertising spread rapidly after Watson himself left the university and entered the advertising field. Endless and massive repetition was regarded as the foundation for advertising success. Habits of buying particular products or brands were to be inculcated in millions of consumers and constant repetition of simple and forthright messages became standard practice in advertising as in the classroom.

However inadequate this view of consumer psychology may seem today, it has a solid core of truth and continues to be manifested in advertising practice. In its extreme form this doctrine makes the consuming public an inert and docile mass without the power of rational decision and subject to manipulation at the will of the advertiser.

At the same time it must be admitted that our daily lives are largely made up of useful habits, which help us to avoid an overwhelming volume of decision-making from moment to moment. A useful habit is not so much irrational as non-rational. It is not opposed to reason but can operate without the active intervention of reason. A rational being can properly make a decision to cultivate useful habits as a way of economizing psychic energy. There are some routines which have the force of habit but never become entirely automatic. This is certainly true of so-called buying habits. Reminders through advertising, even though repetitious, can be of service to consumers in maintaining buying routines without really infringing on the prerogative of rational choice.

Motivation research today attempts to penetrate more deeply and to lay the foundation for strategies other than that of conditioning the consumer through massive repetition. This is an inevitable response to the pressures for advertising efficiency.

Contemporary motivation research has drawn its inspiration from schools of psychology first developed in Europe as compared to the earlier commitment to the native American school of behaviorism. In fact, nearly all that now goes under the name of motivation research is derived from two great schools of European psychology, each with numerous variations and each now firmly established in the United States.

These two schools are in such glaring contrast with each other that the main thing they have in common is their opposition to behaviorism and its faith in the conditioned reflex. This article will attempt to say something about what these two schools are, about the implications for advertising strategy of adopting one view or the other, and about possible reconciliations between the two for motivation research, for advertising strategy, and for management policy.

2. Contrasting Views of Motivation

The two principal schools of motivational theory are derived from Gestalt psychology and psychoanalysis. Gestalt psychology is associated with such names as Wertheimer, Kohler, Koffka, and Lewin, all of whom came to the United States in their prime and published some of their most important work here. In fact Gestalt scarcely became a psychology of motivation until it entered its American phase, having begun as a new approach to the psychological analysis of perception.

Psychoanalysis is associated with such names as Freud, Adler, Jung, Rank, Sullivan and Fromm. Psychoanalysis has also gone through a major transition from the preponderantly biological interest of Freud and his followers to the social and cultural viewpoint of more recent writers such as Fromm, Sullivan, Kardiner, and Horney. Gestalt as compared to behaviorism represented renewed interest in conscious mind and rational decision. Psychoanalysis invented and popularized such concepts as the unconscious or subconscious mind.

Gestalt as a psychology of motivation is pre-eminently concerned with goal-directed behavior and rational use of the resources of the environment to attain conscious ends. Psychoanalysis, at least in its earlier versions, held that behavior is primarily determined by instinctive drives and contended that we are unconsciously motivated, to seek goals which we do not recognize or may be unwilling to acknowledge even to ourselves.

In a general way one may be said to emphasize rational behavior and the other irrational behavior, even though it is not always possible to draw a sharp line between these two categories.

One definition of rational behavior would be the conscious and deliberate pursuit of goals that are consistent with the survival and well-being of the individual. Psychoanalysis would say that much of human behavior lies outside the area of rationality so defined, and that some of the most fundamental aspects of motivation are hidden below the level of consciousness. To the extent that this is true, it obviously complicates the problem of finding out what people really want or what motivates their behavior.

It is also true however, that rationality of goals or behavior would not necessarily mean that the task of motivation research would be easy. While psychoanalysis holds that ideas are repressed because the ego cannot accept them, people also forget because they have achieved a satisfactory adjustment and have had no reason to recall their original motivations. In case after case there seem to be perfectly practical and common sense reasons why consumers should prefer one dishcloth, detergent or depilatory to another. If respondents seem vague when first challenged to explain, it is probably because they have had other things to think about rather than any great inner tensions or anxieties connected with these everyday products.

One of the difficulties about the concept of rationality is that it is not always considered from the viewpoint of the subject whose behavior is under critical scrutiny. The inherent standards of rationality in a field of consumer use may be quite different from imputed standards of rationality existing in the mind of the outsider. All too often some producer assumes that users place a high value on certain technical characteristics of his product only to find upon investigation that they have an entirely different conception of its principal virtues. It seems obvious after the fact, for example, that housewives might consider absorbency a valuable characteristic in a dishcloth. Nevertheless, the first draft of one survey questionnaire omitted this topic entirely, even though the manufacture had made an exhaustive attempt to deal with every characteristic which could possibly interest the consumer.

The two leading schools of thought point to quite different conclusions as to the development of personality. Gestalt in its original version pictured the rational mind as endowed with insights which enabled it to see a solution almost as soon as the problem situation was presented. Later versions make more allowance for learning from experience. The mature personality is one which has become progressively more skilled in the management of the resources of its environment.

The mature personality for psychoanalysis is one which has finally achieved a degree of poise and balance after surviving nearly disastrous incidents along the way. Growing up for psychoanalysts of biological bent is the painful process of recovering from such traumatic experiences as birth, weaning, toilet training and puberty. Even those with social and cultural leanings picture the typical life history as a continuous battle to master the forces of a hostile environment.

Obviously these two views have very different implications as to the way consumers will react toward goods or toward the various appeals presented in advertising. If the first view is correct the consumer might be expected to regard a product as primarily an instrument for obtaining a given end and to judge it in terms of its instrumental efficiency. If the second view is correct the consumer might be expected to be much more preoccupied with the symbolic aspect of goods, to utilize them as means of giving vent to suppressed desires, and to be more interested in symbols of mastery than in working tools.

3.   Consequences of the Instrumental View

If goods are working tools or instruments for gaining specific ends, advertising might be expected to take on an educational character. In a service magazine for housewives, for example, the tone of an advertisement might not be too different from that of an article describing a method for dealing with some household product. Like any other teacher, the advertiser might engage in repetition partly to make sure that each subject had learned the lesson and partly because there is a constant stream of new subjects who have not yet been exposed to the lesson.

Advertising on this view sees consumers in their social roles as members of households, as income earners, and as purchasing agents for the household. It talks to them in terms which they can use in talking to their family and friends. Its appeals are made through public channels and are directed to what may be called the public life of the individual compared to what is peculiarly personal and private.

To proceed as if consumer behavior is fundamentally rational is to assume that behavior patterns will be convergent. That is to say that consumers with precisely the same problem will tend to adopt precisely the same solution after some experience with the various alternatives. Rationality in the form in which it is generally available consists in being able to make comparative judgments among ways of accomplishing the same thing. Thus, at the level of consumer buying it is reflected in a capacity to learn even when there is not enough creative insight to be right the first time.

Some advertisers who have themselves preferred rational appeals have sometimes been discouraged with the apparent results. Some years ago a leading dentifrice advertiser rebelled against what he considered the fantastic claims made by himself and his competitors. He decided to advertise that the sole function of a toothpaste was to clean teeth and that his product could do it as well as any other. About this time his brand began to suffer a serious decline in sales so that he soon returned to less factual and more colorful claims. Interestingly enough, the same manufacturer is today once more treating the consumer as a rational being and is presumably doing all right. Undoubtedly consumers are steadily becoming more sophisticated, but it is also possible that the manufacturer misread the evidence on the first occasion as to consumer reactions.

It has already been pointed out that the supplier sometimes does not really know what the consumer's problem is. If he is familiar with the problem he may not be clear as to the product features which are important to the user. There is also the possibility that even where there is a consumer need there may not yet be a widespread conscious recognition of the problem among consumers. Sometimes the advertiser must establish the fact that a problem exists before trying to show that his product offers a solution. Emotionally colored language directed to this end is not inconsistent with the postulate of consumer rationality. Absorbed as we may be in our daily affairs, each of us may need to be startled into recognizing the urgency of some problem, the importance of being prepared for the eventuality which it represents or the frequency with which such occasions may be expected to arise.

Long experience in consumer research gives one considerable respect for the job done by the consumer buyer. She must consider many things bearing on

This chapter contains 19 propositions about human behavior and the pro
cesses of adjustment to the environment. The postulate of rationality is embod
ied in the fifth proposition which reads as follows: "Behavior is basically the
goal-directed attempt of the organism to satisfy its needs as experienced, in the
field as perceived". The organism strives constantly to actualize, maintain and
enhance itself. This seeking is accompanied by emotion which facilitates the
maintenance and enhancement of the organism.

The concept or image of the self arises out of experience and helps to mediate
the continual process of adjustment to the environment. Any experience which
is inconsistent with the structure of the self image may be perceived as a threat
Maladjustment exists when the individual refuses to admit significant experi
ence into consciousness, or as Rogers says, fails to "symbolize and organize
such experience into the Gestalt of the self structure".

Threats to the cherished self image bring anxiety and defensive behavior
Under favorable conditions therapy can produce a reorganization of the value
system and reduce the incongruity between experience and the structure of the
self. In the normal course of maturation the individual replaces values which
have been taken over from others and achieves an inner harmony through greater
self-knowledge and acceptance.

This statement by Rogers affords a basis for reconciliation between the two
major trends in motivation theory. It also makes a place for the theory of learning
emphasized in the earlier behaviorism but in more dynamic form. We do not
learn by passive acceptance of impressions but by the environment. We make a
more skillful use of our means as we learn more about the available instruments.
We reshape our ends as we learn more about ourselves. Many achieve individual
adjustment without professional counsel because of good family adjustment. A
happy household is not only an end in itself but a fortunate setting for informal
group therapy.

Marketing management solves its problems by helping consumers to solve
their problems. While the good life demands an increasing variety of goods,
it also draws on the realm of ideas and emotions. With becoming modesty
the supplier of goods can recognize that some human problems are beyond
his reach. He can well take account of the social and psychological setting in
which his products will be used. However, half-baked attempts to deal with the
problems of disturbed personalities are likely to end up being both poor therapy
and poor selling.

A perspective such as that sketched by Rogers can provide some useful guide
posts for motivation research. For the rational problem solver his own irrational
impulses or defense mechanisms are part of the problem. We are learning how
to devise experimental procedures which parallel the decision structure of real
life problems. Ways can be found to introduce faulty self-knowledge as an
element in these experimental designs. Progress in experimentation is a goal

which might well attract the exponents of the non-directed interview as well as the advocates of massive sampling surveys. Advances in this type of motivation research should contribute substantially to advertising effectiveness.

Rogers calls his view "phenomenological", a designation shared with other writers such as Snygg and Combs. That means that the environment as perceived by the subject is taken as the behavioral field. Both the world image and the self image of the individual are keys to understanding his behavior. Kenneth Boulding, in his recently published essay "The Image," suggests the term "eiconics", for a science of images cutting across economics, psychology and the other social sciences. Advertising, which is in the business of creating images, has a stake in the outcome of such a project.

Meanwhile advertising strategy wisely shows some restraint in applying the results of motivation studies in the present state of the art. The psychoanalytic view in particular is marked by two quite distinct versions from Freud himself, followed by a profusion of free-wheeling speculation by his many disciples.

So far the major impact has not been on the advertiser's claims concerning his products but on the manner of their presentation. A new aura of interest for a product may be created by a fresh copy approach, but the product still has to compete with other instruments recommended for the same purpose.

There is some warrant in clinical lore for calling a spade a symbol of fertility but it still belongs in the tool shed rather than the boudoir. Every copywriter knows that a man buys suspenders to hold up his trousers and not as a "reaction to castration anxiety". A woman buys a garden hose to water the lawn and not because of the "futility of urethral competition for the female." Possibly we are saved from the solemnities of Freud by the sanity of Rabelais. Any student of the gusty Frenchman will remember a chapter on toilet training that has never been approached in Freudian literature. The five year old Gargantua has some remarkable things to say in this chapter about product testing. As for urethral competition, who can forget Gargantua's first visit to Paris and the flood which drowned 260,418 Parisians, not counting women and children. He may have been visiting the Madison Avenue of that day, since his protest concerned the gullibility of the great crowds which gathered to behold any spectacle from "a mule with tinkling bells" to "a blind fiddler in the middle of a crosswalk."

Advertising strategy must take account of both gullibility and gumption, of human needs both instrumental and symbolic. In the long run the odds are in favor of a strategy which takes rational problem solving as a fundamental aspect of human behavior. Despite all the quirks and foibles revealed by motivation research, rationality and efficiency are universal goals of the maturing individual. For most products the long run advantage probably lies with the kind of advertising appeals which will still make sense to the mature and balanced personalities which most of us are trying to become.

Chapter 21

ETHICS, IDEOLOGIES AND SANCTIONS*

Wroe Alderson

The Committee on Ethical Standards and Professional Practices of the American Marketing Association has undertaken a broad study of ethical problems arising in connection with marketing and advertising. The interests of the Association far transcend the adoption of a code of standards to govern the conduct of research and consulting organizations. The Association is concerned with the role of marketing in modern society, the prevailing ethical standards of American business, and the unique responsibility which the marketing aspect of business assumes in undertaking to modify cultural values. Marketing may be described as applied economics insofar as it is concerned with meeting established demand, but it would be much more accurate to call it applied anthropology when the impact on values in our culture is taken into account.

The Association's objective, through its Committee on Ethical Standards and Professional Practices, is nothing less than to review the foundations of ethics as they pertain to everyone engaged in marketing activities, whether salesmen, advertisers, professional marketing researchers or business leaders. This memo will lay out a broad framework for the consideration of ethics in marketing and then propose a research program and the means for carrying out this research.

1.   Rules Governing Human Behavior

Our discussion should start with a recognition that rules governing human behavior are of several types and that ethics deal with only one form of control which a group imposes on its members. The field might be divided broadly into three parts—namely, law, manners and morals, and ethics. These categories are distinguished by different ways of generating the rules which the members of a society are expected to observe.

Under the law, rules are generated out of legislative research and debate. Under our form of government the enactment of the law generally means that

*From the Report of the Committee on Ethical Standards and Professional Practices, American Marketing Association, December, 1964, pages 1-20.

It is the viewpoint of ambitious and energetic people who want to get ahead bu who associate the acquisition of specialized skills with getting ahead. This, o course, is what is often called "middle-class ethics." The term "middle-clas ethics" is in no sense derogatory, and surveys have shown that the great majorit of American people regard themselves as members of the middle class.

The competitive spirit of this view of ethics carries over into the trainin of the young, with every parent anxious to secure some competitive edge fo his offspring in making a career. This view toward the training of childre tends to contrast sharply with that held by people lower in the social scale wh tend to embrace the equalitarian ethics. The equalitarian father asserts that on man is as good as another and he would prefer that his son become a good soli workman and not become estranged from his family by engaging in the struggl to go ahead.

It was the ethics of emulation, of course, which Max Weber had in mind i his great book, *The Protestant Ethic and the Rise of Capitalism.* It is quite clea that the ethics of emulation has a special relationship to business enterpris and provides the foundation for most of the codes of business and professiona ethics.

The ethics of leadership is the ethics which is characteristically associate with people who have already arrived at the top. In its most advanced form the ethics of leadership applies to the heads of very large organizations, but i can permeate far more deeply into the general population. That is to say, nearl every adult has had some experience in making decisions on behalf of othe people even though it is only his own family, his lodge, or his club or churc committee.

The ethics of leadership is concerned with the relationship between powe and responsibility. At its best, the ethics of leadership takes into account th aspirations of all members of an organization and in major decisions undertake to select alternatives in the light of the benefits which can be generated for al concerned. Leaders differ, of course, as to the level of their own aspiration and the level which they are prepared to impose or try to evoke among other that belong to the organization. Such a leader of a large organization tend to identify his destiny with that of the organization he heads and to be force inevitably to the development of creative plans rather than simple decision as the basis for maximizing benefits for the organization. It is the ethics o leadership which Chester Barnard had in mind when he said that "one functio of the leader is to project a morality which his organization can live by."

The penalty of leadership, on the other hand, is to live under a condition o ethical tension and ambiguity because of the many diverse claims made upo the leader by employees, stockholders, customers, suppliers, his communit and his nation. It would be invidious to select individual business leaders fo mention. Among political leaders of the past, some who represent the fulles personal identification with the welfare of their nations were Abraham Lincoln, Frederick the Great, William the Silent of the Netherlands, and King Henry Navarre of France. (It happens that three of these four were assassinated, while Frederick was a bent and weary old man at fifty. The writer does not believe that these are a representative sample in this respect).

3.   Professional Ethics

Codes of professional ethics which might be created for various functions under the broad classification of marketing would doubtless contain elements of all three of the general ethical views which have been mentioned. Most fundamentally, perhaps, a code of ethics reflects the ethics of emulation and, in a sense, attempts to regulate competition. Codes of ethics sometimes tread on hazardous legal ground because of the attempt to enforce active competition in general under the anti-trust laws.

Codes of ethics are more likely to have legal approval if the rules concentrate on standards of quality of goods or services and do not venture into the area of price. Many individual businessmen are thinking primarily of price-cutting when they speak of unethical practices in their fields. Obviously a code of fair practice could become an instrument of monopoly if the law would permit. The so-called codes of fair practice under the National Recovery Act demonstrated the preoccupation of businessmen with prices during the period when legal immunity was granted. Even when these NRA codes did not mention minimum price schedules, they were often concerned with the way in which price should be calculated.

On the other side of the effort to regulate competition—namely, the maintenance of quality—there is a basic economic marketing concept in evidence. That is the notion that competitors should not be allowed to "spoil the market," delivering inferior goods and services and hence destroying consumer confidence in the product. Even when codes are limited to quality maintenance, however, there are anti-trust questions which may arise.

A code might be used, for example, to restrict activities such as market research to a limited group like members of the American Marketing Association. Such a code would be suspect if any form of threat or coercion was utilized to enforce the code. There is also the sound marketing principle that the notion of quality undergoes changes in the steady adaptation of the market to needs of consumers. Thus, it would be hard to enforce a rule that surveys should be based entirely on personal interviews when studies have shown that under certain circumstances mail questionnaires yield superior results.

But while professional codes of ethics might primarily reflect the ethics of emulation, there is room for other considerations. Codes should be equalitarian in the sense of recognizing the principle of equal opportunity. While it is true, every type of market. Their professional job is to remedy these imperfections insofar as this can be done through private means. In a given type of market, however, a marketing specialist may become convinced that the only possibility of remedying an imperfection of the market so that goods can move is through the enactment of the law. Furthermore, marketing specialists may become convinced that some particular product or service can best be supplied by government so that they favor public performance of a particular activity despite a general reluctance to expand the public sector.

The functionalist viewpoint might tend to favor public activity wherever individual requirements tended to be identical and where there were urgent needs which were difficult to finance through private agencies. Similarly, functionalism would tend to favor the assignment of a function to the private sector and to depend on market processes where there was a great diversity in individual requirements. In this respect one might say that the heterogeneous market provides the ultimate stronghold for the manifestation of the marketing concept and the defense of a free market economy.

Ideologies as well as personal ideals determine the acceptance of the general principles we call ethics. The writer has asserted that economics is the second most culture bound of all academic disciplines because it takes the existing type of economy as its point of departure. The most culture bound discipline of all is marketing because marketing specialists tend to place such a high value on the untrammeled operations of the market. There is all the more need for a marketing specialist to place any assertions about right and wrong in a broad human perspective.

5.   Sanctions

For each type of rule governing human behavior, there is a corresponding type of sanction which may be invoked in enforcing it. Sanctions are rewards and penalties which are presumed to be effective in inducing acceptance of the rule of behavior and conformity with it.

With respect to the law, there are penalties for breaking a criminal statute or damages which may be awarded to a plaintiff in a civil suit. Over the years there has been much discussion as to whether the effectiveness of a legal deterrent increased directly with the amount of the punishment. There is room for doubt concerning this correlation, growing out of the history of law in Great Britain and other countries. At one time there was capital punishment for 200 crimes under English law but, so far as we know, with no noticeable effect on the crime rate.

What is probably most effective with respect to the majority of business and professional people is a general fear or uneasiness about breaking the law regardless of whether the penalty is light or heavy. Certainly the amount of consideration given to the anti-trust laws by businessmen would indicate that the deterrent effect is far greater than that reflected by the number of anti-trust convictions.

There are some interesting ethical issues with respect to the observance of anti-trust or economic statutes generally. In many of these areas the business-man first acts and the courts then decide whether he has violated the law. Should a businessman refuse to take action unless he is absolutely sure that his action is in accordance with the law? In many areas this would mean that he never took action at all because not even the courts will know whether the law has been violated until the case goes to litigation.

Some business executives complain that they have over-conservative legal counsel who stultify action and others say that their only salvation has been the use of legal counsel to tell them what they can do rather than what they cannot do. A recent winner of the Parlin Award said that he had joined the family business in 1917 and that anti-trust prosecution or some Federal administrative action had been going on in every year since that time.

Under the headings of Manners and Morals the sanctions supporting the rules consist largely of the approval or disapproval of relevant groups. In business this can mean members of the same industry, consumers of a company's products, or the general public which may be interested in labor policy or aspects of a company's public relations.

Sometimes social approval is expressed in a positive way through awards and distinctions. There are literally thousands of such awards bestowed annually, ranging all the way from the Nobel Prize to certificates of excellence for performance in various fields. The existence of such awards may exert considerable influence in some fields. Most awards, however, are made for a lifetime of activity while others recognize specific achievements. The award which is made to a man because of his established eminence in a field is quite different in its effect from awards given to encourage the relatively unknown person. In making an award to an established figure, an organization is often seeking to honor itself as much as the recipient of the award. This is a consideration which might be taken into account in reviewing some of the award programs which have been sponsored by the American Marketing Association or its chapters.

6.   Organizational and Ecological Sanctions

There are two kinds of sanctions which are of special importance because they bear primarily on individuals occupying leadership positions. The first of these might be called organizational sanctions. The responsibilities of leadership impose constraints on the individual, limiting his freedom of action. There are situations in which the individual in a responsible position is glad when a legal sanction is imposed because it enables him to take action which his conscience tells him is overdue. When the writer was in the consulting business the possibility of employing a Negro economist was on his conscience for some time. For one reason or another this action did not take place until the state of Pennsylvania passed a Fair Employment Practices Act. It then seemed relatively easy to take this step and to point to the new law as the sanction for this action.

There are many occasions on which considerations of organizational balance and structural soundness provide the executive with sanctions he can point to in justifying the limitations within which the organization must work. An overriding consideration in the management of an organization is securing the basis of its survival in its industry. A very severe sanction inclines the leader to try to maintain the health of the organization because internal disorders can develop with alarming rapidity if there is not a sound internal adjustment.

Finally, there is the concept of ecological sanctions which is concerned with adjustment to the external environment. Looking outward, the executive must be concerned with the habitability of the environment or habitat. The word habitability is meant to convey the concept of the capacity of the environment to support life. Thus, as he surveys the inside of the organization, the leader will be concerned with conditions that insure survival and externally he will be concerned with habitability since a decline in habitability will eventually threaten survival. Ecological sanctions in the long run set severe and fully determined limits on the outlook for habitability and hence for survival.

There are two ecological sanctions which are the most severe of all. One is the threat of atomic warfare and the other the possible consequences of the population explosion. The marketing function is very much involved with both of these ecological sanctions. On the one hand, defense marketers continue to cooperate in the accumulation of nuclear arms. On the other hand, marketers in more peaceful fields continue to make plans as if there would be an unending exponential growth in the number of individuals and families available to buy food, clothing and shelter.

Perhaps we throw up our hands and say that we are too deeply involved to do anything about either of these major threats. On the other hand, there are many occasions which tend to spoil the environment which we could do something about if we were aroused to undertake it. The willful or thoughtless destruction of forests and streams, the mining out or farming out of many areas without any thought for generating new industries to sustain stranded populations, the noxious fumes, traffic hazards and unsanitary conditions that assail the senses in our cities are among the conditions which reduce the satisfactions of living and may eventually threaten survival itself.

More and more the marketing profession will have to be concerned with the kind of goods and services we offer for sale as well as with standards of behavior in selling them. The marketing profession undertakes to change cultural values and hence cannot escape criticism and the bestowal of praise or blame for favorable or unfavorable changes in these values.

There is reason to hope that business and professional leadership is becoming steadily more conscious of ecological sanctions. Ecological sanctions can have the same impact as other sanctions on standards of human behavior. Sanctions can enter directly into the decision taken by an executive because in his own judgment it would be harmful to his organization to violate the sanction. Sanctions can also help the executive in bringing an organization around to his way of thinking when its members become aware of the nature of these sanctions. Organizational and ecological sanctions help to fill the gap between law and morals, on the one side, and ethics proper, on the other, by lending support to the dictates of conscience.

The view which has been called idealistic relativism holds with most cultural anthropologists that there are differences in the way people make up their minds about decisions concerning right and wrong which cannot be ignored. It is fruitless for the philosopher to argue that they would make up their minds in exactly the same way, intelligence, ethical sensitivity and all other things being equal, because of the unique experiences of the individual within his cultural setting.

On the other hand, the writer has been influenced by the philosopher, Edgar Singer, and the viewpoint he called instrumental idealism. An ideal is something you can approach by ever closer stages but never reach. The ultimate ideal would be for every responsible individual to apply exactly the same principles in resolving ethical dilemmas. Surely there is some empirical evidence that this trend is manifested in history . Each epoch finds that it has better technologies and greater control over nature than the last one. Each decade discovers that it must do better because it can do better.

Our version of a brighter future embraces the elements of equal opportunity, the dynamics of competition and the special sanctions which bear upon the responsible leader. But to explain the leader in ethical conduct we must make the further assumption that he hungers and thirsts after righteousness. Such a drive offers a direct parallel with what Singer calls the aims of science—namely, "the progressive reduction of error."

Chapter 22

THE AMERICAN ECONOMY AND CHRISTIAN ETHICS*

Wroe Alderson

There is no reconciliation between dog-eat-dog competition and turn-the-cheek acceptance of humiliation and inferior status. But I do not believe we came here to consider such extremes. The American economy is far from dog-eat-dog and there is much more to Christian ethics than the strategy of non-violent resistance.

American enterprise operates through a peculiar combination of competition and cooperation. Economic theory has emphasized the competitive side of business, and one responsibility of the courts is to enforce the anti-trust laws in the effort to maintain competition. But the courts also recognize the sanctity of contracts and other aspects of business cooperation. Business operates under legal constraints and under rules of conduct which go beyond the law. One aspect of cooperation is the way in which business men cooperate with the courts and with each other to maintain the accepted rules of conduct. But principles of behavior which can be formulated as rules are not the end of ethics in business but only the beginning. Men cannot be ethical by rote but only through a creative approach to problems of action.

The term Christian ethics could be interpreted in several ways. It could apply descriptively to the behavior of professing Christians from the early Christian martyrs down through the Crusades and the Inquisition to the rise of modem industrialism and the crimes against humanity in the 20th century. It could mean an ethical view prevalent among some group of Christians such as that discussed by Max Weber in his great work *The Protestant Ethic and the Rise of Capitalism*. It could mean the ethics of Christ as presented second-hand in the Gospels, or third-hand through the impact on Paul and the other epistolary writers. I prefer to begin with Christ but not for the purpose of deriving a new

---

*Originally published in *Growth and Profit Planner* (1964) 2(August, No.3), whole issue, based on a talk to students at the Christian Association at the University of Pennsylvania, June 1964.

version of the moral law from his teachings. At the moment I only wish to comment on the basic educational methods he employed.

1.   Socrates and Jesus

The teaching methods of Socrates were in sharp contrast with those of Jesus. His use of probing questions gave rise to the concept of the Socratic method. He asked one question after another until his pupils either admitted that they knew nothing or began the slow and painful process of reconstructing a view of life based on more carefully examined premises. Jesus dealt in answers rather than questions, after the manner of the scribes and the Pharisees. But unlike his predecessors, his answers suggested broad principles of action rather than meticulous and detailed regulation of conduct. He supported these principles with brief reasoning here, the analogy of parable there, and complete freedom in stating a new rule even when it seemed in direct conflict with the last one. The high point in this approach is in the chapter in Matthew in which the Golden Rule is stated, a formulation which has some rather obvious shortcomings. Sometimes there is nothing the other fellow would abhor so much as treating him the way I would like to be treated. The Golden Rule takes no account of differences in taste. Later in the same chapter Jesus enunciates what I have called the Platinum Rule since it is an even more sweeping guide to conduct. It says, "Not everyone who saith unto me Lord, Lord shall enter into the kingdom of heaven but he that doeth the will of my father which is in heaven."

Jesus states various rules of conduct which are often in apparent conflict and I think he does it deliberately. Like Socrates, he wants his hearers to reexamine their lives and their beliefs and seek firmer foundations. But his ethical message was more profound than anything we glean from Socrates. To me he seems to be saying that the ethical life begins precisely at the point where the rules run out. If a satisfactory rule can be formulated to govern conduct, it is in the area of law or morals. Ethical decisions are concerned with matters for which no rule exists. Ethics deals with conflicts in the moral law or in the situations where conscience tells us there ought to be a rule. Ethical decisions are not generally decisions between good and evil but between contrasting conceptions of the good. An ethical decision calls for a creative solution or plan of action to actualize as much as possible of the potential good in the situation.

2.   The Life and Teachings of Jesus

A spiritual genius, such as Jesus, exemplified this lofty ethics in his life even more effectively than he taught it. He did not flinch in his later days when he realized that he could accomplish his mission of serving the highest good only through his own death. While he proclaimed that he had come to fulfill the law he often went counter to the established rules. This is what brought him into conflict with the authorities and eventually destroyed him. Growing up in a devout Jewish family he gradually matured his vision of the Kingdom of Heaven, of the holy community ruled by love, and of the sterility of the moral law without love. He taught us to live creatively in the face of conflicting values and with an abiding faith in divine love and the divine spark in every man. This is our Christian heritage rather than any rule, even one which has such general application as the Golden Rule.

Are we suggesting an idealistic ethics here which is totally impractical for application in business? I think not. Much of business conduct is controlled by rules of morality, many of which have the force of law. The mass of decent business men keep their word when they make a promise, do not stoop to lie or cheat, devote many hours to civic institutions and causes, and try to inspire men to give the best within them not only for the sake of the firm but for the sake of themselves and their families. True, there are violators who either actually break the law or sail as close to the wind as possible. But there are also ethical leaders in business who face grave issues of organization and efficiency, of private and public values, who make decisions and adopt plans which are calculated to promote more advanced conceptions of the good life for all. What these men decide today on what may be called the ethical frontier will become the accepted standard for others to follow tomorrow.

3.   Ethical Views in American Society

In order to place the ethics of leadership in its proper setting let us pause to consider the several broad alternatives among ethical views which are prevalent in our culture. They are cogently presented in a little book with the single word "Excellence" as its title, written by Dr. John Gardner, President of the Carnegie Corporation. He mentions first the equalitarian ethics of the frontier and reminds us that we are not very far away from the frontier in the United States. In this simple view all men are treated as equals and no assertion of superiority is tolerated. People stand ready to help their neighbors because mutual aid is essential to survival. Yet each prefers to be free and independent and will only ask for help in case of dire need. Young people are not encouraged to advance beyond their parents but are expected to grow up in the same mold. Rural communities still reflect this general view, particularly where subsistence farming still prevails. The labor unions also have tended toward a version of the equalitarian ethics.

Next is the ethics of emulation under which people are prepared to do what it takes in order to get ahead. They define getting ahead as acquiring material goods and social status, but they are generally aware of the need to conform to standards of behavior in order to progress. There is room for diversity under this view which is not readily accepted by the equalitarian frontiersman. People are allowed to be different but not too different. There is tremendous pressure on young people to make careers and to equal or exceed the accomplishments of their parents. The individual measures himself against his fellows and seeks to develop his special talents and to prevail over his immediate rivals. This is a highly competitive view of life but it is an ethics of regulated or controlled competition. A man ends by being a success or failure in material terms but in either case will insist that his children enter the same race. In fact, preparatory schools or colleges are often chosen with a view of gearing the young person up to the fastest competitive pace he can stand, in the hope of starting him early on the road to success.

Most of us will recognize this as the dominant ethical view of the social environment in which we live. While it has been called middle class ethics, the term is in no sense to be used as an epithet. Some have said that there are no permanent classes in America because all are being absorbed into the great middle class. It was the middle class ethics which Max Weber associated with the rise of capitalistic enterprise and it provides the primary base for business ethics. During the Industrial Revolution and the Commercial Revolution which preceded it, the English common law was steadily forging ahead. The rules of conduct which grew out of the prudence and frugality of the rising middle class often took on the formal status of law. Benjamin Franklin, whom we claim as the founder of the University of Pennsylvania, was a persuasive advocate of the middle class ethics in his Poor Richard's Almanac. But we moved from an acceptance of the prudential maxim of "Honesty is the best policy" to specifying the requirements of honesty by statute as economic life became more complex.

The great value to society of the middle class ethics is in its insistent drive for excellence. A man expects to achieve greater competence as his career progresses, whatever his field. He expects his son to build on what he has provided and to move ahead still further. Business enterprise and the professions are the natural habitat for these ethical views. The ethics of emulation is frequently in conflict with the equalitarian ethics which still has a strong hold on the average American. Many of us like to escape from the "rat race" of emulative effort and return to the simple life of hunting and fishing or the easy fellowship of the countryside for a few weeks at a time.

4.   The Aristocratic Ideal

Dr. Gardner is almost ready to settle for a perspective of American life based on the tension between these two ethical views, but not quite. He acknowledges that there is an ethics of leadership which can have a profound effect at times. He associates the ethics of leadership with such names as Washington and Jefferson and with the aristocratic component in American society. He believes that the aristocratic ethics is a declining factor in our culture, but I would not accept his view. Those who hold to an aristocratic view may be few in numbers but they are large in influence. The term aristocratic ethics must be more sharply defined if it is not to create confusion. To many, aristocracy suggests a privileged class which is interested in nothing but the uninterrupted enjoyment of its privileges. We do not associate the aristocratic ethics with this way of life or with the Nietzchean concept of the Superman. As indicated by Dr. Gardner's reference to Washington and Jefferson, he relates it to the highest sense of social responsibility. It is the ethics of noblesse oblige, of the urgent need to dedicate one's talents to the welfare of humanity through whatever medium is available to us.

Since we are talking about an open aristocracy of talent and not the ethics of a privileged social class, it may be safer to speak of the ethics of leadership. Many of our most influential leaders have emerged into full-fledged leadership as they fought their way up. They have learned step by step to exercise leadership over a broader range of human affairs. Having reached the top in their chosen field, the ethics of emulation is no longer adequate to their needs. In the exercise of their powers and responsibilities they are confronted with ethical problems which are new to them and which no one has faced before in the precise form in which they are presented. The fact that our business leaders reach this stature by the gradual processes of growth gives them a very different perspective from that of a nobility in a closed society who became leaders through hereditary right.

This third ethical view has interesting relationships to the two previously discussed. There is an equalitarian emphasis on freedom and independence among those who have arrived at the top which is not unlike that of the frontiersmen in the simpler society. There is an emphasis on talent which resembles that of the ethics of emulation but with quite a different import. In one case talent is developed for its instrumental value or one might say as a competitive weapon. Under the third view talent is developed because of an inner urge to transcend oneself and to measure up to the highest responsibilities of leadership. These responsibilities pertain especially to creative decision making beyond the reach of the established moral code and in the present of conflicting claims and interests.

5. Training for Responsible Leadership

We like to feel that students at Pennsylvania are being trained for leadership in business and other fields. Some knowledge of the ethics of leadership should perhaps be a formal part of that training. Methods of teaching would be a problem if we started with the proposition that the ethics of leadership begins where the rules run out. Perhaps it could be taught by the case method combined with some attempt to educe general principles. If we can devise effective

ethical training for future business leaders it will accelerate the process by
which new standards are established and then diffused through a large busines
organization. It should be emphasized, however, that the ethical problem
of leadership are encountered in small organizations and in divisions of larg
organizations. The leader is obliged to resolve these problems in one way o
another and subordinates are largely influenced by example.

One's personal faith includes the notion that there is a deep inner urge to
lead an ethical life quite apart from the dictates of prudence in serving our othe
needs. Rufus Jones, the famous Quaker leader, used to say that a man shoul
live as if he hoped to make his life his masterpiece. We are uneasy perhaps a
the thought that we must rely on such noble motives in our business leaders. We
may ask what sanctions exist to insure ethical conduct in the area that transcend
law and the established moral code. For some of us there is support for ethica
principles in religious scruples. West Churchman has suggested that we shoul
act in such a way that future generations will approve of our conduct. I have
tried to point out that there are more immediate sanctions available. These
have called ecological sanctions by which I mean the constraints imposed o
us by the environment and by our desire to maintain the habitability of the
environment. The ultimate sanction today is the prospect of atomic warfare
The threat of atomic missiles is not merely that they would kill millions o
people but that they would destroy the habitability of large regions of the earth
for centuries to come. This continual threat creates an awareness of ecologica
sanctions of greater intensity than ever before.

6.   The Ethical Problems of Marketing and Advertising

Some of my students in the Wharton School have expressed uneasiness abou
reconciling Christian ethics with careers in marketing and advertising. They
have no qualms about designing or producing any type of good but they are
somehow squeamish about selling it. Actually selling can be an honorable and
creative career. The newcomer in a marketing organization must have a firm
grasp of the meaning of consumer sovereignty. One of the most importan
freedoms in the American economy is the freedom of the consumer to decide
what is good for him. It is true that there have been some notorious abuses
but deception is deplored by the majority of business men as well as by the
consumer. It is also true that marketing men in their own interest, should be the
first to identify and criticize abuses when they occur.

For advertising to become corrupt and ineffective could be a crippling blow
to a free market economy. This type of economy feeds on innovation and the
sponsor must communicate with consumers to induce acceptance of innovation
The prospective purchaser does not evaluate the new product in isolation but
relates it to other products and eventually to his vision of the good life. He really

wants help from the advertiser in putting the product in perspective, in picturing it in the setting in which he is expected to use it and enjoy it. But what if the way of life suggested by the advertisement is shoddy and unattractive? Who wants to live in a hypochondriac's world in which the greatest joy is quick relief from headache? Who wants to live in a fool's paradise in which smokers believe that they can indulge in nicotine and yet escape all the hazards of indulgence? Who really wants the dullard's cuisine in which bland and tasteless foods are touted as the gourmet's delight? The consumer cannot believe in the product if the advertiser could not possibly believe in the kind of world he projects as a setting for his product.

Marketing attempts to alter the patterns of contemporary culture and advertising is its primary instrument for this purpose. Some critics charge that advertising is an active agency in the debasement of public taste. It is more likely that advertising has contributed to cultural confusion. Advertising itself is a public art and as an art it deserves and must expect criticism. *The Saturday Review of Literature* has made a beginning in establishing annual awards for advertising. But advertising is not only art but prophecy. Not only advertising but marketing in general is in the business of making promises. Its practitioners set themselves up in the business of dreaming dreams and seeing visions.

The marketing executive should at least stop and consider whether he would like to live in the kind of world his efforts might seem calculated to produce.

Chapter 23

PLANNING AND PROBLEM SOLVING IN MARKETING: A BOOK REVIEW*

Wroe Alderson and Paul Green. Homewood, Ill.: Richard D. Irwin, Inc., 1964. 661 pp. $13.35.

Arnold E. Amstutz
Sloan School of Management, Massachusetts Institute of Technology

This volume contains the beginning of four books:

- a practical philosophy of management by authors' well-acquainted with corporate infrastructures,

- an exposition of Bayesian decision theory by its foremost proponent,

- a how-to guide to executive planning and control,

- a pragmatic review of approaches to marketing strategy formulation and execution

The book begins with Wroe Alderson's sagacious observations on leadership, organizations, and executive personalities and motivations. His comments on the mechanics of power reveal an empathetic understanding of "the type of man who wants to sit at the head of the table." His "six or seven general views of how to manage a business" provide a multidimensional evaluation of alternative management approaches ranging from the well-tuned up business that can run itself to the formal planning and systems approach associated with management by decision rule. Because of his discernment the reader may be disappointed by the lack of discussion in support of the author's commitment to the negotiative process perspective.

Those who matched wits with Alderson will recall the exuberance with which he approached a new puzzle as they read his characterization of problem solving as an aspiration, the too short discourse on "insight—the search for significant

*Originally appeared in the *Journal of Marketing Research* 1968, 5(February, No. 1), pages 109-111.

structure," his synthesis of planning and problem solving, and the careful analysis of the twelve-coin problem and the single corner problem after Chapter 3.

The second section of the book begins discussing uncertainty and decision making in market planning; Green examines the design and planning of purposeful behavior sequences for the firm. Beginning with a general model of a problem situation he presents the maximin, minimax regret, and Laplace criteria of choice as unworthy alternatives to the Bayesian approach to decision making. The fundamentals of Bayesian decision theory are reviewed in a concise presentation of prior, posterior, and preposterior analysis. Assuming only a brief exposure to classical statistics, Green effectively summarizes relevant concepts and theorems preparing the reader to work comfortably within the Bayesian framework. His exposition of value theory as related to decision making takes explicit account of the often ignored difficulties of quantifying and evaluating alternative management objectives. Comparative structural assumptions and relationships are clearly delineated in the text and a technical appendix.

This section gives four applications of the Bayesian approach. New product development decisions are used to effectively contrast a well-structured, if tedious, hypothetical example and a real-world management application. Classical and Bayesian approaches to the pricing decision are outlined in a review of marginal analysis, multiple linear regression, and a Bayesian analysis of price-volume relationships.

Asserting that "the current state of technique development does not permit definitive... (assessment of)... how much to spend for promotion," Green elaborates on budget determination through marginal analysis and dynamic programming under the assumption that suitable response functions are given. The design of market experiments using analysis of variance and a Bayesian decision framework are contrasted.

Distribution channel decisions are deemed to be directly amenable to cost and value analysis if one is willing to accept management's prior assessment of future market conditions, salesmen effectiveness, etc. An evaluation of in-house sales force versus external sales agents using the Bayesian framework and a linear programming approach to the transportation problem conclude this section.

The third section concerns design, techniques of market planning, the end products of planning, and an overview of the planning function. Alderson proposes parallel principles of optimization and structural principles of design. His principles of optimization start from a conception of how an entity functions and name the variables for which a maximum or minimum value is sought. These include campaigns that optimize the use of time, facilities optimize the use of space, organizations optimize decision power, and systems optimize operational effectiveness. His structural principles are concerned with the pattern of activity devised so that a plan may function optimally.

Each of the four end products of planning (campaigns, facilities, organizations, and systems) as associated with three planning levels are discussed. The first step in campaign planning is to consider the order of steps or stages in the sequence of activity. After considering the before-and-after relationships, the planner determines the amount of time required. Finally, he sets starting and closing dates for the proposed activity. "Facility planning is carried through the stages of coping with proximity, area, and site." Organization planning begins with an analysis of the hierarchy or chain of command. From the organization hierarchy the planner proceeds to specify duties for each position and to name the personnel who are to fill the various posts in the hierarchy and to function in accordance with the duties prescribed. System planning begins with the consideration of objectives. Desirability must be balanced against feasibility. Objectives must be stated operationally in terms of expected outputs or in terms of the state of affairs at some future date taken as a target. The next step in system planning is building a model of the system in operation. The practical question is to determine a suitable level of aggregation that will cast more light on the basic structure of the system. The final step is to provide procedures for scheduling and coordinating the specific campaigns which are being executed by the system. These campaigns may be seen as the fundamental outputs of the system.

Alderson views the planning process as a dialogue or interchange between the executive responsible for action and the staff planner. "The expected outcome of the dialogue is that the executive will talk himself into adopting a specific course of action." The planning dialogue, formal interchange, should move progressively toward the visualization of a preferred course of action and its ultimate adoption as the company's official program. Alderson believed that the planner-executive interchange can deal with three broad subjects: the content of the planning assignment, including the situation the plan is expected to meet and the issues to be resolved in preparing a plan; the discipline of planning and the growth of understanding by participation in the planning dialogue; and the planning contract or definition of mutual commitment under which the planner must operate. Alderson hoped this book would make it easier to talk about planning and marketing. The aim in part was to give a kind of "agenda for the conversations in somewhat more organic form than the usual check list."

Four chapters concern the planning of campaigns. The process begins with a preplan audit designed to achieve the double balance fundamental to the marketing audit—the balance between needs and resources and the balance between opportunity and effort. The unique position of the firm in the market is defined by differential advantage with respect to competition. Marketing opportunities are arrayed against the marketing effort expended in the cultivation of opportunity. Statements of corporate profit objectives are examined in light of qualifications based on growth and stability requirements, noneconomic considerations, and short range constraints. The role of forecasting in planning is developed conceptually in terms of factors affecting future fluctuations and growth. Costs associated with forecast error are considered.

Chapter 16 introduces several approaches that may speed up the (creative) process by bringing some measure of system into the search for strategic ideas. Concepts suggested include formulation of strategic interaction as game theory, exploitation of new or unusual opportunities, reactive strategies, life cycle-oriented planning, strategic timing, and triangulation of goals, opportunities, and effort.

Chapters 17 through 20 contain a pragmatic discussion of design principles applicable to campaigns, facilities, organizations, and systems. Topics considered under campaigns include the mechanics of critical path scheduling, market segmentation, product characteristic matching, and new product development. The discussion of facilities design covers merchandise warehouses, display space arrangement, supermarket aisle layouts, store and warehouse location, territorial structures, and market segmentation.

Alderson formulates an approach to organization design based on two optimizing principles and several interrelated structural principles of design. He moves, perhaps too swiftly, through structural attributes associated with functions, products, and customers; centralization versus decentralization; line-staff balance; the effective use of committees; planning internal communication structures; and distinguishing between the static structure of the organization and the structure for decision-making process. A succinct presentation of procedures for dynamic organization planning is the last observation.

The fourth chapter on design considerations presents marketing cost analysis as a primary tool for planning or replanning a marketing system. Methods for structuring, analyzing, and evaluating the marketing operation are considered. Horizontal systems encompassing products, channels, and markets are illustrated with a projectable cost and profit model. Vertical aspects of system structure are represented by an inventory model.

The final chapter in the managerial practice section handles some issues involved in operating under a detailed marketing plan. Tests of the logic of the plan and its underlying assumptions are proposed in addition to the traditional assessments of market and competitive conditions.

The concluding chapter is designed to put the planning function in perspective, from the various viewpoints of the planner, the top executive and his subordinates at the organization's various levels. Alderson returns to the wide angle focus of the first chapters to contemplate foresight as organized hindsight and determination of the optimal amount of time devoted to planning in any given planning problem. He compares the activities of a first-rate executive to those of Hannibal and to twentieth century commanders. Problems of strategy, organization structure, coordination, and top management involvement in the planning process are surveyed.

The chapters end with a paradigm of planning that summarizes the framework and principles introduced earlier. A standard planning outline is presented as a departure point in determining planning methods for any given assignment.

Various aspects of the book's organization and content could be criticized. The lack of footnotes identifying sources referenced only as some theorists or one authority might disturb the scholarly reader. More attention could have been given to measurement problems. Questions of process and response measurement are too often deferred to future research. The quantitative procedures presented are not really adequate for many management concerns qualitatively formulated. A FORTRAN program included as an example of product development simulation is unintelligible because it was prepared on a printer equipped with the wrong type chain.

But these points are not fundamentally significant. The topic considered is global; there is so much that could be said. Under different circumstances it could be concluded that Alderson and Green laid the ground-work for three or four collaborative works that will be eagerly anticipated. As it is we can appreciate the insights and concepts Alderson recorded here and look to Paul Green for further development of the paradigm and associated measures and analytic procedures.

COMMENTARIES ON ALDERSONIAN MARKETING

INTRODUCTION TO PART IV: ALDERSON'S MARKET BEHAVIOR THEORY WITH ITS LINKS TO OTHER THEORIES

Robert D. Tamilia

Over the years, Alderson's theoretical work has encouraged many authors to elucidate his work. A single article cannot ever hope to capture the essence of all of his contributions. When an author elaborates on some parts of his work, it not only helps us better understand his contributions, it also adds to his body of thought that enriches the marketing discipline. Selecting a representative set of previously published material on Alderson was no easy task. One criterion used was to select material that show how Aldersonian thought stood up relative to other management and economic contributions and theories. It was sheer delight to discover that not only is Aldersonian thought still acceptable and respectable in this 21st c., his work can further contribute to theory development not only in marketing but in strategic management and economics as well. For example, his contributions are still consistent with Austrian economics and relevant to value chain analysis, industrial organization economics and the political economy framework applied in marketing.

Portions of the Grether article is reproduced here for the simple reason that Alderson was the person originally responsible for writing a chapter honoring Edward Chamberlin's contributions to monopolistic competition theory. We really do not know what Alderson would have said about Chamberlin's views on competition and their impact on marketing theory development had he not died. We know that the two met on a number of occasions, one in particular at a marketing theory seminar held at the University of Vermont in 1954, where the two exchanged ideas on market discrepancies and related topics. In this shortened version of his article, Grether discusses how the marketing discipline distanced itself from economic theory by stressing managerial decision making to the neglect of marketing theory development. Despite the trend, Grether showed how Alderson was able to offer a more formalized theory of marketing based in part on economic analysis that was in some ways more ambitious and complicated than Chamberlin's theory of monopolistic competition.

The Hunt, Muncy and Ray article attempts to clarify Alderson's marke behavior theory. The approach used was to reconstruct and restate some parts of the theory into a discrete set of statements, each one presented as a proposition. The rationale was that by formalizing Alderson's theory, it would help the uninitiated or those that never really understood him an opportunity to grasp the fundamentals of his theory. Additional readings are needed, of course, if a more thorough understanding of Alderson is sought because the approach does not present the thought behind each proposition.

The Reekie and Savitt (1982) article was selected because of its intellectual rigor and its contributions to theory development in marketing from an Alderson perspective. It is a challenging article to read, especially for students with less than a formal training in economics. This article illustrates well the link of Austrian economics with Alderson's market behavior theory. Austrian economics is a school of economic thought originally developed in the late 19th c. as a reaction to neoclassical economics' emphasis on marginal analysis and has since regained status in the 1970s. It has remarkable links to Aldersonian marketing thought because of the way Alderson treats information, market heterogeneity and the entrepreneurial element in marketing decision making. Moreover, Austrian economists are not concerned about the attainment of market equilibrium as assumed in orthodox economic theory but the attempt to reach it is what's important, in agreement with Alderson's market behavior theory. It is noteworthy that Alderson was familiar with the works of Bšhm-Bawerk a pioneer Austrian economist whom he credits for the notion that a consumer is engaged in building an assortment of goods and to replenish or extend an inventory of goods for use by households (i.e. the potency of assortment concept). Although not discussed in this text, Austrian economists claim that the notion of the sorting process had its origin in the works of Carl Menger, a 19^{t} c. Austrian economist (Reekie 1984). The authors claim that an understanding of market processes by means other than by neoclassical economics may result in a better understanding of market behavior with implications for managers as well as marketing's place in the overall economy.

The article by Dixon and Wilkinson (1989) was selected because of its bold attempt to develop a general theory of marketing based on Aldersonian concepts and a Parsonian view of society. Hunt, Muncy and Ray also presented a general theory of marketing but unlike the macro perspective of Dixon and Wilkinson theirs is more micro. This article is an elaboration of chapter 1 from their 1982 book (*The Marketing System*, Longman, pp. 1-23) as well as Dixon' (1984) formalization of a general theory of macromarketing. Starting from a simple transaction between a buyer and seller in a market, the authors propose a framework such that the cumulative impact of all such transactions can lead to a national economy and where marketing fits in such a macro aspect of society. Their modest attempt is one of first attempts to link micromarketing with macromarketing.

Priem, Rasheed and Amirani (1997) represent recent authors who have discussed Alderson's market behavior theory in light of scholarly advances in the management and economic literature. More precisely, they compare Alderson's theory with Michael Porter's value chain analysis, a theory based on industrial organization economics. What makes this article all the more surprising is that the management literature is even aware of Alderson's work, contrary to present-day marketing academics. They concluded that Alderson's concept of the transvection was richer and ahead of his time than Porter's concept of value chain. They recommended a rapprochement between marketing and strategic management, which hopefully might lead to new theory development and extensions of existing concepts with rewarding research opportunities. One article by Priem (1992), not included due to space limitation, is his discussion of industrial organization economics and how Alderson's theory represents an improvement of the traditional economic theory of SCP (structure, conduct and performance). After all, Alderson believed that function was a determinant of structure. It is interesting to note that the 2001 Nobel Prize winner in economics was awarded based on how information exchanges work in asymmetric markets. Yet Alderson argued decades earlier that information asymmetries between parties to transactions are key factors in heterogeneous markets. Another interesting point by Priem (1992) is that sorts can either increase or decrease heterogeneity, depending on how far the sorts are from supply or demand conditions. This is similar to the postponement and speculation principles. The closer the actual production of the good, the more heterogeneous the product is for the buyer but not for others. Priem and his colleagues concluded that new developments in IOE, Porter's work, Williamson's market hierarchies, TCA, among others, provide amble evidence for further expansion and extension of Alderson's market behavior theory.

These articles illustrate well that when the theory of monopolistic competition, value chain analysis, industrial organization economics, and channel theory, among others, are studied in light of Alderson's marketing thought, it is clear that marketing cannot only be the study of the individual consumers. Marketing is intertwined and interconnected with many other market processes, market functions and market structures such that it forms the backbone of our economic system.

Chapter 25

ALDERSON AND CHAMBERLIN*

E. T. Grether

The late Wroe Alderson had agreed to write this essay on Chamberlin's impact on marketing literature. His untimely death led to the substitution of the present writer on the assignment. Although Alderson's files did not disclose any formal work on the Chamberlin essay, a posthumous book (Alderson, 1965), in conjunction with his earlier writings, does suggest the possible nature of Alderson's interpretation.

Wroe Alderson was without doubt the most influential "marketing theorist" in recent times in the United States. His influence radiated both from his voluminous writings and from his personal force, the latter exerted especially through the annual summer seminars on marketing theory of which he was the architect and continuing intellectual provocateur. Alderson's interests and talents were unique in many respects, including a profound interest in both theory and marketing action. During all of his life he was engaged in active consultation and in private practice for business and government, either on a personal basis or, in later years, through the consulting firm that bore his name. Although he had some interest in theory for the sake of theory, his basic orientation was in theory oriented toward marketing action. His best-known book was entitled *Market Behavior and Executive Action* (Alderson, 1957).

He labeled his approach as "functionalist" or "functionalism"; his posthumous volume *Dynamic Marketing Behavior* bears the subtitle "*A Functionalist Theory of Marketing.*" But this verbiage for him did not merely replicate the "functional" approach and categories of the traditional marketing treatments.

Alderson's basic interest was in problem solving at both the micro and macro-levels, but primarily, at the micro-level (Alderson and Green, 1964). He was concerned first with goals, objectives, and purposes, or "functions." Structure must serve and facilitate the purposes or desired outcome, or function. He conceived of society as a congeries of loose and tight "organized behavior

---

*Originally published as "Chamberlin's Theory of Monopolistic Competition and the Literature of Marketing" in Robert Kuenne, editor (1967) *Monopolistic Competition Theory: Studies in Impact* pages 315-318, John Wiley and Sons, New York.

systems." This conceptualization logically carried him in two directions: (1) the analysis of the internal goals, objectives, and organization of individual systems, and (2) the linkage of individual systems, as subsystems, into some sort of total systems conceptualization. His emphasis on problem solving and action programs led him to stress a normative systems approach, although he was interested also in descriptive or explanatory systems analysis. For him, there was always a gap (representing room for improvement) between descriptive systems analysis and normative systems analysis (Alderson, 1965, p. 319).

Now what has all this to do with Chamberlin? To begin with, Alderson avowedly had the same Weltanschauung in looking at economic society. Like Chamberlin he was impressed by the basic heterogeneity and variety about him, instead of the homogeneity assumed in the economics of perfect and pure competition. In terms of the general functioning of marketing, this led Alderson to stress searching and sorting as basic aspects of the "logic of exchange" (Alderson, 1957, Ch. VII). The exchange processes never culminated in a full equilibrium through a pricing mechanism, but represented ongoing movements under the propulsions of the attempts of various types of enterprises (business or household or others) to solve their problems. These endeavors were analyzed and interpreted in terms of ecological behavior, or adjustments of enterprises to environment. But these "group" adjustments were not deterministic (as under the competitive market system)— there was always a presumption of some amount of genuine free choice and discretion.

Freedom of choice expressed itself basically in a continuing search for differential advantage on the part of all participants in the heterogeneous universe. At this point Alderson again gained sustenance from and joined forces with Chamberlin. Alderson stated his indebtedness as follows:

> The writer has drawn upon E. H. Chamberlin for the treatment of differential advantage although the term has never been used by Chamberlin. At our first meeting in 1933, Chamberlin was amused by questions about his sales experience and how he had acquired his remarkable knowledge of marketing (Alderson, 1965, p. 184).

Alderson characterized the search for differential advantage in terms of six types of strategies for differentiation of a market position; namely, those of market segmentation, selection of appeals, transvection[1], product improvement, process improvement, and product innovation. He compared his analysis of these six types with Chamberlin's and concluded, no doubt incorrectly, that Chamberlin's product differentiation replicated only his product innovation (Alderson, 1965, p. 185).

---

[1] "Transvection" is a concept invented by Alderson in 1958 and was defined by him as follows: "A transvection is the unit of action for the system by which a single end product such as a pair of shoes is placed in the hands of the consumer after moving through all the intermediate sorts and transformations from the original raw materials in the state of nature" (Alderson, 1965, p. 84).

Chamberlin and Alderson, in fact, agreed in one further aspect of their approaches. In his final volume, in a discussion of advertising theory, Alderson noted that

> Chamberlin's analysis largely adopts the viewpoint of the single firm marketing a differentiated product. He makes use of the concept of an industry consisting of a number of firms, but the concept is difficult to define within the framework of his theory. In the strictest sense each seller constitutes a one-firm industry under monopolistic competition (Alderson, 1965, p. 185).

Actually, the stress on the individual enterprise and its uniqueness in a universe of heterogeneity created a more serious problem in terms of macroanalysis for Alderson than for Chamberlin. Chamberlin as an economist consistently considered himself to be engaged in economic analysis. Alderson's stress on the functional behavior of organized behavior systems led him into a broad sociobehavioral type of analysis far beyond that of Chamberlin. Alderson's problem of linking the enterprise-organized behavioral subsystem into a broader framework of systems was much more ambitious and complicated than that of Chamberlin. Chamberlin was still able to link his enterprise into the price system through concepts of group interaction and equilibrium not available or of interest to Alderson.

Alderson's "functionalism" placed its stress on the nature and means of improving the functioning of organized behavior individually. The interrelationships among such systems were handled under a wide-ranging conceptualization of proximate and ultimate ecological environments. On the contrary, economic analysis posits the linkage into a system of competitive adjustments (equilibrium). If the actual going concern doesn't fit into the ideal economic system, then, according to Alderson, it is handled outside as a monopolist or is brought under the system by reducing it to an appropriate abstract form. Ultimately, Chamberlin qua economist was interested in the firm viewed within the totality of the competitive economy. On the contrary, Alderson was basically interested in the total set of relations only as these affected the functional behavior of the firm as an organized behavior system. Alderson's approach would fit into or relate to a rational total system only if the behavior of the individual behavior system were (1) subordinated to or under the aegis of a goal-directed society or (2) determined by impersonal forces, as the competitive market system. Alderson, however, accepted neither of these sets of relationships explicitly. Consequently he was left dangling in a vague form of social environmentalism, under which a variety of general systems concepts appear in diverse contexts en route to a full "science of society." Chamberlin evades all of this by confining himself to economic analysis.

References

Alderson, Wroe (1957). *Marketing Behavior and Executive Action: A Functionalist Approach to Marketing* . Richard D. Irwin Inc, Homewood.

Alderson, Wroe (1965). *Dynamic Marketing Behavior: A Functionalist Theory of Marketing*. Richard D. Irwin Inc., Homewood.

Alderson, Wroe and Green, Paul (1964). *Planning and Problem Solving in Marketing*. Richard D. Irwin Inc., Homewood.

Chapter 26

ALDERSON'S GENERAL THEORY OF MARKETING: A FORMALIZATION*

Shelby D. Hunt
Texas Tech University

James A. Muncy
Texas Tech University

Nina M. Ray
Texas Tech University

Abstract

Wroe Alderson is one of three marketers to attempt a general theory of marketing. Substantial controversy exists concerning this general theory, partially because few understand Alderson and his work. The authors attempt to clarify Alderson's work by "formalizing" his theory.

1. Introduction

There have been several attempts to develop a general theory of marketing: Bartels (1968), EI-Ansary (1979), and Alderson (1965). Bartels (1968) proposed that a general theory of marketing consisted of the following seven component sub theories: 1) the theory of social initiative; 2) the theory of economic separations; 3) the theory of market roles, expectations, and interactions; 4) the theory of flows and systems; 5) the theory of behavior constraints; 6) the theory of social change and marketing evolution; and 7) the theory of the social control of marketing.

---

*Originally published in Ben Enis and K. Koering eds. (1981) *Review of Marketing 1981* pages 267-272, American Marketing Association, Chicago.

Hunt (1971) analyzed the seven sub theories proposed by Bartels, found them to be lacking in lawlike generalizations, and concluded that the seven sub theories were not theories at all but were "an assemblage of classificational schemata, some intriguing definitions, and exhortations to fellow marketing students to adopt a particular perspective in attempting to generate marketing theory." Further evaluations of Bartels' "general theory" were conducted by Pinson, Angelmar, and Roberto (1972) which concluded that more specific criteria for evaluating theoretical constructions were needed. A reply by Hunt (1973) provided further explication of criteria for evaluating theories and concluded that Bartels' conceptualization was "neither a theory of marketing nor a general theory of marketing."

EI-Ansary (1979) proposed that, by definition, the general theory of marketing should be the "broadest theory" explaining marketing phenomena. Further, the general theory of marketing should be the "central theory" or the culmination of all other theories, and should "logically integrate" all other theories in marketing. Although EI-Ansary did not specifically develop a general theory of marketing, he proposed an outline, which if developed, would comprise a general theory of marketing. EI-Ansary suggested that a general theory of marketing would be composed of sub theories involving the following areas: consumer behavior, organizational buyer behavior, interorganizational management, channel member behavior, channel system behavior, channel institutions, micromarketing, macromarketing, and strategic marketing. The conceptualization of a general theory of marketing put forth by EI-Ansary has not yet been subjected to critical analysis.

The works of Wroe Alderson constitute the third approach to developing a general theory of marketing. Although Alderson authored numerous articles, two books summarize the major points of his theory: *Marketing Behavior and Executive Action* (1957) and *Dynamic Marketing Behavior* (1965). The present article will focus on and attempt to formalize Alderson's general theory of marketing.

2.   Background

Substantial controversy exists concerning Alderson's general theory of marketing and its contribution to marketing thought. An early review by Nicosia (1962) suggested that Alderson's theory "merits consideration as a frame of reference." Similarly, Schwartz (1963) concluded that "on the whole, Alderson's concept of an organized behavior system and his theory of market behavior represent a significant contribution to marketing theory." As evidence of continued interest in the works of Alderson, one need only to observe that there were four articles on Alderson in the proceedings of the 1979 American Marketing Association special conference on marketing theory, and three articles on Alderson in the 1980 theory conference. Finally, Blair and Uhl (1976) point out:

> marketing theorists of the 1950's and 1960's hailed Wroe Alderson as a leader in their field. Time has substantiated their judgment; Alderson's works are among the few writings of their period accorded anything more than historical esteem... Alderson was the most powerful author immediately preceding what Kotler has called marketing's shift from applied economics to applied behavioral science... Alderson's writings offer perhaps the most recent general theory of marketing. Also, Alderson was an author of great insight. These facts contribute to Alderson's continued major significance in modern marketing thought.

Nevertheless, many authors have seriously examined the status of Aldersonian theory in current literature. They concluded that "almost none of the concepts pioneered by this leading marketing theorist appear in any of the leading (selling) marketing principles texts." Barksdale (1980) also observed that few marketing books include references to Alderson's work. Barksdale also concluded that Alderson's concepts were "not well developed," his ideas were "not closely reasoned," and his theoretical system never became the organizing concept for the mainstream of marketing thought.

Why are there such widely divergent views on Alderson's general theory of marketing? The thesis of this paper is that a substantial amount of the controversy can be attributed to differences in interpreting Alderson's work. These different interpretations have led to substantial misunderstandings concerning Alderson's theory of marketing. It is sad, but true, that Alderson was a notoriously non-systematic writer. As Hostiuck and Kurtz (1973) point out, "even recognized scholars of marketing groan at the mere mention of Alderson and intimate that they never really understood him."

3. Purpose

The purpose of this paper is to clarify the issues concerning Alderson's work by reconstructing and rigorously stating in propositional format Alderson's entire general theory of marketing. In the philosophy of science this process is referred to as the "formalization" of a theory (Rudner 1966). The complete formalization of a theory consists of a formal language system that has been axiomatized and appropriately interpreted. Such a fully formalized theory would include: elements, definitions, formation rules for elements, axiom, transformation rules for axioms, rules of interpretation. Although very few theories are ever completely formalized, the process of partially formalizing theories is a key step in theory development. As has been observed (Hunt 1976), "the partial formalization of a theory is an absolutely necessary precondition for meaningful analysis of the theory." The remainder of this paper will attempt to rigorously reconstruct, that is, partially formalize, Alderson's general theory of marketing.

A Partial Formalization of Alderson's Theory of Marketing

A Definition of key terms

   1 There are three primitive elements in marketing: sets, behaviors, and expectations (1965, p. 25).

     a sets are aggregates containing some class of components such as points in a line, physical objects or human beings (1965, p. 47).

     b behavior is activity occupying time (1965, p. 48).

     c expectations are attached to what the individual thinks may happen and the favorable or unfavorable results of these future events (1965, p. 50).

   2 Collections are sets which can be taken as inert with no interaction among the components (1965, p. 47).

   3 Conglomerates are collections as they occur in a state of nature (1965, p. 57).

   4 Assortments are collections which have been assembled by taking account of human expectations concerning future action (1965, p. 47).

   5 Systems are sets in which interactions occur that serve to define the boundaries of the set (1965, p. 47).

   6 There are four kinds of behaviors (1965, p. 48).

     a normal behavior is that which is an end in itself or a means to an end,

     b symptomatic behavior is that which is not functional in that it is neither an end nor a means to an end,

     c congenial behavior is that which is chosen because it is presumed to be an end in itself and is directly satisfying, and

     d instrumental behavior is that which is regarded as a means to an end.

   7 A behavior system is a system in which persons are the interacting components (1965, p. 47).

   8 An organized behavior system is one with these minimum characteristics:

     a a criterion for membership,

     b a rule or set of rules assigning duties, and

     c a preference scale for outputs (1965, p. 48).

B Marketing is the exchange which takes place between consuming groups and supplying groups (1957, p. 15).

   1 Exchange in a society results from specialization of the production function (1965, p. 39).

   2 Marketing is fundamentally instrumental behavior (1965, p. 261).

3 Marketing is fundamentally a phenomenon of group behavior (1957, p. 13).

4 Marketing is conducted by organized behavior systems which have the following four subsystems (1957, p. 35):

   a a power system,

   b a communication system,

   c a system of inputs and outputs, and

   d a system of internal and external adjustments.

5 The potency of an assortment is the expected value of an assortment or its anticipated effectiveness in marketing contingencies (1965, p. 50).

6 The Law of Exchange states: if x is an element in the assortment A, and y is an element of the assortment B, then x is exchangeable for y if, and only if, the following three conditions hold:

   a x is different from y,

   b the potency of the assortment A is increased by dropping x and adding y, and

   c the potency of the assortment B is increased by adding x and dropping y (1965, p. 84) .

7 An exchange is optimal if both parties to the exchange prefer the exchange when compared to the set of all other available exchanges (1965, p. 85).

8 A set of exchanges in a series can replace direct sales by the supplier to the ultimate consumer if the exchanges are optimal at each step (1965, p. 85).

C The household is one of the two principal organized systems in marketing (1965, p. 37).

1 The household persists over time because the behavior system offers a surplus to its participants that they would not expect to enjoy outside the system (1965, p. 37).

2 The household purchasing agent enters the market to replenish or extend the assortment of goods needed to support expected patterns of future behavior (1965, p. 144).

3 Household buying behavior is a form of instrumental behavior (1965, p. 146).

4 The household purchasing agent engages in search behavior (1965, p. 50).

   a Search is defined as the sorting of information (1965, p. 50).

   b Searching for goods is largely a mental process involving movement on the part of the consumer but not involving physical movement of the goods (1965, p. 36).

5 The household purchasing agent is guided by two principles in making decisions:

  a the conditional value of the good if used, and

  b the probability of use or the estimated frequency of use (1965, p. 38).

6 Household demand is heterogeneous, that is, households have differences in tastes, desires, incomes, locations, and the uses for goods (1965, p. 193).

D The firm is the second primary organized behavior system in marketing (1965, p. 38).

  1 Firms evolve in a society when specialization of labor results in removing the production function from the household (1965, p. 39).

  2 Firms act as if they had a primary goal of survival (1957, p. 54).

    a The survival goal results from members of the firm believing that they can obtain more in terms of goods and status by working towards the survival of the system than by acting individually or by becoming a member of another system (1957, p. 54).

    b The goal of growth is sought because of the conviction that growth is necessary for survival (1957, pp. 103-108).

  3 In order to survive, firms compete with other firms in seeking the patronage of households (1957, p. 103-108).

  4 A firm can be assured of the patronage of a group of households only when the group has reasons to prefer the output of the particular firm over the output of competing firms (1957, pp. 103-108).

    a Therefore, each firm will seek some advantage over other firms to assure the patronage of a group of households.

    b Such a process is called "competition for differential advantage" (1957, pp. 103-108).

  5 Competition consists of the constant struggle of firms to develop, maintain, or increase their differential advantages over other firms (1957, p. 106). Competition for differential advantage is the primary force leading to innovation in marketing (1957, p. 102).

  6 New firms enter a field because of an expectation of enjoying some differential advantage (1957, p. 102). The success of the new firm creates opportunities for other firms to enter the field through:

    a simulation, that is, copying the marketing strategy of the original entrant,

    b deviation, that is, developing a marketing strategy which deviates in some significant way from the marketing strategy of the original entrant, and c complementation, that is, serving as a supplier to the original entrant (1965, pp. 198-200).

7 The bases of differential advantages are:

   a market segmentation,

   b selection of appeals,

   c transvection,

   d product improvement,

   e process improvement, and

   f product innovation (1965, p. 185).

8 Through time competitors will attempt to neutralize the differential advantage of an entrant (1965, p. 204).

   a The time for neutralization must be sufficiently long to provide an expected reward for innovation (1965, p. 206).

   b The time for neutralization must not be too long or firms will take unfair advantage of households (1965, p. 206).

   c Instantaneous neutralization occurs only in the case of price reductions on homogeneous or very closely competitive products with few sellers (1965, p. 204).

9 The existence of a differential advantage gives the firm a position in the marketplace known as an "ecological niche" (1957, p. 56).

   a The "core" of a firm's ecological niche consists of the group of households for which the firm's differential advantage is most completely suited (1957, p. 56).

   b The "fringe" of a firm's ecological niche consists of the group of households for which the firm's differential advantage is satisfactory but not ideal (1957, p. 56).

   c Firms can withstand (survive) attacks by competitors on its "fringe" as long as its "core" remains intact (1957, p. 56).

   d Firms can survive attacks by competitors on its "core" as long as they exhibit "plasticity," which is the will and ability to find another differential advantage and another core (1957, p. 57).

10 Given heterogeneity of demand and competition for differential advantage, there will be "heterogeneity of supply," that is, firms will produce:

   a a variety of different goods and

   b many variations of the same generic kind of goods (1957, p. 103).

E Given heterogeneity of demand and heterogeneity of supply. the fundamental purpose of marketing is to effect exchanges by matching segments of demand with segments of supply (1957, pp. 195-199).

1 The matching process comes about as a result of a sequence of sorts and transformations (1965, p. 26).

2 A sort is the assignment of goods, materials or components to the appropriate facilities (1965, p. 27). The four kinds of sorts are:

   a sorting out, the breaking down of a heterogeneous collection into smaller homogeneous collections; and

   b accumulation, the building up of a large homogeneous collection into several smaller homogeneous collections; and

   c allocating the breaking down of a large homogeneous collection into several smaller homogenous collections; and

   d assorting, the building up of a large heterogeneous collection from several homogeneous collections (1957, pp. 202-210) (1965, p. 34).

3 The sortability of a collection can be measured by the sortability scale (1965, p. 32)

   a Sortability $= \frac{(\text{number of classes}) - 1}{(\text{number of items}) - 1}$

   b A perfectly homogeneous collection would have a sortability of "zero" (1965, p. 32).

   c A perfectly heterogeneous collection would have a sortability of "one" (1965, p. 32).

4 Transformations are changes in the physical form of a good or its location in time or space (1965, p. 49).

5 A transvection is the unit of action by which a single end product is placed in the hands of the consumer after moving through all the intermediate sorts and transformations from the original raw materials in the state of nature (1965, p. 86).

6 In any transvection the sorts and transformations must alternate, that is, a sort always intervenes between any two transformations (1965, p. 93).

7 A transvection has the optimal number of steps if costs cannot be decreased either by increasing or decreasing the number of sorts or transformations (1965, p. 94).

8 The sum of all transvections during a given period, allowing for time lags, is equivalent to the marketing process (1965, p. 35).

9 Heterogeneous markets may be "discrepant" (1965, p. 27).

   a There may be goods desired by consumers but not produced. This kind of discrepancy is "cleared" by innovation (1965, p. 27).

   b There may be goods produced by firms but not desired by consumers. This kind of discrepancy is "cleared" by information (1965, p. 27).

c Discrepant markets result from failures in communication (1965, p. 29).

d A major problem for marketing is determining the optimal amount of information to clear markets (1965, p. 30).

10 Homogeneous markets may be discrepant. Homogeneous discrepant markets are not "cleared" by innovation, but rather, by adjusting:

a price and

b quantity (1965, p. 28).

11 In heterogeneous markets the role of price is reduced to a datum which is included in the information that households need to know about a good (1965, p. 31).

12 In a perfectly heterogeneous market each small segment of demand could be satisfied by just one unique segment of supply (1965, p. 29). In real world markets there are always partial homogeneities, that is:

a groups of households desiring essentially the same product and

b groups of firms supplying essentially the same product (1965, p. 26).

F A third organized behavior system in marketing is the channel of distribution.

1 The channel of distribution does not qualify as a primary organized behavior system in marketing.

a This is, because in contrast with firms and households, not all channels of distribution are organized behavior systems (1965, p. 44).

b Only those channels of distribution where all participants have a common stake in the survival of the channel should be considered organized behavior systems (1965, p. 44).

2 Indications of whether a particular channel can be considered to be an organized behavior system are:

a whether there is a control group which develops a marketing plan of operation for the channel and

b whether there is cooperation among the members of the channel in adhering to the plan (1965, p. 252).

3 A primary cause of conflict in channels of distribution is the distribution of rewards among the channel members (1965, p. 253).

4 Both large manufacturers and large retailers attempt to be the control group which develops the marketing plan for the channel and turns it into an organized behavior system (1965, p. 257).

5 Marketing intermediaries (and therefore, channels) come into existence because they can effect economies in sorting (1957, p. 211).

a One major economy is the reduction of contactual costs (1965, p. 250).

b The number of contacts between n manufacturers and m retailers is n times m (1965, p. 250).

c The number of contacts between n manufacturers and m retailers, given one wholesaler, is n plus m (1965, p. 250).

6 The assortment of goods which is optimal for any particular manufacturer to produce is seldom the same as the assortment of goods which is optimal for an intermediary to carry. The difference between these two optimal assortments is called the "discrepancy of assortments" (1965, p. 78).

7 The discrepancy of assortments is a major inhibiting factor within channels of distribution.

a It inhibits the forward integration of manufacturers and the backward integration of retailers (1975, p. 217).

b This explains why the successive stages in marketing are so commonly operated as independent agencies (1957, p. 217).

8 A wholesaler is most vulnerable if it purchases only a small part of what the manufacturer supplies and sells to retailers only a small portion of what their customers demand (1965, p. 80). Therefore, wholesalers need to be strongly anchored either to their manufacturers or to their retailers.

9 There are four problem areas calling for decisions in retailing:

a store location and size;

b the assortment;

c store image; and

d form of promotion (1965, p. 212).

10 Every retail store is truly unique in at least one of its fundamental characteristics, namely, location (1965, p. 211).

G Given heterogeneity of demand, heterogeneity of supply, and the requisite institutions to effect the sorts and transformations necessary to match segments of demand with segments of supply. the marketing process will take conglomerate resources in the natural state and bring about meaningful assortments of goods in the hands of consumers (1965, p. 26).

4.   Conclusion

Readers will note that the term "functionalism" does not appear in the preceding formalization of Alderson's general theory of marketing. This absence is by design, not accident. Functionalism is a procedure or perspective which one can adopt in at tempting to create theory. Functionalism is not, of itself, a part of the final theoretical structure. In general, functional analysis seeks to understand a behavior pattern or sociocultural institution by determining the role it plays in keeping the given system in proper working order or maintaining it as a going concern (Hempel, 1965). Unfortunately, Nicosia (1962) and others have continued to refer to "Alderson's functionalism" as if functionalism were an inherent part of the theory itself. It is not.

The preceding formalization of Alderson's general theory of marketing explains at least some of the variance in the differing evaluations of Alderson's work. For example, Blair and Uhl conclude that "Alderson's functionalism will not characterize enlightened efforts in future marketing theory construction." However, their conclusion is based in part on attributing to Alderson such positions as the following: "organized behavior systems were defined through Barnard's model, as collectivities whose organizing glue is economic advantage, and whose members all act to maximize organizational achievement" (emphasis added). As can be clearly seen in the formalization, Alderson did not state that the members "act to maximize organizational achievement." Alderson states that members of an organized behavior system pursue their own goals while attempting to insure the survival of the organized system.

In order to effectively evaluate the theoretical efforts of an author, it is absolutely imperative to be accurate and precise as to exactly what the theorist's position is/was. It is the belief of the present authors that the definitive evaluation of Alderson's general theory of marketing has yet to be undertaken. We hope and believe that the preceding formalization will assist theoretical analysts in their efforts to evaluate Alderson's work.

Assuming that the preceding formalization accurately characterizes Alderson's general theory of marketing, it is, or is it not, a good "general theory?" What is needed are some criteria for evaluating "general" theories. Both Hunt (1976) and Zaltman (1972) have explored the issue of evaluating theoretical construction. For example, Zaltman (1972) suggests that there are four classes of criteria for evaluating theoretical constructions: 1) formal criteria, 2) semantical criteria, 3) methodological criteria, and 4) epistemological criteria. Nevertheless, these works and criteria do not address the issue of whether there are specific criteria which should be applied to "general" theories as compared to ordinary, "garden variety" theoretical constructions. Intuitively, it would seem that the adequacy of a "general" theory of marketing would depend in large part on precisely delimiting the exact nature of marketing phenomena and the marketing discipline. The definitive evaluation of Alderson's general theory of marketing must await the complete explication of the characteristics of a general theory.

References

Alderson, Wroe (1957). *Marketing Behavior and Executive Action: A Functionalist Approach to Marketing*. Richard D. Irwin Inc., Homewood.

Alderson, Wroe (1965). *Dynamic Marketing Behavior: A Functionalist Theory of Marketing*. Richard D. Irwin Inc., Homewood.

Barksdale, H. C. (1980). Wroe Alderson's Contributions to Marketing Theory. In Lamb, Charles and Dunne, Patrick, editors, *Theoretical Developments in Marketing*, pages 1–3. American Marketing Association, Chicago.

Bartels, Robert (1968). The General Theory of Marketing. *Journal of Marketing*, 32(January):29–33.

Blair, Ed and Uhl, Kenneth P. (1976). Wroe Alderson and Modern Marketing Theory. In Slater, Charles C., editor, *Macro-Marketing Distributive Processes from a Societal Perspective*, pages 66–84.

Dawson, Jr., Lyndon E. and Wales, Hugh G. (1979). Consumer Motivation Theory in Historical Perspective: An Aldersonian View. In Ferrell, O. C., Brown, Stephen W., and Lamb, Jr., Charles W., editors, *Conceptual and Theoretical Developments in Marketing*, pages 210–221. American Marketing Association, Chicago.

El-Ansary, Adel I. (1979). The General Theory of Marketing Revisited. In Ferrell, O. C., Brown, Stephen W., and Lamb, Jr., Charles W., editors, *Conceptual and Theoretical Developments in Marketing*, pages 399–407. American Marketing Association, Chicago.

Hempel, Carl (1965). *Aspects of Scientific Explanation*. The Free Press, New York.

Hostiuck, K. Tim and Kurtz, David L. (1973). Alderson's Functionalism and the Development of Marketing Theory. *Journal of Business Research*, 1(2):141–156.

Hunt, Shelby D. (1971). The Morphology of Theory and the General Theory of Marketing. *Journal of Marketing*, 31(April):65–68.

Hunt, Shelby D. (1973). Lawlike Generalizations and Marketing Theory. *Journal of Marketing*, 37(July):69–70.

Hunt, Shelby D. (1976). *Marketing Theory: Conceptual Foundation of Research in Marketing*. Grid, Inc., Columbus.

Nicosia, Francesco M. (1962). Marketing and Alderson's Functionalism. *Journal of Business*, 35(October):403–413.

Pinson, Christian R. A., Reinhard, Anglemar, and Roberto, Edwardo L. (1972). An Evaluation of the General Theory of Marketing. *Journal of Marketing*, 36(July):66–69.

Rudner, Richard (1966). *Philosophy of Social Science*. Prentice-Hall, Inc., Englewood Cliffs.

Schwartz, George (1963). *Development of Marketing Theory.* South-Western Publishing Company, Cincinnati, Ohio.

Zaltman, G., Pinson, C. R. A., and Angelmar, R. (1972). *Metatheory in Consumer Research.* Rinehart and Winston, Inc., New York.

Chapter 27

MARKETING BEHAVIOUR AND ENTREPRENEURSHIP: A SYNTHESIS OF ALDERSON AND AUSTRIAN ECONOMICS*†

W. Duncan Reekie

Ronald Savitt

Marketing is multi-faceted and describes a societal institution and an organisational function as well as prescribing a philosophy of decision making. In all three of these dimensions the main concern is understanding how markets work and how market participants actually behave. As a philosophy of decision making marketing is the process of first determining and then fulfilling consumer wants. It is premised on a recognition of the heterogeneity found in real life markets and on the appreciation of how decision makers go about the matching of market offerings with market demands. Efficiency of want satisfaction is the prime consideration, not Pareto optimality. This, of course, only begs the question.

In brief, marketing analysis assumes *ab initio* that the true state of the world is diversity rather than homogeneity. Hence for decision makers the attainment of efficiency implies some "matching" of the discrepancies between heterogeneous supplies and demands as the source of want satisfaction. This matching is never total. The clearance of markets as described in basic economic theory is viewed as the exception. Hence the role of the decision maker goes beyond that of either a participator in a Walrasian auction for setting price; or that of a selector of quantity as postulated by Marshall. The marketing decision maker must engage in the more complex task of entrepreneurship.

The purpose of this article is to merge the ideas of Wroe Alderson, one of the most original marketing theorists, with the recent works in Austrian economics in order to provide a point of departure for an entrepreneurial-based theory of marketing. The discussion is presented in three sections. The first reviews Alderson's concepts of market behaviour and integrates them with the Austrian perspective. The second section is addressed to an investigation of the nature of information required in dynamic markets. It explores the question "How much information

---

*The authors are grateful to Roger Beck for fastidious and provocative comment. No blame and much credit attaches to his contributions to our views

†Originally appeared in 1982 in the *European Journal of Marketing*, 16(7), pages 55-66.

is enough?". The final section establishes the role of the entrepreneur in the dynamic market as the means of answering this question.

1. Alderson, Austrianism and Market Clearing

Alderson attacked the problems of the market from the point of view of the businessman who requires knowledge of how markets operate (and recommendations of how they may be made to work better). Alderson did not believe that general equilibrium analysis could provide sufficient understanding of the market process: hence, he argued that such an approach must be widely expanded. "Economics as the mathematical logic of scarcity is invaluable for marketers but not sufficient... But the level of taste, the technological functions, and the *flows of information* which the economist takes for granted are the primary business of a science of marketing" (Alderson, 1965, p. 303, emphasis added). This is similar to the view which we now find Austrian economists expressing. "Faulty decision-making is (more than) mistakes in arithmetic... making the 'right' decision... calls for a shrewd and wise assessment of the realities (both present and future) within the context of which the decision must be taken" (Kirzner, 1980, pp. 6-7).

Alderson emphasised the primacy of the *ex ante* entrepreneurial element in decision taking. Decisions in real life are taken today with a view to affecting conditions tomorrow. This in turn implies that decisions must be taken without full information and that the consequences can result in either gains or losses for the decision taker. To the extent that he guesses right he makes profits. If he "makes mistakes" he incurs losses. The profits from guessing right persist only so long as other market participants do not emulate him.

Alderson's approach thus differs dramatically from *ex post* analysis of an existing equilibrium. Explicitly, observation of the market process indicates that in some cases goods are sold at published prices, some goods are not, some consumers know of the offerings and some not, and some suppliers know of buyers and some do not. Since these conditions represent the rule rather than the exception, a theory of market behaviour must focus on this real market behaviour rather than on how markets theoretically should operate.

2. Market Behaviour

Alderson's theory of market behaviour begins by stripping away the assumptions of economic theory. He does this in several ways. His taxonomy replaced homogeneity with heterogeneity. Heterogeneity means that buyers have an infinite range of demands. It also means that the total set of wants is unique for each individual. Because such demands are heterogeneous suppliers in their turn may satisfy them in an infinite number of ways, subject to more or less accurate perceptions of the differences. Hence, simplified concepts of supply and demand have little explanatory value since they ignore the diversity of the real world. In addition, and not unimportantly, the *attainment* of equilibrium is unimportant to Alderson. The attempt to reach it is.

Alderson broadened the concept of demand by focusing on the desired attributes of each of a bundle of items. This makes the consumer's matching process complex. The value of the assortment sought by a demander can be described in terms of potency. "Potency... (is) the probability that the assortment will prove adequate over a planning period. The rational justification for buying (a) product... is that it will narrow the gap between the potency of some ideal assortment and (that of) the actual assortment as it will stand after the purchase" (Alderson, 1965, p. 231). That is, a motivating force for the demander is increased potency or, to put it another way, it is the anticipated achievement of a differential advantage in assortments. Creation of, or search for, this differential advantage is the engine of change on the supply side (Alderson, 1965, p. 29).

Alderson's concept of supply rejected traditional market morphology because aggregate supply is laid out in terms of a homogeneous demand. In the perfectly heterogeneous market, "each market segment of demand can be satisfied by just one unique segment of supply" (Alderson, 1965, p. 29). Hence, it is artificial to link firms together just because they produce similar products since they are actually serving different markets. Competition should not be defined in traditional market structure terms but the emphasis should be shifted to the creation of differential advantage by individual firms in their pursuit of markets. Firms can rarely be sure what price is "right" nor what product offering is "right". They must seek the answer in markets which are usually open to entry from competing suppliers. Alderson stresses that firms actively strive to secure a "unique niche" in the market in pursuit of profits. This competitive striving, however, is taking place, by definition *before* the unique niche is attained.

The search for differential advantage is based on *expectations* about demand. The degree to which a market position can be maintained once attained, is the degree to which it continues to be successful in matching supply and demand. *Ex post* the industrial economist's traditional inclination has been to say that this is the essence of monopoly but the true meaning is exactly the opposite. The ability to find and hold a segment is indicative of competition through successful *ex ante* entrepreneurship. The firm has worked through the informational complexities of the market process. Tastes change, demanders change potency requirements, and some suppliers react. As supply conditions change, other suppliers in their turn offer new goods and information. In short, the market becomes still more heterogeneous. But the knowledge that this is so increases the problem of matching supply with demand. The statement that, "the heterogeneous market can only be cleared by information" (Alderson, 1965, p. 30) is Alderson's acknowledgement of this. The transaction costs of mutually beneficial exchange (information provision and search and sorting costs) have increased.

What does this imply? Both tangible and intangible goods (information) must pass through what Alderson called the sorting process. This involves the transformation of supplies from raw inputs which fail to meet demand into assortments of finished goods which can satisfy wants. Thus exchange can take place creating want satisfaction for both parties. In order for transactions to occur gaps between buyers and sellers and their respective desires and offerings must be bridged. The gaps are those of space, time, technology, form, and most importantly, information.

Want satisfaction in marketing is a much more complex concept than that presented by the interaction of supply and demand curves. Exchange can take place when there is minimum want satisfaction for either participant; in other words, partial congruence of supply and demand is necessary and sufficient to indicate that a transaction has been, or can be, successful. Total congruence is also sufficient, but it is unnecessary and, indeed, implausible. (Although the closer to perfect congruence the market process approaches the higher, for a time, will be some suppliers' profits and the greater, for a period, will be some demanders' satisfaction). It is more appropriate to speak of partial congruence among the various elements in an offering set (O) and a demand set (D) such as:

$$O_1, O_2, \ldots, O_4, \ldots, O_6, \ldots, O_n$$

$$D_1, \ldots, D_3, \ldots, D_6, \ldots, D_8, \ldots, D_n$$

The presence of discrepancies between offering characteristics and demand characteristics, satisfaction available and satisfaction wanted, indicates opportunities for entrepreneurial activities. Such opportunities are grasped by conducting the sorting process (Narver and Savitt, 1971).

3.   Sorting in Macro Marketing

The sorting process has four stages. These can be undertaken by groups of organisations or single organisations. First, sorting out represents the breaking down of heterogeneous collections into homogeneous sub-lots to take advantage of economies of production or handling. This is followed by the accumulation of homogeneous sets of goods in economically viable marketing and production units. Third, allocation represents the breaking down of the homogeneous collections to meet demanders' requirements. Assorting, the final stage, is the building up of a heterogeneous supply which matches as closely as possible the heterogeneity of demand. The process both satisfies consumer wants and creates supplier discrepancies. These discrepancies are the basis for seller want satisfaction in the form of profits from perception of the related opportunities.

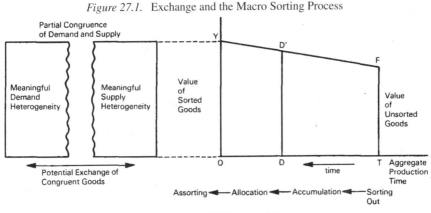

Figure 27.1. Exchange and the Macro Sorting Process

Garrison, 1978, p. 177

In 1978, Garrison illustrated the Aldersonian approach at the macro level by employing a trapezoid version of the Hayekian triangle with axes reversed (Garrison, 1978). Shown in Figure 27.1 is Hayek's "aggregate production time", the equivalent of Alderson's "transaction" or sorting process. The analysis shows how production must be considered part of the marketing process as much as communication, financing and risk-bearing. Because of its temporal element, it demands recognition of the discrepancies which are found and the utilities which are created. Thus Alderson's Austrian perspective becomes apparent at both the micro and aggregate levels.

The summation of all sorting processes on the supply side of an economy begins at point T and proceeds leftwards. At the end of this continuous process, consumption goods with a value of OY emerge. At point T there are no sorted goods only a meaningless heterogeneity of supply which have a potential value only to the entrepreneur who foresees profitable future exchange. They do not reach full value until the completion of sorting at OY. The slope of FY indicates their rate of increase of anticipated value per unit of time. At any given point, meaningful, (i.e., tradeable) heterogeneous supplies will be emerging at O at the same time as incompletely sorted goods will be in existence (e.g., at DD').

Simultaneously consumers will be searching entrepreneurially in their own right. They will be moving from a situation where their wants are meaningless and heterogeneous to one where their demands are meaningful and heterogeneous. In Figure 27.1 an Aggregate Production Time trapezoid could have been constructed on the left of the diagram symmetrically akin to that on the right hand side. Sorting by the consumer is awarded the distinguishing name "searching" by Alderson (Alderson, 1965, p. 36). But he tends, somewhat confusingly, to use the words interchangeably. He does so partly because suppliers often "vicariously search" out demanders in their own sorting process (by advertising and other forms of information provision). In addition, although searching by consumers *vis-à-vis* producers is relatively more often solely "a mental operation" it can still be broken down into the four sorting stages. "Sorts are performed in selecting the (items) which can best be added to the consumer's (basket of wants)" (Alderson, 1965, p. 36).

Decisions made at T on the Aggregate Production Time function are made on assumptions about demander expectations at the time the goods will be in the assorting stage. Given the changing nature of demand sets, there is no assurance that more than partial congruence will result.

Since the process is time, space, form and technologically dependent, there are bound to be discrepancies, as noted previously. For the sorting process to operate, whether at a macro or at a micro level, information must be generated and received by suppliers and demanders at each stage of the process. The critical question is "How much information is enough?" Market clearance, the partial intersection of the two heterogeneous demand and supply sets comes about only through the creation, dissemination and reception of information. The greater the congruence achieved, *ex post*, the greater the profitability of the supplier, the greater the want satisfaction of the consumer. *Ex ante*, however, as noted, full congruence is unlikely. Nevertheless, the task of the entrepreneur (prior to sorting or its completion) is to maximise this expected level of congruence.

4.   Information, Ignorance and Entrepreneurship

Alderson's view that markets can achieve partial want satisfaction only through the production, dissemination and reception of some optimum quantity of information has been considered by economists. In particular, Stigler's seminal work on information can be seen as paralleling and reflecting Alderson's arguments (Stigler, 1961). Lancaster (1966) attempted to breathe new life into the theory of the firm by identifying goods as bundles of characteristics, an insight present for decades in the most elementary marketing textbooks. They attempted to enhance general equilibrium analysis by focusing on the role of information in dealing with risk and uncertainty given heterogeneous supplies and demands. Yet in so doing they failed to deal with a major flaw of standard economic theory: namely that risk, uncertainty and ignorance are three different concepts (Loasby, 1976).

Stigler and others deal skilfully with risk and uncertainty. Ignorance, however, is almost totally neglected. Risk represents a condition where all possible states of the future are assumed known and a probability distribution can be defined for those states. With these data the economist can forecast the equilibrium using the expected value criterion. The analysis of resource allocation can then proceed in the normal manner. When uncertainty is present, all possible outcomes are again known but there are numerous probability distributions with associated subjective weights.

In reality such a full list never is available. This is Loasby's state of "partial ignorance". In such a state general equilibrium analysis and decision taking by purely mathematical techniques is impossible. Managers must seek to overcome "information mismatch" or ignorance without relying on expected value calculations, either objectively or subjectively constructed (Alderson, 1965, p. 60-64). A product is only "adequately identified" for a consumer (i.e., the optimal information is provided) if, in his ignorance "the supplier has guessed right" (Alderson, 1965, p. 61). "Guessing", of course, is simply a way of overcoming ignorance. It is not a computative process; it is intuitive. It is the process of entrepreneurship in which the successful guesser or entrepreneur makes a profit, the unsuccessful a loss.

This entrepreneurial perspective places Alderson directly in the mainstream of Austrian economics. The greater the thrust toward heterogeneity on the part of the demanders and the greater the attempts to satisfy it by suppliers, the more difficult and important the role of the decision maker becomes. The decision maker is faced with the ever increasing importance of ignorance which simultaneously offers difficulties and opportunities in achieving exchange. By contrast the manager in a controlled economy, or in a textbook perfect market is not confronted by this since ignorance, dynamism and heterogeneity are either ignored or not fully recognised. In the transition from the homogeneous market (which is either directed or automatically moved to equilibrium through adjustments in price or quantity) to discrepant markets, which are persistently radical and never static, entrepreneurship replaces bureaucratic management. Alderson indicated this:

> A homogeneous market can be cleared by adjustments of price and quality. A heterogeneous market is cleared by information matching two sets, one ranging over heterogeneous demand and the other over heterogeneous supply. A discrepant market can only be cleared by innovation... If strongly motivated problem solvers face each other... it can never be cleared but only moves in the direction of that equilibrium state. Another state, representing new requirements and new opportunities, has arisen before the last is satisfied (Alderson, 1965, p. 207).

Alderson pointed the way to the study of the successful "guesser" or entrepreneur. Some economists have seen this issue to be at the heart of the market process. Buchanan in his plaintively titled article "What Should Economists Do?" makes just this point (Buchanan, 1964). He wishes to see the "theory of markets" and not the "theory of resource allocation" at centre stage. The process of exchange, not the computation of marginal rates of substitution, is the purpose of a market.

We are ignorant of exchange possibilities because we are dealing with other humans. Robinson Crusoe could rely on static marginal equivalency as his guiding principle but whenever Man Friday came on the scene, inter-personal association and trade were inevitable. The motivations of each to trade were the obvious ones of moving from less preferred to more preferred positions, and doing so voluntarily. But neither Friday nor Crusoe knew what the other had to offer, and even if they (impossibly) do know what the other has to offer *today*, neither could ever know what the other might have or might be willing to offer *tomorrow*. It is to this study of mutually beneficial, voluntary exchange between different people with different resource endowments, different tastes and potentially changing values for each of these parameters, that marketing theory addresses itself. This is the nub of the Aldersonian and Austrian positions. Some economists, such as Buchanan, have agreed that catallactics, the study of exchange in a world of partial ignorance, is the proper subject matter for both economics and marketing. Adam Smith, the father of both subjects, might well have argued that marketing theory should be the core of economics. He asserted that the wealth of nations arises from mankind's "propensity to truck, barter and exchange" (Smith, 1975, p. 117).

5.   Information in the Discrepant Market

In the case of the homogeneous market, price is the clearance mechanism. For the static heterogeneous market, information serves that function (at least in principle). The discrepant market, however, (which is dynamically heterogeneous) is never cleared. Full congruence is never attained. The problem is to ascertain how human beings in the discrepant market place act in order to maximise each other's satisfaction. Although the problem can be simply stated, it is not easily resolved.

In the static heterogeneous market Alderson caught himself in the trap which has entangled others. He tried to reduce the question: "How much information is enough?" to a one variable answer: price. This is not the price of the homogeneous market certainly, but price modified by other factors: viz. actual price = transaction price ÷ other aspects of the product package. In short, he argued that the decision making process of answering how much information is enough, namely which "prices" to charge, is a complex one involving a large number of interacting areas each with numerous vectors (Alderson, 1965, Chapter 12). Whatever discretion firms exercise with regard to any one variable can be expected to influence their decisions with regard to other variables. These decisions produce a stochastic range of expected volumes on turnover. In turn, a range of possible responses by competitors arises and if a sufficiently complex probabilistic model is built, a range of "price" alternatives is present to the manager.

Even in conditions of risk, that is when the objective probabilities of all outcomes are known, the multiplicative rule of statistical probability coupled with the sheer range of alternatives makes it certain that the "correct" choice will have an extremely small expected value. So small that the normal gloss given by managerial economists that "over a run of decisions" the firm will profit maximise, becomes a nonsense. Even in a static heterogeneous market a "run" must be very, if not unacceptably long. In conditions of uncertainty, any calculated outcome would be even less worthwhile because the probabilities used would not even be objective. The notions of "bounded rationality" and "satisficing" would then become the only fallback positions (Simon, 1957).

With these informational problems, how do firms engage in a process of searching for and establishing a differential advantage in the discrepant market? Alderson, despite the weakness of his overall position in this area, identified a variety of ways (Alderson, 1965, pp. 361-362). He cited a combination of product differentiation, information expansion and differentiation, and enterprise differentiation. The sum total of these is the discovery of the ecological niche: "To succeed in competition, each firm, like every blade of grass, must find a separate place to stand" (Alderson, 1957, p. 132). This involves "guessing right" or as Austrian economists would put it, successful entrepreneurship. But Alderson went no further. Just as he was on the brink of answering the question "How much information is enough?" for the area he identified as the most vital both conceptually and practically, the discrepant market, he stopped tantalisingly short.

6.   Entrepreneurship as Dynamic Marketing Behaviour

Alderson's contributions to macro-marketing were ended by his untimely death. Marketers returned to the micro-science and the apparently easier "managerial approach" where partial ignorance is ignored and even the rigours of academic logic can be pushed to one side by the excuse that the polymath, the marketer who draws on many disciplines, cannot be expected to be a master of them all.

Economists in turn generally have overlooked Alderson's contributions. They have resorted to rarefied theory or econometrics based on statistical risk and uncertainty. They have largely ignored the problems of partial ignorance. To quote Scherer: "(they have) characteristic indolence... (it) is hard work to plow through file after file of company documents and to interview dozens of executives, crosschecking each observation to guard against bias and misinterpretation. It is much easier to work with census data punched into IBM cards that can be interrogated in the comfort of one's home, that... answer... without evasion... that will never complain" (Scherer, 1980, p. 7).

Some industrial organisation economists are willing to carry on the Alderson tradition of hard practicality. But even they fail fully to perceive the partial ignorance of the discrepant market, where only thoughtful logic, with on occasion empirical insights, provide the answers. The true current successors to Alderson's intellectual tradition are the members of the small but burgeoning Austrian school which experienced a renaissance in the 1970s. Alderson would certainly have approved of their intellectual approach, if not of their (still present) fear of empiricism.

They argue as follows (and Alderson would surely have agreed): in conventional price theory "efficiency" is found in equilibrium. In the theory of competition as a process, efficiency does not depend on the equality of price with marginal cost or the equivalence of marginal rates of substitution, "rather, it depends on the degree of success with which market forces can be relied upon to generate spontaneous corrections. . . at time of disequilibrium" (Kirzner, 1973, pp. 6-7).

This process of correction is the function of the entrepreneur. "Entrepreneur means man acting in regard to the changes occurring in the market. " (von Mises, 1963, p. 254). When Mises refers to the entrepreneur in this way, he is not referring solely to the capitalist or worker, to the manager or employee, to the producer or consumer. Any of these can be an entrepreneur. "Economics in speaking of entrepreneurs, has in view not men, but a definite function' (von Mises, 1963, p. 252). Therefore by inference, any producer, consumer or resource owner who acts in response to change is, to a greater or lesser degree, an entrepreneur. This is completely in tune with our analysis of both sides of the market in Figure 27.1 above.

In equilibrium there is no place for the function of entrepreneurship. This is the homogeneous market. In equilibrium, or what Mises called an "evenly rotating economy", there are no changes in the given data of endowments, technologies or preferences. In such an imaginary economy in which all transactions and physical conditions are repeated without change in each cycle of time, there is no ignorance. Everything is imagined to continue exactly as before, including all human ideas and goals. Under such fictitious constant repetitive conditions, there can be no net change in any supply or demand and therefore there cannot be any changes in prices (or marginal valuations or marginal contributions). But as soon as these rigid assumptions of given data are abandoned in favour of the dynamic heterogeneous or discrepant market, it is clear that action must be affected by every data change. Since action is directed towards influencing the future, even if "the future" is simply the next instant, then action is affected by every correctly or incorrectly anticipated data change between the initiation of the act and the period towards which the act is directed; ... "the outcome of action is always uncertain. Action is always speculation" (von Mises, 1963, p. 252).

Conventional economic theory has not, of course, repudiated either entrepreneurs, or the concept of uncertainty. What it has failed to embrace is the Misesian entrepreneur and the handling of ignorance in the presence of changes in the underlying (already uncertain) market conditions. The static heterogeneous market may have been tolerated; the discrepant market of Alderson and the Austrians has been ignored.

Conventional theory permits transactors to take decisions using a wide variety of techniques developed explicitly to take account of different contingent outcomes. Moreover, Bayesian decision theory enables transactors not only to take decisions using probability theory (prior analysis) but also enables them to process further information as acquired (posterior analysis).

But as Littlechild points out, none of these elaborations on conventional theory meets the aim of understanding the market process. All of "these models more or less run down as agents discover all there is to know. . . To see why this should be so, let us look more closely at the assumptions in the models. The agents are equipped with forecasting functions and decision functions to enable them to cope with uncertainty. Indeed the agents *are* these functions. But although their specific forecasts and decisions may change over time in response to changes in economic conditions, *the functions themselves remain the same*. The agents never learn to predict any better as a result of their experiences. Nothing can ever occur for which they are not prepared, nor can they ever initiate anything which is not preordained" (Littlechild, 1977, p. 7). Eventually they simply move towards and reach (at least in theory) the questionable Nirvana of equilibrium. The entrepreneur, be he producer, consumer, middleman or resource owner, does far more than merely bring together two parties and facilitate a mutually beneficial exchange between them. The entrepreneur is the person who is *alert* to the presence of such opportunities before anyone else perceives them.

The entrepreneur notes, *ex ante*, that the preferences of consumers are different tomorrow from what they are today. He notes *ex ante*, that the production techniques of firms are not the same tomorrow as they are today. The Misesian entrepreneur foresees these changes in the market data. It is this foresight which is important in the discrepant market. The "strongly motivated problem solver" of Alderson's competitive world continually faces the challenge of "guessing right."

The entrepreneur may make mistakes in his predictions, or he may be correct, in which case he makes respectively losses or profits. The entrepreneur must choose which prediction he believes to be correct. But he cannot simply choose to facilitate a process which equates *current* marginal valuations. Professor Shackle says: "Decision is choice amongst rival available courses of action. We can choose only what is still unactualised; we can choose only amongst imaginations and figments. Imagined actions. . . can only have imagined consequences" (Shackle, 1970, p. 106).

Even without changes in basic market data (consumer tastes, production possibilities and resource endowments) decisions made today generate a new series of decisions tomorrow. Today's decisions (the commencement of the market process) are made in ignorance of these market data. As the market process unfolds, this ignorance is reduced (at least in relation to current and past data) and each market participant revises his actions in the sorting process in the light of what has occurred and what he has now learned about to whom or from whom, he may wish to sell or buy. *The process is inherently competitive* since the outcome of each successive set of sorting actions is designed to be more attractive than the preceding one. That is, every individual product offering (be it in terms of price, quality, place or whatever) is being made with the awareness that all other offerings in their turn are now being made with fuller knowledge of the advantageous opportunities available. Since that is so, each individual participant knows that he cannot offer less attractive trading opportunities than his competitors. He (and they) must continually inch ahead of his (their) rivals. The competitive process of market clearing is "analytically inseparable" from entrepreneurship.

To accomplish market clearing in a discrepant market, the entrepreneur must generally incur costs. But his net profit over costs does not arise through the surplus predicted by simple trade theory (i.e., exchanging something he values for something he values more). It comes about rather because he has been alert enough to discover sellers and buyers with such different valuations. Pure entrepreneurial profit arises from *"the discovery of something obtainable for nothing at all"* (Kirzner, 1973, p. 48, emphasis in original).

In rigid neoclassical orthodoxy, equilibrium already prevails in conditions of perfect competition. In a heterogeneous market, equilibrium pertains when information is adequate. In the discrepant market of Alderson and the Austrians, the market process *potentially* (but in reality never) terminates in a state of long-run equilibrium. In what Shackle called a *"Kaleidic Society"* there are always sooner or later unexpected changes which upset existing patterns, "interspersing its moments or intervals of order, assurance and beauty with sudden disintegration and a cascade into a new pattern" (Simon, 1957, p. 76). Hence in real-life industry, where changes in technologies and consumer tastes occur, the equilibrating effort of the Misesian entrepreneur or the Aldersonian marketer is always overtaken before it has done its work. Individual markets for individual goods may, for a time, find their respective equilibria, but the macro-market system never does.

7. Conclusions

Alderson's arguments culminate in an individualistic stance based on a conviction that the market process can only be understood in terms of choice and perception of opportunity. His view relies on a full comprehension of the constraints imposed by the market, organised by society and influenced by the ecological structure of the environment (Alderson, 1965, p. 321). His approach provides challenges for both economic and marketing scholars who are attempting to understand the market process. What is the source of entrepreneurship? Kirzner (1980) argues that it is alertness to opportunity, and the imagination and vision to capitalise on it. Given that matching is an activity which generates fuller congruence between wants and available supplies, what implications does this have for public policy? Since entrepreneurs are motivated by profit (however defined)) then any suppression or taxation of profits will reduce entrepreneurship, lessen marketing activity and decrease the congruence between wants and supplies. Is this a correct inference? If so, is it normatively unattractive? It will be no mean task to create and implement a body of entrepreneurially based theory. Those who have the quest for fresh perspectives and open minds may well find the tasks challenging. Where Alderson and Austrianism meet is to be found a new theory of market behaviour: a theory which is potentially operational at both public policy and managerial levels.

References

Alderson, Wroe (1957). *Marketing Behavior and Executive Action: A Functionalist Approach to Marketing*. Richard D. Irwin Inc., Homewood.

Alderson, Wroe (1965). *Dynamic Marketing Behavior: A Functionalist Theory of Marketing*. Richard D. Irwin Inc., Homewood.

Buchanan, J. M. (1964). What Should Economists Do? *Southern Economic Journal*, 30(January):213–222.

Garrison, R. (1978). Austrian Macroeconomics: A Diagrammatical Exposition. In Spadaro, Louis, editor, *New Directions in Austrian Economics, Institute for Human Studies*, pages 167–204. Sheed Andrews and McMeel Inc., Kansas City.

Kirzner, I. (1973). *Competition and Entrepreneurship*. University of Chicago Press, Chicago.

Kirzner, I. (1980). *The Prime Mover of Progress*. Institute of Economic Affairs, London.

Lancaster, K. (1966). Change and Innovation in the Technology of Consumption. *American Economic Review*, 56(March, No. 1/2):14–23.

Littlechild, S. (1977). Change rules ok? Inaugural Lecture, Birmingham, Birmingham University Press.

Loasby, B. J. (1976). *Choice, Complexity and Ignorance: An Enquiry into Economic Theory and the Practice of Decision-Making*. Cambridge University Press, Cambridge.

Narver, John C. and Savitt, Ronald (1971). *The Marketing Economy: An Analytical Approach*. Holt, Rinehart and Winston, Inc., New York.

Scherer, F. M. (1980). *Industrial Structure and Economic Performance*. Rand McNally, New York, second edition.

Shackle, G. L. S. (1970). *Expectation, Enterprise and Profit: the Theory of the Firm*. George Allen and Unwin, London.

Simon, H. (1957). *Models of Man*. John Wiley, New York.

Smith, Adam (1975). *The Wealth of Nations*. Penguin Books, London. Edited by A. Skinner.

Stigler, G. J. (1961). The Economics of Information. *Journal of Political Economy*, 69(June, No. 3):213–225.

von Mises, Ludwig (1963). *Human Action: A Treatise on Economics*. Henry Regnery Press, Chicago, revised 3rd edition.

Chapter 28

AN ALTERNATIVE PARADIGM FOR MARKETING THEORY*

D. F. Dixon

I. F. Wilkinson

Marketing theory experienced a scientific "crisis" over thirty years ago, and a new paradigm emerged in the form of "functionalism". However, current work in marketing, or "normal science": reflects an older paradigm. A research agenda rooted in the alternative functionalist paradigm is suggested.

1. Kuhn's Paradigm Concept

A paradigm is an accepted model or pattern which underlies "normal science", that is, research based upon past scientific achievements "that some particular scientific community acknowledges for a time as supplying the foundation for its further practice". This pattern is reported in textbooks, and the "legitimate problems and methods" of research are defined for succeeding generations (Kuhn, 1962, p. 10). Students study the accepted paradigm to prepare for membership in their discipline, and "subsequent practice will seldom evoke overt disagreement over fundamentals" (Kuhn, 1962, p. 11). Consequently, "normal science" is characterized by "mopping-up operations", and it is this "mop-up" work which engages most scientists throughout their careers (Kuhn, 1962, p. 24).

Normal science attempts to bring theory and fact into closer agreement, but there are always some discrepancies. Normal science typically perceives such discrepancies as "puzzles", but they may also be viewed as anomalies in the paradigm. A "crisis" occurs when a discrepancy occurs to be viewed as more than "just another puzzle" or normal science (Kuhn, 1962, p. 82). The recognition that an existing paradigm is inadequate leads to a scientific

*Originally published in the *European Journal of Marketing* (1989), 23(8), pages 59-69.

revolution, in which an older paradigm is replaced in whole or in part by an incompatible new one (Kuhn, 1962, p. 91).

2.   A "Crisis" and a New Paradigm for Marketing

Evidence of a Kuhn "crisis" in marketing theory emerged in a 1948 Journal of Marketing article by Alderson and Cox:

> It has become evident that if the difficulties raised by events in the areas of public and private policy as applied to marketing are to be solved, they must be put into a framework that provides a much better perspective than is now given by the literature (Alderson and Cox, 1948, p. 39).

There is explicit criticism of the existing paradigm as well: "Students of marketing have achieved too little even in setting fundamental and significant problems for themselves, to say nothing of working out procedures for solving such problems." Moreover, there is a recognition of the need for a new paradigm: "What marketing men really seek... a better statement of the problems to be solved and more ingenious methods to be applied in solving them" (Alderson and Cox, 1948, p. 138).

Kuhn argues that when a discipline reaches such a point the scientist will often seem to be "searching at random". Simultaneously, "the scientists in crisis will constantly try to generate speculative theories" (Kuhn, 1962, p. 87). Evidence of such a search is apparent in the Alderson and Cox (1948) article, first in a search for sources for new theory, and second, a suggested approach to an integrated theory. This approach is "group behaviorism as it has been developing in the social sciences", which is seen as allied to the functional approach in marketing. "It would undertake to analyze marketing processes by taking primary account of the objectives they are designed to serve" (Alderson and Cox, 1948, p. 148).

This suggested approach is consistent with the concurrent emergence of interest in General Living Systems Theory which rapidly gained popularity in the early 1950s. Of special significance is an article by Bertalanffy introducing this theory to a wide audience, which emphasises that this "new scientific doctrine" is rooted in "the formal correspondence of general principles, irrespective of the kind of relations or forces between the components" (von Bertalanffy, 1950, p. 28). The emphasis is upon living systems, which are defined as "open systems maintaining themselves in exchange of materials with environment, and in continuous building up and breaking down of their components" (von Bertalanffy, 1950, p. 23).

This framework of analysis was explicitly applied to marketing problems in a symposium sponsored by the American Marketing Association in 1949. Alderson's contribution to this symposium reiterated the need for "the kind of perspective that can guide the selection of methods in specific problem situations and that can facilitate the integration of research findings into a growing body of scientific marketing principles". The suggested integrative concept is the "organized behavior system" (Alderson, 1950, p. 67). The fundamental aspects of Alderson's organised behaviour system are:

1 the organisation of the system into sub-systems and the nature of the bonding among sub-systems,

2 the integration of these sub-systems by means of communication, and

3 the operational behaviour of the system, that is, the input and output of the system.

Emphasis is placed upon the problems of system survival and the system's adjustment to its environment. Alderson's argument is consistent with the perspective of General Living Systems Theory because, although the business firm is taken as the point of reference in his presentation, it is noted that "similar laws are believed to govern survival and adjustment for other types of organized behavior systems, differing only as to details of application" (Alderson, 1950, p. 86).

As General Living Systems Theory developed during the early 1950s its correspondence to Alderson's approach became more apparent. In a lecture delivered in 1955, Ashby provides evidence that the problems noted in the 1948 article by Alderson and Cox were not unique to marketing:

> Until recently the strategy of the sciences has been largely that of analysis. The units have been found, their properties studied, and then, somewhat as an afterthought, some attempt has been made to study them in combined action (Alderson and Cox, 1948, p. 1).

It is noted that a new discipline is emerging in which the system is studied without breaking it into pieces, so that "the internal interactions are left intact, and the system is, in the well known words, studied as a whole" (Ashby, 1958, p. 2).

In the same year the potential application of General Living Systems Theory to the social sciences was explicitly recognised. Miller, defining systems as "bounded regions in space-time, involving energy interchange among their parts, which are associated in functional relationships, and with their environments" notes that living systems extend "roughly from viruses through societies" (Miller, 1955, p. 514). He argues that all behaviour can be conceived of as "energy exchange with an open system or from one such system to another", and that systems are not only kept in equilibrium, but are also usually in balance with their environments, which have outputs into systems and inputs from them. Furthermore, this general statement can be translated into the terminology of several behavioural sciences (Miller, 1955, p. 515). Miller also argues that measurement problems can be overcome, and "there is no reason why all social phenomena cannot be profitably analyzed by formal models" (Miller, 1955, p. 523).

In the first full-scale presentation of his work, Alderson re-emphasised the organised behaviour system as the foundation of marketing theory: "Every phase of marketing can be understood as human behavior within the framework of some operating system". Moreover, "all marketing activity is an aspect of the interaction among organized behavior systems related to each other in what may be described as an ecological network" (Alderson, 1957, p. 1). This focus on the organised behaviour system is the basis of Alderson's "Functionalist" approach: "Functionalism is that approach to science which begins by identifying some system of action, and then tries to determine how and why it works as it does" (Alderson, 1957, p. 16). In his later work, Alderson explicitly recognises the relationship between his work and general systems theory: "Functionalism implies a commitment to what is coming to be known as the total systems approach" (Alderson, 1965, p. 24). But despite his appreciation of the total systems approach, Alderson limited his attention to "the study of small systems, primarily households and business enterprises" (Alderson, 1965, p. 15). This focus neglects an especially important implication of General Living Systems Theory — the interactions among systems theory in Management Science (Boulding, 1956).

The implications of a hierarchy of systems for marketing thought are demonstrated in Fisk's *Marketing Systems* (Fisk, 1967). Here Alderson's scheme is broadened and the emphasis shifted from the management of a small system — the firm — to the study of marketing as a total system in which the firm represents only one level of interest. Explicitly following "the general systems approach" Fisk identifies seven levels of organisation, from the individual, who would constitute a sub-system in Alderson's "small system" to the world economy. Because his analysis involves both interactions within and between system levels, Fisk argues that "General Systems Theory can organize the bewildering interrelationships between production, marketing, and consumption into a coherent and unified perspective from the standpoint of the consumer, the marketing channel commander, the business manager, or the social welfare of the nation" (Fisk, 1967, p. 11).

The extension of systems theory to the marketing channel was formally recognised in AMA symposia in 1968 and 1970 (Bucklin, 1970, Thompson, 1971) with vertical marketing systems. A further extension, to system levels transcending the channel, is apparent in the annual Macromarketing Seminars which commenced in 1976, and which led to the appearance of the *Journal of Macromarketing* in 1981.

Marketing As A "Normal Science"

The contemporary marketing paradigm is apparent in conventional textbooks, which deal not with the study of marketing in the broad sense proposed by the extended functionalist paradigm, but solely with marketing management, or in Alderson's terms, the management of a "small system". For example, McCarthy (1981) specifies: "The main locus of this text will be on micromarketing — as seen from the viewpoint of the marketing manager" (McCarthy, 1981, p. 9). Thus the "total system" becomes the firm itself (McCarthy, 1981, p. 35). The manager's job includes the development of marketing strategies, that is, determining market segments and manipulating four sets of controllable variables which comprise the marketing mix. The emphasis of the text is upon the marketing mix: "Most of this text is concerned with developing profitable marketing mixes for clearly defined target markets" (McCarthy, 1981, p. 53).

The paradigm underlying this approach is that of microeconomics, as it was developed a half century ago, when the focus of economic analysis shifted from the industry to the firm. Joan Robinson (1933) analysed the decisions of an individual seller when "the conditions of demand, which (abstracting from advertisement and other marketing cost) lie entirely outside his control" (Robinson, 1933, p. 15). Given the assumption that demand and cost curves are independent, attention was centred upon opportunities offered by different demand conditions.

It is seen that a seller might be able to divide his market into separate parts because of "a difference between the elasticities of the demands" (Robinson, 1933, p. 185). These differences in elasticity might be due to "natural" causes, such as the location of buyers, as well as the result of the seller's action. "Various brands of a certain article which in fact are almost exactly alike may be sold as different qualities under names and labels which induce rich and snobbish buyers to divide themselves from poorer buyers; and in this way the market is split up" (Robinson, 1933, p. 181). The seller deals with each sub-market differently with respect to price, which is the only marketing variable being considered: "However the market is divided, once the division has been achieved the sub-markets will be arranged in ascending order of their elasticities, the highest price being charged in the least elastic market, and the lowest price in the most elastic market. . . " (Robinson, 1933, p. 187).

It is clear that Joan Robinson's treatment of the issue which today is called "market segmentation" is consistent with that found in current textbooks. McCarthy for example, states that "the basic idea underlying market segmentation is that any market is likely to consist of sub-markets which might need separate marketing mixes" (McCarthy, 1981, p. 224). Each of these sub-markets is represented by a different demand curve, which may be created by the seller's action, such as changes in the physical product itself (McCarthy, 1981, p. 225).

In contrast to Robinson, Chamberlin (1933) centres his attention on supply considerations; emphasis is placed upon the variables which can be manipulated by the seller in his effort to maximise profit. Chamberlin identifies two general categories of such variables, in addition to price. The first, product variation, utilises the term "product" in a broad sense: "Its 'variation' may refer to an alteration in the quality of the product itself — technical changes, a new design, or better materials; it may mean a new package or container; it may mean more prompt or courteous service, a different way of doing business, or perhaps a different location" (Chamberlin, 1933, p. 71). It is clear that the "product" represents a set of variables, and that each might be isolated for analysis. The factor of location is isolated, and developed separately in an appendix.

The second category other than price is "selling cost" — including "advertising of all varieties, salesmen's salaries and the expenses of sales departments, margins granted to dealers (retail and wholesale) in order to increase their efforts in favor of particular goods, window displays, demonstrations of new goods, etc." (Chamberlin, 1933, p. 117).

Thus the whole of the emphasis in the "normal science" of marketing, as presented in conventional textbooks — market segmentation and the "4 Ps" — can be found in Robinson and Chamberlin's work published in 1933. The potential role of microeconomics as a paradigm for marketing was noted in the Alderson and Cox article: "the core of marketing theory might well be modern price theory" (Alderson and Cox, 1948, p. 144), but, as seen above, this was discarded in favour of systems theory. The textbook which Cox co-authored (Vaile et al., 1952) is rooted in economic theory, but it is not narrowed to the theory of the firm. It is the conviction of the authors that "students can best be introduced to marketing by a textbook whose primary point of view is the transcendent importance of this social institution as a vast and complex function of our free-enterprise economy" (Vaile et al., 1952, p. v). The central role of marketing seen here is the allocation of resources: "Marketing, through its organisations and activities, directs the use of the nation's resources" (Vaile et al., 1952, p. 24).

Initially Alderson seemed to be tied to a perspective rooted in microeconomic theory, for in discussing a marketing executive's theory he remarked:

> This theory or set of assumptions in the mind of the executive might be regarded as a special case of what economists call 'the theory of the firm'. A central purpose of this book is to represent a richer and more suggestive version of the theory of the firm which will provide perspective on marketing problems for the market analyst and the marketing executive (Alderson, 1957, p. 11).

But this view was subsequently discarded: "Marketing as a field of study does not rest comfortably under the label of applied economics" (Alderson, 1965, p. 302).

By moving beyond the microeconomic paradigm, Alderson provided a conceptual scheme which links non-economic and economic variables and indicates their combined role in shaping marketing behaviour in the firm. An extension of Alderson's ideas provides a conceptual scheme which places the analysis of marketing behaviour in the firm within the context of a hierarchy of marketing systems, which in turn provides a means of linking the marketing system to the society as a whole. It is to this we now turn.

3. A Functionalist Paradigm for the Study of Marketing

Alderson has stated that the functionalist approach "begins by identifying some system of action" (Alderson, 1957, p. 16). A society is a system of action operating in a material environment which contains the substances useful to man called resources. The economic system of a society has as its function the utilisation of resources to meet the requirements of society through the provision of goods and services. Some goods and services are freely available, but the majority require the application of human effort. This effort typically requires interaction between two or more persons and involves both production processes, i.e. "transformations", and exchange processes, i.e. "transactions". The study of marketing focuses on the transaction aspect of the economic system, in particular market transactions. The market transaction thus becomes the basis for identifying the system of action which is marketing.

While the market transaction is the sine qua non of marketing, sub-transaction level action systems may be identified, as can aggregates of transaction systems. As a result, the system of action which is studied in marketing is not a single system but a nested hierarchy of systems of action in which system levels are differentiated in terms of their functions. Each system is characterised by inputs and outputs, as well as some kind of organisation which converts inputs into outputs. Furthermore lower-level system outputs are the inputs for higher-level systems. For the purposes of this exposition seven system levels have been identified. These are shown in Table 28.1.

The basic units of the system of action are individual marketing roles. The energy, skill and knowledge of individuals is used to do work of various kinds. Marketing focuses on the work individuals do which contributes to market transactions; and this work defines their marketing roles. The work of individuals, including their marketing roles, is organised in primary organisations to produce "activities". An activity typically involves the inputs of work of more than one individual.

Two primary organisations of interest in marketing are the household and the firm. The household, the ultimate source of demand for goods and services in a society, converts these goods and services into satisfaction. The firm, a primary supply unit in society, specialises in some part of the process of

Table 28.1. The Marketing Systems Hierarchy

Level	Input	System	Output
I	Energy SkiII Infor-mation	Individual marketing roles	Work
II	Marketing Work	Primary organisations (households and firms)	Market exchange activities i.e., buying and selling
III	Buying and Selling	Markets	Specialised market trans-actions (contact, material, contract)
IV	Specialised Market Transactions	Unit flow channels	Contact flow, Material flow, Contract flow
V	Marketing Flows	Transvection channels	Transvection
VI	Transvections	Transvection channel groups	Assortments of goods and services
VII	Assortments	Marketing system	Material satisfaction

meeting household demand for goods and services. Marketing activity is a particular type of exchange activity required to bring about market transactions between demand and supply units. The terms "buying" and "selling" are used to refer to this exchange activity and the marketing roles of individuals are organised around these activities. Primary organisations are said to play the roles of buyers and sellers when performing these activities.

The next system level is that of the market, in which market transactions are the output and the buying and selling activities of primary organisations represent the inputs. Market transactions do not result from the action of any single primary organisation but from the joint action of a buyer and seller. The joint action results in three types of transaction outputs, and the corresponding processes which generate these outputs.

(a) *Contact.* If there is to be interaction between the buyer and seller there must be communication processes, which involve a two-way movement of information between the parties involved. The communication of information is the means by which agreement is reached about the terms of a transaction and the basis upon which all activities are planned.

(b) *Material transformation.* In order to meet the requirements of the buyer (and user) a material good or personal service of some kind is required. This in-volves transforming material in form, time and place; and it must be recognised that people, as well as objects, have a material existence.

The first two processes are common to all types of transactions; whether within or between organisations. The third process is peculiar to exchange transactions in which private property is an element of the interaction, such as in a market transaction.

(c) *Contract.* Market transactions involve the transfer of ownership and usership rights between the buyer and seller for the goods and services in question. The transfer of money payments from buyer to seller is one aspect of this process.

In order to meet the requirements of a household for a particular good or service more than one market transaction is generally involved. One reason for this is that the production activities involved are usually divided among a number of specialist producers. Moreover, the contact, contract and material transformation processes linking a producer to a household or another producer are divided up among a number of interrelated specialised market (and non-market) transactions. Each of the specialised market transactions results in contact, material and contract outputs but one or more of these outputs depend on the outputs of other specialised transactions. For example, the material transformation processes taking place as part of the transaction between a wholesaler and a retailer depend on the material transformation processes taking place in the transactions between the manufacturer and wholesaler and between, say, any transportation agency and the final customer.

Three systems of market transactions can be identified linking a producer to a household or another producer, each corresponding to one of the three market transaction outputs. The output of each of these systems is termed a "flow" because the underlying processes involve movement of some kind. The three types of flows are therefore contact flow, material flow and contract flow.

The organisation which converts market transactions into flows is termed a unit flow channel (Fisk, 1967, p. 93) and it comprises a set of dyads or pairs of buyers and sellers which jointly perform the activities required. The total set of interrelated market transactions, involving all three flows, constitutes a transvection; the organisation involved is termed a transvection channel. The transvection channel is thus the aggregation of all the dyads involved in all the flows linking a producer to a household or another producer.

Three systems of transvections may be identified according to the different kinds of inter-relationships that exist among them:

a   the system of transvections that links all the production stages involved in supplying a good or service, from the original source of supply to final demand;

b   the system of transvections that links all producers at a particular stage of production of a good or service to an adjacent production stage (including final consumption);

c   the system of transvections involved in supplying the assortment of goods and services required by a producer or household.

The final system level is that of the marketing system of a society itself. The output of the marketing system may be termed material satisfaction. International marketing systems using inputs from a number of domestic marketing systems could also be identified leading to an eighth level in the hierarchy.

4.   Research Questions

In order to understand how and why a system works as it does, four types of relations have to be considered (Emery and Trist, 1965). These are depicted in Figure 28.1 (a) in which the subscript "1" refers to the system and "E" to the environment.

R_{11} refers to intra-system relations, i.e., processes and interdependencies internal to the system. R_{E1} refers to the actual or potential effects of the environment on the system and R_{1E} to the actual and potential effects of the system on the environment. Finally, R_{EE} refers to interaction among parts of the environment.

Such a framework can be applied to each level in the marketing systems hierarchy. However, the hierarchical organisation of systems introduces additional kinds of relations which are only implicit in Figure 28.1 (a). These concern the relations between a marketing system and the supra-system of which it is a component, and between the system and its sub-systems. Supra-systems and subordinate systems represent special kinds of environmental systems which both affect and are affected by the focal marketing system. The inclusion of relations among systems and sub-systems results in an expanded set of relations as shown in Figure 28.1 (b). In this figure the subscript "1" refers to the focal system, "O" to the sub-system, "2" to the supra-system and "E" to the non-marketing environment. Applying the framework suggested in Figure 28.1 (b) to each level of the marketing systems hierarchy results in a logically complete set of relationships describing the main research questions that constitute the focus of study in marketing. These questions centre on three main types of relations.

(a) System/sub-system relations

The study of interactions among marketing systems at different levels of the hierarchy involves an examination of the nature of the outputs produced by systems and the constraints and opportunities for a system's action which result from inputs derived from the other marketing systems' outputs. These constraints and opportunities arise internally as a result of characteristics of the sub-systems making up the system. The nature of the individuals who are employed by a firm, or who are members of a particular household, affect their respective organisations' action. The nature of the buyers and sellers in a market affect the market transactions that emerge, and the characteristics of market transactions affect the nature of the unit flow channels. Constraints and opportunities also arise externally as a result of the characteristics of the

(a)

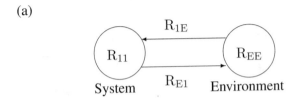

(b)

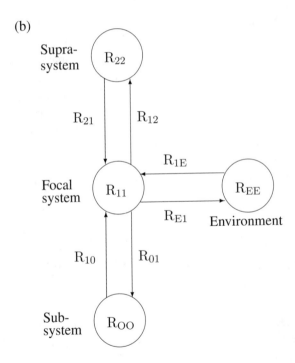

Figure 28.1. System Environment Relations

larger system of which the focal system is a part. For example, an individual's behaviour is constrained by the household and firm to which he or she belongs, a buyer's or seller's behaviour is affected by the characteristics of the markets in which they operate, and the characteristics of market transactions are influenced by the nature of the channel systems of which they are a part.

(b) Intra-marketing system relations

The study of these relations involves considering the structure, operations, control and performance of the system. The study of structure examines the nature of the relationships among system members. The study of operations examines the nature of the tasks required to accept and convert system inputs into outputs and how these tasks are allocated among system members. The study of control examines the way in which the system is co-ordinated and directed. Lastly, the study of performance examines the efficiency and effectiveness of the system and how this may be improved.

An important qualitative difference in the nature of intra-marketing system relations exists between systems at levels below the market transaction and those of the market transaction and above. Intra-marketing system relations below the level of market transactions are abstracted from three types of concrete systems, which are more than marketing action systems, i.e., individuals, firms and households. Higher level systems are pure marketing action systems although they are obviously influenced by and influence non-marketing action systems. Individuals, firms and households are systems in which the marketing and non-marketing outputs are co-produced. The non-marketing aspects of these systems are special types of environmental systems and include other action systems as well as underlying material, chemical and biological processes.

(c) Marketing system — environment relations

The focus of study here is on the constraints and opportunities on the action of a marketing system which arise as a result of the outputs of non-marketing systems. In addition, the constraints and opportunities affecting the action of non-marketing systems which arise as a result of the outputs of marketing systems are examined.

Relations between different parts of the environment ($R_{EE}s$) seem to be more properly regarded as the province of disciplines other than marketing. However, such relations cannot be ignored by students of marketing systems. As Emery and Trist (1965) have shown, these relations, or what they refer to as the "causal texture" of the environment, have profound implications for any system's behaviour and performance.

5. Conclusion

The functionalist paradigm outlined in this article provides a general analytical framework for the study of marketing; one in which the study of the marketing activities within a firm is placed in the context of a hierarchy of marketing systems. A logically complete set of research questions has been developed from the paradigm in terms of different kinds of system relations. These relations can be used to guide research in marketing. Existing contributions can be located in terms of them and relations not previously studied or requiring increased research attention highlighted.

References

Alderson, Wroe (1950). Survival and Adjustment in Organized Behavior Systems. In Cox, Reavis and Alderson, Wroe, editors, *Theory in Marketing*, pages 65–87. Richard D. Irwin, Homewood, Illinois.

Alderson, Wroe (1957). *Marketing Behavior and Executive Action: A Functionalist Approach to Marketing*. Richard D. Irwin Inc., Homewood.

Alderson, Wroe (1965). *Dynamic Marketing Behavior: A Functionalist Theory of Marketing*. Richard D. Irwin Inc., Homewood.

Alderson, Wroe and Cox, Reavis (1948). Towards a Theory of Marketing. *Journal of Marketing*, 13(October):137–152.

Ashby, W. R. (1958). General Systems Theory as a New Discipline. *General Systems*, 3:1–6.

Boulding, K. E. (1956). General Systems Theory — The Skeleton of Science. *Management Science*, 2(April):197–208.

Bucklin, Louis P. (1970). *Vertical Marketing Systems*. Scott, Foresman and Co., Glenview, Illinois.

Chamberlin, E. H. (1933). *The Theory of Monopolistic Competition: A Reorientation of the Theory of Value*. Harvard University Press, Cambridge, Massachusetts. Frequently revised since then.

Emery, F. E. and Trist, E. L. (1965). The Causal Texture of Organisational Environments. *Human Relations*, 18:21–31.

Fisk, George (1967). *Marketing Systems An Introductory Analysis*. Harper&Row, Publishers, New York.

Kuhn, Thomas S. (1962). *The Structure of Scientific Revolutions*. University of Chicago Press, Chicago.

McCarthy, E. Jerome (1981). *Basic Marketing: A Managerial Approach*. Richard D. Irwin, Homewood, Illinois.

Miller, J. G. (1955). Toward a General Theory for the Behavioral Sciences. *American Psychologist*, 10:513–531.

Robinson, Joan (1933). *The Economics of Imperfect Competition*. Macmillan and Co. Ltd, London.

Thompson, D. N. (1971). *Contractual Marketing Systems*. DC. Heath and Company, Lexington, Massachusetts, DC.

Vaile, R. S., Grether, E. T., and Cox, Reavis (1952). *Marketing in the American Economy*. The Ronald Press Company, New York.

von Bertalanffy, L. (1950). The Theory of Open Systems in Physics and Biology. *Science*, 111(January 13):23–29.

Chapter 29

ALDERSON'S TRANSVECTION AND PORTER'S VALUE SYSTEM*†

A comparison of two independently-developed theories

Richard L. Priem

Abdul M. A. Rasheed

Shahrzad Amirani

An instance of independent theory formulation may have occurred recently. Wroe Alderson's concept of the transvection and Michael Porter's concept of the value system are remarkably similar. This situation presents a number of opportunities for management scholars interested in Porter's work, and for marketing scholars interested in Alderson's ideas. It is likely, however, that few strategic management scholars are aware of Alderson's theory. This article presents a brief biographical sketch of Wroe Alderson and outlines the major aspects of his theory. It then compares Alderson's ideas on the transvection and Porter's on the value system, and each author's view of competitive advantage. Next is discussed the relative influence of each author's work, and suggested are other potential areas wherein Aldersonian thought may make unique contributions to strategic management.

Throughout the history of science scholars working independently have often arrived at virtually identical theories or discoveries (Merton, 1957). Instances of simultaneous but independent discovery include: the Periodic Table for classifying elements by Dmitri Mendeleev in Russia and Lothar Meyer in Germany in 1869, the development of differential calculus by Newton and Leibniz, the theory of evolution by Darwin and Wallace, and the postulation of the existence of Neptune based on observations of perturbations in the orbit of Uranus by John Adams in England and Le Verrier in France in 1846 (Fernie, 1995).

*Originally published in the Journal of Management History Bradford (1997) 3(2), pages 145-165.
†The authors wish to thank Ken Bahn, Roger Dickinson, and Chuck Lamb for helpful comments on earlier versions of this paper.

In economics, both Chamberlin (1933) and Robinson (1933) are credited witl independently developing the theory of imperfect competition. Kuhn (1959 similarly describes the discovery of the principle of energy conservation by a many as twelve different scientists in the years 1830-1850, and explains thi case of independent multiple discovery as resulting from the extant structure o scientific ideas as well as other aspects of cultural tradition.

Another instance of independent theory formulation may have occurred mucl more recently. Wroe Alderson's (1965) concept of the transvection and Michae Porter's (1985) concept of the value system are remarkably similar. Both ar at the macro (i.e., business system) level of analysis. Both the value systen and the transvection are conceptualized as the activities required to move from raw materials in their natural state to finished goods in the hands of consumers Both conceptual schemes are suggested as useful planning tools for achievinj sustainable competitive advantage (Alderson, 1965, Porter, 1985). The devel opment of each was also influenced by economic theory. Alderson (1965), fo example, acknowledges the influence of Chamberlin's (1933) theory of imper fect competition on the development of his own ideas on differential advantag (Grether, 1967, Savitt, 1990). Similarly, Porter's recent ideas were influence by his early training in industrial organization economics (e.g. Caves and Porter 1977, Porter, 1974).

This situation presents a number of opportunities for management schol ars interested in Porter's (1980, 1985, 1990) work, and for marketing scholar interested in Alderson's (1957, 1965) ideas. It is likely, however, that few strate gic management scholars are aware of Alderson's theory. Biggadike's (1981 review of marketing's potential influence on strategy research, for example doesn't mention Alderson. It is precisely the fact that remarkably similar idea evolved independently, but were received differently in two fields separated by several disciplinary boundaries including lack of a common vocabulary, whicl offers us some exciting possibilities. First, a synthesis of Alderson's and Porter' work may help to advance theory in both marketing and strategy. Second, sucl a synthesis may pave the way for a long overdue increase in interaction betweer the two fields. Third, identifying differences between Porter's and Alderson' formulations and reconciling them theoretically or resolving them empiricall may offer rewarding research opportunities.

In the sections that follow, we present a brief biographical sketch of Wroe Alderson and outline the major aspects of his theory. We then compare Alder son's ideas on the transvection and Porter's on the value system, and eacl author's view of competitive advantage. We next discuss the relative influence of each author's work, and suggest other potential areas wherein Aldersonia thought may make unique contributions to strategic management.

1. Alderson as theoretician and practitioner

Marketing scholars generally recognize Wroe Alderson as the premier marketing theorist of his day (e.g. Grether, 1967, Brown and Fisk, 1984, Goodman, 1986). His on-going work to develop a general theory of marketing (Alderson, 1965, Alderson, 1957) persisted until his death in 1965. Few marketing scholars, however, continued his work in subsequent years (Barksdale, 1980). Nevertheless, Alderson's existing work "presents what many consider the most comprehensive theory of marketing that has been constructed up to the present time" (Barksdale, 1980, p.1). Sheth, Gardner and Garrett, for example, argue that Alderson's theoretical contribution remains a "most likely" foundation for the eventual development of a general theory of marketing, due to its "comprehensive view of marketing that includes the environment, and all relevant actors, as well as nontraditional elements like global competitors" (1988, p. 202).

Alderson is also lauded as a pioneer in bringing theory, and its importance, to the attention of the marketing discipline (e.g. Barksdale, 1980, Baumol, 1984). In an advocacy role, he initiated and hosted an annual series of marketing theory seminars. A seminar was held each summer from 1951 through 1963, with the location alternating each year between Colorado and Vermont (Sheth et al., 1988). Influential participants in these seminars included invited marketing scholars and guests from outside the discipline. For example, the economist Edward H. Chamberlin attended several of Alderson's theory seminars (Dawson and Wales, 1979). "The goal was an open non-discipline-limited forum for exposing/ reacting to ideas and concepts of possible relevance to marketing theory" (Goodman, 1986). Alderson began marketing's move from an almost purely applied discipline to one that demands theory-based research.

Alderson was simultaneously a marketing theoretician and a marketing practitioner, and was equally at home in each role (Barksdale, 1980). He believed that theory should inform action, and action should inform theory (Alderson, 1957). Throughout his life he engaged in the practice of marketing for either business or government (e.g., at Curtis Publishing and the U.S. Department of Commerce), or as head of his consulting firm, Alderson & Sessions (Grether, 1967). This work continued during his scholarly tenure at the University of Pennsylvania, from 1959 until his death, and during visiting appointments at MIT and NYU (The New York Times, 1965).

Alderson constantly employed theory in his practice of marketing. For example, *Cost & Profit Outlook*, the monthly newsletter of the Alderson & Sessions consulting firm, provided the initial exposure for a number of important ideas in marketing theory, including Wendell Smith's (1955, 1956) concept of market segmentation (Goodman, 1986). *Cost & Profit Outlook* was quite influential; it was used in university classes, it was circulated among executives, it was quoted in editorials and by marketing specialists, and it had articles reprinted in full by other publications (Dawson and Wales, 1979). Alderson also used his practice to inform his theory development. His well-known study of the Philadelphia supermarket industry in 1960 (Alderson, 1965), for example, formed the basis for his theory of consumer behavior. His empirical work is regarded as both creative and rigorous for his time (Dawson and Wales, 1979).

Alderson read widely across disciplines, and drew from many sources in developing his general theory of marketing (Monieson and Shapiro, 1980). His thinking was influenced, for example, by the sociologists Merton and Parsons regarding behavioral systems, by the anthropologists Malinowski and Steward regarding biological theories and cultural ecology, and by the economists Chamberlin, Baumol and Clark regarding, among other things, heterogeneity of firms and resources (Alderson, 1965, Monieson and Shapiro, 1980). The influence of the day's economic thinking can be expected to have been particularly strong. Alderson discussed economic theory with Chamberlin during several of the marketing theory seminars, and he worked closely with Baumol for a period that included the Philadelphia supermarket study (Alderson, 1965, Baumol, 1984). A number of Alderson's ideas concerning market heterogeneity and dynamics are similar to those from Austrian economics (Reekie and Savitt, 1982).

2.   Alderson's general theory of marketing

Alderson's general theory revolves around the interactions of firms and households, each of which he views as organized behavior systems. The goal of such systems is survival. Individuals join these systems because they expect that, through participation, they will more likely achieve their individual goals. Organized behavior systems exist within a heterogeneous market. Market heterogeneity is seen both on the demand side, in the heterogeneity of assortments desired by households, and on the supply side, in the heterogeneity of resources in their natural state.

The basic functions of firms in Alderson's theory are to perform sorts and transformations. Sorts alter heterogeneity, and transformations add space, form, or time utility. Sorts and transformations are typically followed by transactions that take place between firms and, ultimately, between firms and households. The complete sequence of sorts and transformations required to convert raw materials in nature into finished goods ready for consumption is called a transvection. The typical transvection thus encompasses the activities of multiple firms.

Each of these building blocks of Alderson's general theory is described in more detail in this section. In so doing, we have drawn from Alderson's 1965 book, *Dynamic Marketing Behavior*, and from Barksdale (1980), Hunt, Muncy and Ray (1981) and Priem (1992), each of whom have provided detailed and very accessible summaries of Alderson's theoretical scheme.

3. Market heterogeneity

One of the basic assumptions behind economic models of perfect competition is market homogeneity. Even when economists recognize that real world markets are not perfect, these are analyzed as deviations from the ideal (e.g. Kenney and Klein, 1983). Alderson starts with a diametrically opposite ideal, namely, the perfectly heterogeneous market. In a perfectly heterogeneous market, each small segment of demand can be completely satisfied by only one unique segment of supply. Markets are cleared only when the naturally-occurring heterogeneity of resources can be altered to match the heterogeneity demanded by consumers. Thus, markets are heterogeneous with respect to both demand and supply. Pricing is the key mechanism that clears homogeneous markets. Alderson asserts that heterogeneous markets are discrepant by their very nature, and pricing alone will not be able to clear them. "Some goods are left over which nobody wants. Some wants remain unsatisfied for the lack of corresponding goods. Some consumers accept goods which only partially satisfy their wants. This market imperfection results from a failure in market communication" (Alderson, 1965, p. 29).

Alderson argues that discrepant, heterogeneous markets can be cleared by either innovation or information. Innovation includes producing goods to satisfy needs currently unmet, or inducing demand for existing products through marketing efforts. Alternately, if buyers can unambiguously communicate what they need, there will be no production of unwanted goods. Although inefficiencies in the market can be reduced through better information exchange between suppliers and buyers, this information is not free. The information search costs and dissemination costs involved in creating a perfect market would be prohibitive. Thus, the most important issue becomes determining the optimal amount of information to clear markets.

4. Organized behavior systems

A fundamental concept in Alderson's general theory is that of the organized behavior system. An organized behavior system is any system with a criterion for membership, a rule or set of rules for assigning duties, and a preference scale for outputs (Alderson, 1965). The two principal organized behavior systems in marketing are households and firms. Each persists over time because it offers its members a surplus that they would not be able to enjoy outside the behavior system. Households engage in purchasing in the marketplace in order to build up an assortment of goods that would support expected patterns of future consumption behavior. Each household attempts to increase what Alderson calls the potency of its assortment. The demand patterns of households tend to be different, however, due to differences in tastes, desires, incomes, and locations. The acquisition of an Early American-style lamp, for example, would be desirable for a household that already holds Early American furniture in its assortment, but would not increase the assortment potency of a household which owns Danish Modern furniture.

Firms are behavior systems that evolved as a result of the specialization of labor, although originally the firm "was scarcely more than a household producing a surplus of some class of goods" (Alderson, 1965, p. 38). The primary goal of firms is survival, and firms seek growth out of the belief that growth is necessary for survival. Firms tend to persist over time because members realize that their benefits in terms of goods and status can be protected only if the firm survives. Thus, the underlying objectives of firms are those of their participants. Further, firms can survive only by ensuring the patronage of a group of households. This results in a continuing competition among firms for "differential advantage". Alderson's view of firms as organized behavior systems parallels the development of the theory of the firm in economics (Seth and Thomas, 1994). Alderson, however, goes beyond traditional theories of the firm by viewing firms as ecological systems operating in ecological niches defined by the heterogeneous market (Lockshin, 1993). Information search and physical sorting are the processes by which firms adapt to their environment.

5.   Sorts and transformations

In heterogeneous markets, the matching between differentiated segments of supply and differentiated segments of demand is effected through a series of sorts and transformations. Sorting is the physical process through which goods, materials, or components are assigned to appropriate segments of demand. Once a sort is completed, it cannot be reversed without some risk of loss. Alderson identifies four different types of sorting. The process of breaking down a heterogeneous collection into smaller homogeneous collections is called "sorting out." The opposite of this is "assorting," which is the building up of a large heterogeneous collection from several homogeneous collections. Each household is engaged in building up an assortment of goods. "Allocation" is the breaking down of a large homogeneous collection into several smaller homogeneous collections. The reverse of this is "accumulation" which involves the building up of a large homogeneous collection from several smaller homogeneous collections. A perfectly homogeneous collection of goods is one which cannot be sorted any further, whereas a perfectly heterogeneous collection is one in which each item is different from all other items.

Alderson argues that there must always be a transformation between two successive sorts. He defines a transformation as a "change in the physical form of a product or in its location in time and space which is calculated to increase its value for the ultimate consumer who adds the product to his assortment" (Alderson, 1965, p. 93). As described by Priem (1992, p. 138), Alderson's sorting-transformation process occurs when

> A consumer purchases unlike items to build an assortment based on that consumer's use desires. Alderson calls this process assorting, and considers it of greatest interest to marketers. The consumer selected, however, from among relatively homogeneous groupings of products (as might be found, for example, in a hardware store). These relatively homogeneous groupings were allocated (broken down) from larger, more homogeneous accumulations that may have been built up through, for example, factory production. To initiate this process, the factory producer was likely faced with heterogeneous natural resources that were sorted and transformed to become a differentiated segment of supply.

Even a non-manufacturing firm such as Federal Express is engaged in successive sorts (sorting out-accumulation-assorting) and transformations (change in locations).

6. Transactions and transvections

Transactions and transvections are the two basic units of action suggested by Alderson (1965). A transaction is the "product of a double search in which customers are looking for goods and suppliers are looking for customers" (Alderson, 1965, p. 75). Transactions can be further divided into "fully negotiated transactions" or "routine" transactions. Fully negotiated transactions may either be large transactions or controlling transactions that define the framework within which a number of subsequent future transactions will take place. These subsequent transactions are referred to as routine transactions. Every transaction involves an exchange. An exchange between x and y takes place if and only if x is different from y and if each of the parties to the exchange end up with assortments of higher utility as a result of the exchange.

Using a term he coined from the Latin roots *trans* and *vehere*, meaning "flowing through," Alderson defines a transvection as a unit of action "by which a single end product such as a pair of shoes is placed in the hands of the consumer after moving through all the intermediate sorts and transformations from the original raw materials in the state of nature" (Alderson, 1965, p. 86). A transvection is the outcome of a series of transactions, sorts, and transformations that creates meaningful heterogeneity from meaningless heterogeneity. Alderson notes that "instead of matching buyers and sellers who are in immediate contact, it matches an original producer and an ultimate consumer through a series of sorts and transformations" (1965, p. 22). A transvection has the optimal number of steps if costs cannot be decreased by either increasing or decreasing the number of sorts and transformations.

7.   A comparison of Alderson and Porter

This section compares Alderson's ideas with those of Michael Porter (1985). First, we provide a direct comparison between the transvection and the value system. Second, we evaluate the way each author uses his concepts to identify sources of competitive advantage.

The Transvection and the Value System

The two units of action suggested by Alderson (1965) for marketing systems are the transaction and the transvection. The transaction involves negotiation leading to an exchange, with many such exchanges taking place at many levels of the marketing system. The transvection is a broader concept that is related to the inputs and outputs of the entire marketing system. A transvection "is consummated when an end product is placed in the hands of the ultimate consumer, but the transvection comprises all prior action necessary to introduce this final result, going all the way back to conglomerate resources" (Alderson, 1965, p. 92). Transvections, then, can be seen as the sequence of sorts and transformations that occur in the marketing process. Transformations add space, form or time utility, and sorts either decrease (generally closer to the supply side) or increase (generally closer to the demand side) heterogeneity.

Porter's (1985) value system also traces products from the original producer to the ultimate consumer. He suggests that competitive advantage can best be understood by disaggregating the firm into the many discrete activities (not simply functions) it performs. A firm's activities "that are performed to design, produce, market, deliver and support its product" (Porter 1985, p. 36) are called its value chain. Porter also suggests that each firm's value chain "is embedded in a larger stream of activities" (1985, p. 34) that he calls the "value system." The value system might consist, for example, of the upstream raw material supplier's value chain, the focal firm's value chain, the downstream distributor's value chain and, finally, the ultimate buyer's value chain. Porter notes that either industrial firms or households may be the ultimate buyer, and explicitly discusses special characteristics of household value chains. Figure 29.1 provides representations of the transvection and value system concepts.

Similarities

Table 29.1 shows the strong similarities exhibited by the transvection and value system. Both concepts represent the sequence of activities required to take a product from raw materials to the ultimate consumer. Both are suggested as planning tools that may allow firms to attain sustainable competitive advantage. The actors in Alderson's (1965) general theory are members of "organized behavior systems;" these systems may be firms, households, or (when their goal is survival) marketing channels. Although Porter's (1985) work emphasizes strategic business unit value chains, he also asserts that firms (or SBUs), households and marketing channels have value chains. He specifically notes that either industrial firms or households may be the ultimate buyer, and explicitly discusses the special characteristics of household value chains as part of the value system.

Alderson's "discrepant" markets never wholly clear due to market communication problems. Thus, the information problem, key in Alderson's view of marketing, asks the fundamental question "How much sorting is enough?" (1965, p. 31). Consistent with Alderson's general theory, Porter notes that "exploiting (value chain) linkages usually requires information or information flows that allow optimization or coordination to take place. Thus, information systems are often vital to gaining competitive advantages from (value chain) linkages" (1985, p. 50).

Alderson (1965) sees the degree to which the number of sorts and transformations in a transvection are optimized as the source of what he calls differential advantage. Such advantage can be achieved through transvection cost minimization or through a transvection that better matches heterogeneous segments of supply and demand. Porter (1985) suggests that the primary value chain activities (inbound logistics, operations, outbound logistics, marketing and sales, and service), and secondary activities (procurement, technology development, human resource management and firm infrastructure) that support the primary activities, are the potential sources of competitive advantage. These categories are the basis for evaluating the value produced by an activity, as seen by the household or industrial consumer, and the cost of the activity itself. Such cost-benefit information can then be used by the firm in resource allocation decisions.

Differences

The partial formalization of Alderson's general theory by Hunt, Muncy and Ray (1981) identifies a well-defined conceptual foundation and consistent linking rules. Thus, Alderson's (1965) transvection concept is part of a larger general theory of marketing that appears to meet the requirements of a theoretical structure (Hostiuck and Kurtz, 1973). Porter's recent work, on the other hand, has been criticized for the "lack of precision ... apparent in the woolly definitions of some of the key concepts ... and in the specification of relationships between them" (Grant, 1991, p. 541). An example of this lack of precision is found in the definition of "value activities" as "the physically and technologically distinct activities a firm performs" (Porter, 1985, p. 38, emphasis added), thus defining these activities in terms of the activities themselves.

Figure 29.1. The Value System and the Transvection

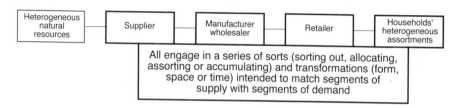

| Raw materials | Upstream supplier's value chain | Focal firm's value chain | Marketing channel value chain | Household value chain |

Focal firm's value chain
Primary activities
Inbound logistics
Operations
Outbound logistics
Marketing and
sales service
Support activities
Procurement
Technology development
Human resource management
Firm infrastrucure

Porter's (1989) value system

| Heterogeneous natural resources | Supplier | Manufacturer wholesaler | Retailer | Households' heterogeneous assortments |

All engage in a series of sorts (sorting out, allocating, assorting or accumulating) and transformations (form, space or time) intended to match segments of supply with segments of demand

Alderson's (1965) transvection

Table 29.1. Similarities of the transvection and value systems

Concept	Transvection	Value System
Scope	Marketing System	Marketing System
Use	Planning Tool	Planning Tool
Actors	Organised Behavior Systems: Firms Channels Households	Strategic Business Units: Firms (Business Level) Channels Households
Key to Competitive Advantage	Information	Information
Actions	Sorting Transforming	Value Chain Activities as cost drivers
Strategic Approaches	Differentiation Low Cost Market Segmentation	Differentiation Low Cost Focus
Theory Orientation	Positive	Normative

Grant (1991) does note, however, that some lack of clarity is almost inevitable given the scope and relevance of Porter's work.

Porter's (1985) work provides a detailed typology of activities and relates distinctive competence in various activities to sustainable competitive advantage. Alderson's (1965) approach is, however, more parsimonious in classifying activities as either sorts or transformations, and may be more rich conceptually with its emphasis on heterogeneity/homogeneity. Finally, Alderson's theory is primarily positive (i.e., descriptive), attempting to explain and predict marketing phenomena. Porter's approach is more normative (Grant, 1991), offering prescriptions for how firms' value chains, and the value systems of which they are a part, should be evaluated and altered to improve competitive position. Thus, Porter's (1985) work produces a typology of activities that results in strong prescriptions for practitioners. Alderson's (1965) parsimonious theory may be more descriptive of actual marketing systems, although its prescriptive implications are apparent.

Sources of competitive advantage

Alderson and Porter also propose similar strategies for building competitive advantage. Alderson (1965) argues that the search for differential advantage explains the dynamics of competition. He proposes market segmentation, the transvection itself, and advertising or product and process innovation as potential sources of differential advantage. Porter (1985, 1980) identifies three generic business-level strategies for achieving competitive advantage: differentiation, cost leadership, and focus. He argues that comparison of the value chains of competing firms exposes the factors that result in differing levels of these strategies for achieving competitive advantage.

Thus, each author's strategies involve 1) cost savings (in sorting activities of the transvection process or value activities of the value chain); 2) differentiation (by creating a unique product, technology, appeal, or process); or 3) focus (market segmentation through emphasis on a particular product line or market segment). The means each author suggests for achieving these strategies, based on transvection analysis in Alderson's case or value system analysis in Porter's case, are outlined in the sections that follow.

Cost advantage

Alderson regards the transvection as an all-embracing concept, "representing a unit of action for the marketing system as a whole" (1965, p. 22). He sees the transvection as an analytical tool, useful in making a marketing system work better by finding the "shortest" path to the market. For repetitive operations, the shortest path to market is the one that results in minimum cost; either adding or subtracting a sort or transformation would increase the total cost of the transvection. Thus, the lowest total cost can be found by minimizing the expression $Y = C_s + C_t$, where C_s represents the cost of sorts and C_t the cost of transformations.

Porter (1985) argues that a firm's value activities, and how they are performed, determine the overall cost position of the firm relative to other firms in its industry. He views interrelationships among value activities, both within and outside the firm, as important influences on each value activity's contribution to total cost. "Cost advantage results if the firm achieves a lower cumulative cost of performing value activities than its competitors" (Porter, 1985, p. 64). Firms emphasizing this approach are pursuing Porter's "cost leadership" strategy. He recommends that cost analysis using the value chain proceed by first identifying those activities that "represent a significant or rapidly growing percentage of operating costs or assets"(Porter, 1985, p. 64). These activities are then investigated in greater detail. A firm's important "cost drivers," such as economies of scale resulting from reduced value activity unit costs at higher volumes, are identified. These cost drivers are then incorporated into operational and strategic plans. A firm is believed to have cost advantage if 1) its overall value activities cost is lower than that of competing firms, and 2) the bases of these lower costs are hard for competing firms to copy. A cost advantage that is easily replicated by competitors will not produce competitive advantage that is sustainable.

Alderson (1965) also recognizes that sources of cost advantage can be imitated or attacked by competitors. He argues that firms are continually trying to neutralize competitors' cost advantages. He suggests that the first step in improving a firm's own cost position should include analysis of possible economies of scale in marketing channels. In Alderson's view, study of the manner in which a firm performs its functions will likely identify scale economies that may result in greater efficiency.

Porter's generic business strategy of cost leadership is quite similar to the Aldersonian notion of the shortest path to market (total cost minimization). In this case, each author applies his planning tool in similar ways. For example, Porter sees achieving economies of scale in performing value activities as a means of gaining advantage over competitors. Alderson proposes attainment of economies of scale in the marketing process as a device for neutralizing the differential advantage of market entrants. Thus, both the planning tools of each author and their proposed application to gain competitive advantage are quite similar.

Market segmentation

Alderson sees the search for differential advantage as requiring the development of strategies for differentiation of a market position. "The simplest base for differentiation reflects nothing more than the selection of certain customers from a market in which heterogeneous demand has already become established" (Alderson, 1965, p. 185). Thus, market segmentation involves identifying consumers who have similar needs from among the diverse needs of the overall population. The firm then attempts to serve a limited number of relatively homogeneous groups rather than the entire market. Alderson (1965) argues that such a strategy can help firms achieve lower costs through standardization; economies in production and marketing may be achieved through focus on fewer product models than would be required without segmentation.

Porter (1985) presents the "focus" strategy as an approach to gaining a competitive advantage in an industry. When properly implemented, this strategy results in competitive advantage by matching a firm's abilities with the needs of a particular market segment. Porter suggests that segmentation may be achieved based on either marketing-related or any other value chain activity, and introduces the term "industry segmentation." "Industry segmentation combines buyer purchasing behavior with the behavior of costs, including both production costs and the costs of serving different buyers. Industry segmentation is viewed as encompassing the entire value chain, exposing differences in structural attractiveness among segments as well as conflicts in serving segments simultaneously" (Porter, 1985, p. 232). The goal of the focused firm is to configure its value chain in a manner that is optimal for the targeted segment; the desired value chain configuration may attempt to achieve either cost leadership or differentiation relative to other firms serving the segment. Porter notes that, while some economies of scope may be realized by attempting to serve more than one segment, the danger for a focused firm considering expansion into other segments is loss of the original advantage achieved through focus. Compared to cost leadership and differetiation, there have been relatively few empirical studies on focus strategies. In one study, however, economies of scope were found, overall, to be negatively associated with performance for service firms when quality cannot be determined prior to purchase (Nayyar, 1993). These results are consistent with Alderson's emphasis on information as the key mechanism for clearing markets.

Both Alderson (1965) and Porter (1985) view segmentation as a basis for obtaining competitive advantage by achieving lower total cost, evaluated either through the value chain and its activities or the transvection and its alternating sorts and transformations. Porter, however, extends Alderson's ideas by including the behavior of costs, as well as buyer purchasing behavior, as a basis for segmentation.

Differentiation

Alderson (1957) argues that each firm must seek to fulfill a function that is in some way unique (e.g., through product, customer, operations or location). This search for functional uniqueness is seen as the basis for competitive advantage Alderson is careful to note, however, that absolute improvements which may be easily imitated by others do not provide competitive advantage. Any superiority must be relative to the capabilities of other firms to produce a truly differential advantage.

Alderson (1957) asserts that differential advantage may be developed based on legal, locational, or technological factors, but that technological factors are becoming increasingly important.

> The various aspects of technological advantage are, in general, related to use requirements, production processes, and marketing methods. An advantage may be obtained by styling a product to meet a particular consumer taste or desire... Advantages based on production processes may be exploited by the use of unique assembly-line methods, new equipment, or application of results from a time and motion study. Marketing methods offer an ever-widening basis for exploiting an advantage. A differential advantage may be obtained by a new and different distribution system, or by a revised warehousing or inventory control system" (Alderson, 1957, p. 107).

Thus, Alderson views differentiation as frequently tied to production at lower cost and total cost minimization. He also sees cooperation with others in the same marketing channel as a potential source of differential advantage, particularly where channel members may work together for a common end (e.g., survival).

Differentiation is Porter's third proposed generic business strategy. He argues that

> a firm differentiates itself from its competitors when it provides something unique that is valuable to its buyers beyond simply offering a low price. Differentiation allows the firm to command a premium price, to sell more of its product at a given price, or to gain equivalent benefits such as greater buyer loyalty during cyclical or seasonal downturns. Differentiation leads to superior performance if the price premium achieved exceeds any added costs of being unique. A firm's differentiation may appeal to a broad group of buyers in an industry or only to a subset of buyers with particular needs (Porter, 1985, p. 120).

He suggests that the effects of the firm's value chain activities on the buyer form the basis for differentiation. Porter argues that uniqueness can be created through technology-based product innovation or marketing innovation, or via activity linkages throughout the value system.

Value system linkages can produce uniqueness if they allow more exact satisfaction of consumer needs. Uniqueness in meeting buyers' needs may be the result of coordination with suppliers. Examples of channel linkages that can lead to uniqueness include: training channel members in key business procedures, joint sales programs, and subsidizing sales- or service-related investments by channel members. Porter acknowledges that such steps toward differentiation are costly, since "a firm must often incur costs to be unique and uniqueness requires that it performs value activities better than competitors" (1985, p.127).

Both Alderson and Porter perceive differentiation as a competitive advantage strategy that involves the creation of unique products, technologies, services, or marketing efforts, or unique, cooperative relationship among a firm, its suppliers, and other channel members. Both see the important distinction between segmentation and differentiation (Smith, 1956). Both also acknowledge the role of cost factors in successful differentiation, but they disagree on how the sources of competitive advantage may be employed to attain high performance. This difference will next be used to provide an example of how the interaction among the two conceptual frameworks may be beneficial in interating and extending the theories.

An example of an interaction among the theories

The validity of scientific theories is primarily evaluated in terms of their ability to explain observed phenomena and predict future phenomena. There has been a vigorous effort in the past one and a half decades to evaluate, confirm or falsify Porter's generic strategy framework. On the other hand, there has been little, if any, effort to validate or disconfirm the propositions that follow from Alderson's general theory. A direct comparison of the two theories and an examination of the empirical results that have accumulated over the years can provide researchers with valuable insights in addressing some of the controversies and unresolved issues relating to Porter's generic strategy framework. One controversy has centered around the mutual exclusivity of the generic strategies (Dess and Rasheed, 1992).

Porter has generally described the competitive advantage strategies of cost leadership and differentiation as mutually exclusive; the cost reduction commitment required to achieve cost leadership and the expense necessary to achieve differentiation simply preclude the successful pursuit of both simultaneously. He argues that a firm "must make a choice about the type of competitive advantage it seeks to attain and the scope within which it will attain it. Being 'all things to all people' is a recipe for mediocrity and below-average performance..." (Porter, 1985, p. 12). Thus, firms pursuing multiple sources of competitive advantage are said to likely be "stuck in the middle," with no distinctive competence and little ability to compete.

Alderson (1965) views simultaneous pursuit of low cost and differentiation as both compatible and synergistic. He argues that differentiation is frequently achieved through technological advances that result in cost improvements in production processes or physical distribution, in addition to through expenditures for advertising or research and development. Alderson's approach is derivative of his transvection concept; the goal of the marketing system is to minimize the costs of the sorts and transformations necessary to bring the desired good into the hands of the consumer. Alderson sees differentiation as critically dependent on the cost-quality relationship, and therefore low relative cost as important in achieving differentiation.

Porter's (1985) view that low cost and differentiation are discrete ends of a continuum that may never be associated with one another has sparked much conceptual debate and empirical research. This debate may have been encouraged in part because of the absence of conceptual "building blocks" supporting his value system theory. Scholars have since developed theory counter to Porter's view, suggesting that low cost and differentiation may actually be independent dimensions that should be vigorously pursued simultaneously (e.g. Hill, 1988, Jones, 1988, Murray, 1988). Empirical research using the PIMS database by Miller and Dess (1993) suggests that the generic strategy framework could be improved by viewing cost, differentiation and focus as three dimensions of strategic positioning rather than as three distinct strategies. The idea that pursuing multiple sources of competitive advantage is both viable and desirable has also been supported by other researchers (Philips et al., 1983, White, 1986). Thus, the research in strategic management following from Porter (1980, 1985, 1990) does not provide unequivocal support for Porter's original formulation. Although many firms pursuing cost and differentiation simultaneously may become stuck in the middle, there is clear evidence to suggest that at least some firms have been successful in achieving superior economic performance by pursuing both advantages. Since Alderson's formulation developed from his transvection ideas does not require cost and differentiation advantages to be incompatible, the empirical evidence that has accumulated over the years can be viewed as providing strong support for Alderson's approach.

8.   Evaluation and discussion

Theoretical frameworks are often evaluated on criteria such as the degree to which they: simplify complex phenomena, predict accurately, are generalizable, and stimulate research interest (e.g. Anderson, 1983, Weick, 1979). When compared to Porter's (1985) theory, Alderson's (1965) ideas fare quite well on the criteria of simplicity and generalizability. Alderson's (1965) work is more formally developed than Porter's (1985) and, with its emphasis on the well-defined sort and transformation as building blocks, considerably more parsimonious. This parsimony results in a simpler and more generalizable theory that can, perhaps, be applied more effectively to "real world" problems. Paraoxically, however, there have been few direct empirical tests of Alderson's 1965) work.

In one effort to test a portion of Alderson's (1957, 1965) general theory, hapiro (1964) evaluated the survival orientation of members of a non-profit rganized behavior system, with inconclusive results. More indirectly, Priem 1992) has found considerable support for the basic concepts of Alderson's 1965) general theory in recent empirical work from industrial organization conomics. The tests of Alderson (1965) are quite sparse and tangential, however, when compared to the work that has gone on evaluating Porter (1985, 980).

Porter's (1985) theory has been particularly successful on the criterion of timulating research interest, and researchers have found support for the predictive accuracy of his early models (e.g. Dess and Davis, 1984, Kim and .im, 1988, Miller and Friesen, 1986a, Miller and Friesen, 1986b). Clearly, a igorous evaluation of Porter's (1985) ideas is underway.

. Relative influence

Although their theories are quite similar, it is clear that the type of influence ach author's work has had on practitioners and scholars in his own field has een quite dissimilar. Alderson contributed to marketing thought both as a theorist and as an advocate of theory (Goodman, 1986). Some feel that Alderson's najor contribution comes from his overall emphasis on the importance of theory to scholarship and to practice, however, rather than from the substance of he theories he developed (Barksdale, 1980). A number of Alderson's concepts ave been extended or tested by marketing scholars. For example, conceptual vork has been undertaken recently using Alderson's ideas of core/niche competitive advantage (Lockshin, 1993, Evans et al., 1993) and marketing cooperation (Larson and Lusch, 1992), and Shapiro (1964) has empirically examined he organized behavior system (Alderson, 1957). Even so, Alderson's conceptualizations, and particularly the transvection concept that is central to his general theory of marketing, seem to have had relatively little influence on the ubstance of marketing theory over the past thirty years. Barksdale has noted hat Alderson's "theoretical system never became the organizing concept for he mainstream of marketing thought" (1980, p. 3). Few of the 150 falsifible propositions offered in Alderson's 1965 work have been tested, and little conceptual work has been undertaken to refine or extend his general theory Barksdale, 1980, Dawson and Wales, 1979). In a comprehensive book Houson (1994) recently edited on exchange relationships, for example, Alderson is ited regarding assortment potency, but not for his transvection ideas.

This lack of attention to Alderson's theories by marketing scholars may be lue in part to his somewhat nonsystematic writing style (Hostiuck and Kurtz,

1973), and in part to the absence of a tradition or school of researchers to continue his work. It does not appear that a "particular coherent tradition of scientific research" (Kuhn, 1959, p. 10) has sprung from Alderson's general theory. The situation, however, may be akin to that of Coase's (1937) work on the nature of the firm; it took many years before the true value of Coase's contribution was widely recognized by the academic community (Macharzina and Oesterle, 1994).

Porter's work (1980, 1985, 1990), on the other hand, has had considerable influence on practitioners and scholars. *Business Week* notes, for example, that "Porter's model of the 'value chain' has become one of the bag of tools every MBA should graduate with. . . Management consultants have made millions by applying the author's competitive logic to one company after another" (1990, p. 12). Management researchers have undertaken empirical work to evaluate Porter's generic strategies (e.g. Dess and Davis, 1984, Miller and Friesen, 1986a, Miller and Friesen, 1986b). Porter's framework has been empirically assessed for generalizability, accuracy and simplicity (Miller and Dess, 1993) and context specificity (White, 1986, Calingo, 1989, Miller, 1992a) and evaluated theoretically for its adequacy and accuracy (Chrisman et al. 1988, Jegers, 1993, Miller, 1992b). In recent years, Porter's value-based ideas have been extended via the "resource-based" approach to strategic management (e.g. Barney, 1991, Dierickx and Cool, 1989, Rumelt, 1984). The value system is receiving increasing attention in both the practitioner (e.g. Normann and Ramirez, 1993, O'Sullivan and Geringer, 1993, Reimann, 1989) and academic (e.g. Armistead and Clark, 1993, Durand, 1993, Hergert and Morris, 1989, Roth, 1992) literatures. Porter's 1990 work may be expected to have a similarly strong influence on international trade theory (Grant, 1991). Marketing researchers have even begun to make some use of Porter's concepts (e.g. Dickinson and Cooper, 1992, Kotabe and Duhan, 1993, Wright et al., 1991), but have generally not focused on the macro-level value system.

10.   Potential for extending Alderson's theory to strategic management

The strong similarities between the concepts of the transvection and the value system, and in their application to issues of competitive advantage, may be useful for extending Alderson's (1965) general theory for application to other strategy-related issues. Alderson's work may be helpful, for example, in aiding in a shift from static to dynamic models, and in validating the context-specificity and discriminating ability of Porter's (1985, 1980) generic strategies.

Alderson's notions of differential advantage receive considerable support from empirical work in strategic management testing for the existence of Porter's (1980) generic business-level strategies (e.g. Dess and Davis, 1984, Miller and

Friesen, 1986a, Miller and Friesen, 1986b). This early work by Porter (1980) was built, however, on static models (Grant, 1991). Alderson's 1965 book, *Dynamic Marketing Behavior*, is one of the first dynamic theories to be proposed in a management-related discipline, and Porter (1991) has acknowledged the need for more dynamic theories. His model of competitive advantage of nations (1990) is a truly dynamic model, although it has been criticized by some for treating international strategy primarily as "an issue of geographic scope" (Rugman and Verbeke, 1993). Generally, however, Porter's more recent work (1990) shifts from a static to a dynamic theoretical frame (Grant, 1991) that is more consistent with Alderson's (1965) approach. This newer work may be similarly useful in potentially extending Alderson's (1965) theory to encompass a global perspective.

Although Porter's (1980) generic strategies have been presented as universal strategies equally applicable in all environmental contexts, there has been some debate about the context specificity of these strategies (Miller and Friesen, 1986a, Hambrick, 1983, Day, 1984). Empirical studies by Calingo (1989), Miller (1992) and Miller and Dess (1993) suggest that the generic strategies may possibly be more contingent than generic. Porter acknowledges that "cost advantage and differentiation in turn stem from industry structure" (1985, p. 11). Strong theoretical reasons for such context specificity have been proposed by Murray (1988). While the generic strategy framework in isolation may be independent of environmental conditions, Porter and the IO tradition in which his work is based place paramount importance on industry analysis. Fundamental contributions of Porter (1980) include the structural analysis of industries and the development of generic industry environments. Alderson's general theory, on the other hand, does not develop a formal methodology for analyzing and classifying industry environments. A possible reason for this lack of development in his general theory may well be that in the 1950s, research in IO economics had not accumulated to the point that a comprehensive methodology for industry analysis could be developed.

Chrisman, Hofer and Boulton (1988) found Porter's classification scheme of generic strategies to be mutually exclusive, stable, parsimonious, and timeless. They, however, suggest that the classification scheme is not sufficiently internally homogeneous. That is, a category such as differentiation may contain several dissimilar forms of differentiation. Miller (1992), for example, identifies three distinct forms of differentiation based on innovation, marketing, and quality. A recent study of focus strategies in service firms suggests that, from a performance standpoint, a focus on selected customer segments is superior to a focus on either internal capabilities or geographic regions (Nayyar, 1992). A comparison between Alderson and Porter on this issue is difficult since Alderson's work was not aimed at creating a classification system at all. Instead, his focus is on creating "differential advantage." A possible reason for lack of empirical research based on Alderson's general theory may well be the absence of a classification system in his theory; classification is a prerequisite for effective theory testing (McKelvey, 1982, Rich, 1992). From the point of view of the strategist, however, a functionalist theory that suggests multiple means for attaining differential advantage may be more appealing than the development of a parsimonious typology.

11. Conclusion

An understanding of the history of management thought is important for current management scholars (e.g. Perrow, 1973). For strategic management scholars, an understanding of the history of thought in the additional disciplines from which they may now be borrowing may be equally beneficial. We believe that Alderson's (1957, 1965) work provides an illustration of the potential importance of past theories. Although marketing has had little recent influence on strategic management thought, Alderson's general theory, developed more than thirty years ago, has the potential to make a unique contribution. Alderson's emphasis on resource heterogeneity, the transvection and sustainable competitive advantage may offer a bridge between Porter's theories and the resource-based view of strategic management. His concepts of sorting and building up or breaking down assortments may bring new perspectives to strategy scholars evaluating competitive advantage. Controversies over aspects of Porter's (1985, 1980) work may be informed through reference to Alderson. The 150 "testable propositions" offered by Alderson in his 1965 book may be useful for empirical researchers. The formalized nature of Alderson's work may aid in the further formalization of Porter's ideas and the resource-based view of strategy.

Smith (1966) lauded Alderson's contributions to marketing: his insistence on an interdisciplinary approach; his demonstration of the usefulness of theory through his own work as a practitioner; his leadership in bridging the academic and business communities to identify substantive research opportunities for the discipline; and the specific theoretical contributions of his general theory, including the concepts of differential advantage and the transvection. Our discussion of Alderson's (1957, 1965) and Porter's (1985) use of their theoretical frameworks in assessing approaches to achieving competitive advantage cannot fully capture the richness and subtleties of each theorist's ideas, due in part to the broad scope of each theory. Although the terminology is somewhat different, the similarities in the two theoretical frameworks are remarkable. Given the strong similarities between Alderson's theories and recent work in strategic management, we believe that closer consideration of Alderson's ideas by strategy scholars is warranted.

References

Alderson, Wroe (1957). *Marketing Behavior and Executive Action: A Functionalist Approach to Marketing*. Richard D. Irwin Inc., Homewood, Ill.

Alderson, Wroe (1965). *Dynamic Marketing Behavior: A Functionalist Theory of Marketing*. Richard D. Irwin Inc., Homewood, Ill.

Anderson, P. F. (1983). Marketing, Scientific Progress, and Scientific Method. *Journal of Marketing*, 47(Fall):18–31.

Armistead, C. G. and Clark, G. (1993). Resource Activity Mapping: The Value Chain in Service Operations Strategy. *The Service Industries Journal*, 13:221–239.

Barksdale, H. C. (1980). Wroe Alderson's Contributions to Marketing Theory. In Lamb, Charles and Dunne, Patrick, editors, *Theoretical Developments in Marketing*, pages 1–3. American Marketing Association, Chicago.

Barney, J. B. (1991). Firm Resources and Sustained Competitive Advantage. *Journal of Management*, 17:99–120.

Baumol, W. J. (1984). Preface to "On the role of marketing theory". In Brown, S. W. and Fisk, R. P., editors, *Marketing Theory: Distinguished Contributions*, page 60. John Wiley & Sons, New York.

Biggadike, E. R. (1981). The contributions of marketing to strategic management. *Academy of Management Review*, 6:621–632.

Brown, Stephen W. and Fisk, Raymond, editors (1984). *Marketing Theory: Distinguished Contributions*. John Wiley & Sons, New York.

Business Week staff writer (1990). A Classic Business Bookshelf. *Business Week*, March 5:10–12.

Calingo, L. R. (1989). Environmental Determinants of Generic Competitive Strategies: Preliminary Evidence from Structural Content Analysis of *Fortune* and *Business Week* articles (1983-1984). *Human Relations*, 42:353–370.

Caves, R. E. and Porter, M. E. (1977). From entry barriers to mobility barriers: Conjectural decisions and contrived deterrence to new competition. *Quarterly Journal of Economics*, 91:241–261.

Chamberlin, E. H. (1933). *The Theory of Monopolistic Competition: A Reorientation of the Theory of Value*. Harvard University Press, Cambridge, Massachusetts. Frequently revised since then.

Chrisman, J. J., Hofer, C. W., and Boulton, W. R. (1988). Toward a System for Classifying Business Strategies. *Academy of Management Review*, 13:413–428.

Coase, R. H. (1937). The Nature of the Firm. *Economica*, 4:386–405.

Dawson, Jr., Lyndon E. and Wales, Hugh G. (1979). Consumer Motivation Theory in Historical Perspective: An Aldersonian View. In Ferrell, O. C., Brown, Stephen W., and Lamb, Jr., Charles W., editors, *Conceptual and Theoretical*

Developments in Marketing, pages 210–221. American Marketing Association, Chicago.

Day, G. S. (1984). *Strategic Market Planning: The Pursuit of Competitive Advantage*. West, St. Paul, MN.

Dess, G. G. and Davis, P. S. (1984). Porter's (1980) Generic Strategies as Determinants of Strategic Group Membership and Organizational Performance. *Academy of Management Journal*, 27:467–488.

Dess, G. G. and Rasheed, A. (1992). Commentary on Generic Strategies: Classification, Combination and Context. In Shrivastava, P., Huff, A., and Dutton, J., editors, *Advances in Strategic Management*, pages 409–416. JAI Press, Greenwich, CT. Volume 8.

Dickinson, R. and Cooper, B. (1992). The Emergence of Cost-based Strategies in Retailing. *Journal of Marketing Channels*, 2(1):29–46.

Dierickx, L. and Cool, K. (1989). Asset Stock Accumulation and Sustainability of Competitive Advantage. *Management Science*, 35:1501–1511.

Durand, T. (1993). Economy of Scope, Added Value Chain and Cost Dynamics: A Tentative Optimization Model. *International Journal of Product Economics*, 29:237–247.

Evans, K. R., Barnes, J. W., and Schlacter, J. L. (1993). A General Systems Approach to Retail Evolution. *The International Review of Retail Distribution and Consumer Research*, 3:79–100.

Fernie, J. D. (1995). The neptune affair. *American Scientist*, 83(2):116–119.

Goodman, Charles (1986). The Transformation of the Marketing Discipline 1946-1986. *The Wharton School of the University of Pennsylvania*, Working Paper No. 88-010R.

Grant, R. M. (1991). Porter's 'Competitive Advantage of Nations': An Assessment. *Strategic Management Journal*, 12:535–548.

Grether, E. T. (1967). Chamberlin's Theory of Monopolistic Competition and the Literature of Marketing. In Kuenne, R., editor, *Monopolistic Competition Theory: Studies in Impact, Essays in honor of Edward H. Chamberlin*, pages 307–329. John Wiley & Sons, New York.

Hambrick, D. C. (1983). High Profit Strategies in Mature Capital Goods Industries: A Contingency Approach. *Academy of Management Journal*, 26:687–707.

Hergert, M. and Morris, D. (1989). Accounting Data for Value Chain Analysis. *Strategic Management Journal*, 10:175–188.

Hill, C. W. L. (1988). Differentiation versus Low Cost or Differentiation and Low Cost: A Contingency Framework. *Academy of Management Review*, 13:401–412.

Hostiuck, K. Tim and Kurtz, David L. (1973). Alderson's Functionalism and the Development of Marketing Theory. *Journal of Business Research*, 1(2):141–156.

Houston, F. S., editor (1994). *Marketing Exchange Relationships, Transactions, and Their Media*. Quorum Books, Westport, CT.

Hunt, Shelby D., Muncy, James A., and Ray, Nina M. (1981). Alderson's General Theory of Marketing: A Formalization. In Enis, Ben M. and Roering, Kenneth J., editors, *Review of Marketing 1981*, pages 267–272. American Marketing Association, Chicago.

Jegers, M. (1993). Methodological Limitations of Porter's Three Generic Strategies Framework. In Rugman, A. M. and Verbeke, A., editors, *Global Competition: Beyond the Three Generics*, pages 43–50. JAI Press, Greenwich, CT.

Jones, D. G. Brian (1988). Origins of the Functional Approach in Marketing. In Shapiro, Stanley J. and Walle, A. H., editors, *Marketing: A Return to Broader Dimensions: Proceedings of the 1988 AMA Winter Educators' Conference*, pages 166–170. American Marketing Association, Chicago.

Kenney, R. B. and Klein, B. (1983). The Economics of Block Booking. *Journal of Law and Economics*, 26:497–540.

Kim, L. and Lim, Y. (1988). Environment, Generic Strategies, and Performance in a Rapidly Developing Country: A Taxonomic Approach. *Academy of Management Journal*, 31:802–827.

Kotabe, M. and Duhan, D. F. (1993). Strategy Clusters in Japanese Markets: Firm Performance Indicators. *Journal of the Academy of Marketing Science*, 21:21–31.

Kuhn, Thomas S. (1959). Energy conservation as an example of simultaneous discovery. In Clagett, M., editor, *Critical problems in the history of science*, pages 321–356. University of Wisconsin Press, Madison.

Larson, P. D. and Lusch, R. F. (1992). Functional Integration in Marketing Channels: A Determination of Product Quality and Total Cost. *Journal of Marketing Channels*, 2:1–28.

Lockshin, L. S. (1993). The Role of the Biological Model in Marketing Strategy. In Varadarajan, R. and Jaworski, B., editors, *Marketing Theory and Applications, AMA Winter Educators' Conference Proceedings*, pages 226–233. American Marketing Association, Chicago.

Macharzina, K. and Oesterle, M. J. (1994). International Comparative Evaluation of North-American and German Research Output in Business and Management. *Management International Review*, 34:255–265.

McKelvey, B. (1982). *Organizational Systematics*. University of California Press, Berkeley, CA.

Merton, Robert K. (1957). Merton, R.K., "Priorities in scientific discovery: A chapter in the sociology of science. *American Sociological Review*, 22:635–659.

Miller, A. and Dess, G. G. (1993). Assessing Porter's Generic Strategies in Terms of Generalizability, Accuracy, and Simplicity. *Journal of Management Studies*, 30:553–585.

Miller, D. (1992a). Generic strategies: Classification, combination and context. In Shrivastava, P., Huff, A., and Dutton, J., editors, *Advances in Strategic Management*, pages 391–408. JAI Press, Greenwich, CT. Volume 8.

Miller, D. (1992b). The generic strategy trap. *Journal of Business Strategy*, 13(1):37–41.

Miller, D. and Friesen, P. H. (1986a). Porter's (1980) generic strategies and performance: An empirical examination with american data, part i: Testing porter. *Journal of Management Studies*, 7:37–55.

Miller, D. and Friesen, P. H. (1986b). Porter's (1980) generic strategies and performance: An empirical examination with american data, part ii: Performance implications. *Journal of Management Studies*, 7:255–261.

Monieson, D. D. and Shapiro, Stanley J. (1980). Biological and Evolutionary Dimensions of Aldersonian Thought: What He Borrowed Then and What He Might Have Borrowed Now. In Lamb, C., editor, *Theoretical Developments in Marketing*, pages 7–12. American Marketing Association, Chicago.

Murray, A. I. (1988). A Contingency View of Porter's 'Generic Strategies'. *Academy of Management Journal*, 13:390–400.

Nayyar, P. R. (1992). Performance Effects of Three Foci in Service Firms. *Academy of Management Journal*, 35:985–1009.

Nayyar, P. R. (1993). Performance Effects of Information Asymmetry and Economies of Scope in Diversified Service Firms. *Academy of Management Journal*, 36:28–57.

Normann, R. and Ramirez, R. (1993). From Value Chain to Value Constellation: Designing Interactive Strategy. *Harvard Business Review*, 71(4):65–77.

O'Sullivan, L. and Geringer, J. M. (1993). Harness the Power of Your Value Chain. *Long Range Planning*, 26:59–68.

Perrow, C. (1973). The Short and Glorious History of Organizational Theory. *Organizational Dynamics*, 2(1):2–15.

Philips, L. W., Chang, D. R., and Buzzell, R. D. (1983). Product Quality, Cost Position, and Business Performance: A Test of Some Competing Hypotheses. *Journal of Marketing*, 47:26–43.

Porter, Michael E. (1974). Consumer behavior, retailer power, and market performance in consumer goods industries. *Review of Economics and Statistics*, 56:419–436.

Porter, Michael E. (1980). *Competitive Strategy*. The Free Press, New York.

Porter, Michael E. (1985). *Competitive Advantage*. The Free Press, New York.

Porter, Michael E. (1990). *The Competitive Advantage of Nations*. The Free Press, New York.

Porter, Michael E. (1991). Towards a Dynamic Theory of Strategy. *Strategic Management Journal*, 12(Winter):95–118.

Priem, Richard (1992). Industrial Organization Economics and Alderson's General Theory of Marketing. *Journal of the Academcy of Marketing Science*, 20(2):135–141.

Reekie, W. Duncan and Savitt, Ronald (1982). Marketing Behavior and Entrepeneurship: A Synthesis of Alderson and Austrian Economics. *The European Journal of Marketing*, 16(7):55–66.

Reimann, B. C. (1989). Sustaining Competitive Advantage. *Planning Review*, 17(2):30–48.

Rich, P. (1992). The Organizational Taxonomy: Definition and Design. *Academy of Management Review*, 17:758–781.

Robinson, Joan (1933). *The Economics of Imperfect Competition*. Macmillan and Co. Ltd, London.

Roth, K. (1992). International Configuration and Coordination Archetypes for Medium-sized Firms in Global Industries. *Journal of International Business Studies*, 23:533–549.

Rugman, A. M. and Verbeke, A. (1993). Generic Strategies in Global Competition. In Rugman, A. M. and Verbeke, A., editors, *Global Competition: Beyond the Three Generics*, pages 3–16. JAI Press, Greenwich, CT.

Rumelt, R. P. (1984). Towards a Strategic Theory of the Firm. In Lamb, R. B., editor, *Competitive Strategic Management*, pages 556–570. Prentice Hall, Englewood Cliffs, NJ.

Savitt, Ronald (1990). Pre-Aldersonian Antecedents to Macromarketing: Insights from the Textual Literature. *The Journal of the Academy of Marketing Science*, 18(4):293–301.

Seth, A. and Thomas, H. (1994). Theories of the firm: Implications for strategy. *Journal of Management Studies*, 31:165–191.

Shapiro, Stanley J. (1964). The Survival Concept and the Nonprofit Behavior System. In Cox, Reavis, Alderson, Wroe, and Shapiro, Stanley J., editors, *Theory in Marketing*, pages 109–124. Richard D. Irwin, Homewood, Illinois, second series edition.

Sheth, Jagdish N., Gardner, David M., and Garrett, Dennis E. (1988). *Marketing Theory: Evolution and Evaluation*. John Wiley and Sons, Inc., New York.

Smith, Wendell R. (1955). Imperfect competition and marketing strategy. *Cost and Profit Outlook*, 8(10):1–3.

Smith, Wendell R. (1956). Product Differentiation and Market Segmentation as Alternative Marketing Strategies. *Journal of Marketing*, 21(July):3–8.

Smith, Wendell R. (1966). Leaders in Marketing: Wroe Alderson. *Journal of Marketing*, 30(January):64–65.

The New York Times (1965). Wroe Alderson, 66, of Wharton School. Obituary column, June 2.

Weick, K. (1979). *The Social Psychology of Organizing*. Addison-Wesley, Reading, MA, second edition.

White, R. E. (1986). Generic Business Strategies, Organizational Context and Performance: An Empirical Investigation. *Strategic Management Journal*, 7:217–231.

Wright, P., Kroll, M., Chang, P., and Hamel, K. (1991). Strategic Profiles and Performance: An Empirical Test of Select Key Propositions. *Journal of the Academy of Marketing Science*, 19:245–254.

V

COMMENTARIES ON ALDERSON THE MARKETER

Chapter 30

INTRODUCTION TO PART V: ORIGINAL CONTRIBUTIONS TO THIS PUBLICATION

Stanley J. Shapiro

The final section of any publication of this type should complete the picture its authors or editors wish to provide their readers. In this case, previous parts have included a brief biography of Wroe Alderson (Part I), a fairly extensive set of Alderson's more theoretical writings (Part II), and a number of his more applied contributions in the areas of marketing management and marketing ethics (Part III). Also, previously published material by others about Wroe Alderson has been included for two reasons. First, this was done because it was felt such literature (see Lusch and Amstutz in Part III) would provide additional insights into Alderson's work. Also, previously published material was included in Part IV to demonstrate how other scholars had subsequently employed and/or built upon Aldersonian thought.

All of the material found in Parts II, III, and IV has been previously published. Ben Wooliscroft's biography of Alderson found in Part I, though written for inclusion in this publication, draws very heavily upon that author's recently completed doctoral dissertation. In contrast, the six contributions in this Part (Part V) were commissioned expressly for inclusion in this publication. The six articles are very different in nature but, nevertheless, they collectively flesh out the picture of Wroe Alderson the editors wish to provide.

Mike Halbert was for many years both personally and professionally very close to Wroe Alderson, closer perhaps than any other still living marketing practitioner or academic. For this reason, Halbert was invited and he agreed to write on the Wroe Alderson he knew. His contribution shows, among many other things, that Alderson was, in many different respects, a "larger than life" figure. The Halbert article provides us with otherwise unavailable insights into Wroe Alderson the man, Wroe Alderson the consultant, and Wroe Alderson the philosopher. It also adds useful personal insights that do indeed complete the intellectual picture the many other contributions provided in Part V.

The second new contribution, by Stan Shapiro with the assistance of Jim McKeon and Bob Rothberg, provides a detailed account of Wroe Alderson's accomplishments in his less than six years as a member of the Wharton School's

ALDERSONIAN MARKETING THOUGHT

Marketing Department. Originally, the article was going to focus exclusively on Alderson's Wharton-related research activities. However, these initiatives were only a part of all that Alderson had undertaken during that period. In order to provide a more complete picture, the scope of the article was expanded to include, as well, discussions of Wroe Alderson's involvement with the Marketing Science Institute, of the extensive amount of publishing that he did while at Wharton and, of the Behavior Systems consulting firm he established in the early 1960s.

The editors of this publication believe Alderson's work can still serve as an important point of departure for those currently concerned with theory building in marketing. However, our merely asserting this position seemed inadequate. To prove this was indeed the case, we invited Shelby Hunt and Dennis Arnett to discuss how "Resource-Advantage Theory," a very important and very contemporary intellectual development, was an extension of Alderson's theory of market processes. The editors believe, of course, that the intellectually exciting Hunt and Arnett paper is but one illustration of how Alderson can still provide a foundation or launching platform for contemporary theory building in marketing.

Robert Tamilia's article is an especially ambitious one in that it attempts to put Wroe Alderson's contributions to marketing in historical perspective. Tamilia discusses Alderson's market behavior theory with its many sub-theories and conceptual components. He then highlights some of the weaknesses and omissions of Alderson's theoretical contributions, especially when these are viewed from a modern-day business perspective. In doing so, Tamilia also presents the reasons why he believes the current generation of marketing academics no longer pays adequate attention to Alderson's work or, for that matter, to the many other contributions to the marketing discipline that were made by Alderson's contemporaries. In addition, Tamilia discusses the individuals, the schools of thought and the many different disciplines which Alderson used as his own intellectual points of departure.

Alf Walle's paper also explores reasons for declining late twentieth century interest in Alderson and his work. He attributes this decline, in part at least, to the fact that the previously dominant models of classical theory upon which Alderson's functionalism is based themselves fell out of intellectual favor in the second half of the twentieth century. However, Walle goes well beyond providing a marketing-related history of ideas. He also shows how, were such contemporary concepts as conflict and change incorporated into it, Alderson's structural/functional approach could again become an important conceptual tool with renewed relevance to marketing theory and practice.

The final contribution to Part V by Ian Wilkinson and Louise Young has a pedagogical focus. It discusses ways that Aldersonian concepts can be taught and, indeed, have been taught, in contemporary classrooms to current students of marketing. A number of very specific examples of how this can be done are provided. We believe the Wilkinson and Young approach to Alderson is one that others could effectively use in their own classrooms. We also believe that teaching Alderson in this fashion has just become administratively much easier since all of the Aldersonian concepts that professors might wish to employ are now to be found in this publication. However, all that we as editors of the volume can do is strongly recommend that Alderson again be taught. The current generation of marketing scholars must decide if, in fact, this will be done.

Chapter 31

THE WROE ALDERSON I KNEW

Michael Halbert

mike-halbert@juno.com

1.   Introduction

Wroe was an exceptionally good conversationalist who could and would discuss almost any subject at almost any length with depth, knowledge, skill, and humor. Yet I do not remember hearing Wroe ever go on about his religious or ethical values or about his specific personal philosophy. What I remember about him on those topics is what I learned or inferred from his behavior and from the ethical and philosophical content in our discussions on other topics. For example, while he often talked about the Quakers and his experiences as an active member of the Meetings he attended, the tenor of his conversation was seldom specifically about theology or about his personal theological beliefs. Therefore, most of what I think I know about Wroe's ethics and philosophy is deduced from our many and close interactions — the memories of which I still cherish.

This chapter, then, contains mostly such memories and reminiscences of my relationship with Wroe. Now, memory is not the most reliable source for information, especially about one's friends, and I am sure that my memory is less so than that of many others. I have heard it said that the function of memory is to create a history that is at least tolerable to the historian. It is selected bits of my history with Wroe that I find tolerable that I offer you here. I am sure that I recall those pieces of information that confirm my image of Wroe far more readily than I recall those that might contradict it.

Even an accurate memory makes choices of what to include and what to leave out. The cumulative effect of my making these kinds of choices about my experiences with Wroe almost half a century ago is certain to color and distort the picture I present to you here. Still, I hope it will interest you and give you a view of what Wroe looked like to someone who was his employee, colleague, associate, and friend.

This volume contains two papers in Section III by Wroe, himself, on ethics. One is The American Economy and Christian Ethics; the other is Ethics, Ideologies and Sanctions. These both show some of Wroe's views about ethics. Neither of them shows much about Wroe's own ethics. My attempt in this chapter is to share my views of what his ethics and philosophy actually were as embodied in his speech, his actions and his personality.

Since the picture I here share with you of Wroe is my personal picture it is, of course, incomplete, biased, and, in some of its details, I am sure, incorrect. The only way I know to acquaint you with my view of Wroe's philosophy and ethics is to recount many of my impressions and the experiences on which those impressions are based. This chapter is much nearer to a memory dump than to an organized exposition. It is the best I can do.

It probably will help you understand and evaluate my views for you to know something of the various twists and turns in my history with him and some of the biases I developed while living through that history.

In 1952, a few years after I graduated from Penn, one of my teachers, C. West Churchman (who had become a good friend), gave a talk here in Philadelphia about "Operations Research", a topic I had never heard of. I went and found myself fascinated by his subject. Afterwards, I asked West how I could get into that OR stuff.

West thought that his friend Wroe Alderson, who along with Bob Sessions, ran a market research and management consulting firm (A & S) here in Philadelphia might have a place for me. West gave me an introduction, and Wroe and I met. We hit it off immediately and Wroe hired me.

I worked with Wroe at A & S from 1952 until 1956. It was there that I learned all I know about marketing, business, and management consulting. It was also where I had one of the finest career experiences of my life.

Several years later, in 1962, while I was with DuPont in Wilmington, Wroe, who had moved to the Wharton School at Penn, was helping Tom McCabe Sr., Chairman of Scott Paper Co., set up the new Marketing Science Institute which was to be housed next to the Penn campus. Wroe was on MSI's Board and was helping Tom staff the new organization. Wroe suggested that I be its Technical Director. Tom McCabe interviewed me, approved Wroe's recommendation, and I became MSI's first Technical Director, a position I held until 1967 when the whole MSI moved to Harvard. Since Wroe was at Wharton and on the board of MSI he and I frequently met and often worked together. It was during this stint that I joined Wroe as a member of the annual Marketing Theory Seminars.

Wroe and I had become friends. My wife and I were often his guests at his home in Haverford and, later, at "One Hand Clapping", his retirement home on the Eastern Shore of the Chesapeake. The day he died in May 1965, Elsie, his widow, called me at home and asked me to phone some of his many friends in academia and from the Marketing Theory Seminar and tell them about his passing.

I grieved Wroe's death then and still miss him. I had two wonderful mentors in my professional life — Wroe Alderson and C. West Churchman. By coincidence, just a few months ago, on my birthday in 2004, West died at the age of 90.

In this chapter you will certainly see evidences of my appreciation and love for these two giants who employed me, advised me, and helped me become a professional. Of even more value, they also graced me with their friendship.

2.   The Role of Philosophy in Wroe's Life

Everyone has some sort of a model of the reality in their mind, and that model guides their perceptions, attentions, evaluations, memories, and behaviors. Somewhere in that model is a piece we can call their philosophy of life, and, perhaps another piece, nearby, we can call their ethics.

Many people have rather fragmented and disconnected world models with some of the pieces more or less isolated and independent from many of the other pieces. Some people, on the other hand, have well integrated models, with strong and complex dependencies and interconnections among most, if not all, of the various parts. Wroe's model was of this latter ilk. His views on almost any topic were internally consistent, robust, and consonant with almost all of his views of the rest of reality. He would never say, as some people can, "Well, ethics and morality are OK for Sunday, but you know, business is business." or "Not in my back yard!"

His general philosophy and his ethical values informed all of his business and consulting activities, as well as his daily behaviors and his everyday speech. I don't mean that he talked or acted like a professor or a preacher, but what he did and what he said were in keeping with his deeply held values and his worldview. In Carl Rogers' sense, Wroe was an authentic personality. His feelings and his behavior were congruent. What you see is what you get. This does not mean that Wroe was simple, naïve, or transparent. He was extremely complex, always sophisticated, and often hard to read. It does mean that his motives were rarely in conflict with each other. He most often knew his own mind quite well, and his internal complexities were almost always in harmony. I remember him only very rarely to have been unsure about what he wanted to do or why he wanted to do it.

Since Wroe's inner worldview was well integrated, it is not surprising that his philosophical and his ethical positions were not separate and distinct but were interdependent and merged at more than just their edges. As an example of the influence of that merging Wroe immediately saw the potential for the concept of "absorptive capacity" that I had brought back one day from a meeting at the Agency for International Development. This concept was commonly used by geo-politicians to refer to the amount and kind of technological aid that underdeveloped cultures could comfortably absorb, install, and profit from.

Wroe adapted that idea to mean that the nature, depth, and even the style of the recommendations we would give to a consulting client should depend, in part, on how much change that client and his organization could accept and put into practice. As brilliant experts in all aspects of business conduct (our view of ourselves) we often saw remedies for our client's problems that were far beyond that client's ability or willingness to adopt, even with all the help we could give in explaining, designing adaptive organizational procedures and techniques, and in training and support for his staff. If so we backed off and made recommendations that we thought had a real chance of actually being implemented. It became usual for us to include a formal absorptive capacity analysis in our planning for any major engagement from then on. In part, this was based on Wroe's respect for the client's abilities, integrity, and understanding of his own business.

Wroe often said that the measure of our success in a consulting assignment was whether the client was strategically better off a year after the end of our work with him. He also held that we were change agents; that our role was not only to solve the presenting problem, but to upgrade the client's ability to solve the problems he would face after we were gone. Wroe was great for installing formal problem solving and planning procedures in the client's organization. This was often seen by the client as a minor adjunct to the solution of the major presenting problem, but was often the part of our work with the client that gave Wroe the greatest satisfaction. Wroe always felt that our underlying role as consultants was to make the free enterprise system work better. Sometimes we felt that we did.

One of Wroe's successful uses of the absorptive capacity concept is illustrated by one client who came to us in desperation. His bank had grudgingly extended his credit only on his agreement to hire a consultant to help get his costs under control. This client was relatively unsophisticated about modern management methods (this was in the late 50's).

One of the client's problems was that his product inventory was far too large and badly unbalanced. When I saw this, I was eager to set up some automatic inventory controls using reorder points, linear programming (a brand new technology at that time), and computer modeling. When I enthusiastically presented this program to Wroe in an early planning session, he told me, "Mike, when you see a guy with his thumb caught in the car door, open the door before you simonize the hood." I found that to be good advice then and for the rest of my consulting career.

Many of our clients stayed with us for many years and through many different projects. One factor that contributed to that loyalty may have been our use of absorptive analysis to guide us in setting the scope of the ways we felt we could provide realistic help. It was Wroe's insistence that we focus our work on really making a difference to our client. We never had any potboiler or boilerplate projects. Wroe just wouldn't treat clients (or his own staff) that way. We always took the client's problems seriously and the client's concerns as important. Much of that attitude flowed from Wroe's ethical recognition of the importance and dignity of every individual.

Wroe appreciated his own intellect, knowledge, and creativity, but he also respected everybody else's: clients, colleagues, students, employees, and the waiters in the restaurants where he ate. I have never seen Wroe insult or put anybody down — client, employee, or cab driver. It was just not in his nature. Although Wroe had extraordinary intellectual capabilities, he had the skill and the patience to take his less gifted audience (even an audience of one) through the logical path that had led him to his often somewhat startling conclusions.

I remember one occasion in an interview with a new prospect. The prospect's Marketing VP, with a smirk, had plopped a thick internal document down on the conference table right in front of us. It had many multi-page tables showing shipments, sales, returns, and profits by calendar quarter, by product line, and by market territory. I was pretty good at reading tables and graphs, but I was still trying to determine whether the percents were summed across or down the table, when Wroe looked up at the prospect (the President) (with a side glance at the marketing VP) and said, "I see you've been losing your ass since midyear on your two main products in the Chicago market." Wroe then referred to several of the nested table sections to show that the rate of growth in market share in Chicago had fallen behind most of the other main market areas, and that the profit margins had also been eroding.

Two other remembered conversational tidbits show Wroe's attitudes about egotism and about ignorance. In the first, he and I were discussing Bob, a well-known and highly regarded marketing professional. I mentioned that while Bob certainly was egotistical, he had a great deal to be egotistical about. Wroe replied with a remark we both heard and liked that had come from Jay Minos, a mutual friend and professional philosopher, "Oh, no. He mistakes his attributes for his worth." Wroe never mistook his own attributes for his worth.

While Wroe was not egotistical; he was not overly modest either. Although he had only a bachelor's degree he more than once rejected offers from Universities to award him honorary doctorates. He said that he felt honorary doctorates were unfair to those who had worked for and earned their degrees and would only demean their extensive academic accomplishments.

I once was deploring to Wroe the ignorance of a particular client's market researcher by calling him stupid. Wroe blunted my tirade with the new-to-me aphorism, "Remember, ignorance is temporary. Stupidity is forever. We are all ignorant, only about different things." Wroe had a lifelong mission to reduce his own ignorance as well as that of the whole rest of the world, a mission at which he was remarkably effective. It was one of the reasons he was such a great teacher. He really believed in the value of teaching.

3.   Wroe's Ethics

Wroe was a well-known committed Quaker, was on the Board of their American Service Committee, and was an active member at various Friends' Meetings. When he decided to "retire" to the Eastern Shore, he told me that a major factor in his selection of Royal Oak, a small town near Easton, MD, was that he had visited most of the Meetings around there and that the Easton Meeting was the one he thought was the most suitable for him. Wroe was known to be so eloquent and poetic that often when he spoke at Meeting, someone in the congregation would take down his words. One such occasion was when Wroe was moved to speak at the Haverford, PA Meeting in the Fall of 1960. The result, The Autumn Prayer, is shown on page 10.

As an active Quaker Wroe was one of six men who, as a Quaker mission, were let into Russia in June 1955, shortly after that country opened its borders to westerners. The mission's goals were to look at the quality of life in Russia, particularly with regard to individual and religious freedom. Because of Wroe's marketing orientation, he, of course, also took notice of the economic conditions he saw there.

He told me that he had met a farmer in one of the outlying areas who raised oranges. That farmer, each week in season, took a few crates of oranges, flew them in his private plane to Moscow, and sold them on the street market, then flew back home. Wroe remarked that Russia had a long way to go to get reasonable efficiencies into its primitive marketing and distribution systems. He said that they had so far to go in economic, business, and marketing development that they would never, or not for a long, long time at least, constitute any appreciable threat to the US in world affairs.

There is much more about this Quaker mission to Russia in the 1956 book by Alderson, Cary, et al, *Meeting the Russians: American Quakers Visit the Soviet Union.* I have not read that book, so I am here still relying on my personal reminiscences.

While he was on the Penn faculty, Wroe lived in a house on a hill right next to the Haverford campus and was on their Board. A footbridge crossed the small street that separated his property from the University. He often guest lectured at Haverford and told me that on his death, he was leaving his theology books to the Haverford University library. He then would remark that his religious library was larger than that of Haverford's.

Although Wroe seldom talked directly of his religious beliefs, I got from him the strong feeling that his wonder and appreciation of the beautifully harmonious complexity of the universe, and the general rightness of that complexity supported his conviction that there was purpose and guidance from some higher source. Far better than anything I might remember, Wroe's own words, the last line of his Autumn Prayer, eloquently provide the best insight to his faith. "Our faith in a loving and eternal God is faith in the abundance of life."

I felt that Wroe did not believe in a paternalistic white-bearded god on a throne amongst the clouds who continually stares down at people to reward or punish them. Rather I saw Wroe's position to be that we are each responsible for our own destiny. This leads directly to his emphasis on individual self-reliance and economic, political, and social interdependence. Thus he was always optimistic, though always a realist. He believed fairness to be an absolute good. It is good for the society and good for the individual who practices it. When someone was deploring aggressive cutthroat competition, especially in marketing and advertising, Wroe would remind them that there is far more cooperation in the production, distribution, and marketing of goods and services than there is competition. It is the cooperative framework that sets and moderates the competitive arena. The very genius and foundation of civilization is the cooperation among groups who do not have family or clan ties. Wroe would have loved the internet.

It was not that he was a Pollyanna nor was unaware of sham and deceit or that he detested them as sinful and evil. Rather it was that he saw through those superficial poses and tricks so readily that he just ignored them. He once told me that he did not think everybody was a good person. It was just that he always saw that there was good in everyone. It was Wroe who explained to me that the reason Buddhists clasped their hands and bowed to another person rather than shaking hands was that they were acknowledging the divinity in each person. This, of course, is part of the Quaker doctrine.

Wroe once was discussing West Churchman's teaching style with me and complimented West by saying that when he was asked a rather stupid question he would often respond by answering the question the student would have asked if only he only had known what he was talking about. Wroe had that ability, too. He often made the person he was talking with feel smarter than they knew themselves to be by responding as though they knew more than their remarks showed. He called that talking up to people. It was never done from any position of superiority, but always with the intent to raise the level of the dialogue. Wroe loved to learn and just assumed that everyone else did, too. If somehow they didn't, Wroe felt a duty to try to raise their sights. Wroe often said that a good conversation was one in which both parties came away having learned some things they hadn't known before.

Wroe's innate optimistic future orientation was well shown one year at a national marketing meeting. That meeting was set up to give some of the "great old timers" awards and honors for their major lifetime contributions to the development of marketing thought. At that meeting each recipient of the award presented a prepared paper. The other "greats" each recapped the ideas he was most known for, one in channels of distribution, one in pricing theory, another in consumer behavior. Wroe's paper was entirely devoted to his insights, forecasts, and expectations for developments in the coming hundred years. He always believed that the best was yet to come and he always acted on those beliefs.

4.   Wroe's Philosophy

As I mentioned earlier, Wroe seldom focused any of our discussions on either his general philosophy or his specific business philosophy, but I naturally gained some feel for his thinking in both of these extensive and serious areas. For instance, Wroe had a strong interest in logic, and he delighted in solving convoluted and often abstruse puzzles. I tried to help him learn some elementary symbolic logic, but he preferred, as he said, "to puzzle things out rather than to reduce them to a mechanical process like long division." I think it was partly the pleasure he got from the mental exercise.

It was the same with any mathematics past algebra or geometry. He liked to listen to discussions involving advanced statistical concepts (and often contributed remarkably cogent insights), but he resisted adding those formal tools to his own repertory. He would have made a good mathematician, in part, because of his ability to hold and manipulate quite complex systems in his mind, but he always considered himself an artist rather than a technician. Besides, he had excellent access to the best technicians in academia and in the business community and used that access well. When Paul Green introduced multidimensional scaling to marketing research, Wroe was one of the first to adopt it, and he often explained it to our clients in much more understandable ways than I could. He loved to learn about new things. It was part of his position that knowledge was always preferable to ignorance. He was fond of quoting one of our clients whose favorite saying was "It aint what we don't know that gets us in trouble; it's what we know that ain't so."

Wroe was an omnivorous reader. I have seen six or more books on the night table next to his bed, each of them partly read, with bookmarks keeping his places. They were on economics, history, politics, exploration, poetry, art, biography, and many other diverse subjects. I don't know how he kept them all straight as he read a piece of one then a bit of another.

I have a memory about Wroe that I have not been able to corroborate with the little research I have done, but it might be true, so I offer it for your interest. I think I recall Wroe telling me once, with obvious pleasure, that he had been (for a year, I think) the president of the (a) Philomathian Society. I know that there is a nationwide (maybe worldwide) Philomathian philosophical society, with chapters at most Universities. I checked the few that I thought it might have been, with no luck.

In philosophy Wroe was against the strong emphasis on reductionism, a general philosophy of explanation that was widely espoused during much of his life. Briefly, reductionism holds that complex phenomena are best explained by referring (reducing) them to definitions at more basic levels of science. According to the reductionist view, social behavior is best explained by psychological principles. Psychology can best be understood by the concepts of biology, biology by chemistry, chemistry by physics, and that perhaps, by mathematics (the queen of sciences).

Wroe held that relativism, the notion that there is no hierarchy of science to begin with, and that, in West Churchman's words, "In order to answer any question completely, one must answer all possible other questions completely." Wroe adopted the position that each level of explanation was appropriate to certain sets of questions. For example, he held, along with many others, that the appropriate questions of faith and of science were in different domains, and thus could not be in conflict. They clashed only when religion attempted to answer scientific questions, such as, "What is the genetic relation of humans to other animals?" or when science strayed into faith areas, e.g., "explaining" miracles. Much of the apparent conflict comes from questions about religion that are treated as scientific by anthropologists or social scientists.

Wroe's views on organizational design owed much to this relativistic philosophy. He felt that strong hierarchal designs were seldom the best way to get an organization to reach its goals. He often said that the ideal organization was one that was fluid and adaptive. At any stage, he felt, the goals and rewards of each organizational unit should be such, that if every employee attempted to maximize his own measure of effectiveness, the entire organization would continually move toward optimum. This was, of course, an ideal, but we used it in many consulting assignments where we were making recommendations about organizational dynamics. This position of Wroe's naturally led him to emphasize the collection and use of information as a major corporate activity. Wroe made good use of the Military Intelligence distinctions between data, information, and intelligence. Many times when we were called in to evaluate a company's Market Research Department we would find that the product managers and most of the senior marketing executives held MR in rather low repute and tended not to use their output well.

Wroe would point out that most of market research's output was data, factual descriptions of macro-market behavior. He would show how to process those data into information, which is summarized, analyzed, and interpreted data. Then he would show the need for intelligence MR officers who would take the information and focus it at specific problems and produce action recommendations. This usually would get the attention of the senior staff. This whole approach derived from Wroe's conceptual view of the organization as a behaving organism rather than as a collection of staff functions.

We occasionally would kid a client when we wanted to focus some of our work (and the client's resources) on the information management function. An example from DuPont is an experience we had with a senior executive near the start of a major project. The client had just shown us, proudly, some of the detailed records DuPont had of its inventories. They had dollar figures, for each of their thousands of products, by each of thousands of different storage locations, by product age, and by calendar quarter.

We said, "As you took us around your two large high-rise buildings here in downtown Wilmington, we saw thousands of people hard at work. The only ones we saw who directly handled chemicals were the medical technicians who analyzed the urine samples from prospective employees. The rest handled miles and miles of filing cabinets where they put folders full of information in and took folders out. Do you have any dollar numbers on the value of all that information you have in inventory? Do you know the age of the information? Do you have procedures for scrapping it when it loses its usefulness? Do you have a classification scheme that lets you know how much you have? And what, after all, is the measurement unit for the value of information and how do you convert those measures to dollars so that you can evaluate the efficiency of your huge information system?"

We got the client's enthusiastic support for our investigation of their information processes.

Part of Wroe's integrated view of the way things work included the development and behavior of organizations. He often used an organic model in which he likened the systems in the organization that collected, analyzed, stored and manipulated information to an animal's nervous system, and the systems that made and moved product to the muscles. We often found that we were dealing with organizations that were dinosaurs — lots of muscles, little brains. This was especially true of those whose information systems were mostly concerned with internal behaviors (personnel, sales, accounting, inventories etc.). Wroe believed that many companies were lacking adequate information about the outside world (customers, competitors, government, suppliers, research, etc.). He tried to get our clients to have a balanced development. He has said that it is better to have an organization with approximately equal quality and depth in all its parts than to have one that was wonderful in one function, but only mediocre in many others.

Wroe was often in the forefront of adopting and espousing new developments in philosophy. In discussing these with colleagues, students, clients or others, he never denigrated any other opinions, and was always willing, even eager, to hear different opinions ("If you only listen to people who agree with you, you'll never learn anything"). But he was a great debater. I think I recall that he was

fied —academically, professionally, and by reputation, corporate contacts, and interests. The Marketing Science Institute (MSI) was set up as a research corporation. I was hired away from DuPont to be its Technical Director (at Wroe's recommendation), and McCabe (sometimes with me as second banana) met with the heads of 50 major US corporations. Tom twisted arms, when necessary, and got them each to commit $50,000 a year for a minimum of five years to support MSI. MSI's Board of Directors was formed with Tom as Chairman, Wroe as a member, and representatives from some of the supporting companies. Tom also got the supporters to agree to cooperate with MSI's research agenda by allowing us access to their economic and market research data, their personnel, and their internal workings.

As I interviewed prospects for our staff, I would honestly and enthusiastically tell them that this was exactly the way I would choose to spend my time, if I didn't have to work for a living. Wendell and I, with Wroe's help, assembled a great staff, and for the next four years we tried to develop the foundations of a true science of marketing. Wroe was always a supporter and a colleague; our only limitations were those imposed by our own shortcomings. We certainly did not produce a science of marketing, but we did help make that goal more acceptable. It is seldom that one meets someone who has deep knowledge and interest in both the realms of science and of marketing. Wroe was such a man. He and Tom McCabe took a step into the future of marketing thought that provided a path that some still follow, and more will certainly travel.

7.   Wroe as a Man

In this chapter I have tried to share with you some of my recollections and feelings for what kind of a person Wroe was. Or, at least, what kind of a person I remember him to be. I tried to show how his ethics and philosophy pervaded and shaped everything he did — his ideas, his work, his conversation, how he related to others, his total personality.

But to keep my picture of Wroe from being a paean to a paragon, I need to show you some more whimsical and playful examples of his nature. Wroe's enjoyments were on the same scale as his intellectual attainments. He was a gourmand (as well as a gourmet). You could name almost any major city and Wroe would tell you its best restaurant (and often the name of his friend, its executive chef). He was good friends with Jack Rosenthal, the Director of The Culinary Institute of America at Hyde Park, and had my wife and me as his guests at a Faculty Club Thanksgiving dinner that Jack put on at Penn. It was the best turkey I ever had. Wroe had three helpings.

The first meal I ever had with Wroe was two days after I joined A & S. Wroe took me with him to a client meeting in New York and, naturally, picked the restaurant for our evening meal. Being a new employee, I ordered the same meal as Wroe. It was roast beef, baked potato, etc. Both platters came at the same time. By the time I had cut, buttered, and salted my potato, Wroe had finished his entire platter and was drumming his fingers on the table waiting for his coffee. When it came, it was so hot that Wroe had to wrap his napkin around the cup to pick it up, so he could drain it in one long draught. One of Wroe's colleagues described Wroe's eating habits as "He unhinges his lower jaw and just shovels it in."

I have mentioned that Wroe snored. One time, he was the guest of honor at a national marketing meeting, seated at the head table, waiting to be introduced to receive yet another lifetime award. I watched, as did the entire audience, as Wroe's head tilted slowly to one side and he started to snore while the toastmaster was lauding Wroe's achievements as part of the introduction. He woke up in time and the program continued.

At one consulting visit to St. Louis, when I was still quite new with the firm, there were about six of us from A & S on the project team. In the evening we all gathered in Wroe's hotel room to report on the various interviews we had each conducted with the client's staff that day. While I was making my report, Wroe, who was sitting on the bed, leaned back and started to snore. I was embarrassed and didn't know what to do. I looked around at the others. They were smiling and gestured for me to continue. Just as I finished, Wroe sat up with a snort and asked me a question as though he had heard everything I had said in my whole report. Somewhat testily I told him that I had already covered that point. He laughed and ate some more peanuts.

Wroe was always almost late for trains and planes. Once I was with him when we actually missed a flight, but usually we made our connections at the last possible minute by dashing frantically. Wroe had had a heart attack and carried nitroglycerin pills with him for angina attacks. I remember both of us running down a train platform to catch a train and seeing Wroe pull his pills out of his coat pocket, pop one in his mouth, and keep on running. We made that train.

Another St. Louis adventure occurred when Wroe and I were taking a cab from our hotel to our client's offices. Wroe instructed the driver on the route to take (Wroe was proud that he knew the geography of many US cities) and the driver turned onto a street, not the one Wroe had recommended. Wroe told the driver that it would be longer and cost more if we didn't go the way he had described. The driver ignored him. When we arrived at the client's, it was obvious that the driver had been right and his way had been much shorter, quicker, and cheaper. Wroe was furious and when he paid the driver, he ostentatiously pulled out a single bill and handed it with a flourish to the driver as the tip. As we left the cab and it pulled away, Wroe noticed that he had given a ten-dollar tip instead of the one-dollar he had intended. I kidded him that we could make it up by increasing the cost to the client by at least ten thousand. He wasn't tempted, but it lightened his mood and the rest of the day went well.

Wroe was not a good car driver. He has been described as having a binary driving style, either full down on the accelerator or full down on the brake. At one of the Marketing Theory meetings at Boulder, five of us were in Wroe's large rented car. My wife and I were up front with Wroe, who was driving, and three other attendees were in the back. We were going up a narrow, twisting mountain road to a picnic site right above the campus. We felt it was getting dark and too late and decided to turn back and go down.

Wroe tried to make the turn by backing the car around on the narrow road with the mountain wall on one side and a sheer drop with no guardrail on the other. He roared the car around, slammed it into the rock wall, threw it into reverse, gunned the engine, and just managed to stop before the rear wheels went over the cliff edge. I pulled up on the hand brake, stopping the car. We all piled out. Wroe stubbornly refused to get out and let one of us drive and make the turn. He stayed at the wheel while we all yelled instructions to him from the road outside. We all (but not Wroe) almost had heart attacks as he barely managed to avoid the apparently inevitable disaster and finally got the car turned around. I have forgotten the talks on marketing theory at that meeting, but not our turn around adventure on that mountain road.

Because of his stature in marketing Wroe was often asked to review new marketing books. His method was to read the introduction, look at the Table of Contents, glance at a few pages here and there in the text, and then look at the author index in the back of the book to see how many references there were to Alderson, Wroe. Overall, this was probably not too bad a rating technique.

This section would not be adequate if I left out an example of my total misjudgment of Wroe's character. It happened at one of the Theory Seminars, a time after I had gotten to know Wroe quite well, or so I thought. One evening we were having a presentation of a 35 mm slide talk by one of our attendees who had just come back from a safari in Africa.

We met in the dorm lunchroom, sat on hard wooden folding bridge chairs, and prepared for the slide show. Wroe was sitting just ahead and a little to my right. Leo Aspinwall was to his immediate left; my wife was immediately to my left. The lights were turned off, the projector was turned on, and the speaker began his talk.

I noticed that very soon after it got dark Leo reached over and put his hand lightly on Wroe's upper thigh. I was more surprised than shocked. I had known that Wroe and Leo were old and good friends. I just hadn't thought their friendship was that good. In about a minute Wroe slumped a bit in his chair, started to snore, and Leo squeezed Wroe's leg. Wroe gave a snort, a grumble, and sat up. Five minutes later that sequence was repeated. Leo kept waking Wroe up during the entire talk, which lasted about an hour. When it was over, we all got up and went to the snack bar. I was left with the impression that this was an old accommodation that Wroe and Leo had worked out long ago and had used through many boring slide talks in the past. I abandoned my earlier snap judgment. Wroe and Leo were no more than good friends.

Wroe was easy to be with, to work for, and to discuss with. He never talked at you; it was always with you. He listened attentively and well, not a common ability among those with a great deal of knowledge and an active intellect. I enjoyed my times with him and I hope this chapter has enabled you to see him somewhat as I did.

Chapter 32

WROE ALDERSON AS ACADEMIC
ENTREPRENEUR: THE WHARTON YEARS*

Stanley J. Shapiro
Simon Fraser University

Wroe Alderson was associated with the Wharton School for just under six academic years. He started teaching there in the Fall of 1959 and remained at Wharton until his death in late May of 1965. I, in turn, was associated with Wroe for most of that period — first as a student in his Marketing Theory class, then while writing a dissertation testing Alderson's survival and behavior systems concepts for a de facto supervisory committee on which he served and, finally, as a junior colleague responsible for administering a number of the projects Wroe was conducting under Wharton School sponsorship. However, the projects I administered on Alderson's behalf were only a part of Wroe's activities during what, in retrospect, appears to have been an incredibly productive six year period. These wide ranging activities, as best I and others concerned can now recall them, are discussed below.

1.   The Wharton Research Initiatives

Shortly after arriving at Wharton, Wroe Alderson became Chair of that School's Management Science Center. Most of Wroe's Wharton-related activities were conducted using the very modest resources of this Center. The then Dean of the Wharton School, Willis Winn, used Ford Foundation funding to underwrite core secretarial and related expenses and some project costs. With that support and more specifically targeted funding sources that Wroe generated, the Management Science Center carried out a number of activities involving conference administration, research and publication. These undertakings included the three major activities as discussed next.

---

*The author wishes to thank Dr. James C. McKeon of the School of Business, Western New England College, and Dr. Robert Rothberg, Faculty of Management, Rutgers Business School for writing the section on the Behavior Systems consulting firm found in this chapter.

The Administration of the Annual Marketing Theory Seminars

Since 1951 Wroe Alderson had been the driving force behind an annual gathering of marketing professors and those from other disciplines whose ideas and presence, Wroe felt, could contribute to the further development of marketing theory. The only known history of these meetings is to be found in an unpublished manuscript that E. D. McGarry had prepared for the last of the regular Theory Seminars, the one held in Boulder in late August of 1965, less than three months after Wroe Alderson's death (McGarry, 1965). McGarry discusses the informal launch of the meetings and the intellectual excitement associated with bringing together, in an informal setting at which all present were expected to contribute, many of the leading marketing academics of the period. Those specifically mentioned as being present at early Marketing Theory Seminars included Paul Converse, Hix Huegy, Roland Vaile, Wenzel Dolva, Ralph Cassady, Reavis Cox, Larry Lockley, Hugh Wales, Wendell Smith and, of course, the co-founders with Alderson of the Seminars, McGarry himself and Leo Aspinwall.

McGarry mentions the interdisciplinary visitors at the various seminars and Alderson's response to them. In 1953, Wroe discussed Puzzles and Problem Solving in an Operations Research context and then West Churchman followed up with a discussion of the philosophical background of the underlying theories. Edward Chamberlin attended in 1954 and related his theory of Imperfect Competition to marketing theories—an effort which led Alderson in reply to develop his thesis of Imperfect Rationality in Consumer Behavior. In 1955, McGarry reports that, partly intellectually inspired by the presence of his friend Kenneth Boulding, Wroe developed his concept of heterogeneity of demand. At the 1956 meeting, the invited interdisciplinary guest was William J. Baumol, then a promising young economist who had done some consulting for Alderson & Sessions. It was at this meeting that Alderson presented to the group some of the other material subsequently published in *Marketing Behavior and Executive Action.*

McGarry indicates that by the end of the 1950s the seminar had changed drastically since its early years.

> Much as we tried to limit the attendance to those who had some theories to discuss, we found an increasing number of well recommended teachers and researchers who wanted to attend. We realized that we needed a continuous stream of younger men into our ranks to keep the undertaking alive. Moreover, as Wroe pointed out, there were new values not contemplated in our original plans which would result from having more people attend. It would provide a larger audience in which to disseminate our ideas. It would (also) give an opportunity (for others) now entering our profession to express and expand their ideas.
>
> With the growth in attendance, changes had to be made in the programming. No longer could we have the type of spontaneous give and take discussions with

everyone taking part. The program had to be planned with a central theme as a focus. Topics had to be assigned. In order to allow as many as possible to participate and at the same time to keep some measure of informality, panels were set up in advance of the meetings.

Over the years the subject matter of our discussions had also changed. We began with programs devoted to (1) refinements of the functions of marketing as originally conceived by Arch Shaw; (2) an elaboration of how marketing activities were inter-related with types of goods marketed and the geography to be covered; and (3) the problem of adjustment and survival in the market complex. The development of new techniques of management, with their emphasis on decision making and operational control, has had an increasing influence on our discussions. Techniques of measuring customer reaction to marketing pressures have become more and more the grist of our mill. The search for a "scientific" method of market prediction has reoriented our entire approach. Our programs have more and more tended toward the practical approach of the business man or consultant rather than the exploratory or developmental approach of the academician. The entire subject matter has become more sophisticated, more segmented and more highly specialized (McGarry, 1965, pp. 11-13).

I have quoted at length from McGarry for two reasons. The first, and most relevant, is the importance of the information he conveys. This is, unfortunately, the only opportunity there will be to put his observations on the record. Also, the time of the change in focus of the Theory Seminars roughly corresponds to the period that these Seminars began to be administered out of Alderson's Research Center at Wharton rather than from the offices of Alderson & Sessions. It was then that a greater degree of formalization was introduced and a real effort made to attract the" next generation" and even the generation after that of marketing academics. Among those attending at the "next generation" level were Bill Lazer, Gene Kelley, George Fisk, Bill Davidson, Danny Monieson, Perry Bliss and Hans Thorelli, all of whom subsequently went on to have very distinguished academic careers. Bringing together younger academics in this supportive environment led to a variety of academic friendships and publishing alliances among individuals who had never even previously met. For example, the Shapiro and Doody readings book, *Marketing In America: Settlement to Civil War* grew out of discussions I had with Al Doody, then at Ohio State University, at two of these early 1960s Theory Seminars (Shapiro and Doody, 1968).

The Penjerdel Metropolitan Data Bank Project (Alderson and Shapiro, 1963a)

During the 1959-60 academic and organizational year, the Economics Committee of the Greater Philadelphia Chamber of Commerce surveyed the demand for an area statistical service. The results of the study suggested a need for a more detailed analysis of the feasibility and cost of establishing and operating such a service. The Chamber obtained funding for a follow up project from

Pennsylvania-New Jersey Delaware Metropolitan Inc (Penjerdel) in order that a research team under Alderson's general supervision could prepare the necessary design (Alderson and Shapiro, 1963a). Penjerdel was a nonprofit, nongovernmental agency established to research and promote the potential of the region. In September of 1961, the University of Pennsylvania and Penjerdel signed a contract that involved both parties contributing to the financing of the data bank project. The objective of the area data bank was described in the contract as follows:

> The general purpose of the proposed Service is to provide systematic current data on pertinent economic activity and other significant phenomena in the Penjerdel area as a central service to business firms and public agencies in that area. The data to be made available will be those required for sound and knowledgeable decision making by such firms or agencies in planning their future programs, and will include data on changes in the size and composition of the population, personal and family income, residential and other construction, consumer expenditures, employment, and other statistical series widely used by such firms and agencies (Alderson and Shapiro, 1964).

The contract also specified that the Wharton team would, among other duties, "design alternate services to meet current and foreseeable future demands, private and public". Charged with such a mandate, it was eventually decided to concentrate upon developing five different components of an area data service, each of which would meet a major informational need of the three state, 4,500 square mile Penjerdel region with its then population of just under 5,000,000.

The core data utilization center was designed to be both freestanding in its own right and, as well, to be an essential component of the four other approaches, all of which would require marked improvement in the quality, availability and comparability of existing data. The Wharton report recommended that the Penjerdel data utilization center perform two sets of activities. The first activity was designed to deal with the just mentioned quality and related issues. How this might be done was spelled out in some detail. This type of activity would greatly increase the value of secondary data and require only relatively minor expenditures. In contrast, the second major data utilization center function included all those steps intended to facilitate the more economical use of existing data. The objective was to centralize and thus to reduce the cost of performing data-oriented tasks now being carried out with unnecessary duplication by a number of firms and agencies. A program for achieving this objective was also spelled out. Finally, the Center was expected to prepare an annual state-of-the-region report.

Establishment of a data utilization center, it was argued, would meet some but not all of the requirements of those with an interest in improved metropolitan statistics. Consequently an effort was made to design the "add on" services that would fill the remaining gaps. Four such major needs were identified. The first was for a land use, parcel card inventory which would provide accurate up-to-date information on the uses and condition of land, the important features of all existing structures, and the characteristics of the people who live or work at each location. The proposed location and traffic service, in contrast, by reporting on the movement of individuals and goods both within and outside the region, was proposed as a way of locating activities in the more favorable sites and developing better channels for travel, transportation, and communication. The third proposed "add on" service involved the development of regional economic indicators similar to those available on the national level. Data would be collected and analyzed in a way that allowed for the preparation of a set of regional accounts every third year. The fourth and final proposed service involved the development of a capital expenditure evaluation model that might be used in locating both public and private facilities.

The above summarizes the design components of the Metropolitan Data Bank project. However, the Wharton contract with Penjerdel also emphasized the importance of exploring the relationship between the business community and the proposed data bank. Consequently, the concluding sections of both the research team's formal report to Penjerdel and the subsequently published article in *Business Horizons* demonstrated that: 1) a properly designed area data service would satisfy many but not all the data needs of business; 2) researchers would be provided with a better factual starting point for the highly specialized studies firms will continue to require; 3) a metropolitan data center would not be a federally subsidized competitor of private consultants and commercial research firms; and 4) the financial support provided by private industry would be more than justified by the benefits that each firm would receive.

Towards A Theory of Retail Competition — An Intellectual Odyssey

The Retail Competition Study that Alderson directed in the early 1960s was an attempt to contribute to the development of retailing theory (Alderson, 1963). A Wharton School research team focused in great detail on the competitive interdependence among food chains active in the Philadelphia area. This three year undertaking was financed by one of the many grants made by the "Green Stamp" company, Sperry & Hutchinson, to further basic research in retailing. A detailed report on what turned out to be a long and somewhat intellectually frustrating three stage project appeared in the second edition of *Theory In Marketing* (Alderson and Shapiro, 1964). The opening paragraph of that report discusses these frustrations and the "avenues of false promise that eventually lead to intellectual impasses." It then provides a very detailed record of just what was done.

For the project's first stage, Alderson recruited not only Reavis Cox but also Professors William Baumol and Richard Quandt, both of Princeton's Department of Economics. Dr. George Fisk was also a team member not only in this first stage but throughout the entire project. The Baumol and Quandt involvement followed from the fact that the focus of empirical testing in Phase I was the possible relevance of the Cournot oligopoly model to pricing behavior as revealed by a study of advertised prices. To make a long story short, no such relevance could be established. However, Stage I did provide a number of insights into the nature of the competitive behavior that was occurring. These insights in large part shaped Stage II of the project where an attempt would be made to determine the adequacy of monopolistic competition as an explanation of the structure of competition among Philadelphia area food chains.

In an article that appeared in the March 1963 issue of the *Journal of Advertising Research*, Alderson summarized the research team's conclusions at the end of Stage II. In retrospect, the following two of the five propositions he formulated at the time appear the most significant:

1 Competition among supermarket chains in a metropolitan area does not conform very closely to any of the standard models for competition among the few such as oligopoly or monopolistic competition. There is some evidence of oligopolistic interaction but only on a fraction of one per cent of the thousands of items carried. Monopolistic competition, to the extent that it appears to be present, is reflected in ways that are peculiar to retailing rather than by product differentiation, as in competition among manufacturers.

2 The conviction still stands that the search for differential advantage is central to the competition of large retailers or any other large organization. Further development of the concept of administered prices seems to offer the best hope of interpreting some of the peculiar variations in the competitive behavior of these chains: . . . the concept will lead to more fruitful questions about promotional pricing in retailing than the theories of oligopoly or monopolistic competition. . . Promotional pricing does not comprise the whole range of price policy problems but it should be possible to deal with all aspects of price policy within the framework of administered prices (Alderson, 1963).

After setting out his propositions, Alderson used the term promotional pricing to describe the various methods employed by supermarkets in using price as a promotional tool. An attempt was then made to explain the promotional pricing strategy of the competing chains in light of the administrative costs of the promotional devices they had employed. This being so, it's not surprising that the focus in Stage III of the project was on empirical pricing patterns. What was learned from a series of Stage III studies is discussed in the second edition of *Theory in Marketing* and, in greater detail, in a subsequent *Journal of Advertising Research* article (Fisk et al., 1964). Nonprice competition was also studied at this time with the focus being on competitive interaction with regard to enterprise and merchandise differentiation. Other studies on the costs and benefits of promotional pricing had been planned as part of Stage III but these were never carried out. At the time (late 1963) the *Theory in Marketing* article was written, the following was identified as a revised program for basic research in retailing.

1 A social and managerial appraisal of the locational aspects of food chain competition

2 A study of the authority and autonomy, in theory and in fact, of branch store managers and regional executives.

3 The design of a retailing information system which would provide real time (current) rather than historical data on changing market conditions and the actions of competitors.

4 The development of measures which would indicate the relative competitiveness of market areas and the effect on competition of proposed mergers.

5 An examination of the influence of consumer store images, government policies, and supplier practices on the efforts of food chains to establish a measure of differential advantage.

The above suggests how the retail competition study evolved and how it ended. The report on the project in the Second Edition of *Theory in Marketing* is not easy reading but even today it should be of interest to those concerned with retail competition. The closing paragraph of that article remains especially relevant because it so closely reflects Alderson's approach to marketing theory.

> The fact that an interest in retailing theory has pointed up the need for more information on the operating problems of business executives should not be surprising. Any aspect of marketing theory must serve two masters. It should simplify the task of those concerned primarily with obtaining some understanding of the myriad of events occurring in the marketplace. It must also, however, provide a broader framework within which marketing practitioners can deal with problems they encounter in their day-to-day operations (Alderson and Shapiro, 1963b, pp. v-vi).

2. The Three Major Publications that Alderson Co-edited

In a very real sense, Alderson's Center at Wharton was also in the publishing business. Wroe had a number of ideas he wished to share both with fellow academics and with his other natural constituency, thoughtful members of the business community. On three occasions he did this by bringing together leading academics and practitioners on his subject of interest, in either a lecture or conference format. At the same time, he arranged to have edited versions of these conference or seminar presentations subsequently published not in a Proceedings volume, but in books he would co-edit either for Richard D. Irwin or for Prentice-Hall. The first of these publications was *Marketing and the Computer*, the next, *Theory in Marketing: Second Series*, and the third, *Patents and Progress: The Sources and Impact of Advancing Technology*. The nature and scope of each of these publications is discussed, in turn, below.

Marketing and the Computer (1963)

The following material taken from the Introduction to this volume, material which I wrote over forty years ago, discusses first the "why" and then the "what" of this publication.

This book is an outgrowth of the senior editor's belief that marketing executives and students of marketing are not fully aware of computer applications in their field. Although computers are playing an important role in business, marketing executives have been slower than their counterparts in finance, accounting or production to make use of this new and valuable piece of equipment. This delay may be due to the marketing executive's fear of a strange and unfamiliar tool, a wide spread belief that marketing problems do not lend themselves to computer-oriented management science techniques or the monopolization of existing computer facilities by executives from the other functional areas of the business. In any case, the present volume is designed to overcome fears that might exist, to reveal how computers can and are being used in marketing, and to show the very real value of such computer applications. Since the prospective audience for this book was clearly defined, each contributor has directed his remarks and shaped his presentation to meet the needs of present and potential marketing executives.

Emphasis is placed on three major difficulties which plague a decision maker: lack of information, inability to draw meaningful conclusions from and to base operating decisions on adequate information of unquestioned accuracy, and uncertainty as to the consequences associated with possible future strategies or alternate plans. The first three of the volume's five sections contain materials which indicate ways of overcoming or dealing with these problems. The chapters in the first section review the related flows of goods and information and the computer's role in facilitating these flows... In the second section of the book, certain important considerations in decision making are set forth, and techniques used to solve a number of marketing problems are explained and illustrated. The authors contributing to the third section discuss a number of computer-based approaches to various aspects of business planning... Inclusion of case studies in the fourth section of the book seemed logical since one of the volume's previously stated objectives was to show that computers are being used as well as talked about in marketing circles.

The editors believe that the book has some additional uses not fully appreciated at the time this venture was first undertaken. In the first three sections, some of the most important research presently being conducted in marketing is discussed. A volume designed to acquaint marketing managers with recent developments of great significance might be expected to include a review of Bayesian decision theory, civilian applications of military planning techniques, Industrial Dynamics, simulation, and inventory theory... These same topics are treated in this volume in a way that gives present and potential executives a grasp of the essential aspects of such techniques (Alderson and Shapiro, 1963b, pp. v–vi).

Theory in Marketing: Second Series (1964)

Reavis Cox is listed as the first of three Editors of this publication. However, I recall this project as essentially an Alderson initiative. Most of the contributors were either Marketing Theory Seminar regulars or younger scholars who were invited to participate because Wroe felt they had something to contribute. Indeed, initial drafts of many of the contributions were reviewed at the 1963 Marketing Theory Seminar. I am not sure, however, which of my senior colleagues arranged for AMA sponsorship of the publication My job as junior editor was to keep the project on track by seeing that the contributors met their deadlines and that the publisher's needs were met.

What Cox did do, and quite well, is write a lengthy Introduction to the volume in which he attempted both to assess each of the various contributions and to place them in a theoretical perspective. His comments are still available to those who wish to read them as the book itself remains readily accessible through interlibrary loan if no other way. For present purposes, only Cox's comparison of this second series with its 1950 predecessor and his comments regarding Alderson's seminal contribution to the development of theory in marketing are presented.

> The appearance of a second volume of essays concerned with theory in marketing offers a welcome opportunity to see how far and in what directions we have moved since the first volume appeared in 1950. Of course students have been developing theories of marketing for a much longer period. Perhaps the most influential single contribution thus far made—Shaw's first statement of the functional approach to marketing—dates back half a century. But the conscious effort to establish a sophisticated theory or set of theories as a joint effort of students in the field is about twenty years old. What have we achieved in that time?. . . (Cox, 1964, p. 1)

> Inasmuch as the material appearing in this volume is a fair sample of the work being done throughout the profession, we can come to some conclusions. Unquestionably the level of sophistication of this volume is much higher than that of the first volume. The persistence of efforts to obtain respectable and defensible theories in marketing provides continued evidence of the richness of this area of human behavior and experience as a field for study. Nevertheless, our discipline is still characterized by the presence of much uncertainty and confusion. We are far from having formulated a body of theory as impressive as that achieved by the theoretical economists and, even more importantly, by the theoretical physicists. Not settled as yet is the question of whether we seek a theory for operating managers, for their staff associates and advisors, or for the academicians. Perhaps we seek all three but need to define them as three different jobs to be done.

> A final, more personal comment needs to be made. If there is any one individual who deserves the credit for stimulating, encouraging, and goading us into struggling as best we can with the formidable problems the various authors touch upon, it is Wroe Alderson. As a coeditor of this volume, he will no doubt object to being singled out in this way for attention and praise. However, nothing is more striking about this volume of essays than the frequency with which his name comes up as the source of some idea or the stimulator of the work that led to some idea. Not only in his own writings and in the specific articles he has encouraged others to write, but also in his general support of theory as a field of study and in his organization of a long series of seminars concerned with the

subject, he has unquestionably been the dominant force keeping us to the task of working out an effective body of theory (Cox et al., 1964, pp. 14-15).

Patents and Progress (1965)

Alderson as a young man had spent a few months in the U.S. Patent Office and the Patent system apparently remained an intellectual interest throughout the rest of his career. Toward the end of that career, he obtained funding from a pharmaceutical firm to present a series of seminars by leading authorities in the area and then to have these presentations published. The following excerpts from the Foreward to that publication briefly summarize the scope of that publication, touch upon the role of marketing innovations and show how Alderson believed technological change was a key factor in making competition dynamic.

This volume is the first in a series designed to deal with various aspects of modern competition. . . The special subject of this first volume is technological change. The contributors approach the subject from various perspectives. The essays in Part I are largely concerned with the sources of technological change; the forces which produce it; the industrial climate which favors it; and the special incentives which encourage the inventor and the innovator. The essays in Part II emphasize the impact of technological change on the nature of competition and on public policy with respect to competition. The areas of public policy which are affected by the acceleration of technological change include policy in granting patents, policy with respect to government support or participation in projects resulting in patentable ideas, anti-trust policy, and policies of the Federal government designed to foster or favor small business enterprise. . .

The marketing analyst has never been able to ignore the advances in marketing technology because it has been his business to help produce them. These marketing advances are often quite as impressive as the improvements in products or production techniques. Some regard it as a paradox that marketing improvements are occurring at an accelerated rate despite the fact that there is no patent protection available in marketing. There are several reasons why this happens, only one of which need be mentioned here. Marketing innovations are internal to the process of moving goods to market and are a direct expression of market competition. The advantages of operating at or near capacity in mass production and mass distribution make the pressure for marketing innovation irresistible. Even though these advantages may be quickly eroded away, the aggressive competitor hopes to maintain his lead by pioneering further improvements in marketing.

A dynamic view of competition emerges naturally from a book concerned with technological change. Modern competition is largely concerned with deliberate efforts to improve products and to improve the methods of marketing them. Passive adaptation in the market place has given way to a systematic and continuous drive to solve problems. Competition among problem-solvers is inherently dynamic (Alderson et al., 1965, p. vi).

3.   Alderson's Publications While at the Wharton School

The projects and publications mentioned above were the ones with which I was directly involved. However, they represent only some of the activities in which Wroe was involved during his less than six full years at Wharton.These included two trips to lecture in Japan, involvement in planning the Annual Parlin Award Dinners and a series of guest lectures at New York University. During the period in question, Wroe Alderson also wrote and published at a truly amazing pace, while engaging in a very significant amount of institution building. He was also actively involved, first, in the final years of the firm that by then had become Alderson Associates and, then, in the launching of a second consulting organization, Behavior Systems. In this and the following two sections, these three facets of Alderson's Wharton career, publishing, institution building, and consulting, are briefly discussed.

Until quite recently, there was no definitive list of Alderson's publications during a publishing career that began in 1928. That gap in our knowledge has, fortunately, now been filled by the Bibliography that appears at the end of this publication. I have drawn on this source to prepare the kind of publication summary of the Wharton years that one would find in a contemporary scholarly vita. What emerges is a truly staggering record of achievement characterized by quantity, quality, depth and breath. If ever one should require confirmation of the wide ranging Alderson intellect, it is reflected in what he published during this relatively brief period. These writings by Alderson include not only material with a managerial and theory focus but also literature that reflected his quantitative, behavioral and ethical interests.

4.   Wroe Alderson's Authored, Co-Authored or Edited Publications 1960-1968

Authored Books

1 Wroe Alderson & Paul Green, *Planning and Problem Solving in Marketing*, (Homewood, Il., Richard D. Irwin, 1964).

2 Wroe Alderson, *Dynamic Marketing Behavior* ,(Homewood, Il., Richard D. Irwin, 1965) Alderson died before his draft copy of the manuscript could be reworked by him. Paul Green, Mike Halbert and Pat Robinson prepared that manuscript for publication but limited their efforts to "modest editing and stylistic changes".

3 Wroe Alderson & Michael Halbert, *Men, Motives and Markets*, (Englewood Cliffs, N.J.: Prentice Hall, 1968) Along with Mike Halbert, Paul Green and Ron Frank helped ready Alderson's draft material for publication.

Edited Books

1 Wroe Alderson & Stanley J. Shapiro, (eds.) *Marketing and the Computer*, (Prentice Hall, Englewood Cliffs, N.J.: 1963).

2 Reavis Cox, Wroe Alderson & Stanley J. Shapiro, (eds.) *Theory in Marketing: Second Series*, (Richard D. Irwin, Homewood, Il.: 1964).

3 Wroe Alderson, Vern Terpstra, & Stanley J. Shapiro (eds.) *Patents and Progress: The Sources and Impact of Advancing Technology*, (Richard D. Irwin, Homewood, Il.: 1965).

Alderson's Contribution to Edited Books

1 Wroe Alderson, "Introduction" in Frank, Kuehn, and Massy (eds.) *Quantitative Techniques in Marketing Analysis: Text and Readings*, (Richard D. Irwin, Homewood, Il.: 1962), pp. xi-xvii.

2 Wroe Alderson, "An Overview, Marketing and the Computer", in *Marketing and the Computer*, pp. 2-13.

3 Wroe Alderson, "A Normative Theory of Marketing Systems" in *Theory in Marketing: Second Series*, pp. 92-108.

4 Wroe Alderson and Stanley J. Shapiro, "Towards a Theory of Retail Competition" in *Theory in Marketing: Second Series*, pp. 190-212.

5 Wroe Alderson, "A Marketing View of the Patent System" in *Patents and Progress*, pp. 225-243.

Journal Articles

1 Wroe Alderson, "Mass Audience Capable of Improvement in Taste", *Business and Society*, Vol. 3, No. 1 (Autumn, 1962), pp. 25-28.

2 Wroe Alderson, "Administered Pricing and Retail Grocery Advertising", *Journal of Advertising Research*, Vol 3, (March 1963), pp. 2-6.

3 Wroe Alderson and Stanley J. Shapiro, "A Metropolitan Data Bank for the Business Community", *Business Horizons*, Vol.5 (Summer 1963), pp. 53-62.

4 Wroe Alderson and Miles Martin, "Toward a Formal Theory of Transactions and Transvections", *Journal of Marketing Research*, Vol. 2, (May 1965), pp. 117-127.

5 Wroe Alderson, "Mercury Yes, Mars, No!", *Columbia Journal of World Business*, Vol 1 (Winter, 1966), pp. 9-14.

Published Proceedings, Seminars, Speeches, Commentaries and Book Reviews

1 Wroe Alderson, "New Concepts for Measuring Productivity in Marketing" in *Productivity in Marketing: Its Measurement and Change* University of Illinois Bulletin, Vol. 58 (August, 1960), pp. 3-11.

2 Wroe Alderson, " Marketing Research Breakthroughs of the 1960's— Discussion" in Wenzil Dolva ed., *Marketing Keys to Profits in the 1960's*, (Chicago: American Marketing Association, 1960), pp. 300-303.

3 Wroe Alderson, "Possible Impact of the Soviets Upon World Trade in the 1960s-Discussion" in Wenzil Dolva ed., *Marketing Keys to Profits in the 1960's*, (Chicago: American Marketing Association, 1960), pp. 485-491.

4 Wroe Alderson, Review of West Churchman Prediction and Optimal Decision, *Management Science*, Vol. 8 (April, 1962). pp. 375-381.

5 Wroe Alderson, Review of Alfred Kuhn, The Study of Society—A Unified Approach, *Journal of Marketing Research*, Vol. 1 (February, 1963), pp. 72-74.

6 Wroe Alderson, "An Approach to a Theory of Planning", in William Decker, ed., *Emerging Concepts in Marketing*, (Chicago: American Marketing Association, 1963), pp. 257-264.

7 Wroe Alderson, "Marketing Systems in the Ecological Framework" in Harvey Huegy ed. *The Conceptual Framework for a Science of Marketing*, University of Illinois Bulletin, Vol. 61 (October, 1964), pp. 29-43.

8 Wroe Alderson, "Ethics, Ideologies and Sanctions, " for the *Report on the Committee on Ethical Standards and Professional Practices*, (Chicago: American Marketing Association, 1964), pp. 1-20. Subsequently reprinted in Robert Lavidge and Robert Holloway, eds. Marketing and Society: The Challenge (Homewood, Ill., Richard D. Irwin, 1969), pp. 74-85.

9 "The American Economy and Christian Ethics" This was a presentation by Alderson to a student group at the Christian Association of the University of Pennsylvania in June of 1964. It subsequently appeared in the August 1964 issue of the Behavior System newsletter, *Growth and Profit Planner* and was later reprinted in John Wright and John Mertes, eds., *Advertising's Role in Society*, (New York: West Publishing, 1969), pp. 252-258.

10 Wroe Alderson, "Commentary on Churchman and Scheinblatt, "The Re-
    searcher and the Manager—A Dialectic of Implementation", *Manage-
    ment Science*, Vol. 12 (October, 1965), pp. B 6-9. This was originally
    a letter from Wroe Alderson to West Churchman on Churchman's paper
    that was subsequently published as a Commentary.

11 Wroe Alderson, "Marketing Innovations and the Problem Solver" in
    Frederick Webster, Jr., ed., *New Directions in Marketing* (Chicago: Amer-
    ican Marketing Association, 1965), pp. 53-61. This paper was presented
    posthumously by Mike Halbert.

In addition to the above, Wroe Alderson also authored the Stage I report on
the Retail Competition Study, co-authored the Penjerdel report and contributed
articles both to the last three issues of *Cost and Profit Outlook* and to at least
seven issues of *Growth and Profit Planner*, the Behavior Systems successor to
that earlier newsletter. More information on these publications is to be found
in Dr. Tamilia's complete listing of publications by and about Wroe Alderson
at the end of this volume. None of this additional material is at the moment
readily available. Interestingly enough, in 1980 the American Association had
tentatively agreed to publish a complete set of the *Cost and Profit Outlooks* along
with some material by Robert Sessions on the history of Alderson and Sessions
and of its then widely read publication. The proposed editorial team at that time
consisted of Reavis Cox, Hugh Wales and Leslie Dawson. Unfortunately, the
AMA changed its mind and the proposed book was never published. Hopefully,
in the current era of web sites and online publishing, it will soon be possible to
make full sets of both newsletters available to interested individuals.

5.   Wroe Alderson as Institution Builder

During his stay at Wharton, Alderson also engaged in activities that can best
be characterized as "institution building". One such institution was, of course,
Behavior Systems, his second consulting firm which will be discussed in some
detail in the next section of this paper by those who worked there at the time.
Wroe was also organizationally active during the period in both the AMA's
ethics initiative and, more generally, in The Institute of Management Science,
especially when it was headed by Dr. Tibor Fabian, another longtime Alderson
colleague. In retrospect, however, perhaps his most significant organizational
efforts related to the establishment of the Marketing Science Institute.

Wroe was involved long before the official launch of MSI and, along with
such other then titans of academic marketing as Neil Borden, E.T. Grether and
Maynard Phelps were outside (non-corporate sponsor) Trustees. Alderson also
had a tremendous influence in MSI's Wharton period given that MSI's first
President was Wendell Smith, a former partner in Alderson and Sessions and
such Alderson colleagues as Paul Green, Mike Halbert, and Pat Robinson were

involved with MSI during that period. Indeed, Alderson had recruited all three for MSI. Unfortunately, MSI's official history of its first 25 years says relatively little about either its Philadelphia-based launch or Alderson's involvement at that time (Bloom, 1987). The original MSI research program is also not discussed in that history in any great detail. All one finds is the following; "The initial activity of MSI focused on rather large research projects that produced several long books. These were done primarily by full-time MSI staff, with Wharton marketing faculty members making substantial contributions in a few cases" (Bloom, 1987, p. 9). However, there is far more detailed information available as to MSI's initial research focus. This is to be found in a Foreward that Wendell Smith wrote for one of the early monographs in the McGraw-Hill Marketing Science Institute Series.

> The basic function of the Marketing Science Institute is to conduct research and educational activities designed to contribute to the emergence of a science of marketing, and to stimulate increased application of scientific techniques to the understanding and solving of marketing problems. In order to perform this function properly, it has been necessary that all research undertaken by the Institute staff—or initiated and supported by the Instute although conducted by others—be integrated into a broad long-range program.
>
> The initial research activity has involved the conducting of "position studies" in four specific areas. The major purpose of these position studies is to bring into focus the current state of knowledge and practice in marketing. Only in this way could it be made certain that the specific substantive and theoretical research projects now being conducted or supported by MSI would be relevant to the Institute's long-range objectives. In essence, these four initial study areas comprise four different approaches to the study of marketing phenomena. They are inter-related although each bears a different emphasis.
>
> The first study area involves an examination of the structure and functions of marketing institutions as a means of observing and understanding the interrelationships between marketing and socioeconomic developments, as well as the effect of change at each level of distribution on other levels.
>
> The second study area deals generally with the conduct of marketing activities and specifically with the making of marketing decisions within an organizational framework. It is oriented toward marketing management and decision making in the allocation of marketing funds and effort among the available marketing tools.
>
> The third study area is generally concerned with the impact of major changes in international trade on marketing management, marketing structuire and marketing organization.
>
> The fourth study area has as its purpose the relating of the theoretical content of the other three, and the providing of a continuing compilation and assessment of the developments in language, concepts and theory that form the basis for understanding and improving marketing practice (Smith, 1964, pp. xi-xii).

That original research program not only generated several books that were published in the McGraw-Hill Marketing Science Institute Series but also a number of journal articles. In retrospect, the "new task", "modified rebuy", and "straight rebuy" characterization of industrial purchasing appears to have been the most widely accepted and adopted MSI finding of that period (Robinson et al., 1967). Indeed, for decades this classification has been an almost required component of any text book chapter on business-to-business marketing. However, all of this early MSI output was of high quality and much of the research was conducted by those in the Alderson orbit.

In addition to helping launch MSI in a way that somewhat linked it to Wharton, Alderson made other contributions to that School which proved to have an impact for a much longer period of time. Wroe was instrumental in attracting first Paul Green and then Russ Ackoff and his entire Operation Research unit to the Wharton School. Both Green and Ackoff had a previous association with the University of Pennsylvania. However, Wroe's offering Paul Green the Deputy Directorship of his Management Science Center and the associated opportunity to work closely together obviously helped facilitate that move. Similarly, Wroe, with the assistance of Pat Robinson, negotiated the movement of Ackoff, with whom he was already well acquainted, and his entire Operations Research Center from Case Western Reserve University.

Ackoff was at Wharton for over twenty years during which period he continued to build on his already significant academic accomplishments. Those he either brought with him or subsequently recruited continued to make important contributions even after his retirement in 1986. Paul Green has been associated with the Wharton Marketing Department for over forty years and his publications over that period made him for a very significant period marketing's most widely cited academic. He also contributed in any number of ways to the further development of both the marketing discipline and of the Wharton Marketing Department.

6.   Behavior Systems

Wroe Alderson wore a great many hats during his relatively short tenure at Wharton (1959-1965) but both during this period and for many years before it, he had an extraordinary impact on the development of marketing theory, through his own writings and through the works of others with whom he interacted as friend, teacher, consultant, colleague, convenor of conferences and seminars and organizer of research organizations.

We pay special attention here to Wroe's influence on us and on marketing practice through Behavior Systems, Inc., the private consulting firm he owned during his Wharton years. Both of us originally met Wroe as graduate students. We came to know him well as Behavior Systems consultants and as friends and teaching colleagues at Wharton.

Wroe had a good many fans among business executives who were interested in what his approach could contribute to improving their understanding of their companies' own marketing efforts. Repeated inquiries in this regard led Wroe to set up his own firm, Behavior Systems, in 1961. The name itself was taken from one of the ecological concepts he introduced to the business literature in his 1957 book. In this context, he used behavior systems to explain how organizations, like individual species, would adjust, adapt, and even attempt to change their environments in order to survive and to grow.

Behavior Systems was an early version of what was later to become known as a "boutique" consulting firm. It became well known for the special quality of the conceptualization it brought to bear on a wide variety of marketing problems. It was also highly regarded for the quality of its "macro" insights in *Growth and Profit Planner*, its periodic newsletter.

Behavior Systems' Executive Director was Dr. Ken Middleton, whose special expertise was statistics and experimental design and whom Wroe had known at Alderson & Sessions. Most of the senior staff were Wharton MBAs or Phd graduate students selected personally by Wroe. Jim McKeon and Bob Rothberg are cases in point. Other graduate students serving in a professional capacity at different points in time included Jim Mercer and Marty Grosjean, Filemon Berba, Almadrones Eduardo, Pravin Shah and Kahandas Nandola, among many others. Jackie Lewis ran the office. Various Wharton faculty members and others of Wroe's acquaintance were called in as their expertise was needed. Wroe's main role here, as implied earlier, was that of rainmaker, selector of professionals, and occasional reviewer of sensitive client proposals, work in progress, and recommendations.

The clients themselves tended to be larger firms operating on a national and international scale. A number of good-sized firms operating primarily in the Delaware Valley region were also serviced.

One should also add that Behavior Systems did not stand alone as a marketing consultancy close to Wharton. A Dupont-funded entity, Behavior Research Associates, rented adjoining space. It specialized in advanced consumer behavior research using tachistiscopes and related instrumentation to measure consumer reactions to different marketing stimuli. This operation was headed up initially by Dr. Malcolm McNiven and later by Dr. Abraham Wolf.

Working at Behavior Systems

As noted earlier, Wroe's main role at Behavior Systems was that of rainmaker and selector of key personnel. Ken Middleton's role also included that of rainmaker, but, given his background, he also oversaw the project design of all of the empirical studies. Jim McKeon, as a full-time Behavior Systems professional, was the first among equals as a consulting project leader and a project-flow coordinator. Bob Rothberg was also a project leader but less intimately involved in day-to-day affairs during the school year because of his obligations to Wharton in the classroom and as a Ph.D candidate.

Overall, Wroe gave senior people at Behavior Systems unusual latitude in the design and execution of its studies and reports. While hypotheses might be advanced in particularly challenging situations, explicit directives on his part were few and far between. Even then, these took the form of subtle suggestions more than anything else.

A Sampling of Marketing Studies

Behavior Systems became known for its willingness to tackle especially challenging marketing assignments. Client satisfaction with the work done was high, if this can be inferred from the amount of repeat business. Three examples of specific projects should suffice to illustrate the kind of work around carried out: a) a pharmaceutical client interested in improving its advertising and promotional effort productivity; b) a motor vehicle manufacturer interested in redefining its competitive space in the utility vehicles sector; and c) a highly-integrated meat packing/leather tanning operation concerned with the future of its leather products in the shoe industry.

Pharmaceuticals.   This client was primarily concerned about how best to promote its drugs, first in terms of its choice of physician-directed magazines in general; and second, in terms of its advertising content and positioning within specific periodicals.

The problem in the first instance was that physicians receive a bewildering variety of advertising-laden magazines, journals and tabloids sent to their homes and offices, generally free of charge. Circulation numbers thus provided very little indication of readership and hence of the cost of physician exposure.

The research task here was to ascertain the likelihood of physician readership of these various periodicals. Several different types of mail questionnaires (un-aided and aided recall) were used, along with one highly-detailed and extended series of personal interviews with matched panels of physicians. The former, dramatically cheaper, were to be used on an ongoing basis but with "corrective" factors reflecting response differentials compared to the findings from personal interviews.

The pattern of these differentials could be readily explained in terms of the foibles of professional egos. The same foibles, incidentally, also helped to explain the differences between unaided and aided recall results, particularly when the latter was based not simply on the names of the various publications but incorporating the logotypes used in their titles. Physicians are like the rest of us: They respond more reliably in terms of pattern recognition than to magazine titles printed with the same type face. This research was, to the best of our knowledge, the first of its kind. The use of a series of premiums to boost completion of these physician survey sets was also a first.

The second problem here was, given exposure to the periodical, to ascertain the likelihood of physician readership of a given advertisement. While standard measures have long existed to gauge the depth of readership of a given advertisement, the challenge here was to incorporate this with the physician's reading habits for different kinds of periodicals. To improve the reliability and validity of the physician responses, a host of checks were used here including both faux advertisements and faux editorial matter. The use of these devices was also, to the best of our knowledge, a research first at the time.

Still another research effort for the same pharmaceutical client required Behavior Systems to ascertain whether physician "innovators" existed and could be identified as far as early product acceptance and advocacy of new drugs and delivering systems were concerned. We think this was a "first" in marketing research insofar professional markets were concerned. It involved the close examination of the new drug delivery system in a large but relatively isolated section of the country. Physicians, hospitals and other institutions and retail drug outlets were all the subject of study. We found that professional "innovators" could be readily identified and their influence patterns documented. Special targeting to such groups is now standard practice in new professional product introductions.

Utility Vehicles.　This was a competitive intelligence study for a Behavior Systems client. Long a dominant factor in this sector, our client now had to confront a new vehicle entry from a much larger competitor. The challenge here was to ascertain how well this rival's marketing tactics were working in the domestic nonfleet market sector. Given the strengths and weaknesses of this competitor, the next step was to identify an appropriate range and sequence of product-development responses for our client.

This research was remarkable in what it revealed about the details of consumer purchase and use behavior. It also uncovered (quite legally) the competitor's own analyses of our client's product weaknesses. Overall, this research led to a significant number of changes in our client's product line, including the acceleration of mechanical changes already underway, "cosmetic" modifications to current offerings, and to the successful development and introduction of an entirely new range of utility vehicles to tap into markets it heretofore had not served.

The nature and extent of this competitive intelligence work was novel at the time as was the comprehensive time-phased series of recommendations.

Leather.　Our client here was a large meat packer with significant leather tanning operations, the principal end market for which was shoes. It was upset over the consistent overestimates of demand it felt were being made by the shoe industry and by the Census Bureau. It was even more distressed by the market threat it felt it faced from DuPont's Corfam. This was a synthetic material that threatened to displace leather from the lucrative shoe "uppers" market. Earlier, other synthetics had displaced leather in other sectors of the shoe market such as soles.

Behavior Systems first looked into the matter of shoe sales trends over an extended period of time. According to Census records, per capita consumption of shoes had been essentially flat for the past 10-15 years. This finding was consistent neither with our expectations nor our experience. Closer study, however, revealed that what the Census Bureau and the industry called shoes was limited to products made on traditional shoe-making machinery— a definition going back to the days of the United Shoe Machinery Trust. Forty years earlier, shoe manufacturing equipment could only be rented, not purchased. Royalties were based on the number of pairs of shoes produced! Redefining shoes as footwear for this client brought into play a host of alternatives such as sneakers, sandals and other leather shoe substitutes. Virtually all of the growth in the footwear sector over the past decade had been in non-leathers.

The principal beneficiaries of this shift had been textile producers and importers of finished footwear. Dupont's Corfam, and a host of other synthetics we discovered also to be under development, when perfected, were also expected to make significant inroads in leather shoes by virtue of the major economies they promised in materials cutting and shoe assembly. While this latter development was not expected to directly impact the market for higher-quality leather uppers, sales to this sector was not be expected to grow any faster than the general population. Our recommendation to this client to sell its leather operations was acted upon quickly. A lot has happened to the domestic footwear industry and its leather suppliers over the past four decades. However, the advice given to this client at the time still looks good if not prescient.

Summing Up

How do you summarize a life as rich intellectually as that of Wroe Alderson? It is certainly clear that Wroe had a profound effect on these who came in contact with him personally and professionally.

Wroe certainly was a person who viewed life itself as a continuous process of learning. He was constantly pushing himself and others to reach deeper levels of knowledge and insight. He was much more than a simple theoretician content to rest on a given set of elegant conceptualizations. Wroe believed theory in and of itself was insufficient. It had to have a practical business application to be of any value. This view was reflected in Behavior System's projects. Most of these began with extensive exploratory work, followed by the development of general hypotheses. The empirical research was then designed to test these hypotheses in the specific product/market situation. Overall, we think Wroe saw life as one grand scheme or system, with everything related to everything else. He was a great explorer and charted much new conceptual territory in the realm of business ecology.

Wroe was also a visionary, who saw opportunities, intellectual and otherwise, where others did not. He was aggressive in the pursuit of goals, decisive in his choices of staff and generous to a fault in both his willingness to share credit and to delegate real responsibility to others.

Wroe was also an academic entrepreneur without peer. There are others who will celebrate his role in developing Penn's Management Science Center, the Marketing Science Institute and the host of invitation-only conferences and retreats he convened to address the challenge of defining business problems generally and marketing problems in particular. The point to be made here is that Wroe was a builder, not for himself so much as for the common good, as he sought a deeper understanding of the marketing systems in which we all find ourselves imbedded.

What do the authors remember most about Wroe? The McKeon recall is to be found in the closing section of this chapter. What follows, then, are Rothberg's remembrances. I have a cascade of images, experiences, and emotion in front of me from which to choose. I see him physically, with Falstaffian girth and subtle sense of humor relentlessly probing those around him on the most improbable of subjects from Japanese purchasing habits with respect to men's shirts to the merits of using ductile iron pipe as opposed to competing materials for municipal water systems. I see him intellectually in the give-and-take of scholarly exploration and discussion, stimulating all, but also occasionally putting someone down in the gentlest manner possible. Above all, however, I think I see him as a decent, sharing and compassionate human being whose singular contributions to our understanding of marketing today are reflected in the number of people who have something to say about Wroe in this book forty years after his passing.

7.   In Closing — Assessments of a Remarkable Man

What appears above in one sense describes all that Wroe Alderson did and accomplished while a member of Wharton's Marketing Department. However, not enough has been said about how it was to work for and with Wroe. All of those involved at the time have favorite Alderson stories. Mine involves after a busy morning his rushing out of the office on a Friday afternoon to catch a plane to Montreal for an important weekend meeting of TIMS. When he returned, I politely asked about the meeting only to hear him grumble "got there but it's next weekend". More than one of his associates have commented on the fact that Wroe was not a particularly good lecturer but at his intellectual best after a few beers at the Faculty Club of the University of Pennsylvania. But even this sort of story tells us nothing about the high regard in which he was held at the time by his colleagues and associates. One finds that reflected in the closing part of the eulogy that Orin Burley delivered at Wroe's funeral.

> Wroe was an extraordinary person. In the words of one of his colleagues, "One of a very small handful of men I have known who have come close to realizing all the potentials of a human being." His enormous capacities for life and work left its impression on both individuals and institutions. Despite his relatively few years at the University, and the Wharton School, the impact of his personality, abilities, and interests is apparent in many ways that can be understood fully only by those who were on the campus before he came.
>
> Wroe Alderson had a rare quality for lasting friendships. Literally, he had no former friends. His colleagues at the University were proud to be numbered among his many friends—both socially and professionally. Despite his busy life, he always had time to discuss problems representing a wide variety of interests, and the insights he developed were of extreme value. Intuitively—but really based on his able mind and broad experience—he seemed to envision the central problem at issue and to bring clarity to its solution.
>
> Wroe's name, so long and favorably associated with Marketing and allied areas, will always stand for solid and mature contributions to the literature, research and teaching in his field. He was a pioneer in distribution cost analysis and marketing theory. In addition, his many contributions to the advancement of management in marketing are especially well known. Even in his last year of life, he was the author of two books, destined to be outstanding in lasting contribution, and the editor of another.
>
> Wroe had the unique quality of the true teacher who took his greatest pleasure from helping others to help themselves. His like is not soon to come again. We shall miss him deeply but are profoundly happy that he shared his life with us (Burley, 1965).

Those were words written forty years ago shortly after the death of this remarkable man. I believe they adequately reflect both his defining personal characteristics and the way he was viewed by his associates at the time. His impact has been a lasting one and Wroe Alderson forty years later is still remembered as a larger-than-life figure who greatly influenced all of those with whom he closely worked. As evidence of this fact, I close with the following comments, sent to me by Jim McKeon almost forty years after Wroe Alderson's death.

> As I look back, the time I knew Wroe Alderson seems so short, but at the same time I feel I knew him forever. In 1960 I applied to and was accepted by the Wharton School. At the time I was unaware of what the future held for me. I had intended to return to engineering after I earned an MBA degree. In 1961 I met Wroe Alderson and from that moment in time my life took an abrupt turn. This professor somehow captured my mind. As I recall he was not a great platform teacher, often struggling for words, but his book, "Marketing Behavior and Executive Action", contained some business concepts I found fascinating.

He gave me a binder of his writing in past "Cost and Profit Outlooks". Wroe had the ability to take concepts from sociology, psychology and the physical sciences and combine them into marketing concepts. This cross-fertilization of ideas, perhaps his most important contribution, intrigued me.

Wroe was an individual who saw life as a continuous process of learning and expansion of knowledge. He seemed to possess a sense of self-dissatisfaction in that he was constantly pushing himself and others to the next level of knowledge. He was more than a conceptual theoretician. He believed that theory was insufficient in itself: theory had to have a practical business application to have value. Many of his firms' consulting projects began with a theoretical hypothesis with the ensuing project then designed to test that hypothesis. I believe that Wroe saw life as one grand scheme with everything related to everything else. He was a great innovator of business concepts and interrelationships. He used the printed word to educate his clients, former students, associates and anyone else that shared his passion for learning.

Wroe was more than my mentor, business associate and friend. He was the person that had the greatest impact on my business life. I remember our lunches at the Faculty Club, his fondness for Balantine India Ale, his chuckle, his energy, and his giving nature. I think of him often, used his concepts throughout my business career and still use them today in my classroom (McKeon, 2004).

All of us who knew Wroe Alderson at Wharton did so in different contexts and at different stages of our careers. However, we all have Alderson stories similar to Jim McKeon's to tell and I believe we all continue to hold Wroe's memory in equally high regard.

References

Alderson, Wroe (1963). Administered Prices and Retail Grocery Advertising. *Journal of Advertising Research*, 3(March):2–6.

Alderson, Wroe and Shapiro, Stanley J. (1963a). A Metropolitan Data Bank for the Business Community. *Business Horizons*, 5(Summer):53–62.

Alderson, Wroe and Shapiro, Stanley J., editors (1963b). *Marketing and the Computer*. Prentice-Hall Inc., Englewood Cliffs.

Alderson, Wroe and Shapiro, Stanley J. (1964). Towards a Theory of Retail Competition. In Cox, Reavis, Alderson, Wroe, and Shapiro, Stanley J., editors, *Theory in Marketing*, pages 190–212. Richard D. Irwin, Homewood, Illinois, second series edition.

Alderson, Wroe, Terpstra, Vern, and Shapiro, Stanley J., editors (1965). *Patents and Progress: The Sources and Impact of Advancing Technology*. Richard D. Irwin Inc., Homewood.

Bloom, Paul N. (1987). *Knowledge Development in Marketing: The MSI Experience*. Marketing Science Institute and Lexington Books, Lexington, Massachusetts.

Burley, Orin E. (1965). Eulogy read by Dr. Burley at Wroe Alderson's funeral in early June. Made available to the editors by Dr. Lyndon Dawson.

Cox, Reavis (1964). Introduction. In *Theory in Marketing*, page 1. Richard D. Irwin, Homewood, Second Series edition.

Cox, Reavis, Alderson, Wroe, and Shapiro, Stanley J., editors (1964). *Theory in Marketing*. Richard D. Irwin, Homewood, Second Series edition.

Fisk, George, Nein, Lawrence, and Shapiro, Stanley J. (1964). Price Rivalry among Philadelphia Food Chains. *Journal of Advertising Research*, 4(June):12-20.

McGarry, E. D. (1965). Wroe Alderson's Marketing Theory Seminar, an Experiment in Higher Education. This unpublished paper, a presentation by Dr. McGarry to the August, 1965 Marketing Theory Seminar, was made available by Dr. Lyndon Dawson.

McKeon, Jim (2004). Personal communication [email] from Dr. McKeon to Stan Shapiro in early December, reproduced with permission.

Robinson, Patrick J., Faris, C. W., and Wind, Y. (1967). *Industrial Buying and Creative Marketing*. Allyn and Bacon, Boston.

Shapiro, Stanley J. and Doody, Alton F., editors (1968). *Readings in the History of American Marketing: Settlement to Civil War*. Richard D. Irwin, Inc., Homewood, Illinois.

Smith, Wendell (1964). Foreward. In Robinson, Patrick J. and Luck, David J., editors, *Promotional Decision Making: Practice and Theory*, pages xi–xii. McGraw-Hill, New York.

Chapter 33

TOWARD A GENERAL THEORY OF MARKETING: RESOURCE-ADVANTAGE THEORY AS AN EXTENSION OF ALDERSON'S THEORY OF MARKET PROCESSES

Shelby D. Hunt
Texas Tech University

Dennis B. Arnett
Texas Tech University

Abstract   Wroe Alderson influenced considerably the development of marketing theory and practice. This article explicates how Alderson's differential advantage theory of competition grounds his theory of market processes. It then shows how resource-advantage (R-A) theory incorporates and extends Alderson's key concepts and generalizations. Consequently, we argue, R-A theory is toward a general theory of marketing.

Wroe Alderson's theoretical efforts spanned numerous marketing subjects, including theories related to pricing, advertising, consumer behavior, innovation, and retailing (Alderson 1957, 1965). However, it is his functionalist theory of market processes that justified his 1965 book's subtitle, "A Functionalist Theory of Marketing." This theory, partially formalized in Hunt, Muncy, and Ray (1981), enabled Alderson to explain how market processes can take conglomerate resources in the natural state and bring about meaningful assortments of goods in the hands of consumers. Indeed, Alderson's theory of market processes is widely acknowledged to be the theory that comes closest to being a general theory of marketing (Hunt, 1983).

A key component of Alderson's theory of market processes is his theory of competition for differential advantage, which was drawn from the works of Clark (1954, 1961). This theory explains the forces that motivate firms in the marketplace by positing that, in order to survive, firms compete with other firms for the patronage of households. A firm can be assured of the patronage of particular groups of households (i.e., market segments) only when members of the groups have reasons to prefer the output of the particular firm over the output of competing firms. Therefore, each firm will seek some advantages over other firms to assure the patronage of groups of households. This process, known as "competition for differential advantage," consists of the constant struggle of firms to develop, maintain, or increase their differential advantages over other firms.

In the Preface to Alderson's posthumously published final book, *Dynamic Marketing Behavior* (1965), Paul Green, Michael Halbert, and Patrick Robinson poignantly remark: "It is with a deep sense of honor that three of us—Wroe's students in the broadest sense of the word—introduce this book, a legacy from an eminent scholar and challenge for other theorists to take up and extend" (1965, p. vi). Unfortunately, Alderson's theory of market processes has lain fallow for decades. It is time (indeed, past time) to seed the field that Alderson prepared, to develop further his theory of market processes.

The purpose of this article is to respond, albeit belatedly, to the "take up and extend" call of Green, Halbert and Robinson. Specifically, we argue in this article that resource-advantage (R-A) theory, a general theory of competition that was first articulated in Hunt and Morgan (1995) and then developed in scores of publications thereafter, extends Alderson's theory of market processes. Consequently, we argue, R-A theory is toward a general theory of marketing. The first section of this article reviews Alderson's theory of market processes. The second provides a brief overview of R-A theory. The third section argues that R-A theory, by accommodating and integrating key concepts of Alderson's theory of market processes, extends Alderson's work and is, therefore, toward a general theory of marketing[1].

1.   The Theory of Market Processes

Alderson (1957, 1965), in developing his functionalist theory of market processes, drew heavily on several sources. Most notably, he was influenced by Clark's (1954, 1961) theory of effective competition. To understand Alder-

---

[1]This article draws extensively on Hunt (2002a, Chapter 9), which argues that R-A theory is toward a general theory of marketing on three grounds. First, because marketing takes place within the context of competition, a general theory of marketing should be consistent with the most general theory of competition. Accordingly, Hunt (2002a) argues that because R-A theory is the most general theory of competition, it is an appropriate foundation for working toward a general theory of marketing. A second argument is that R-A theory is toward a general theory of marketing because it provides a positive foundation for normative marketing strategy. A third argument—and the one discussed in this article—is that R-A theory is toward a general theory of marketing because it accommodates key concepts and generalizations from Alderson's theory of market processes and integrates them into the broader, R-A theoretical framework.

son, therefore, requires an understanding of Clark. Hence, before discussing Alderson's theory, we first review Clark's effective competition theory.

Effective Competition Theory

In the 1930s and 1940s, Clark (1940) developed the concept of workable competition. Later, Clark (1954, 1961) abandoned the label *workable* competition and replaced it with *effective* competition for reasons he states clearly:

> I am shifting the emphasis from "workable" to "effective competition" because "workable" stresses mere feasibility and is consistent with the verdict that feasible forms of competition, while tolerable, are still inferior substitutes for that "pure and perfect" competition which has been so widely accepted as a normative ideal. And I have become increasingly impressed that the kind of competition we have, with all its defects—and these are serious—is better than the "pure and perfect" norm, because it makes for progress. Some departures from "pure and perfect" competition are not only inseparable from progress, but necessary to it. The theory of effective competition is dynamic theory (Clark, 1961, p. ix).

Because a dynamic theory of competition would have different standards of appraisal, Clark inquires as to the objectives society would want competition to accomplish. He suggests that competition should provide or promote an adequate variety of products (including low priced products, high quality products, and new products), economic opportunity, social mobility, a productive economy, rewards to innovators, low search costs, a diffusion of the gains of progress, high and stable employment, business freedom, the elimination of process inefficiencies, and an appropriate balance of desirable and undesirable effects on individuals (Clark 1954, pp. 323-4; 1961, pp. 63, 74, 77, 78, 81, 82, 86).

Taken collectively, the desirable outputs of competition would seem to be a tall order. Yet Clark maintains that effective, dynamic competition could come tolerably close to achieving all his suggested goals. But effective, dynamic competition does not imply that firms would be price-takers, or that they would seek to maximize profits, or that competition is a struggle with only one winner (1961, p. 18). What, then, does effective competition imply? Acknowledging his "kinship" with Schumpeter's "creative destruction," competition is:

> a form of independent action by business units in pursuit of increased profits . . . by offering others inducements to deal with them, the others being free to accept the alternative inducements offered by rival business units. Active competition consists of a combination of (1) initiatory actions by a business unit, and (2) a complex of responses by those with whom it deals, and by rivals (Clark, 1954, p. 326).

Clark's definition of dynamic competition is remarkably compact. Indeed, his entire 1961 book is devoted to "unpacking" it. A good starting point for us is his view that firms pursue increased profits rather than maximum profits.

Clark (1961, p. 9) specifically alerts readers that his "profit minded" firms are not profit maximizers. He argues that firms do not maximize profit because all firms at all times face such conditions of uncertainty as to consumers' and rivals' actions that they lack the necessary information to maximize (pp. 93, 471). He further argues that some firms at some times (1) sacrifice profits for growth (p. 96), (2) sacrifice profits in favor of community responsibilities (p. 91), and (3) sacrifice profits because of following the "morals of trade" (p. 479). By substituting "increased profits in the face of uncertainty" for the neoclassical "maximum profits in the face of perfect information," Clark makes competition dynamic. That is, the continuing pursuit of increased profits, *more* profits, prompts changes in the "inducements to deal."

When firms are successful in effecting changes in inducements targeted at specific customers, e.g., by providing market offerings of higher quality or lower prices, such firms have a "differential advantage" over rivals (1954, p. 327). It is the pursuit of differential advantages over rivals that prompts the innovations that constitute "aggressive competition" (1961, p. 14). For Clark, the sum of innovations that result in differential advantages over rivals constitutes the technological progress required for a "dynamically progressive system," that is, for economic growth (1961, p. 70). Therefore, mandating the homogeneity of demand and supply—as argued for by many defenders of perfect competition theory—would necessitate the "stoppage of growth and progress, a price we should be unwilling to pay" (1961, p. 70). Indeed, "perfect competition . . . define[s] a model from which competitive progress would be ruled out; progress could come only by government fiat" (1954, p. 329).

For Clark, the innovations resulting from aggressive competition can come from small firms, as stressed by Marshall (1890), or from large firms, as stressed by Schumpeter (1950). Contrasted with Schumpeter (1950), however, the innovations by firms large and small can be such that they only modestly improve quality or lower costs. Cumulatively, however, Clark points out that small innovations are important to the firm and economy. Whether an innovation is brought about by small firms or large ones, whether it is industry-shaking or only a modest improvement, "the life history of a successful innovation is a cycle. It is developed, profitably utilized, and ultimately loses its value as a source of special profit" (1961, p. 189).

An innovation loses its value to produce superior profits when it is either superseded by something better (i.e., Schumpeter's "creative destruction") or when it is diffused among rivals and becomes standard practice by "defensive competition." Thus, when an innovation is diffused among rivals, it becomes— rather than a differential advantage for the originator—much like the "ante" in a poker game. Both aggressive and defensive competition are required for effective competition: "without initiatory moves, competition does not begin, without defensive responses, it does not spread" (1961, p. 429). Aggressive competition creates innovations and differential advantages; defensive competition diffuses innovations and neutralizes such advantages. As to the speed of neutralization:

> If a potential innovator expects neutralization to be complete before he has recovered the costs of innovation, his incentive vanishes . . . On the other hand, if neutralizing action were permanently blocked, the initiator would have a limited monopoly, in the sense of a permanent differential advantage. . . . The desirable case lies somewhere between too prompt and too slow neutralization. I will not call it an 'optimum', because that term suggests a precision which no actual system could attain (Clark, 1954, pp. 327-8).

Clark's hope was that his dynamic theory of effective competition would provide a framework for understanding actual forms of competition and for fostering those forms most conducive to a dynamic welfare ideal. He knew, however, that "the threat of failure looms large, in that readers whose conception of theory is identified with models of determinate equilibrium are likely to decide that no theory has been produced" (1961, p. x). He was prescient, to say the least. Both his 1954 article and his 500-page 1961 book—having not a single differential equation or geometrical representation—were not incorporated into mainstream economics. However, Clark's work did significantly impact Alderson's (1957, 1965) functionalist theory of market processes.

Alderson's Functionalist Theory

Alderson (1957, 1965) was strongly influenced by Chamberlin's (1933) heterogeneous demand theory and by Clark's (1954, 1961) theory of effective, dynamic competition. Also, he was impressed by Merton's (1949) functionalist, systems approach to theory development. Furthermore, his background in marketing, with its historical interest in groups of manufacturers, wholesalers, and retailers that form channels of distribution, pointed him toward developing a theory of marketing systems. Accordingly, his functionalist theory of market processes may be viewed as a functionalist, systems approach to integrating theories of heterogeneous demand, differential advantage, and channels of distribution.

Alderson (1957, p. 16) views functionalism as "that approach to science which begins by identifying a system of action, and then tries to determine how and why it works as it does." He identifies (1) firms as the subsystems that produce goods and (2) households as the subsystems that constitute the basic consuming units. He (1965, p. 39) notes that firms evolve in a society when specialization of labor results in removing the production function for some goods from the household. Extending Chamberlin's (1933) view that intra-industry demand is substantially heterogeneous, he notes that the particular assortment of goods that is viewed as meaningful or desirable by any one household is likely to differ greatly from those of others. Thus, the macro-systems that he seeks to understand and explain are those that involve firms taking tangible resources in their natural state and transforming them into a variety of marketplace goods. These various goods ultimately wind up as meaningful assortments of goods in the hands of particular households.

Although firms pursue profit, Alderson (1957, p. 54) maintains that they do so as if they had a primary goal of survival. The survival goal results from firm owners and employees believing that they can obtain more in terms of financial and nonfinancial rewards by working toward the survival of their existing firms than by acting individually or by becoming members of other firms. Firm growth, therefore, is sought because of the conviction that growth is necessary for survival (1957, pp. 103-108). In a market-based economy, however, survival depends crucially on a firm's ability to compete with other firms in seeking the patronage of specific (1) intermediate buyers and/or (2) ultimate households.

A firm can be assured of the patronage of intermediate buyers and/or groups of households only when buyers have reasons to prefer its output over that of competing firms. Therefore, each competing firm will seek some advantage over other firms to assure the patronage of some group of either intermediate buyers or ultimate households. Citing the work of Clark (1954), Alderson labels the process "competition for differential advantage" (1957, p. 101). Indeed, "no one enters business except in the expectation of some degree of differential advantage in serving his customers, and . . . competition consists of the constant struggle to develop, maintain, or increase such advantages" (1957, p. 106). Therefore:

> The functionalist or ecological approach to competition begins with the assumption that every firm must seek and find a function in order to maintain itself in the market place. Every business firm occupies a position, which is in some respects unique. Its location, the product it sells, its operating methods, or the customers it serves tend to set it off in some degree from every other firm. Each firm competes by making the most of its individuality and its special character. It is constantly seeking to establish some competitive advantage . . . [because] an advanced method of operation is not enough if all competitors live up to the same high standards. What is important in competition is differential advantage, which can give a firm an edge over what others in the field are offering (Alderson 1957, pp. 101-2).

Alderson (1957, pp. 184-197) identifies six bases of differential advantage for a manufacturing firm: market segmentation, selection of appeals, transvection, product improvement, process improvement, and product innovation. By market segmentation having the potential for a differential advantage, Alderson means that firms may have an advantage over competitors when they (1) identify segments of demand that competitors are not servicing (or rivals are servicing poorly) and (2) they subsequently develop market offerings that will appeal strongly to those particular segments. On the other hand, by "selection of appeals" he means that some firms can achieve advantage by the images that are conveyed to consumers through advertising and other promotional means. Similarly, by "transvection" he means an advantage in reaching a market segment through a unique channel of distribution.

The existence of a differential advantage gives the firm a position in the marketplace known as an "ecological niche" (1957, p. 56). The "core" and "fringe" of a firm's ecological niche consists of the market segments for which the firm's differential advantage is (1) ideally suited for and (2) satisfactorily suited for, respectively. A firm can survive attacks by competitors on its "fringe" as long as its "core" remains intact; it can survive attacks on its "core" as long as it has the will and ability to find another differential advantage and another core (1957, pp. 56-57). Therefore, given heterogeneity of demand and competition for differential advantage, heterogeneity of supply is a natural phenomenon. That is, manufacturers will respond to heterogeneity of demand by producing a variety of different goods and many variations of the same generic kind of good (1957, p. 103).

To reach households, however, manufacturing firms require market intermediaries, that is, channels of distribution. Market processes involving intermediaries are essentially "matching" processes, that is, matching segments of demand with segments of supply. In a perfectly heterogeneous market, each small segment of demand, that is, each household, could be satisfied by just one unique segment of supply (i.e., one firm) (1965, p. 29). In most markets, however, there are partial homogeneities. That is, there are groups or segments of households desiring substantially similar products and there are groups of firms supplying substantially similar products.

The major job of marketing intermediaries is to effect exchange by matching segments of demand with segments of supply. The matching process comes about as a result of a sequence of sorts and transformations (1965, p. 26). A sort is the assignment of goods, materials, or components to the appropriate facilities. A transformation is the change in the physical form of a good or its location in time or space.

With the preceding as backdrop, Alderson (1965, p. 26) can provide an answer to the question that prompted his functionalist theory. Given heterogeneity of demand, heterogeneity of supply, competition for differential advantage, and the requisite institutions (intermediaries) to effect the sorts and transformations necessary to match segments of demand with segments of supply, market processes will take resources in the natural state and bring about meaningful assortments of goods in the hands of households.

2.   An Overview of R-A Theory

We turn now to a brief overview of resource-advantage theory. R-A theory is an evolutionary, process theory of competition that is interdisciplinary in the sense that it has been developed in the literatures of several different disciplines. These disciplines include marketing (Falkenberg, 2000, Foss, 2000, Hodgson, 2000, Hunt, 1997a, Hunt, 1999, Hunt, 2000a, Hunt, 2000b, Hunt, 2001, Hunt, 2002a, Hunt, 2002b, Hunt and Arnett, 2001, Hunt and Arnett, 2003, Hunt et al., 2002, Hunt and Morgan, 1995, Hunt and Morgan, 1996, Hunt and Morgan, 1997, Morgan and Hunt, 2002), management (Hunt, 1995, Hunt, 2000d, Hunt and Lambe, 2000), economics (Hunt, 1997b, Hunt, 1997d, Hunt, 1997e, Hunt, 2000c, Hunt, 2002c), ethics (Arnett and Hunt, 2002), and general business (Hunt, 1998, Hunt and Duhan, 2002). R-A theory is also interdisciplinary in that it draws on and has affinities with numerous other theories and research traditions, including evolutionary economics, "Austrian" economics, the historical tradition, industrial-organization economics, the resource-based tradition, the competence-based tradition, institutional economics, transaction cost economics, and economic sociology. As will be argued in the next section, R-A theory also draws on and has affinities with Alderson's theory of market processes.

Resource-advantage theory is a general theory of competition that describes the process of competition. Figures 33.1 and 33.2 provide schematic depictions of R-A theory's key constructs, and Table 33.1 provides its foundational premises. Our overview will follow closely the theory's treatment in Hunt (2000b).

The structure and foundations of R-A theory

Using Hodgson's (1993) taxonomy, R-A theory is an evolutionary, disequilibrium-provoking, process theory of competition, in which innovation and organizational learning are endogenous, firms and consumers have imperfect information, and in which entrepreneurship, institutions, and public policy affect economic performance.

Evolutionary theories of competition require units of selection that are (1) relatively durable, that is, they can exist, at least potentially, through long periods of time, and (2) heritable, that is, they can be transmitted to successors. For R-A theory, both firms and resources are proposed as the heritable, durable units of selection, with competition for comparative advantages in resources constituting the selection process.

At its core, R-A theory combines heterogeneous demand theory with the resource-based theory of the firm (see premises P_1, P_6, and P_7 in Table 33.1). Contrasted with perfect competition, heterogeneous demand theory views intra-industry demand as significantly heterogeneous with respect to consumers'

Figure 33.1.

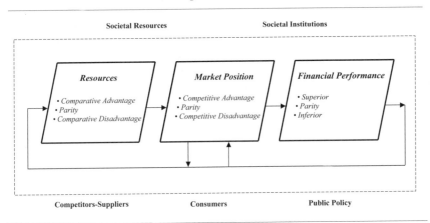

Read: Competition is the disequilibrating, ongoing process that consists of the constant struggle among firms for a comparative advantage in resources that will yield a marketplace position of competitive advantage and, thereby, superior financial performance. Firms learn through competition as a result of feedback from relative financial performance "signaling" relative market position, which, in turn signals relative resources.

Source: Adapted from Hunt and Morgan (1997)

tastes and preferences. Therefore, viewing products as bundles of attributes, different market offerings or "bundles" are required for different market segments within the same industry. Contrasted with the view that the firm is a production function that combines homogeneous, perfectly mobile "factors" of production, the resource-based view holds that the firm is a combiner of heterogeneous, imperfectly mobile entities that are labeled "resources." These heterogeneous, imperfectly mobile resources, when combined with heterogeneous demand, imply significant diversity as to the sizes, scopes, and levels of profitability of firms within the same industry. The resource-based theory of the firm parallels, if not undergirds, what Foss (1993) calls the "competence perspective" in evolutionary economics and the "capabilities" approaches of Teece and Pisano (1994) and Langlois and Robertson (1995).

As diagramed in Figures 33.1 and 33.2, R-A theory stresses the importance of (1) market segments, (2) heterogeneous firm resources, (3) comparative advantages/disadvantages in resources, and (4) marketplace positions of competitive advantage/disadvantage. In brief, market segments are defined as intra-industry groups of consumers whose tastes and preferences with regard to an industry's output are relatively homogeneous. Resources are defined as the tangible and intangible entities available to the firm that enable it to produce efficiently and/or effectively market offerings that have value for some marketing segment(s). Thus, resources are not just land, labor, and capital, as in neoclassical theory. Rather, resources can be categorized as financial (e.g., cash resources, access

Figure 33.2.

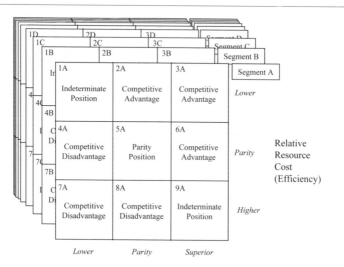

Lower   Parity   Superior

Relative Resource-Produced Value
(Effectiveness)

Read: The marketplace position of competitive advantage identified as Cell 3A in each segment results from the firm, relative to its competitors, having a resource assortment that enables it to produce an offering that (a) is perceived to be of superior value by consumers in that segment and (b) is produced at lower costs than rivals.

* Each competitive position matrix constitutes a different market segment (denoted as segment A, segment B, …).

Source: Adapted from Hunt and Morgan (1997).

Table 33.1. Foundational Premises of Resource-Advantage Theory (Hunt, 1997c)

P_1:   Demand is heterogeneous across industries, heterogeneous within industries, and dynamic.

P_2:   Consumer information is imperfect and costly.

P_3:   Human motivation is constrained self-interest seeking.

P_4:   The firm's objective is superior financial performance.

P_5:   The firm's information is imperfect and costly.

P_6:   The firm's resources are financial, physical, legal, human, organizational, informational, and relational.

P_7:   Resource characteristics are heterogeneous and imperfectly mobile.

P_8:   The role of managment is to recognize, understand, create, select, implement, and modify strategies.

P_9:   Competitive dynamics are disequilibrium-provoking, with innovation endogenous.

to financial markets), physical (e.g., plant, equipment), legal (e.g., trademarks, licenses), human (e.g., the skills and knowledge of individual employees), organizational (e.g., competences, controls, policies, culture), informational (e.g., knowledge from consumers and competitive intelligence), and relational (e.g., relationships with suppliers and customers).

Each firm in the marketplace will have at least some resources that are unique to it (e.g., very knowledgeable employees, efficient production processes, etc.) that could constitute a comparative advantage in resources that could lead to positions of advantage (i.e., cells 2, 3, and 6 in Figure 33.2) in the marketplace. Some of these resources are not easily copied or acquired (i.e., they are relatively immobile). Therefore, such resources (e.g., culture and processes) may be sources of long-term competitive advantage in the marketplace.

Just as international trade theory recognizes that nations have heterogeneous, immobile resources, and it focuses on the importance of comparative advantages in resources to explain the benefits of trade, R-A theory recognizes that many of the resources of firms within the same industry are significantly heterogeneous and relatively immobile. Therefore, analogous to nations, some firms will have a comparative advantage and others a comparative disadvantage in efficiently and/or effectively producing particular market offerings that have value for particular market segments.

Specifically, as shown in Figure 33.1 and further explicated in Figure 33.2, when firms have a comparative advantage in resources they will occupy marketplace positions of competitive advantage for some market segment(s). Marketplace positions of competitive advantage then result in superior financial performance. Similarly, when firms have a comparative disadvantage in resources they will occupy positions of competitive disadvantage, which will then produce inferior financial performance. Therefore, firms compete for comparative advantages in resources that will yield marketplace positions of competitive advantage for some market segment(s) and, thereby, superior financial performance. As Figure 33.1 shows, how well competitive processes work is significantly influenced by five environmental factors: the societal resources on which firms draw, the societal institutions that form the "rules of the game" (North 1990), the actions of competitors, the behaviors of consumers and suppliers, and public policy decisions.

Consistent with its Schumpeterian heritage, R-A theory places great emphasis on innovation, both proactive and reactive. The former is innovation by firms that, although motivated by the expectation of superior financial performance, is not prompted by specific competitive pressures—it is genuinely entrepreneurial in the classic sense of *entrepreneur*. In contrast, the latter is innovation that is directly prompted by the learning process of firms competing for the patronage of particular market segments. Both proactive and reactive innovation contribute to the dynamism of R-A competition.

Firms (attempt to) learn in many ways—by formal market research, seeking out competitive intelligence, dissecting competitor's products, benchmarking, and test marketing. What R-A theory adds to extant work is how the process of competition itself contributes to organizational learning. As the feedback loops in Figure 33.1 show, firms learn through competition as a result of the feedback from relative financial performance signaling relative market position, which in turn signals relative resources. When firms competing for a market segment learn from their inferior financial performance that they occupy positions of competitive disadvantage (see Figure 33.2), they attempt to neutralize and/or leapfrog the advantaged firm(s) by acquisition and/or innovation. That is, they attempt to acquire the same resource as the advantaged firm(s) and/or they attempt to innovate by imitating the resource, finding an equivalent resource, or finding (creating) a superior resource. Here, "superior" implies that the innovating firm's new resource enables it to surpass the previously advantaged competitor in terms of either relative costs (i.e., an *efficiency* advantage), or relative value (i.e., an *effectiveness* advantage), or both.

Firms occupying positions of competitive advantage can continue to do so if (1) they continue to reinvest in the resources that produced the competitive advantage, and (2) rivals' acquisition and innovation efforts fail. Rivals will fail (or take a long time to succeed) when an advantaged firm's resources are either protected by such societal institutions as patents or the advantage-producing resources are causally ambiguous, socially or technologically complex, tacit, or have time compression diseconomies.

Competition, then, is viewed as an evolutionary, disequilibrium-provoking process. It consists of the constant struggle among firms for comparative advantages in resources that will yield marketplace positions of competitive advantage and, thereby, superior financial performance. Once a firm's comparative advantage in resources enables it to achieve superior performance through a position of competitive advantage in some market segment(s), competitors attempt to neutralize and/or leapfrog the advantaged firm through acquisition, imitation, substitution, or major innovation. R-A theory is, therefore, inherently dynamic. Disequilibrium, not equilibrium, is the norm. In the terminology of Hodgson's (1993) taxonomy of evolutionary economic theories, R-A theory is non-consummatory: it has no end-stage, only a never-ending process of change. The implication is that, though market-based economies are *moving*, they are not moving toward some final state, such as a Pareto-optimal, general equilibrium.

3.   The Theory of Market Processes and R-A Theory

With respect to the nature of competition, both Alderson's functionalist theory and Clark's effective competition rely on the concept of competition for

Table 33.2. Differential-Advantage Theory and Resource-Advantage Theory (Hunt, 2004)

Differential-Advantage Theory	Resource-Advantage Theory
1. Perfect competition is not an appropriate welfare ideal.	**1.** Perfect competition is not an appropriate welfare ideal. However, R-A competition is desirable because it promotes resource allocation, resource creation, productivity, and economic growth.
2. Industry demand is heterogeneous.	**2.** Industry demand is heterogeneous (P_1 in Table 33.1).
3. Competition matches segments of demand and supply.	**3.** R-A competition is segment by segment and matches segments of demand and supply.
4. Firm motivation is not profit max, but *increased* profits and survival.	**4.** Firm motivation is superior financial performance, which equates with "more than" and "better than" some referent (P_4 in Table 33.1). Superior rewards to stakeholders result from firm superior performance (P_3 in Table 33.1).
5. Competition is dynamic.	**5.** The objectives of "more than" and "better than" imply dynamic competition.
6. Markets are discrepant (products wanted, not produced; products produced, not wanted).	**6.** Markets are discrepant (products wanted, not produced; products produced, not wanted).
7. Competition is evolutionary, with ecological niches.	**7.** Competition is evolutionary, nonconsummatory, with niches. The units of the evolutionary selection are firms and resources. Competition is the selection process.
8. Firms seek differential advantages.	**8.** It is comparative advantages in resources that lead to marketplace positions of competitive advantage and, thereby, superior financial performance (Figures 33.1 and 33.2).
9. Competition neutralizes advantages.	**9.** Competition can neutralize competitors' advantages by acquisition of similar resources and/or can leapfrog competitors by reactive innovations that result in superior resources. When resources are tacit, causally ambiguous, socially or technologically complex, interconnected, or have mass efficiencies or time compression diseconomies, they are more difficult to neutralize or leapfrog.
10. Competitive actions may be aggressive or defensive.	**10.** Proactive and reactive innovations constitute aggressive and defensive competitive actions, respectively.
11. Firms sort (sort out, assort, allocate, and accumulate).	**11.** When firms sort (sort out, assort, allocate, and accumulate), they may develop sorting competences that become firm resources.

differential advantage. Therefore, we use the label *differential advantage theory* ("D-A theory") to refer to the combination of their respective views. This section argues that R-A theory accommodates and integrates key concepts and generalizations of D-A theory into its general theory of competition. Table 33.2 compares D-A theory and R-A theory on several attributes. As is readily apparent, R-A theory both draws on, has numerous affinities with, and extends D-A theory. Here we focus on five areas for discussion.

First, both differential advantage theory and R-A theory maintain that competition is dynamic (see 5 in Table 33.2). Indeed, they share a similar propulsion mechanism. For D-A theory, the mechanism is increased profits; for R-A theory, it is the more general concept (and more completely explicated concept) of superior financial performance. That is, R-A theory proposes that the firm's primary objective of superior financial performance (P_4 in Table 33.1) is pursued under conditions of imperfect (and often costly to obtain) information about extant and potential market segments, competitors, suppliers, shareholders, and production technologies (P_5 in Table 33.1). Superior financial performance is indicated by such measures as profits, earnings per share, return on investment, and capital appreciation. Here, "superior" equates with both "more than" and "better than" (see 4 in Table 33.2). It implies that firms seek a level of financial performance exceeding that of some referent. For example, the referent can be the firm's own performance in a previous time-period, the performance of rival firms, an industry average, or a stock-market average, among others. Affecting the process of competition, both the specific measure and specific referent will vary somewhat from time to time, firm to firm, industry to industry, and culture to culture (see the five environmental factors in Figure 33.1).

Firms are posited to pursue superior financial performance because superior rewards—both financial and nonfinancial—will then flow to owners, managers, and employees (consistent with the view of human motivation identified in P_3 of Table 33.1). However, superior financial performance does not equate with the neoclassical concepts of "abnormal profits" or "rents" (i.e., profits differing from the average firm in a purely competitive industry in long-run equilibrium) because R-A theory views industry long-run equilibrium as such a rare phenomenon that "normal" profits cannot be an empirical referent for comparison purposes. Furthermore, the actions of firms that collectively constitute competition do not force groups of rivals to "tend toward" equilibrium. Instead, the pursuit of *superior* performance implies that actions of competing firms are disequilibrating, not equilibrating. That is, R-A competition is necessarily dynamic because all firms cannot be superior *simultaneously*.

As a second point of similarity, neither D-A theory nor R-A theory is defended on the ground that its theory of competition represents "second best" or "workable" approximations of perfect competition. Instead, both theories deny that the equations of general equilibrium, relying as they do on perfect competition, represent the appropriate welfare ideal (see 1 in Table 33.2). For both D-A and R-A theory, the appropriate welfare ideal must accommodate, at the minimum, competition-induced technological progress. The more general R-A theory, contrasted with D-A theory, explicates in detail how R-A competition produces increases in productivity and economic growth (see Hunt 2000b).

Third, both D-A and R-A theory share the view that competition involves both initiatory and defensive actions (see 10 in Table 33.2). The "aggressive competition" and "defensive competition" of D-A theory parallel the "proactive innovation" and "reactive innovation" of R-A theory. Thus, competition-induced innovations, whether large or small, by huge corporations or solitary entrepreneurs, play a major role in both theories.

Fourth, both D-A and R-A theory share the view that competition involves the struggle among rivals for *advantages* (see 8 in Table 33.2). For D-A theory, the concept of the kinds of advantages that firms pursue are of an unspecified (or only limitedly specified) nature. For R-A theory, firms pursue two kinds of advantages: advantages in resources and advantages in marketplace position. Specifically, they pursue comparative advantages in resources that will yield marketplace positions of competitive advantage and, thereby, superior financial performance (see Figures 33.1 and 33.2). Furthermore, R-A theory explicates the nature of resources that will make effective neutralization by rivals less likely or at least more time-consuming: when resources are imperfectly mobile, inimitable, and imperfectly substitutable, they are more likely to thwart effective neutralization (see 9 in Table 33.2). That is, when resources are tacit, causally ambiguous, socially or technologically complex, interconnected, or they exhibit mass efficiencies or time-compression diseconomies, they are *less* likely to be quickly and effectively neutralized and more likely to produce a sustainable competitive advantage.

Finally, both D-A theory and R-A theory are developed in a natural language, that is, English. They are not developed in the language of mathematics. But R-A theory's preference for natural-language exposition should not be interpreted as being anti-equation. Rather, unlike D-A theory, the more general R-A theory is argued to be a theory of competition that incorporates perfect competition theory as a special case and, thereby, explains when the equations in the neoclassical tradition will predict accurately (see Hunt 2000b and Hunt 2002a).

4. Conclusion

Wroe Alderson influenced considerably the development of marketing theory and practice. Indeed, his functionalist theory of marketing processes (Alderson 1957, 1965) incorporates many concepts that are integral to current marketing strategies. For example, Alderson's theory argues that both supply and demand

ALDERSONIAN MARKETING THOUGHT

are heterogeneous and that markets are discrepant. These concepts form the basis for market segmentation strategy, for segmentation, viewed as a strategic option, involves (1) identifying segments of demand, (2) targeting specific segments, and (3) developing specific marketing "mixes" for each targeted segment (Hunt and Arnett, 2004).

This article explicates how Alderson's differential advantage theory of competition grounds his theory of market processes. It then shows how R-A theory incorporates and extends Alderson's key concepts and generalizations. Specifically, we explicate in detail five major ways in which R-A theory draws on, has affinities with, and extends differential advantage (D-A) theory. Among other things, both theories: (1) maintain that competition is dynamic, (2) eschew the notion that its theory of competition represents a "second best" or "workable" approximation of perfect competition, (3) share the view that competition involves both initiatory and defensive actions by firms, (4) view competition as a constant struggle among rivals for advantages, and (5) are developed in a natural language, that is, English, rather than the language of mathematics. We succinctly present the affinities between the D-A and R-A theories of competition in Table 33.2.

Because it extends Alderson's theory of market processes, resource-advantage theory is argued to be toward general theory of marketing. Therefore, our article shows how Alderson's work continues to influence marketing theory. Clearly, though, Alderson's ideas have much more to offer current marketing scholars, and there still is much work to do. Therefore, we close by repeating the "take-up and extend" call of Green, Halbert, and Robinson (Alderson 1965, p. vi). The resource-advantage theory of competition is an important step forward, but it, we argue, should be only the beginning of our discipline's efforts to advance Alderson's vision of what the marketing discipline should be. Furthering that vision is our discipline's duty. If not us, who? If not now, when?

References

Alderson, Wroe (1957). *Marketing Behavior and Executive Action: A Functionalist Approach to Marketing* . Richard D. Irwin Inc, Homewood.

Alderson, Wroe (1965). *Dynamic Marketing Behavior: A Functionalist Theory of Marketing*. Richard D. Irwin Inc., Homewood.

Arnett, Dennis B. and Hunt, Shelby D. (2002). Competitive Irrationality: The Influence of Moral Philosophy. *Business Ethics Quarterly*, 12(3):279–303.

Chamberlin, E. H. (1933). *The Theory of Monopolistic Competition: A Reorientation of the Theory of Value*. Harvard University Press, Cambridge, Massachusetts. Frequently revised since then.

Clark, John M. (1940). Toward a Concept of Workable Competition. *American Economic Review*, 30(June):241–256.

Clark, John M. (1961). *Competition as a Dynamic Process*. Brookings Institution, Washington, DC.

Clark, Lincoln H., editor (1954). *Consumer Behavior (Volume 1): The Dynamics of Consumer Reaction*. New York University Press, New York.

Falkenberg, Andreas W. (2000). Competition and Markets. *Journal of Macromarketing*, 20(June):8–9.

Foss, Nicolai (1993). Theories of the Firm: Contractual and Competence Perspectives. *Journal of Evolutionary Economics*, 3(2):127–144.

Foss, Nicolai (2000). The Dangers and Attractions of Theoretical Eclecticism. *Journal of Macromarketing*, 20(June):65–67.

Hodgson, Geoffrey M. (1993). *Economics and Evolution*. University of Michigan Press, Ann Arbor, Michigan.

Hodgson, Geoffrey M. (2000). The Marketing of Wisdom: Resource-Advantage Theory. *Journal of Macromarketing*, 20(June):68–72.

Hunt, Shelby D. (1983). General Theories and the Fundamental Explanada of Marketing. *Journal of Marketing*, 47(Fall):9–17.

Hunt, Shelby D. (1995). The Resource-Advantage Theory of Competition: Toward Explaining Productivity and Economic Growth. *Journal of Management Inquiry*, 4(December):317–332.

Hunt, Shelby D. (1997a). Competing through Relationships: Grounding Relationship Marketing in Resource-Advantage Theory. *Journal of Marketing Management*, 13(5):431–445.

Hunt, Shelby D. (1997b). Evolutionary Economics, Endogenous Growth Models, and Resource-Advantage Theory. *Eastern Economic Journal*, 23(4):425–439.

Hunt, Shelby D. (1997c). Evolutionary Economics, Endogenous Growth Models, and Resource-Advantage Theory. *Eastern Economic Journal*, 23(4).

Hunt, Shelby D. (1997d). Resource-Advantage Theory: An Evolutionary Theory of Competitive Firm Behavior? *The Journal of Economic Issues*, 31(March):59–77.

Hunt, Shelby D. (1997e). Resource-Advantage Theory and the Wealth of Nations. *The Journal of Socio-Economics*, 26(4):335–357.

Hunt, Shelby D. (1998). Productivity, Economic Growth, and Competition: Resource Allocation or Resource Creation? *Business and the Contemporary World*, 10(3):367–394.

Hunt, Shelby D. (1999). The Strategic Imperative and Sustainable Competitive Advantage: Public Policy Implications of Resource-Advantage Theory. *The Journal of the Academy of Marketing Science*, 27(2):144–159.

Hunt, Shelby D. (2000a). *A General Theory of Competition: Resources, Competences, Productivity, Economic Growth*. Sage, Thousand Oaks, California.

Hunt, Shelby D. (2000b). A General Theory of Competition: Too Eclectic or Not Eclectic Enough? Too Incremental or Not Incremental Enough? Too neoclassical or Not Neoclassical Enough? *Journal of Macromarketing*, 20(1):77–81.

Hunt, Shelby D. (2000c). Synthesizing Resource-Based, Evolutionary and Neoclassical Thought: Resource-Advantage Theory as A General Theory of Competition. In Foss, N. J. and Robertson, P., editors, *Resources, Technology, and Strategy*, pages 53–79. Routledge, London.

Hunt, Shelby D. (2000d). The Competence-Based, Resource-Advantage, and Neoclassical Theories of Competition: Toward A Synthesis. In Sanchez, R. and Heene, A., editors, *Competence-Based Strategic Management: Theory and Research*, pages 177–208. JAI Press, Greenwich, CT.

Hunt, Shelby D. (2001). A General Theory of Competition: Issues, Answers, and an Invitation. *European Journal of Marketing*, 35(5/6):524–548.

Hunt, Shelby D. (2002a). *Foundations of Marketing Theory: Toward a General Theory of Marketing*. M. E. Sharpe, Inc., Armonk, New York.

Hunt, Shelby D. (2002b). Marketing and a General Theory of Competition. *Journal of Marketing Management*, 18(1-2):239–247.

Hunt, Shelby D. (2002c). Resource-Advantage Theory and Austrian Economics. In Foss, N. J. and Klein, P., editors, *Entrepreneurship and the Firm: Austrian Perspectives on Economic Organization*, pages 248–272. Edward Elgar Publishing, Inc., Cheltenham, U.K.

Hunt, Shelby D. (2004). Incorporating Aldersonian Thought into Resource-Advantage Theory. working paper. Texas Tech University, Rawls College of Business, Marketing Department, Lubbock, TX.

Hunt, Shelby D. and Arnett, Dennis B. (2001). Competition as an Evolutionary Process and Antitrust Policy. *Journal of Public Policy and Marketing*, 20(1):15–25.

Hunt, Shelby D. and Arnett, Dennis B. (2003). Resource-Advantage Theory and Embeddedness: Explaining R-A Theory's Explanatory Success. *Journal of Marketing Theory and Practice*, 11(1):1–16.

Hunt, Shelby D. and Arnett, Dennis B. (2004). Market Segmentation Strategy, Competitive Advantage, and Firm Performance: Grounding Market Segmentation Strategy in Resource-Advantage Theory. *Australasian Marketing Journal*, 12(1):7–25.

Hunt, Shelby D. and Duhan, Dale F. (2002). Competition in the Third Millennium: Efficiency or Effectiveness? *Journal of Business Research*, 55(2):97–102.

Hunt, Shelby D. and Lambe, C. Jay (2000). Marketing's Contribution to Business Strategy: Market Orientation, Relationship Marketing, and Resource-Advantage Theory. *International Journal of Management Reviews*, 2(1):17–44.

Hunt, Shelby D., Lambe, C. Jay, and Wittmann, C. Michael (2002). A Theory and Model of Business Alliance Success. *Journal of Relationship Marketing*, 1(1):17–36.

Hunt, Shelby D. and Morgan, R. M. (1995). The Comparative Advantage Theory of Competition. *Journal of Marketing*, 59(April):1–15.

Hunt, Shelby D. and Morgan, Robert M. (1996). The Resource-Advantage Theory of Competition: Dynamics, Path Dependencies, and Evolutionary Dimensions. *Journal of Marketing*, 60(October):107–114.

Hunt, Shelby D. and Morgan, Robert M. (1997). Resource-Advantage Theory: A Snake Swallowing Its Tail or a General Theory of Competition? *Journal of Marketing*, 61(October):74–82.

Hunt, Shelby D., Muncy, James A., and Ray, Nina M. (1981). Alderson's General Theory of Marketing: A Formalization. In Enis, Ben M. and Roering, Kenneth J., editors, *Review of Marketing 1981*, pages 267–272. American Marketing Association, Chicago.

Langlois, Richard N. and Robertson, P. L. (1995). *Firms, Markets and Economic Change: A Dynamic Theory of Business Institutions*. Routledge, London.

Marshall, Alfred (1890/1949). *Principles of Economics*. Macmillan, London.

Merton, Robert K. (1949). *Social Theory and Social Structure*. The Free Press, New York.

Morgan, Robert E. and Hunt, Shelby D. (2002). Determining Marketing Strategy: A Cybernetic Systems Approach to Scenario Planning. *European Journal of Marketing*, 36(4):450–478.

North, Douglass C. (1990). *Institutions, Institutional Change, and Economic Performance*. University of Cambridge, Cambridge.

Schumpeter, Joseph (1950). *Capitalism, Socialism, and Democracy*. Harper and Row, New York.

Teece, David and Pisano, Gary (1994). The Dynamic Capabilities of Firms: An Introduction. *Industrial and Corporate Change*, 3(E):537–556.

Chapter 34

PLACING ALDERSON AND HIS CONTRIBUTIONS TO MARKETING IN HISTORICAL PERSPECTIVE*

Robert D. Tamilia
University of Quebec at Montreal

Abstract   Alderson's contributions to marketing (management) thought and theory are so far reaching that they are considered by some to be essential in building an understanding of marketing. Given the importance of his contributions, it is indeed surprising that he is but a name to current marketing students. The chapter attempts to find out why by analyzing the intellectual milieu in which he lived. An analysis of the environment will not only shed light as to why he has been forgotten but will also reveal where his seminal contributions came from, what their inherent weaknesses are and what's missing. The world of academic marketing began to change toward the end of Alderson's life, in part due to his unprecedented efforts to make marketing more theoretical and scientific. Current trends in marketing scholarship and education and how these trends transformed the marketing discipline in this post Aldersonian era are also discussed.

1.   Aldersonian Marketing Thought: An Introduction

Alderson has been all but forgotten in contemporary marketing scholarship. While earlier marketing textbooks (pre-1980s) readily acknowledged his ideas, insights and theories, this is no longer the case. For example, early editions of Philip Kotler's marketing management textbooks had numerous pages discussing Alderson, yet none remain after the 9th (1997) edition. Alderson was the first and perhaps the only marketing scholar who modified and extended economic theory to meet the needs of marketing students and practitioners. The social sciences also gave his inquisitive mind new ideas. His creative genius adapted all of this information to the needs of marketing theory development. He is considered to have been the most vocal promoter and 'agent provocateur'

---

*The number of references cited has been reduced to save space, given the extent of the material presented.

for marketing theory development and is known as the outstanding marketing theorist of the second half of the twentieth century.

Sadly, despite his achievements, he belongs to a class of academics that hardly exists today. Current marketing academics can no longer identify with his work. This is largely due to a lack of focus in contemporary education on marketing thought and theory at both the graduate and undergraduate level. Education plays a formidable role in the transmission of marketing knowledge from one generation of academics to the next one. If there are weaknesses in the transmission process, then a generation of authors could potentially be forgotten. They remain outside our consciousness until someone again recognizes their scholarship. For example, Ben Wooliscroft's efforts to reintroduce Alderson to the marketing community have spurred a new interest in his contributions. It has also resulted in this book being available for current and future academics to explore, contemplate and enjoy.

Alderson is the founding father of the interdisciplinary approach to the study of marketing. He could also be considered to be the founding father of marketing management, largely due to both his market behavior theory as well as his other managerial contributions (Alderson 1957, 1965). Consumer research and marketing management have become academic marketing's *raison d'être* ever since. He coined many new terms in marketing, redefined existing concepts and elaborated extensively on others. These terms, now taken for granted include:

> Product differentiation, positioning, enterprise differentiation, potency of assortment, routinized transactions, competitive advantage, core market, fringe market, discrepancy of assortments, discrepancy of quantity, matching, marketing audit, information search, double search, demand heterogeneity, supply heterogeneity, meaningful and meaningless heterogeneity, transvection, sorts, ecological niche, perishable distinctiveness, plasticity, and principle of postponement.

It is rather ironic that marketing management is now an overwhelming focus in marketing education and, yet, mainstream academic marketers have largely forgotten this key figure. We need to ask the question why this seminal contributor to marketing theory has been neglected and even eliminated from the marketing discipline? What has happened to Aldersonian marketing thought in mainstream marketing? Why is it that contemporary marketing textbooks and published articles no longer cite Alderson and his contributions, as was the case a generation ago? In this twenty-first century, he is still being studied and cited, but not in mainstream marketing but rather in the management literature, Austrian economics, and management science.

This disturbing trend is not unique to the marketing discipline. Fragmentation of the business disciplines and proliferation of an ever-growing number of specialized research topics and journals are partly responsible. The marketing education process certainly shares part of the blame, as will be shown.

Some have even suggested that Alderson was too difficult to read and few could actually understand his work (Sheth et al., 1988).

Alderson had his own unique style for developing marketing thought. He was also a product of the intellectual environment in which he lived. We cannot fully understand Alderson's contributions or why he is all but forgotten unless more is known about that environment and about the man himself. Certain authors fade away from a given discipline over time perhaps because their work was judged to be minor. On the other hand, why would an author, such as Alderson, be largely forgotten when he was considered to be seminal during his life? The very discipline he helped to legitimize and to theorize fails to recognize and even acknowledge his contributions a short time later. This chapter will explore possible explanations of the current neglect of one of marketing's premier scholars of the twentieth century.

2.   Alderson as a Marketing Generalist

Alderson was a marketing generalist committed to theory development and research in marketing. Alderson felt that real advances in marketing knowledge could only come from the interaction of theory and empirical research. His deductive approach toward an understanding of marketing necessitated the creation of numerous new terms that reflected his ideas and understanding of marketing. Theory development through deductive reasoning demands a very creative mind, as was the case with Alderson. He developed his general theory of market behavior at the time the notion of a general theory in management preoccupied some academics (e.g. Alderson and Cox, 1948, McInnes, 1954, Frederick, 1963, Green and Redmond, 1957).

Today's marketing academics, for better or for worse, live in an inductive world where hypothesis testing is de rigueur and the formulation of a theory of marketing, let alone a general theory, preoccupies few academics. In this age of publish or perish, being a marketing generalist à la Alderson is no longer a viable alternative for promotion, tenure and peer recognition. Today, there are few marketing thinkers and philosophers, unlike the greater number of marketing empiricists and experimenters. As Leonard Berry, a past President of the American Marketing Association, once said:

> Specialization is a natural and healthy response to an increasing complex discipline. There are, however, some dangers. One is that too many of us become 'super specialists' leaving too few generalists. Marketing needs generalists as well as specialists; it needs scholars whose specialty is marketing rather than a subset of marketing (1986, p. 1).

Alderson's publications cover a wide range of topics and issues such as advertising, channels, ethics, pricing, research methods, consumer behavior, market planning, retailing and wholesaling, patents and the computer, productivity and distribution cost analysis, and of course theory development, among others.

Given this range of interest, current marketing academics would be inclined to label Alderson as an author in search of an identity. Unlike too many of today's academics, he was not topic or issue-bound. His intellectual curiosity and inquisitive mind nurtured in him a need to read voraciously material that broadened his understanding of the many facets of marketing. Today's academic world is unlike the one that existed during his lifetime. Increased specialization through topic fragmentation has made it much harder for marketing generalists to emerge and to succeed.

Other scholars of his time were also generalists, that is scholars who were interested in developing knowledge for the benefit of their field and not just for a specialized sub-field (e.g. Talcott Parsons, Chester Barnard, and Peter Drucker, among others). Alderson was a contributor to the development of a general theory of marketing, referred to as his market behavior theory.

Previously, the textbook was more likely to be the vehicle used to disseminate new marketing knowledge. Today the outlet is the journal article. Writing and publishing an article is a faster and more economical way to develop and disseminate knowledge than through a textbook, which can take years of hard work and patience. Moreover, the article is ideally suited for the current research emphasis on publishing empirically-based studies. A case in point, the Journal of Marketing's original mission was to offer authors an opportunity to present marketing thought and theory issues of importance to the marketing community at large. Currently, the Journal, as most others, seems to have narrowed its focus and prefers publishing only empirically-based articles.

Alderson's strength was to provide a broader and richer view of marketing. Research specialization has fragmented the marketing discipline so much that Aldersonian types have disappeared. The tendency to focus on a narrow set of issues and problems is not unique to marketing. Many other disciplines also have experienced the same phenomenon. When only a micro part of the discipline is known, it becomes more difficult to have a general sense of what marketing is. By the same token, theory development is that much more difficult to achieve.

3.   Alderson and His Contemporaries

Typical of many scholars of the time, Alderson's publications usually contained relatively few references, unlike today where an article usually cites a large number of them. He was an unconventional and creative thinker writing his own material and he did not need to tell his reader who influenced him or where he got some of his ideas. It is the hallmark of an original thinker and few authors today fall in that category. It is no coincidence that such authors are also theorists, more specifically, practicing theorists in search of developing theories, even a general one.

Most of Alderson's writings were single authorship, indicating his preference to work alone. For whatever reason, he seemed to be somewhat isolated from the world of mainstream marketing that existed during his career. His publications did not reflect or build upon the work of his contemporaries (see Bartels, 1962). Yet, during his lifetime, he could not but be influenced by the ideas of others. Many of his closest colleagues were also non-marketers, such as Kenneth Boulding, William Baumol, and Russell Ackoff, among many others. Perhaps Alderson and Sessions, his consulting firm, provided him with sufficient contacts and intellectual stimulation to satisfy his need for marketing theorization and research opportunities.

For most academics, the dissertation advisor is often a person of major influence for the student. Given that Alderson did not experience this process, it is difficult to tell who was the person who most influenced his thinking, or the book that stimulated him the most. For Alderson, there were many. Moreover, Alderson came into the academic world near the end of his life. He had little time to build a solid base of future disciples to continue his work after his death. As the founding father of the marketing theory seminar held from 1951 until his death, he was more likely to be the one who influenced others than be influenced by those present at these annual meetings. As an advocate of the interdisciplinary approach to the study of marketing, many invited scholars at those meetings were non-marketers and included such renowned scholars as Edward Chamberlin and Kenneth Boulding (McGarry, 1965).

Alderson did not accept the marketing wisdom of his time. Notwithstanding the annual marketing theory seminar which be initiated, he did not seem to have that many contacts with established marketing academics of his period, especially with those who did not share his interests in marketing theory development, at least as reflected in the citations of his published writings. His career as a full member of the academic world was short-lived, lasting about six years near the end of his life. He may also have been too busy reading and studying material from non-traditional sources to keep abreast of what his colleagues were doing in academic marketing. For example, the functional approach to marketing was the dominant paradigm of his day (Hunt and Goolsby, 1988). When functionalization in marketing was suggested by Arch Shaw in the mid 1910s, it transformed not only the nature and content of the marketing discipline, but also the way textbooks were written and the way it was taught, until the 4Ps paradigm took over in the 1960s and beyond.

Alderson's marketing functions were of a different type and were fewer in number and broader in scope. They were also purposeful, such as his sorting and searching functions, unlike the functional analysis advocated by many of his contemporaries. In fact, he did not care much for classifying marketing functions as exchange, supply and facilitating. He thought they lacked goal orientation, and they gave the illusion that marketing theory was taking place while in reality all that was done was the listing and classifying of marketing functions. According to Monieson and Shapiro, Alderson viewed the various lists of marketing functions as being of limited value for they lacked

> usefulness to the various behavior systems that conducted marketing operations. His concern was with a view of marketing as a system, how it works and how the system can be made to work better (1980, p. 7).

On the other hand, Dixon felt that marketing functions were more activities than functions, and they could be regarded as sub functions of the functions of marketing "because the relevance of the behavior to the system as a whole is not demonstrated" (1984, p. 13).

Alderson acknowledged that these functions were the beginning of marketing theory development but not the end (Alderson 1957, p. 23). Yet the introduction of marketing functions in the marketing literature in the early part of the twentieth century

> has been hailed as one of the most significant theoretical developments of early contemporary marketing thought. Indeed, it has been compared with the discovery of atomic theory (Jones, 1988, p. 166).

While this may be an exaggeration, Alderson, nevertheless, failed to see that the functional approach enabled marketing to distinguish itself as a science separate from economics. It also contributed toward a greater understanding of the field. It provided a means to analyze distribution costs and measure marketing productivity and provided a better understanding of the institutional structure and organization of channel members. Otteson suggested that "a valid argument might be developed that a student does not achieve complete understanding of marketing without an orderly study of each of its functions" (1959, p. 437). In other words, functional analysis was not simply a listing of functions as Alderson thought; it was analytical and useful to managers and to students of marketing. Let us not forget that the 4Ps are really nothing more than marketing management functions, albeit simplified and reduced for pedagogical and managerial purposes.

4.   Alderson and Marketing Textbooks

After the 3rd edition of Marketing (1953, with Alexander and Surface), Alderson's textbooks were no longer pedagogically-oriented and they were more like reference books for the very serious student of marketing. The two theory books he co-edited, along with his discussion of market behavior theory, functionalism, the OBS (organized behavior system), and the functions of searching and sorting made the study of marketing that much more difficult than when presented under the functional approach. After all, the functional and the marketing and the economy approaches simplified the learning process and provided textbook writers with a ready-made table of contents. The material was presented to students in a logical step-by-step way, albeit lacking excitement and glamour.

The functional approach to the study of marketing (as well as the institutional and commodity approaches), were displaced by the modern marketing management approach of the 4Ps about the time Alderson was publishing his last series of books. The marketing management approach (4Ps) was so much more interesting and fun for students. After all, the 4Ps put students in the driver's seat and enable them to act vicariously as VP of marketing responsible for managing the 4Ps. On the other hand, Alderson's two textbooks (1957, 1965) and others in between were not ones that would have excited the typical undergraduate student. The textbooks lacked visual appeals with no colors or illustrations, with few tables and were lacking in pedagogical material such as exercises or questions at the end of each chapter to help students learn the material. Alderson was less in the textbook publishing business to make money but more in the business of developing and disseminating marketing theory.

Possibly his scholarly work would be more widespread today if his textbooks had been better structured to meet the pedagogical needs of marketing students. Unfortunately, Alderson's textbooks are out of print and many libraries do not have access to any of them. The same can be said for his numerous published articles. He is a challenge to study and seems to be in a niche available for serious students only.

5. Alderson and the Practitioner-Academic Interface

Alderson believed that contributions to marketing theory were derived from the interactions of practitioners and academics. It was natural (perhaps expected) for business and academics to interact and for both to develop marketing knowledge for the benefit of all students of marketing, including practitioners. Before he became a marketing professor, Alderson worked for the government (U.S. Department of Commerce), a private firm (Curtis Publishing), and had established his own management consulting firm (an entrepreneur). He had attended meetings, given presentations and actively interacted with numerous well-known academics such as John Kenneth Galbraith, Kenneth Boulding, Edward Chamberlin, C. West Churchman, Russell Ackoff, Reavis Cox, and E. T. Grether.

By the time Alderson officially joined the Wharton School of Business of the University of Pennsylvania in 1959, he had already published at least five textbooks, over forty articles, including eleven in the *Journal of Marketing*, and numerous industry studies as well as his prolific contributions to *Cost & Profit Outlook*, the newsletter he founded in 1947 for the management consulting firm known as Alderson and Sessions. That is quite an accomplishment for a person whose full time academic career began at the age of 59. He was also a past President of the American Marketing Association (1948) and had won the Charles Parlin Award in 1954 and the Paul D. Converse Award in 1955. In brief, his contributions to the marketing discipline had already been firmly established by the time he joined Wharton and he had proven his worth many times over to both the academic world and the business community. His contributions after he joined Wharton were no less significant. Unfortunately, they were never fully realized due to his untimely death in May 1965, only six years after he joined the faculty. One can only imagine what his contributions would have been had he lived longer!

Alderson's academic accomplishments prior to becoming a full faculty member are the exception today rather than the rule. Yet Alderson's career path was not unique during that time frame. Prior to the 1960s, the business community and academics mingled more frequently than is usually the case today, as illustrated by such businessmen as L. D. H. Weld, C. C. Parlin, Paul Mazur, Malcolm McNair, William Davidson, Edward Filene and of course, Arch Shaw, all outstanding marketing scholars. In other words, the development of marketing thought and theory was not considered to be the exclusive domain of academics. The business community was also involved in the academic process, unlike today where the two groups are drifting farther apart, as if they were living in different worlds. This interaction was not unique to marketing and was also evident in other business areas such as finance, credit, accounting, and human relations.

Alderson believed that the task of marketing is a never-ending one due to the dynamic nature of the market. If answers to important marketing problems were to be found, Alderson reasoned that new types of investigations and research approaches were needed, not only to upgrade the existing marketing knowledge of the time but also to generate new developments in marketing theory. Schwartz summarized well the Aldersonian research philosophy:

> The continuing development of marketing science will aid marketing practition-
> ers through the discovery of principles of action and the development of scientific
> techniques for the orderly investigation and solution of concrete marketing prob-
> lems (1963, p. 103) .

Business and academics previously intermingled far more frequently than is now the case. The gulf between the two is currently considered one of academic marketing's major weaknesses, often referred to as the practitioner/academic gap. While a full discussion of this issue is beyond the scope of this paper, it is well known that today's typical marketing academics are far more removed from the issues and problems facing the business community, with fewer interactions than before. Some have actually asked if marketing professors are even relevant today (Peterson, 1995) or if marketing professors really know what marketing is (Morris, 1995).

At least three reports sponsored by the American Marketing Association have recognized this gap problem, as well as many other problems facing marketing education (Myers et al., 1979, AMA Task Force on the Development of Marketing Thought, 1988, Lehmann and Jocz, 1997). No doubt, doctoral education plays a crucial role in the marketing knowledge development process. Yet Peterson (1999) questioned the obvious notion that doctoral programs should teach marketing. If doctoral programs teach material other than marketing per se, than one can be assured that Alderson will not be taught.

The gap problem has reappeared indicating once more that the issue still exists and probably has worsened (e.g. Baker and Holt, 2004, Tapp, 2004). Shapiro's glib "third generation idiot savant" expression captures the gap issue, and illustrates well the type of training and subsequent research orientation many doctoral students in marketing obtain today:

> Twenty-five year old doctoral candidates without any administrative experience whatsoever are often the academic protégés of thirty-two year old professors also lacking real world contact... Existing PhD programs have long been criticized for emphasizing rigor rather than relevance and for graduating model builders who could not make change... With the tendency of business professors to publish a steady stream of increasingly esoteric articles on ever more specialized topics. This procedure guarantees both tenure and an international reputation as a leading authority on next to nothing at all (1982, pp. 2-3).

In brief, why Alderson is no longer studied maybe due in part to the current approach to marketing education and academic research priorities. As explained by Bartels (1983) and others (i.e. Monieson, 1981), what is taught and the nature of research undertaken may no longer reflect issues and problems confronting business. Concomitant with the gap issue is the tendency of the marketing discipline to limit its teaching responsibilities to only a handful of topics, "devoted largely to promotion and merchandising of consumer products" (Bartels 1983, p. 35), while simultaneously permitting traditional areas of marketing to be taught by "those whose domain has been regarded as complementary to marketing" (Bartels 1983, p. 34). Bartels added that the discipline's "product line has through the years been narrowed to that which offered the highest short-term payoff" (p. 35). Additionally, the popularity of business programs has put a strain on finding qualified faculty members to teach marketing courses, such that many schools now depend on part-time faculty and sessional instructors to fulfill their pedagogical obligations.

6. Alderson and the Transformation of Marketing Education

Alderson (and others such as Paul Green, John Howard, Jerome McCarthy and Philip Kotler) spearheaded a movement in the 1950s and 1960s that radically transformed marketing education, with consequences that Alderson never could have imagined. Some of the changes he initiated were very positive, while others actually disrupted the diffusion of his contributions as well as those of many others, thus resulting in fundamental changes in the way marketing is understood and researched.

The 1959 Ford Foundation and Carnegie Corporation reports on business education stated that business education needed to be reexamined (Pierson, 1959, Surface, 1960). The world of business had changed after the Second World War and business education was suffering from

> an interrelated set of deficiencies: low academic standards, low admission requirements, low-caliber students, inadequate facilities, superficial teaching, excessive vocationalism, and a proliferation of specialized courses that have no place in colleges or universities, and a consequent crowding out of the liberal arts and sciences, a neglect of research, and a general atmosphere of stagnation and directionlessness (as quoted in Weil 1962, p. 5).

Moreover, courses were not analytical enough with few focused on developing decision-making skills. Business education was deficient in quantitative methods as well as in the behavioral sciences.

Alderson answered the call to action. His commitment to the behavioral sciences via the interdisciplinary approach was a hallmark of his approach toward the development of better marketing theory. Moreover, soon after he joined Wharton, he became the school's most vocal proponent of management science in order to make marketing more scientific. As argued by Saas (1982, p. 320) "Alderson's genius served as a catalyst in the introduction of advanced quantitative methods and the return of marketing to a practical, technical orientation." Saas added:

> Using mathematical models and quantitative techniques, Alderson would attack such problems as how to analyze consumer tastes, how much to spend on advertising, how big a sales force to maintain, how to allocate salesmen to accounts, and how to apportion marketing messages across media. To enhance the scientific rigor of his program, he brought onto the faculty young scholars who were superbly trained and extremely talented in things quantitative (1982, pp. 310-311).

Alderson's faith in marketing science to solve practitioners' problems is understandable. He made no distinction between academic and practical marketing research. Alderson never admitted of an intellectual gulf separating marketing managers and academicians. Marketing science was useful to both theory development and as an aid for practitioners. Little did Alderson know that Monieson (1981) would argue later that making academic marketing more scientific (i.e. more hypothesis-testing using sophisticated analytical approaches) might not lead toward solving practical business problems. Monieson further added that emphasizing rigor over relevance in research might not contribute much to marketing scholarship to the point that such an approach might actually provide knowledge that would seem to be useless to the practitioner.

Soon after joining Wharton in 1962, Alderson established the Management Science Center. He was the appropriate man to head this new organization, given his previous involvement with ORSA (Operations Research Society of America) and TIMS (The Institute of Management Science). He also played a key role in the creation of MSI (Marketing Science Institute). He was instrumental in the transformation of marketing education from a branch of 'institutional economics' to a more managerial perspective, at least at Wharton (Saas 1982). Obviously, this transformation was not unique to Wharton because many other schools changed their curricula along similar lines but not necessarily in the same time frame. Unfortunately, Alderson died before he had a chance to judge if this approach to marketing education and research proved to be in the best interest of the discipline in the long run.

As the founding father of the interdisciplinary approach to the study of marketing, little did Alderson know that his innovative approach would serve as an impetus for moving marketing education and research away from the economics literature (i.e. from price/cost/profit/competitive considerations), and more into the social sciences (i.e. the social-psychological study of consumers). Unknowingly, Alderson and other marketing scholars of his time started a revolution that would transform both marketing education and academic research priorities in the 1960s and beyond. Marketing went from an economics-based discipline in which the study of the market prevails to a more decision-making behavioral one, where quantitative and measurement skills dominate the study of the consumer's cognitive makeup. These behavioral priorities now seem to be the hallmark of the marketing educational process, rather than a focus on marketing knowledge per se, at least for some aspects of mainstream marketing.

The consequence of this educational transformation was a movement toward hiring many non-marketing trained academics, at least non-trained in the pre-Aldersonian established wisdom (Peterson, 1984, Heritage and Weinrauch, 1984). Of course, a shortage of marketing professors in the 1970s coupled with the more appealing working conditions in schools of business relative to other university departments also attracted this new breed of marketing academic. There is nothing inherently wrong with this practice as long as marketing education does not suffer. But what happens to marketing education when economics and previous accumulated marketing knowledge is deemed secondary to the newly emerging areas of marketing fragmentation and specialization? Alderson also failed to foresee the growing acceptance of the 4Ps paradigm. This pedagogical approach to the study of marketing began to dominate marketing education during his academic career and has become the fundamental approach to marketing education ever since.

Moreover, the 4Ps approach led to a broadened field of marketing — the application of the 4Ps in non-traditional areas — a consequence he could not have anticipated. Broadened marketing fueled a debate about marketing's identity as a business discipline. Bartels (1983) argued that methodology had to some extent replaced substance as the bulk of marketing knowledge. Broadening marketing gave the illusion of marketing expanding its academic wings. In reality, what was expanding was not marketing knowledge or theory development but rather the application of the 4Ps in non-business areas, to the neglect of traditional market issues. Bartels warned that too much broadening would hurt marketing scholarship and marginalize the discipline to the point that marketing might be supplanted by another discipline whose domain would include more of what academic marketing should be. Numerous authors have since voiced their concern about the state of marketing scholarship and the role of marketing in today's business world. For example, Day said:

> Within academic circles, the contribution of marketing, as an applied management discipline, to the development testing and dissemination of strategy, theories and concept has been marginalized during the past decade. . . The prognosis for marketing management based on present trends and past behavior is not encouraging (1992, p. 324).

Brown went much further and said "we continue to be treated with disdain by the hard social sciences, we are little more than the laughing stock among the humanistic social sciences and liberal arts" (1996, p. 260). More recently, Holbrook and Hulbert argued that it is questionable if marketing is needed today and concluded, "Let us therefore give marketing the dignified burial it deserves" (2002, p. 727). Alderson (and many others) would no doubt turn over in his grave upon hearing such brazen comments. In this post Aldersonian era, the understanding of marketing has changed drastically. An analysis of these disturbing and controversial comments cannot be provided here. Academic marketing's raison d'être shifted its focus during Alderson's tenure (as already discussed), with the effects still reverberating today.

Despite one's lack of prior training in the subject area, the 4Ps approach made it a lot easier for anyone to learn and to teach marketing within a relatively short period of time. As a result, the likelihood of being exposed not only to Aldersonian marketing thought but also to many other scholars that preceded him has become increasingly tenuous. The laissez-faire trend in marketing education seems to be accelerating, especially with e-commerce in all its facets (Heckman, 1999, Tapp and Hughes, 2004). Many other disciplines such as law, psychology, and accounting are reluctant to allow those not trained in their respective field to teach. What turned out to be a rather novel and exciting experiment in marketing education, has resulted in a paradigmatic shift in the way marketing is now being taught, researched and understood. If Alderson is no longer known today, perhaps part of the blame can be put on the new approach to marketing scholarship of the 1950s and 1960s, which he so strongly advocated.

7.   Alderson and Marketing History

Marketing thought seminars were once considered essential for the preparation of a scholarly career in marketing. Harold Maynard and Robert Bartels, both at the Ohio State University, are considered to be some of the pioneers in this branch of marketing education. However, with the new breed of marketing academics, there was a slow disappearance of marketing thought and history seminars at the doctoral level. Most marketing history seminars in the 1980s and beyond were replaced by more methods courses, many emphasizing research techniques applied in consumer behavior, as an example. Others focused more on philosophy of science issues of the Kuhnian type, sprinkled with discussion of positivism, relativism, constructivism, empiricism, falsificationism, post-modernism, and other issues.

Few schools in the U.S. now offer marketing thought courses at any level (Kurtz 1997). If current faculty do not know much about Alderson or for that matter know little about the numerous other marketing scholars who have contributed to the discipline since the early part of the twentieth century, marketing education is to blame. Other disciplines pay homage to some of their founding fathers by ensuring current and future generations of students will understand the scholars who helped mold and shape their discipline. For example, Heilbroner's (1999) seminal book on the intellectual contributions of past economists has been a must for students of economics and has helped them understand and appreciate the origin of their discipline. In contrast, the marketing discipline has few disciples of the Aldersonian faith.

Obviously, this book on Alderson is a step in the right direction. It is our modest attempt to pay homage to such an outstanding contributor to our discipline. In fact, this Aldersonian book is the very first ever in the discipline entirely dedicated to the intellectual contributions of a previous marketing scholar. Many other disciplines from sociology, philosophy, psychology, and medicine, and even architecture and engineering, value their founding fathers. This tradition is sorely lacking not only in marketing but also in many other business disciplines. Recently, to remedy this weakness in current management doctoral programs, a group of concerned business professors supported the addition of a history component to the AACSB International standards for business accreditation (Van Fleet, 2004). The proposed change simply wanted students to be exposed to the founding fathers in each of their respective disciplines. In December 2004, however, AACSB declined to make any changes to the current doctoral accreditation standards.

Despite the lack of historical scholarship in mainstream marketing, since 1983, a small group of marketing historians has been holding a bi-annual Conference on Historical Analysis and Research in Marketing (CHARM). This conference led to the creation of the Association for Historical Research in

Marketing, now called the CHARM Association. Similarly, an annual Macro-marketing Seminar since the late 1970s has also led to the formation of the Macromarketing Society, a group which is also interested in marketing history but more importantly, the study of "marketing in society," an area that was also of considerable interest to Alderson.

Marketing historians and macromarketing aficionados are few in numbers relative to more specialized areas of marketing. Membership in these two groups will increase one's chance of being exposed to Alderson as compared to other SIGs such as consumer behavior, advertising, relationship or Internet marketing. CHARM and the Macromaketing Seminar groups cannot ever hope to match the interest and the influence of those academics whose raison d'être reside in other areas of the discipline. The trend in marketing is to view material published more than a decade ago as being ancient history. Marketing knowledge does not accumulate in the same way as in the hard or natural sciences, where new knowledge displaces known facts. The sad consequence is that current marketing scholarship too often reflects what is current or faddish, forgetting that like any other social discipline, marketing has a past and Alderson is a major component of that past.

8.   Alderson and Economics

Economics was important to the development of marketing thought and theory from its early beginning until the 1970s. Prior to the curricula changes in the 1960s and beyond, marketing education had a strong economics orientation, no doubt due to the fact that the founding fathers of the marketing discipline were primarily economists. Moreover, the first professional marketing meetings were under the aegis of the American Economic Association. Bartels concluded "economic theory has provided more concepts for the development of marketing thought than any other social discipline" (1962, p. 195). In addition, economics departments were the forerunners of schools of business. With the new type of academics teaching marketing, it was just a matter of time before mainstream marketing would pay less attention to economics as its main source for thought development and research priorities. With the changing of the guard, economics lost its status in schools of business and eventually those trained in more specialized areas replaced economics faculty, resulting in a paradigm shift for marketing thought development, a shift still evident today.

Alderson was one of the first "new" breed of academics to break free from pure microeconomic theory as the sole basis for marketing thought and theory. Alderson provided the means by which the marketing discipline could evolve from its economics origin in order to secure its rightful place in the realm of the social sciences having its very own set of concepts, ideas, terminology, research approaches and theories. In spite of economics' tremendous contributions to marketing, Alderson was uncomfortable with labeling marketing as 'applied economics.' While "economics had some legitimate claim to being the original science of markets" (1958, p. 15), Alderson felt marketing went beyond the economics of meeting demand because of marketing's impact on society. He added that the economist's theory of the firm could not "satisfy the growing demand for marketing theory" (Alderson, 1950, p. 66). Alderson concluded that, "marketing theory may eventually be recognized as part of the theoretical framework for a general science of behavior" (Alderson, 1964, p. 92).

In his attempt to place marketing more as an applied science of human behavior, Alderson became the first marketing academic of the twentieth century to dwell deeply on the social sciences (mainly sociology, anthropology and psychology). Marketing theory could thus be elaborated upon and/or enriched based on the ideas and concepts derived from the interdisciplinary approach. After all, marketing deals with consumers as people behaving in the market. Economists, on the other hand, tended to study price, quantity or markets, all very important marketing concepts, but lacking in their relationship with every day consumers. To Alderson, marketing was a phenomenon of group behavior where the OBS, one of the corner stones of his theory of market behavior, is engaged in buying, selling, searching, sorting and pricing. The two marketing theory textbooks he co-edited reflected his change in orientation from the use of economics as a means to generate marketing theory (Cox and Alderson, 1950), to more of an interdisciplinary focus fifteen years (Cox et al., 1964).

Grether argued that too much emphasis on the social sciences, to the neglect of economics, was not the answer to marketing scholarship:

> Markets and the market systems, instead of being considered in the environs or outside the playing field, can continue to be the first base. Therefore marketing as a discipline should continue and strengthen its nexus with formal and applied macro and microeconomics, rather than to rush ahead pell-mell into an unjelled social behaviorism (1965, p. 194).

Current academics may have less training in micro and macroeconomics than the previous generation, at least for mainstream marketing. While no study exists, one would find that current doctoral programs no longer require advanced courses in economics (or history of economic thought) as was once required. Likely, the only economics courses students learn are those offered in MBA programs.

This state of affairs may not be all that surprising given the emphasis on the consumer as the center of the universe in marketing education and research. Marketing is suffering from an exaggerated focus on the consumer, a focus Alderson would have disagreed with because he viewed marketing as the study of group behavior (i.e. problem solving for the household), and not of the individual consumer. Moreover, the functioning of any complex modern economy cannot depend exclusively on the consumer. Market participants, such as manufacturers, wholesalers and retailers, also influence and educate consumers and other buyers in the marketplace with their aggressive and omnipresent marketing programs. Thus, the organizational structure of our economic system is more seller-oriented rather than completely buyer-oriented. Why has marketing almost abandoned economics and opted more for other social sciences, mainly psychology and sociology, as its main source for theory development and research focus? The answer lies partly with Alderson as a pioneer contributor to marketing's shift away from economics.

9.   Alderson and Systems Theory

Alderson played a major role in the introduction of systems thinking in marketing, even though systems theory had earlier beginnings. In his market behavior theory, he proposed a systems approach to the behavior of consumers, firms and channels. The formulation of his systems theory came from ecology, functionalism, cybernetics, Austrian economics, microeconomics, statistics, and even philosophy. Systems contributions also came from Edgar Singer, the University of Pennsylvania philosopher who, according to Saas (1982, pp. 326-327), inspired Alderson to define the OBS's organizational structure as well as his survival concept. Chester Barnard (1938) might have had an even greater influence on Alderson.[1]

Systems thinking in the post-Aldersonian era is evident with the works of such authors as Fisk (1967) and Dixon and Wilkinson (1982). It is also embodied in the "modern" marketing concept where the implementation of its two main components (market focus and profits) requires an integrated company approach. Moreover, the marketing mix, marketing planning, consumer decision-making, integrated communications, relationship marketing, vertical marketing systems, and e-marketing, all require a systemic perspective.

Mainstream marketing focuses much of its attention on demand stimulation (advertising and promotion) rather than on physical supply as if distribution were not part of the marketing process. Notwithstanding the integrated communications approach, systems thinking in mainstream marketing has never been widely used for conceptual thinking or managerial action. Much of demand stimulation is managed and evaluated more from a discrete functional perspective rather than from a systemic one. The application of systems analysis did, however, revolutionize logistics and channel management, from the 1960s and beyond. The logistics channel, composed of numerous distribution activities, forms a quasi-closed system with its various parts being interconnected and intertwined. The arrival of the electronic age further crystallized the domain

---

[1] A comparative analysis of Aldersonian marketing thought with Barnard's management contributions would be most interesting.

of logistics which, by its very nature, cuts across numerous functional areas of the firm, including storage, sorting, order processing, billing, packaging, transportation and delivery, production scheduling, purchasing, inventory management, accounting and even sales and customer service. A systemic view led logistics managers to seek the "least" total cost approach to distribution. That is, systems analysis gave rise to the idea that trade-offs between distribution activities could be achieved, through lowered operating costs for the firm as well as for suppliers and distributors, upstream and downstream along the distribution chain (i.e. the transvection). More importantly, these activities could be accomplished while increasing product and service availability and adding customer value.

Systems thinking never really took off in mainstream marketing, except in the channels and logistics areas, where supply chain management now dominates the way many companies manage their operations. Interestingly, logistics and channels management are academic preoccupations outside of mainstream marketing. In fact, Stern and Weitz expressed disappointment in marketing academics' lack of attention to distribution in schools of business, where the majority of schools do not offer a course in channels management. They concluded that no scholar or teacher of marketing today could ignore the major developments taking place in distribution "because they are creating massive new challenges for marketing managers in all organizations" (1997, p. 824). The irony is that the study of distribution at the turn of the twentieth century was what created marketing as a distinct academic field of study a hundred years ago.

Distribution has contributed a great deal to the marketing theorization process and Alderson's market behavior theory emphasizes distribution with its sorts and transformations, routinized transactions, and the transvection. Alderson was one of the first scholars to introduce in marketing the need to manage channel conflict and to seek cooperative strategies among channel partners rather than emphasize competitive behavior, the dominant economic approach toward more efficient resource allocation (Nielsen, 1988). In a sense, Alderson was one of the first in marketing to advocate the formation of strategic alliances and partnerships as a means for the OBS to achieve differential advantage and assure its survival. The literature on strategic alliances is now voluminous not only in marketing and logistics, but also in management, finance, international trade, governments at all levels, and even in NGO administration.

Other theoretical contributions stemming from distribution can be found in vertical integration in marketing (i.e. vertical marketing systems), the depot theory of distribution, the characteristics of goods theory, the theory of functional spin-off, the theory of market gaps, the political economy theory, the principles of postponement and speculation, among many others. Alderson's four sorts (sorting out, accumulation, allocation and assorting) aptly describe the typical marketing work done in wholesaling. But wholesaling, logistics, and channels are located in subject areas considered to be of secondary importance for marketing scholarship today. Those trained in distribution are often puzzled when told that marketing does not have any theories, and that most of marketing's body of knowledge is derived elsewhere. If Aldersonian marketing thought is not well known today, perhaps it is because many of his contributions can be found in areas no longer considered to be fundamental in marketing education and research, except for those in channels, logistics and related areas.

10.   Alderson and the Theory of Market Behavior

A full discussion of Alderson's market behavior theory is beyond the scope of this chapter but can be found elsewhere (e.g. Nicosia, 1962, Hunt et al., 1981, Sheth et al., 1988). His theory will be presented here in the context of microeconomics and functionalism, followed by a discussion and appraisal of some aspects of his thinking.

In spite of Alderson's repeated claims that marketing theory is to be found in areas other than economics, he was still very much a marketing economist. Atwater, an invited economist who attended a special AMA session on Aldersonian marketing theory, went further:

> He himself was a first rate economist. Wroe knew and cited more economic theories in his work than any marketing professional before him or since. He also knew psychological theories well, but found them less useful (1979, p. 195).

Much of his understanding of marketing, especially his market behavior theory, is derived from microeconomics. He was a product of the intellectual environment of his time, despite his venture into areas other than economics. For that matter, neoclassical economics dealing with monopolistic competition, as first proposed by Alfred Marshall in the 1890s, then elaborated by Joan Robinson and Edward Chamberlin in the 1930s, has been a fundamental building block of modern marketing management. The marketing manager manipulates the firm's supply function (i.e. the 4Ps) in order to obtain demand (i.e. sales) and the firm reaches an equilibrium state with the market, all notions analogous to microeconomics. Chamberlin (1953, p. 3) provided a detailed description of what amounts to an analysis of the 4Ps. Chamberlin even admitted that he had developed the idea in the 1930s, and Alderson (1957) mentions the marketing mix concept as well. This is a startling revelation, given that the origin of the 4Ps is usually attributed to Neil Borden or to Jerome McCarthy for their work in the late 1950s and early 1960s.

There is no doubt that Alderson was an ardent follower of microeconomic theory because his market behavior theory has an uncanny resemblance to it, albeit with extensive additions and ramifications. As a practitioner-theorist, Alderson was more concerned with helping managers make better decisions than in attempting to build macromarketing theory or to help consumers be better buyers. His theory has links with macromarketing, in sharp contrast with microeconomics, but only on a limited basis mainly due to his emphasis on sorting, searching and the transvection. Alderson's main objective was not to view marketing as a means for society to solve market problems, but

> To present a richer and more suggestive version of the theory of the firm which will provide perspective on marketing problems for the market analyst and the marketing executive (1957, p. 11).

Alderson recognized the importance of a hierarchy of systems such that the output of one system served as the input to a higher order one, and so forth. However, he presented his theory of marketing as a system with no apparent external links to society's other institutions. He did not explore the relation of marketing to other subsystems in society, such as the school, the church, the culture, and the government. His focus was the firm, and the theory failed to link the firm (a small system) to the economy (a larger system). His theory was more micro, that is a managerial theory of the firm, rather than a macro one. Alderson did not fully recognize that marketing as a process affected society's values, attitudes, roles and relationships, and consumption habits. Not only do social institutions affect marketing but these are also affected by marketing, which explains why marketing is often controversial. The marketing process touches upon questions of social responsibility, ecology, culture, values, materialism, and even the productivity of our market economy (i.e. resource allocation).

Alderson viewed technology and innovation as processes within the firm, as part of the firm's entrepreneurial spirit. Of course, inventions can also come from sources external to the firm. Notwithstanding his interest in how innovation is related to marketing, his theory only examined how technology was linked to the firm as an internal process. He therefore did not show how inventions could improve the cost efficiency of the various sorts and transformations because they were external to the firm (i.e. in the market). Additionally, consumer information is also subjected to innovative forces making it easier and less expensive for consumers to search for and acquire information to make purchase decisions. His theory did not show how improvements in existing information sources or the addition of new media could affect search behavior and other market processes.

We also need to add that Alderson neglected to mention other OBSs in society, such as NGOs, advocacy groups and nonprofit organizations. He preferred to limit his attention to traditional market participants. Alderson would have probably been uncomfortable with the broadened marketing movement of the 1970s. Development issues facing poor countries are also not discussed, nor are similar issues within the U.S. economy (marketing to the poor or to other disadvantaged consumers). Thus, his theory is a limiting one and is better suited to one reflecting a U.S.-style free market economy, but only for those having disposable income sufficient to make rational choice decisions. He seemed to avoid discussing the complex realities of a modern capitalistic market economy with its controversial and unequal wealth distribution.

Grether (1965) observed that the state played no part in Aldersonian marketing, such that unfair trade practices, misleading advertising, monopoly formation, price discrimination, and many other uncompetitive market practices that impact on the efficiency of a modern society and on distributive justice were absent from his discussion. Major legal requirements of a market transaction in a free and democratic society, such as the importance of transaction rights, property rights and individual rights, were also unexplored. His notion of marketing as a system in an ecological framework (i.e. evolution) had little to do with today's concern with protecting the environment, conserving energy and resources and reducing waste (i.e. ecological marketing).

However, in all fairness to Alderson, this was a period of rising living standards, where increases in consumption were viewed as beneficial to the economy and the key to wealth creation and happiness. More importantly, there was an unfettered faith in the ideals of a U.S.-style market economy, which made it all possible. Alderson, like many of his contemporaries, was a firm believer in a free market system with the state playing a minimal role. Too much government was not good for the economy, a philosophy still evident in the U.S., in marked contrast to many other nations of the world.

11.   Alderson and Market Information

One of Alderson's famous statements is that the market is cleared by information, and not by price adjustments in supply and demand conditions, as was assumed by economists. Alderson's key point was that reducing information to price was not satisfactory in explaining market behavior. There is heterogeneity on both sides of the market, and not the homogeneity assumed in microeconomics. Alderson attributed market imperfections to a failure in information between buyers and sellers. Sellers cannot always find buyers for their products and buyers cannot always know what is available. Consequently, some goods go unsold and some wants go unfulfilled. Alderson believed that this mismatch could be corrected with information.

The importance of information in Alderson's market behavior theory reflected the reigning economic philosophies of his time. It was the era of interventionist economists such as Paul Samuelson and John Maynard Keynes. They advocated government-imposed instruments to shape the direction of the economy. In the same spirit, Alderson's "interventionist" approach believed that firms could plan their marketing activities better and consumers could better plan their purchases if only they had enough information. Thus, the mismatch (i.e. a market failure) could be overcome if only sufficient information were available on both sides of the market. It should be noted that Alderson's theory is a seller's oriented one, that is more managerially-based, such that information for managers was more of a concern than consumers having access to information.

Yet, other economists, such as Ludwig von Mises and Friedrich Hayek, argued that in a market economy, it is almost impossible for both buyers and sellers to have enough information to make rational purchase decisions. Buy and sell decisions emerge not only on the basis of price but also because of many other factors that are often beyond anyone's ability to understand, let alone predict. The capacity to understand let alone control complex interdependent systems, such as a market system, is rather limited, even today. We now see why Alderson considered information to be so vital in his market behavior theory. He simply accepted the economic wisdom of the time. Nevertheless, it is unclear why he had such faith in the value of information given his penchant for Austrian economics when some of its most ardent supporters, such as Hayek and von Mises, did not believe it was the only means by which market behavior and market processes could be explained.

Information is a much more complex process in society than assumed by Alderson. Even perfect information will not necessarily result in a sale, as assumed under pure competition, unless consumers have access to the product (time and place constraints) and the means to buy. Too much information may actually dissuade buying. How much information is needed is still a moot question in marketing. Moreover, only part of the information comes from market sources. Alderson did not discuss the role played by other information sources or the interactions that take place among and between them (e.g. friends and family, church, school, reference groups, media and government). Neither did he specify how information could increase the efficiency of sorts and transformations. Besides, information by itself, even if price is considered a piece of information, will not result in a market transaction unless followed by a legal transfer of ownership rights from the seller to the buyer.

12. Alderson and Functionalism

Functionalism, a social science paradigm, was the source of some of Alderson's theoretical foundations. Moreover, microeconomic theory is also functionalist. Alderson stands out as the marketing scholar who introduced the functionalist paradigm into marketing, even though it was prevalent in other social sciences (e.g. psychology, anthropology and sociology). The use of the term functionalism, even by Alderson himself, no doubt has confounded many scholars who have attempted to understand his theoretical contributions to marketing. As discussed by Hunt (1991, pp. 68-75) and Fraedrich (1987), the logic of functionalism and functionalist explanation can be complex and confusing, requiring multiple explanations and as well, raising ontological and epistemological issues, among other concerns. As previously discussed, few in mainstream marketing today know much about Alderson, let alone about functionalism, which was the source of some of his ideas. Moreover, functionalism in the social sciences lost its academic appeal as a social paradigm because it viewed social structure as being too fixed within a given social order.

It is best for this chapter to avoid a detailed discussion on functionalism. Suffice it to say that functionalism is not a theory but a means by which a theory can be structured, similar to the manner by which Alderson elaborated his market behavior theory. Thus, we cannot refer to Alderson's functionalism anymore than we can refer to Shelby Hunt's logical empiricism, as if Hunt had a special "brand" of logical empiricism. Alderson's use of the term may have contributed to this erroneous conclusion. Additionally, the marketing discipline has a history of using terms or expressions borrowed from other disciplines and giving them different meanings. For example, functionalism for Nicosia represented an important step in the evolution of marketing theory because it "effectively merges and broadens the commodity, institutional and functional approaches" (1962, p. 406) to the study of marketing. Was functionalism in other disciplines a rallying point unifying other study approaches, as was allegedly the case for marketing?

To add to the confusion, institutionalism or the institutional approach has been employed in marketing to refer to something other than its meaning in other social sciences. If the term 'functionalist approach' was used when referring to Alderson rather than 'functionalism,' perhaps that would help reduce the confusion. Moreover, some scholars confuse functionalism with the functional approach to the study of marketing (i.e. the marketing functions). To make this distinction, Bartels proposed the term 'functionism.' The systems perspective is an integral part of functionalism but not of the functional approach (functionism) and for a good reason. The marketing functions were proposed in the early part of the twentieth century, decades before systems theory had yet to be introduced not only in the social sciences but in the marketing literature as well. Finally, too much is made of functionalism in Aldersonian marketing, often leading to a long discussion far removed from his market behavior theory and its contributions to marketing thought.

Notwithstanding his long introduction to micro and macrofunctionalism in his 1965 book (Alderson 1965, pp. 1-22), perhaps it is far simpler to go back to his 1952 explanation that functionalism was just another name for studying the problem solving behavior of consumers (Alderson 1952, p. 120). In general, he viewed the functionalist approach as a means to study and understand market and marketing processes. The study of market processes such as competition, pricing, consumer motivation, channels of distribution or advertising could all be studied from a functionalist perspective. He also acknowledged that his functionalist approach was not tied to a particular body of thought (i.e. a discipline) but was by definition eclectic and called for the interdisciplinary approach. Functionalism for Alderson was fundamentally problem-oriented. If a solution to a market problem was to be found, Alderson would ask what is the market process underlying the problem and what is its purpose? In other words, "the functionalist in marketing engages in the study of systems with the aim of understanding how they work and how they can be made to work better (Alderson 1964, p. 106).

Some aspects of his "functionalist" theory will be briefly discussed and some of their limitations shown. Alderson's market behavior theory viewed marketing as a biological system, which acts in harmony (or in equilibrium) with its environment until disruptions from outside the system force the organization to change and adapt to new competitive conditions. Adaptation is an internal process that enables the OBS to reach a new equilibrium with the environment and achieve a homeostatic state for survival. Of course, competitive forces result in a constant struggle to find the right differential advantage that will allow the OBS (here the firm) to maintain, increase, or develop its niche in the market. In microeconomics, competition is the force that guarantees resource allocation optimization.

Alderson's contribution was to add cooperation, as previously discussed (Nielsen 1988). Economics stressed goal attainment through optimization, as in profit maximization. Alderson also believed in optimization, but his pragmatic side favored a more realistic approach to decision making in the real world. The search for optimization is what counted for Alderson, and not actually achieving it. That is why there was always room for improvement in marketing decision-making and Alderson believed the search for better ways to market was a never-ending task for the manager. Alderson was a believer in the Darwinian survival of the fittest (evolutionary theory) with survival coming from within the organization. In modern terms, the firm is continuously adjusting its resources via the 4Ps in order to seek harmony with the environment. Of course, some limitations exist because the firm cannot always use the differential advantage mechanisms he outlined (such as market segmentation, product innovation or product improvement, or promotional appeals) which would enable the firm to adjust its internal structure in order to respond to market disruptions.

Many situations exist where achieving differential advantage by internal means will either not be possible or may not be the only methods available. Mergers and acquisitions, hostile takeovers, outsourcing, new state and foreign laws, selling of assets or subsidiaries, R&D partnerships, or the purchase of patents must also be considered. The firm simply cannot control all of the exogenous factors that may impede its ability to make decisions and survive. Modern management principles would even argue that the firm could influence its own competitive environment by lobbying efforts, trade group alliances, political contributions, public relations efforts and so forth.

Finally, Alderson did not explore the interactions between the firm and its environment. For Alderson, the environment simply existed out there and was treated as a constraint for the rational manager. Such external factors were of analytical interest only when they impacted the efficiency and effectiveness of the firm and its need to survive. The kinds of competitive environments (stagnant, disruptive, or turbulent) or the typology of environments (micro and macro) were unknown concepts at the time he formulated his theory. Most modern marketing and (strategic) management textbooks usually devote chapters discussing the various components of the microenvironment (e.g. competition, resellers or buyers) and the macroenvironment, as in PEST, a mnemonic expression for classifying the macroenvironment (e.g. political, economic, social and technological).

13.   Alderson and the Sorting Process

Alderson's sorting process with its four sorts are considered to be one of marketing's major functions (the other being searching) and represented the marketing system as a complex series of distribution activities in the economy. Marketing is to Alderson a process that begins with meaningless resources in their natural state and ends with meaningful heterogeneous assortments in the hands of final buyers. The sorts refer to the necessary work required to bring raw materials (e.g. iron ore) or goods in their natural state (fish, trees, and agricultural products) having little or no economic value to where such goods are in demand by industrial users or households. The sorts are also subjected to various transformations (time, place, form), in which successive OBS channel members add value on their way to final consumers.

Alderson used the fundamental notions of market supply and demand, combined them with economic utility theory and arrived at his vision of the role of marketing in the economy. Of course, searching is an important function because as goods move through the distribution system on their way to the consumer, not only is information required (the searching function) but a matching function one between buyers and sellers as well. The sorting, searching and matching occurred on both sides of the market (supply and demand), according to Alderson, unlike the prevailing economic wisdom of the time, which focused almost exclusively on the supplier side.

For Alderson, marketing was essentially a sorting process, with four sorts arranged in a sequence. Alderson (1957, p. 201) stated that each of the four sorts (sorting out, accumulation, allocation and assorting) occurred most frequently in that order. He then said that sorting out, the first sort, could also be grouped with assorting, the last sort, depending on "the qualitative aspects of collections." Logically, accumulation should precede sorting out. After all, if supplies need to be broken down in categories, there is a need to have an accumulation of supplies in order to achieve the required classification. Assorting should be the last sort, as Alderson stated, because of its close proximity to buyer's needs. The conclusion is that the sequence priority of each sort is not set and, on the following pages, Alderson discussed various market problems associated with each sort.

His discourse on the functioning of each sort is one of the longest chapters in the 1957 book. For some unexplained reason, his presentation lacked reference to any previously discussed ideas or concepts pertaining to the sorting process. If previous market processes similar to his sorts had been presented, perhaps a better understanding of his sorting process would have ensued along with a greater appreciation of the market problems of each sort. The only hint given was on p. 200 and in particular on p. 227, when Alderson said:

> The earliest treatment of sorting as an economic function is apparently the cited article by Shove. He recognized the problem of heterogeneity on both the demand side and the supply side of the market.

Alderson thus credits Shove (1930), a British economist, for having inspired him to develop his sorting process. However, a study of Shove's article did not reveal much and only one line in that article (p. 99) was found to be somewhat related to the sorting process. If it was not Shove who influenced him, then who did?

To answer this question, we need to consider why the four sorts were not even discussed in conjunction with the traditional marketing functions. After all, the sort processes are intimately linked with distribution. Arch Shaw said, in the 1910s, that marketing was matter in motion, which links the sorting process with distribution activities. The supply functions, such as bulk making and bulk breaking, are part of the sorts, while others are facilitating ones, such as grading and standardization. Moreover, other supply functions indicate that products need to be packaged, packed, wrapped, bundled, crated, braced, assembled, stored, warehoused, loaded, unloaded, shelved, and displayed. Yet no mention is made by Alderson of any of these existing market processes.

Alderson also failed to mention the Clark and Clark (1942, pp. 4-7) marketing functions of concentration, equalization and dispersion. He also did not refer to the functions of collecting, sorting and dispersing proposed by Vaile, Grether and Cox (1952). With all due respect to Alderson, many of these functions reflect similarities to his sorting process and the four sorts. It is unfortunate that he did not show how and why his four sorts were better or more advanced market processes for explaining marketing than the functions suggested by others. To this day, it is still unclear exactly where his four sorts fit with the functions proposed by others.

Apart from this shortcoming, this author fortuitously obtained one reference source not cited by Alderson. An unpublished paper written by Mertes (1971) presented sufficient evidence to conclude that Vaughan (1942), a University of Oklahoma marketing professor, influenced Alderson. Mertes met Alderson at the annual meeting of the AMA in December 1949, at the Waldorf Astoria in New York City. The two discussed Vaughan's work and Mertes added that Alderson thought the Vaughan book did not get the academic attention it deserved because it was published during the Second World War. Thus, Alderson was familiar with Vaughan's work. Mertes concluded:

> Alderson knew of this work that was to become the intuitive springboard in his concept of matching and sorting. Alderson pursued the idea that sorting enhanced the utility of an assortment. He used the word supply in the same sense as Vaughan to refer to 'a collection of identical or similar products' (1971, p. 9).

A close examination of Vaughan's book revealed that indeed, Chapter 3 "Rearranging" (1942, pp. 39-49), presented some basic ideas of Alderson's sorting process. Unlike Alderson, Vaughan's approach was based on the traditional list of marketing functions but presented in a rather novel way. His terminology was also unique, similar to Alderson's. For example, Vaughan used terms such as rearranging, assembling, dividing, redividing and reassembling. These terms seem to have some similarity with Alderson's sorts.

However, the depth and breath of Alderson's description of each sort is far more complete and richer than Vaughan's treatment of the material. For one thing, Vaughan did not combine various transformations with the four sorts, as Alderson did. Moreover, Vaughan considered assembling to have both legal and physical aspects (p. 39), while Alderson discussed transactions as changes in ownership separate from the sorts or even the various transformations of time, place or form.

Unlike Alderson, Vaughan's practical market experience was in the marketing of agricultural products. Vaughan had intimate knowledge of the distribution of agricultural products from their points of origin at the farm to their destination to ultimate consumers. He had a working relation with such groups as the California Fruit Growers Exchange, the American Fruit and Auction Association, the Chicago and Kansas Boards of Trade, and others. His consulting work enabled him to theorize about the rearranging process, which was made up of assembling and dividing, his version of the sorting process. Similar to Alderson, Vaughan argued that "some products require more assembling and dividing than others" (p. 47). He added that producers engage more in assembling their products than in the dividing process. Similar to Alderson, Vaughan argued that the sequence of his stages was not set:

> The number of steps or stages in rearranging varies greatly as between commodities, enterprises, places, and periods of time. Between the producer and

consumer some products require no rearranging, while others are assembled and reassembled, then divided and redivided (1942, pp. 42-43).

The last quote has some notions of the transvection, even though no mention was made of the various transformations required along the steps. Vaughan was also very concerned about market efficiency and of the need to limit the number of stages if costs were to be lowered. This is analogous to Alderson's notion of an optimal set of sorts through which an increasing volume of transactions could be executed at the same or lower cost. It is interesting that Vaughan did not refer to his market processes as marketing functions as was done by most other textbook writers. He always referred to them as 'functions of marketing,' similar to Alderson's functions of marketing of sort and search.

It begs the question as to why Alderson provided an obscure reference from a non-U.S. author and not Vaughan for the initial idea of the sorting process. The answer will probably never be known. This lapse in memory in no way diminishes the value of Alderson's sorting process for his explanations far outweigh Vaughan's initial attempt. For that matter, Reekie said that Alderson's sorting process was "simply Menger's movement from higher to lower order goods" (1984, p. 110). Carl Menger was a nineteenth century economist and one of the founding fathers of the Austrian school of economics. There was no evidence, as Reekie pointed out, that Alderson had ever read Menger's 1871 *Principles of Economics*.

Market behavior à la Alderson involves a host of requirements other than just sorting, searching and matching that were not discussed, unless assumed under ceteris paribus. These include access to market information, good transportation facilities such as roads, water, air, and railway, availability of warehouses of all types, sufficient disposable income, the presence of media channels of all types, access to banking services and credit, and the rule of law needed for the proper transfer of ownership rights. Some have questioned Alderson's sorts as lacking behavioral content. Any OBS is goal-oriented by definition, and the sorts are always arranged for the purpose of satisfying buyer needs at any level. Some of the sorts can be intervening (i.e. repeated) on their way to the consumer. Moreover, an intervening sort must follow every transformation in time, form or space of a product.

The repeated nature of sorts prompted Alderson to favor routinized transactions because of their cost saving potential. He borrowed John Commons' (1934, p. 365 and p. 632) ideas of seeking fully negotiated transactions (change in ownership) because the time and effort saved could now be better spent on improving the efficiency and effectiveness of the various sorts and transformations. Alderson realized that transactions were not costless, as assumed in microeconomic theory. He may also have been the first marketing scholar to recognize TCA (transaction cost analysis) in marketing. This is not very surprising, given his award winning studies in distribution cost analyses done much earlier, at the time he worked for the U.S. Department of Commerce.

14.   Alderson and the Transvection

The transvection is one of Alderson's remarkable contributions to marketing. It is a simple concept that describes a rather complex process. A transvection is one in which a series of transactions (changes in legal ownership through a sale) and transformations (changes in sorts and other transformations: place, time and form) take place in the market to meet buyer needs, from points of production to points of consumption. In modern terminology, a transvection can be analogous to both an industry's supply chain as well as a firm's supply chain. A supply chain for some firms can be very complex, especially for those selling hundreds of thousands of products, as is the case for certain manufacturers, wholesalers, and retailers. Analyzing a transvection from an industry's perspective seems to be more logical and appropriate than from a firm's point of view (going from the macro to the micro), a perspective ignored by Alderson.

He simplified the transvection as if it were for a single product. But even for a single product destined to consumers, many sorts and transformations requiring the supply of other components or sub-assemblies could occur along the way to final buyers. Another point deals with the wide range of channel participants. Given that all transvections are part of an industry, how does one define an industry, a topic not covered by Alderson? Even today, the definition of an industry is no easy task. A firm selling tens of thousands of products, some outsourced and some produced and sub-assembled in a multi-plant arrangement, will necessarily belong to many industry groups. How one then selects the appropriate set of products, competitors, buyers, or resellers for a particular transvection is still unclear, even under Porter's competitive model.

Moreover, Alderson did not consider an internal transvection, as in the case of a vertically integrated firm performing some of the sorts and transformations. A transvection is by definition, both internal and external to the firm, even in a vertically integrated firm, again a point not made explicit by Alderson. The participation and cooperation of other channel participants, however minimal, is a sine qua non in channels. Consequently, the transvection needs to be linked with many other OBSs, which in turn could then be further linked to the whole of the economic system. The micro vision of his theory prevented him from linking the sum of all transvections to the overall economy, a formidable task both then and even now.

The task of linking a simple market transaction to the overall organizational structure of the economy and society was left to Donald Dixon, one of the leading marketing theorists of the post Aldersonian era. In his seminal 1984 article, Dixon elaborated on Alderson's theory and combined it with Parsons' view of society, to suggest a general theory of macromarketing from a social systems perspective, in contrast to Alderson's more micro marketing theory (Dixon, 1984).

Following microeconomic theory, a transvection can have an optimum number of sorts and transformations if costs cannot be decreased either by increasing or decreasing steps. A cost analysis of the various sorts and transformations could point out which ones could be eliminated or added to improve efficiency. Of course, such cost analyses are possible in theory but not necessarily in practice because of the difficulty of identifying the appropriate channel members of the industry, among other reasons. Many channel members lie outside the influence of the firm and these cannot be controlled in the same way a firm manages its internal operations.

More importantly, Alderson's view of achieving distribution efficiency by costs alone is rather unrealistic. Channel efficiency and organization not only depend on costs, as assumed in microeconomics. Many other factors affect channel structure and channel organization such as the nature of the market, buyer type, product characteristics, the firm itself, competition, labor and state laws, and contracts, among others. Alderson either assumed ceteris paribus, or he did not take into consideration all of the uncontrollable factors in the macro and microenvironments that constrain a manager's ability to make optimum channel decisions. In fairness to Alderson, understanding channel structure and organization is one of the most complex topics of modern business.

Finally, Mallen (1977) argued that the term 'sorting out' as one of Alderson's four sorts and part of the sorting process created some semantic confusion. Perhaps the three functions of marketing as presented by Vaile, Grether and Cox (1952), collecting, sorting and dispersing, may be easier to understand from a pedagogical perspective than Alderson's sorting process. Economic theory recognized allocation as the only sort while Alderson felt that his four sorts, which included allocation, were more relevant to the economy than the simple process of allocation as described by economists.

Alderson's market behavior theory uses a vocabulary of new and unusual terms not seen anywhere else. It is not so much his writing style that has hindered greater access and understanding of his theory but his vocabulary. Despite some of those shortcomings, what he did was to present known concepts in economics and gave them new meaning, more from a marketing perspective than an economic one. His unique vocabulary may explain in part why the proposed research agenda for his market behavior theory, which consisted of 150 propositions, did not generate much subsequent research interest to test them (1965, chapter 15). His late arrival in the world of academia and his untimely death may also have contributed to this lack of interest.

15.   Alderson and Marketing Organization

Apart from borrowing heavily from microeconomics, Alderson was also into the sociology of marketing and how the OBS is organized, that is the firm's internal organizational structure. This is somewhat analogous to what some now call "internal marketing." This aspect of his market behavior theory is not often mentioned in the literature. One of Alderson's premises was that function determines structure, that is, an OBS's organizational structure is related to the functions it performs. In order for an OBS to perform its economic activities (i.e. its functions of sorting and searching), appropriate relational structures must be in place. Alderson recognized a number of relational structures such as power, communication, control mechanism (internal/external adjustments), and operations (input/output). Their functioning needs to be understood in order to achieve efficiency and effectiveness (performance structure), as well as the requirements for organizational survival and growth, which are implicit goals of the OBS.

Of course, such a view of the marketing process is what we would refer to today as the sociology of organizations, part of organizational behavior and/or organizational theory (OB/OT), discussed extensively in the strategic management literature. No doubt Alderson borrowed these views of an organization from Chester Bernard, one of the leading management theorists of the period. Is this premise still valid today? Is the structure of an organization related to its success in the marketplace or its level of profitability? Are the functions of an organization only concerned with sorting, searching and matching? That would depend, of course, on the type of organization. The distributive trade sector of the economy relates well to Alderson's functions. But that is not necessarily the case for financial or professional services organizations such as banks, marketing research firms, advertising agencies, consulting or legal firms where the application of the sorting process, transformations or even the notion of a transvection are more difficult to conceptualize.

The structure of organizations today is a far more complex process than fifty years ago, due to the larger scale of operations and multiple organizational units ranging from world headquarters, to regional, national and local divisions. The extent of world trade, the larger number of products and markets of any one firm, mergers and acquisitions, these and other factors have drastically changed the nature of organizational structure. The relation between function and structure and the types of relational structures Alderson proposed may be too simplistic with respect to the need of the organization to exploit existing markets, to seek new opportunities, to innovate, to introduce new technologies and to establish new procedures and policies. In brief, an organization needs to change and adapt much faster today due to the ever-changing market conditions.

16. Alderson and Rational Consumer Behavior

A functionalist approach to consumer motivation, according to Alderson, assumes that the consumer is a problem solver with limited resources faced with making a choice among alternatives, consistent with some objective. The consumer needs to be convinced that the offer will solve his or her market problem. Alderson's view of consumer behavior was derived from microeconomics and assumed rational decision-making as consumers sought to maximize their utilities. Alderson (1957, pp. 232-33) argued that consumers allocate purchases according to the marginal theory of consumer behavior. In other words, he accepted the principle of diminishing marginal utility. This makes sense in theory, but in practice, the consumer does not always have access to all the information, time and costs involved in making the calculations required to optimize choice. It would just be too inconvenient, if not impossible. At the time of developing his theory, the modeling of consumer (or managerial) decision-making using a decision science approach was just beginning.

An understanding of consumer information processing was in its infancy. As such, we cannot blame Alderson for drawing on established economic theory to understand consumer behavior. The act of purchase, and that act alone was considered to be evidence of how consumers behaved. Alderson, on the other hand, argued that a sequence of behaviors motivated consumers to buy and underlay the act of final purchase. This view of buyer behavior is far closer to current theory where the act of purchase is considered to be the last step in a hierarchical series involving internal cognitive processing (i.e. exposure, attention, comprehension, retention, behavior, post purchase behavior). Alderson's steps are more action-oriented (overt behavior) than cognitive ones. Nevertheless, he needs to be recognized as the first author in marketing to consider the consumer as a problem solver and a learner engaged in a purchase decision process, notions which now overlay much of consumer research.

One of the serious flaws in Alderson's theory of consumer behavior is his suggestion that the problem solving activities of the housewife were largely similar to those of a rational industrial purchasing agent, and that up to two-thirds of U.S. families behaved in this matter (Alderson 1957, pp. 179-181). We know that Alderson understood the difference between industrial and consumer marketing as a result of his own consulting experience and writings (i.e. B2B vs. B2C). However, his buyer behavior theory did not clearly distinguish between the two, leading to the conclusion that his theory is more B2C than B2B.

Following his penchant for consumer rationality, Alderson went so far as to propose to practitioners that the use of rational appeals were much more effective than emotional ones when communicating with consumers, a point well summarized by Schwartz:

> The consumer is a rational problem-solver, advertising copy which regards the consumer as a creature of habit, or as having emotions which influence her buying decisions is relatively less effective in producing sales than advertising which informs and persuades the consumer buyer of the importance of certain needs and the efficacy of certain products and brands in satisfying needs (1963, p. 113).

Alderson felt that consumers based their purchase decisions more on functional features than on emotional ones. Perhaps his suggestion might be more valid in B2B, but not necessarily so in B2C. If he were to make such a recommendation to advertisers today, his views would most certainly be rejected. His understanding of advertising goes against not only current advertising research (both academic and practical), but also the advertising shown in all media. No matter the type of goods or their prices, consumer goods today are sold more as symbols and emotions, through aural, visual and sensory stimulation, and less on functional features and economic performance factors. Alderson would be uncomfortable with the current emphasis placed on brand perception and brand equity. He would no doubt disapprove of the heavy emphasis placed in consumer research on information processing and cognitive modeling of the consumer.

To Alderson, the informational content of advertising was more significant to consumers than appeals based on symbolism. While he accepted that consumers had non-rational motives when making purchases, he felt uneasy with some of the prevailing approaches to the study of consumer behavior such as motivation research, Freudian psychology and other psychoanalytical theories. Alderson's understanding of how advertising worked on consumers was too rational and reflected his economic bias. Advertising is considerably more than an information search process for consumers. Alderson's interdisciplinary approach to the study of the advertising process was not followed to the same degree as he had studied other marketing topics. Advertising has a rich history and over the years, an understanding of this influence process has preoccupied and intrigued both academics and business people.

Alderson's focus on the value of information content is also tied to his view of the family (i.e. the household) as the fundamental unit of analysis in consumer research. He viewed the household as a basic unit of consumption, an economic OBS through which society satisfies its needs. In other words, his functionalist approach to consumer motivation viewed the structure and functions of the household as the deciding factors of consumer buying. Today, the emphasis in consumer research is on studying individual consumers' purchase choice decisions (i.e. the buying process) and not those of the household. Moreover, the behavior of consumers is not really studied, as would be the case in consumption research. What is studied is consumer buying, that is the analysis of cognitive or mental processes leading to purchase choice. Consumer research for Alderson was more oriented toward consumption research (i.e. panels, dairies and shopping situations), a focus others shared with him at the time.

Alderson's focus on the family led him to believe that family purchase decisions and those of individual family members were the same. The study of the organization of household units is what mattered to Alderson and not the cognitive structure and organizational map of individual members of the family. Not surprisingly, Chester Barnard shared similar views with respect to organizational goals and goals of individual members. As Nicosia (1962, p. 406) explains:

> An ecological system comes into being and persists as long as its members satisfy their individual goals. Thus Alderson denies the existence of group or system goals apart from the goals of each member.

Yet, family and individual product choices often cannot be treated as equivalent decision situations. He was preoccupied with developing a topology of families because the structure of a family unit (an OBS) was related to the functions it performed in marketing, i.e. its goals (Alderson 1957). His family topology was based on family income levels and not on the plurality of family structures. Alderson did not foresee the demographic changes that were beginning to take place in the U.S. economy. After all, the family arrangement of the husband at work and the wife minding the home and caring for the children was a cultural icon during his time.

After the Second World War, dramatic changes in family organization such as the rise in the number of one-person households and the increasing participation of working wives, working mothers, and of women in general in the labor market began to occur. These demographic changes along with the rise in the divorce rate substantially reduced the role and importance of the traditional stay at-home housewife as the sole purchasing agent for all family members. Moreover, Alderson could not have imagined the rise in importance of the children and young adult markets, as well as the growth of the preteen market (the 'tweens' market) with children now having considerable disposable income to spend on goods and services.

In an Aldersonian world, a household, an OBS, acts in a rational problem-solving manner and is viewed as making product assortment decisions from an economic theory perspective. The purchase is made not in isolation but in the context of an existing household assortment of goods. Any new purchase needs to fit in with an existing assortment such that the new addition will maintain (replenish) or increase the potency of assortment, that is, it will benefit the household in some future consumption activity. But is that the only reason why consumers buy and accumulate goods? Goods replenishment behavior is obvious for many frequently bought and rapidly-consumed items, i.e. convenience goods. As well, the potency of assortment makes sense for certain purchases such as clothes (color, coordination or style) or household furniture. But not all purchases are made with this in mind, such as gifts, personal items, or impulse purchases.

Alderson never considered the case in which a household may no longer have any use for some products. These goods need to be stored, given away, or thrown away, even when they are in good condition. Product obsolescence of certain goods forces a household to manage living space efficiently. There is a limit on the extent to which goods are allowed to accumulate in a household, beyond which they can reduce the potency of assortment, a case not entertained by Alderson. Besides, a consumer can get tired of a current set of assortments because of changes in taste, boredom, even changes in one's personal appearance (i.e. weight gains or losses). Briefly, the purchase and accumulation of goods for a household or for an individual consumer may be related, to personality factors, to status, or to culture. In other words, it's a far more complex process than the one presented by Alderson.

17.   Final Comments

Alderson's "interdisciplinary, systems-theoretical perspective" to marketing scholarship dramatically changed the very nature of the discipline and its research orientation. Yet he has been all but forgotten in contemporary marketing. Before Alderson, the marketing discipline was somewhat unreceptive to research that lacked immediate practical application. Alderson made marketing theory development more respectable and acceptable and helped elevate the scientific status of marketing. Alderson laid the foundation for the establishment of marketing science as a means to develop or refine marketing theory. Alderson may have been the first to say "we must become more theoretical in order to become more practical."

Most theoretical work that is recognized today appears to be more empirically-based, thus allowing for the use of sophisticated statistical techniques. Alderson would have supported the use of powerful quantitative measurement analyses, but only if such analyses contributed to marketing theory development. His interest would have been more on theory development than on the methodology used to analyze the data. Progress in marketing theory development today is too often intertwined and interrelated with methodology, such that methodology (rigor) takes precedence over theory (relevance) because it is much easier to master the former than the latter.

The world of marketing scholarship has changed drastically since Alderson's contributions to the discipline. The multivariate revolution in the 1970s caught marketing and all of the social sciences by storm. Then came the PC, the Internet and e-commerce. Mainstream marketing has an infatuation with attempts to measure every known marketing phenomenon, as if the measurement itself legitimizes researching the marketing problem at hand. The illusion is that the more scientific marketing is, the more it will be recognized as a legitimate and worthy member of the social sciences, the same goal Alderson sought to achieve by making marketing more theoretical.

The marketing discipline needs more Aldersonian-type thinkers and theorists to deliver marketing from this methodological quagmire. The marketing discipline has not been blessed with world-famous and well-known deductive theorists and philosophers that exist in most other fields of human inquiry, notably in the hard sciences (Isaac Newton, Albert Einstein), in philosophy (Aristotle, Socrates), in economics (Adam Smith, John Maynard Keynes, John Kenneth Galbraith), in the social sciences (Max Weber, Thorstein Veblen, Robert Merton, Karl Polanyi), and even in management (Frederic Taylor, Peter Drucker). These scholars are remembered and are often immortalized in some way by their discipline for future generations of students to honor. Similarly, this book is our attempt both to thank Wroe Alderson for what he has contributed to marketing knowledge, to marketing science and to marketing education, and to try to see that these contributions are again widely recognized and appreciated.

References

Alderson, Wroe (1950). Survival and Adjustment in Organized Behavior Systems. In Cox, Reavis and Alderson, Wroe, editors, *Theory in Marketing*, pages 65–87. Richard D. Irwin, Homewood, Illinois.

Alderson, Wroe (1952). Psychology for Marketing and Economics. *Journal of Marketing*, 17(October):119–135. Paper was originally presented at the second Marketing Theory Seminar August 1952, University of Colorado.

Alderson, Wroe (1957). *Marketing Behavior and Executive Action: A Functionalist Approach to Marketing*. Richard D. Irwin Inc., Homewood, Ill.

Alderson, Wroe (1958). The Analytical Framework for Marketing. In Duncan, Delbert J., editor, *Proceedings: Conference of Marketing Teachers from Far Western States*, pages 15–28, Berkeley. University of California.

Alderson, Wroe (1964). A Normative Theory of Marketing Systems. In Cox, Reavis, Alderson, Wroe, and Shapiro, Stanley J., editors, *Theory in Marketing*, pages 92–108. Richard D. Irwin, Homewood, Illinois.

Alderson, Wroe (1965). *Dynamic Marketing Behavior: A Functionalist Theory of Marketing*. Richard D. Irwin Inc., Homewood, Ill.

Alderson, Wroe and Cox, Reavis (1948). Towards a Theory of Marketing. *Journal of Marketing*, 13(October):137–152.

Alexander, Ralph S., Surface, Frank M., and Alderson, Wroe (1953). *Marketing*. Ginn & Company, Boston, 3rd edition.

AMA Task Force on the Development of Marketing Thought (1988). Developing, Disseminating, and Utilizing Marketing Knowledge. *Journal of Marketing*, 52(October):1–25.

Atwater, Thomas V. (1979). 'Lost' or Neglected Components of a General Equilibrium Theory of Marketing. In Ferrell, O. C., Brown, Stephen W., and Lamb, Jr., Charles W., editors, *Conceptual and Theoretical Developments in Marketing*, pages 184–196. American Marketing Association, Chicago.

Baker, Susan and Holt, Sue (2004). Making Marketers Accountable: A Failure of Marketing Education? *Marketing Intelligence and Planning*, 22(5):557–567.

Barnard, Chester I. (1938). *The Functions of the Executive*. Harvard University Press, Cambridge.

Bartels, Robert (1962). *The Development of Marketing Thought*. Richard D. Irwin, Homewood, Ill.

Bartels, Robert (1983). Is Marketing Defaulting Its Responsibilities? *Journal of Marketing*, 47(Fall):32–35.

Berry, Leonard (1986). 'Dream' of serving AMA educators can become a reality. *Marketing Educator*, 3(Fall):1,5.

Brown, Stephen (1996). Art or Science? Fifty Years of Marketing Debate. *Journal of Marketing Management*, 12:243–267.

Chamberlin, E. H. (1953). The Product as an Economic Variable. *Quarterly Journal of Economics*, 67(February):1–29.

Clark, Fred and Clark, Carrie (1942). *Principles of Marketing*. Macmillan, New York, third edition.

Commons, John R. (1934). *Institutional Economics*. Macmillan Co., New York.

Cox, Reavis and Alderson, Wroe (1950). *Theory in Marketing*. Richard D. Irwin, Chicago.

Cox, Reavis, Alderson, Wroe, and Shapiro, Stanley J., editors (1964). *Theory in Marketing: Second Series*. Richard D. Irwin, Homewood, Ill.

Day, G. S. (1992). Marketing's Contribution to the Strategy Dialogue. *The Journal of the Academy of Marketing Science*, 20(Fall):323–330.

Dixon, Donald (1984). Macromarketing: A Social Systems Perspective. *Journal of Macromarketing*, 4(Fall):4–17.

Dixon, Donald and Wilkinson, Ian F. (1982). *The Marketing System*. Longman Cheshire, Sydney, Australia.

Fisk, George (1967). *Marketing Systems An Introductory Analysis*. Harper&Row, Publishers, New York.

Fraedrich, J. (1987). Marketing Functionalism The Enigma Explained. In Belk, Russell, editor, *Marketing Theory*, pages 376–379. American Marketing Association, Chicago.

Frederick, William (1963). The Next Development in Management Science: A General Theory. *Academy of Management Journal*, 6(September):212–219.

Green, Edward and Redmond, Gomer (1957). Comments on a General Theory of Administration. *Administrative Science Quarterly*, 2(September):235–243.

Grether, E. T. (1965). An Emerging Apologetic of Managerialism?: *Theory in Marketing*, 1964. *Journal of Marketing Research*, 2(May):190–195.

Heckman, James (1999). Everybody's teaching marketing these days. *Marketing News*, 33(October 25):4.

Heilbroner, Robert (1999). *Wordly Philosophers: The Lives, Times and Ideas of the Great Economic Thinkers*. Simon and Schuster, New York.

Heritage, Jeannette and Weinrauch, J. Donald (1984). A Retraining Program of Non-Business Professors: A Case Study for Meeting Excessive Demand for Collegiate Marketing Positions. In Lindquist, Jay, editor, *Developments in Marketing Science, Vol. 7*, pages 216–220. Academy of Marketing Science, Kalamazoo, Michigan.

Holbrook, Morris B. and Hulbert, James M. (2002). Elegy on the death of marketing: Never send to know why we have come to bury marketing but ask what you can do for your country churchyard. *European Journal of Marketing*, 36(5/6):706–732.

Hunt, Shelby and Goolsby, Jerry (1988). The Rise and Fall of the Functional Approach to Marketing: A Paradigm Displacement Perspective. In Nevett, Terence and Fullerton, Ron, editors, *Historical Perspectives in Marketing*, pages 35–51. Lexington Books, Lexington, Massachusetts.

Hunt, Shelby D. (1991). *Modern Marketing Theory: Critical Issues in the Philosophy of Marketing Science*. South-Western Publishing Co., Cincinnati.

Hunt, Shelby D., Muncy, James A., and Ray, Nina M. (1981). Alderson's General Theory of Marketing: A Formalization. In Enis, Ben M. and Roering, Kenneth J., editors, *Review of Marketing 1981*, pages 267–272. American Marketing Association, Chicago.

Jones, D. G. Brian (1988). Origins of the Functional Approach in Marketing. In Shapiro, Stanley J. and Walle, A. H., editors, *Marketing: A Return to Broader Dimensions: Proceedings of the 1988 AMA Winter Educators' Conference*, pages 166–170. American Marketing Association, Chicago.

Kotler, Philip (1997). *Marketing Management: Analysis, Planning, Implementation, and Control*. Prentice Hall, Inc., Upper Saddle River, New Jersey, 9th edition.

Kurtz, David, Velliquette, Anne, Garretson, Judith, Dhodapkar, Subhas, and Olson, Jeanne (1997). An evaluation of the marketing theory seminar in ph.d. programs: Teaching alternatives and future directions. *Marketing Education Review*, 7(Summer):1–15.

Lehmann, Donald and Jocz, Jatrine, editors (1997). *Reflections on the Futures of Marketing, Practice and Education*. Marketing Science Institute, Cambridge, Massachusetts.

Mallen, Bruce (1977). *Principles of Marketing Channel Management*. Lexington Books, Lexington, Massachusetts.

McGarry, E. D. (1965). Wroe Alderson's Marketing Theory Seminar, an Experiment in Higher Education. This unpublished paper, a presentation by Dr. McGarry to the August, 1965 Marketing Theory Seminar, was made available by Dr. Lyndon Dawson.

McInnes, William (1954). A general theory of marketing. Unpublished Ph.D. Dissertation.

Menger, Carl (1871/1950). *Principles of Economics.* Free Press, Glencoe, Il. Translated and edited by James Dingwall and Bert F. Hoselitz, with an introduction by Frank H. Knight.

Mertes, John (1971). Marketing Thought: The Use of Historical Concepts. *Southern Journal of Business,* 7(May):76. Abstract of a paper presented to the Southern Marketing Association, November, Miami FL.

Monieson, D. D. and Shapiro, Stanley J. (1980). Biological and Evolutionary Dimensions of Aldersonian Thought: What He Borrowed Then and What He Might Have Borrowed Now. In Lamb, C., editor, *Theoretical Developments in Marketing,* pages 7–12. American Marketing Association, Chicago.

Monieson, David (1981). What Constitutes Usable Knowledge in Macromarketing? *Journal of Macromarketing,* 1(Spring):14–22.

Morris, David (1995). Do Marketing Professors Really Know Marketing? *Marketing News,* 29(3):4–5.

Myers, John, Greyser, Stephen, and Massey, William (1979). The Effectiveness of Marketing's R and D for Marketing Management: An Assessment. *Journal of Marketing,* 43(March):17–29.

Nicosia, Francesco M. (1962). Marketing and Alderson's Functionalism. *Journal of Business,* 35(October):403–413.

Nielsen, Richard (1988). Cooperative Strategy. *Strategic Management Journal,* 9(5):475–492.

Otteson, Schuyler F. (1959). Marketing. In Pierson, Frank C., editor, *The Education of American Businessmen: A Study of University-College Programs in Business Administration,* pages 423–451. McGraw-Hill Book Company, New York.

Peterson, Robin (1984). Short Retooling Programs Lower Prestige of Marketing. *Marketing News,* 18(July 20):6.

Peterson, Robin (1995). Relevancy of Marketing Professors. *Marketing News,* 29(March 13):2.

Peterson, Robin (1999). Ph.D. Pitfalls Doctoral Programs Should Teach Marketing. *Marketing News,* 33(August 2nd):12.

Pierson, Frank C. (1959). *The Education of American Businessmen. A Study of University-College Programs in Business Administration.* McGraw-Hill Book Company, Inc., New York.

Reekie, W. Duncan (1984). *Markets, Entrepeneurs and Liberty: An Austrian View of Capitalism.* Wheatsheaf Books Ltd., Brighton, Sussex.

Sass, Steven A. (1982). *The Pragmatic Imagination. A History of the Wharton School 1881-1981.* University of Pennsylvania Press, Philadelphia.

Schwartz, George (1963). *Development of Marketing Theory.* South-Western Publishing Company, Cincinnati, Ohio.

Shapiro, Stanley J. (1982). North American Ph.D. Programs: Omissions and Imbalances. In *AACSB Conference on Life Long Learning, March 14-17,* Racine Wisconsin. An invited paper.

Sheth, Jagdish N., Gardner, David M., and Garrett, Dennis E. (1988). *Marketing Theory: Evolution and Evaluation.* John Wiley and Sons, Inc., New York.

Shove, G. F. (1930). The Representative Firm and Increased Returns. *Economic Journal,* 40(March):94–116.

Stern, Louis and Weitz, Barton (1997). The Revolution in Distribution: Challenges and Opportunities. *Long Range Planning,* 30(6):823–829.

Surface, James (1960). The Carnegie and Ford Foundation Studies and Marketing Education. In Hancock, Robert, editor, *Dynamic Marketing for a Changing World,* pages 219–225. American Marketing Association, Chicago.

Tapp, Alan (2004). The Changing Face of Marketing Academia. *European Journal of Marketing,* 38(5/6):492–499.

Tapp, Alan and Hughes, Tim (2004). New Technology and the Changing Role of Marketing. *Marketing Intelligence and Planning,* 22(3):284–296.

Vaile, R. S., Grether, E. T., and Cox, Reavis (1952). *Marketing in the American Economy.* The Ronald Press Company, New York.

Van Fleet, David (2004). Personal communications, October to December.

Vaughan, Floyd (1942). *Marketing Functions, Mediums, Practices, Variations, and Appraisal.* Farrar and Rinehart, New York.

Weil, Rolf (1962). Business Schools Adjusting Focus in Face of Criticism. *Business and Society,* 2(2):4–8.

Chapter 35

WROE ALDERSON'S VISION RENEWED AND REHABILITATED: SOCIAL STRUCTURES AND MARKETING THEORIES*

Alf H. Walle

Erskine College, Due West, South Carolina

Abstract   Wroe Alderson, whose influence peaked in the late 1950s, embraced classic struc-
tural/functional social theory. Around the time of Alderson's death in the 1960s,
however, the homoeostatic (self regulating) nature of the then-dominant models
of the social sciences declined in influence. In addition, the 4 Ps marketing management approach arose as a powerful and unifying orientation within marketing. Due to these developments, the influence of Alderson's structural/functional
model withered. Using Kenneth Boulding's general systems framework, the
value of Alderson's vision and its ability to be rehabilitated are discussed. Because a revised Aldersonian perspective can deal with how social structures
evolve, change, and respond to an evolving world, it has a bright future in marketing theory and practice.

1.   Introduction

The purpose of this paper is to review Wroe Alderson's structural/functional
model and suggest ways in which it can be rehabilitated for use in the 21st
century[1]. The updating that is suggested acknowledges social change, stress,
and conflict. So revised, Alderson's macro structural/functional perspectives
are poised to enjoy a renaissance. As a result of this situation, the time is ripe
for a retrospective analysis of Alderson's contributions with an eye towards how

---

*Many individuals, such as Robert Tamilia and Ben Wooliscroft have helped me and encouraged me regarding
this contribution. While I want to thank them all, I do not want to draw attention away from those such as
Donald Dixon, George Fisk, and Stanley Shapiro who actually knew and worked with Alderson and have
helped me over the years.
[1]Due to space limitations my arguments must be phrased in an abbreviated form. As a result, various topics
(such as the existential tradition) may not be adequately developed. Reference to other work that amplified
the discussion of various topics is provided within the text.

they can be usefully updated and returned to service within marketing theory and practice.

In order to accomplish its goal, this paper begins with a discussion regarding how Alderson was indirectly impacted by 19th century German philosopher Fredrich Hegel as well as being directly influenced by mid 20th century social theory. Having provided this framework, the classic structural/functional framework of the social sciences that formed the foundation for Alderson's work is discussed. The term "structural/functional", as used here, is inspired by the anthropological writings of the 1930s and the term is used to depict the breadth and variation of such perspectives. As will be discussed, in the 1960s classic structural/functional theory became passé as the interest of social science turned away from an examination of stability and cooperation in order to focus upon change and conflict. In tandem with the decline of the classic structural/functional approach, the influence of Alderson's work (that was built upon this model) also faded. In a nutshell, faced with significant challenges in the 1960s, the classic structural/functional approach was unable to adapt to changing intellectual tastes and it was replaced by other alternatives such as the 4 Ps marketing management approach and alternative paradigms, including those that stem from the existential tradition.

This paper argues that, in spite of decades of neglect, Alderson's structural/functional approach can (and should) be updated and invigorated by acknowledging cultural change and the tensions that exist between different social groups. The dynamic structural/functional model that results from doing so will be able to respond to the issues of the contemporary era (such as those that are hinged around conflict and change). As a result, Alderson's vision can be revised, updated, and returned to prominence within marketing.

2.   Hegel and Beyond: An Intellectual Legacy

A good place to begin an appreciative discussion of Wroe Alderson's structural/functional approach is a retrospective analysis of the intellectual influences upon which he based his work. Initially, the indirect impact of 19th century German philosopher Fredrich Hegel is discussed. Hegel's influence upon marketing thought is increasingly being recognized; those desiring a broader discussion of his impact upon marketing are referred to "Fredrich Hegel: Social Structures as Overarching Monolith" (Walle, 2002, pp. 27-41). This analysis is followed by an examination of how classic structural/functional social theory, as it existed in the mid 20th century, influenced Alderson.

An understanding of Hegel and his influence are facilitated by considering the impact of the Enlightenment. Embracing a rational way of viewing the world, the leaders of the Enlightenment assumed that inherently superior strategies of life, culture, and social relationships could be extrapolated through a process of empirical observation and, once discovered, these discoveries could be embraced to the benefit of all mankind. The leaders of the Enlightenment believed that by identifying what we now call "best practices", all people would benefit from universal solutions to the problems of life. The work of these 18th century intellectuals mirrors the perspectives of contemporary marketing theorists such as Theodore Levitt. Thus:

> In some ways,.... [the Enlightenment] is similar to the notion of "globalization" that has been advanced by contemporary marketing theorists such as Theodore Levitt; Levitt theorizes that due to the impact of science and technology all the world's cultures are evolving in homogeneous ways that are destined to reduce cross-cultural variation (Walle, 2002, p. 33).

The legacy of the Enlightenment was eventually challenged on the grounds that because of cultural differences no universal models of social life exist. An early advocate of such an approach was Johann Herder who greatly influenced what came to be called the Avolksgeist perspective which insisted that specific cultures possess a unique spiritual and intellectual ethos. Writing within the marketing literature, Walle (2002, p. 33) has observed that Herder emphasizes that there are no universal models or patterns that can be applied to all human behavior. In contrast, every society/culture possesses a distinctive volkgeist (spirit of the people/national character) and, as a result, it responds in a unique and distinctive manner.

Hegel largely embraced these ideas and he worked them into his vision of culture and society. In doing so, he metaphorically depicted society as a living organism that has a synergistic existence that is bigger, more significant, and longer lasting than its constituent parts (individual people and circumscribed groups). This led Hegel to emphasize the culture as a collective entity and to de-emphasize specific individual components. As is widely recognized, Hegel was influenced by the theories of biology that were emerging in the early 19th century. These models emphasized that living creatures are composed of different parts that cooperate with each other in ways that lead to what we now call synergism. Hegel adopted this perspective as a metaphor that he used when describing and conceptualizing specific cultures. This means of representation has survived into our era (Walle, 2002, p. 30).

As time went on, an emphasis upon the structure of society became institutionalized within the social sciences. The resulting model emphasizes the stability of the social system (when it is operating "normally"). As a result, this kind of analysis does not center upon social stress, tension, and cultural change in order to concentrate upon homogeneity and cooperation. While other models of society and culture might deal with rivalries and competition as a natural state of affairs, the classic structural/functional model is not designed to do so.

The success of this paradigm led to the dominance of models that emphasized the self-regulation and the maintenance/stability of a system. A simple mechanical "homeostatic system" that maintains stability is the thermostat of a furnace or air conditioner that functions to maintain a constant temperature. The thermostat turns the unit on and off in order to keep the temperature within a predetermined range. As a result, stability is maintained.

Homoeostatic models are also useful when studying culture and society. The socialization process, for example, helps the next generation to master the culture and preserve it as an ongoing tradition. Laws and law enforcement methods maintain the equilibrium of society. Institutions, such as religions, help maintain belief and ethical structures over time. Many social and cultural institutions can be usefully viewed from this kind of homoeostatic perspective. Classic structural/functionalism tends to emphasize such modes of analysis. While embracing such an approach is often useful and legitimate, by doing so the focus upon change, tension, and cultural stress is largely eliminated.

3.   Alderson and Homeostatic Social Analysis

In the 1950s and 1960s, largely under the leadership of Wroe Alderson, marketing was greatly influenced by these classic structural/functional theories. Embracing such a focus allowed Alderson (and those influenced by him) to usefully transcend the ad hoc functional orientations of marketing (such as those of Paul Converse, etc.). In accordance with the dominant social theory of his era, Alderson focused upon the macro social system and viewed it as an overarching structure that was typically modeled as a static phenomenon. Although Alderson accepted micro-oriented responsibilities when he worked as a consultant, his scholarly and theoretical work emphasized structural/functional theories that embraced a holistic macro (not a micro) perspective (Alderson, 1957, p. 16).

Besides being structural/functional in nature, Alderson's model was homeostatic and, as a result, he centered upon how systems maintain themselves. In line with the social theories of the era, Alderson's models tend to concentrate upon how the status quo of the social system is maintained through the functioning of its parts. As a result, Alderson's model does not focus upon change, stress, and social tensions, even though he could hardly have been unaware of these phenomena.

Adapting relevant ideas from the leaders of other fields is the usual strategy of cross-disciplinary scholarship; Alderson employed this age-old technique in the usual way by embracing perspectives that mirrored the thinking of the experts from whom he borrowed. This method, while fruitful in the short-term, proved to be a time-bomb that eventually undercut Alderson's work. Around the time of Alderson's death, social scientists became interested in social change, stress, and tension between various groups that were competing for resources. Due to changing scholarly fashions, the intellectual foundations upon which Alderson based his work were rendered passé and his theoretic perspectives fell from favor. Under these circumstances, it is hardly surprising that Alderson and his contributions were quickly neglected except among a minority of marketing scholars, many of whom are identified with the macromarketing subdiscipline.

In a nutshell, Alderson's work is geared towards modeling stability, homogeneity, and cooperation within culture and society. But by the 1960s scholars were becoming increasingly concerned with change, distinctiveness, and tension. Thus, the theories that Alderson championed collided with changing intellectual tastes. This emphasis upon stability and cooperation, for example, is clearly emphasized in writings such as his posthumous *Dynamic Marketing Behavior* (1965) and the work of other scholars who Alderson supported and showcased. As already emphasized, classic social structural/functional theory emphasizes stability and de-emphasizes tensions within the social system. Alfred Reginald Radcliffe-Brown (1935), as others, drew an analogy between a living organism and a society. He observes:

> An animal organism is an agglomeration of cells and interstitial fluids arranged in relation to one another not as an aggregate but as an integrated whole... The system of relations by which these units are related is the organic structure. As long as it lives, the organism preserves a certain continuity of structure.

Such models did not emphasize change or conflict. Radcliffe-Brown (1935) continues:

> Over a period of time its constituent cells do not remain the same. But the structural arrangement of the constituent units of the organism does remain similar... The life of the organism is conceived as the functioning of the structure.

Although the social theorists of the mid 20th century recognized that conflict and change exist, they found it useful to employ models that focus upon stability and cooperation as the normal state of affairs. In embracing this approach, Alderson implicitly emphasizes equilibrium and cohesion, not evolution and conflict. The fact that Alderson always strove to help marketing institutions (and ad hoc practitioner strategies) to change for the better does not totally eclipse the covert implications of the static model that formed an intellectual foundation for his work.

Indeed, an almost identical analogy to that used by Radcliffe-Brown crops up in the work of Edmund D. McGarry (1950) in an article anthologized by Alderson:

> The function of the heart is not simply to beat, but rather to supply the body with a continuous supply of blood... In like manner, "functions of marketing" should denote a purposefulness.

Thus, Alderson's structural/functional models (and those of other marketing scholars to whom he was sympathetic) focus upon the stability of the macro system, the cooperation of its parts, and the universal benefits it provides. This focus led to ignoring (or at least de-emphasizing) change, conflict, and the distinctiveness of specific parts of the macro social system. Nonetheless, this perspective proved to be fruitful for many years.

4.   The Decline of Alderson's Vision

Around the time of Alderson's death in 1965, his macro perspectives began to fall from favor. In 1964, for example, Donald Dixon complained about the tendency of marketers to use structural/functional methods to deal with specific/micro concerns, not to examine broader issues. Dixon went on to observe that the broader macro vision (that was needed to explore marketing's relationship to humanity and society) was becoming less and less prominent within the discipline.

Dixon argues that relevant, broad-based marketing theory was not being developed, because of:

> the narrowness of the concept of functionalism which now underlies much marketing theory. This narrowness can be traced to the practice of marketing writers viewing marketing as a how-to-do-it area of study. . . Marketing theory has been unduly restricted by a narrow concept of functionalism and the coincident view that the ultimate objective of a theory is to understand how firms and households attempt to solve problems in the marketplace (Dixon, 1964, p. 28).

Dixon attempted to develop an interest in general systems theory in his "A Social Systems Approach to Marketing" (1967), but his efforts were unable to turn the tide away from the marketing management approach that was coming to dominate.

Combining observations, such as Dixon's, with the timing of Alderson's death, the decline of macro-structural/functionalism within marketing seems to have resulted from two distinct influences:

1 Wroe Alderson, the guru and mastermind of the macro structural/functionalist movement within marketing, did not leave a disciple who was able to immediately follow in his footsteps and continue to establish a macrostructural analysis within the mainstream of marketing (although various advocates of Alderson, such as Stanley Shapiro, George Fisk, and Donald Dixon, etc. continue to work towards a renaissance of Aldersonian thought).

2 Marketing, which has always been an applied, practical, and practitioner-oriented science, has tended to gravitate towards micro issues which can be applied to solving short-term pragmatic problems.

Without doubt, these two factors influenced marketing to adopt the micro orientation that arose after 1960 and has dominated the field ever since. Indeed, the rise of "4 Ps" micromarketing, prompted by the publication of E. Jerome McCarthy's *Basic Marketing: A Managerial Approach* (1960), quickly transformed the discipline in ways that overshadowed the structural/functional approach that Alderson was developing in the last years of his life. Thus, Alderson died just as a rival practitioner-oriented paradigm of marketing was being established. In the transformation that resulted, Alderson and his work were lost in the shuffle.

While this restructuring of the field was taking place, some marketers, such as Donald Dixon, continued to advocate a theoretical perspective that was largely based upon structural/functional principles; Dixon (1964) argues, for example, that marketing must be broadened beyond mere pragmatic "cookbook" status in order to expand its theoretical base. He observes,

> One way of doing this is to reexamine the concept of functionalism in marketing, stressing its relationship to functionalism in other disciplines.

Dixon's potential impact is significant but still currently largely unrecognized. Those seeking a broader perspective on Dixon are referred to Tamilia and Reid's "An Introduction to Dixonian Thought" (1999) which provides a thoughtful analysis and a bibliography of works by and about Dixon.

This paper, in tandem with Dixon's orientations, seeks to revive Alderson's structural/functional model in ways that mesh with the needs of the contemporary world. In order to do so, key issues faced by today's social scientists and cultural observers will be addressed.

5. The Paradigm of Social Change and Tension

As discussed above, the classic structural/functional theories that Alderson embraced are closely identified with mid 20th century social thought that focused upon stability and cooperation. Although these models possess many useful applications, they are not designed to conveniently deal with (1) social change and (2) the tensions that often exist between different social groups. The 1960s, however, was an era in which social tensions (such as the civil rights struggle, the anti-war movement, anti-colonial perspectives, etc.) were coming to a head. Under these circumstances, social theorists became dissatisfied with paradigms that emphasized harmony, unity, and the universal benefits provided by the social system.

Many social theorists went so far as to depict the classic structural/functional model as a reactionary apology for the status quo. If the forceful tactics of a dictatorship maintain the social system, for example, a traditional structural/functional analysis could easily give the regime a positive evaluation because of the stability that it provided. Even though a classic structural/functional analysis might legitimately point to benefits enjoyed by society as a whole, the method is not designed to easily deal with the inequities faced by certain groups and/or the tensions that exist between various segments of society. As social scientists and cultural critics became increasingly concerned with treating all groups with equity and with analyzing and resolving social tensions in fair and harmonious ways, the classic structural/functional model came to be viewed as passé and it was discredited accordingly.

In her polemical analysis of sociologist Talcott Parsons, for example, Betty Friedan (1964) wrote:

> functionalism began as an attempt to make social science more "scientific" by taking from biology the idea of studying institutions as if they were muscle or bones in terms of their "structure" or "function" in the social body. By studying an institution only in terms of its function within its own society the social scientists intended to avoid unscientific value judgements. . . (but). . . "The function function is" was often translated "the function should be." By giving an absolute meaning and a sanctimonious value to the generic term "woman's role", functionalism put women into a kind of deep freeze.

Overstating her case in a polemical way, Friedan points to one of the dark potentials of focusing upon stability and cooperation: if an observer interprets behavior simply as part of an on-going and stable system, criticizing that behavior becomes difficult.

The classic structural/functional method was under such attack by 1961 that influential anthropologist Edmund Leach (1961) referred to its practitioners as little more than butterfly collectors who rip living things out of their proper context and position them in displays according to some typology that probably fails to reflect "reality".

Fredrik Barth (1966) (one of the few anthropologists to do fieldwork among Western businesspeople) was even more pointed and pessimistic, observing:

> The [Radcliffle-Brown/classic structural/functional] model does not depict any intervening social processes between the moral injunction and the pattern [of behavior]. There is indeed no science of social life in this procedure, no explanation of how actual forms, much less frequency distributions of how behavior came about. . . The study of social anthropology cannot today be much advanced by sophistication and refinement of the current stock of concepts and ideas.

Thus, to use the model presented by Thomas Kuhn in his *Structure of Scientific Revolutions* (1962), Barth believed the old paradigm of a static structural/functionalism had become so passé it that could not updated and refined through the interjection of superficial refinements.

Alderson's use of this paradigm can be criticized on similar grounds. As early as 1944, Alderson had emphasized the equilibrium of the system. Revising this homeostatic model somewhat in the 1960's, Alderson (1965), nevertheless, continued to integrate such concepts into his structural/functional model.

Just as Radcliffle-Brown tended to strategically deal with social change as an abnormal phenomenon, Alderson (1965) dealt with disequilibrium as essentially pathological, he states:

> The several basic elements [of a structure] will be in precise adjustment if the system is in equilibrium. There are several ways in which such a system can

> go into a state of disequilibrium. The pathology is somewhat analogous to the pathology of the human body. . . [When it is in a state of disequilibrium] a system is running out of control, and unless control can be established, it will eventually disintegrate as a system.

Alderson's theoretic work was based on the classic structural/functional method that emphasized stability. The fact that he was personally interested in change does not alter this fact. Alderson informally resolved this issue by being eclectic and by adopting an ad hoc stance. Thus, he embraced a rather static structural/functional model as a theoretic foundation, while supplementing this paradigm with dynamic perspectives that dealt with the issue at hand in an eclectic and ad hoc manner.

Towards the end of his life, Alderson apparently attempted to resolve the conflicts between stability and cooperation vs. change and tensions through the use of neo-Marxist theories, such as those provided by Julian Steward (Alderson, 1965). Marxist analysis, of course, deals with social tension, cultural evolution, and conflict between different people and groups. The neo-Marxist "cultural materialists" school of anthropology provides a means of divorcing Marx's scholarly theories of cultural stress and change from his partisan political rhetoric and propaganda. Although such an approach might have provided Alderson with a means of (1) overcoming the static limitations inherent in the classic static structural/functional model and (2) acknowledging tensions that exist between different social groups, he died before he made much progress in that direction. Today, incidentally, marketing scholars are again looking towards Marxist theory as a means of dealing with the dynamics of the marketplace. See, for example, "Marxist Theory and Marketing/Consumer Research: An Anthropological Perspective" (Walle, 2002, pp. 43-63).

Nevertheless, since the 1960s classic structural/functional thought has faced the dilemma of how to deal with social change and cultural stress. Initially unable to respond in a decisive manner, the method fell from favor. This decline of classic structural/functional analysis within the social sciences is paralleled by a similar response within marketing thought. As the classic structural/functional method lost ground, other alternatives rose to prominence and dominance.

6. Transcending Stability and Cooperation

As indicated above, Wroe Alderson was greatly influenced by the classic structural/functional social research of his era: a research stream that was largely framed in a static and deterministic mold. This type of thought largely parallels what Kenneth Boulding calls a "clockworks" model because it concentrates upon internal harmony and how all members of a social group tend to interact in predictable, static, and mutually beneficial ways.

According to such an approach, the various elements of culture and society (including marketing relationships) are viewed in terms of how they fit with and contribute to the greater social structure in ways that benefit all. This perspective also assumes that when a system is behaving "normally", its actions and responses function in largely predetermined ways.

Due to changing intellectual tastes and the issues that came to dominate social thought after 1960, the classic social structural/functional model fell from favor. This trend took place within marketing research and elsewhere.

Kenneth Boulding, however, envisioned a series of interrelated paradigms (including some that are deterministic/static and others that are dynamic/deal with strife and change). Because Boulding argues that these different components blend into each other, the deterministic nature of classic structural/functional analysis (that is at a lower level of the hierarchy) can be revitalized by merging them with later components that acknowledge change and tension. So viewed, Alderson's theories can be updated in order to restart them on "a new product life cycle."

In a nutshell, Boulding states that the analysis of a phenomenon typically begins with an investigation of the static structure, progresses to examining completely determined motions (clockworks models), and graduates to "cybernetic" models that acknowledge the existence of control mechanisms that regulate and stabilize the system. These are the basic levels of social structural/functional analysis that were available to Alderson in the mid 20th century.

Building upon this foundation, Boulding presents additional paradigms that deal with "open systems" and employ biological analogies (similar to those used by early social theorists). This style of thought leads to Boulding's 7th level, which examines the individual human being. This individual focus, incidentally, corresponds with existential analysis (and advances to it such as poststructuralism and postmodernism) that centers upon the individual (and/or groups that are depicted as surrogate individuals).

In level 8, the center of attention returns to an interest in larger systems and their functioning. Thus, while one method examines human beings in isolation, another focuses upon larger, macro social systems. This was the arena of investigation that Alderson advocated.

Boulding clearly believed that the system of paradigms he presents has an important role to play in business and strategic research. He states:

> The above scheme might serve as a mild word of warning even to management science. . . [that] represents an important breakaway from overly simple mechanical models. . . Its emphasis upon communication systems and organizational structure, on principles of homeostasis and growth, on decision processes under uncertainty, is carrying us far beyond the simple models [of previous levels of analysis] (Boulding, 1956, p. 10).

Not only does the Boulding formulation provide a way to update Alderson's static structural/functional approach, "the two were friends" (Shapiro, 2005). As a result, there is every reason to believe that Alderson was overtly familiar with Boulding's general system theory hierarchy (because it was one of his major contributions and it was widely discussed in the last years of Alderson's life). As Shapiro (2005) also reports, some of Alderson's ideas, such as his heterogeneity of demand model, were "intellectually inspired by the presence of his friend Kenneth Boulding".

In the years immediately following Alderson's death, furthermore, those influenced by his work continued to make use of Boulding's system theory orientation. Thus, George Fisk and Donald Dixon gave Boulding's seminal article on general systems theory the lead position within their book *Theories for Marketing Systems Analysis* (1967).

The key concept of Boulding's article is that old paradigms are not rendered completely passé; instead they form the foundation for future advances. Viewing Alderson's effort from this perspective, it emerges as pioneering work to build upon, not as an obsolete method to be discarded as alternatives (such as 4 Ps marketing management and methods deriving from the existential tradition) are developed.

The key issue is that although Alderson employed a fairly static structural/functional paradigm, he also believed that this work was merely one rung on a ladder of general systems theory analysis. He apparently got this idea from his friendship from Kenneth Boulding. Alderson's growing interest in neo-Marxist analysis is evidence that towards the end of his life he was beginning to transcend his static methods of analysis by dealing with change, stress, competition, and cultural/economic transformations. When analyzed from this perspective, Alderson's view of marketing exhibits robustness and complexity. In today's world of multiple influences and stakeholders, this macro view is much needed.

The paper acknowledges that Wroe Alderson embraced the classic social structural/functional paradigm of his day: a model that tended to be static and did not adequately deal with change and social conflict. Nonetheless, this retrospective analysis of his work focuses upon the fact that towards the end of his life Alderson attempted to adopt more dynamic models (such as non-political forms of Marxist analysis) in order to acknowledge change, stress, and conflict within society. Alderson, however, died before he made significant progress in this direction. And, yet, he laid the groundwork for future advances.

The work of those who carried on Alderson's work in the years immediately following his death further underscores the link with Alderson's marketing theory and Boulding's systems theory approach. George Fisk and Donald Dixon (two marketing scholars who affirm an intellectual debt to Alderson) writing only 2 years after his death, for example, observe that "Marketing systems are confined largely to what Boulding refers to as social systems at the eighth level of complexity" (1967, p. 3). Level 8, as we have seen, concerns itself with social organization. This, of course, is the way that Alderson sought to frame marketing theory.

Being envisioned and constructed with a general system theory perspective in mind, Alderson's work possesses a robustness and a flexibility that can be rehabilitated for use by contemporary scholars in the 21st century. Thus, while Alderson's actual work is niched at a certain level of the general systems theory that emphasized stability and cooperation, he was keenly aware that more sophisticated system theory models existed and, no doubt, he anticipated that at some point they would be needed.

Fate did not allow Alderson to be involved in this process, even though he left hints of how he might have proceeded (by briefly pointing to neo-Marxist social theory, for example). Fortunately, the legacy that Alderson left can be reformulated and updated in ways that that transcend stability and cooperation.

7.   Operationalizing Contemporary Aldersonian Thought

While an intellectual justification of Alderson's vision is useful and appropriate, a nuts and bolts discussion regarding how to operationalize and update his macro vision is also needed. A preliminary step in this process involves underscoring the value of structural/functional analysis within marketing thought. Many marketing scholars who embrace a macromarketing perspective, for example, are deeply interested in studying the impacts and influences of various social and marketing structures. One way to do so is to emphasize that social systems evolve over time in ways that impact marketing and consumption.

Such an approach is able to explore marketing management issues because, as cultures change, marketers strategically adjust products to meet consumer's evolving expectations and demands. Thus, marketing can be seen are responding to cultural and social changes. By analyzing this situation, marketing scholars can deal with social structures in terms of change, not stability. This is the whole thrust of Alf H. Walle's *The Cowboy Hero and its Audience: Popular Culture as Market Derived Art* (2000). That monograph also demonstrates that marketing scholarship and consumer research can be usefully merged with humanities disciplines such as literary and film criticism in order to deal with changes in the culture over time.

Calling for cross-disciplinary research, Walle observes:

> [Those who create products of popular culture such as films and TV series] have long employed strategies, tactics, and methods that are remarkably similar to modern business disciplines such as marketing. . . in large measure, the field of consumer behavior parallels the discipline of popular culture since both seek to predict and explain how and why people either embrace certain aspects of culture or, in contrast, reject them. . . Today the fields of marketing/consumer behavior and popular culture are converging. These disciplines come from different roots, but increasingly focus on the same phenomena (Walle, 1996, pp. 185, 195).

Analyses that embrace this kind of perspective deal with general trends and transformations that resonate through the culture at large. Such investigations while recognizing that discernable patterns of response do exist, acknowledge that not all people respond in an identical manner. Such a methodology is elegantly accomplished via a structural/functional analysis that acknowledges change, difference, and tension. This is exactly the type of analysis that results from an updating of Alderson's structural/functional analysis so that it operates at Level 8 of Boulding's general system theory hierarchy.

Thus, a first step in operationalizing a revised Aldersonian structural/functional model is to recognize the significance of investigating the collective responses of a significant percentage of a social group while recognizing that these responses evolve over time. This perspective stems from the ideas of Hegel and it emphasizes that cultures have an essence that can be isolated, examined, and discussed. According to Boulding's general systems theory approach, such investigations take place at level 8 of the hierarchy, while individual-centered analysis takes place at level 7. Thus, both methods are useful, appropriate, and make distinct contributions to make to marketing thought.

As a result of this situation, a second step in operationalizing a revision of an Aldersonian structural/functional model is to position the approach as a specialized method that is ideal for certain types of research questions. Advocates need to affirm that even though the structural/functional method has limitations, it is ideally suited for certain types of investigations and it can be justified accordingly. In the example presented above, a structural/functional method was used to analyze the evolution of popular culture over time. Using this method was explicitly justified as useful in this particular context. All scholars need to justify their choice of methods. Those who employ some form of structural/functional analysis are no different.

The third step in operationalizing a revised Aldersonian structural/functional analysis is to look to modern structural/functional scholars within the social sciences in order to see how they have updated their work in light of the criticisms that have beset the method during the last 40 years. By doing so, likeminded marketing scholars can embrace these revisions and benefit accordingly.

One illustrative research stream that has revitalized social structural/functional analysis is conflict theory. Writing in the marketing literature, Walle has observed that conflict theory in sociology rose to prominence because social life is not always harmonious and that not all groups benefit in an equitable manner from the social arrangements that typify a society. As a result, conflict theory provides a way to deal with the fact that societies evolve in response to internal and external pressures (Walle, 2002, p. 217). This development demonstrates that structural/functional theory can be updated and adjusted to current needs and conditions. As a result, it does not need to be replaced outright.

Having presented this overview of the rise and role of conflict theory, Walle explores a number of precedents for modern conflict theory such as the work of Karl Marx, Max Weber, Georg Simmel, C. Wright Mills, etc. This leads to a brief analysis of some of the pioneers of modern conflict theory such as Randall Collins and Jonathan Turner. The purpose of the discussion is to demonstrate how current advances in modern conflict theory provide structural/functional analysis with a means of transcending the classic structural/functional approach that declined in the 1960s. Because structural/functional analysis has the ability to be transformed in ways that respond to change and stress, it can be usefully revived and employed by contemporary marketing scholars. For a fuller discussion of conflict theory and its implication to marketing see "Conflict Theory: Individualism Within a Social Context" (Walle, 2002, pp. 215-228).

Thus, advances in modern structural/functional research have met the challenges of rivals and detractors (such as those whose models stem from the existential tradition). As a result, the tools needed to update and operationalize Alderson's structural/functional paradigm exist and they can be embraced with a minimum of difficulty.

In summary, an updating of Aldersonian thought depends upon at least the following three developments and responses:

1 Recognizing the significance of social groups and envisioning them as such, not as an aggregate of individuals.

2 Positioning and justifying an updated structural/functional analysis as a specialized method that is ideal for certain types of analysis.

3 Incorporating advances within contemporary structural/functional analysis into a revised Aldersonian model in order to keep it up to date and state of the art.

By doing so, those who seek to justify and rehabilitate Alderson's structural/functional model will offer the discipline a robust alternative to other models, such as those that stem from the existential tradition (that focuses upon the individual or circumscribed social groups that are depicted as surrogate individuals).

Dealing with social groups as holistic entities is a complicated method of analysis. In today's world, nonetheless, dealing with the actions and influences of larger, overarching groups is vital to the questions asked by social scientists, in general, and by marketing scholars, in specific. Modern structural/functional methods are nuanced and sophisticated, and they are poised to serve in a variety of roles. Marketing scholars need the options that these models provide.

As we have seen, one of the complaints routinely leveled against structural/functional analysis is that it is not well equipped to deal with change and conflict within the system. While this may have been a problem during an earlier era, it is no longer a stumbling block because advocates of the structural/functional school are reframing their model in ways that overcome these limitations. As a result, social structural/functional analysis is well equipped to return to prominence within marketing thought. Since Alderson was a major proponent of this approach, his star is rising.

8. Conclusion

Wroe Alderson is the pioneer of marketing theory who went beyond the ad hoc functionalism of earlier marketers (such as Paul Converse) by embracing the classic structural/functional models of mid 20th century social science. Doing so gave Alderson's work a breadth that has proved appropriate within the context of macromarketing (a subdiscipline that also deals with overarching social structures and their impacts).

Due to the static nature of classic structural/functional theory, however, that paradigm from the social sciences fell from vogue around the time of Alderson's death. In addition, the micro-oriented 4 Ps marketing management approach rose to prominence at exactly the same time. As a result, Alderson structural/functional model rapidly declined.

Today, however, advances in the structural/functional models coupled with the need to deal with society at large are re-invigorating the structural/functional approach. Coupled with a variety of issues involving (1) the impact of society upon consumption and vice versa and (2) normative issues regarding ecology, societal marketing, etc., the need for the type of vision presented by Alderson's structural/functional style of analysis is sorely needed.

A rehabilitated structural approach, inspired by Alderson, can also provide an alternative to 4 Ps marketing management and paradigms that stem from the existential tradition. As a result it has a significant role to play when certain kinds of issues are being examined.

As a result, Alderson and his structural/function model are poised to return to prominence with marketing theory and practice.

References

Alderson, Wroe (1957). *Marketing Behavior and Executive Action: A Functionalist Approach to Marketing*. Richard D. Irwin Inc., Homewood, Ill.

Alderson, Wroe (1965). *Dynamic Marketing Behavior: A Functionalist Theory of Marketing*. Richard D. Irwin Inc., Homewood, Ill.

Barth, Fredrick (1965). *Models of Social Organization*. Royal Anthropological Institute, London.

Boulding, K. E. (1956). General Systems Theory — The Skeleton of Science. *Management Science*, 2(April):197–208.

Dixon, Donald F. (1964). Functionalism as an Approach to Marketing Theory. *Economics and Business Bulletin*, pages 28–34.

Dixon, Donald F. (1967). A Social Systems Approach to Marketing. *The Southwestern Social Science Quarterly*, 48(September):164–173.

Fisk, George and Dixon, Donald, editors (1967). *Theories for Marketing Systems Analysis*. Praeger Publishers, New York.

Freidan, Betty (1964). *The Feminine Mystique*. Dell Publishing, New York.

Kuhn, Thomas S. (1962). *The Structure of Scientific Revolutions*. University of Chicago Press, Chicago.

Leach, Edmund (1961). *Rethinking Anthropology*. Athlone Press, London.

McCarthy, E. Jerome (1960). *Basic Marketing: A Managerial Approach*. Richard D. Irwin, Homewood, Illinois.

McGarry, E. D. (1950). Some Functions of Marketing Reconsidered. In Cox, Reavis and Alderson, Wroe, editors, *Theory in Marketing*, pages 263–279. Richard D. Irwin, Chicago.

Radcliffe-Brown, A. R. (1935). On the Concept of Function in Social Science. *American Anthropologist*, pages 394–402.

Shapiro, Stanley J. (2005). Personal communication.

Tamilia, Robert D. and Reid, Susan (1999). An Introduction to Dixonian Thought. In Cunningham, Peggy and Bussiére, David, editors, *Marketing History: The Total Package, Proceedings of the 9th Biannual Conference on Historical Research in Marketing and Marketing Thought*, pages 77–95. Michigan State University, East Lansing.

Walle, Alf H. (1996). Hack Writing and Bell Letters: The Strategic Implications of Literary Achievement. *Journal of Popular Culture*, 30(3):185–196.

Walle, Alf H. (2000). *The Cowboy Hero and Its Audience: Popular Culture as Market Derived Art*. The Popular Press, Bowling Green, Ohio.

Walle, Alf H. (2002). *Exotic Visions In Marketing Theory and Practice*. Quorum, Westport, Connecticut.

Chapter 36

TO TEACH OR NOT TO TEACH ALDERSON? THERE IS NO QUESTION*†

Ian Wilkinson
University of New South Wales

Louise Young
University of Technology Sydney

1. Introduction

There is a lack of acknowledgment and inclusion of the writings of Wroe Alderson in most marketing courses, even though many of our basic marketing concepts and principles may be traced back to him. Fewer and fewer students, including trainee academics, encounter his work directly in their studies. A web-based search for "Wroe Alderson" on Google (10 February, 2005) uncovered only 652 references and only a few of them directly relate to teaching (e.g. subject outlines, discussions of the importance of teaching Alderson) plus a few more given over to resources that might be intended for use in teaching. And marketing texts that take a more Aldersonian functionalist or systems type approach (e.g. Dixon and Wilkinson, 1982, Fisk, 1967, Narver and Savitt, 1971) are long out of print.

Does this mean Alderson's ideas are no longer relevant or are they appropriately incorporated indirectly in modern texts and research without the need to refer to original sources? If relevant, what should we teach about Alderson and to whom? To what parts of a marketing curriculum do his ideas belong? And in what ways might we best communicate them to students? This chapter

---

* Acknowledgments — we would like to thank the students from the over three decades of our cumulative experience in teaching marketing theory for teaching us how to effectively help others to learn about Alderson. In particular we would like to thank Tamsin Agnus-Leppan, Monali Hota, Daniel Kwasnica, and Victoria Smith whose essays for their marketing theory studies were mentioned in this chapter.
† Authors are listed alphabetically, corresponding author is Louise Young, School of Marketing, UTS, P.O. Box 123, Haymarket, NSW, Australia (louise.young@uts.edu.au)

addresses these issues. We argue that Alderson should be taught throughout the university curriculum, and perhaps beyond, and should incorporate a wide range of his descriptive and normative theories of both micro and macro marketing.

It needs to be made plain at the outset that our views on the role and value of Alderson's work are biased. We were both required to read Alderson's two main books, *Marketing Behavior and Executive Action* (1957) and *Dynamic Marketing Behavior* (1965), at the beginning of our doctoral studies and were strongly influenced by systems thinking and functionalist theory. Ian Wilkinson (one author) also studied and worked with Don Dixon for a number of years in the USA, indirectly benefiting from Don's experience in studying with Alderson at Wharton and Don arguing with him at the annual Marketing Theory Seminars Alderson ran (later to reemerge in the form of the Macromarketing Conferences). Don and Ian combined to write an introductory marketing text, structured along Aldersonian lines, that was eventually published in Australia in 1982 and which was used to teach undergraduate and graduate classes in the USA and Australia for some years with mixed success. Louise Young (the other author) was one of the students who used their text in her first marketing subject and she went on to teach the subject. Later Louise and Ian combined to teach a development of marketing thought seminar for research students, including a substantial portion on Alderson, which has been taught at various universities in Australia over the last 15 years. Hence we are both fans of Alderson, having been exposed to his ideas throughout our careers and we continue to see links to much of what is taught in marketing today. In the following discussion we draw first on our experience in teaching Alderson's theories to postgraduate research students and then consider those beginning their marketing studies.

2.   Teaching Alderson as part of the History of Marketing Thought

Alderson's ideas have a natural place in any history of marketing thought course. Moreover, we would argue that study of our intellectual history is important for doctoral students in particular. As George Day argued in the 60th anniversary edition of the *Journal of Marketing*: "Histories serve many functions. They reveal our origins, celebrate our successes, and remind us of our debts to our intellectual ancestors. A history also helps interpret the past by identifying the reasons for important transitions" (Day, 1996, p. 14). We believe that a better understanding of the way marketing ideas have evolved help us to avoid reinventing concepts and ideas, promotes the accumulation rather than the recycling of knowledge, and contributes to the credibility of the discipline as a science. Unfortunately, stand-alone marketing history subjects are rare in business schools, although there are signs of a growing interest in the area. This is reflected in articles reviewing the development of ideas on particular aspects of marketing (e.g. Wilkinson, 2001, Dixon, 1990, Dixon, 1999, Dixon, 2002), more general reviews of the development of marketing thought (e.g. Jones and Shaw, 2002), as well as the emergence of conferences and conference tracks devoted to the history of thought, such as the bi-annual Conference on Historical Analysis and Research in Marketing (CHARM) which began in 1983.

Our experience with teaching the history of marketing thought is via a seminar we co-developed and have each run on the nature and evolution of marketing theory. About half of this subject is devoted to Alderson and his impacts. We begin with an introduction to scientific method and the philosophy of science; including a sampling of the debate about research philosophies that took place in the marketing literature in the 1980s and 1990s (see Wilkinson and Young, 2002b for more details). We do not start with the idea that marketing thought began in the 20th century with the advent of courses of that name in the USA, which is the impression one gets if you begin with the various editions of Bartels' (1962, 1976, 1982) book on the history of marketing. Instead we start with the rise of early marketing thought in Ancient Greece and sample the development of marketing thought as reflected primarily in the writings of Dixon (e.g. 1978, 1979, 1981, 2002). We consider such things as St. Thomas Aquinas on ethical selling behavior, normative theories of merchants prior to the industrial revolution and 19th century macromarketing thought. Moving to more modern times we consider the development of marketing leading up to Alderson and Cox's (1948) *Journal of Marketing* article, which critiques the state of marketing theory and sets forth an agenda for change. We then proceed to consider the main ideas and contributions of Alderson and his contemporaries and the nature and extent to which marketing theory has progressed since.

The subject reveals Alderson as an important watershed in contemporary marketing thought. His extensive business experience and wide reading allowed him to appreciate the potential contribution to marketing thought of a number of other disciplines, not just economics. These include sociology, psychology, ecology, geography and institutional economics. It is easy to conclude that these few decades when he was publishing his work were part of a Golden Age of marketing theory development. Apart from studies of Alderson's own writings, reviews and commentaries at the time (e.g. Clewett, 1958, Revzan, 1951, Vaile, 1949) as well as later interpretations (e.g. Nicosia, 1962, Blair and Uhl, 1976, Dixon and Wilkinson, 1989, Smalley and Fraedrich, 1995) help frame and position his many contributions and highlight their potential relevance to current thinking (e.g. Gadde and Hulthen, 2003).

Students are set the following essay topic for this part of the course: "There has been no significant progress in marketing thought since Alderson. Discuss." They are allowed considerable latitude in how they interpret the topic and how they define "significant," "progress" and "marketing thought." Students often chose to write on the way one or more of his theories of marketing management are reflected in introductory marketing subjects and texts they have encountered. For example, a typical submission is a doctoral student analyzing the ways in which theories of differential advantage are reflected in Kotler et al's text (2004). Not surprisingly, she concluded that discussion of differential advantage is embedded throughout the material on differentiation and positioning and that the theory described had not developed much beyond Alderson's original ideas. What little augmentation there has been was judged as largely cosmetic. A similar approach was taken by a student who explored contemporary consumer behavior theory as reflected in an introductory textbook (Neal et al., 2002). It was concluded that organized behavior systems, an Alderson concept though not attributed to him in the text, is the basic theory that drives the discussion throughout the text. While this approach leaves the evaluation and interpretation of Alderson's theories at a fairly elementary level it does indicate to students (most of whom will themselves soon teach introductory university-level subjects) the extent to which Alderson's theories are an integral part of the contemporary bedrock of marketing management theory, the failure of textbook authors to know and/or to acknowledge this, and the extent to which his theories have stood the test of time.

A more challenging approach to the essay topic is taken by students who explore theories of Alderson in relation to their research topics. One student, studying the demise of group decision making in household purchasing due to the rise of on-line purchasing, considered the extent to which Alderson's theories could guide the development of his theory and research. Using Wolfinbarger and Gilly (2001) as a point of comparison, he concluded that even though Alderson had no knowledge of the Internet or even personal computers, his theories on individual decision-making were entirely applicable to this context and had not been fundamentally extended in the focal or other, similar, modern works. Here a higher level analysis of theory has occurred and again the robustness of Alderson's ideas are confirmed in the mind of the student.

An interesting variant is one student who became interested in the extent to which Alderson's theories reflected the practices of the firm she had worked for. She was able to match the ways the focal firm had been seeking long and medium term competitive advantage to the various sources of differential advantage proposed by Alderson. The case she developed was set against this theoretical framework and included reflections of her personal involvement, interviews with managers, archival materials and stories in the popular press (Hota and Young, 2003). This takes the teaching of Alderson to another level, where it becomes the basis of additional, original research. We will encourage other students to take this approach in future offerings of this subject.

Students tend to focus on micro marketing applications of Alderson's theories, as this is the dominant subject matter of most marketing programs. More problematic is engendering in students an appreciation of his macro-marketing concepts, even though many of the pre 20th century readings discussed do address these types of issues. As a result we have included additional readings focusing on the importance and relevance of contemporary macromarketing research (e.g. Fisk, 2001). This awakens in students a recognition that the wider social issues of marketing continue to exist and in a few cases this has led to a redirection of their own research.

3.   Alderson in Introductory Marketing Subjects

This section is based on our experience in using a marketing systems text (Dixon and Wilkinson, 1982) designed around Alderson's ideas, to teach introductory graduate and undergraduate classes. In the early 1980s the School of Marketing at the University of New South Wales had a strong systems and theory orientation at both the micro and macro level. The research focused on marketing systems and economic development in developing countries, channel system structure, systems theories and strategy and the structure and evolution of marketing systems (reviewed in Wilkinson, 2001). This was also the focus of the introductory courses.

In "our" introductory marketing we started by focusing on the generic activities required to bring about market exchange and how and why this is and should be divided up between sellers, buyers and other participants in the market. The analysis included consideration of Alderson's concepts of the transaction as the primary unit of action and the work involved in bringing about a transaction, using the concepts of discrepancy of assortments and sorting and linking them to the concepts of marketing flows and utilities and even to the 4Ps. This work is carried out by people performing individual marketing roles in firms and households, the primary units of the marketing system. Following Alderson, we considered larger units of work, such as transvections and marketing flows, which arise out of interrelated sets of transactions which are brought about by higher level systems made up of interdependent firms and households such as channels and networks and industries. These marketing processes and systems were then considered within social, economic, political and physical processes and systems, which affect the role marketing plays in any society.

The next part of the course examined marketing in households and firms. Both firms and households were presented as organized behavior systems, comprising power, communication and operating structures which carry out marketing activities. This means organizational and household buying behavior are analysed in similar ways and showed students the parallels between consumer and industrial buying behavior theories as well as to the organization and processes of the selling side of the firm. A firm's marketing function was examined in more depth and seen in the context of the larger marketing system of which it is a part. The fundamental problem facing the firm is, as Alderson characterized it, the continual search for differential advantage. Traditional concepts of planning, positioning, implementation and control fit within this overall orientation.

The next parts of the course focused on macro systems such as channels and networks and the marketing system as a whole, including their evolution and history, the work they do, why the work is organized the way it is, and how they enable and constrain individual action by firms and households. In this way distribution channels and networks can be visualized as part of the extended organisation of a firm or household (on the supply and demand side) and the means by which all marketing activities are carried out. Finally, we returned to the way a marketing system is embedded in larger social, economic, political and physical systems and considered the positive and negative effects of marketing on these environmental systems.

We still believe this is a good approach pedagogically, but the problems we encountered highlight many of the issues that we have referred to already. Although this was their first marketing class students already had strong pre-conceptions of what marketing was or should be and what they wanted to learn about it; and this did not correspond to a systems approach. Already indoc-trinated — perhaps through secondary school and/or the media — students then and now see marketing primarily in micro normative terms: as selling, as something done by firms to customers. What they want to learn is how-to-do-it, recipes to succeed in the marketplace. Furthermore, it is not just the students' resistance that must be overcome it also that of our colleagues'. In many parts of the world, several generations of marketing academics have been brought up on an exclusive diet of marketing management and associated technologies, it is threatening to them to have core curriculum that use different organizing frameworks.

If we believe education involves more than recipes, how can we deal with this resistance? Rather than hold off considerations of Alderson and his sys-tems approach to marketing until higher level undergraduate, postgraduate or doctoral work we could consider going further back and introducing them in high school. Business studies courses in Australia, for example, have taken over from economics in many high schools and require a more systematic and balanced consideration of the nature and role of marketing in society than is portrayed in a typical marketing management text. This is where some of Alder-son's ideas can be of use. There is at least a segment of the youth who are keenly concerned with these issues and feel that it should be part of the primary and secondary curriculum (e.g. Angus-Leppan et al., 2004a, Angus-Leppan et al., 2004b discusses interviews with young adults who feel that business ethics, corporate responsibility and the like should be part of high school and perhaps primary school curriculum). So while the history of marketing and Alderson himself might not be taught until the university or postgraduate years the ground could be seeded much earlier.

4. Conclusions

Some might argue that a systems approach, built around Aldersonian concepts, is beyond the capability of introductory students and would be likely to discourage further study. Indeed some prepublication reviews of the Dixon and Wilkinson (1982) text we used suggested it was more appropriate for doctoral courses! Our experience suggests that the subject matter is no more difficult than introductory economics or science books (and in many cases students entering marketing courses have better academic records than many entering the sciences). We have not found that Alderson's ideas are difficult to read and understand, as others have argued (e.g. Holbrook, 2001), though they certainly go beyond the more common laundry lists and cookbook approaches of many existing texts. For example Alderson's "Analytical Framework for Marketing" paper delivered originally at the Conference of Marketing Teachers from Far Western States in 1958 (reproduced in Kernan and Sommers, 1968) stands the test of time as a masterly original integration and overview of the nature of marketing in society. Others also comment that mastering his ideas is not a major issue; his work is not semantically complex and thus is accessible (e.g. Brown, 2002, Wooliscroft, 2004). One problem with understanding him, which has been at least indirectly the focus in past critiques, is that Alderson paints his theory pictures almost exclusively with words, which is problematic in an age when so much theory is presented in terms of flow charts and schematic models. In addition, the macro level of analysis in parts of Alderson's work is foreign to most students and academics brought up on firm-focused marketing management texts. Yet the relevance and value of this level of analysis is becoming ever more apparent to business and government as the complexities, dynamics and interactions of modern day business systems increase and undermine traditional concepts of planning and strategy (e.g. Wilkinson and Young, 2002a, Wilkinson and Young, 2005).

We end this chapter with some issues to consider in designing contemporary offerings to inspire present and future students about the nature and role of Alderson. The following should be kept in mind:

- Alderson first hand versus second hand: Material that discusses Alderson is important in exposing students to theoretical analysis but it is no substitute for reading some of his original work.

- Description and analysis: Lists of Alderson's contributions are not enough. The interconnections of theories and different levels of analysis are required. Using mapping and other visualization techniques may be particularly valuable.

- Debating his Contribution: The literature includes diametrically opposed points of view which require consideration, analysis and comparison.

- Contemporary material: Quality and relevance is often equated by students to the presence of recently published material. Without the inclusion of some newer material a message is sent that the ideas are no longer seen to be relevant by the mainstream. There is little modern writing about Alderson, hence this volume is important and will send the message that some "old stuff" continues to be important.

References

Alderson, Wroe (1957). *Marketing Behavior and Executive Action: A Functionalist Approach to Marketing*. Richard D. Irwin Inc., Homewood, Ill.

Alderson, Wroe (1965). *Dynamic Marketing Behavior: A Functionalist Theory of Marketing*. Richard D. Irwin Inc., Homewood, Ill.

Alderson, Wroe and Cox, Reavis (1948). Towards a Theory of Marketing. *Journal of Marketing*, 13(October):137–152.

Angus-Leppan, Tamsin, Benn, Suzanne, Daniel, Kerry, and Young, Louise (2004a). CSR: The Australian Consumers' Perspective. In *Proceedings of the Australian and New Zealand Marketing Academy*, Wellington, New Zealand. Victoria University. CD-ROM.

Angus-Leppan, Tamsin, Benn, Suzanne, Daniel, Kerry, and Young, Louise (2004b). Individualised Reflexivity and CSR: Perspectives on the Consumer. In *Proceedings: Australian and New Zealand Academy of Management*, Dunedin, New Zealand. University of Otago.

Bartels, Robert (1962). *The Development of Marketing Thought*. Richard D. Irwin, Homewood, Ill.

Bartels, Robert (1976). *The Development of Marketing Thought*. Richard D. Irwin, Homewood, Ill., second edition.

Bartels, Robert (1982). *The Development of Marketing Thought*. Richard D. Irwin, Homewood, Ill., third edition.

Blair, Ed and Uhl, Kenneth P. (1976). Wroe Alderson and Modern Marketing Theory. In Slater, Charles C., editor, *Macro-Marketing Distributive Processes from a Societal Perspective*, pages 66–84.

Brown, Stephen (2002). Reading Wroe: on the biopoetics of Alderson's functionalism. *Marketing Theory*, 2(3):243–271. [a paper with many factual errors].

Clewett, Richard M. (1958). Book Reviews: Market Behavior and Executive Action. *Journal of Marketing*, 23(1):343–345.

Day, George S. (1996). Using the Past as a Guide to the Future: Reflections of the History of the Journal of Marketing. *Journal of Marketing*, 58:14–17.

Dixon, Donald and Wilkinson, Ian F. (1982). *The Marketing System*. Longman Cheshire, Sydney, Australia.

Dixon, Donald F. (1978). The Origins of Macromarketing Thought. In Slater, Charles, editor, *New Steps on the Learning Curve, Proceedings of the Third Macromarketing Seminar*, pages 9–28, Rhode Island. Business Research Division, University of Colorado.

Dixon, Donald F. (1980). Medieval Macromarketing Thought. In Slater, Charles, editor, *Macromarketing: Evolution of Thought, Proceedings of the Fourth Macromarketing Seminar*, pages 59–70, Boulder Colorado. Business Research Division, University of Colorado.

Dixon, Donald F. (1981). The Role of Marketing in Early Theories of Economic Development. *Journal of Macromarketing*, 1(Fall):19–27.

Dixon, Donald F. (1990). Marketing as Production: The Development of a Concept. *Journal of the Academy of Marketing Science*, 18(Fall):337–344.

Dixon, Donald F. (1999). Some Late Nineteenth Century Antecedents of Marketing Theory. *Journal of Macromarketing*, 19(December):115–125.

Dixon, Donald F. (2002). Emerging macromarketing concepts: From Socrates to Alfred Marshall. *Journal of Business Research*, 55:87–95.

Dixon, Donald F. and Wilkinson, I. F. (1989). An Alternative Paradigm for Marketing Theory. *The European Journal of Marketing*, 23(8):56–69.

Fisk, George (1967). *Marketing Systems An Introductory Analysis*. Harper&Row, Publishers, New York.

Fisk, George (2001). Reflections of George Fisk: Honorary Chair of the 2001 Macromarketing Conference. *Journal of Macromarketing*, 21(2):121–122.

Gadde, Lars-Erik and Hulthen, Kajas (2003). Aldersonian Sorting: An 'Old' Concept for a 'New' Reality. In *19th IMP Conference*, Lugano, Switzerland.

Holbrook, Morris B. (2001). Wroe Alderson (1957) Marketing Behavior and Executive Action. *ACR News*, pages 37–38.

Hota, Monali and Young, Louise (2003). Is Aldersonian Theory Relevant in Today's Contexts? — An Illustrative Case. In *ANZMAC 2003 Conference Proceedings*, pages 593–599, Adelaide. ANZMAC.

Jones, D. G. Brian and Shaw, Eric H. (2002). A History of Marketing Thought. In Weitz, Barton A. and Wensley, Robin, editors, *Handbook of Marketing*, pages 39–65. Sage Publications, Thousand Oaks, Ca.

Kernan, Jerome and Sommers, Montrose, editors (1968). *Perspectives in Marketing Theory*. Appleton-Century-Crofts, New York.

Kotler, Philip, Brown, L., Adam, S., and Armstrong, G. (2004). *Marketing*. Pearson Prentice Hall, Engelwood Cliffs, sixth edition.

Narver, John C. and Savitt, Ronald (1971). *The Marketing Economy: An Analytical Approach*. Holt, Rinehart and Winston, Inc., New York.

Neal, C., Quester, P., and Hawkins, D. (2002). *Consumer Behaviour*. McGraw-Hill/Irwin, Sydney, Australia, third edition.

Nicosia, Francesco M. (1962). Marketing and Alderson's Functionalism. *Journal of Business*, 35(October):403–413.

Revzan, David (1951). Review of *Theory in Marketing* by Reavis Cox and Wroe Alderson eds. *Journal of Marketing*, 15(1):102–109.

Smalley, Roger and Fraedrich, John (1995). Aldersonian Functionalism: An Enduring Theory in Marketing. *Journal of Marketing Theory and Practice*, 3(4):1–16.

Vaile, Roland S. (1949). Communications: Towards a Theory of Marketing — A Comment. *Journal of Marketing*, 14:520–522.

Wilkinson, Ian (2001). A History of Network and Channels Thinking in Marketing in the 20th Century. *Australasian Journal of Marketing*, 9(2):23–53.

Wilkinson, Ian and Young, Louise (2002a). On Cooperating: Firms, Relations and Networks. *Journal of Business Research*, 55(2):123–132.

Wilkinson, Ian and Young, Louise (2002b). The Role of Marketing Theory in Studying Marketing. In Cadeaux, J. and Pecotich, A., editors, *Macromarketing in the Asia Pacific Century, Proceedings of the 27th Macromarketing Conference*, pages 161–169, Sydney. School of Marketing, University of New South Wales.

Wilkinson, Ian and Young, Louise (2005). Towards a Normative Theory of Normative Marketing Theory. *Journal of Marketing Theory*, 4. In Press.

Wolfinbarger, Mary F. and Gilly, Mary C. (2001). Shopping online for freedom, control and fun. *California Management Review*, 43(2):34–55.

Wooliscroft, Ben (2004). *Paradigm dominance and hegemonic process: the loss of Wroe Alderson's theories of marketing*. PhD thesis, University of Otago, Dunedin, New Zealand.

VI

ALDERSONIAN BIBLIOGRAPHIES

Chapter 37

LIST OF PUBLICATIONS BY WROE ALDERSON

From 1928 to 1968

Robert D. Tamilia
University of Quebec at Montreal

Ben Wooliscroft
University of Otago

with the assistance of Stanley J. Shapiro
Simon Fraser University

This bibliography presents Wroe Alderson's published and unpublished material. Finding Alderson's published material was no easy task for the simple reason that the archival materials on his publications at the Wharton School of the University of Pennsylvania, in other university libraries, and in private files were incomplete. Library as well as electronic searches were necessary. The electronic searches involved using his name in Goggle. The catalogues of many university libraries in the U.S. were electronically searched, including the Barker Library at Harvard, University of California at Berkeley, the University of Pennsylvania as well as the Wharton library site. The Library of Congress site was also searched.

Various data banks were consulted with the most useful one being JSTOR. In fact, a number of new publications were discovered in early 2005 by using in JSTOR combinations of key words along with his name. The UMI dissertation services, a data bank that archives doctoral dissertations, was also consulted. A library search of the available Proceedings of the American Marketing Association from the 1950s up to 1966 was conducted. Unfortunately articles published in the AMA Proceedings are not yet available electronically. Also, and somewhat unexpectedly, reviews by Alderson were found in the book review sections of many academic journals, some of which were available electronically, while others had to be examined at a library. Pagination of some articles was also an issue, given that page numbers were often missing from some citations or, when cited, were sometimes incorrect. Confirming the volume number of certain journals also posed similar problems.

Extensive use was made of interlibrary loans in preparing this bibliography. However, Alderson's earlier published materials were not available, especially those written when he worked for the Department of Commerce (pre-1935). Some references were obtained from David Revzan's (1951) *A Comprehensive Classified Marketing Bibliography*, Part 1 and Part 2, the Supplements to Part 1 and Part 2, published in 1963, as well as his 1968 *A Geography of Marketing: Resource Bibliography*, all published by the Institute of Business and Economic Research, University of California, Berkeley. The referencing of *Cost and Profit Outlook* also posed problems. Many marketing-related articles published in C&PO were not included because it was discovered other authors had written them. In spite of the thoroughness of all these searches, this list might still not be exhaustive. Additional material written by Alderson may still exist out there. If readers come across such material, the compilers of this list look forward to being informed of such discoveries.

Alderson, Wroe (1928). *Advertising for Community Promotion.* Technical Report Domestic Commerce Series, No. 21, Office of Domestic Commerce, Bureau of Foreign and Domestic Commerce, Washington, DC: Superintendent of Documents, Government Printing Office.

Alderson, Wroe (1929). Cost Accounting for Distribution in Retail Grocery Stores. *NY: Bulletin of the National Association of Cost Accountants*, 11(October 1, No. 2):119-128.

Alderson, Wroe (1930). *Louisville Grocery Survey: Wholesale Grocery Operations*, Part 1, Distribution Cost Studies no. 6. Office of Domestic Commerce, Bureau of Foreign and Domestic Commerce, Washington, DC: Superintendent of Documents, Government Printing Office.

Alderson, Wroe and Bromell, John R. (1930). Problems of Wholesale Paint Distribution. Technical Report Distribution Cost Studies No. 8a, Office of Domestic Commerce, Bureau of Foreign and Domestic Commerce, Washington, DC: Superintendent of Documents, Government Printing Office.

Alderson, Wroe with Nelson A. Miller (1930). Problems of Wholesale Dry Goods Distribution. Distribution Cost Studies No. 7, Bureau of Foreign and Domestic Commerce, Washington, DC: Superintendent of Documents, Government Printing Office.

Alderson, Wroe (1931). *Allocating Distribution Costs to Commodities and Customers.* Office of Domestic Commerce, Bureau of Foreign and Domestic Commerce, DC: Superintendent of Documents, Government Printing Office.

Alderson, Wroe and others (1931) *Merchandising Characteristics of Grocery Store Commodities,* Louisville Grocery Survey, Distribution Cost Studies No. 11, Part 111-A, U.S. Bureau of Foreign and Domestic Commerce.

Alderson, Wroe and others (1931) *Merchandising Characteristics of Grocery Store Commodities, Perishables,* Distribution Cost Studies No. 12, U.S. Bureau of Foreign and Domestic Commerce.

Alderson, Wroe and others (1931), *Merchandising Characteristics of Grocery Store Commodities, Dry Groceries,* Distribution Cost Studies No. 13, Part 111-C, U.S. Bureau of Foreign and Domestic Commerce.

Alderson, Wroe and Haag, Frederick, Jr. (1931). *Problems of Wholesale Electrical Goods Distribution.* Technical Report Distribution Cost Studies No. 9, Office of Domestic Commerce, Bureau of Foreign and Domestic Commerce, Washington, DC: Superintendent of Documents, Government Printing Office.

Alderson, Wroe and Aiken B. B. (1932). *Merchandising Requirements of the Drug Store Package.* Technical Report Domestic Commerce Series, No. 73, Office of Domestic Commerce, Bureau of Foreign and Domestic Commerce, Washington, DC: Superintendent of Documents, Government Printing Office.

Alderson, Wroe and B. B. Aiken (1932). Survey of 1,000 Drug Store Packages. *Consumer Marketing Series No. 10,* American Management Series. NY: American Management Association:27-36.

Alderson, Wroe and Meserole, William H. (1932). *Drug Store Arrangement, Technical Report Domestic Commerce Series, No. 57,* Office of Domestic Commerce, Bureau of Foreign and Domestic Commerce, Washington, DC: Superintendent of Documents, Government Printing Office.

Alderson, Wroe and Miller, Nelson A. (1934). *Costs, Sales, and Profits in the Retail Drug Store.* Technical Report, Domestic Commerce Series No. 90, Office of Domestic Commerce, Bureau of Foreign and Domestic Commerce, DC: Superintendent of Documents, Government Printing Office (184 pages).

Alderson, Wroe with Ralph Alexander and others (1935). *Report of the Committee on Definitions.* National Association of Marketing Teachers, May. Alexander was Chairman with George Collins, John Wingate, and Paul Converse who resigned before the report was finished.

Alderson, Wroe (1936). Product Differentiation and the Integrating Price. *The American Marketing Journal*, 3(April, No. 2):118-126. Reprinted in Larry Rosenberg editor, (1978). *The Roots of Marketing Strategy A Collection of Pre-1950 Readings.* Arno Press, NY.

Alderson, Wroe (1937). A Marketing View of Competition. *Journal of Marketing*, 1(January):189-190.

Alderson, Wroe (1937). The Effect of Price Controls on Non-Price Competition. *Law and Contemporary Problems*, 4(June, No. 3):356-362.

Alderson, Wroe (1940). The Consumer Market-Income, Expenditures, and Savings. *Annals of the American Academy of Political and Social Science*, 209(May, No. 1):1-13.

Alderson, Wroe with Ralph Alexander, Frank Surface, and Robert Elder (1940). *Marketing.* Ginn and Co., Boston.

Alderson, Wroe (1941). A Critical Analysis of Recent Literature Dealing with Marketing Efficiency: Discussion. *Journal of Marketing*, 5(April, No. 4):365-370. Alderson (along with others) made comments on two papers published in the same issue (by Nathaniel Engle and by Roland Vaile) on marketing efficiency.

Alderson, Wroe (1941). Marketing Classification of Families. *Journal of Marketing*, 6(October, No. 2):143-146.

Alderson, Wroe (1943). The Marketing Viewpoint in National Economic Planning. *Journal of Marketing*, 7(April, No. 4):326-332. Reprinted in Larry Rosenberg editor, (1978). *The Roots of Marketing Strategy A Collection of Pre-1950 Readings.* Arno Press, NY.

Alderson, Wroe (1944). Conditions for a Balanced World Economy, *World Economics.* Bulletin of the Institute of World Economics, 2(May, No. 7-8):3-25.

Alderson, Wroe (1944). Full Employment Through Market Organization. In Dykstra C., Mitchell, W. C., Ruml, B. and Whitney A. F., editors, *The Winning Plans in the Pabst Postwar Employment Awards*, pages 16-20. Pabst Brewing Company, Milwaukee, WI.

Alderson, Wroe (1945). An Outline of Marketing Research Procedures for Industrial Products. *Industrial Marketing*, 30:46, 104, 106.

Alderson, Wroe (1945). Establishment of the Charles Coolidge Parlin Memorial Lecture (and) Some High Points of the First Parlin Memorial Lecture. In George Lundberg *Marketing and Social Organization*, First Charles Coolidge Parlin Memorial Lecture, presented on May 15, pages 3-7. Franklin Institute, Philadelphia.

Alderson, Wroe (1946). Trends in Public Opinion Research. In Blankenship, Albert B., editor, *How to Conduct Consumer and Opinion Research: The Sampling Survey in Operation*, chapter 23, pages 289-309. Harper and Brothers, NY.

Alderson, Wroe (1947). New Applications for Market Research-Determination of an Effective Selling Price. *Sales Management*, February 1:46.

Alderson, Wroe (1947). The Marketing Audit and the Ad Budget. *Industrial Marketing*, 32(December):50, 130.

Alderson, Wroe (1948). A Formula for Measuring Productivity in Distribution. *Journal of Marketing*, 12(April):442-448.

Alderson, Wroe and Cox, Reavis (1948). Towards a Theory of Marketing. *Journal of Marketing*, 13(October):137-152. Comments by Roland Vaile (1949). Towards a Theory of Marketing? A Comment. *Journal of Marketing*, 13(April): 520-522.

Alderson, Wroe and Sessions (1948). Better Questions and Better Answers in Marketing. *Cost and Profit Outlook*, 2(December, No. 3):1-3.

Alderson, Wroe (1949). Scope and Place of Wholesaling in the United States. *Journal of Marketing*, 14(September):145-155.

Alderson, Wroe with Ralph Alexander and Frank Surface (1949). *Marketing*, revised edition. Gin and Company, Boston.

Alderson, Wroe and Sessions (1949). Foundations of Marketing Science: A Proposal for Basic Research. *Cost and Profit Outlook*, 2(May-June, No. 7), 4 pages.

Alderson, Wroe and Sessions (1949). Consumer Choice and Free Markets. *Cost and Profit Outlook*, 2(December, No. 9).

Alderson, Wroe (1950). Survival and Adjustment in Organized Behavior Systems. In Cox, Reavis and Alderson, Wroe, editors, *Theory in Marketing*, Chapter 4, pages 65-87. Richard D. Irwin, Chicago, IL.

Alderson, Wroe (1950). The Concentration of the American Market in Metropolitan Areas. *Printers' Ink*, 233 (October 27, No. 4):27-31, 56. A new population study is presented based on 149 metropolitan area Census figures, reemphasizing the basic importance of urban markets. A preview of the addition of 22 new metropolitan areas by the Census to Alderson's 149, was published in 1951 as Census Data for 22 New Standard Metropolitan Areas. *Printers' Ink*, 234 (February 9, No. 6):29.

Alderson, Wroe (1950). Book review: Donald Hobart editor, (1950). *Marketing Research Practice*. Ronald Press, NY. *Journal of Marketing*, 15(July):112-114.

Alderson, Wroe (1950). Let's Look at the Cost of Distribution. address before the National Marketing Conference, Chamber of Commerce of the United States of America, Detroit, MI February 28 (mimeographed). Reference from Vaile, Grether and Reavis Cox (1952, page 643).

Alderson, Wroe with Cox, Reavis, editors, (1950). *Theory in Marketing: Selected Essays*. Richard D. Irwin, Chicago. The book review essay by David Revzan (1950) *Journal of Marketing*, 15(July, No. 1):101-109 is very insightful.

Alderson, Wroe and Sessions, Robert E. (1950). *'Unjustly Discriminatory or Promotive of Monopoly', Defined and Applied to Tire Distribution: An Economic Study of Tire Marketing*. Alderson and Sessions, Philadelphia, Penn, January.

Alderson, Wroe and Sessions (1950). The Alderson and Sessions Basic Research Program. *Cost and Profit Outlook*, 3(July).

Alderson, Wroe and Sessions (1950). Marketing Efficiency and the Principle of Postponement. *Cost and Profit Outlook*, 3(September, No. 4).

Alderson, Wroe (1951). A Systematics for Problems of Action. *Philosophy of Science*, 18(January, No. 1):16-25.

Alderson, Wroe (1951) Progress in the Theory of Marketing. In Wales, Hugh G., editor, *Changing Perspectives in Marketing*, 1949 Marketing Symposium, pages 77-90. The University of Illinois Press, Urbana, IL.

Alderson, Wroe and Kent, Leonard (1951). The Concentration of the American Wholesale and Retail Markets in Metropolitan Areas. *Printers' Ink*, 235(April 13):29-32, 54, 55.

Alderson, Wroe and Kent, Leonard (1951). Major American Markets. *Printers' Ink*, 235(May 25):31-35.

Alderson, Wroe and Sessions (1951). The Strategy of Business Growth. *Cost and Profit Outlook*, 4(April). Reprinted in Kelly, Eugene and Lazer, William, editors, (1958). *Managerial Marketing: Perspectives and Viewpoints A Source Book*, pages 137-143. Richard D. Irwin, Homewood, IL. Reprinted in Lazer, William and Kelly, Eugene, editors, (1962). *Managerial Marketing: Perspectives and Viewpoints A Source Book*, revised edition, pages 295-301. Richard D. Irwin, Homewood, IL.

Alderson, Wroe and Sessions (1951). Searching and Sorting in the Market Place. *Cost and Profit Outlook*, 4(June, No. 6).

Alderson, Wroe and Sessions (1951). Communication in a Marketing System. *Cost and Profit Outlook*, 4(August). Reprinted in Kelly, Eugene and Lazer, William, editors, (1958). *Managerial Marketing: Perspectives and Viewpoints A Source Book*, pages 369-378. Richard D. Irwin, Homewood, IL. Reprinted in Lazer, William and Kelly Eugene, editors, (1962). *Managerial Marketing: Perspectives and Viewpoints A Source Book*, revised edition, pages 541-549. Richard D. Irwin, Homewood, IL.

Alderson, Wroe and Sessions (1951). Perspectives for Marketing Planning. *Cost and Profit Outlook*, 4(September).

Alderson, Wroe and Sessions (1951). The Meaning of Market Potential. *Cost and Profit Outlook*, 4(December, No. 12).

548   ALDERSONIAN MARKETING THOUGHT

Alderson, Wroe (1952). Psychology for Marketing and Economics. *Journal of Marketing*, 17(October, No. 2):119-135. Paper was originally presented at the second Marketing Theory Seminar August 1952, University of Colorado.

Alderson, Wroe (1952). Quantity Limits and the New Economic Policy. *Journal of Marketing*, 17(July, No. 1):56-60. This is a reprint of an article, which appeared in *Cost and Profit Outlook*, 5(January, No. 1) in the same year. It was reprinted because of the importance of the subject to business executives and teachers.

Alderson, Wroe and Sessions (1952). Principles of Market Planning. *Cost and Profit Outlook*, 5 (June, No. 6). Reprinted in Kelly, Eugene and Lazer, William, editors, (1958). *Managerial Marketing: Perspectives and Viewpoints A Source Book*, pages 209-215. Richard D. Irwin, Homewood, IL. Reprinted in Lazer, William and Kelly, Eugene, editors, (1962). *Managerial Marketing: Perspectives and Viewpoints A Source Book*, revised edition, pages 326-332. Richard D. Irwin, Homewood, IL.

Alderson, Wroe and Sessions (1952). Marketing Initiatives and Price Policy. *Cost and Profit Outlook*, 5(August, No. 8).

Alderson, Wroe (1953). Social Adjustment in Business Management. *Explorations in Entrepreneurial History*, 6(October, No. 1):20-29.

Alderson, Wroe (1953). Statistical Training for Marketing Research. *American Statistician*, 7(February):9-11.

Alderson, Wroe with Ralph Alexander, and Frank Surface (1953). *Marketing*, 3rd edition, Gin and Company, Boston.

Alderson, Wroe (1953). A Theory of Puzzles and Problem Solving. Unpublished paper presented at the Marketing Theory Seminar, Dartmouth College.

Alderson, Wroe and Sessions (1953). Consumer Motivation and the Economics of Consumption. *Cost and Profit Outlook*, 6(February, No. 2).

Alderson, Wroe and Sessions (1953). How to Solve Marketing Problems. *Cost and Profit Outlook*, 6(August, No. 8), whole issue 4 pages.

Alderson, Wroe (1954). A Functionalist Approach to Competition. In Huegy, Harvey, editor, *The Role and Nature of Competition in our Marketing Economy*, pages 40-49. 1953 Marketing Symposium, University of Illinois Bulletin, 51

No. 76, Bureau of Economic and Business Research, College of Commerce and Business Administration, University of Illinois, Urbana, IL.

Alderson, Wroe (1954). Factors Governing the Development of Marketing Channels. In Clewett, Richard, editor, *Marketing Channels for Manufactured Products*, pages 5-34. Richard D. Irwin, Homewood, IL. Reprinted in Mallen, Bruce, editor, (1967). *The Marketing Channel*, pages 35-40. John Wiley and Sons, NY. Reprinted in Moller, William, Jr. and Wilemon, David, editors, (1971). *Marketing Channels A Systems Viewpoint A Book of Readings*, pages 15-24. Richard D. Irwin, Homewood, IL.

Alderson, Wroe (1954). The Crisis in Urban Development. *Cost and Profit Outlook*, 7(September, No. 9), whole issue 4 pages. From a talk before the Mayor's Conference on Philadelphia's Future, September 22, 1954.

Alderson, Wroe (1954). Search Theory in the Analysis of Consumer Shopping. *Journal of the Operations Research Society of America*, 2(February, No. 1):78. The abstract was found under the article The Third National Meeting of the Society as a paper presented at the meeting.

Alderson, Wroe (1954). Evaluation of Acquisitions in Antitrust Cases. *Cost and Profit Outlook*, 7(November, No. 11), whole issue 4 pages. From a talk before the Association of the Bar of the City of New York. The approval of J. J. Smith, of Hogan and Hartson, Washington, is acknowledged.

Alderson, Wroe (1954). Problem Solving and Marketing Science, Charles Coolidge Parlin Memorial Lecture, Philadelphia, as announced in *Cost and Profit Outlook*, 7(June, No. 6):4. Available at: http://www-marketing.wharton.upenn.edu/news.info/wroe_alderson.html.

Alderson, Wroe and Sessions (1954). The Motivation of Consumer Buying. *Cost and Profit Outlook*, 7(January, No. 1):1-3.

Alderson, Wroe and Sessions (1954). Buying Motives and Consumer Shopping. *Cost and Profit Outlook*, 7(February, No. 2):1-4.

Alderson, Wroe and Sessions (1954). Experimental Methods in Motivation Research. *Cost and Profit Outlook*, 7(March, No. 3), whole issue 4 pages.

Alderson, Wroe and Sessions (1954). An Audit of Marketing Methods and Channels. *Cost and Profit Outlook*, 7(October, No. 10), whole issue 4 pages.

Alderson, Wroe and Sessions (1954). Reflections on the Executive Function. *Cost and Profit Outlook*, 7(December, No. 12), whole issue 4 pages.

Alderson, Wroe (1955). Here's How Stores Will Face It. *Nation's Business*, 43(November, No. 11):85-90. Reprinted in Seelye, Alfred, editor, (1958). *Marketing in Transition*, pages 69-77. Harper and Brothers, NY. Reprinted in Kelly, Eugene and Lazer, William, editors, (1958). *Managerial Marketing: Perspectives and Viewpoints A Source Book*, pages 349-358. Richard D. Irwin, Homewood, IL.

Alderson, Wroe (1955). Operations Research and Management Problems. *Advanced Management*, 20(4):14-17.

Alderson, Wroe and Sessions (1955). Personality and Function in Motivation Research. *Cost and Profit Outlook*, 8(February, No. 2):1, 3-4.

Alderson, Wroe and Sessions (1955). A Marketing Approach to Organization Planning. *Cost and Profit Outlook*, 8(March, No. 3):1-3. Reprinted in Kelly, Eugene and Lazer, William, editors, (1958). *Managerial Marketing: Perspectives and Viewpoints A Source Book*, pages 237-242. Richard D. Irwin, Homewood, IL. Reprinted in Lazer, William and Kelly, Eugene, editors, (1962). *Managerial Marketing: Perspectives and Viewpoints A Source Book*, revised edition, pages 365-370. Richard D. Irwin, Homewood, IL.

Alderson, Wroe and Sessions (1955). How to Use Marketing and Management Counsel. *Cost and Profit Outlook*, 8(May, No. 5), whole issue 4 pages.

Alderson, Wroe and Sessions (1955). Interaction Levels in Consumer Motivation. *Cost and Profit Outlook*, 8(June, No. 6):1-4. The second article, The Expanding Frontiers of Marketing Research, pages 1-3.

Alderson, Wroe and Sessions (1955). Marketing and World Peace. *Cost and Profit Outlook*, 8(July, No. 7), whole issue 4 pages.

Alderson, Wroe and Sessions (1955). Supermarkets and Marketing Efficiency. *Cost and Profit Outlook*, 8(August, No. 8), whole issue 4 pages. The second article, The Changing Pattern of Food Marketing, pages 1 and 4.

Alderson, Wroe and Sessions (1955). The Psychology of Consumer Behavior. *Cost and Profit Outlook*, 8(September, No. 9):1 and 3-4.

Alderson, Wroe and Sessions (1955). Needs, Wants and Creative Marketing. *Cost and Profit Outlook*, 8(September, No. 9):1-3. Reprinted under Alderson Associates Inc. in Westing, Howard and Albaum, Gerald, editors, (1964). *Modern Marketing Thought An Environmental Approach to Marketing*, pages 18-21. Macmillan, NY.

Alderson, Wroe and Sessions (1955). Imperfect Competition and Marketing Strategy. *Cost and Profit Outlook*, 8(October, No. 10):1-3. The second article, Advertising in the National Economy is on page 4.

Alderson, Wroe and Sessions (1955). A Marketing View of Business Policy. *Cost and Profit Outlook*, 8(December, No. 12), whole issue 4 pages.

Alderson, Wroe (1956). Biography of Charles Coolidge Parlin. *Journal of Marketing*, 21(July, No. 1):1-2.

Alderson, Wroe (1956). A Functionalist Approach to Consumer Motivation. In Cole, Robert, editor, *Consumer Behavior and Motivation*, pages 6-24. Marketing Symposium, University of Illinois Bulletin, 53 No. 45, Bureau of Economic and Business Research, College of Commerce and Business Administration, University of Illinois, Urbana, IL.

Alderson, Wroe, Gary, S. G., Edgerton, W. B., Moore, H. W., Pickett, C. E., and Zelliot, E. (1956). *Meeting the Russians: American Quakers Visit the Soviet Union*, American Friends Service Committee, Philadelphia, PA.

Alderson, Wroe and Sessions (1956). Experimental Research in Consumer Behavior. *Cost and Profit Outlook*, 9(February, No. 2), whole issue, 4 pages.

Alderson, Wroe and Sessions (1956). Planning as a Component of Leadership. *Cost and Profit Outlook*, 9(March, No. 3). 4 pages, 1-3.

Alderson, Wroe and Sessions (1956). Consumer Information and Rational Choice. *Cost and Profit Outlook*, 9(March, No. 3):1, 3-4. Notion of low information gathering discussed (i.e. low involvement).

Alderson, Wroe and Sessions (1956). Advertising and the Pursuit of Happiness. *Cost and Profit Outlook*, 9(June, No. 6), whole issue 4 page. The use of hedonomics and other expressions are mentioned.

Alderson Wroe and Sessions (1956), Selecting the Location for a New Supermarket. *Cost and Profit Outlook*, 9(July, No. 7): 1, 3-4.

Alderson, Wroe and Sessions (1956). Advertising Strategy and Theories of Motivation. *Cost and Profit Outlook*, 9(December, No. 12), whole issue, 4 pages. Reprinted and adapted in Ferber, Robert and Wales, Hugh, editors, (1958). *Motivation and Market Behavior*, pages 11-21. Richard D. Irwin, Homewood, IL.

Alderson, Wroe (1957). *Marketing Behavior and Executive Action A Functionalist Approach to Marketing Theory*. Richard D. Irwin, Homewood, IL. The book was translated and published in Japanese in 1984. The book was reviewed by Richard Clewett (1958). *Journal of Marketing*, 23(July, No. 1):343-345. Daniel Feinberg (1957) *American Economic Review*, 47(December):1058-1060. Glen Mitchell (1959). *Journal of Farm Economics*, 41(4):853-855. Donald Mulvihill, (1958/59). *Southern Economic Journal*, 25(1/4):113-114. The 1957 issue of *Cost and Profit Outlook*, 10(February No. 2), presented a brief summary of the book on page 1.

Alderson, Wroe (1957). Competition for Differential Advantage, chapter 5 from *Marketing Behavior and Executive Action*, pages 101-109.Richard D. Irwin, Homewood, IL. Reprinted (with deletion) in McCarthy, E. Jerome, Grashof, Johnand and Brogowicz, Andrew, editors, (1978). *Readings in Basic Marketing*, revised edition, pages 52-59. Richard D. Irwin, Homewood, IL.

Alderson, Wroe (1957). Advertisers Urged to Follow Path of Rational Problem Solving Rather Than of Instinctive Drives. *Advertising Age*, 28(March 4):83-84.

Alderson, Wroe (1957). A Marketing View of Business Policy. In Lawrence, R. J. and Thomas, M. J., editors, (1971). *Modern Marketing Management Selected Readings*, pages 17-39. Penguin Books, Middlesex, England. Excerpts from *Marketing Behavior and Executive Action*, pages 444-463. This article has the same title as the 1955 one.

Alderson, Wroe (1957). Major Issues in Motivation Research. In Clewett Richard, editor, *Marketing's Role in Scientific Management*, pages 271-281. American Marketing Association, Chicago. Also in Alderson, Wroe (1957). Major Issues in Motivation Research. *Cost and Profit Outlook*, 10(July No. 7), whole issue, 4 pages. Paper presented at the National Conference of the American Marketing Association, June 19.

Alderson, Wroe with Donald Longman and others (1957). The Values and Uses of Distribution Cost Analysis, American Marketing Association Committee on Distribution Costs and Efficiency. *Journal of Marketing*, 21(April No. 4):395-400. Reprinted in Lazer, William and Kelly, Eugene, editors, (1962). *Managerial Marketing: Perspectives and Viewpoints A Source Book*, revised edition, pages 213-220. Richard D. Irwin, Homewood, IL. Longman was the chairman of the Committee and other members were Donald Blankertz, E. J. Carroll, Donald Cowan, Thomas McGann, Robert Miner, Charles Sevin, and Charles Smith.

Alderson, Wroe (1957). Basic Research and the Future of Marketing Theory. In Bass, Frank, editor, *The Frontiers of Marketing Thought and Science*, pages 170-178. American Marketing Association, Chicago.

Alderson, Wroe (1957). Areas for Basic Research in Marketing. A mimeographed paper, dated September 17, Alderson Associates. Inc., Philadelphia.

Alderson, Wroe and Sessions (1957). The Challenge of Marketing Management. *Cost and Profit Outlook*, 10(January, No. 1), whole issue 4 pages. Reprinted in Kelly, Eugene and Lazer, William, editors, (1958). *Managerial Marketing: Perspectives and Viewpoints A Source Book*, pages 199-208. Richard D. Irwin, Homewood, IL. Also reprinted in Lazer, William and Kelly, Eugene, editors, (1962). *Managerial Marketing: Perspectives and Viewpoints A Source Book*, revised edition, pages 317-326. Richard D. Irwin, Homewood, IL.

Alderson, Wroe and Sessions (1957). Operations Research Applied to Marketing Problems. *Cost and Profit Outlook*, 10(March, No. 3):1-4.

Alderson, Wroe and Sessions (1957). Automation and Marketing Orientation. *Cost and Profit Outlook*, 10(August, No. 8):1-4.

Alderson, Wroe and Sessions (1957). What is Industrial Marketing. *Cost and Profit Outlook*, 10(November, No. 11):1-4.

Alderson, Wroe and Sessions (1957). Management Support for Marketing Planning. *Cost and Profit Outlook*, 10(December, No. 12), pages 1-4.

Alderson, Wroe (1958). The Analytical Framework for Marketing. In Duncan, Delbert, editor, *Proceedings: Conference of Marketing Teachers from Far Western States*, pages 15-28. University of California, Berkeley. Reprinted in Bliss, Perry, editor, (1963). *Marketing and the Behavioral Sciences Selected Readings*, pages 25-40. Allen and Bacon, Boston, as well as in the 2nd edition (1968), pages 565-580. Reprinted in Barksdale, Hiram, editor, (1964). *Market-*

ing in Progress: Patterns and Potentials, pages 84-97. Holt, Rinehart and Winston NY. Reprinted in Kernan, Jerome and Sommers, Montrose, editors, (1968). *Perspectives in Marketing Theory*, pages 69-82. Appleton-Century-Crofts, NY. Reprinted in Lawrence, R. J. and Thomas, M. J., editors, (1971). *Modern Marketing Management Selected Readings*, pages 58-74. Penguin Books, England, Middlesex,. Reprinted in Brown, Stephen and Fisk, Raymond, editors, *Marketing Theory Distinguished Contributions*, pages 45-53. John Wiley and Sons, NY. Reprinted in Enis, Ben and Cox, Keith, editors, (1969). *Marketing Classics A Selection of Influential Articles*, pages 2-15. Allyn and Bacon, Boston, as well in the 2,nd, 3,rd and 4th editions (1973, 1977, 1981) pages 24-37, 31-44, 24-34. Reprinted in Enis, Ben, Cox, Keith and Mokwa, Michael, editors, (1990). *Marketing Classics A Selection of Influential Articles*, 8th edition, pages 22-32. Prentice-Hall, Upper Saddle River.

Alderson, Wroe (1958) A Basic Guide to Market Planning. *Industrial Marketing*, 44(July):53-57. Reprinted in Shultz, William and Mazze, Edward, editors, (1963). *Marketing in Action Readings*, pages 398-405.Wadsworth, Belmont, CA.

Alderson, Wroe (1958). The Productivity of Advertising Dollars. *Cost and Profit Outlook*, 11(February, No. 2), whole issue 4 pages. Reprinted in Sandage, C. H. and Fryburger, Vernon, editors, (1960). *The Role of Advertising A Book of Readings*, pages 381-390. Richard D. Irwin, Homewood, IL. Based on a talk presented at the AAA Research Workshop, Eastern Annual Conference.

Alderson, Wroe (1958). Consumer Reaction to Product Innovation. In Clark, Lincoln, editor, *Consumer Behavior Research on Consumer Reactions*, pages 3-9. Harper and Brothers, NY.

Alderson, Wroe (1958). Theory and Practice of Market Planning. *Cost and Profit Outlook*, 11(July-August, No. 7-8), whole issue 6 pages. Reprinted in Britt, Steuart Henderson and Boyd, Harper, editors, (1963). *Marketing Management and Administrative Action*, pages 154-164. McGraw-Hill, NY. Reprinted in Britt, Steuart Henderson and Boyd, Harper, editors, (1968). *Marketing Management and Administrative Action*, second edition, pages 245-255. McGraw-Hill, NY.

Alderson, Wroe Associates Inc. (1958). Introducing Behavior Research. *Cost and Profit Outlook*, 11(January, No. 1).

Alderson, Wroe (1959). A Marketing View of Business Policy. In Stockman, Lynn, editor, *Advancing Marketing Efficiency*, pages 114-119. American

Marketing Association, Chicago. Reprinted in Lazer, William and Kelly, Eugene, editors, (1962). *Managerial Marketing: Perspectives and Viewpoints A Source Book*, revised edition, pages 28-34. Richard D. Irwin, Homewood, IL. Reprinted in Holloway, Robert and Hancock, Robert, editors, (1969). *The Environment of Marketing Behavior Selections from the Literature*, second edition, pages 260-262. John Wiley and Sons, NY.

Alderson, Wroe (1959). Perspective on the Planning Process. *Journal of the Academy of Management*, 2(December, No. 3):181-196.

Alderson, Wroe (1959). Administered Prices Reconsidered-Discussion. *American Economic Review*, 49(May, No. 2):451-461.

Alderson, Wroe (1959). Product-Line Policy And the Marketing Audit. In *Analyzing and Improving Marketing Performance 'Marketing Audits' In Theory and Practice*, AMA Management Report No. 32, Marketing Division, pages 61-64. American Management Association, NY.

Alderson, Wroe Associates Inc. (1959). Top Management Support and Market Orientation. *Cost and Profit Outlook*, 11(January, No. 1).

Alderson, Wroe (1960). New Concepts for Measuring Productivity in Marketing. In *Productivity in Marketing: Its Measurement and Change*, Department of Marketing, University of Illinois Bulletin, 58 August, Bureau of Economic and Business Research, College of Commerce and Business Administration, Urbana, pages 3-11. The University of Illinois, IL.

Alderson, Wroe (1960). Marketing Research Breakthroughs of the 1960's: Discussion. In Dolva, Wenzil, editor, *Marketing Keys to Profits in the 1960's*, pages 300-303. American Marketing Association, Chicago.

Alderson, Wroe (1960). Possible Impact of the Soviets Upon World Trade in the 1960's?Discussion. In Dolva, Wenzil, editor, *Marketing Keys to Profits in the 1960's*, pages 485-991. American Marketing Association, Chicago.

Alderson, Wroe et al. (1960). *The Structure of Retail Competition in the Philadelphia Market*, Wharton School of Finance and Commerce, Philadelphia.

Alderson, Wroe (1960) Marketing and Management Decision. *Cost and Profit Outlook*, 13(January., No. 1):1, 3-6. Reprinted in Lazer, William and Kelly, Eugene, editors, (1962). *Managerial Marketing: Perspectives and Viewpoints A Source Book*, revised edition, pages 213-220. Richard D. Irwin, Homewood,

IL. Based on a talk before the National Association of Accountants.

Alderson, Wroe with Ralph Alexander and others (1960). *Marketing Definitions A Glossary of Marketing Terms*, American Marketing Association, Chicago, IL. A 23-page AMA publication. The other members of the Committee were John Albright, W. F. Crowder, W. A. Cullman, Robert Prather, William Shultz, Hugh Wales, J. W. Wingate, H. D. Wolfe, and Vergil Reeditor, Wroe Alderson was a member of two of the three Definitions Committees, all chaired by Ralph Alexander, which published the 1935 and 1960 reports. He was not a member of the second Report of the Definitions Committee (1948). *Journal of Marketing*, 13(October):202-217.

Alderson, Wroe with Ralph Alexander and others (1960). Key Marketing Words? What They Mean. *Small Business Administration*, August (Ralph Alexander, and The Committee on Definitions of the American Marketing Association). Reprinted in Dirksen, Charles, Kroeger, Arthur and Lockley, Lawrence, editors, (1963). *Readings in Marketing*, pages 60-66. Richard D. Irwin, Homewood, IL.

Alderson, Wroe with Stanley J. Shapiro (1961). Book Review: *An Introduction to Electronic Data Processing for Business*, by Hein, Leonard, D. Van Nostrand, Princeton. *Management Science*, 8(October, No. 1):109-110.

Alderson, Wroe (1961). A New Approach to Advertising Theory. *Cost and Profit Outlook*, (Spring):1-2, 6-8. Reprinted in Holmes, Parker, Brownlie, Ralph and Bartels, Robert, editors, (1963). *Readings in Marketing*, pages 371-378. Charles E. Merrill Books, Columbus, Ohio.

Alderson, Wroe (1961). Advertising in a Free Society. *Cost and Profit Outlook*, (Summer):1-2, 6-8.

Alderson, Wroe (1962). Mass Audience Capable of Improvement in Taste, *Business and Society*, 3(Autumn, No. 1):25-28.

Alderson, Wroe (1962). Discussion-on Fisk's 'The General Systems Approach to Marketing', and David Hertz 'Marketing as a Social Discipline', in Stevens, W. D., editor, *The Social Responsibilities of Marketing*, pages 219-221. American Marketing Association, Chicago.

Alderson, Wroe (1962). Introduction. In Frank, Ronald, Kuehn, Alfred and Massy, William, editors, *Quantitative Techniques in Marketing Analysis Text and Readings*, pages xi-xvii. Richard D. Irwin, Homewood, IL.

Alderson, Wroe (1962). Book Review: *Prediction and Optimal Decision* by Churchman, C. W., *Management Science*, 8(April, No. 3):375-380.

Alderson, Wroe Associates (1962). Basic Research Report on Consumer Behavior: Report on a Study of Shopping Behavior and Methods for Its Implication. In Kuehn, Alfred and Massy, William, editors, *Quantitative Techniques in Marketing Analysis*, pages 129-145. Richard D. Irwin, Homewood, IL. This is an edited version of a mimeographed report dated April 1957, when the firm was known as Alderson and Sessions.

Alderson, Wroe and Shapiro, Stanley J., editors, (1963). *Marketing and the Computer*, Prentice-Hall, Englewood Cliffs, NJ. Reviewed by Bass, Frank (1964). *Journal of Marketing Research*, 1(August):84-85.

Alderson, Wroe (1963). Administered Prices and Retail Grocery Advertising. *Journal of Advertising Research*, 3(March, No. 1):2-6. Reprinted in Ryans, John, Donnelly, James and Ivancevitch, John, editors, (1970). *New Dimensions in Retailing*, pages 263-273. Wadsworth, Belmont, CA.

Alderson, Wroe (1963). An Approach to a Theory of Planning. In Decker, William, editor, *Emerging Concepts in Marketing*, pages 257-264. American Marketing Association, Chicago.

Alderson, Wroe (1963). An Overview, Marketing and the Computer. In Alderson, Wroe and Shapiro, Stanley, editors, *Marketing and the Computer*, pages 2-13. Prentice-Hall, Englewood Cliffs, NJ.

Alderson, Wroe (1963). Ford Foundation Archives: Application for Ford Foundation funding to support PhD students under Wroe Alderson, Reel R1643, Grant number PA 64-14.

Alderson, Wroe (1963). Growth and Market Planning. *Growth and Profit Planner*, 1(February, No. 1):1, 3. The first issue of Behavior Systems, a new consulting firm.

Alderson, Wroe (1963). Consumer Questions and Advertising Answers. *Growth and Profit Planner*, 1(August, No. 3):1, 3-6.

Alderson, Wroe (1963). Planning in Japan. *Growth and Profit Planner*, 1(November, No. 4), whole issue 4 pages.

Alderson, Wroe and Shapiro, Stanley J. (1963). A Metropolitan Data Bank for the Business Community. *Business Horizons*, 5(Summer):53-62.

Alderson, Wroe (1964). The American Economy and Christian Ethics. *Growth and Profit Planner*, 2(August, No. 3), whole issue, 4 pages. From a talk to students at the Christian Association at the University of Pennsylvania, June. Reprinted in Wright, John and Mertes, John, editors, (1974). *Advertising's Role in Society*, pages 252-258. West Publishing, NY, St. Paul, Minn.

Alderson, Wroe with Reavis Cox and Stanley Shapiro, editors, (1964). *Theory in Marketing*, Second Series. Richard D. Irwin, Homewood, IL. A book review essay by Grether, E. T. (1965). An Emerging Apologetic of Managerialism?. *Theory in Marketing*, 1964, *Journal of Marketing Research*, 2(May):190-195. Also reviewed by Seymour Banks (1966). *Journal of Business*, 39(July, No. 3):420-421.

Alderson, Wroe (1964). A Normative Theory of Marketing Systems. In Cox, Reavis, Alderson, Wroe and Shapiro, Stanley, editors, *Theory in Marketing*, pages 92-108. Richard D. Irwin, Homewood, IL.

Alderson, Wroe (1964). Marketing Systems in the Ecological Framework. In Huegy, Harvey, editor, *The Conceptual Framework for a Science of Marketing*, Marketing Symposium, October 1963, University of Illinois Bulletin, 61(February, No. 57). Bureau of Business Management, College of Commerce and Business Administration, pages 29-43. University of Illinois, Urbana, IL.

Alderson, Wroe (1964). Ethics, Ideologies and Sanctions, for the Report on the Committee on Ethical Standards and Professional Practices, American Marketing Association, pages 1-20. Reprinted in Lavidge, Robert and Holloway, Robert, editors, (1969). *Marketing and Society The Challenge*, AMA Reprints Series, pages 74-85. Richard D. Irwin, Homewood, IL.

Alderson, Wroe (1964). Book Review *The Study of Society: A Unified Approach*, Alfred Kuhn 1963, Irwin Dorsey Press, Homewood, IL, *Journal of Marketing Research*, 1(February, No. 1):72-74.

Alderson, Wroe (1964). Management Counsel in Sickness or in Health. *Growth and Profit Planner*, 2(May No. 1), whole issue, 4 pages.

Alderson, Wroe (1964). Forecasting Structural Change in Long Range Planning. In Robert Kaplan ed. *The Marketing Concept in Action*, pages 146-153. American Marketing Association, Chicago.

Alderson, Wroe and Green, Paul (1964). Operating Under a Formal Marketing Plan. *Growth and Profit Planner*, 2(November No. 4):4. Reprinted from *Planning and Problem Solving*, pages 72-73. Richard D. Irwin, Homewood, IL.

Alderson, Wroe (1964). The Strategy of Marketing Research. *Growth and Profit Planner*, 2(December 5):1, 3.

Alderson, Wroe and Shapiro, Stanley J. (1964). Towards a Theory of Retail Competition. In Cox, Reavis, Alderson, Wroe and Shapiro, Stanley J., editors, *Theory in Marketing*, pages 190-212. Richard D. Irwin, Homewood, IL.

Alderson, Wroe with Reavis Cox and Stanley J. Shapiro, editors, (1964). *Theory in Marketing*, Richard D. Irwin, Homewood, IL.

Alderson, Wroe and Green, Paul (1964). Growth vs. Profit Maximization in Market Planning. *Growth and Profit Planner*, 2(1). Behavior Systems, Philadelphia, Pa. This reference may be incorrect.

Alderson, Wroe and Green, Paul (1964). *Planning and Problem Solving in Marketing*, Richard D. Irwin, Homewood, IL. Reviewed by Amstutz, Arnold (1968). *Journal of Marketing Research*, 5(February, No. 1):109-111. Part of chapter 11, Bayesian Decision Theory in Channel Selection, pages 311-317 is reprinted in Mallen, Bruce, editor, (1967). *The Marketing Channel: A Conceptual Viewpoint*, pages 199-203. John Wiley and Sons, NY.

Alderson, Wroe (1965). *Dynamic Marketing Behavior A Functionalist Theory of Marketing*, Richard D. Irwin, Homewood, IL. Especially chapter 3, Transactions and Transvections, chapter 8, The Search for Differential Advantage and Research Agenda for Functionalism, pages 345-374. Chapter 13, Cooperation and Conflict in Marketing Channels, reprinted in Stern, Louis, editor, (1969). *Distribution Channels: Behavioral Dimensions*, pages 195-209. Houghton Mifflin, Boston. The Heterogeneous Market and the Organized Behavior System, pages 23-51. Reprinted in Hunt, Shelby, (1983). *Marketing Theory The Philosophy of Marketing Science*, pages 292-313. Richard D Irwin, Homewood, IL.

Alderson, Wroe (1965). A Marketing View of the Patent System. In Wroe Alderson, Terpstra, Vern and Shapiro, Stanley, editors, *Patents and Progress*

The Sources and Impact of Advancing Technology, pages 225-243. Richard D. Irwin, Homewood, IL.

Alderson, Wroe (1965). Marketing Innovations and the Problem Solver. In Frederick Webster Jr. editor, *New Directions in Marketing*, pages 53-61. American Marketing Association, Chicago. Michael Halbert presented the paper due to his death on May 31.

Alderson, Wroe (1965). Commentary on 'The Researcher and the Manager: A Dialectic of Implementation'. *Management Science*, 12(October, No. 2):B-6 to B-9.

Alderson, Wroe and Martin, Miles (1965). Toward a Formal Theory of Transactions and Transvections. *Journal of Marketing Research*, 2(May):117-127. Reprinted in Mallen, Bruce, editor, (1967). *The Marketing Channel: A Conceptual Viewpoint*, pages 50-55. John Wiley and Sons, NY. Reprinted in Fisk, George and Dixon, Donald, editors, (1967). *Theories for Marketing Systems Analysis Selected Readings*, pages 71-80. Harper & Row, NY. Reprinted also in Kernan, Jerome and Sommers, Montrose, editors, (1968). *Perspectives in Marketing Theory*, pages 340-360. Appleton-Century-Crofts, NY.

Alderson, Wroe, Terpstra, Vern and Shapiro, Stanley, editors, (1965). *Patents and Progress The Sources and Impact of Advancing Technology*, Richard D. Irwin, Homewood, IL.

Alderson, Wroe (1966) Mercury, Yes; Mars, No!. *Columbia Journal of World Business*, 1(Winter, No. 1):9-14.

Alderson, Wroe and Halbert, Michael (1968). *Men, Motives and Markets*, Chapter 3, pages 45-51. Prentice Hall, Englewood Cliffs, NJ. Reprinted as The Mission of Marketing in Wish, John and Gamble, S. H., editors, (1971). *Marketing and Social Issues: An Action Reader*, pages 49-59. John Wiley and Sons, NY.

Chapter 38

A SELECT LIST OF AUTHORS WHO HAVE COMMENTED ON ALDERSONIAN MARKETING THOUGHT

From 1951 to 2005

Robert D. Tamilia
University of Quebec at Montreal

Ben Wooliscroft
University of Otago

with the assistance of Stanley J. Shapiro
Simon Fraser University

This bibliography lists many of the publications of authors who have commented upon and/or elaborated upon Alderson's contributions to marketing thought, or who have built upon his ideas in making their own theoretical contributions to marketing. Numerous readings books in marketing, retailing, advertising and other topics from the 1940s to the present were consulted. In addition, the indices of a large number of marketing textbooks published from the 1940s to the present were searched for the Alderson name. Non-American Marketing Association sponsored Conference Proceedings were also examined.

The references included here represent a solid sample of what many authors have discussed in their textbooks or in articles on Alderson. However, it would be an almost impossible task to look at every edition of every marketing textbook published since the 1940s to see if the authors had discussed Alderson. Such a task would be formidable especially for textbooks that were published on other continents or languages other than in English. Thus, there may well be additional authors who have either commented upon or have used Alderson's theoretical ideas whose work is not listed in this bibliography. The compilers of this listing look forward to being informed of any and all omissions of what our colleagues consider important material on Alderson.

Atwater, Thomas (1979). 'Lost' or Neglected Components of a General Equilibrium Theory of Marketing. In Ferrell, O. C., Brown, Stephen and Lamb, Charles, editors, *Conceptual and Theoretical Developments in Marketing*, pages 184-196. American Marketing Association, Chicago.

Banks, Seymour (1951) Comments on Alderson's Index of Sorting Balance. *Journal of Marketing*, 15(January):331-335.

Barksdale, Hiram (1980). Wroe Alderson's Contributions to Marketing Theory. In Lamb, Charles and Dunne, Patrick, editors, *Theoretical Developments in Marketing*, pages 1-3. American Marketing Association, Chicago.

Bartels, Robert (1970). *Marketing Theory and Metatheory*, pages 21-22, and 24-25. Richard D. Irwin, Homewood, IL.

Bartels Robert (1988). *The History of Marketing Thought*, 3rd edition. Publishing Horizons, Columbus, OH. Alderson is discussed on pages 156-157, 177, 178, 181, 234, 236-238, and 249. Alderson is also discusses in Bartels (1962). *The Development of Marketing Thought*, Richard D. Irwin, Homewood, IL., pp, 178, and 181-182, and in the 2nd edition (1976). *The History of Marketing Thought*. Grid, Columbus, OH, with the exact same page numbers as in the 3rd edition, except for page 249.

Baumol, William (1957). On the Role of Marketing Theory. *Journal of Marketing*, 21(April):413-418. The last few pages of the article are on Alderson.

Beckman, Terry (2005). Alderson's Contributions to Marketing, or: The Wroe River: The Canyon Carved by Alderson. In Neilson, Leighann C., editor, *The Future of Marketing's Past*, Proceedings of CHARM, Conference on Historical Analysis and Research in Marketing, pages 2-10. Association for Historical Research in Marketing, Long Beach, CA.

Bell, Martin (1966). *Marketing Concepts and Strategy*, chapter 3, The Systems Concept in Marketing, pages 56-77. Houghton Mifflin, Boston.

Blair, Ed, and Uhl, Kenneth (1977). Wroe Alderson and Modern Marketing Theory. In Slater, Charles C., editor, (1977). *Macro-Marketing*, pages 66-84. Business Research Division, Graduate School of Business Administration,

University of Colorado, Boulder, Colorado. Also published as working paper #326 August 1976, Faculty Working Papers, College of Commerce and Business Administration, University of Illinois at Urbana-Champaign.

Borden, Frederick (1955). Marketing consultant takes a first-hand look at distribution in the U.S.S.R. *Industrial Marketing*, 40(October, No. 10):71, 73. The article is based on Alderson's 30-day visit in June 1955 as one of a six-member delegation representing the American Friends Service Committee whose task was to look at the status of religious groups in the U.S.S.R. There's a neat photo of Alderson with a Polaroid camera.

Brown, Stephen (2002). Reading Wroe: On the Biopoetics of Alderson's Functionalism. *Marketing Theory*, 2(3):243-271. Also as a working paper, School of Marketing, University of Ulster, 2001.

Bruce, Grady Jr. and Dutton, Richard (nd). A Résumé of *Marketing Behavior and Executive Action* by Wroe Alderson, a 19-page mimeographed report. Both are graduates of the University of Texas.

Burley, Orin E. (1965). Wroe Alderson, Eulogy read to the Wharton School Faculty.

Business Week (1955). A Red Revolution in Marketing. No. 1353(August 6):114, 116-118, 120. An interview with Alderson following his visit to the Soviet Union, along the lines of the Borden (1955) article. This article contains much more marketing information compared to the Borden one. It should be noted that this article predates the Borden one by several months.

Buzzell, Robert (1964). Introduction to Alderson. In Huegy, Harvey, editor, *The Conceptual Framework for a Science of Marketing* University of Illinois Bulletin 61 (February, No. 57), pages 27-28. Bureau of Business Management, College of Commerce and Business Administration, University of Illinois, Urbana, IL.

Cooke, E. F. (1983). Wroe Alderson's Model of Marketing Competition. In Summey, John, et. al., editors, *Marketing Theories and Concepts for an Era of Change*, pages 161-163. Proceedings of the Southern Marketing Association.

Cox, Reavis, Dawson, Lyndon and Wales, Hugh (nd). Preface. The 9-page document including a table of content, with the McGarry (nd) and Sessions (nd) papers, were to be published in an AMA-approved book in the early 1980s containing all issues of *Cost and Profit Outlook*. (May 1947 to May-June 1958).

Unfortunately, the AMA never published the book.

Dawson, Lyndon and Wales, Hugh (1979). Consumer Motivation Theory in Historical Perspective: An Aldersonian View. In O. C. Ferrell, Brown, Stephen and Lamb, Charles, editors, *Conceptual and Theoretical Developments in Marketing*, pages 210-221. American Marketing Association, Chicago.

Dixon, Donald (1964). Functionalism As an Approach to Marketing Theory. *Economics and Business Bulletin*, pages 28-34.

Dixon, Donald (1965). Dynamic Marketing Behavior-The End or a Beginning? A Review Article of Wroe Alderson *Dynamic Marketing Behavior. Economic and Business Bulletin*, Temple University (December):35-41.

Dixon, Donald (1965). The Emergence of Marketing Systems *Economic and Business Bulletin*, (June):3-8.

Dixon, Donald (1967). A Social Systems Approach to Marketing. *The Southwestern Social Science Quarterly*, 48(September):164-173.

Dixon, Donald (1982). Universal Marketing Functions: A Systems Perspective. In John Summey, Bergiel, Blaise, and Anderson, Carol, editors, *A Spectrum of Contemporary Marketing Ideas*, Proceedings, pages 241-244. Southern Marketing Association.

Dixon, Donald and Wilkinson, Ian (1982). *The Marketing System*, Chapter 1, pages 1-23. Longman Cheshire, Melbourne, AU.

Dixon, Donald (1988). Preliminary Design Work for a Bridge Between Micro and Macromarketing, A Review of Some Nineteenth Century Blueprints. Paper presented at the 1988 Macromarketing Conference, San Jose, California, August.

Dixon, Donald and Wilkinson, Ian (1989). An Alternative Paradigm for Marketing Theory. *European Journal of Marketing*, 23(8):59-69.

Dixon, Donald (1996). Alderson's Austrian Antecedents: A Missed Opportunity for Macromarketing. In Droge, Cornelia and Calantone, Roger, editors, *Enhancing Knowledge Development in Marketing* AMA Educators' Conference, pages 172-173. American Marketing Association, Chicago. Updated in 1999 as Some Late Nineteenth Century Antecedents of Marketing Theory.

Journal of Macromarketing, 19(December):115-125.

Dixon, Donald (1999). Some Late Nineteenth Century Antecedents of Marketing Theory. *Journal of Macromarketing*, 19(December):115-125. The author discusses Alderson's theory in relation to 19th c. Austrian economists.

Fisk, George (1967). *Marketing Systems An Introductory Analysis*, pages 12, 61, 94, 222, 258, 337, and numerous other pages. Harper and Row, NY.

Fisk, George (2001). Reflections of George Fisk: Honorary Chair of the 2001 Macromarketing Conference. *Journal of Macromarketing*, 21(December, No. 2):121-122.

Fraedrich, J., (1987). Marketing Functionalism The Enigma Explained, In Russell Belk et al, editors, *Marketing Theory*, pages 376-379. American Marketing Association, Chicago.

Friedman, Jon (1980). Alderson's Impact on Marketing. Independent study research paper, University of Pennsylvania, Management Department, May, referenced in Steven Sass (1982). *The Pragmatic Imagination A History of the Wharton School 1881-1981*, University of Pennsylvania Press, Philadelphia, note 17 page 338.

Gadde, Lars-Erik and Hulthen, Kajas (2003). Aldersonian Sorting: An 'Old' Concept for a 'New' Reality. In 19th IMP Conference, Lugano, Switzerland.

Glaser, S. and Halliday, M. (1980). A Systems Foundations for Alderson's Functionalism. In George Fisk, Nason, Robert and White, Philip, editors, *Macromarketing: Evolution of Thought*, pages 71-82. Business Research Division, Graduate School of Business Administration, University of Colorado, Boulder.

Green, Paul (2001). The Vagaries of Becoming (and Remaining) a Marketing Research Methodologist. *Journal of Marketing*, 65(July, No. 3):104-108.

Green, Paul and Goodman, Charles (2003). About Wroe Alderson. Wroe Alderson Distinguished Lecturer Series, Available at:
http://www.marketing.wharton.upenn.edu/news/info/wroe_alderson.html
A three-page paper on Alderson with a list of former speakers of the Wroe Alderson Distinguish Lecturer Series.

Grether, Ewald T. (1967). Chamberlin's Theory of Monopolistic Competition and the Literature of Marketing. In Kuenne, Robert, editor, *Monopolistic Competition Theory: Studies in Impact*, pages 315-318. John Wiley and Sons, NY.

Hernandez, Sigfredo Augusto (1988). The Division of Housework: A Social Exchange Framework. Unpublished doctoral dissertation, Temple University.

Hewitt, John (1983). A Guide to Alderson: His Marketing View of Economic Competition. Working paper, University of Scranton, May.

Holbrook, Morris (2001). Wroe Alderson (1957) *Marketing Behavior and Executive Action*. *Association of Consumer Research News*, pages 37-38. Winter.

Hollander, Stanley (1957). Looking Around: New Marketing Concepts. *Harvard Business Review*, 35(September-October):151-152. Reprinted in Kelley, Eugene and Lazer, William, editors, (1958). *Managerial Marketing: Perspectives and Viewpoints A Source Book*, pages 460-466. Richard D. Irwin, Homewood, IL. Alderson is discussed with an emphasis on his 1957 book.

Hostiuck, K. Tim. and Kurtz, David(1973). Alderson's Functionalism and the Development of Marketing Theory. *Journal of Business Research*, 1(Fall):141-156.

Hota, Monali and Young, Louise (2003). Is Aldersonian Theory Relevant in Today's Contexts? An Illustrative Case, Proceedings of the New Zealand Australia Marketing Academy Conference (ANZMAC), pages 593-599. Adelaide, AU.

Hunt, Shelby, Muncy, James and Ray, Nina (1981). Alderson's General Theory of Marketing: A Formalization. In Ben Enis and Koering, K., editors, *Review of Marketing 1981*, pages 267-272. American Marketing Association, Chicago. Reprinted in Hunt, Shelby (1983). *Marketing Theory*, pages 314-324. Richard D. Irwin, Homewood, IL.

Hunt, Shelby (2002). Alderson's Functionalist Theory. In *Foundations of Marketing Theory Toward a General Theory of Marketing*, pages 263-266. M. E. Sharpe, Armonk, NY.

Jones, Brian, D. G., and Shaw, Eric (2002). A History of Marketing Thought. In Weitz, Barton and Wensley, Robin, editors, *Handbook of Marketing*, pages 39-65, especially pages 55-56. Sage Publications, Thousand Oaks, CA.

Kane, James (1964). Marketing Behavior and the Environment: An Ecological Study of the Adaptive Behavior of Marketing Agencies. In Smith, L. George, editor, *Reflections on Progress in Marketing*, pages 101-109. American Marketing Association, Chicago.

Klein, Tom (2003). Assessing Our Ancestors: Alderson and the Development of Marketing Thought. Presentation delivered at the special Panel Session on Alderson at the Macromarketing Conference, August 2003 Foxwoods, CT.

Lambert, Douglas M. (1978). *The Distribution Channels Decision*, pages 12-19. National Association of Accountants, NY

Lewis, Edwin (1968). *Marketing Channels: Structure and Strategy*, pages 139-146. McGraw-Hill, NY.

Lusch, Robert (1980). Alderson, Sessions and the 1950s Manager. In Lamb, Charles and Dunne, Patrick, editors, *Theoretical Developments in Marketing*, pages 4-6. American Marketing Association, Chicago.

Mallen, Bruce (1977). *Principles of Marketing Channel Management*, Appendix 3 Functionalism and Distribution Structure, pages 89-115. Lexington Books, Lexington, Mass.

McGarry, Edmund (1965). Wroe Alderson's Marketing Theory Seminar, an Experiment in Higher Education. Unpublished paper presented at the 1965 Marketing Theory Seminar, Boulder, Colorado, August.

Mertes, John (1971). Marketing Thought: The Use of Historical Concepts. Paper presented to the Southern Marketing Association, November, Miami FL. Abstracted in *Southern Journal of Business*, 7(May):76.

Millman, R. William (1962). A General Systems Approach to the Analysis of Managerial Functions. Unpublished doctoral dissertation, University of Florida, June. Abstracted in the 1963 *The Academy of Management Journal*, 6(September, No. 3):246-247.

Monieson, David and Shapiro, Stanley(1980). Biological and Evolutionary Dimensions of Aldersonian Thought: What he Borrowed Then and What he Might Have Borrowed Now. In Lamb, Charles and Dunne, Patrick, editors, *Theoretical Developments in Marketing*, pages 7-12. American Marketing Association, Chicago.

Narver, John and Savitt, Ronald(1971). *The Marketing Economy*, Holt, Rinehart and Winston, NY. Comments on Alderson on pages 42-49, 55. The book has many other short comments on Alderson.

Nicosia, Franco M. (1962). Marketing and Alderson's Functionalism. *Journal of Business*, 35(October):403-413. Reprinted in Kernan, Jerome and Sommers, Montrose, editors, (1968). *Perspectives in Marketing Theory*, Chap. 8, pages 83-96. Appleton-Century-Crofts, NY.

Nicosia, Franco (1969). Marketing Systems: Toward Formal Disciplines and Structural Properties. In King, Robert, editor, *Marketing and New Science of Planning*, pages 14-23. American Marketing Association, Chicago.

Panschar, William (1958). Discussion of the Analytical Framework for Marketing. In Duncan, Delbert, editor, *Proceedings: Conference of Marketing Teachers from Far Western States*, pages 29-31. University of California, Berkeley.

Priem, Richard (1992). Industrial Organization Economics and Alderson's General Theory of Marketing. *Journal of the Academy of Marketing Science*, 20(Spring, No. 2):135-141.

Priem, Richard and Amirani, S. (1992). The Transvection and the Value System: A Comparison of Alderson and Porter. In Leone, Robert and Kumar, V., editors, *Enhancing Knowledge Development in Marketing*, AMA Educators' Proceedings, page 473. American Marketing Association, Chicago.

Priem, Richard, Rasheed, Abdul and Amirani, Shahrzad (1997). Alderson's transvection and Porter's value system: a comparison of two independently developed theories. *Journal of Management History*, 3(2):145-165.

Reekie, W. Duncan (1984). *Markets, Entrepreneurs and Liberty: An Austrian View of Capitalism*, Chapter 5, pages 107-117. Wheatsheaf Books Ltd, Brighton, Sussex.

Reekie, W. Duncan and Savitt, Ronald (1982). Marketing Behaviour and Entrepreneurship: A Synthesis of Alderson and Austrian Economics. *European Journal of Marketing*, 16(7):55-66.

Rethans, Arno (1979). The Aldersonian Paradigm: A Perspective for Theory Development and Synthesis. In Ferrell, O. C., Brown, Stephen and Lamb, Charles, editors, *Conceptual and Theoretical Developments in Marketing*, pages

197-209. American Marketing Association, Chicago.

Rewoldt, Stewart, Scott, James and Warsaw, Martin (1969). *Introduction to Marketing Management*, pages 254-263. Richard D. Irwin, Homewood, IL.

Rutledge, Daniel P. (1989). Strategy, Competition and Differential Competitive Advantage: Examination in the U.S. Nonrubber Footwear Market. Unpublished doctoral dissertation, Michigan State University.

Sass, Steven A. (1982). *The Pragmatic Imagination A History of the Wharton School 1881-1981*, pages 304-313. University of Pennsylvania Press, Philadelphia. The author discusses the adoption of systems theory at Wharton and the hiring of Alderson.

Savitt, Ronald (1990). Pre-Aldersonian Antecedents to Macromarketing: Insights from the Textual Literature. *Journal of the Academy of Marketing Science*, 18(4):293-301.

Schwartz, George (1963). *Development of Marketing Theory*, Chapter 7 Organized Behavior Systems and The Theory of Market Behavior, pages 101-114. South-Western Publishing, Cincinnati, OH.

Sessions, Robert (nd). A Brief History of Cost and Profit Outlook. Unpublished paper. 12 pages.

Sessions, Robert (nd). Alderson and Sessions A Consulting Business on Professionalism in Management. Unpublished paper, 17 pages.

Shapiro, Stanley (1963). Decision Making, Survival and the Organized Behavior System: A Case Study of the Ontario Hog Producer Organization. In Decker, W., editor, *Emerging Concepts in Marketing*, pages 438-442. American Marketing Association, Chicago.

Shapiro, Stanley (1964). The Survival Concept and the Nonprofit Behavior System. In Cox, R., Alderson, W. and Shapiro, S., editors, *Theory in Marketing*, pages 109-124. American Marketing Association, Chicago.

Sheth, Jagdish, David Gardner, and Dennis Garrett (1988). Marketing Theory, John Wiley and Sons, NY. The Functionalist School of Thought, pages 86-96. This is a very good review of Alderson's theory, albeit incomplete.

Sirgy, Joseph (1984). *Marketing as Social Behavior A General Systems Theory*, pages 3-25 and 27-74. Praeger, NY.

Smalley, Roger and Fraedrich, John (1995). Aldersonian Functionalism: An Enduring Theory in Marketing. *Journal of Marketing Theory and Practice*, 3(4):1-15.

Smith, Wendell (1966). Wroe Alderson-Leaders in Marketing. *Journal of Marketing*, 30(January):64-65.

Staudt, Thomas, Taylor, Donald and Bowersox, Donald (1976). *Managerial Introduction to Marketing*, 3rd edition, Chapter 13: Marketing Channel Structure, pages 273-285. Prentice-Hall, NY.

Stern, Louis and El-Ansary, Adel (1977). *Marketing Channels*, pages 219-226. Prentice-Hall, Englewood Cliffs, NJ.

Svensson, Göran (2002). The Theoretical Foundations of Supply Chain Management a Functionalist Theory of Marketing. *International Journal of Physical Distribution and Logistics Management*, 39(9):734-754.

Thorelli, Hans (1967). Ecology in Marketing. *The Southern Journal of Business*, 2(October):19-25.

University of Pennsylvania, *A Brief Guide to the Wroe Alderson, 1898-1965 Papers*. The University Archives and Records Center, 7 Cubic ft., UPT 50 A362. A three-page document briefly describing the content of each of the seven boxes. Available at:
http://www.archives.upenn.edu.

Wales, Hugh and Dawson, Lyndon (1979). The Anomalous Qualities Between Present-Day Conferences and Alderson's Marketing Theory Seminars. In Ferrell, O. C., Brown, Stephen and Lamb, Charles, editors, *Conceptual and Theoretical Developments in Marketing*, pages 222-227. American Marketing Association, Chicago.

Walle, Alf (1984). Alderson's Functionalism: A Phoenix Rising from Its Ashes. In Anderson, Paul and Ryan, Michael, editors, *Scientific Method in Marketing*, pages 78-80. American Marketing Association, Chicago.

Walle, Alf (2003). Rethinking Macrofunctionalism: Rehabilitating Wroe Alderson for the 21st Century. Unpublished working paper, November.

Wind, Yoram and Green, Paul(2004). Continuing the Alderson tradition. In Wind, Yoram (Jerry) and Green, Paul, editors, *Marketing Research and Modeling: Progress and Prospects A Tribute to Paul E. Green*, pages 293-298. Kluwer Academic Publishers, Boston. Page 293 is a poem by Wroe Alderson, dated October 9, 1960.

Wooliscroft, Ben (2000). Examining a Case for Quaker Influence in Modern Marketing Theory. In Shultz, C. J. and Grbac, B., editors, *Marketing Contributions to Democratization and Socioeconomic Development*, Proceedings, pages 326-336.

Wooliscroft, Ben (2001). Too Hard to Read? Wroe Alderson's Theory of Marketing. In Rahtz, Don and McDonagh, Pierre, editors, *Proceedings of the 26th Macromarketing Conference*, pages 435-446. University of Rijeka.

Wooliscroft, Ben (2003). Getting to Know Wroe: A Short Biography of Wroe Alderson. In Redmond, Bill, editor, *Marketing to Diverse Cultures*, Proceedings of the 28th Annual Macromarketing Conference, Connecticut, August 11-14, pages 126-139.

Wooliscroft, Ben (2003). Wroe Alderson's Contribution to Marketing Theory Through His Textbooks. *Journal of the Academy of Marketing Science*, 31(Fall, No. 4):481-490.

Wooliscroft, Ben (2004). Paradigm Dominance and the Hegemonic Process: The Loss of Wroe Alderson's Theories of Marketing. Unpublished doctoral dissertation, University of Otago.

Index